Praise for this book

"This book documents and explores an important time in US history, and does so with a depth and intelligence that make it irresistibly compelling."

—Scott Turow, author, *Presumed Innocent*

"Florence Kelley is a forgotten American hero. Independent-minded and tough, Kelley at the turn of the last century led the fight for a minimum wage and decent working conditions, especially for women and children. In these pages, Leigh Bienen offers a worthy tribute to Kelley and draws intriguing parallels to the struggles of today."

—Alex Kotlowitz, author, *There Are No Children Here*

"In *Florence Kelley, Factory Inspector in 1890s Chicago, and the Children*, Leigh Buchanan Bienen has written an audaciously original hybrid fashioned from parallel narratives, from public records and private diaries, from history and memoir. The book remains scrupulously rooted in historical fact even as it explores the subjective fluidity between past and present."

—Stuart Dybek, author, *The Coast of Chicago*

"Too few people know what a huge place Florence Kelley holds in labor history, but in addition to setting out her record, Leigh Bienen gives us added perspective on her heroic accomplishments: through her own journal entries she draws out parallels—similarities and contrasts—that make us question what has changed and what has, lamentably, stayed the same in more than a century of legal, economic, and personal drama. This is a fascinating book, abundant, useful, and important."

—Rosellen Brown, novelist, author of *Before* and *After Tender Mercies*

FLORENCE KELLEY, FACTORY INSPECTOR IN 1890S CHICAGO, AND THE CHILDREN

Florence Kelley, a lifelong advocate for women and children, came to Chicago with her three children fleeing an abusive husband. She lived at Hull-House in the 1890s and was appointed state factory inspector by Governor John Peter Altgeld, becoming the first woman to hold that post in the United States. As factory inspector she and her colleagues worked to place children in school and remove them from tenement factories and dangerous industrial environments. With colleagues she conducted a wage and ethnicity census of the slums of Chicago at the time of the World's Fair, resulting in the publication of *Hull-House Maps and Papers* (1895). Its findings and astute observations are relevant today. This book braids together three narratives: the story of Florence Kelley's life as a mother and reformer in the tumult of 1890s Chicago; the story of the author's arrival in Chicago a century later and her new life and work here; and references to wrongful convictions and exonerations over the course of a decade leading finally to the abolition of capital punishment in Illinois.

Florence Kelley

Factory Inspector in 1890s Chicago

and the children

by **Leigh Buchanan Bienen**

Published in the United States by Open Books
213 W. Institute Place, Chicago, Ill. 60610
Stacy Ratner, founder
This book is a publication of Open Books Ltd., a Chicago-based nonprofit social venture that provides literacy experiences for tens of thousands of readers each year through inspiring programs and creative capitalization of books. Learn more about how we transform lives through reading, writing, and the power of used books at www.open-books.org.

Catalog Information: Bienen, Leigh Buchanan
Florence Kelley, Factory Inspector in 1890s Chicago, and the Children
Women's History; Women and the Law; Nineteenth Century History; Chicago History; Progressive Philosophy; Urban Studies; Hull-House; Jane Addams
Includes bibliographic references and photographs
Printed in the United States of America
Photo Credits:
   Cover/Interior: Library of Congress Chicago Daily News, 1902-1933, courtesy Chicago History Museum
   Photo of Florence Kelley: Wikipedia (public domain)
   Nationalities Map No. 1 - Polk Street to Twelfth, Halsted Street to Jefferson, Chicago. From *Hull House Maps and Papers,* published in 1895

ISBN-13: 978-0692291184
ISBN-10: 0692291180

Typeset in Minion.
Book design: Mark Swindle
Front and back cover design: Mark Swindle

Printed by Createspace, an Amazon.com company.

For Henry

Bird's eye view of "Tall Buildings", Chicago, IL. Source: ICHi-30045. Chicago History Museum. Reproduction of photograph, photographer - J. W. Taylor. Date: 1895.

Contents

Interior of Board of Trade, the pit; Chicago, IL. Source: ICHi-18146. Chicago History Museum. Reproduction of photograph, photographer unknown. Date: 1896.

Introduction

In January 1995, we moved from Princeton, New Jersey, where we had lived for twenty-eight years and raised our three daughters, to Evanston, Illinois—my husband, Henry Bienen, to be the fifteenth president of Northwestern University, and I to continue teaching and writing about the law at Northwestern University School of Law. And, surprisingly, as it turned out, I would continue in another state as an advocate and participant in the ongoing national challenge to the reimposition of capital punishment in America.

In 1995, the official president's residence was a large, gracious, draughty stone house at 639 Central Street in Evanston, a few blocks from the undergraduate campus, in a leafy, quiet suburban neighborhood. The campus of the Northwestern School of Law was in a set of adjoining buildings, Levy Mayer Hall, the Rubloff Building, and the Mc-Cormick Building at 357 East Chicago Avenue in downtown Chicago, fifteen miles and a lifetime away from Evanston.

Evanston was like the suburban university town we had just left, and except for the multifaceted university, little engaged me there. Besides, it was my husband's territory. Chicago, on the other hand, was another world, the world of a great city, a legal center with its many courts, its bustling noise and dirt, its theatre and places of music, its velvet hotels and the people, so many different kinds of people, doing so many different things, beginning with everything that was going on at our law school and our medical school. The medical school and the law school were side by side, with the medical school surrounded by hospitals which would grow and sprout into new high-rise buildings in the next decade and a half during our tenure. When the dust had settled, I looked from the fourth floor of the law school library and found myself in the middle of everything that was happening in Chicago.

In 1995 I had not lived in a city, a real city—unless you count Ibadan, Nigeria, certainly a real city—I had not lived in a real American city since I lived in New York City as a young working woman recently graduated from Cornell University. Our children were grown and living elsewhere. My husband was fully occupied from dawn to midnight, and there was no reason to stay home, especially since our house from the moment of arrival was filled with sawing and hammering, and exceptionally friendly carpenters and plasterers and painters. And this house, our house, was something else, certainly not a home, but the official residence of the president of the university.

When we arrived in 1995, I knew no one in Evanston or Chicago except a former student who became a close friend, and an acquaintance from homicide conferences, a fellow homicide researcher. We had no grandchildren, and all three of our daughters lived a plane ride away. By the time we left the Evanston residence in August 2009 to go to a high-rise apartment in downtown Chicago, we had six grandchildren, and our expanded family considered themselves part of the large and wonderfully welcoming Northwestern community, which extended to both coasts and around the globe.

During these fifteen years at Northwestern and after, we were part of and witnessed surprising and momentous developments, at our educational institutions, in the courts and legislatures, and in national and international politics. Some of these we could participate in, for others, we were simply, like everyone else, witnesses. Often, it seemed as if everything was speeding up and then happening much too quickly, going by too soon, and that events and their consequences were spinning out of control.

Meanwhile we continued doing what we were here to do, to be stewards of a great American university with its multitude of institutional traditions and present identity. Along the way, unexpectedly, and by a circuitous route, I fell in love with the city of Chicago and its history.

In 1998 when I had been teaching law students for several years, I came across a set of original handwritten police records of homicide cases in Chicago from 1870-1930. As a longtime homicide researcher, I knew immediately that this was an important new data set, and it had to be made public. These cases led me to the extraordinary archives, legal records, documents, and photographs relevant to the set of handwritten police records of fourteen thousand homicides in this period.

This data set of homicides had to be transcribed from a microfilm of the original bound set of handwritten records, then coded and analyzed, and transcribed in what eventually turned into a multi-year collaborative research project, with an interdisciplinary academic conference in 2000, followed by a set of scholarly papers in the *Journal of Criminal Law and Criminology*. Eventually, the website, Homicide in Chicago 1870-1939 (homicide.northwestern.edu), was launched in 2004, making all 14,000 police cases available online. The site included an interactive search engine, which allowed anyone to search the 14,000 case records and the hundreds of contemporaneous photographs and thousands of pages of legal documents and commentary. The website also included a set of in-person interviews with lawyers, law professors, and capital punishment researchers.

The Homicide in Chicago website continues to attract thousands of visitors every month, after initially attracting more than 77,000 visitors on the day of its launch, June 7, 2004, when it crashed the Northwestern server hosting it. Many of these visitors were and are finding records of ancestors and family members, for these simple police clerks' files of murders include name of victim and defendant, date of arrest, location of homicide, and other details of the crime and its adjudication. As of 2013 more than a million people have come to this website.

The wealth of historical records and archival materials from the period of the homicide project led to another web-based collaborative, educational enterprise, centered on the history of Chicago. The Florence Kelley website, based upon the work of Florence Kelley, state factory inspector in the 1890s, was launched in 2008, making thousands more pages of court records, letters, documents, books and commentary, photographs, and other materials available to the farthest reaches of the world: The Life and Times of Florence Kelley in Chicago, 1891-1899 (florencekelley.northwestern.edu).

Still, it wasn't enough. I decided I must write a book about Florence Kelley and her time in Chicago, although there were already three excellent, very different biographies of her, and she had written her autobiography. I became convinced there was more to be said about her time in Chicago, when she lived at Hull-House, the people surrounding her, the legal and historical context, and Florence Kelley's own accomplishments as the first statewide factory inspector in the country, appointed by Governor John Peter Altgeld in July 1893.

Florence Kelley's legal authority came from the Factory and Workshop Inspection Law (or Factory Inspection Law), which was enacted in 1893 after years of advocacy by Hull-House residents and many others in that active and diverse legal community. Her personal authority and the role she played were uniquely her own. The political opposition to the efforts of the factory inspectors and their allies was also formidable, I was to discover. They did not go away quietly after her appointment, but fought the implementation of the statute with all their considerable political and economic resources.

As excellent as the three biographies of Florence Kelley were, none, in my opinion, conveyed the richness of the historical context of the effort to reform the conditions in the city sweatshops and tenements, and the people who fought that fight. There was the ever-present mystery of the interplay between the actions and personalities of public figures, such as Florence Kelley and Jane Addams, their role in historic events and the role of chance, circumstance, and unpredictable externalities, such as the World's Columbian Exposition, the massive immigration to Chicago of the 1880s and 1890s, the depression of 1893, and the nature of the determined political opposition. A different time, a different place, and different individuals, and none of this would have happened in quite the same way. In other words, it was just like the present.

This unique array of energetic and talented individuals who came to Chicago in the 1890s and played a role in the Herculean efforts to clean up the sweatshops and slums of Chicago—Henry Demarest Lloyd, Jane Addams, John Peter Altgeld, Carroll Wright, Abraham Bisno, and Florence Kelley—began speaking to me in their own voices. I came to recognize Florence Kelley's handwriting in the archives, and that of her mother, son, father, and brother. The pictures of Chicago during the 1890s were richly evocative, but the photographs of the family and the public occasions did not match the power of their words. They were remarkable writers. The more I read about them, about what they and others said about themselves and each other, the more I wanted to know about their families and their lives.

A photograph found while working on the homicide site haunted me. There are three men, working men, heavily dressed, wearing several layers of thick wool clothing, standing next to a cart and a pony shaggy in its full winter coat. One man holds the reins. They are standing on ice next to the first Chicago water intake crib, built in 1867, four miles from the shore of Lake Michigan. They must have taken the cart and the pony over the ice for four miles, which means that the lake must have frozen for four miles out. Were the winters that much colder then? Elsewhere I came across reports of large parts of the lake freezing over, and of the unemployed being sent to cut ice through the winter for cooling in the winter and the summer.

Perhaps the photograph dated from the devastatingly cold winter of 1893, when Florence Kelley had just been appointed factory inspector. Like so many of the remnants in the archives, the picture was mesmerizing, and raised more questions than it answered. Now I was really drawn in. In addition to that devastating winter and the economic depression of 1893, what else was happening in Chicago during 1893 and the few years when Florence Kelley was state factory inspector?

From the outset of our time here, I was continuing to teach law at the Northwestern University School of Law, from which, I discovered to my astonishment, Florence Kelley had received a degree in 1895. I was doing what I always did: attending death penalty conferences and writing about developments in capital punishment, publishing fiction and nonfiction, writing for the academic legal community, and becoming increasingly involved with advocacy surrounding capital punishment in Illinois. And we were getting to know the extraordinary community of Chicago theatre artists, many of whom, most notably those at Lookingglass Theatre and Steppenwolf Theatre, had deep and abiding connections to Northwestern University, and commitments to social justice and the city of Chicago.

Still I kept returning to 1890s Chicago and Florence Kelley, finding new reports and transcripts, traveling to New York to read the family letters in the New York Public Library Archives, driving through the snow to New Hampshire to look at the only existing original print copies of the *Chicago Tribune* for the period, part of the remarkable American Newspaper Repository established by Nicholson Baker and his wife, Margaret Brentano. What was I looking for, and whom did I find?

These 1890s people were crusaders, reformers, lawyers. They were like us, and not like us. They wanted justice, and to do good. Or, they wanted things to stay the same and to hang on to what they had, or they wanted both. There seemed to be no public issue they hadn't considered and discussed, often with a degree of sophistication and depth beyond what could be found in our present public discourse. And so the subject of the book kept shifting.

All of us—lawyers, judges, legislators, governors, students, teachers, journalists, academic administrators—we were and are all living in the middle of another extraordinary time, and it is another revolutionary time. In Chicago we are once again in the middle of it: the steamy politics, the torrent of unresolved issues around national and city economics, unprecedented international challenges, political history and anarchy, all of it inescapably steeped in the law. The more I watched what was happening from 1995 to 2011, the more it started to look like America in the 1890s and at the turn of the century.

The political and social boundaries of our world were tilting before our eyes. In the short time since 1995, when we arrived in Chicago, less than an eye blink in history, our world was transformed. I kept asking myself: What would Florence Kelley and her intelligent, articulate companions have said about this? Could they have kept steady their moral compass?

In Chicago, politics remains our principal preoccupation, entertainment, and the scourge of our struggle to create a responsible, accountable civil society. Remarkable people walk on stage, disappear into the wings, and what happened when and where and to whom becomes a matter of dispute, sometimes in the courts. And so it was in the 1890s. The hands on the levers of power may have changed, but many patterns and synchronicities remain. There has indeed been a revolution, and it has changed our world, most notably but not only in our employment. It wasn't the revolution Florence Kelley and her colleagues kept talking about, waiting for, and writing about. And as in many other disruptive upheavals, many are left out, and many have had their expectations upended. Perhaps it is always the case, that no one's life turns out exactly as expected, and this is just another version of that theme.

Now, as in Florence Kelley's time, all questions, big and small, are on the national agenda. And all of us—parents, children, grandparents, lawyers, government officials, teachers—try to leave things a little better and to make sense of our world, our lives, our work. As best we can we educate and provide for and protect our families and children, for a future which will certainly be different from the world we know, and yet we can do no more than extrapolate from our experience.

The law continues to be primary, portentous, pretentious, stubborn, often wrong, too frequently plagued by corruption and conflict of interest, and the waste and fraud in government are tolerated and perpetuated by our own inertia, incompetence, and fear. The rule of law is a principle honored with shallow allegiances. The lawyers and the judges hide behind their titles, behind the formalities of the law, crouch behind their professional armor, and live in fear of unpredictable democratic politics. And so it is elsewhere.

Yet the law for all its faults is all we have, and within the institutional structures of the law, important changes do sometimes happen, in legal institutions, in the formal law, in educational institutions, and in politics. And, life goes on, for the lawyers, for the reformers, for those who oppose the reforms, for the teachers and students, and for everyone else, for all the people who are just standing there, just sitting there, doing the best they can with limited control of their circumstances, at this time and at that place. Those who can read and write, have shelter and food and water, and the possibility of employment, and live in a stable political environment are the lucky ones, and the few. If the law, or the illusion of the rule of law, can create the structure for a stable civil society, it does its most important job.

Those of us charged with supporting the institutions of law and education do the best we can under the circumstances. We drive our cars through the ice and snow, run through the rain when we forget our umbrellas, shiver in the cold when the heat falters, and walk along the streets of Chicago and look at the deserted lots and the tall buildings and wonder. People are brave and energetic, commit unspeakable acts of cruelty and brutality, unpredictably sacrifice themselves for others, and we watch, pray and listen as the music plays.

Then we pick ourselves up and move on to the next square. A death occurs, a child is born, a law is repealed, another law is passed, an important court decides a landmark case, the judges change, for better or for worse. Maybe an appellate court opinion stands, maybe it doesn't. And still we stare down the city streets, ride the elevators up the tall buildings, and continue on, rapidly becoming part of the historical past ourselves.

Actors give themselves in performances, and the audience laughs, or cries. A football is thrown, a baby learns to crawl and then stand up and walk, and then learns to run, and to drive. And so it goes on and on, although we all wonder how long it can go on like this. How can it all just go on, where there was, and is, so much injustice, foolishness, and greed, so much stupidity and incompetence, in high places and low? Some little bit is accomplished, and then things slide back to where they were before. Why can't someone do something about it, whatever it is, and sometimes they do.

The more I read about Florence Kelley, her companions and compatriots, and their concerns, the closer they seemed to us, although with each passing year they were more distant in time. So I kept coming back to the 1890s, looked deeper, found more records, letters, court documents, all the while asking myself how later generations, even our children and grandchildren, would find us, judge us. Because these people were mostly lawyers and reformers, and held public offices, they appeared in litigation, made public statements and left records of themselves. They were public figures. I tracked their public lives and looked for their private lives. The more I learned, the deeper the mysteries.

They certainly seemed to know who they were and what they were doing. Their clarity of purpose had the far-reaching call of a church bell tolling across the fields of the decades. Their shining intelligence, their command of language, their depth of thought, and what they said about what they saw and lived through were arresting. They seemed to have faith that some part of what they said and thought and did would be remembered. They were all passionate about the law. They all believed the law could change something, change society. There were many versions of their public lives, as well as of their private lives.

If I could make sense of their world—as it came down to us in newspapers, the haphazard remaining documents, court records, letters, and photographs—then perhaps I could make sense of our world. I kept coming across pieces of communications, which were as vivid as the night lightening over the lake. Other writings were just news about events which were no longer news. So I started to copy down what I found meaningful, or true, about their world without any idea of how these bits and pieces of writing might be put together.

As the time in Evanston came to a close and we moved into the city, I kept copying down their words. I collected government reports and transcripts of hearings, remarks against the backdrop of some of the historic events of their time—Pullman, the passage of the Factory Inspection Law, Haymarket, the great depression of 1893, the World's Columbian Exposition, the founding of Hull-House, the government study "The Slums of Great Cities"—without trying to construct a single coherent, synchronous narrative of Florence Kelley's period in Chicago, 1891-1899. Others had already done that.

Meanwhile in our new century we lived our lives, talked about the weather, wrapped ourselves up and stripped down, ate and slept, and the days turned into weeks and years.

We switched to new computers and phones, greeted one another, rarely doubting that the sun would rise and the world we knew would be there. The great Chicago institutions of culture and government went on, more or less efficiently, sometimes effectively. People came and went in positions of elected or appointed authority, and lawyers and public officials made pronouncements. The law students complained about too much work, the faculty complained they were underappreciated, some graduated or left, new people came. The lawyers said the profession wasn't what it used to be; the few remaining unions threatened to strike and demanded higher wages, the city and the state were strapped financially, and no one was satisfied with what the legislators, the regulators and the courts said or did, at the same time that everybody talked about it. The courts were open for business: crimes were committed, people were arrested and put in jail, other people sued one another, the firms got bigger and bigger, and then the financial crisis came.

Still, several truths could not be denied: we live in a society where there is the rule of law in spite of its many imperfections. There is corruption in judicial institutions, and greed and chicanery in government and in the private and public sectors. Yet by and large, by some miracle, the courts, the statutes, the regulatory agencies, the legislatures, the universities, the states, the churches, the cities survive as institutions, even if it sometimes seems they do not act justly or within their constitutional mandate. The other overwhelming reality which remains is the persistence of family attachments and the enduring quality of love.

As I became more hypnotized by these people, absorbed in their stories, listening to their voices as those were preserved in a written record, I reimagined their world: what remained? If I could make sense of their lives, I could make sense of my own a hundred years later. It is unlikely there will be a stash of permanent paper records in fifty or a hundred years. The record of who we were and what we did may all be out in the cloud. But how will those who come later, especially those who care about the law and what our society was, find us—what we did and what we hoped for in the institutional structure of our flawed, variegated civil society in Chicago.

July 2014

Image of men walking on the partially frozen ice of Lake Michigan, with a steamship or tugboat in the background in Chicago, Illinois. DN-0001833, Chicago Daily News negatives collection, Chicago History Museum.

1

The Real Business of the Law Is Education

In this autobiography it is my purpose to wander wherever I please and come back when I get ready. . . . Finally in Florence, in 1904, I hit upon the right way to do an Autobiography: start it at no particular time in your life; wander at your free will all over your life; talk only about the thing that interests you for the moment; drop it the moment its interest threatens to pale, and turn your talk upon the new and more interesting thing that has intruded into your mind meantime.

Mark Twain, *Autobiography*, quoted in *Mark Twain*, Charles Neider, editor

"Chicago, Chicago!" called the brakeman, slamming open the door. They were rushing into a more crowded yard, alive with the clatter and clang of life. She began to gather up her poor little grip, and closed her hand firmly on her purse. . . . "Chicago!" called the brakeman, drawing the word out long. They were under a great shadowy train shed, where the lamps were already beginning to shine out, with passenger cars all about and the train moving at a snail's pace. The people in the car were all up and crowding around the door.

Sister Carrie by Theodore Dreiser

When Florence Kelley arrived in Chicago, as she described it later in her *Autobiography*, "on a snowy morning between Christmas 1891 and New Year's 1892," her first destination, but not the first place she went, was Hull-House, the settlement house recently founded by Jane Addams and Ellen Gates Starr. Her later description is of the seemingly predestined, enchanted, idyllic journey through the streets of Chicago to get to Hull-House:

On a snowy morning between Christmas 1891 and New Year's 1892, I arrived at Hull House, Chicago, a little before breakfast time, and found there Henry Standing Bear, a Kickapoo Indian, waiting for the front door to be opened. It was Miss Addams who opened it, holding on her left arm a singularly unattractive, fat, pudgy baby belonging to the cook, who was behindhand with the breakfast. Miss Addams was a little hindered in her movement by a super-energetic kindergarten child, left by its mother while she went to a sweatshop for a bundle of cloaks to be finished.

The Florence Kelley who came to Hull-House was at that moment Florence Kelley Wischnewetzky, mother to three children under six, whom she had left at the Women's Building, the magnificent new headquarters of the Woman's Christian Temperance Union. She was fleeing New York City to escape her husband, Lazare Wischnewetzky, whom she would soon meet in a court in Chicago.

Florence Kelley's biographers argue about the actual date of her arrival in Chicago, noting that the recorded weather did not show a large new snowfall between Christmas and New Year's Day.

The most authoritative of her biographers suggests that the crucial journey with Jane Addams to visit the writer Henry Demarest Lloyd and his family at his country home, Wayside, in Winnetka occurred perhaps a few days later than the date in Florence Kelley's *Autobiography.*

After all, her recollection was written more than 25 years after the events, so a few lapses in memory or errors might be expected. Better to have that vivid, re-created moment than some more accurate or precise but boring chronicle of the fact of her arrival, without the bright recollection of this narrative. Somehow the memory of a momentous arrival is always imprinted, even if inaccurately.

This is how another writer, Theodore Dreiser, in *The Titan* described the approach to Chicago by train in the early 1890s:

He had spent two nights in the gaudy Pullman then provided—a car intended to make up for some of the inconveniences of its arrangements by an over-elaboration of plush and tortured glass—when the first lone outposts of the prairie metropolis began to appear. The side-tracks along the road-bed over which he was speeding became more and more numerous, the telegraph-poles more and more hung with arms and strung smoky-thick with wires. In the far distance, cityward, was, here and there, a lone working-man's cottage, the home of some adventurous soul who had planted his bare hut thus far out in order to reap the small but certain advantage which the growth of the city would bring. . . . The tracks, side by side, were becoming more and more numerous. Freight-cars were assembled here by thousands from all parts of the country—yellow, red, blue, green, white. (Chicago, he recalled, already had thirty railroads terminating here, as though it were the end of the world.) The little low one and two story houses, quite new as to wood, were frequently unpainted, and already smoky—in places grimy.

At grade-crossings, where ambling streetcars and wagons and muddy-wheeled buggies waited, he noted how flat the streets were, how unpaved, how sidewalks went up and down rhythmically—here a flight of steps, a veritable platform before a house, there a long stretch of boards laid flat on the mud of the prairie itself. What a city! Presently a branch of the filthy, arrogant, self-sufficient little Chicago River came into view, with its mass of sputtering tugs, its black, oily water, its tall, red, brown, and green grain-elevators, its immense black coal-pockets and yellowish-brown lumber yards.

Although Hull-House itself, the physical place, where Florence Kelley brought herself, was not new, Hull-House the institution was. Founded in 1889, it was a brand-new experiment in collective living, a new design for social work, a new venture in philanthropy, in a newly dedicated place, although Jane Addams insisted that "we would always pay our own expenses, and that at any moment we might decide to scatter through the neighborhood and live in separate tenements." And indeed, the residents of Hull-House did all pay their way: the ordinary fee for residents was twenty-one dollars per month for a room and board during the ten years of the 1890s. Florence Kelley paid it, often with a struggle, and sometimes she was in arrears. And the residents and visitors did indeed scatter all over the neighborhood. And the idea of Hull-House spread all over the country, and the world.

Hull-House was unique, but it was also a continuation, a variation, on other similar institutions, both in America and abroad. It was a home, and a home for Florence Kelley and her children in the 1890s. She became a lawyer here, a real lawyer admitted to the Bar of Illinois in 1895, a lawyer and a public servant, the head of a state agency, who understood that the law was inextricably entwined with the politics and history of the state, the city and the country. The law was the deep red, coursing blood of the society, and it had and still has no independent existence outside of the civic body politic.

January 1, 1995: Officially I began my life in Chicago today, having arrived in late December on a cold, grey, hopeless-feeling day, with a little snow. Actually we have lived in Chicago before, as graduate students. Two of our children were born here, and we lived in a series of dark brick-walled walk-ups, and then in a beautiful pale stone building, a copy of a nineteenth-century British building, now torn down, when we returned from Africa with our three children.

I am beginning a new phase of my professional life—at age 57—as a senior lecturer at Northwestern University School of Law. I suspect that will not be my principal occupation, although I am glad to be teaching still. I have a new identity as the wife, spouse of the president of this university, which I don't know at all. My three grown daughters, my mother, my sister, and my brother all live in other cities. I have no friends or colleagues here.

We are required to live in this big, cold, empty stone house where all but two rooms are filled with boxes. Our first view of this house was a few months ago when we were taken on a quick tour and told we were going to live here. I didn't like the house then and I don't like it now, although admittedly it is rather grand and has its own style.

We can make coffee in the kitchen, and wash in an incredibly contorted shower. That is about all we can do. Except go to work. But everyone is wonderfully welcoming, and in the huge stone entrance hall is a great red poinsettia. I can hardly complain that we are living in conditions of destitution. We live in a mansion. Only it isn't home.

My professional life is in the law; I have been a public defender, and an advocate, a researcher working on rape and homicide and capital punishment for decades. I will not be doing any of those things here. I will be teaching law. And pouring tea, I suppose. I will be an observer, here. Actually I am glad to be finished with capital punishment. I did my service in New Jersey and nothing is happening here. And there is always the writing.

In *Twenty Years at Hull-House* Jane Addams describes how she and her companion, Ellen Starr, found the house which was to become Hull-House:

Another Sunday afternoon in the early spring, on the way to a Bohemian mission in the carriage of one of its founders, we passed a fine old house standing well back from the street, surrounded on three sides by a broad piazza which was supported by wooden pillars of exceptionally pure Corinthian design and proportion. I was so attracted by the house that I set forth to visit it the very next day, but though I searched for it then and for several days after, I could not find it, and at length I most reluctantly gave up the search.

Three weeks later, with the advice of several of the oldest residents of Chicago, including the ex-mayor of the city, Colonel Mason, who had from the first been a warm friend to our plans, we decided upon a location somewhere near the junction of Blue Island Avenue, Halsted Street, and Harrison Street. I was surprised and overjoyed on the very first day of our search for quarters to come upon the hospitable old house, the quest for which I had so recently abandoned. The house was of course rented, the lower part of it used for offices and storerooms in connection with a factory that stood back of it. However, after some difficulties were overcome, it proved to be possible to sublet the second floor and what had been the large drawing-room on the first floor.

The house had passed through many changes since it had been built in 1856 for the homestead of one of Chicago's pioneer citizens, Mr. Charles J. Hull, and although battered by its vicissitudes, was essentially sound. Before it had been occupied by the factory, it had sheltered a second-hand furniture store, and at one time the Little Sisters of the Poor had used it for a home for the aged. It had a half-skeptical reputation for a haunted attic, so far respected by the tenants living on the second floor that they always kept a large pitcher full of water on the attic stairs. Their explanation of this custom was so incoherent that I was sure it was a survival of the belief that a ghost could not cross running water, but perhaps that interpretation was only my eagerness for finding folklore.

The photograph of Hull-House from 1892 shows a square-cornered, brown, hulking building, large, imposing with solid lines, dwarfing the figure of a unidentified man, looking incidental in a long coat poised next to a horse and carriage parked in front of the building, and not a tree, shrub, or flower in the picture. It was a hulk, this building, and not beautiful.

January 26, 2012, Chicago Tribune: "Hull House Sets Friday for Closing, Bankruptcy."

Jane Addams' Hull House Association will be out of business Friday, leaving employees and clients scrambling to fill a void the 122-year-old organization will leave.

Despite announcing last week plans to close in March, Board Chairman Stephen Saunders said Wednesday that the organization will fold this week because it can no longer afford to stay open. He also said Hull House plans to file Friday for bankruptcy. . . .

The organization, first formed in 1889, has provided foster care, domestic violence counseling, child development programs and job training to 60,000 children, families and community groups each year.

In Chicago, Florence Kelley introduced herself to Jane Addams and Henry Demarest Lloyd not as Mrs. Lazare Wischnewetzky, but as Mrs. Florence Kelley, an inauthentic name, a made-up name, a name which had no meaning, since there was no Mr. Kelley.

When Florence Kelley arrived in Chicago on that reimagined, remembered snowy December day, she had a husband, and his name was Dr. Lazare Wischnewetzky. When she came to Chicago, she had taken their three children under six and left him behind in New York.

In the 1890s, a woman with three children in tow required a name which designated her as a married woman. If coming to Chicago and Hull-House meant a new beginning, a new identity, it required a new name. And why not go back to her unmarried name, since she was returning to her unmarried self, and she had an identity in that name. But there was the obstacle of having three children and being a public person. Miss Florence Kelley could not have three children, but Mrs. Florence Kelley could. And so that was the name she took for herself, and it served her well indeed.

January 6, 1995: I have an office, downtown in our law school. And I will have students, or so I assume. At the moment it is all I can do to drive my flimsy New Jersey car downtown and avoid skidding on the ice. The weather is unremittingly grim, the roads and sidewalks ashen and dirty, and grit permeates everything. Getting from the car to the office is an athletic feat.

When Florence Kelley arrived in Chicago in late 1891, whatever the precise date, whatever the weather, she was not an unknown person in Chicago. Florence Kelley was known in Chicago as a writer, an activist, a reformer, a translator of Frederick Engels's *Die Lage Der Arbeitenden Klasse in England in 1844* and as someone who had long been devoted to improving the living and working conditions for women and children through the law. She went first to the Woman's Christian Temperance Union headquarters, from which it regularly published a newspaper and many other publications. She was going to an institution which had published her work, a place where she knew people and where she was known. She was going to a place where she knew she would find people to help her.

January 26, 2013: The temperature remains in the low teens, and even down to zero. So much for global warming. The lake, ever beautiful, cracked blocks of ice, giant trapezoids showing on the surface and making an uneven plane, of greys and blues. A visit to John Peter Altgeld's university yesterday, in the cold, where there are still people dedicated to its future.

Then Florence Kelley became one of the newcomers, one more in the ocean of immigrants, people who came to Chicago, for whatever reason, and fell in love here and stayed, fell in love with the city, with the work here, with the tumult, the possibilities, the hurry, the everything-going-on-at-once city, the city of too much of everything—too much money, too much destitution, too much hope and too much despair—the "let's do it" spirit which was and is the essence of Chicago. Dreiser, *The Titan*, again:

This singing flame of a city, this all America, this poet in chaps and buck-skin, this rude, raw Titan, this Burns of a city! By its shimmering lake it lay, a king of shreds and patches, a maundering yokel with an epic in its mouth, a tramp, a hobo among cities, with the grip of Caesar in its mind, the dramatic force of Euripides in its soul. . . .

From New York, Vermont, New Hampshire, Maine had come a strange company, earnest, patient, determined, unschooled in even the primer of refinement, hungry for something the significance of which, when they had it, they could not even guess, anxious to be called great, determined so to be without ever knowing how. Here came the dreamy gentleman of the South, robbed of his patrimony; the hopeful student of Yale and Harvard and Princeton; the enfranchised miner of California and the Rockies, his bags of gold and silver in his hands.

For Florence Kelley, Jane Addams, Henry Demarest Lloyd—all of whom came from elsewhere—and the others, some who passed through, some who came and stayed for years, as Florence Kelley did, Hull-House was home and the headquarters for plans: plans to clean up and close the sweatshops, plans to outwit and throw out the corrupt politicians, plans to put the illiterate children in school, to get the poor women into jobs where they weren't chained sixteen hours a day to a sewing machine, schemes to improve life for the starving families in the neighborhood. Hull-House was embedded in its neighborhood, one of the worst slums in America, the Nineteenth Ward, when Florence Kelley arrived in 1891. God pitched his tent in the place of excrement.

February 15, 1995: It is cold, a cold which is more settled in than we are. We are still surrounded by boxes, large boxes, small boxes, drop cloths, boards, grates for heaters. The heating system is entombed in the basement and has many imposing large, separate parts, none of them quiet, most of them metal. I have hired two people: a woman to work in the house, an elegant young Polish artist who has just returned to Chicago, and an older woman, a designer, also very elegant, who has lived here her whole life. Both will, I hope, put some light, and some life, into these spaces.

The rooms are empty, rectilinear without purpose or identity, except when they are full of cheerful, busy painters and wallpaper hangers, carpenters, and other banging and clattering handy people, who do things. The thick walls are papered with the lives of former occupants. I will never be at home here, but my husband loves the house, even in its awkward, unfinished state, loves his job, and he has thrown himself and me into the new world. The children promise to visit.

Many people are telling me earnestly about how things are to be done here and what is expected of me. At the law school there are other expectations. They don't smile at me often at the law school, although I always make a point of smiling and saying hello, even when I can't remember anyone's name.

The Hull-House people, mostly women, but some men, were conspirators in their efforts to make life better for their neighborhood and their city. They were determined to make Chicago live up to its promises, to push the City Council to live up to the legal requirement for universal education enacted in 1867, a requirement to teach literacy in English and create schools for the cascades of immigrants in the 1880s and 1890s from Russia, Sweden, Italy, Ireland, and Bohemia who were Hull-House's neighbors.

The Hull-House community was made up of lawyers, writers, advocates—some had grand theories about society and what was right and wrong for the polity, and some of them had no particular ideology. They just wanted to do the work. What they had in common was that they were people who did things. They spent less time talking about what to do than they did doing it. And there was lots to do: people—millions of them— had poured into Chicago in the 1880s, looking for work, looking to escape where they were before, looking for and finding a new life. And they needed help from the people who were already there.

June 9, 1995: The failure of the imagination. The person who imagines, really does imagine, herself in the future, in this or that context, and then because it is imagined, thinks that the thing is done, when it is not and cannot be.

Improvement was clean water, fresh air, uncontaminated food, sanitation and sewers, protection from smallpox, the garbage being picked up, and the opportunity to learn to read and do sums. This was not radical, this was not revolutionary, it was not anarchist or communist or socialist, it was just what needed to be done. And always there was the question of education.

March 1995: One thing is clear: nothing is happening in Illinois with regard to capital punishment. In Illinois there are no ongoing, systemwide challenges to the death penalty, and there are no institutions strong enough to stand up to a system of elected state judges, elected county prosecutors and a system of capital punishment which has been firmly and enthusiastically entrenched since statehood and before. Nor am I a member of the Bar of Illinois. I am grateful to be out of the fray, just to teach.

Accomplishing these improvements in the lives of others was done through the law, through the institutions of the law, by enforcing existing laws, by persuading the state legislature and the City Council to enact new laws and regulations, by writing reports and taking testimony, by bringing the facts to the attention of lawmakers and courts, by telling policymakers about how bad it was, and then by trying to carry out the mandates of the law. And by getting new laws. The fact that the method of improving society was through the laws does not mean that there weren't already lots of lawyers, courts, and laws in Chicago. When Florence Kelley arrived, there was already plenty of law, well-established legal institutions, and every kind of lawyer in Chicago.

Here is how one observer, Dreiser, in *The Titan* again, described the politically powerful lawyer in 1890s Chicago:

> *The old soldier, over fifty, had been a general of division during the Civil War, and had got his real start in life by filing false titles to property in southern Illinois, and then bringing suits to substantiate his fraudulent claims before friendly associates. He was now a prosperous go-between, requiring heavy retainers, and yet not over-prosperous. There was only one kind of business that came to the General—this kind; and one instinctively compared him to that decoy sheep at the stock-yards that had been trained to go forth into nervous, frightened flocks of its fellow-sheep, balking at being driven into the slaughtering-pens, and lead them peacefully into the shambles, knowing enough always to make his own way quietly to the rear during the onward progress and thus escape. A dusty old lawyer, this, with Heaven knows what welter of altered wills, broken promises, suborned juries, influenced judges, bribed councilmen and legislators, double-intentioned agreements and contracts, and a whole world of shifty legal calculations and false pretenses floating around in his brain. Among the politicians, judges, and lawyers generally, by reason of past useful services, he was supposed to have some powerful connections. He liked to be called into any case largely because it meant something to do and kept him from being bored.*

The momentum for these reform efforts coming out of Hull-House was national and within the state, yet individuals—Florence Kelley, William Stead, John Peter Altgeld, Jane Addams and Henry Demarest Lloyd—were more than incidental. Their adversaries were not pushovers: Marshall Field, George Pullman, Levy Mayer, Philip Armour, and the business leaders who lunched regularly at the Millionaires Table at the Chicago Club. The Hull-House advocates were mostly women, but not only women; they were true advocates, although few were lawyers. Elections were important to their work, yet these women didn't even have the vote.

Jane Addams and Ellen Starr had deliberately founded Hull-House as a settlement in the middle of one of the worst slums in America, next door to the most crowded, filthy sweatshops and the most desperate tenements. As reformers, their inspiration came from their families, the people they grew up with, their education, and from institutions such as Toynbee Hall in London, which set out to apply principles of Christian socialism to the needs of the London poor, in order to train men for service in the ministry. Toynbee Hall still exists and probably still claims that mission. Hull-House itself still exists as a museum and a center for advocacy. Jane Addams and Ellen Starr had as their goal to start a movement of social service, without the component of religion. And they did just that.

January 26, 1995: My professional office is on the second floor of the old law school building Levy Mayer Hall—which I first found with difficulty, and only getting into the electronically guarded parking lot with the help of an ambling, round Northwestern police officer. My office overlooks Chicago Avenue and is annexed to the newer law school building with the library.

When Florence Kelley came to Chicago in 1891, she was a writer, an accomplished public speaker, an advocate, and an educated person. Her father, William Darrah Kelley, a self-made man whose father had died when he was two years old, had been a member of the US Congress for thirty-five years, as well as a judge and a state's attorney in Philadelphia. He was himself a powerful writer, a voracious reader, and until his death passionately involved in what they didn't then call "reform politics." Most years of his thirty-five years in Congress William Darrah Kelley introduced a bill for women's suffrage. Each time the bill did not pass.

As his second wife, he married a woman from a prominent family of Quakers, long-standing, active, vociferous abolitionists and advocates for women's suffrage. Their advocacy was often carried on at great personal risk of bodily harm. Florence Kelley's father taught her to read with school primers illustrated with black-and-white drawings of piteous slaves. Before university, Florence Kelley taught herself what others thought by reading all the books on the high shelves of her father's large private library, reading through all of the shelves from top to bottom, beginning in the far right corner. As she also recalled in her *Autobiography*:

> *Father built in 1850 a house in an ample square in West Philadelphia, four miles as the crow flies from Independence Hall, near what became, long after, Fairmount Park West. In that home I was born in September, 1859. It is now a hospital for women and children at Forty-first and Parrish streets. . . .*

> *Because I never went regularly to school, and encouraged by his interest I began then, at the age of ten years and wholly without guidance, to read Father's library through.*

April 24, 1995: At last the spring, and at last my first semester of teaching at the law school is coming to a close. The sun is even shining occasionally. I have given up on trying to remember everyone's name. They will just have to think that I am dull. They know my name, and for some reason the university event planners always include my unmarried name on name tags and in announcements.

I distance myself from all the squabbling at the law school, purposely, and because I am too,

too scheduled. Most days I drive home and we go out immediately, sometimes driving right back downtown again.

Congressman William Darrah Kelley was called "Pig Iron Kelley" because of his fierce protectionist position on behalf of the steel industry in his home state of Pennsylvania. Florence Kelley's father took her as a child at two in the morning to watch the Bessemer steel processing plant, and then in the middle of the night to see the Pennsylvania glass works in operation. Industry was a wonder. He took her to see the stunted boys, covered in dust, boys no bigger than she was then, running to and from the great red maw of the glass furnace, carrying shining globs of molten glass over hot floors sprinkled with shining spilled glass, carrying tin dippers with water to the sweating glass blowers, the men sweltering in the stare of the furnace, the ashen boys trotting with the fiery molten glass on a stick held forward, like the lance of a medieval knight. Little figures moving swiftly in the shadows, carrying trays of hot glass, cutting their bare feet on the spilled bits of hot liquid glass, quickly turning to shards on the floor, the boys scarred by molten glass dripping on their arms and legs.

January 30, 1995: In my new office downtown, there are medallions, crests embedded in the white plaster walls. There are ghosts here. There is a dirty closet with an old sink. Alumni come by and tell me they remembered a former dean as having this office. Levy Mayer Hall has, since the 1926 inauguration of the Chicago campus of Northwestern University, been the home of the School of Law. The building is old-style academic, dark paneling, oil portraits of famous male legal luminaries. The mood of the portraits: scholarly, pensive, serious.

One floor down, in the chilly stone entry hall, hangs a large portrait of Levy Mayer himself, in a dark suit, his arm on a book, a law book presumably, a distinguished, authoritative figure, the personification of the social stature conferred by the building's name and our law school. Levy Mayer looks out from a dark and somber background. The painting has the patina of an old master. On the facing wall is a smaller portrait of an unprepossessing woman in an unbecoming light dress, Levy Mayer's wife, Rachel Meyer Mayer.

William Darrah Kelley was a formidable prose stylist himself, largely self-taught. Florence Kelley's father, her mother, her aunts, and their community of like-minded people in Philadelphia were the education which lasted a lifetime. Florence Kelley did attend Cornell University for formal training, matriculating in letters and sciences and graduating after an interruption caused by illnesses, among one of the first classes of women in 1882. But her real education, the education which lasted a lifetime, she got at home.

March 21, 2008: The second day of spring. The branches of the fir tree shake. I am in the middle of a cloud in my third-floor studio in the house, my haven.

When Florence Kelley arrived in Chicago, she had been a graduate student in economics, law and political theory at the University of Zurich for two years, after trying unsuccessfully to enter a postgraduate program at the University of Pennsylvania and Oxford University. The University of Zurich was an educational institution of high intellectual seriousness, in the German tradition. Florence Kelley ended up in Zurich after graduating with honors from Cornell, not by design, but after she was hastily conscripted by her family and the doctor to accompany her brother on a convalescent trip to Europe.

February 10, 1995: Then there is the house, which is supposed to be our home, built for a rich business family in 1918. The house is in Evanston, a desultory suburb fifteen miles north of downtown Chicago. This heavy house will never feel like home. Our meager furniture and inherited art disappear into its corners.

Only the master bedroom with its graceful windows opening onto the street and garden is now recognizable as a place where people might actually live. Our heavy, inherited, dark family furniture leans securely against the thick walls and fits right in to the somber environment, as do our threadbare oriental rugs. This is the only room I am glad to return to. Our bedroom furniture is from the same period as the house. The ornate smoky mirror is firmly screwed into the wall, nailed in like a battlement, so that we can look at ourselves in the morning in the same mirror we have seen ourselves in for more than twenty years after the family got rid of it, the mirror others saw themselves in for decades before us.

Somehow this house has to be ready for the officials of the university to come to a reception in the spring. The garden is dormant. Our bedroom window is above a frozen, hazardous porch leading to a heavy, ornamented wooden front door, the door in a castle wall.

Florence Kelley's older brother, William Darrah Kelley Jr., who later was to play several roles in her life—head of the family after the death of the father, personal advisor, the lawyer who managed the family affairs, counselor, partner in the care of their aging mother, the same brother who traveled to Chicago to testify on her behalf at the 1892 legal proceeding later in Chicago—was the brother whom she accompanied after her graduation from Cornell, to France and the Riviera. He was ordered to take a sea voyage to rest and recuperate after becoming suddenly afflicted in Philadelphia with periodic bouts of complete blindness. The fact that people's lives were suddenly, and often catastrophically, interrupted by unexplained illness is characteristic of the period.

Their father, the congressman, arranged for the secretary of state of the United States to provide a letter of introduction to the French minister of instruction—which is what that post was called then—for the two young people traveling abroad, the recent college graduate and her older brother with the mysterious ailment, but the trip in that winter of 1883 was not one of glamorous socializing in European capitals.

Brother and sister left Philadelphia abruptly by boat immediately after Thanksgiving in 1882, their destination the French Riviera via Liverpool and Paris. Much of the long, dreary European winter was spent in depressing Avignon, where there was no doctor in the town and William Jr.'s illness required twenty-four-hour care, with his sister hand-feeding him all of his meals, dressing him, and even sleeping in his room at night. This was a cheerless, friendless winter in Avignon where the mistral settled in for the duration, and the locals claimed they could not understand Mademoiselle's elegant and fluent French.

April 29, 2013, Chicago Tribune: "Fatal Building Collapse in Bangladesh Brings Arrests: Owner of Structure Where Hundreds Died Caught Near Border."

NEW DELHI—The owner of a collapsed building in Bangladesh was arrested Sunday near the border with India as the death toll rose to at least 370 in the nation's worst garment industry disaster. Fire broke out in the ruins of the building, further dimming hope for more than 800 missing people.

Mohammed Sohel Rana, landlord of the pancaked Rana Plaza, was trying to flee the country when he was detained in the border town of Berapole, police said. Rana is reportedly an official with the ruling party.

The one bright spot for Florence Kelley during that claustrophobic winter in Avignon was a visit from her old Cornell friend, M. Carey Thomas, who had just earned a PhD from the University of Zurich, the only university in Europe to grant graduate academic degrees to women. This was around the time when President Charles William Eliot of Harvard was boasting of successfully resisting for another year the pressure for the admission of women to Harvard. Later presidents of Harvard and other elite Eastern institutions in the United States were to continue to resist successfully the admission of women well into the next century. The flagship state universities in the West and Midwest admitted women earlier, or had never excluded them. In the western United States and Midwest the tradition of excluding women, long established in the Eastern universities and their preparatory schools, with the older British universities as their models, never took hold. Cornell was the Eastern exception in admitting women along with men to pursue any field of study almost from the outset, and to have all women in classes with men.

February 15, 1995: At the Northwestern School of Law there are some two hundred first-year students, pretty much an equal number of men and women. As law students they follow a prescribed course of study—taking first-year courses in criminal law, property, contracts, torts and civil procedure—and engage in a process of professional certification recognizable across the rest of the country, a process governed by the Bar of the state.

When I was a law student in the 1970s I was surprised to find my law school, Rutgers-Newark School of Law, had more women in the entering class than any other law school in the country. Having spent too many of the previous few years in Africa, I was oblivious to the fact that every middle-class married or divorced or unemployed woman who looked around her and wanted more had decided to go to law school.

I am admitted to the bar in four states; I don't need to bother with getting admitted to the Bar in Illinois. I will never practice here.

William Jr.'s illness that winter in Avignon in 1883 was referred to as temporary blindness, but Dr. M. Carey Thomas, in a letter to a friend, described William Jr. as "a cad and dissolute," someone who had been shot at by a laboring man in a streetcar in Philadelphia. Perhaps William Jr.'s illness was a form of hysterical blindness, or the result of venereal disease or alcohol poisoning, but whatever the hypothetical diagnosis a century after the fact, William Jr. eventually fully recovered, became fully reconciled with his sister after the bitter family disputes over money following the congressman's death, and lived what appeared to be a mostly happy, ordinary and uneventful family life as a lawyer working in the insurance business. William Darrah Kelley Jr.'s letters are businesslike, warm, competent, rather lackluster; however, that must not have been his personality, from the scraps of his life we know from other episodes.

It was nine years after Avignon when William Darrah Kelley Jr. came to Chicago to testify on behalf of his sister in the child custody matter. He was then the oldest son, but not the executor, of the estate of William Darrah Kelley, the congressman, and consequently had something to say about what monies had recently been advanced to the Wischnewetzky household in New York at 110 East 76th Street. Money—this family was not a family where people primarily cared about or talked about money—would be an irritant and a preoccupation for Florence Kelley, in her work and throughout her marriage and her life. As is too often the case in families, money was later the occasion for bitter dissension. It is as if it is the one tangible, measurable, concrete thing, seeming to be serious and important enough, which people can get a hold of and fight about in their frustration and grief.

March 15, 1995: Levy Mayer Hall itself covers an entire block from Chicago Avenue to Superior Street. My office has a cheesy plasterboard lowered false ceiling to conserve the heat, and has recently been painted. I smell paint both at home and at the office. A set of cheap industrial grey metal bookcases has been installed for me, and is insufficient.

The stone entryway to the law school building is imposing, as is the deep wood paneling and the hand-painted ceiling in the lobby of Levy Mayer, one floor down. The paint is peeling on the ornamented ceiling. The entrance hall looks out on a small courtyard covered with snow. The faculty offices, with heavy wooden doors mostly shut, including my own, are scattered throughout the old and new buildings, attached by a large, light-filled atrium. The new building houses the law library with its magnificent view of the lake.

When my new world is most confusing, or exhausting, I retreat to the third floor of this law library, sit behind a shelf of books, and look at the sky and the lake, where the wind, water and ice fight for control of the shore, as cars creep along the highway at its edge.

M. Carey Thomas, this same old friend from Cornell, described the young people's circumstances in Avignon as "abject in the extreme." No one spoke English, and the French would have nothing to do with the two young people. They assumed Florence Kelley was her brother's mistress, since sisters and brothers of that age would never have traveled alone together in France or have been living together under similar circumstances. And she was sleeping in his room. The good news that M. Carey Thomas brought to the ailing brother and his depressed caretaker was that there was a university in Europe which accepted women for graduate study.

Florence Kelley's inquiry about pursuing graduate education at Oxford University had been politely rebuffed: "little offered there for an American woman student," she was told. At the University of Pennsylvania her inquiry about graduate study had been turned down flat, and rudely, by a trustee, an old friend of the family, who wrote to William Darrah Kelley that he hoped he would "never see the day when women students would be in the same classroom with men at the University of Pennsylvania." Women had been receiving medical degrees from the women's medical college in Pennsylvania at least since the 1860s, but the classes and colleges were separate. Cornell was unique among Eastern establishment institutions. Northwestern University had founded a medical school for women in 1870, but it was closed in 1902.

In spite of views such as those expressed by its then trustee, the University of Pennsylvania graduate school did begin admitting women in 1885, three years after Florence Kelley's inquiry, and by 1889 ten American universities were granting doctorates to women, including Northwestern, which later, and surprisingly, was to become the only educational institution to grant Florence Kelley a graduate degree.

January 30, 1995: My first course at the School of Law is titled: "Persuasion—The Art of Writing, In, For and About the Law." We read documents of the law together, and of course they must write legal research papers. The course is designed around the reading of what I have called "real books," books by people who are not lawyers, that is, books which place the reader in a completely foreign world, where the rules of society have been taken for granted at this time and place, and then are not in place, for external reasons, such as civil destruction and disorder of war. I have a favorite corner now on the third floor of the law school library. It is quiet. The shelves are filled with state reports and bound copies of the law journals. I look out at the ice, and dream.

The University of Zurich was unique in Europe in the 1880s and a godsend for Florence Kelley, as was the visit of her old friend. M. Carey Thomas had just received a PhD in philosophy summa cum laude from the University of Zurich. She described the requirements for the degree as "savage," but noted that if others had done them, she was determined to do so.

In Zurich, in addition to writing a publishable dissertation in German on *Sir Gawayne and the Green Knight* and a qualifying paper in German on the poet Swinburne, for her doctorate M. Carey Thomas had to pass a three-day written examination in her designated field, German philology, and take a three-hour oral examination in German before the entire assembled faculty of the University of Zurich, whose vote that she had passed all the examinations was required to be unanimous.

February 1, 1995: From underneath a wrinkled, filthy carpet on the third floor of the house in Evanston, a dirty maple floor has been uncovered, once a dance floor apparently with narrow blond slats. Most of these grand houses built at the turn of the twentieth century had what they called a "ball room." We will see what the floor looks like sanded and polished. The third-floor room is cavernous, with old-fashioned dormer windows and a smell of mold, but the leaded windows open onto the back garden and the front walk. I like that the space has been lying unused, fallow.

Earlier M. Carey Thomas had sought to obtain a graduate degree first from the University of Leipzig and then from the University of Gottingen, then and long after considered the most prestigious of German universities. In answer to her application for a graduate degree after she had amply demonstrated that she was academically qualified to do the work, Gottingen told M. Cary Thomas that the university would give no degree to a woman, although she had passed courses there and written acceptable papers for her professors. M. Carey Thomas was later to become a founding dean and then president of Bryn Mawr College and a longtime national leader in American higher education, especially the education of women.

M. Carey Thomas described William Darrah Kelley Jr. as a "pill" after her visit in Avignon, and said that she thought his condition, the periodic blindness, was caused by "dissipation," which may have meant sex, venereal disease, alcohol, or drugs.

November 6, 2008: Rain, and cold, miserable weather. But the jubilation is not dampened—only exhausted, only incredulous.

In *Twenty Years at Hull-House* Jane Addams continued the description of the beginning of the settlement:

> *The fine old house responded kindly to repairs, its wide hall and open fireplaces always insuring it a gracious aspect. Its generous owner, Miss Helen Culver, in the following spring gave us a free leasehold of the entire house. Her kindness has continued through the years until the group of thirteen buildings, which at present comprises our equipment, is built largely upon land which Miss Culver has put at the service of the Settlement which bears Mr. Hull's name. In those days the house stood between an undertaking establishment and a saloon. . . .*
>
> *We furnished the house as we would have furnished it were it in another part of the city, with the photographs and other impedimenta we had collected in Europe, and with a few bits of family mahogany. While all the new furniture which was bought was enduring in quality, we were careful to keep it in character with the fine old residence. Probably no young matron ever placed her own things in her own house with more pleasure than that with which we first furnished Hull-House.*

After graduation from Cornell, Florence Kelley came home to Philadelphia and taught at the New Century Working Women's Guild. In the Philadelphia of the 1880s, young, undernourished girls aged fourteen to seventeen flocked to the Women's Guild for the newly offered classes, and because their numbers were unexpected, students overflowed to all available spaces. Classes were held on the stairways and in the halls. Mill hands and domestic servants sought to better themselves—always domestic service and unskilled labor are the first place for immigrants to find work. Dressmakers and shop girls came to the guild, eager to increase their wages of a dollar and a half a week by learning simple arithmetic and becoming literate. Then they wanted to learn French as an accomplishment, to better themselves. This teaching in Philadelphia was Florence Kelley's first extended contact with working women, she said later. The result was a published article titled: "Need Our Working Women Despair?"

In Chicago, the testimony from the working women and girls in the factory inspection cases in 1894 indicated that their principal concern was the same: how to increase their paltry wages, for that was all they had. Yet they, too, wanted to better themselves. Most believed that their employment in the factory or tenement sweatshop was temporary and that they would soon move to something better. Most supported family members.

March 16, 1995: My students are confident, expecting to earn over $100,000 when they graduate, most at private firms. The school is searching for a new dean, and there is much chatter. People are wary of me and leave me alone. I am purposefully staying out of it, holed up in the library with my course materials and papers, or trying to find what I will next be working on since my experience doing research on homicide and the death penalty and working with the Supreme Court of New Jersey seems to have little relevance here. There is still all of the rest of criminal law. This spring the point is to survive until graduation. Something promising is happening on the third floor of the old home. Between classes we go to look at drapery fabric, or lampshades. I am tearfully grateful to rely on the expertise of others and let them fuss about the cost.

Florence Kelley's university education had been interrupted by a misdiagnosed, nearly fatal illness, which delayed her graduation from Cornell but resulted in her taking time off to recover her health while doing research on child labor laws at the Library of Congress for her Cornell senior thesis and living with her father. The effects of this misdiagnosed illness, diphtheria, followed by its mistreatment—the application of brandy every two hours followed by the repeated administration of strychinia and other poisons—were long lasting. When she survived the illness, she had to recover from the well-meaning mistreatment, which almost killed her. Her brother William Jr. came to Ithaca to help her recover.

Florence Kelley graduated from Cornell in June 1882. The senior thesis was eventually published in August 1882 by the *International Review*, described as a highbrow New York periodical on public affairs.

In 1882 when she was teaching at the Women's Guild in Philadelphia, Florence Kelley's suggestions for improving the conditions of the working women who were her pupils included: self-help, regular exercise, suitable work clothing (no corsets), and the establishment of associations to provide legal protection to working women, noting that "the facts of... human relations must be studied as they exist, with patient care; but exact tabulation of facts is the beginning only; afterwards comes the work of interpretation."

She had just outlined her life's work.

May 6, 1995: The weather perfect, ideal. Yesterday was the official inauguration, although sometimes it feels as if we have been here for years. Finally the carpenters are gone, the painters are gone, the boxes are gone, and the house is supposedly finished. The trustees will come to a reception at the house for the first time at graduation in June.

The question of what to wear has been settled by going to New York for clothes and paying too much money for acceptable outfits which I would never wear, were I not unexpectedly in this position. Now when I dress for official events I feel as if I am becoming another person, which I am. The women who are part of this community have been wonderfully under-standing, and if they have opinions, which I am sure they do, about the way I dress, or my appearance, or what I do, or say, they say nothing to me, which I appreciate.

After graduation from Cornell, leaving her teaching job in Philadelphia, and then being unsuccessful at attempts to continue her graduate education there, it was a long, lonely winter in Europe and Avignon with William Jr. requiring all her attention, and for Florence Kelley no prospects for employment or further education. No one to talk to in Avignon until M. Carey Thomas came and offered a first-person example of the possibility of a woman earning an advanced degree at the University of Zurich. Even the irrepressible Florence Kelley called this time in Avignon a lonely sojourn.

April 20, 1995: The search for a new dean reveals much division among the faculty.

My course this spring has been modeled upon my courses at Princeton and elsewhere, being a course on reading and writing. For the past twenty years at various universities I have taught advanced legal research and writing, the teaching interspersed with my own research and writing.

There is little interest here in my former New Jersey research or in the work I did in Africa. The faculty is preoccupied by the politicized battle for the deanship. I will never be accepted here by the faculty as a colleague, as an equal. I get along fine with the students.

Mostly I steer my way downtown, distracted, on slippery roads through the snow and ice and come to rest in the cold stone quiet of my office. Then I seek a table and my view of the always-changing lake on the third floor of the law library. I look out the window and wonder what my life is going to be here. First lady is a term I dislike intensely.

By the time Florence Kelley arrived in Chicago, at the age of thirty-two in 1891, she was an accomplished public speaker, fundraiser, political organizer, and writer, was fluent in five languages, was known as a translator of the prominent European socialist Frederick Engels, and was well-traveled, observant and sophisticated about people, society and the law. She had long honed her intellectual skills.

May 17, 1995, Chicago Tribune: "Edgar Rejects Clemency Plea: Governor Won't Stop Execution for 'Heinous Crimes.'"

... Edgar received nearly 1,200 e-mail letters requesting clemency for Davis since the convict established an Internet forum late last month. But in denying Davis' request for clemency late Tuesday afternoon, Edgar said: "These were heinous crimes and brutal murders. I'm convinced he is responsible for that which

he received the death penalty and at least three other murders
for which he was convicted."

These paths to Chicago in the 1890s were long, varied, sometimes tortuous, often characterized by chance encounters, and luck for the survivors. Abraham Bisno, who made his way from Russia to Chicago and later worked with Florence Kelley in Illinois, recalled in his memoir:

The family fortunes in those years—I must have been then about twelve or twelve and a half—were very low indeed. There was very little work for Father to do; we had very little merchandise in the store to sell, and what little we had our neighbors, the peasants, seemed to have no use for.

There were additional misfortunes befalling our family. The wife of my older brother, who had been married only a year and a half or so, had a baby. They lived with us. My brother was recruited in the army and ran away, was caught, and there was a serious threat that he would go to the punitive regiment, where he was almost sure to be killed because of the very severe treatment by way of incarceration and physical punishment that the soldiers were subjected to in that regiment. In order to save Brother from what my poor father and mother considered almost a death sentence, it was necessary to have a couple of hundred rubles to bribe the authorities and get him out, as they called it. . . .

I had a cousin in Fastov, a ladies' tailor, and it was to that cousin I made up my mind to go. He may be able to employ me, and if not, he'll probably find something for me. I had no money for railroad fare; shoes were torn, practically no laundry and no clothes other than those on my back. But I thought, I'll go anyway; I was told that a kid like myself could hide under the benches in Pullman cars, [that] normally the people in the railway car would sympathize with a kid and would cover him up with some clothes or put bags around him so that they would hide him from the conductor, which was true. The people in the car, mostly Jews, going to Kiev, which lay along the same route, beyond Fastov, did advise me to get under a bench and put a lot of handbags and stuff all around me so that I thought I was safe. One of the passengers was a Gentile who evidently thought that I ought to pay my fare and he informed the conductor that I was hiding under the bench. The conductor pulled me out, asked me whether I had any money, and when I told him I didn't, he wouldn't believe me, searched me carefully, both through my pockets and on the body, and when he found that I had no money he promised to have me locked up in Fastov but evidently didn't want to bother with me, for when we came to Fastov, he gave me a kick and threw me off.

May 17, 1995, Chicago Tribune: "Edgar Rejects Clemency Plea; Appeals Denied; Davis Executed by Lethal Injection."

... "We did our best to get the facts out," Davis, who continued to maintain he was victimized by police, said in a call to his lawyer about an hour before his execution. "The Lord must have meant for me to come home."

October 26, 2009: A fall day. In the morning, lying in bed at six in the morning with the sun streaming into the apartment, improbably we seem to be settled now in downtown Chicago.

The narrative of Abraham Bisno's journey to Chicago continues:

Kiev, the capital of the province, was my next destination, a city of some 200,000 population, but Kiev was a city where Jews were not allowed, especially a Jew that had no passport. But I took a chance. Nothing was worse than to go back home, so I came to Kiev in the same way as I did to Fastov, under a bench, covered up by the passengers, with their clothes and handbags and what not. There were two cousins living in Kiev, both of whom I had never seen. Neither of them knew of my existence; both of them sympathized with me but could give me very little help, since under the law it wasn't legal for a family to furnish shelter to anybody illegally residing in Kiev.

Under the laws of Russia, no man could leave his birthplace without taking with him a birth certificate which served as a passport in travel. So, when I finally came to Kiev it was necessary for me to first register myself by showing my passport. I had no passport. Government documents could only be secured by paying for them, and one had to spend much time in getting them. Since I had no money, I could not make application for a certificate, and so took no passport along on leaving home. All my relatives could not very well shelter me without endangering their freedom and right to live in Kiev at all. There was one way out of my difficulty. One might bribe the local officials, but that sort of bribery required more money than I could raise. I was, in fact, penniless, and so found myself in a big city among strangers.

March 22, 1995, Chicago Tribune: "17 Years After Crimes, 2 Killers Die an Hour Apart."

Nearly 17 years ago, James Free and Hernando Williams committed brutal sex-related murders little more than a month apart. Early Wednesday they were strapped to hospital gurneys, wheeled into a small room at Stateville Correctional Center and executed by lethal injection, little more than an hour apart. The executions

31

marked the first time since 1952 that Illinois has put two convicts to death on the same day, and increased to four the number of inmates executed in the state since the death penalty was reinstituted in 1977.

June 30, 1995: At last the academic year is over. The summer should be glorious. We will go to Montana for a respite.

Abraham Bisno continues:

My first night in Kiev was spent at my cousin's blacksmith shop without his knowledge of my being there. His shop was simply a shed outside in a yard; while some of the tools were locked away, the shed itself had even no door, and its boards were mostly rotted away, or knocked out of the walls. I came in late at night, after walking through the city for a long time, and fell asleep in a corner there. Even before lodging there, I looked a sight, and the dirt and soot there finished my unrespectable appearance. So, dirty, unwashed, I went out to look for a job in the morning. I was then little over twelve, dressed very raggedly and of an extreme thinness, encrusted with dirt, and haunted by fear of any passers-by, especially of policemen who might ask me for my passport. It was, therefore, not surprising that most tailor shops turned me down, but after a long day's search I was finally hired.

I was told by this particular tailor that I wasn't greatly needed, but he had five small children, his wife was kept busy with a stand on the market-place selling cooked beans, and the children had to be taken care of in her absence. He thought I might make a nurse to these children and also carry the pails of beans to and from the market-place. . . . However, on inquiry, he discovered I had no passport and promptly said he could not keep me at all without it.

For two weeks, I stayed, jobless, in Kiev. I slept wherever I could. Sometimes a poor tailor would let me sleep in his shop; sometimes I would wander around all night and sleep during the day at my cousin's; sometimes I had to beg for food where I looked for work. By that time I was covered with vermin, completely exhausted, and in despair left Kiev to Wasilkow in order to visit an uncle of mine, my mother's brother, who was fairly well-to-do, in the hope that he might place me somewhere.

My uncle received me very generously; made me some clothes, cleaned me up, and kept me there for two weeks—but no tailor could be found who wanted an apprentice and I had to go home to Belayacerkow. At home, conditions were somewhat bettered. Father had gotten work, and took me as a helper. Not long afterwards, things again became very difficult for us. Both myself and Father could only get partial employment and did not earn enough to live on. We then planned that the whole family go to Kiev, which we did.

April 1996: Coming from Carmel, California, to be an undergraduate at Cornell University in the middle of the 1950s, I was startled to discover that whether or not you were Jewish was the first thing many wanted to know about you. The sororities and fraternities were openly identified as Jewish and Christian. Several of my friends told me I was the first Christian they had known.

Cornell kept out Jews less than the other Ivy League schools then, but it did discriminate. A distinguished professor of English—himself a Jew—told me the college "had to" discriminate against Jews or else the entire entering class would be made up of those smart Jewish girls from New York! Nor did he seem to think there was anything wrong with this.

At Cornell then there was an openly admitted quota on the number of women admitted to the College of Arts and Sciences, no more than 25 percent. In other words if they had admitted students strictly on academic merit—as they purported to do—they would have had many more women and many more Jews and many more Jewish girls from New York (and presumably elsewhere). At Harvard and Princeton, no women at all were admitted, and there were almost no Jews.

Abraham Bisno continues:

In Kiev, Father did find work for my brother, himself, and myself, but after living in Kiev for half a year, there was a pogrom, or riot against the Jews by the Gentiles [in the spring of 1881]. Times were then very bad. The poor population was suffering great hardship and there were a great many unemployed. Wages were very low; even when there was employment they were very low. Unrest and dissatisfaction were general, and in order to allay this unrest, the Gentile government found it politic to blame the Jews for the general poverty—the Jews were heathens and Christ-killers, they cried—Russia was a holy land, Kiev was a holy city, the Jews contaminated the country, contaminated the city. "Drive them out," these priests cried, "get rid of them."

While the wealthier Gentiles did not want to do this themselves, the more ignorant and poor were only too ready to riot against the Jews. Bands of Russians assaulted the Jewish quarters, broke out doors and windows, destroyed all the furnishings, and stole whatever could be of any use to them. Not all the Russians participated in these pogroms. Some even sympathized with the Jews and sheltered and fed them—but comparatively, these were only a few. In those days it was not safe for a Gentile family to so befriend a Jew, accursed as they were. There were cases where Gentile homes were fired because the owners had sheltered Jews.

Those who participated in the pogroms were mostly drunk, since the first buildings to be wrecked were saloons owned by Jews. The vodka found there was speedily consumed, so that before the pogrom was a day old, most of the rioters were drunk, and completely unresponsible for their conduct. A number of Jews were killed, there were innumerable cases of rape, property was either stolen or destroyed, and the Jewish population was completely terrorized. The building we lived in and the place we worked in were assaulted at the same time. Mother ran for her life while we struggled for ours; we were all separated by the mob—the shop was destroyed, the goods carried away, and we all looked to find shelter with a Gentile family.

January 12, 2012: A Chicago blizzard, but not as fierce as was predicted. Only four inches. The snow is blowing sideways against my window. First in one direction off the lake, then the other. Hundreds of flights canceled, and people ordered to stay off the streets and highways. The airports are campgrounds.

The chronicle of the path to Chicago from Russia continues and was replicated by thousands of others:

I hid myself in a clay hole in an old brickyard on a hillside. Below, in the valley, was a large Jewish population. On the hill lived those whom we had lived among, and while in the clay hole, I witnessed the mob coming down the hill to assault the Jewish settlement. I saw children and old people beaten—buildings burned—I heard women screaming—it was an experience that one never can forget. After [I had been] four hours in that clay hole, the mob returned up the hill. One of the drunkards pulled me out of my hole. I pleaded for life and was finally thrown to the ground and released. My impression is that I ran continuously for at least five hours on the highway until exhaustion. I stopped at the house of a peasant Gentile family along the road. The women in the house had heard of the pogrom, took pity on me, gave me cabbage soup and bread, and put me to sleep in the attic.

June 20, 1995: I am getting used to people mispronouncing my married name, misspelling that name, the way they never did with my Scots maiden name and middle name. The name I miss the most is my old middle name, my father's mother's maiden name. I considered using that as a pseudonym, but eventually decided against it.

I am now used to being taken for Jewish. My father, a Scots Canadian, with black hair and dark eyes, used to comment that so many Jews had changed their names to Scottish names in the 1930s and 1940s, including many academics and economists, that he was usually taken for Jewish, to his annoyance. Now, I have made the transition the other way, from being a WASP to consistently being mistaken for being a Jew, because I go by my husband's Jewish name.

In the late 1950s, I remember the wife of a Princeton academic saying that people assumed she and her husband were Jewish, because he was an economist with a German surname. And, she said, she had to explain to hotel clerks and restaurant managers that they were not Jewish, thus a reservation could be taken. Sorting though my stepmother's papers, I found a small proper note on high-grade stationery, a bill for the golf club they belonged to—on university-owned property—on which the words had been carefully typed on the bottom: "No Jews admitted." And so it went on, decade after decade, century after century, with the groups changing, the continuing urge to discriminate, deny, keep out, step on another, crush a fellow human being, tolerated by the law, allowed by law.

The consequences of who is who, and how people identify themselves—by religion, race, class, neighborhood, name—never go away. When the mass immigration of Russians and Europeans to Chicago took place, people were fleeing. The brutality was escalating.

The narrative of Abraham Bisno's journey to Chicago continues:

The old peasant was very religious, and considered it a great sin to do violence to the Jews, and said he would stay up all night to watch so that no rioters could snatch me away. Over and over again, during the night, I heard people pass asking in loud voices whether Jews did not live here. Always the old man, with a great many oaths, declared there were no Jews at his house. When they persisted, the peasant woman came to her husband's aid, crossing herself again and again, swearing there were no Jews at her home. At two in the morning, I heard someone climb the ladder to the attic, and was almost certain there was someone after me. Every sense and conception of pain and torture at the hands of drunken Gentiles formed in my mind until these climbers started to prowl around in the darkness and to talk among themselves. Then I knew they were Jews like myself.

These people had been permitted to come in by the Gentile peasant, also. After considerable consultation on the part of the family and myself, we all agreed that we Jews must leave before sunrise since we had already troubled the farmer enough, and it would be dangerous to leave in broad daylight. So in the early morning, before light, we went out. One of the men told us that the governor of the state had assigned a powder cellar on the church hill to the refugee Jews, and that if we circled around the town carefully avoiding the roads on which the peasants usually traveled, we might evade the drunken populace and safely get to this underground cellar. This family of Jews had little ones with them who could travel only slowly and I made up my mind to run ahead of them.

November 19, 2012: The lecture hall is crowded, full of anticipatory chatter. A writer, a very public Jew, is the honored lecturer. He reads, brilliantly. After the reading a woman stands to tell the story of her parents' survival from the camps. No one interrupts, although they didn't come to hear her, and her self-description is not relevant, or particularly interesting.

This child who escaped Russia became the man, Abraham Bisno, a union organizer for the garment trades in Chicago and New York. What he remembered about Florence Kelley, with whom he worked closely on the factory inspections, was that she always "treated me as an equal, although I was an immigrant Jew and she was a Yankee."

Actually, it wasn't quite right to call her a Yankee. Although the family were Easterners, Philadelphians, Christians, they were not of the powerful Eastern elite by inheritance or identification, and not wealthy although her father for a brief period was one of the richest men in Philadelphia. They were Quakers, her father not by birth, which meant they advocated for unpopular causes and mostly didn't care what other people thought of them. And they did not seek wealth or riches.

March 10, 1995: In one of the stranger coincidences since our arrival here, the former chairman of the board of the university is a friend and former colleague of an African American lawyer and fiction writer whom I haven't heard news of for more than thirty years. This is someone we were once close to, a friend of another friend, and after leaving Chicago we corresponded for several years, and then lost contact when we went to Africa. We have a small reunion, with this writer, as surprised as we are to meet again. His wife has since died. We all marvel at the coincidence of our being reunited after all of these years. He tells me is he sure I am the sister of a conservative politician with the same name, laughs when I deny the connection. Indeed this person and his politics would be an anathema to me.

William Darrah Kelley, Florence Kelley's father, born on North Second Street in Philadelphia on April 12, 1814, was a self-educated man. Like John Peter Altgeld and many others, he had been taken out of school and sent out to work as a child. His father, a well-established watchmaker and jeweler, dropped dead on the street after being forced into bankruptcy during an economic downturn, the coup de gras being a brother-in-law defaulting on a note which he had endorsed.

July 20, 1995, Bozeman, Montana: The sunshine is worshiped here. The current heat wave in Chicago has caused more than 60 deaths. Mostly the elderly, who could not get out of their old walk-up apartments, which were not air-conditioned.

William Darrah Kelley fathered eight children with his second wife, Caroline, known as Carrie to the family. Three, William Jr., Florence, and Albert, survived to adulthood. The congressman always said he remembered his mother being put out on the street with all of their belongings, three little girls, and himself. When everything was sold the family hid the father's tools, and later his son apprenticed in his father's trade as a jeweler and watchmaker, using those tools hidden from the creditors. He won a juried prize in Boston for the artistry of his designs in gold. His father would have been proud. William Darrah Kelley always said he remembered the trauma of being put on out the street, and he remembered hiding his father's tools. He was two. The trauma was often told as a repeated memory. As an adult Florence Kelley remembered those prized tools.

April 15, 1995: The stone stairs to the front door from the street, have been slippery all winter. The house still feels cavernous and empty, but now that our furniture is placed, and our oriental rugs on the floor, there is some color and beauty. It rains often, but the cold is gone. And new furniture has come to fill in the empty rooms.

The arrival of the mail is announced with footsteps on the front porch and the sound of the mailbox latch snapping closed. Letters and envelopes are placed into a wooden box set in stone directly to the left of the front door. Recently there have been threats from the Unabomber, who is rumored to be back in our town. Since the bomber's specialty is mail bombs, why are we still receiving unopened and unexamined packages? I wait for the mail every day. The security officers tell me to "examine all the packages carefully." This is not reassuring. This bomber killed a man with a mail bomb.

Many people are telling me what they expect and what I should expect. The house is to be a formal house, a place for visitors to the university, especially donors. Why do I need to be here, if I am just a prop, a door post?

I have no friends here. My family is far away. My children rarely visit. My professional associates and my writer friends are in New Jersey and New York. I live in a huge, pretentious house, and everyone assumes that I should be happy and grateful to be here. I seek out a former student, making her way in Chicago. My home is being lived in by strangers more than a thousand miles away.

William Darrah Kelley had a daughter by his first marriage—his first wife dying soon after the second child was born, their second child dying too. That half-sister sometimes lived at the gracious Philadelphia family home with the big library, The Elms, when Florence Kelley was a child, as did one of William Kelley's own sisters. When his father dropped dead, William Darrah Kelley's mother opened a boarding house with her three little girls and small son, and with the help of her husband's brother kept the family together.

The son, William Darrah Kelley, left school at eleven and went to work as soon as he was able, first for a dollar a week in a lottery office, then as an errand boy in a bookstore. Next the boy worked for an umbrella maker, and finally as a copy reader in a printing house, where in winter he read proof from six in the morning until eight at night, and in summer during all of the daylight hours, chewing green tea leaves to keep himself awake, a habit he later claimed resulted in a lifelong condition of nervous stomach and indisposition. He was to die of some sort of cancer which spread to the abdomen.

At thirteen William Darrah Kelley was apprenticed with his father's fine metal working tools to a large jewelry manufacturing firm in Philadelphia for seven years. There he not only could send his mother his monthly wage, but also established a Youth Library and began organizing workmen and promoting the recognition of the ten-hour system, ten hours a day being less than children and adults regularly worked then.

March 1, 1995: A large British bank, Baring Brothers, has collapsed after a trader in Singapore amassed $1.3 billion in losses. The bank had been around for more than two hundred years.

Lobbying for the ten-hour day was considered dangerously political, and eventually the success of William Darrah Kelley's political organizing shut him out of work in Philadelphia after an election where he actively and publicly supported the loser. He came out strongly against Andrew Jackson and the creation of the National Bank in the presidential election of 1832. So the young man left town, or was hounded out of town, and went to work for a large jewelry maker in Boston. There he was recognized for the artistic superiority of his designs.

December 28, 1995: It is cold, snowing, and the family has just left. A stately Christmas fir tree still stands in the corner of the bright sunroom, looking out on the garden. It is decorated with our old Chinese ornaments and paper chains made by our children in school. And football, the university is poised to go to the Rose Bowl. There is much excitement on campus. Of course Christmas made us homesick, but the campus was lovely in the snow. For the moment all is quiet elsewhere. To have everyone together for the holidays was unusual, wonderful.

In his spare time in Boston, after being run out of Philadelphia for his politics, William Darrah Kelley taught himself to write by reading everything he could, especially great literature and philosophy, and generally educating himself, since his formal schooling had ended when he was eleven. Soon he was giving political speeches in Boston, mostly to young working men like himself. Anyone could go to the public halls and talk about the world around him, and politics, or religion, or free love, or hypnotism, or the communication with the dead, or propose changing whatever was wrong with the world.

William Darrah Kelley soon made a friend of an important and rich man, the collector of the Port of Boston, who opened his extensive personal library to the young man. The great American free public library system did not yet exist. The New York Public Library wasn't founded until 1895. If universities had libraries, they were not extensive, except for a Harvard or a University of California. Nor would a free public library system be established anywhere else in the world.

In William Darrah Kelley's time, few had the advantage of an undergraduate college education or even an academic high school education. Only a few colleges and universities, and a few churches or individuals, had extensive library holdings. A private library was often the only access to education. To visit the Library of Congress, or a great university library, was a privilege. When he became a member of Congress and could afford it, William Darrah Kelley established his own extensive private library of literature, philosophy, science, and religion. And in Washington he had the use of the great Library of Congress. It was there that Florence Kelley came to do her first research on child labor laws, and found her calling.

May 31, 2013: The research assistants check the quotes on Google Books, or on ProQuest, on some website where someone has posted an article, or a book, perhaps without permission.

Like many others then prominent in public life, William Darrah Kelley took responsibility for his own education. That meant he read books, newspapers, speeches, novels, poetry, history, plays, and anything printed he could lay hands on. And he talked to people. Private libraries were in some ministries, in some lawyers' chambers, in some courthouses, and in a few homes. People inherited libraries. That was why young people went to school, to have access to the books there. Distinguished lawyers and judges and some courts had their own libraries of the law. That was how young lawyers were trained: they read law in the chambers of a lawyer or judge with an extensive library of cases and commentary, and learned the practice. Certain lawyers with extensive libraries and experience in practice became mentors for upcoming lawyers, although that was not the term they would have used. Judges of higher courts served that function, educating their clerks, teaching them to read the law and to understand institutions.

The collector of the Port of Boston offered his private library to the young William Darrah Kelley. When he saw what an apt student the young man was, how eager he was for knowledge, the collector of the port suggested that the young man might enroll in Harvard College. And the collector of the port offered to assist him with that, even to pay his tuition.

William Darrah Kelley considered the opportunity, but decided he preferred to return to Philadelphia, to read law there, and again become involved in Democratic politics, where he hoped things had settled down. And so he did, and in 1841 he was admitted to the Pennsylvania Bar. A few years later he was appointed as a county prosecutor, and in 1847 he was appointed as a judge at the Court of Common Pleas, the lowest rung of the judiciary.

April 24, 1995: I am not admitted to practice law in Illinois, although I am admitted in four other states, and am a member of the Bar of the Supreme Court of the United States. The Illinois application for admission is pages and pages of background information. You must have practiced for five of the past seven years, in addition to being a resident of Illinois. Every place of residence since high school, every employer since college graduation. Does anyone even read this? Or verify it? Why should I bother? I have lived and worked in many places, at least fifty.

William Darrah Kelley was one of those Democrats who left the party after the Kansas Nebraska bill repealed the Missouri Compromise, the dispute over whether the laws of slavery would be upheld in the as-yet-unadmitted territories. In 1856 during the middle of this political turmoil, he lost his first attempt to be elected to Congress as a Fremont Republican, Fremont being the controversial general who disobeyed Lincoln. William Darrah Kelley went on to play a prominent part in the 1860 Republican convention at the Wigwam in Chicago, was a supporter and friend of Abraham Lincoln, and later became a confidant of Lincoln as president and a self-described habitué of the executive chamber.

In 1860 William Darrah Kelley won a seat in Congress as a Republican by a narrow margin, beginning a distinguished forty-year career which included serving on the House Ways and Means Committee (including being chair for a period), consistently and vigorously supporting women's and Negro suffrage, and becoming a passionate advocate for the protection of American natural resources and infant industries, especially the steel industry in Pennsylvania. He was long identified as a supporter of tariffs on imports, especially to protect America's primary industries, and this was why he was called "Pig Iron Kelley."

November 16, 2008: Grey now and soon dark. The red leaves of the tree outside my third-floor window, defiant. Our new president will face economic devastation challenging the fabric of the society. This Thanksgiving will be the last one in the big house, with all the children and grandchildren together. Our departure from the university is firmly set now: at the end of the academic year 2008-09, next summer. Strange when you know you must leave, when something is over. The impulse is to sum up, to say where we are now, to hurry up to get everything in, to savor the moment. Meanwhile, many unfinished projects, and nothing is packed.

A lifelong abolitionist, William Darrah Kelley was deeply disturbed by the social and economic devastation in both the North and the South following the Civil War. Like many of those who came from the defeated South to resettle in the boom town of Chicago, William Darrah Kelley never forgot what he saw during and after the Civil War. On a postwar speaking engagement in Mobile, Alabama, he was almost lynched for giving a speech about the necessity of the country going forward together. On that occasion one man was killed, another wounded, and William Darrah Kelley fled.

He had come to Mobile as a member of Congress to say that the North should not impose punishing economic conditions upon the South: the two sides should now put down their arms and rebuild. This was not a message received in peace in the South. In Congress William Darrah Kelley supported reconstruction legislation and the expansion of property rights for former slaves.

March 31, 2007: An exceptionally grey and gloomy spring day. Few green shoots. These little bright shoots will turn into tulips and daffodils. It is pleasant to be home, to be quiet in my studio, surrounded by books and papers, to be writing. The homicide project has resulted in a website with 15,000 pages of documents and publications on it, available to anyone in the world with access to the Internet. It is a new kind of library.

Perhaps the most important fact about Florence Kelley's immediate family background is that she was one of eight children, including six girls, and that she was the only girl to survive. Most died as infants, and seemed to have died of the "summer illness," diarrhea or an illness caused by bad milk. Florence Kelley's older half-sister did come and live with, or at least visit, the family at The Elms. When William Darrah Kelley died, and his body was brought in a special train car back to Philadelphia, this other daughter held the post-burial reception at her home in Philadelphia.

February 1996: The darkness of winter descends, again. Hard to remember that it does end, and spring will come. My course on homicide and the death penalty goes along. I miss my legal community in New Jersey, even my dingy office in the state capitol with all of its political nonsense. To get to know the community here, I have agreed to come to some meetings and to give talks when asked. So when people earnestly ask: What would you like to be called? My instinct is to reply: As long as you don't call me "Fool" my ordinary married name is fine. I have long since become used to that name being both misspelled and mispronounced. At least in Chicago, not everyone registers its other half.

One of Florence Kelley's sisters who died was the much-beloved Anna, who died at the age of six when Florence was twelve. After Anna's death Florence Kelley's mother, Caroline, could hardly let her only remaining daughter out of her sight, to go to school or anywhere. Mostly Florence Kelley studied at home, teaching herself, reading always and everything voraciously, including from her father's extensive private library, under the tutelage of not only her father and mother, but also an array of talented and politically sophisticated aunts, grandparents, and politically active friends of the family, with her education and reading being always watched over by her father.

Custom House, San Francisco, Cal. July 2, 1869

My dear child,

I have seen a great many things that I thought would interest you and about which I would write you. But we are so busy that I can not find much time for correspondence. At one of the stations on the plains we saw a group of Indians. Several of the women had little children which they call Papooses tied on their backs. One had a nice leather case which was laced as you lace your shoes from the bottom nearly to the top where it was spun as a great 6 and looking then to on what it contained were two black eyes looking out of a sweet pretty baby face. The little tot looked at us as quietly as if it had known us all.

There are a great many Chinese men here, but very few women and children. But in probing them of their houses I have girls about your size with a little baby brother or sister wrapped in a shawl and tied on their backs one of its little feet under each of their arms. They are very industrious and thus very little girls are made to their share of the work.

Today we visited the Simpson woolen building Smith where 1000 Chinamen are employed in making cloth blankets and such goods. Some of the blankets were the finest I have ever seen. But what I want to tell you about when we got there the men were at dinner and we were invited to come there. It was a curious sight. They were seated four at a table one on each side. Each one had a small blue china bowl of rice. They do not use spoons or forks, but take between their fingers two sticks called chop-sticks. Besides the rice there were on each table three plates, one of which contained a number of little fish of the size of those which Willie stocked his aquarium on fully. Another contained some green beans shells & all cooked with lots of fat pork just about the size of the fish and the other a vegetable the seed of which comes from China and which looks like a huge white radish of which they cook the green tops and pieces of the body together. Between the plates stands a little one like our butter plates which contains a pungent sauce of soy. The dexterity with which they feed themselves with the sticks is very remarkable. They have their own cooks, seem to be very cheerful and happy and were chattering like monkeys.

I received pleasant letters from your mother and Sister Nanette this morning. I get a little home sick sometimes I am so anxious to see you all. I think Anna will be interested to hear about the babies and I will try and find time to write her a letter. I expect to enjoy Cousin Sup and Willie next Sunday week and then to start for home. Give your mother and brother and sister a kiss from me and believe me to be fondly, Your father WmDKelley

With the exception of the relatively brief period of estrangement after her marriage, Florence Kelley was always close to her family. Caroline Bonsall Kelley's letters to her beloved husband, William Darrah Kelley—whom she exhorts "to write as often as you can for it is my only consolation for your absence"— are reports of the weather, the beginnings and ends of journeys, who arrived and left, who was delayed and for how long, what their impressions were of the countryside on their journey, what they ate, how they slept, and that she is fond of the hot chocolate in Switzerland.

November 10, 1996: Always the plans and the journeys, the packing up, the coming home, the suitcases, the cars, the airplanes, the hotels, the tickets, the reservations. Are we late, are we early? We go, we come back, and now we are always coming back to the big stone house in Evanston. The drive to Levy Mayer Hall and the silent whitewashed walls of my office are now familiar. All of a sudden there seems to be a large number of head scarves being worn by female students. A young man tells me he is so proud of his friend for wearing the Muslim head scarf to school, in class. Always the hair, the shoes, the clothes express something: some women wear stiletto heels to class; almost no one wears jeans; some wear very short skirts; the men don't wear suits, unless it is interview day. All this would have not been seen in my law school a few decades ago. And their speech, their way of standing is an attitude, as we say now. A silent kind of defiance; I am here, and I am different.

It was Caroline, Florence Kelley's mother, who was raised by the Quakers. When Caroline's mother died, and then her father died four years later, Caroline Bonsall was adopted by a childless couple: educated, prominent Quakers, Isaac and Elizabeth Pugh. She kept her name. Over the years this couple had taken four little orphaned girls into their home. These were then Florence Kelley's adopted grandparents and aunts, and she spent quantities of time in their company, and remembered them and who they were, and how they lived their lives, all of her life.

September 6, 1995: All students in the class must be on email. We break into groups, one devoted to complex litigation. This week the juror questionnaires, and non-unanimous verdicts.

A family friend who emigrated from England with Elizabeth Pugh's family was one of the first American scientists of international reputation, Joseph Priestly. Like many others then, he was both a scientist and a minister. He left England in 1791, losing his chapel and his laboratory and almost losing his life because of his support for the American Revolution. He was often a guest at the Pugh table and spoken of with affection and respect at that family table, where conversation was important and of a serious nature. Religion and science and social reform were overlapping commitments for these people. The church had a monopoly on education in many communities, and the town minister might have the best or only library.

The maiden Quaker aunts in Philadelphia, as well as their friends, the vocal and highly visible women abolitionists and advocates for suffrage whom Florence Kelley and her mother and aunts kept company with, stood up to authority, and stood up to be counted for what they believed was right, in the face of threats, beatings, jail, and even in some cases threats of murder. With the Quakers, their unstinting devotion to the public good was not accompanied by a crusading Christianity. They were abolitionists, against capital punishment, designed prisons, were advocates for universal suffrage, promoted literacy especially for freed slaves and women, and were devoted to social justice.

Susan B. Anthony was an old family friend of William Darrah Kelley who in London offered Florence Kelley, then a recent college graduate, the opportunity to come and work as her secretary. That was what promising young women did, work for a prominent public figure as a secretary, to learn how they did what they did, then that person would help them move on to another appropriate position.

November 22, 1995, Chicago Tribune: "Final Appeals Denied, DelVecchio Dies by Injection for '77 Murder."

Convicted murderer George DelVecchio became the fifth inmate in Illinois to be put to death this year after he died by lethal injection early Wednesday for the 1977 killing of a 6-year-old Northwest Side boy.

DelVecchio, 47, was pronounced dead at 12:30 a.m. When asked if he wanted to say any last word, witnesses at the Stateville Correctional Center near Joliet heard him mumble several words and say the name of God.

Aunt Sarah Pugh, the sister of Florence Kelley's grandfather by adoption, was more than an ordinary Quaker. She was a teacher at the Philadelphia Friends School at the Twelfth Street Meeting House, and later at her own Girls School on Walnut Street in Philadelphia. Unlike her niece who was not much of a joiner as an adult, nor active in the suffrage movement, Sarah Pugh was an active member of the Female Anti-Slavery Society until it disbanded in 1870, and a leader in women's suffrage organizations.

In 1838 the proposed Philadelphia meeting place of the Anti-Slavery Convention of American Women was burned down by a hostile mob. Facing down the continuing threats, Sarah Pugh reconvened the Anti-Slavery Convention meeting at her own school, and proceeded.

June 26, 1995: Spring is glorious. There are flowers and green everywhere. The house, if not a home, is at least no longer filled with strangers. The first-year markers have been passed. The trees are various shades of green, bright green for the new growth, a deep green for the old fir trees, and the flowers and bushes are white and pink and deep red. A skunk family has taken up residence under the front porch beneath our bedroom window. When the sash is raised, a small, odorous puff wafts up to the second-story window. Finally, my third-floor office is a real workplace. Teaching is over for the semester, and winter is months away. My husband complains happily about his busy calendar, overschedules himself gleefully, and to my surprise, I am happy too. Perhaps it is just the relief of the first bit being over, the joy of spring.

The Quaker women of Florence Kelley's family, some of whom would not use sugar or wear cotton because both were made with slave labor, were the women who filled the benches in the young Judge William Darrah Kelley's courtroom in 1855 as he conducted the trial in a case of a runaway slave challenging the claim to her ownership by a Virginia slaveholder passing through Philadelphia on his way to take up a position as the US minister to Nicaragua.

```
September 18, 1996, Chicago Tribune: "Ray Stewart Executed for
Killing Spree."

Convicted serial killer Ray Lee Stewart was put to death early
Wednesday in Joliet, 15 years after admitting he murdered six
people in the Rockford and Beloit, Wis., area.

Stewart, 44, of Rockford, was pronounced dead at 12:30 a.m.
Wednesday, moments after he was administered a lethal injection
by authorities at Stateville Correctional Center. He was the
eighth person to be executed in Illinois since the state rein-
stituted the death penalty in 1977.
```

The legal question in Judge William Darrah Kelley's court in 1855 was one of Pennsylvania's jurisdiction over the runaway slave and her children. The woman escaped into the countryside after the young Judge Kelley ruled that she did not have to return to slavery with the Virginia emissary. She was spirited out of the courtroom by the Quaker women and hidden until she could run away with her children. She was not returned to the slaveholder.

Florence Kelley's aunt Sarah Pugh was considered a rebel because she cut her hair short. Always and everywhere for women the hair, the covering of the hair, the dressing of the hair, the ornamentation of the hair is a political signifier. None of the women in head scarves at the law school have turned up in my classes.

December 8, 1995, Chicago Tribune: "No 4th Trial for Hernandez."

Alejandro Hernandez, the last remaining defendant in the murder of Jeanine Nicarico, was jubilant after the announcement in court Friday morning.

"After 12 years my mom is able to put up a Christmas tree," he said. "She never put one up for 12 years. And now we're going to celebrate Christmas together, like a family should."

Friday's action marked the latest chapter in a long legal battle that reached a turning point last month with the acquittal of Hernandez's co-defendant, Rolando Cruz.

Hernandez was released from prison on bond after Cruz's acquittal.

In 1840 Sarah Pugh represented the Pennsylvania Female Anti-Slavery Society at the World Anti-Slavery Convention in London, a long title for an important political event. The women delegates, joined by an indignant Lloyd Garrison, were denied entry to the floor of the House of Commons and were made to sit in the gallery behind a bar and a curtain. What began for her as a short jaunt to London turned into a speaking tour which lasted two years, as Sarah Pugh traveled around the country speaking to large gatherings on behalf of the abolitionist cause.

In 1859 there were riots and protests and threats in Philadelphia when abolitionists came to speak, and Sarah Pugh and other women persisted in carrying on with their meetings. During and after the Civil War, Sarah Pugh and other like-minded women stayed for months in the communities of freed men and women in the Sea Isles near the Carolinas, helping these communities learn to farm and teaching them other aspects of husbandry and survival.

September 1997: Always coming back from somewhere, going somewhere, New York, Washington, California, Florida, running downtown, away to football. In class I can sit for a couple of hours and talk about one thing, and not worry about representing something, myself, my husband, our school. Selling the law, only. Selling the idea of research. And now a revived legal research project and publication going back to my old preoccupations: sex offenses, incest. And so it goes, one thing leads to another, in ways not always expected.

January 16, 1996, Chicago Tribune: "Edgar Commutes Sentence: Guinevere Garcia, Killer of Abusive Husband, to Serve Life Without Parole."

. . . Last summer she urged officials to go forward with her execution, lashing out at death penalty opponents, including celebrity activist Bianca Jagger, who had urged Edgar to spare Garcia's life. Garcia said she was responsible for her crimes and was prepared for the punishment. . . .

Jagger said Tuesday that she was pleased with Edgar's decision but concerned about how Garcia would react.

"I hope that she will see we had her well-being at heart and that we all cared that an injustice was not committed against her, a victim." . . .

In a statement, Edgar said that while the evidence did not support a battered-woman defense, the circumstances surrounding the case did not merit the death penalty.

"Guinevere Garcia should never be free again, but I have concluded that the punishment decreed for her was not typical," Edgar said. "Horrible as was her crime, it was an offense comparable to those judges and jurors have determined over and over again should not be punishable by death."

Lazare Wischnewetzky, Florence Kelley's future husband, had been a medical student at the University of Zurich since 1880, when Florence Kelley arrived in 1883. He was from Taganrog, Russia, that part of Russia which was fought over and traded back and forth between Russia and the Austro-Hungarian empire for a century. The young people met in a Political Economy lecture course.

January 15, 1996: A bone-chilling cold. The madness of football is over, at least for this season. Faculty members whom I didn't remember meeting asked for tickets to the big football game. We have a new dean of the School of Law, a new person at the wheel. And so the great chariot of the sun arcs through the sky, time passes, and we follow at a gallop.

The University of Zurich, the Polytechnikum, was a place of instruction which bore little resemblance to the undergraduate College of Arts and Sciences at Cornell

University, then or now, having no dormitories, residence halls, sororities or fraternities, athletic events, university chapel, dance halls, or boat races.

When Bismarck expelled the socialists from Prussia, many came to Zurich. When the pogroms in Russia and Poland expelled or killed the Jews, those who could ran away to Zurich, or people bought tickets to the unknown land across the sea, sometimes ending up somewhere they didn't anticipate, in this time of no passports or visas.

Teaching at the University of Zurich was by lecture, and progress toward the degree was measured by formal examination. Teaching was similar to the method used in teaching law in the United States then, a carrying over of the German tradition of teaching philology, philosophy and science. There was a senior professor, and he was the source of knowledge. He lectured. Students copied what he said. The examination was a recitation and perhaps a bit of reflection on those words or a demonstration that the student could imitate the professor.

Florence Kelley was admitted to the University of Zurich to attend classes on politics, economics, and law. The examination was on the subject of the lectures, as defined by the lecturer. This model of graduate education based upon German educational principles and standards was not broken in America until well after World War II, when all things German came to be viewed differently.

American academic curricula and the structure of university departments remain dominated by German categories of the disciplines today. Legal scholars, historians, philosophers, scientists, engineers, and others have traditionally considered German academic institutions and degrees to be of the highest value, because of the reputation of German universities for their rigor, precision, discipline, and intellectual challenge. Florence Kelley's courses the first semester included lectures in Contemporary History Since 1852, Theoretical Economics, Political Science, and Communist Ideas and Movements to 1848.

February 1, 1997: I can hardly believe that long relationship, that life, is over. So many stories, so much heartache, finished. Now the law will do its clumsy clean-up.

There may not have been interaction or equality in the classroom between professor and student; however, there was much debate and discussion outside of the classroom. If there were no dormitories, there were pensiones, rooming houses, newspapers, journals, shared apartments, and a cultural life with music, cafes, restaurants, a resident theatre and dozens of independent political groups and publications. The university and the city of Zurich were a haven for dispossessed, educated professionals.

February 27, 1996: The teaching is comfortable, my students familiar, and the great law library with the third-floor tables by the windows a place of peace, especially when the dark sky looms and the ice piles up in giant cubes along the shore. Beautiful, when you are inside. Terrifying when you are outside driving. My third floor is my own now, a destination at both ends of the commute now.

Initially Florence Kelley was worried she would not be admitted to the University of Zurich since a trunk containing her Cornell degree had been mistakenly left on a train platform in England and, despite her calls and frantic waving from the window, it was not loaded on the train with the other luggage. The copy of her degree and the trunk remained lost forever. The registrar at the University of Zurich, however, admitted her for lectures after a conversation, an admissions interview of a sort, telling her that the loss of her paper degree was not important since at the University of Zurich they thought American degrees had no value. And, when she was settled, her mother, Caroline, and her younger brother, Albert, came to visit:

I have not enjoyed Christmas so much in many years. I did not seem to see the little absent faces at every turn reminding me of sorrow and grief. I thought of the children but in a new place the sense of loss was less keen. I have lived alone with my own thoughts so much in that great rambling house, that I carry around with me my own recollections, but it is well to have a change, and this one is complete.

On New Year's Day in 1884 when a very formal, very proper medical student first presented his calling card to Florence Kelley in the apartment in Zurich, both Caroline and Albert approved, although Caroline wrote her husband that the medical student "consumes too much time." Later, he would become a full-time job, one without remuneration. He came bearing rare books and passionate conversation. Florence Kelley never wanted to marry, had told him and her friends she would never marry. Their marriage on June 1, 1884, in a simple civil ceremony, surprised many, including her father, who did not give his approval, nor was it solicited.

December 15, 1996: Coming back to quiet. Coming back to the cold. Yet it is welcome. Another class, another event. And on the planes traveling, always the airports; the rhythm of the airport procedures. The destination not what I want or decide. Back and forth with family matters. No good outcome there.

At the time of their marriage—which the couple kept secret from their friends—Florence Kelley and her husband were attending fourteen hours a day of lectures in law and economics at the University of Zurich. She was reading Karl Marx and Frederick Engels in German, since translations of their work into English had not been published. It was in Zurich and later in Heidelberg that Florence Kelley began to translate into English

Frederick Engels's *Die Lage de Arbeitenden Klasse in England in 1844*, or *The Condition of the Working Class in England in 1844*, the translation being a work of devotion to doctrine which began a largely epistolary relationship with Frederick Engels continuing into her time in Chicago. Though his first name is spelled variously today, the spelling of his first name in the English translation of *Die Lage* is Frederick.

Florence Kelley's correspondence with Frederick Engels languished in sealed Russian archives in Moscow throughout the Cold War. After the archives were opened, the letters were discovered by one of Florence Kelley's three biographers, Dorothy Blumberg, herself a prominent socialist, the only person, apparently, to actually go to prison for a violation of the Smith Act in the 1950s. She was imprisoned for two years in the Women's Federal Penitentiary in Virginia, where Martha Stewart was later to serve time.

January 12, 2011: The storm continues, becomes more serious. The airports are closed. No cars on the streets, or people. I will stay inside. The law school buildings are empty, dark, except for an eerie line of corridor lights.

May 8, 1996, Chicago Tribune: "Lawmakers Approve Bill Limiting Outside Interference in Executions."

Almost five months after Gov. Jim Edgar commuted a convicted murderer's death sentence to life in prison, legislators approved a bill Tuesday to limit outsiders' intervention in Death Row appeals.

The legislation was offered in January shortly after Edgar commuted the death sentence of Guinevere Garcia, a Bensenville woman convicted of murder in the death of her former husband.

Under the legislation sent to Edgar's desk on a 46-5 Senate vote, inmates would have to provide written consent for appeals or clemency petitions filed on their behalf. Such papers could be filed on behalf of prisoners deemed mentally incompetent. It's unclear what Edgar will do with the legislation.

During their courtship, Lazare Wischnewetzky's gifts were materials from a private library of rare books to which he had access. Lazare Wischnewetzky was, in spite of what appeared to be a privileged background of wealth, dedicated to the revolution.

March 20, 1995: The rain has settled in, seemingly forever. The students and the faculty together are panting as we come up on the spring break. The women students here are offered six-figure salaries at private law firms. They wear stylish shoes and the standard interview suit, dark blue or black, a simple blazer, a plain skirt. The skirts usually are mid-

knee. Few wear pantsuits. Some of the interviewers look at their legs. The women law students are different from the men, want different things, although they say they don't.

In 1867 the Senate of the University of Zurich had decided as a matter of principle to admit women on an equal basis with men, becoming the first European university to do so, and immediately attracting women who were barred from higher education by statute in Russia, and by statute, tradition, and practice elsewhere, for example, in most institutions of higher education in Britain and the United States. In Russia in the 1870s and 1880s there was a cadre of prominent Jewish women lawyers. Then the czar's government decided that there were too many Jews in the professions. So they were all expelled.

The University of Zurich attracted women who wished to study law, medicine, and economics, and it was particularly attractive to Russian and Eastern European women. Only one other American woman was in the graduate school then, a medical student. Many of the educated exiles were Jews.

Zurich was a city awash in talk of reform, of the politics of all the places people had come from, been pushed out of, all the politics of expulsion, with displaced, angry intellectuals speaking and writing in many languages. Economics at the time, as now, was statistics, legal argument, philosophy and what we would term political studies or social science. It wasn't the manipulation of complicated mathematical models, or the theory of statistics, but the facts were real numbers.

The theory was the theory of markets, labor and capital, class conflict, and the dynamics of socialism. Economics earned its reputation as the dismal science. Adam Smith, Frederick Engels and Karl Marx unpacked the same intellectual suitcase, and Florence Kelley and Henry Demarest Lloyd, as well as Jane Addams, shared a common education based upon political and economic philosophy, mostly of European origin. They also shared a familiarity with recent national history, and a lexicon for how to talk about what they wanted to do when they worked together in Chicago in the 1890s. They wanted reform, they dreamed of change, and their ideas for this came from the same sources.

October 3, 1995: Last night at our dinner with many women attorneys, including many in public life, only one predicted the acquittal of O.J. Simpson. Today a huge television screen is set up in the atrium of the law school for the televised announcement of the verdict. The black students cheered, some white women students wept. His smile said he knew in advance.

Henry Demarest Lloyd's pen had made him famous, especially among the circle of reformers and socialists who read one another's work and shared a passion and energy for change. Henry Demarest Lloyd's book about the Spring Hill Valley miners strike was published in 1890. The miners strike in Illinois, which was a lockout, was a matter of public discussion throughout the country. Eventually Henry Demarest Lloyd would testify about the events before Congress. His writing made the confrontation a matter of class conflict and national attention. Eventually the matter was settled, although the mine owners gave up little.

It was analogous, Henry Demarest Lloyd said in *A Strike of Millionaires Against Miners*, to the methods used by the Iroquois to starve out the Illinois Indians at Starved Rock:

Where the Illinois sweeps its placid way to the Mississippi between the wooded bluffs of La Salle, and over the sandstone which makes many a picturesque shelf in the valley, stands Starved Rock.

Rising straight from the water-side 125 feet, it can be ascended only by a narrow winding path from the shore. Like one of the mediaeval castles which of old threatened but now adorn the lochs of Scotland, Starved Rock once pushed forth from all surroundings, proud of itself as a sure refuge and defense. To-day none but associations of ruin and defeat are intertwined with the beauty of its crumbling head . . . a remnant of one hundred men, women and children—on the ample summit of the rock, which rises as a natural castle from the edge of the water. There was room enough for them, and there was timber for their fires. From the broad river a hundred sheer feet and more below no surprise or attack was possible; the narrow pass upward on the side of the land was a Thermopylae, where a handful could defy a host. There the Illinois stood their last, the Iroquois gathered about. When the besieged lowered their cups for water the strings were cut; when they stole forth for food, they never came back. . . . A few demoniac days of wrath and agony, and the Iroquois stood upon the wide top of the castle of rock, and there were no Illinois—except the dead.

Florence Kelley, Jane Addams, and Henry Demarest Lloyd were heavily influenced by German philosophy, Marxism, and social theory, and were conversant with the stream of mid-nineteenth-century commentary on working conditions, the relationships between capital and the labor. The rhetoric developed around economic and political crises in England, Germany and other parts of Europe. Bismarck banned the socialists from government jobs and educational institutions, but could not keep them from writing and publishing elsewhere and keeping the discussion going on for decades, well into the next century and vigorously among American intellectuals.

July 3, 1996, Chicago Tribune: "3 Convicted of Murders Are Finally Exonerated: No Apology as Judge Dismisses 1978 Case."

Poor lawyering, overzealous police and prosecutors, a dishonest witness and a public uproar over a brutal crime created a mixture that sent four men to prison for a rape and murder they didn't commit.

But it took until Tuesday for the legal system to acknowledge as much.

After spending nearly two decades in prison, three men were finally exonerated in a brief hearing devoid of any new revelations on the brutal crime or the convoluted case.

Chief Criminal Court Judge Thomas Fitzgerald dismissed murder and rape charges against Dennis Williams, William Rainge and Kenneth Adams. There was no apology from the bench.

Florence Kelley's devotion to the translation of Frederick Engels's *Die Lage*, which would last several years, was a characteristic American fealty to European intellectual traditions, a deference which she would only outgrow when she was immersed in the actuality of legal reform in Chicago in the 1890s.

February 28, 1996: Basically what I teach in all of my courses is reading and writing, how to read, and then how to write about what you have read. Reading the law, making sense of the law is just another kind of reading. Writing about the law is just writing for another audience, in another context. The writing may be drenched in subject, in a legal subject, but it is still just writing, good or bad writing.

In the 1880s and 1890s, as now, the question of private profits, unregulated capitalism, the statistical and quantitative measurements of wealth and property were at the center of the public discussion of the role of government and the possibility of reform, only without our vast, churning ocean of daily statistics and financial data, and without the capability to manipulate and broadcast all the numbers immediately, electronically, and without attribution.

In Zurich and New York and Chicago, the discussion was of employment, the stability of banks, financial manipulations, the outsize profits of corporations, the trade balance, the money supply, the stubbornness of economic depression, and the political repression of dissent. Who gets what when and where and how was the subject, ever the subject, still the subject. The highly visible disparities in wealth, the extremes of the working conditions, and the destitution in the tenements simply provided a different occasion for the discussion.

Henry Demarest Lloyd framed *A Strike of Millionaires Against Miners* as a letter to the stockholders of the mining company owning the Spring Hill mine at the time of the lockout:

Great difficulties block the way of the thorough investigation of the facts of any particular case of the social problem by persons as ordinarily circumstanced, even when like you to whom these pages are addressed they are stockholders, and, unlike you, are trying to find out what their own directors are doing. It is hoped that this communication—a part of which was first printed in the Chicago Daily Herald—may be of service not only to you to whom it is specially addressed, "accessories before and after the fact" of Spring Valley, but to all who want to understand the "works and days" of their brothers and sisters. It was agreed at the National Convention of the American Federation of Labor in Boston, in 1889, that as their secretary put it, "Miners were worse off than any other workmen in the country." This gives these results of several months' almost constant study of their lot, at a place given world-wide celebrity by their suffering in a peculiarly interesting crisis, some special value. From one learn all.

Florence Kelley had not met Henry Demarest Lloyd when she arrived at Hull-House in the winter of 1891, but her brother had known his sister, and she would have known his writings, as he would have known hers. And they met soon after her arrival.

April 1996: A wedding, the first in the immediate family, and everyone came. I did none of the work. The bride did it all. I did buy a wedding suit. The wedding was beautiful and went off without any difficulty. The bride and groom, handsome, appropriately serious, joyful. The families happy, all are grateful that a wedding can take place in a time of peace. What is always first reported from a war zone: a family wedding, a beacon of hope for the future from the young, as it is here.

A second article by Henry Demarest Lloyd, on the monopolistic practices of the Standard Oil Company published in the *Atlantic Monthly* in 1881, generated enough excitement for seven printings of the issue. The *Atlantic Monthly* had initially refused to publish the article, and continued to refuse to do so until Henry Demarest Lloyd paid the printing costs, which were several thousand dollars. This article caused John D. Rockefeller to call Henry Demarest Lloyd "the bane of my existence," a view perhaps shared by others who were the target of his writings.

Henry Demarest Lloyd and his wife, Jessie Bross, welcomed Florence Kelley's three children into Wayside, their family home in Winnetka, and the children stayed there on and off for years, initially with a servant, identified only as Celera with no surname, brought from New York. Another servant arrived in Chicago with the trunk full of clothes and toys. Then there were other nursemaids. It is not clear how these women were paid, since Florence Kelley, until she became factory inspector, frequently had trouble meeting the twenty-one dollar residence fee for Hull-House, about $540 in present dollars. Upon arriving in Chicago, after borrowing money for the train fare for herself and the three children, Florence Kelley promised her mother that she would not borrow money any longer.

May 1996: "Chicago is a village," my former student, the law professor and anthropologist now here, now an anthropologist of the present, commented. Or, the relationships between the people who run the big-city institutions, public and private, resemble the elaborate kinship relationships maintained among generations of tribal elders and their children in a traditional African or South Seas village (those worlds gone now), places where people are cut off, and live and stay, and their children stay, and everyone knows exactly who everyone else is, who their parents are, who their grandparents were, and everyone casts a watchful eye over the younger generation. The Chicago daily newspapers still report on the Armours, the Marshall Fields, the McCormicks. Respect must be paid to the elders. And there are expectations for the young who carry the name, sometimes causing difficulties for them. I am told that kind of kinship analysis anthropology is not done any longer, is considered invalid, out of date. It has a truth here. A map could be drawn of these interlocking relationships.

The Lloyd family's welcoming response to Florence Kelley's straitened circumstances was as spontaneous as it was generous. Henry Demarest Lloyd knew who she was, and he served on the board of the newly established Hull-House. Florence Kelley and her children were brought to Wayside by Jane Addams within days of her arrival, although again the biographers dispute the exact date.

The immediacy of the family's warm welcome was characteristic of Henry Demarest Lloyd and his wife, Jessie Bross Lloyd.

A graduate of Columbia University and Columbia Law School, Henry Demarest Lloyd was a writer, an intellectual, a reformer, and an activist. Jessie Bross was the daughter of former lieutenant governor and publisher of the *Chicago Tribune* William Bross. He and Joseph Medill hired Henry Demarest Lloyd for the *Tribune* when he was a bright young newcomer to Chicago, and watched as Henry Demarest Lloyd became first a distinguished literary critic and commentator, then the financial editor of the *Tribune*, and a man of parts who was everywhere in Chicago. Finally he was someone whose political actions could no longer be tolerated by his editor and publisher.

What is to be remembered about this time is that Haymarket was in 1886, with the trial in August 1887 and the quasi-public executions on November 11, 1887. The riot on May 4, 1886, which wasn't a riot at all but a public political event where eight policemen died, most by their own bullets. The occasion was a desultory, peaceful gathering in the rain where socialists and anarchists spoke, and which 176 police officers were ordered to disperse.

The Haymarket events were the culmination of a national movement for the eight-hour day, following the bitter repression of strikes and socialist meetings by manufacturers immediately before. Someone, but not one of the four defendants who were hanged a year later, threw a bomb, killing one police officer and setting off a volley of gunfire. And the aftereffects of those events lingered for years, decades, its long-lasting impact, unanticipated.

Karl Marx, Frederick Engels wrote Florence Kelley soon after the events, would be pleased that the revolution and class war had finally come to America.

The revolution came, but it wasn't the revolution these people expected.

The Haymarket verdict, after a show trial presided over by Judge Joseph E. Gary, was predictable. The jurors were all preselected for conviction. On the other hand some of the defendants, at least, were involved in bomb making and in inciting rebellion. They probably would have been convicted in Russia or Prussia and sentenced to death, and shot, but perhaps not in Britain. The death sentences for the crime of conspiracy to commit murder, imposed upon the defendants some of whom were not present at the bombing, were the new principle of law which has never been overturned on appeal. It was a conviction applauded throughout the country.

September 10, 1996: Teaching has begun again. Really I am grateful that people have welcomed us with such generosity. There are plenty of cities where it would be a long time before you would be invited to people's homes, that people would want to hear from an outsider. Perhaps it is the Midwest, perhaps it is the culture of our university. Whatever the reason, people in the community go out of their way to welcome us, to inquire about our welfare, our adjustment. Fine, everything is fine, I say.

Benjamin R. Magruder of the Supreme Court of Illinois issued a unanimous opinion upholding the death sentences imposed by the trial court judge in Haymarket: four defendants were hanged in a bizarre, orchestrated public execution attended by 180 invited guests, one committed suicide in prison, a defendant who was under eighteen was not sentenced to death, and two had their death sentences commuted to life imprisonment after they recanted and publicly admitted guilt to avoid execution. Those two were later pardoned by Governor John Peter Altgeld.

After the hangings, more than 100,000 people lined the sidewalks of Chicago in police-imposed silence to witness the parade of the caskets of the hanged men in the funeral procession which wound its way slowly through the city, on a carefully prescribed route, and with strict rules imposed (no singing, no cheering, only silence) on November 11, 1887. The shadow of the Haymarket trial and executions was still hanging over Chicago, New York and other American cities when Florence Kelley arrived in Chicago in 1891. The Haymarket executions are remembered as a symbol of the state demonstrating its authority through the very public imposition of the death penalty. After Haymarket, labor organizers and anarchists were lumped together, and the eight-hour movement, which had brought more than a hundred thousand demonstrators to the streets of Chicago to march on May 4, 1886, was dead.

March 16, 1995, Chicago Tribune: "Edgar Rejects Clemency for 2 Who Face Execution Next Week."

Gov. Jim Edgar on Wednesday denied the clemency petitions of convicted murderers James Free and Hernando Williams, clearing the way for their double execution at Stateville Correctional Center near Joliet next week.

"I have consistently believed the death penalty is an appropriate punishment for heinous crimes," Edgar said in a news release announcing his decision.

Henry Demarest Lloyd had become heavily engaged in the Haymarket appeals and the clemency efforts to set aside the death sentences of the remaining defendants before the executions. He published his negative opinion about the conduct of the trial and the behavior of Judge Gary to the great annoyance of his father-in-law. Joseph Medill supported William Bross and was equally disapproving of Henry Demarest Lloyd's criticism of Judge Gary, the trial, and the hangings.

When he was governor, John Peter Altgeld was to publish an even more scathing analysis of Judge Gary's conduct during the Haymarket trial. Joseph Medill and William Bross managed to ease Henry Demarest Lloyd out of the *Tribune*, although Henry Demarest Lloyd was a well-regarded and successful editor and writer before and after his association with the *Tribune*.

January 15, 1996: And the winter is settled in for the long haul. "Persuasion," again. Again the reading of books which create a world different from the world of the student's experience. Books which take you to another time, another place, and what law is in that world.

William Bross disinherited his daughter in retaliation for her husband's political views. Between Jessie Bross's inheritance from her mother and Henry Demarest Lloyd's own income from writing and speaking, however, there was sufficient money to maintain the gracious family home in Winnetka, which was then the country. The Lloyd children were close in age to the Kelley children, and the Lloyd family entertained a constant stream of visitors.

Their home was unpretentious, rambling and gracious, its main building converted from a former rectory. Friends as well as visitors from around the world were welcomed to their table. It was there that Florence Kelley first met John Peter Altgeld and many others who became critical allies in the factory inspection advocacy. Henry Demarest Lloyd and Jessie Bross became lifelong friends, not only of Florence Kelley, but the friendship continued into the next generation.

After Florence Kelley had moved to New York, her oldest son, Nicholas, and sometimes the other Kelley children would visit the Lloyds during the summer in Rhode Island or over the school holidays.

Boxing Day, December 26, 1995: The entire family is absorbed in the most immediate details of trip planning, after what was a new holiday locale for the family. There are babies and a wedding in the future, much to celebrate. The winter hasn't been as severe as predicted, although it is cold, cold, and the roads are black and treacherous. We make fires, and feast on roast meats and sweet pies.

Although writing was his principal method of persuasion, Henry Demarest Lloyd was no armchair intellectual. The night before the executions of the Haymarket defendants, November 10, 1887, Henry Demarest Lloyd traveled to Springfield to plead with Governor Richard J. Oglesby to commute the Haymarket death sentences, as he had promised. The governor had promised but was persuaded not to commute the sentences by Marshall Field and other prominent businessmen. After the public panic caused by the gruesome suicide of one of the defendants, Louis Lingg, in his cell just before the scheduled executions of the others, the governor refused to commute the sentences of those who did not admit guilt and recant. A petition, urging clemency, signed by thousands, including sixteen thousand union members in London, had been hand-carried to Governor Oglesby, along with additional petitions from lawyers, judges, and members of the legal community in Chicago and around the country.

Like Florence Kelley, Henry Demarest Lloyd was a critic of the privileged social group to which he belonged by profession and marriage. After his outspoken published criticisms of the conduct of the Haymarket trial, the judge, police, and prosecutors, Henry Demarest Lloyd was cut dead by many former friends and colleagues. Men crossed the street to avoid facing him and meeting his eyes, and at the city clubs, where so much political and social business was done, and still is done, members greeted him with silence.

After the executions, and his failed mission to the governor, Henry Demarest Lloyd fell into what sounds like a depression. He and his wife traveled abroad for months, and he moved his family out of the city and to Winnetka, which soon was to be connected by streetcar to the city.

Since he had lost his job and his wife had been disinherited by her father, the reason for the move was in part to save money. It was cheaper to live in Winnetka, although they kept a small place in town. By the time Jane Addams brought Florence Kelley and her children to Wayside, the Lloyd family had lived in Winnetka for several years and had just added a wing of children's rooms to the old rectory.

February 6, 1996: Class No. 4. A law case takes place in its own world, where unique rules, its own practices apply. The law makes analogies between circumstances in cases at different times. The law tries to smooth out the differences between circumstances and people by slapping on a label, a technical name. The class is about how the law demarcates human events, so that there is a before and after: an indictment, a trial, a judgment, a final appeal, a marriage, a death. The law then draws a line and will hear no dispute about it.

Henry Demarest Lloyd was the son of a dour Protestant minister named Lloyde, a man with no talent for saving or accumulating money. Like Florence Kelley, he created a new name for himself. Early in his career he dropped the last letter from his surname. As a university student he announced that his goal in life was to be "all that is musical, humanitarian, muscular, imaginative, brainy, poetic, powerful with men and material." And he did become such a person. There must have been love in the family home, perhaps contributed by his mother, since he remained full of hope in the face of circumstances which would make many despair. There must have been some joy and laughter as they were growing up, for there was much of it in his own family home. Henry Demarest Lloyd himself consistently showed a gentle, warm and tender spirit and a sympathy for his fellow man.

Trained as a lawyer at Columbia University, considered the best law school in the country at the time, a member of the New York Bar, he found the ordinary practice of law too limiting and traditional, although, like Florence Kelley, he was ever knocking on the institutional doors of the law to do justice. The work he did was in the most essential way the practice of law, albeit in an unconventional way, bringing facts and circumstances of injustice to the attention of a court or a legal body capable of acting, and asking for something to be done. He argued before the US Congress, petitioned governors and presidents, and worked to persuade legislators. Legal process and the levers of the law were for him mechanisms to influence the political system. In this he was no different from his adversaries.

Like John Peter Altgeld, Henry Demarest Lloyd married for love, and his wife was his equal, his caretaker during periods of delicate health, and his life partner. His powerful father-in-law, William Bross, the former lieutenant governor of Illinois, was the founder of the Republican Party in Illinois and a friend of Abraham Lincoln. William Bross must have at least met William Darrah Kelley, Florence Kelley's father, who was one of several who introduced Lincoln at the Republican convention in Chicago in 1860.

March 1996: The months pass too quickly. There is always an event, where showing up is required. So much busyness, and much of it not busyness which produces anything. Yet I seem to have found a way to continue writing, a place to write, at the law library and on my wonderful third-floor sanctuary in the house. I will never have another writing place as commodious as this one.

Henry Demarest Lloyd's marriage to William Bross's daughter was no opportunistic career move. It was initially blessed by the Bross family. And when the couple went to Europe, the Lloyds left their three children, with their nursemaid, in the care of the Bross parents. Political differences didn't entirely trump family relations.

March 20, 1997: Taiwan, and a visit to the premier university and to its law school. I am graciously welcomed by the dean of that law school and give a talk on the practice of capital punishment in the United States to a small group of faculty and one or two graduate students. They are appropriately astonished to hear about what we do in America. Law is a graduate degree here. Most of the students will be judges and civil servants. The campus has been modeled after an American undergraduate campus, with heavy, square buildings facing one another across a large, grassy midway. They publish professional journals simultaneously in English and Mandarin. The walls of the faculty library are lined with volumes in German, German philosophy, sociology, legal theory. The students must pass an examination in German and read the nineteenth-century German philosophers of law before being awarded a doctorate. The advanced students travel to German universities to study. I am persuaded to publish a piece of my fiction in their bilingual literary journal. But where will I find a translator?

Like Florence Kelley, Henry Demarest Lloyd's pen, his magnetic personality, his rhetorical skills and passion for justice, his shining intelligence, and his personal charm were powerful in the public arena. His handsome face, his slender, neat figure, his zeal and confidence, all made him an attractive and formidable opponent. He well knew he needed all of these attributes to persuade.

Henry Demarest Lloyd's health was precarious—he suffered from lifelong insomnia and other ailments—especially after what sounds like a nervous breakdown following the execution of the four Haymarket defendants. Henry Demarest Lloyd personally delivered the message of commutation to the cells of the two who were spared the night before the hangings. And then he went home.

June 15, 1996: At least that reception at our house is over, and all went well. A lot of money and time spent. More than four-hundred reporters camped in our garden for an event where nothing happened. Should the clothes have a room of their own with a view of the lake for thousands of dollars a night? The events seem to be primarily about the clothes, which gives the newspapers something to write about. At least nothing unfavorable made the news and there was no disaster, and no other news. The money flowed along with the champagne. It was a lucky opportunity and came about in an unlikely way.

Henry Demarest Lloyd did not start out his career as a journalist and writer as a supporter of labor, or as an advocate for the unions. He started investigating the monopolies when he came to the *Tribune* in 1884. His research and what he found out about the financial ownership of the railroads and their ties to Standard Oil and other companies, the ongoing drama of the streetcar franchises in Chicago and elsewhere, as well as the ill-concealed corruption in city and state government, shocked him and put him in conflict with the business elite and the owners and publishers of the *Tribune*. Lloyd's support of the Haymarket defendants, and his exposure of fraud and stock manipulations by bankers and the financial community, did not make him popular with the business elite in Chicago. As long as things were quiet, people were supposed to be quiet.

February 13, 1996: Two guests in class. The subject: torture. The doctor who treats children who are child soldiers in Africa. How does he fit this work into the medical framework? How does he continue in the face of such brutality? The grey outside is unrelenting. In Seattle the plum trees are blooming.

The marriage between Lazare Wischnewetzky and Florence Kelley might not have ever taken place if Florence Kelley's mother, Caroline, and younger brother, Albert, had not left Zurich for several weeks in May and June because there was an outbreak of an infectious disease considered especially dangerous to children. Albert at that time was twelve. William Jr. had recovered enough to go home.

Florence Kelley was grieving over the recent death of her closest friend from Cornell, Margaret Hicks. Caroline writes her husband detailing what a good time she is having at the Christmas parties in Zurich, except that Florrie did not feel like enjoying the occasion, her Christmas having been saddened by the news of Margaret's death:

> *She withdrew without dancing to the great regret of the students who counted upon having her for a partner, not that she allowed herself to give way to violent grief.*

The bomb at Haymarket and the hanging of the anarchists in Chicago in 1887 after the Haymarket trial, and the eventual pardoning of those not hanged by Governor John Peter Altgeld on September 26, 1893, would have a lasting effect upon Florence Kelley and her work in Chicago, upon her political beliefs, her marriage, and her involvement in the politics of the 1886 election in New York, and even reach forward to the suspicion of her expressed by the Daughters of the American Revolution and others, decades later.

But in the spring of 1884 two young people were in love, and to the surprise of many, including Florence Kelley's mother and her father, Florence Kelley and Lazare Wischnewetzky were married on June 1, 1884.

In the fall, the newlyweds went to Heidelberg, where their studious routine continued. Florence Kelley wrote to her friends, several of whom expressed surprise at her change in status, saying that in Heidelberg her husband vanished at nine in the morning to spend three hours in his medical clinic. Then, dinner at a nearby club, followed "by reading and chatting over coffee in their sun filled sitting room. Then lectures again from 4pm to 7pm, followed by the work of studying, reading and translating."

Florence Kelley filled her days by not only translating *Die Lage*, but also doing hack work, the translation of cheap novels into English or one of the European languages, and then perhaps writing an article or letter for a newspaper back in America. Her mother was visiting and was staying at a nearby pensione. Then tea in the evening followed by a long evening of reading aloud.

And soon she was pregnant. . . .

Image of job seekers, men standing in front of the Chicago Daily News building, looking at newspapers with pedestrians walking nearby. The building was located at 15 North Wells Street (formerly 123 Fifth Avenue) in the Loop community area of Chicago, Illinois. DN-0051332, Chicago Daily News negatives collection, Chicago History Museum.

2

The Ides of March: We Are Women – Lawyers

With a pen in hand the narrative stream is a canal; it moves slowly, smoothly, decorously, sleepily, it has no blemish except that it is all blemish. It is too literary, too prim, too nice; the gait and style and movement are not suited to narrative. That canal stream is always reflecting; it is its nature, it can't help it. Its slick shiny surface is interested in everything it passes along the bank—cows, foliage, flowers, everything. And so it wastes a lot of time in reflection.

Mark Twain, *Autobiography*, in *Mark Twain*, Charles Neider, editor

The heart and center of Chicago is the huge pile of masonry which reminds the visitor . . . of the cathedrals and palaces of St. Petersburg. The City Hall and Court House form one immense building, in which all the city and county business is transacted, both judicial and administrative.

William Stead, *If Christ Came to Chicago*

Date: March 24, 1892, and March 25, 1892
Place: The Honorable Judge Baker's courtroom in the Cook County Courthouse.

The weather in Chicago on that day: a clear day in the 50s, if there ever were any clear days in Chicago in those days when the burning of coal left a permanent sooty, particulate cloud over the city on the lake. Approaching travelers knew their destination was near by the smell of burning wood and coal, the reek of garbage and the acrid odor of the slaughterhouses, and by the black cloud over the city, only occasionally washed away by the weather.

There is always something to talk about with the weather in Chicago: is it too hot, is it too cold. Is there a storm coming which will interfere with travel. The weather is always better somewhere else, more temperate, cooler, warmer. Chicago weather can present dangers, the slippery sidewalk, the loss of electricity, the freezing of the water pipes, so much snow the streets are hazardous. Or, if you were traveling in a horse-drawn carriage, the horse could die or stand still and refuse to move. Still, driving headlong through the dancing snow, when it is blowing, when it is alive, driving by the lake as the waves crash on the breakwater and fling up spray, is exhilarating, with anxiety sharpening the senses, and enjoyed in recollection when safely home.

Florence Kelley, who spent August at what became her summer home in Brooklin, Maine, toward the end of her life, was reported to march out into the Maine summer storms, to walk out of the house and into the middle of the wind, the thunder, the lightning, the rain, to disappear into the storm and shout at the wind and the circling rain, and then to return soaked to the skin, her heavy, drenched skirt wrapped around her.

September 5, 1998: I am now teaching in the area of my expertise, the death penalty. Illinois law is still unknown territory. The state has 102 separate legal jurisdictions, unlike New Jersey's twenty-one. That means 102 county prosecutors. And the Supreme Court of Illinois has categorically rejected proportionality review. Our law school during term is a beehive; this year my course will concentrate on an area of law I know little about: federal law, the review of state capital convictions by federal courts under principles of habeas corpus. At the end of the semester, the students and I will know more.

Legal action: state habeas corpus proceedings in the Honorable Judge Frank Baker's courtroom on the blustery days, March 24 and 25 of 1892, these proceedings being a matter of public record and reported in the *Chicago Tribune*, the *Chicago Inter Ocean* and some other publications and records which have since vanished. These proceedings were also the subject of comment in private correspondence, and perhaps recorded in diaries and journals which have been destroyed or disappeared. There is a transcript of the legal proceeding.

In the Florence Kelley collection at the New York Public Library Manuscripts and Archives Division, the extensive collection of her papers and documents established by her oldest son, Nicholas Kelley, there is no record of this proceeding.

The key to all legal proceedings is the procedural posture of the case before the court, as Florence Kelley herself came to understand, if she did not know it already on that day and when she signed up to be what we would call a mature age entry at the Northwestern University School of Law later that year.

The first woman to graduate from a law school was from Chicago. The Supreme Court of the United States case denying women admission to the bar also originated in Chicago, Bradwell v. Illinois (1873). The rules for admission to the Bar in Chicago were well-established when Florence Kelley appeared in Judge Baker's court in March 1892.

As previously noted, the first educational and training prerequisites for licensure were established in 1858 when applicants from the northernmost district which included Chicago were required to furnish "a certificate to the effect that the applicant for examination has studied two years continuously, one year of which must have been with an attorney in their state." And slightly modified, this rule was extended to applicants from the entire state in 1871, they being required to "have pursued a course of law studies in the office of some lawyer of general practice for at least two years." This rule further provided that "the time employed at any law school as a law student shall be considered as part of the two years" of law office study.

Sup. Ct. R. 85, 53 Ill. xvii (1871) cited by James D. Heiple, *Legal Education and Admission to the Bar the Illinois Experience*, 12 S. Ill. U. L.J. 1987-1988, 123-151. 135.

The key for opening the next door in the legal labyrinth is the nature and power of the court itself, its jurisdiction. Who is making the decision being asked for, and who is controlling the argument and framing the questions. Some judicial proceedings are not final. They are just a hurdle to be crossed before reaching the next court, before getting to the next decision maker. Some judgments are subject to later reversal or even eradication, in spite of their air of finality at the proceeding, and sometimes the lawyers will want that.

April 23, 1996: On a beautiful spring day, I have finally received my certificate of admission to the Bar of Illinois. And what a ridiculous process it has been. Pages of forms, my hands covered in ink from the fingerprints freshly taken by the campus police, and this at a time when fingerprint evidence has been largely discredited. The address of every place I have lived since graduating from high school. Every place I have ever worked. Letters, affidavits. Many of my former employers are dead, or certainly don't remember that young woman who briefly came to work for them.

Fortunately I have the help of a respected city attorney and my conscientious faculty assistant. The Bar of Illinois had to be convinced that I worked for seventeen years for the New Jersey Department of the Public Advocate.

For the actual swearing-in ceremony, I am called into the chambers of a retired Supreme

Court of Illinois justice. Like everyone else he is mostly interested in talking about my husband and the university football team, and not interested in my future or past legal career.

Now I hold in my hand a piece of paper, which came in the mail today, saying I am a member of the Bar in Illinois. I will probably never use or need it.

One thing is clear: the Bar of Illinois does not want lawyers from other states coming in to compete with them.

On these two days in March 1892, it was a legal proceeding not of Florence Kelley's choosing, nor was it a legal proceeding she could use to her advantage. She was being dragged into court by her husband under a writ of habeas corpus.

On March 24 and 25 of 1892 in Judge Frank Baker's courtroom, the legal action of state habeas corpus was precipitated by Lazare Wischnewetzky from New York. On these cool days, when some rain was reported, an outraged husband from New York, who had been deserted by his wife, brought a habeas corpus action demanding that his wife, Florence Kelley Wischnewetzky, surrender to him the bodies of his three children. It was, in short, an action for custody of his children, Nicholas, called Ko, then age six, Margaret, age five, and John, four. A state habeas corpus filing was a legitimate and favored action for custody, for getting into court. The exact same form of action for the same purpose can and is used at the present time.

March 2, 2005: Today the snow is alternately slanting, blowing horizontally, and then dropping straight down. The branches of the tall pine sway outside of my third-floor window, the storm a moving image framed in the leaded windows. I am postponing venturing out. So it is March in Chicago. Tomorrow is predicted to be in the 50s. I can work inside if we don't lose electricity.

A new project, coming right out of the historical homicide project: another website, this time based upon a single person, a woman, a writer. Florence Kelley, factory inspector in Illinois, whatever that was.

The reported temperature on March 24, 1892, was mild on the day the writ of habeas corpus was brought before the court by Dr. Lazare Wischnewetzky. He alleged that when Florence Kelley Wischnewetzky fled the family home in New York City (an apartment on East 76th Street) on a dark December night in 1891, taking the three children with her, she deserted him. We don't know the exact date she fled, but we do know it was a desperate day for Florence Kelley when she boarded the train in New York for Chicago with her three babies, a few suitcases, and nothing else.

August 27, 1998: It is hot. Summer, but not the beautiful big sky of Montana, or Seattle. First class for Homicide, the Unlawful Killing of Another. If we can sort through the levels of available appeals for state capital defendants, and how the federal courts have effectively foreclosed such appeals in federal courts, that is enough. The students will write research papers.

At what point does a woman realize that she is married to a crazy person, that the father of her children, the man whose bed she shares and whom she loves, or at least once loved, is not rational, indeed that he intends her harm, perhaps even would kill her? When Florence Kelley Wischnewetzky ran away to Chicago with her three children, she had come to that realization. She was also acting illegally unless a court held that she had legally justifiable reasons to leave her husband's bed and board.

March 8, 2007: Perfectly bright sun, but very cold, in the 20s, but with such glorious sunshine who cannot laugh into the morning. The residents of Hull-House would have smiled to see such a day.

On March 24, 1892, a petition for divorce was not what was being brought before Judge Frank Baker. Dr. Lazare Wischnewetzky did not have the standing nor did he meet the legal residency requirement for a divorce action. Nor could Florence Kelley Wischnewetzky, who had not yet been an Illinois resident for a year, ask for a divorce on that day, although she would have had legal grounds to seek a divorce in Chicago had she met the residency requirement. She had been in Chicago for less than three months.

The habeas corpus action was assigned to Judge Frank Baker, Chancery Division, Circuit Court of Cook County. The Chancery Court in Cook County, Chicago, was a direct descendant of the Chancery Court in England, whose delays and denizens were immortalized in Charles Dickens's *Bleak House*. Florence Kelley and her brother William Jr., who would testify at this trial, had visited the house where Charles Dickens wrote *Bleak House*, as an act of homage, during their trip to Europe.

The court hearing this action was the court which then had jurisdiction over matters of equity, those emotional, messy, imprecise matters of family and the care of children, and the family property, since a Juvenile and Domestic Relations Court, which was to be first founded in Chicago in 1899, did not yet exist.

March 3, 2007: And a typical March Chicago day, gun metal grey, with minute variations of grimy grey in the sky. The snow is temporarily in abeyance. No wind, and the chill right at the freezing mark. The beginning of March is always welcome in Chicago, even if there is no visible sign of spring, and the weather is inclement. At least the cold, short days of February are finished for another year.

Judge Frank Baker came from a long line of distinguished, highly educated public servants, judges and lawyers. His progenitors emigrated from Kent, England, in 1639, settling in one of the original six towns of the New Haven colony, then moving to East Hampton, Long Island. Judge Baker's ancestors served as judges, magistrates, and as the representatives of dukes, in elected and appointed positions. One of them, perhaps his great-great-great-grandfather, was foreman of the first grand jury in the province of New York at the first Court of the Assizes in 1665. That man's son was a member of the council of the first English governor of New York in 1665. That man's son married a Huguenot, moved to Connecticut, and became a merchant engaged in the West Indian trade, a euphemism for the slave trade.

February 19, 1997: Joy! A baby is born, and mostly healthy, although unhappily not living near Chicago. A baby in February lifting the dreary sky of winter all by himself, even though he is not here, and I cannot hold him. If only I could reach across the country and hold him.

The Connecticut Baker married to the Huguenot had a son, Samuel Baker, who was captured by Indians during the Revolutionary War and sold off to General John Burgoyne's camp for twelve dollars, whereupon he remained as a mess boy on the general's staff until the surrender to General Horatio Gates at Saratoga. At that point the young hostage mustered out and went home, where he stayed just until he was eighteen in 1781, whereupon he immediately reenlisted in the Revolutionary army and saw considerable fighting. After the war he was the first non-native settler in the Tioga Valley in Pennsylvania.

In 1794 this man was elected assessor of the town of Bath, Pennsylvania, and held other government positions before being commissioned as the first judge of the Court of Common Pleas in Steuben County, New York, where he remained until 1817. The Court of Common Pleas was the court which heard writs, such as the great common-law writ of habeas corpus, and other actions under the common law of England, as carried over to the colonies and enacted typically by the passage of a declaration of law stating the common law of England was to be in effect in the colonial jurisdiction. Such a statute was enacted in Illinois in 1819.

That Judge Baker, the grandfather of the Judge Frank Baker hearing the habeas corpus petition involving the three children of Dr. Lazare Wischnewetzky and Florence Kelley Wischnewetzky, died in 1842.

June 25, 1996, Chicago Tribune: "Death Row Inmate Exonerated: Charges Dismissed Against Man in '78 Rape, Killings."

. . . By Monday, Jimerson no longer had to worry about making deals. Characterizing the case against Jimerson as an "egregious denial" of due process, Cook County Circuit Judge Sheila Murphy dismissed the charges.

Murphy said the case was littered with prosecutorial misconduct, most notably when the evidence was brought before a grand jury in 1984. Not only did prosecutors present misleading information to the grand jury that led to Jimerson's indictment, the judge said, but they also failed to disclose key information.

The maternal grandfather of that Judge Baker sitting in the Circuit Court of Cook County on March 24 and 25, 1892, had been a member of the state legislature of New York. The father of this same Judge Baker was a prosperous farmer whose desire it was to prepare his six sons for public service. Judge Baker, one of those sons, responded to President Lincoln's call for volunteers in the Union army, served out his term, and then entered the Albany Law School in New York (currently the repository for the National Death Penalty Archive), having graduated from Ohio Wesleyan University.

This Judge Baker initially opened a law office in Tiffin, Ohio, where he served as a prosecuting attorney and had a general practice until 1873, when he set off for Chicago, becoming part of the great wave of people, including many lawyers, arriving in Chicago after the fire. Perhaps it was the outpouring of sympathy and support for Chicago, as well as the expectation of easy cash, which washed ashore on the lake so many lawyers and builders and bankers and crooks and workers and women with a sense of themselves. Some came to leave where they had been, many were chased out or exiled, others came to find what was here and themselves.

November 19, 1997, Chicago Tribune: "State Executes 2 After Appeals Fail: Clemency Denied in South Side, Berwyn Murders."

The state carried out back-to-back executions for the second time in three years early Wednesday morning, putting to death by lethal injection convicted double murderer Walter Stewart, 42, and murderer and rapist Durlyn Eddmonds, 45.

As protesters outside Stateville Correctional Center near Joliet denounced the death penalty and the state's executioner stood behind a one-way mirror inside the death chamber, a physician pronounced Stewart dead at 12:30 a.m. Eddmonds died at 1:35 a.m. He declined to make a final statement before his death. . . .

"The two cases are entirely different, but the death penalty is an appropriate punishment for both of these murderers," the governor said in a written statement.

In 1887 our Judge Baker was elected judge on the Democratic ticket, the party affili-ations being the reverse of the present identifications. The Democrats were conservative and antiabolitionist before the Civil War. The Republicans were the party of the assassi-nated Lincoln. The Democrats, however, controlled some Chicago elections. In the 1890s the Democrats split into various groups with socialist and progressive agendas, some-times attracting reformers such as Florence Kelley's colleague and Hull-House regular, Henry Demarest Lloyd. It was the various splits and feuds among the Democrats which got the young William Darrah Kelley into trouble in Philadelphia, requiring him to leave for a while and go to Boston.

November 20, 1997: No one was executed by the state when I worked for the State of New Jersey. No one, not the governor, not the legislature, and certainly not the State Supreme Court under the leadership of the then-Chief Justice Robert Wilentz, would have gone forward with the order to kill. No one in that hierarchy wanted executions in New Jersey. Now I live in a state where the governor signs five execution orders in a single day.

Judge Frank Baker, with the notable colonial heritage and impeccable judicial cre-dentials, was reelected as a judge in 1891 and again in 1897, allowing him to preside over two matters involving Florence Kelley: the habeas corpus proceeding and her ex parte divorce proceeding in June 1899. Judge Baker was said to have distinguished himself with his opinions while on the Illinois appellate courts and to be so widely respected that the Republicans, not his party, also endorsed his judicial reelection. An excellent scholar and a conscientious and kindly jurist, he was never put forward for the Supreme Court of Illinois.

April 24, 2012: A beautiful spring day. I am so lucky, lucky to be alive, to be in good health. A little breeze today, a sweet breeze. I think I will never get out of this manuscript. Becoming enmeshed in Chicago history is a sentence to life without parole.

It remains unanswered how the original judge in 1892, the esteemed Judge Frank Baker, heard the ex parte divorce proceeding seven years later. Perhaps jurisdiction sim-ply continued to attach to the case. Perhaps the case remained open as a child custody proceeding, and it continued to be his case, so that it was his case for the divorce as well. Perhaps some maneuvering or calendar manipulation was required to keep the matter before this judge. Florence Kelley did not seek a divorce prior to 1899 for reasons which can only be a matter of speculation.

April 30, 1996: A wedding. The weather was perfect, sunshine, cool, in every way beauti-ful. The first formal wedding of this generation in the family. And it was celebrated in our old hometown, the place where all three daughters grew up, went to high school, and some to college, although none was born there. The place we still all think of as home. A joyful celebration, in a garden, with just a hint of rain, and another daughter pregnant. We are fortunate, so fortunate. There is nothing more to be prized than the peace and stability that allow families to be families, to be together, to have babies, and protect them in conditions of safety, of civil order, of peace.

The verbatim record of a legal proceeding is some kind of a truth; it is a record of what people said or what was recorded that they said at a particular point in time, at a particular place. It is not a record of "what happened." It is not a record of what they thought or felt, although some of the statements are revelatory or at least suggestive of that, and some others are deceptive, as people in court mask their intentions or lie outright. At the very least the legal transcript is a record of a highly formalized social interaction, a proceeding in which more than one person speaks. In theory everyone understands the rules of who speaks and when. This social interaction may take place in opulent surroundings, in wood-paneled courtrooms, or in a dingy, dusty room where a tired man sits behind a cigarette-strewn table surrounded by a stack of case files.

The judge decides who can ask and who must answer the questions, and in what order, because that is how a court of law proceeds, first by determining who is in the room and then the order in which the people present may speak. The words of some speakers are valued more, carry more authority, than the words of others. Sometimes what occurs within those rooms is surprising. Just as a game has to be played at a particular time and place, and then there will be an outcome, so in a court of law the game must be played at a particular time and place, and the outcome is not a certainty, or else the parties would not be in court.

May 15, 1997: There are flowers, purple tulips, hundreds of them, in our garden. I will take a large basket of purple tulips to the dean for the celebration of our Law School graduation. There are signs that there will be little pink roses in the garden later this month.

The habeas corpus proceeding brought by Dr. Lazare Wischnewetzky was reported on page 9 of the Chicago Tribune on March 25, 1892. It was raining that day, or there was said to be a light rain, and the skies may have been the stiff grey recognized by all true Chicagoans, that hard gun metal tone which tests one's loyalty to the city. Perhaps the overhanging black cloud of soot was temporarily rinsed away by the rain for Florence Kelley Wischnewetzky as she made her way, probably once again by a horse-drawn cab, from Hull-House, the social settlement at 335 South Halsted Street, as it identified itself by its original address, to the Cook County Courthouse—so prominent in the life of the city that it didn't need an address, the building whose grand Greek-columned exterior promised more justice than may actually have been delivered within its dark, wood-paneled courtrooms.

This same Cook County Courthouse was described in *If Christ Came to Chicago* by the British journalist William Stead, a sometime resident at Hull-House, during the great depression in the winter of 1893:

The heart and center of Chicago is a huge pile of masonry which reminds the visitor by its polished granite pillars and general massive and somber grandeur of the cathedrals and palaces of St. Petersburg. The City Hall and Court House form one immense building in which all city and county business is transacted, both judicial and administrative. . . .

In this building, crammed with invaluable documents, the seat and the center of the whole civic machinery, for want of any better accommodation, there were housed night after night through the month of December from one to two thousand of the most miserable men in Chicago.

If Christ Came to Chicago caused an uproar among the civic community in 1893 and became the occasion for the founding of the Civic Federation, still in operation and still asking questions today about what the City of Chicago should be and do, most recently preparing an analysis of the financial situation of the public schools.

August 19, 1998: The sun is strong on the back porch. August is a wonderful, quiet month. Little traveling, many people gone. To simply sit outside and read the newspaper is contentment.

August 19, 1998, Chicago Tribune: "Crime Chicago Style" by Charles M. Madigan.

. . . The Archives got the books from the Chicago Police Department at 11th and State Streets, where it found them sometimes in the 1980s when it was making a routine visit. . . . They were in terrible shape. The paper crumbled in your hands, Hopkins [Dorothy Hopkins, the conservator from the State Archives] said, and certainly would not have been able to withstand much more handling. As she removed each of the old pages, cleaned them, de-acidified them, sealed them and prepared them for remounting, she found herself reading more and more about bloody murder in Chicago and wondering what it must have been like.

In theory there was no place for children, or for women with children, to be residents at Hull-House. In fact Florence Kelley's children, especially the older ones, Nicholas and Margaret, spent many weeks, months, and years at Hull-House, becoming the children of Hull-House. The Hull-House residents became their surrogate mothers and aunts and fathers and grandparents, as their mother traveled the country for Hull-House, or to go to a conference of factory inspectors, or to visit or give a lecture and sell her articles. And so Florence Kelley replicated the atmosphere at her own mother's house, and at her grandparents' home, where the young people met a variety of gregarious, active, and intelligent people, passionate about reform, and so they learned to talk and listen.

Later, Nicholas Kelley said:

I remember the buildings that were at Hull House when I came. There was the original house, with McGeeny's Livery Stable filling up the space from the house to the corner of Polk Street. I cannot remember what stood on the other side, where now stands that art gallery that the architects Alan and Irving Pond, friends of the House, designed. The crèche was in a little white one-story building in the alley on that side, and the Jane Club, living quarters for young working women, was in a brick tenement building facing on Ewing Street.

Within the original house, the kinder-garten was in the back parlor in the right, and the corresponding room on the left was the dining-room. Opening to the left from the front parlor was the octagon that was then Miss Addams' office.

I remember some of the things that happened in the alleys that ran through the middle of the blocks. Once an elephant went astray from a circus. After he had been lost for two days, he was found in an alley in which, he had become so wedged between the houses that he could not get himself out.

Nicholas became close to Hull-House resident Alice Hamilton, and Jane Addams became very fond of Margaret, mediating between mother and daughter during the difficulties of adolescence, as did Florence Kelley's mother, Caroline. The children spent school holidays at Hull-House or came there when Florence Kelley was traveling, and she was always traveling, bringing the children when they were older, going to New York, or attending a conference with like-minded reformers, or taking a train to Portland, Oregon, or giving a speech in Iowa, or advising all of the people somewhere who wanted her advice on how to start something, or keep it going, or turn people out or get people in. These trips served her in good stead later, as she knew people everywhere.

The Hull-House records show the children spending large parts of their summers there, as well as other school holidays. And they were welcome there. Nicholas had a key to the front door, which he would not give up for years even though his mother had long since moved to New York to live in another settlement house which did not allow children.

After leaving Hull-House Florence Kelley complained she was no longer listed as a resident, and Jane Addams immediately put her back on the roster, although she was in fact no longer living there. Years later Jane Addams wrote Florence Kelley: "I have never gotten used to your absence," missing the sound of her laughter on the stairs.

In March 1892 the Cook County Courthouse—described by William Stead, whom Florence Kelley may not have yet met but would later meet when he came to stay at Hull-House while writing his book—was that large, pretentious building, the classical pile, remnants of which exist today in what is now called the Court House District, where there are many restaurants and plaques for the tourists. The alley behind the old courthouse, where the Haymarket defendants were hanged, is not memorialized with a sign.

June 10, 2010: The great columned courthouse described by William Stead was rebuilt and eventually replaced with a large, modern and singularly unattractive court building at 26th and California streets, and an attached jail. The old criminal courthouse was bought by a private real estate developer who restored parts of it and converted the building to law offices.

My research assistants and I go to 26th and California, as it is called, to pull indictments for capital murder and death-eligible murder from the case files of the Cook County Clerk's office. We sit in a rectangular bland conference room, bring sandwiches, and go through surprisingly well-organized Cook County case files pulling indictments. There is nothing grand or hopeful about this criminal courts building, beginning with the parking on the street where you worry about the safety of your car, to the metal detectors and pat-down when you enter, most of these procedures implemented by men and women who give the appearance of wishing they were anywhere else but here.

Florence Kelley would not recognize this world, although what has not changed and what she and John Peter Altgeld both would have immediately registered is that most of the people who are coming to the criminal courts are poor people, shabbily dressed, and they look anxious, nervous, afraid. Except the lawyers, who are easily recognized in their suits and by their air of distraction. The lawyers, too, look as if they would prefer to be elsewhere.

Florence Kelley would have entered the grand columned front entrance, now gone, of the old courthouse on her way to Judge Baker's courtroom for the legal standoff against the husband she had deserted less than three months earlier, the man whom she was seeking to rid herself of and to deprive of his children. In this building—as she would have been well aware—behind the courthouse, in the narrow alley a special construction had been made between two buildings. The special execution chamber was built for the Haymarket defendants in the alley with an entrance from the jail, so that the four prisoners could be led out, stood on a platform and publicly hanged.

April 25, 2012: And the rain has come, at last. Perhaps my car will get washed in the rain. The death penalty, still, is a symbol of the power of the state. It is as if the law must assert its authority by the symbol of its ability to take a life. That decision, and how it is carried out, still demands our attention, and challenging it is a fundamental act of rebellion against the state.

The six remaining Haymarket defendants, Albert Parsons, George Engel, Michael Schwab, Samuel Fielden, Adolph Fischer, and August Spies, listened in the Cook County jail to the building of the scaffolding for their hangings the night before the executions. Louis Lingg, the seventh defendant sentenced to death, committed a miserable suicide in his cell a few days before the hangings by swallowing a smuggled-in blasting cap and blowing off part of his face, then lingering in pain for days.

The authorities who ordered the building of this special execution chamber next to the jail must have been very afraid that if these defendants were transported to another place for their executions, they would be rescued by their supporters or lynched by a mob, that riots would break out in the streets. And so the authorities arranged for them to be hanged without leaving the building.

On November 11, 1887, a carefully selected audience of 180—journalists, members of the legal community, a favored few observers, and no family members of the defendants—sat in formally arranged chairs in the alley between the Cook County Courthouse and the jail and watched the hanging of four of the Haymarket defendants. Then there was the carefully orchestrated funeral procession to their place of burial.

August 21, 1997, Chicago Tribune: "Edgar Bows Out . . . Then Stampede Begins; Governor Says He Wanted to Leave While Still on Top."

. . . Gov. Jim Edgar finally decided that in the end, he simply wanted to go out on top.

By uttering the words, "I will not be a candidate in the upcoming election," Edgar on Wednesday set off a political chain reaction of massive proportions among Republicans who now hold all major statewide elected offices and caused spillover effects on the 1998 Democratic ticket. . . .

Brenda Edgar has been the governor's closest political confidant. But she said she had thought since January that her husband would run for the Senate. She said she would have supported him had he made the race. . . .

He leaves behind the only life he has known without concrete prospects for the future. "I don't have a job," he said. "I have no real wealth."

He implored GOP legislative leaders to pass school-funding reform as his legacy, a wish they have previously denied. . . . "Our system of funding schools remains fundamentally unfair," Edgar said, vowing to continue pushing for a dramatic overhaul in the way Illinois' property-tax-dependent schools are funded. . . .

Edgar said he would not convert to personal use his $3.5 million campaign fund, but instead was planning to use the money to support GOP candidates and to assist social causes supported by his wife, especially children's issues. He left little room for a return to politics.

October 1998: In my course on capital murder, we read the 1986 Supreme Court of Illinois opinion in People v. Porter (489 N.E. 2d 1329 Filed 2/21/1986). It is a boring case, a straightforward case. This is a good example of how state supreme courts review the facts supporting a murder conviction and post-conviction appeals from death sentences. Basically the opinion shows a state supreme court simply going along, doing what it usually does, in a routine case, with a routine result, affirmance of the death penalty. You can hear the judges yawning as they fill up the opinion with recitations from the police report. We read the case in class, and it arouses little interest or discussion.

The police report reminds me of all the police reports I read in New Jersey. They are as formulaic as a teenage romance novel.

. . . Officer Dennis T. Dwyer and his partner also responded to the call. As they approached the pools from the north, Williams walked out from the bleachers and told them that a man had been shot up in the bleachers. Dwyer observed Hillard on the top step of the bleachers lying on his back and bleeding from the head. Hillard was taken to a hospital where he underwent surgery and later died.

Cook County Deputy Medical Examiner Joanne Richmond performed autopsies on both Marilyn Green and Jerry Hillard. Green had received three "through and through" gunshot wounds. She was shot twice in the right side of the neck at close range; within approximately 1 to 1-1/2 feet. She was shot a third time in the left hand. Green died from massive bleeding due to multiple gunshot wounds. . . .

On August 18, 1982, Taylor viewed a lineup at a police station and again identified the defendant.

The defendant was sentenced to death after a penalty trial with a jury. That sentence was upheld and then after collateral review upheld again by the Supreme Court of Illinois.

September 1998: Apparently, there is no place in Chicago which has an uninterrupted print run of the Chicago Tribune during the entire time, 1870-1930, of the homicide data set. A digital edition is promised, but in the meantime, microfilm is inaccurate and a torture. There is a place in New Hampshire, the American Newspaper Repository, where there is a complete, bound sequential set of the Chicago Tribune for the entire period of the Chicago homicide data set, as well as other complete runs of major papers in the US and Britain.

The Supreme Court of Illinois considered the murder conviction and the death sentence imposed in the Porter case again in 1995 (647 NE 2d 972 [1995]). The legal challenge was based upon an error in the admission of hypothetically exonerating evidence from a witness who wasn't called. The opinion is couched in an appellate court's usual tone of certainty:

The evidence against defendant was considerable. The unaffected findings include the testimony of two eyewitnesses, Henry Williams and William Taylor. The unaffected findings also include the testimony of Anthony Liance, a Chicago police officer who responded to reports of the shootings. Liance's testimony placed defendant in the park near where the shootings occurred shortly after 1 a.m.

The error in not generating the proposed testimony deprived the jury of evidence complementing the alibi defendant presented at trial. But accounting for the error's effect shows no real prejudice could have resulted. . . . Considering the collective effect of the testimony, as well as Davis' alone, we do not conclude a different trial outcome was reasonably likely. . . .

For the above reasons, we affirm the judgment of the circuit court. We direct the clerk of this court to enter an order setting Tuesday, May 9, 1995, as the date on which the sentence of death, entered by the circuit court of Cook County, shall be carried out. Defendant shall be executed in the manner provided by law (Ill. Rev. Stat. 1991, ch. 38, par. 119-5). The clerk of this court shall send a certified copy of this mandate to the Director of Corrections, to the warden of Stateville Correctional Center, and to the warden of the institution where defendant is now confined.

And so it was another death sentence affirmed.

October 15, 1998: These are not the words of a court; it is the tone of a Supreme Being speaking from above. Their judgment is not to be questioned. The police reports quoted include statements from the defendant which have a familiar ring, a predictability. In New Jersey I saw the same kind of police statements reproduced in the court opinion: always detailing the wounds, usually quoting the defendant using foul language, with the defendant expressing hatred or a lack of remorse for the victim, so that the person reading the police report would be immediately disgusted and have no sympathy. This is why the court quotes the police report, for its certainty, for its crude brutality. I mention this to the students. They don't say anything.

Along with the story about Florence Kelley Wischnewetzky's tribulations on page 9 of the *Chicago Tribune* on March 25, 1892, there was a story about the end of the life of a murderer sentenced to ninety-nine years after asking for the death penalty (his conviction based upon a confession which he later renounced), reports of the economic hardships imposed by tariffs on imports and exports (an ever and ongoing intense national debate), a report of police complaining that the streets were being used as dumping grounds by janitors and others, that sweepings, trash, and all manner of garbage, including whatever fell off of overloaded wagons, ended up on the street.

September 24, 1998: The lawyer for Anthony Porter says no one has ever suggested he was innocent. The Supreme Court of Illinois will never hold that Porter cannot be executed because of mental incompetence, I say in response. In class, we read the Texas case of Penry and its progeny, and wring our hands. A court will drown you in detail when it is making a mistake.

During the time Florence Kelley lived at Hull-House the following daily newspapers were published in English: the *Chicago Daily Tribune* (now online), the *Chicago Journal*, the *Chicago Mail*, the *Chicago Daily News*, the *Chicago Evening Post*, the *Chicago Times*, the *Chicago Herald*, the *Chicago Record* (after 1900 to become the *Record-Herald*), the *Inter Ocean*, the *Chicago Daily Law Bulletin*, the *Chicago Daily Drovers Journal*, the *Daily Calumet*, the *Chicago South Side Sun* (earlier simply the *Sun*), and the *Chicago Specialist*.

November 18, 1998: Driving through the snow and wind in New Hampshire and Vermont, I wonder if I will ever get there. Then the little inn has a soft bed, and I can barely get out of it and walk. And then there is the drive back to Boston in the snow.

In addition, in the 1890s there were the uncounted dozens of newspapers, bulletins, pamphlets, broadsheets, and fugitive papers and journals published in German, Swedish, Russian, Czech, Polish, Norwegian, Yiddish, Italian, French, and more. Newspapers were read aloud to the people who couldn't read. Political allegiances could be quickly identified by what newspaper a person regularly read. You could follow the fortunes of the political opposition by reading their newspapers.

November 1998: Back in Chicago, from Vermont/New Hampshire happily. It was cold, cold and isolated in Vermont, and the driving alone along deserted, snowy roads unsettling. The American Newspaper Repository in Vermont is a work of love, a collection of newspapers, bought from the British Library's holdings of print newspapers. They were saved from destruction and then kept at great expense and with great care by two people who love literature, love newspapers, and love print. The newspapers are kept in a huge building which was once a New England mill, built near the water to harness the power of a small waterfall. Now the damp protects the papers.

The repository includes a complete print run of the Chicago Tribune and the New York Times for the period of the Chicago homicide data set, 1870-1930. In every way it was worth it to travel all the way to see those original newspapers, in a bound collection which includes many of the fugitive socialist newspapers of Britain and Europe kept by the British Library, journals and newspapers Florence Kelley, Henry Demarest Lloyd, and William Darrah Kelley would have known. The collection was auctioned off by the British Library.

The founders of the American Newspaper Repository could not have been more gracious. Without them all of these newspapers and journals would have been destroyed. The awful period between print and digitalization, when libraries microfilmed papers, creating ugly, unreadable copies which are guaranteed to cause a headache, and where the haste and lack of care of the filming means missing pages, undecipherable text with heavy black slashes across the page, as if scribbled over by a spiteful child.

Chicago's first newspaper was the *Chicago Weekly Democrat*, founded by John Calhoun in 1833. The *Chicago Tribune* was founded in 1847. Joseph Medill bought it in 1855. The *Chicago Inter Ocean*, an "upper class arbiter of cultural tastes," went into decline after 1895 when it was bought by Charles Yerkes to use as another lever in his battles for control of the street rail franchises. The *Daily News* was founded in 1876, and the morning *Daily News* was renamed *The Record* in 1893. In 1900 Chicago had nine general-circulation newspapers in English when William Randolph Hearst's sensationalist *Chicago American* appeared. The *Chicago Defender* was founded in 1905 and became the nation's most influential and widely read African American newspaper, regularly reporting on lynchings and other news of interest to African Americans in the South and North and around the country, and on the great migration.

November 1998: Nicholson Baker and his wife are regarded with suspicion by the community of librarians and archivists, because they sued to stop the destruction of newspapers. But they saved the sole print copies of many newspapers and journals for us and pointed out that libraries lied about the deacquisitions.

Nor does microfilm display the advertisements, or the layout of the page, or other aspects of a newspaper which allow us to see what someone actually read in 1892. The incidental ads, the reports on what people wore and said, and the unexpected bits of news are the heart of the experience of reading a newspaper, preserved for us from the 1890s only in the print copies of its newspapers.

There is no report of what Florence Kelley wore to the habeas corpus proceeding. Given her astute sensitivity to the social requirements of the moment, she probably wore a conservative, formal, correct long black silk dress, the kind of outfit which could never be criticized as improper, and which called no attention to itself but announced to whoever saw her that its wearer was a member of a certain social class, a person not to be trifled with or treated lightly.

March 12, 2008: Today the sun is shining, and if it is not warm, at least there is blue sky, even if not a leaf or the suggestion of green appears in the tapestry of branches against the sky. The fir tree steadfast, cloaked in its thick bark, another winter survived, for that tree, for this house, for us.

On those damp March days Florence Kelley was probably dressed in a manner similar to that of the women who appear in the 1890s photographs of Chicago's reformers and suffragists, tall women, large or thick to present eyes, straight-backed, severe women, dressed invariably in black, who in the winter sometimes wore fur-trimmed coats, fur hats and carried a fur muff, women who always wore a hat and gloves when they went out in the street, sometimes elaborate hats with ribbons and the plumage of now-extinct birds. The gloves, the heavy coats, even the hats were a kind of protection, as well as an announcement of who they were.

June 5, 1996: Another class at the law school over, another academic year finished. Many official events, much bustle.

The women whose husbands are on our university board wear beautiful clothes. I have never known women who actually bought their clothes in Paris and wore them as they were expected to do, comfortably with that much familiarity.

Wardrobe rescue has come for me in the person of a professional assistant in New York who knows far better than I do what I should wear on what occasions—to a formal dinner, or the opening of the opera, or a trip to California. She also knows what can be packed and emerge without wrinkles during a week of living out of a suitcase in Asia.

There is always the question of what to wear at the many official occasions. The same people go to the football games, to the theatre, to the opera, to the galas and balls, and to the charity runs along the lake. And they have the right clothes for each activity.

The hard part is to find something appropriate to wear for those occasions where I am basically supposed to be present but invisible, but correctly invisible. Hundreds of journalists and photographers from all over the world are scheduled to come for an event which is a non-event. The journalists will be very interested in what is being worn, but not by me.

The *Chicago Tribune* in the 1890s did report on what the fashionable women wore, and featured many clothing advertisements—elegant line drawings of dresses, shirtwaists, cloaks, umbrellas, hats, and shoes. What the fashionable women wore for the many reported social events, and what visiting dignitaries wore, was dutifully reported in the newspaper every day. Minor royalty, dukes and princesses, regularly arrived and there were breathless reports of what they wore.

All items of clothing, including corsets and underwear, could be bought from the large print Sears Roebuck catalog, or from its competitor, the Montgomery Ward catalog, another Chicago company, although the clothes would not have been fashionable enough for the ladies in Chicago society: bloomers, shirtwaists, long skirts, fitted jackets, long coats. These were clothes for working girls or farmers' wives.

What everyone wore to work was an underlayer that could be easily washed without machines. Every large city had hundreds of laundry workers, almost always women. The 1913 statistical abstract of the United States lists 533,697 laundry workers (excluding operatives) of which 520,004 were women in 1910. The very rich sent their fine linens and lace-trimmed items by ship to China or France to be washed and ironed and returned three months later. For the rest, an army of washerwomen washed and ironed and starched the family's clothes inside and outside of the home.

Once again, Theodore Dreiser in *The Titan* imagines the 1893 social scene where his main character, Frank Cowperwood, based upon Charles Yerkes, the street rail magnate, will do his business:

Life passes from individuality and separateness at times to a sort of Monticelliesque mood of color, where individuality is nothing, the glittering totality all. The new house, with its charming French windows on the ground floor, its heavy bands of stone flowers and deep-sunk florated door, was soon crowded with a moving, colorful flow of people.

. . . The adjacent side streets and the open space in front of the house were crowded with champing horses and smartly veneered carriages. . . . The caterer, Kinsley, had supplied a small army of trained servants who were posted like soldiers, and carefully supervised by the Cowperwood butler. The new dining-room, rich with a Pompeian scheme of color, was aglow with a wealth of glass and an artistic arrangement of delicacies. The afternoon costumes of the women, ranging through autumnal grays, purples, browns, and greens, blended effectively with the brown-tinted walls of the entry-hall, the deep gray and gold of the general living-room, the old-Roman red of the dining-room, the white-and-gold of the music-room, and the neutral sepia of the art gallery.

In the 1890s in the prairie it was possible to buy a whole house from the Sears Roebuck catalog, as well as small guns and rifles, entire buggies and a harness, tables, chairs, lumber, aprons, tools, and seeds for planting the crops. You could buy everything but the horse. There was a special culture of its own for the buying and selling of every kind of horse, depended upon for most of the getting to where you were going until the railroad came.

There would be no easy recourse, however, if you were in the middle of the plains and the seeds did not grow, or if the shirtwaist was too tight, or had a tear in its flounced sleeve, or was sewn badly, perhaps by an eight-year-old in the Nineteenth Ward.

Florence Kelley's clothes were thrown on haphazardly, even as her stockings were mismatched or sometimes had holes, as if, Jane Addams said, she were Athena hurrying into battle, which she was.

Florence Kelley herself was never fashionable, and for most of her life had no money. If she had had money she would not have spent it on clothes. Her mother, Caroline, sewed, probably made her daughter's clothes as she was growing up, and embroidered underwear for her granddaughter, Margaret, over her daughter's objection. The archives in the New York Public Library include several unpaid New York bills, including some for clothes. The local dressmaker served many, but it was the revolution of ready to wear, the clothing manufactured in the sweatshops of the Nineteenth Ward, which changed everything and made it possible to go to work in store-bought clothes.

The pictures of Florence Kelley from Philadelphia and Cornell—there are only a few group pictures of her from the time she lived in Chicago—show a pretty, rather prim young person, upright, staring confidently at the camera for the long exposure. The picture of her which is usually reproduced is probably the picture taken for her graduation or matriculation at Cornell. The reports of her as a young woman are of her radiant energy, which belied accounts of her sickly childhood and the months and years spent in bed. In Switzerland and at Cornell she apparently loved dancing, and went to dances held in the Old Red Barn next to Sage Hall, a building which stands today.

June 1997: Our third graduation. Always a relief. And the ceremony has been successfully changed to be outside.

It was said when Florence Kelley left Hull-House to become the secretary of the National Consumers League in New York City in 1899 that the rooms and stairways echoed with the memory of her laughter.

As a girl Florence Kelley's father was her teacher, her closest friend, her mentor, and intellectual soul mate. When she married, if the marriage was to be a true marriage, it was inevitable that the bond between father and daughter would be loosened, and even for a time undone, and only with great pain on both sides.

If the bitterness of the divorce is an index of the former intimacy and the strength of the vanished love between husband and wife, then Lazare Wischnewetzky's fight for his children in the courts, and particularly in this court in March 1892, a fight which continued for years, was a measure of his extreme outrage, or desperation, his anger at being left, his sense of loss, and the depth of his former love.

On March 24, 1892, Dr. Wischnewetzky testified in court that when they married his wife had worshiped the ground he walked on, and the first five years of their marriage were idyllic. A newspaper reporter at the habeas proceeding said that he never once looked at his wife during the proceedings.

Jane Addams was not in court that day, although she had offered to testify. Perhaps it was decided between the women that Jane Addams's appearance would be a distraction, or just attract additional unwanted attention from the press.

The column headline in the *Chicago Tribune* on March 25 reads: "Mrs. Wischnewetzky Pleads for Her Children." The next line identifies her in smaller type as the daughter of Pig Iron Kelley and promises details on the couple's life in New York, noting that the case involved "New York people of prominence and infelicities of a distressing nature." Chicago is ever eager to read about infelicities of a distressing nature involving prominent people from New York, or Europe.

The children were present in court because in a habeas corpus action theirs were the bodies which would have to be produced in response to the legal action. And so the law, a court, in the person of the judge, carries out its stipulated obligations, here to turn over, produce the bodies, or not. And so the children were there to be produced, having been brought down, probably by horse-drawn carriage, from Winnetka, from Wayside, the Lloyd family home, with their nursemaid from New York, whose name is not reported in the newspaper accounts.

March 4, 2007: The sun has appeared, blue sky and a few wisps of clouds, but cold. A perfect March day. Five-toed footprints in the snow on the walk this morning. The branches of the evergreen outside are restless. Today it is possible to believe there will be spring.

As the daughter of a congressman Florence Kelley knew when to put on proper clothes, when the wearing of social class was required, when one is arguing on behalf of the poor, for example.

February 1997: Virginia Woolf castigates herself and anyone reading for writing letters during her designated writing time. She is right. Enough of an indulgence to spend the writing time on a diary.

The Quakers may have eschewed luxury and finery, but their parsimonious simplicity and cleanliness were principled, and their speech and manners impeccable. They did not consider themselves inferior or superior to anyone. Their behavior toward all, rich, poor, suffering, and triumphant, was the same.

The Quakers pulled those around them into the fiery circle of their unwavering moral certainty, not of any one belief, but that there were standards for behavior, that there was right and wrong, and that those mattered. From their earliest colonial beginnings in America, the Quaker cause was the fight to abolish capital punishment. They also developed a theory for the creation of the penitentiary system in America, built on the principle that wrongdoers could change. Wrongdoers must be incarcerated in solitary confinement and in silence. The first prison model developed in America in Pennsylvania by Quakers was shaped like a wheel with spokes, with a single guard at the center able to look down all the silent corridors at once.

May 13, 2013: Finally the spring has come. The death toll from the factory collapse in Bangladesh has passed one thousand. The familiar expressions of outrage, surprise. The factory workers, when they saw the cracks in the building, said they were afraid to come to work, the building was unsafe. The managers said: come to work or don't bother to come the next day. They came to work, and no one came to work the next day.

William Darrah Kelley Jr., Florence Kelley's older brother, recuperated from whatever ailed him as a young man in Philadelphia and Avignon, fully recovered from his episodes of complete blindness, came to testify on behalf of his sister at the habeas corpus proceeding on the second day, March 25, 1892.

March 5, 2006: Apparently much of the Nicholas Kelley archives was originally left to Columbia University. Later the Nicholas Kelley archives, which then included the Florence Kelley archives, moved to the New York Public Library archives. At the Columbia University archives, long-distance communication is cumbersome and time-consuming, and the librarians are not particularly helpful or friendly. They are all very busy. I had better go up and see what they have in the way of original letters and records.

Henry Demarest Lloyd, in the Columbia University class of 1867, aspired to be the class poet, inspired by a vigorous professor who used poetry and fiction to teach history. When he entered Columbia University Law School, it offered a two-year course qualifying graduates for admission to the bar without any further examination.

Henry Demarest Lloyd, however, eager to begin his real life and to start to practice law early, took and passed the New York Bar in the spring of 1867 without waiting to graduate, and went out into the world immediately to right some wrongs.

This is what lawyers are trained to do: to first articulate and define the wrongs, then persuade a court or legislature to recognize rights or wrongs. The people in the sweatshops and tenements in the Nineteenth Ward didn't know until a factory inspector told them that the conditions under which they were living and working could be seen as a violation of law, as a violation of some sort of right.

This Columbia University, these buildings, in the Wischnewetzkys' time in New York City, may have looked much as they do today, as Sage Hall on the Cornell University central campus retains much of the same look as when Florence Kelley lived there as a Cornell undergraduate in 1882, as some of the old buildings on the central campus of Northwestern University remain. The library was the centerpiece of the traditional campus in the nineteenth century.

June 11, 2006: On a glorious day in New York, I take the Broadway bus to the Columbia library to see what is in the Kelley collection. There are more librarians than customers at the desk in the Columbia University archives. There is little of what I have been looking for—not that I know what that is—among the requested files. No one seems very interested in helping me find letters to or from Florence Kelley in the Nicholas Kelley papers. Perhaps I didn't present my request with sufficient formality or self-importance. The librarians cannot be pulled away from their screens.

The beauty of the Columbia University central quadrangle rescues the trip. These American universities, what strange institutions they are. Their survival is some kind of a miracle.

The central Columbia quadrangle sports a large white tent, no doubt from recent graduation festivities. The scale of the buildings and then bold architecture put me into a soporific daydream. How little of the surrounding neighborhood remains from when Henry Demarest Lloyd was a student here in the 1860s. Yet the institution has survived.

Without the island of the university, the entire neighborhood would have been turned into buildings with cheap plastic facades and low-rise dark apartments. While the American universities have built and rebuilt and torn down their foundational buildings, in some few places—Cornell, Columbia, Northwestern, the University of Pennsylvania—the central quadrangle, the grand granite and marble buildings from the eighteenth and nineteenth century, remain: temples to the aspirations of education. They look the same because no one can sell the real estate dedicated to their educational, not-for-profit enterprise.

There was in the Columbia University archives, in addition to unidentified letters and scraps of paper from 1845 and 1865, a lock of golden hair, perhaps from the baby Nicholas, some receipts for clothing, miscellaneous bills, and one small quotation from Jane Addams, said to be from the dedication of a labor museum:

The best education cannot do more than constantly reconstruct daily experience and give it a relation to the past as well as an understanding of contemporary life.

June 11, 2010: We have been gone from the university house for a year now. On the campus everything is green, everything blooming, yet few students or people walk about. The library is silent. Perhaps all the keeping of paper will not be necessary in the future, but in the meantime, it is a comfort to know that a copy of the Chicago Tribune *published on a specific day in 1892, if I can put my hands on a print copy, is the same as the* Chicago Tribune *which Florence Kelley and Jane Addams would have read in the sunlit octagon of Hull-House on that day.*

The medical student Lazare Wischnewetzky first formally came calling on his fellow student Florence Kelley on New Year's Day 1884. Caroline Bonsall Kelley reported to her husband that Lazare Wischnewetzky brought gifts, rare books, works of philosophy, and political theory from a private library.

March 6, 2007: A light snow blowing in little curlicues up from the speckled sidewalk, a dull, metallic sky and a blunt cold. Tenements in 1893 often had no heat in the grim winter of 1893, or were mildly warmed by a sulphurous coal-burning stove. This 1890s Chicago has taken a hold and won't let go. Sometimes I think that I live there. They left so much writing, and the quality is high. The writings they left are like the buildings: monumental, substantial, beautiful, requiring a great deal of skill and intelligence to create, and time and money to preserve.

The *Tribune* report of the habeas corpus action on March 24, 1892, promised to reveal a long series of domestic infelicities between the daughter of Pig Iron Kelley and her husband.

Two paragraphs down the lead caption reads: "A Highly Educated Woman." The story reports that Mrs. Wischnewetzky was fluent in five languages, Italian, German, French, Swedish, and, of course, English, and that during the marriage, and especially in New York, she supported the doctor, a fact he denied under oath.

June 27, 2011: Evanston. My library carrel is filled with boxes, books, and papers from the third floor. Florence Kelley had the right idea. Not to have possessions. But your own writings? Not like the furniture, your own words, the only record that you lived then.

The Northwestern University Library on the Evanston campus is now a place where anyone can walk in and get on a computer and do whatever it is they do on the computer. The high ceilings, inspirational, for what is learning but aspiration, create a cave-like atmosphere, as the students and others crouch forward and stare into the machines.

The desks and tables are not rectilinear. People sit at angles to one another, not talking, not in rows, their heads and bodies leaning forward as if they would fall into the screens.

The librarians also are falling into their computer screens; they can hardly be persuaded to look away to answer a question.

The screen saver on the idling computers is a historic map of an island, a small island in the Pacific, colored frog green, drawn by someone who wanted to know where something was, and now in the university's archives. The university library itself is an island of quiet and calm, as is the university itself, an oasis of green beside the lake, easy to spot and looked for from the returning airplane, circling over the lake before landing.

Florence Kelley's income in Zurich at that time was from her writings for American newspapers and journals, and she seemed to have had to fight for every penny. While Florence Kelley was acting as an educated correspondent for American newspapers and journals, she was also doing the hack work of translating French, Italian, and German popular novels from one language to another. That translating of popular novels served her well when she was factory inspector, and not just because of her language fluency. In New York she was once again the freelance writer and editor, peddling her translation of Engels's *Die Lage*, a work apparently not very many people wanted to read and no mainstream publisher wanted to publish

The marriage must have been, at least for a time, a partnership in work as well as family, and the dissolution of that joint and passionate mutual commitment was not without pain. A friend later remarked that Florence Kelley "drank deep from the cup of bitter disillusionment."

January 20, 1997: At least her last days and nights were not spent suffering. All the stories forgotten, and not written down or recorded. Now no one will tell of those days a hundred years ago in Indiana, in Brooklyn, in California. No one remembers. Even if an imagined grievance was the reason for remembering, it was a recollection, caught in a story.

On March 24, 1892, when Florence Kelley entered Judge Baker's chancery proceeding through the faux majestic columns of the Cook County Courthouse, she was bereft of previous sources of strength. The painful disentanglement of her lifelong relationship with her father, followed by their brief reunion when he was very ill, then his death in 1889, left her now permanently without him.

Relations with her mother and brothers were broken and severely strained during the marriage, which she later referred to as the period of "my cruel ingratitude." Letters and diaries from this period are not to be found anywhere in the family archives, not at Columbia University, nor at the New York Public Library archives: oblique references suggest the quarrels were bitter.

February 1, 1997: Then there is the question of my name. For reasons unknown, many people here insist upon calling me by my unmarried name, or insist upon using my unmarried name as my middle name, which I have not done professionally or in print for decades.

When I was in law school in New Jersey in the 1970s, a court had to declare that a married woman or a divorced woman could use her unmarried name, as opposed to her legal name, her married name, when appearing in court. After my marriage, ten years before entering law school, I never again used my maiden name, not as a byline for journalism—although I could have—or for fiction, nor as a lawyer.

When I began publishing in the law, years later, when I had three children all with their father's name as their surname, there seemed to be little reason to take a different name. The name under which I was admitted to the Bar of New Jersey was my married name, and the name under which I was admitted to all additional jurisdictions was always my married name. Briefly, decades later I considered using a pseudonym for a piece of subversive fiction, but by the time the piece was published the possibility of professional awkwardness had become moot.

By the time I arrived in Chicago, I was always and everywhere, in print, in my byline, to the family, in my professional publications and in my social life, I was everywhere identified by my married name. And, therefore, most people assumed I was Jewish.

Even a failing marriage—a source of pain and depression like a dying tooth—is a pillar of identity, especially if it was once a real marriage and there is hope for it being so again. As her father weakened—he had a series of illnesses, mostly stomach complaints, operations, cancer presumably, and partial recoveries over the course of years—and as father and daughter became estranged, her husband, who was if nothing else a domineering personality, must have been central to her life, especially as the children were born.

William Darrah Kelley never resigned from the Congress during his long illness; however, he was already not strong enough to join Florence Kelley and her brother William when they were traveling in England prior to Avignon. He never came to visit in Zurich, nor is it clear he was invited. His heart must have been breaking not to be in contact with his beloved daughter when she returned to America with his grandson. He probably knew his days were numbered.

When the secret reconciliation between father and daughter came, it must have been accompanied by hot tears, heartbroken embraces, and sighs. After the reconciliation Florence Kelley wrote that her husband was especially pleased to see the family. Probably no one believed that. By the time the reunion occurred, however, William Darrah Kelley was very ill, and the sweetness of this reconciliation was short-lived, clouded by impossible promises, broken hopes, and the knowledge that no one would ever forget the cavernous abyss of the breaking apart of family, and that his death was near.

March 7, 2007: Snow starting and white everywhere and in the 20s, beautiful from my high window in a room where there is heat. Even beautiful on the street where the tire tracks are beginning to be etched in black. What was it like to live in a room without heat?

It is a sad day when a proud parent, a family, has devoted themselves to a favorite child, nursed her through childhood illnesses, nurtured her education, supported her vast ambitions—which mirrored her father's—and then that parent, that family can no longer help to realize the child's ambitions or make the child happy, or fix something which is terribly wrong in the child's life.

And life goes on, and so Florence Kelley wrote:

[New York City] Jan 19th, [1901] It is bitterly cold, but clear and fine. . . . As I write the air is full of sunshine and snow—the first snow of the season—both together. It is a wonderful winter.

What went wrong with that marriage is irretrievable one hundred years later, if ever knowable. Florence Kelley herself left no written record of it. Her friends at Hull-House said little. She always said she did not regret the marriage. Much sadness to be washed away when the family was reconciled in New York. Strange that the congressman and his wife felt the necessity of registering in a New York hotel under an assumed name for their privacy when the reconciliation between father and daughter did eventually take place.

October 3, 2007: Class today. We are so aware of the fragility of life, two months after the surgery. The university imposes a rhythm on our life, in the fall the new students, a new class, the papers, the exams, then the holidays, and a new semester, and finally graduation as a demarcation.

While in Switzerland Florence Kelley gathered her courage and asked Frederick Engels for permission to translate *Die Lage*. He was perhaps surprised and pleased that someone, an unlikely American woman, would wish to translate into English from German— no copy of the original English edition apparently being available—a book about the working class in England many decades ago which had been largely forgotten since its original publication.

January 3, 2009: The trees are still. A light snow in the forecast. The ever-present stone grey of the Midwestern winter. Not as cold as the nineteen below of Christmas. At least the solstice is now behind us.

Many maneuvers, frustrations, and aborted negotiations between Florence Kelley and various socialists and Marxists, self-appointed, jealous guardians of the socialist canon, ensued from the initiation of her project to translate *Die Lage* to its end, which was Florence Kelley finding a publisher for the English translation in America. Engels was at the time living in London, and held the rights to the publication and translation of his own works and the works of Marx, and made a cottage industry of their publication and translation and supported the enterprise with his own money.

October 2, 2007: It is a new world this Internet, and I had to be persuaded to use it for the fourteen thousand homicide cases. It is a miracle.

Both Marx and Engels had small armies of acolytes, fellow travelers, many of whom had emigrated from Germany to Britain at the time of the Bismarck decree. *The Communist Manifesto* by Marx and Engels had been published in 1848. These followers, hangers-on, and admirers allied themselves with Engels and Marx and various other labor and political organizations in the 1880s after Marx's *Das Kapital* became an international phenomenon. After Marx's death, Engels was Marx's literary executor and became the person who dispensed the privilege of translating his own and Marx's work. As the translator of *Die Lage*, Florence Kelley became one of the many seeking the approval and attention of Engels, and later found herself in the crossfire of disputes involving the promotion and distribution of official publications of works by the masters of the doctrine.

Engels carefully nourished the legacy of Marx, watched over the welfare of Marx's reputation and his children, especially one of his two daughters, Eleanor Marx Aveling, whom Engels had promised to protect on Marx's death bed and whom he considered as his own daughter.

The childless Engels had inherited a business and money from his father, a businessman, perhaps a capitalist, and was as a result able to support a number of people and projects related to the socialist cause. Sometimes these publications and translations made money. Certainly Florence Kelley made no money from the translation of *Die Lage*.

March 8, 2004: Such bright sun, but still very cold, in the 20s. The homicide website has a new technical problem: we can't translate the word transcription of the cases into a format that people can use to search for dates, names, or addresses. This is a major objective, to make accessible to anyone all of the data in those handwritten police records which now have been carefully copied and transcribed over the course of a year and a half.

At the habeas corpus proceeding in Chicago eight years and a lifetime after Heidelberg, there would be a dispute over who was paying the bills for the idyllic family enterprise of reading and writing, the routine of scholarship and professional training in Europe.

No one seems to have documented or mentioned the source of Lazare Wischnewetzky's income. There must have been some family transfers, since there is no indication he was ever working or getting paid. There are references of his acting as a doctor in New York, but no indication that he was getting paid or that he was licensed in New York.

June 20, 1999: Another Northwestern graduation, this time outside. All the worry about the weather, for nothing. It was glorious, and a relief to have it over. So much time and planning and expense spent on one day.

Caroline, Florence's mother, and her younger son, Albert, came to Heidelberg to visit and stayed in a nearby German pensione, presumably paying their own way, and dined with the newlywed couple at their pensione almost every day. Florence Kelley would say later to Jane Addams and others at Hull-House: the question of domestic labor has not yet been addressed. She meant, presumably, that life can be very pleasant for those who can afford to take advantage of cheap domestic labor and have others take care of their physical well-being.

March 9, 2007: The sun bright and warm enough for the snow to be melting. People are concerned that the setting forward of the clocks three weeks earlier, this year for the first time scheduled for March 11, will disrupt the automatic calendars and clocks in computers and hand-held organizers. In Chicago the geographic time zones were introduced in the inventive nineteenth century, to synchronize the local time with the arrivals and departures of trains from both coasts. It was confusing to have the porters shouting out the arrival of the trains by their departure time from another place. Train agents would shout each other down announcing the eight o'clock from New York, or the six o'clock from California.

In December of the first year of her marriage Florence Kelley wrote her first letter to Engels. She approached him through an intermediary, asking for permission to translate *Die Lage*. There followed a correspondence which lasted for more than a decade. Florence Kelley's letters to Engels include a running commentary on politics and economics and social issues in New York, with a few veiled references to her own domestic affairs.

110 E 76th St., New York, Dec. 29, 1887, to Frederick Engels

. . . We see a good deal of some of the more wide awake, progressive and influential men among the English speaking organizations (for instance [Samuel] Gompers, President of the Federation of Labor with its 600,000 members). He is perfectly fuddled upon the subject [of protectionist tariffs] and so are most of the rest of them.

It is not a question of polemic against the protectionists but of your defining your posi-

tion explicitly towards <u>protection</u>. . . .

The Federation of Labor held its annual convention in Baltimore a short time ago. It voted in favor of maintaining the internal taxes upon cigars; upon improvements in the methods of oyster culture and other equally urgent matters; but of the improvement of the Factory Acts, prohibition of the employment of children etc. not one word could I find. The Congress voted <u>against</u> the resumption of the Eight Hour Movement; and <u>against</u> independent labor politics; and <u>against</u> a strike funds. [emphasis in the original]

The Federation of Labor, awash in its own politics, briefly supported the eight-hour movement from 1888-91.

The correspondence between Florence Kelley and Frederick Engels discovered by Dorothy Blumberg consisted of some forty letters, primarily concerned with questions about technicalities of the translation, questions of distribution. Florence Kelley also comments to Engels upon the American progress toward socialism, the organization of workers, and the United States elections of 1886. The correspondence begins during the period of early married life in Heidelberg and Zurich, and continues until the translated book is published in 1886, with sporadic letters after her move to Chicago. Both Florence Kelley and Engels believed *Die Lage* was relevant to conditions in America in the 1880s. This is how the project is described in Engels's new preface:

This book, an English translation of which is here republished, was first issued in Germany in 1834. The author, at that time, was young, twenty-four years of age, and his production bears the stamp of his youth with its good and its faulty features, of neither of which he feels ashamed. It was translated into English in 1885 by an American lady, Mrs. F. Kelley Wischnewetzky, and published in the following year in New York . . . the state of things described in this book belongs to-day, in many respect, to the past, as far as England is concerned. . . .

The pettifogging business tricks of the Polish Jew, the representative in Europe of commerce in its lowest stage, these tricks that serve him so well in his own country, and are generally practiced there, he finds to be out of date and out of place when he comes to Hamburg or Berlin; and, again, the commission agent, who hails from Berlin or Hamburg, Jew or Christian, after frequenting the Manchester Exchange for a few months, finds out that, in order to buy cotton yarn or cloth cheap, he, too had better drop those slightly more refined but still miserable wiles and subterfuges which are considered the acme of cleverness in his native country.

In the conclusion Engels notes:

But this I maintain, the war of the poor against the rich now carried on in detail and indirectly will become direct and universal. It is too late for a peaceful solution. The classes are divided more and more sharply, the spirit of resistance penetrates the workers, the bitterness intensifies, the guerilla skirmishes become concentrated in more important battles, and soon a slight impulse will suffice to set the avalanche in motion. Then, indeed, will the war-cry resound though the land: "War to the palaces, peace to the cottages!"—but then it will be too late for the rich to beware.

The revolution did come, and it was a true revolution in work and working conditions, and in the relation between the employed and employers, and between capitalists and machines.

September 28, 2007: Another cool fall day. The air clean. Football tomorrow, and the anticipation is in the air on the campus. Why am I upstairs poring over old letters, looking for something, what, why, I don't even know. Well, tomorrow will be different; it will be the present of the game.

Given that German socialists and German immigrants were prominent in American political and intellectual circles, especially in New York, it is surprising how many times Florence Kelley's English translation of *Die Lage* was rejected by American publishers and magazine editors, especially since Florence Kelley herself had published in America.

After Haymarket, socialists, labor organizers, and anarchists were all lumped together by many into the category of dangerous foreigners who made bombs and incendiary speeches. The fear of strikes, violence, the power of unions, and the fear of immigration crystallized into panic. There were real anarchists, and they did blow up people and buildings. Most notably they succeeded in assassinating President William McKinley in 1905 and arguably the mayor of Chicago at the time of the World's Fair; however, the public's fear of anarchists was disproportionate.

June 10, 2013: The toll of the dead in Bangladesh makes it the worst factory disaster in history, if we can assume all such disasters were recorded.

When energetic, ambitious Eastern intellectuals, such as Henry Demarest Lloyd, came to Chicago in 1872, being admitted to the Illinois Bar in 1875 on the basis of his graduation from Columbia University School of Law, he did not bring the fierce political allegiances debated in New York and London.

Although echoes of the politics of Germany, Russia, Poland, and New York can be heard in speeches and weighty, intellectual prognostications in Chicago, the politics of Chicago was what went on in Chicago. The history of reform in Chicago, of socialism in Chicago, was its own story. Chicago's money was made in Chicago. Chicago's politics stayed in Chicago and kept everyone in Chicago paying attention, and when outsiders came to Chicago they learned Chicago rules.

The newlyweds returned to the bourgeois peace of Zurich for the delivery of their first child, Nicholas, born on July 12, 1885. Florence Kelley's letters from Zurich at the time of the birth of her first child refer to the coming socialist revolution, her own immersion in the writings of scientific socialism, and the philosophy of the German economists. If she believed, or perhaps simply hoped, the socialist revolution was on the verge of coming to America, she was not alone. She wrote to a sympathetic friend that "every American paper . . . [contains] tidings of the coming revolution, which you, who are long among the volcanoes, probably do not recognize as such."

The publication of *Die Lage* in America was planned to coincide with the publication of Engels's own English translation of *Das Kapital*. Florence Kelley wrote to Engels: "I think it would be especially fortunate if 'Die Lage' could appear not very long after the English translation of 'das Kapital.'"

But, when Florence Kelley contacted American publishers, first from Switzerland and later when she lived in New York, she found a skeptical and highly competitive group of publishers, some from the gutters where newspapers were sold, some from the elite wood-paneled offices of educational institutions, and everywhere in between. None of these publishers of newspapers, magazines, pamphlets, books, and journals seemed to be interested in publishing an English translation by an American socialist of Frederick Engels's *Die Lage*.

George Putnam, the brother of Florence Kelley's college friend, found the work dated, although Engels argued that conditions in industrial America in 1885 had many similarities to those in industrial England at the time of Engels's earlier work.

At the time it was common for writers of serious works to pay a subvention for the printing of their own books. Henry Demarest Lloyd's attack upon the Standard Oil cartels and John D. Rockefeller, *Wealth Against Commonwealth*, sold out seven printings of *The Atlantic*, yet he could not persuade the magazine to publish the piece without putting up his own cash for the printing cost, a not-inconsiderable sum of several thousand dollars.

Rachel Foster, a friend of Florence Kelley's who was actively involved with the National American Woman Suffrage Association, promised to pay for the costs of publication of *Die Lage*, and with that subvention Florence Kelley finally secured the promise of publication from the Socialist Labor Party in New Jersey.

By the time Florence Kelley arrived in Chicago, Henry Demarest Lloyd had been the financial and literary editor of the *Chicago Tribune* for several years, with a well-known byline for his writings on political and economic matters. Andrew Dixon White, the president of Cornell and later ambassador to Berlin; Florence Kelley's father, the congressman; and Henry Demarest Lloyd traveled to England and Europe and sent back for publication letters and essays about their observations on economic and social conditions in Europe.

These accounts chronicled conversations with European political figures and intellectuals and were much anticipated and widely read. Europe marked the limits of their world, although there was an awareness of the giant Russia, because of the extraordinary people it had expelled and because of its literature. References to Asia were rare, and to Africa infinitesimal.

Writers, ministers, anarchists, journalists, politicians, and public figures such as Florence Kelley, Jane Addams, Henry Demarest Lloyd, William Stead, Clarence Darrow, and John Peter Altgeld could support themselves in lean times by giving lectures open to the public, usually for a small fee, and then selling for a few cents more their other publications, journal reprints, pamphlets, or broadsides on a particular issue. And so they got their work out and directly addressed the public as well.

March 1, 1999: Our famous Chicago painter is so very generous, offering me an image of one of his paintings for the cover of my book. I go to his studio where in the middle of piles of partly completed paintings, easels, drawings, he and his pals are having a sandwich, taking a break. Should they order me a tuna fish sandwich?

Many immigrants could not read or write in English, or at all, and their education was, along with the daily newspapers which were read aloud, public lectures and fugitive writings. The audiences at such lectures were often workers, or people involved with organizing workers, people such as the young William Darrah Kelley, who left school to be an apprentice and yet was eager to learn and apt, and became an organizer and teacher of young workers. Each generation had to be educated anew.

And so Florence Kelley soon after her arrival in Chicago wrote to Henry Demarest Lloyd on Illinois Bureau of Statistics letterhead:

June 30, 1892 [Hull-House]

It rains, every single day. It is rarely uncomfortably hot, but a trifle depressing. . . . Bessie Nahinsky comes two evenings a week to read English with me (and with a class of twelve of her compatriots). She is going to a Grammar School next year, living with her brother meanwhile. Pascha some thingorother, her pretty blonde cousin— Shapira, with all her brothers and cousins are laboring through the third reader with me and when they have finished I mean to have them read William Morris' News from Nowhere and More's Utopia and then Engels' Development of Socialism from a Utopia to a Science. They are really intellectual, the whole dozen, and it is delightful to teach them.

The birth of their first child and the rapture of being a new mother did not interfere with the rhythm of writing and studying for the newlyweds. Florence Kelley wrote to a friend that she was well, well and happy, in Zurich, and working six to eight hours a day on her dissertation, the translation of *Die Lage*, and newspaper correspondence.

The letters to friends from this time do not seem to mention who was supporting the household. There is no mention of a wet nurse or of whether she was nursing her baby, although at one point when Nicholas is a few months old she writes to a friend that she and her husband have dismissed the nursemaid and are taking care of the baby entirely themselves, which implies that she was breastfeeding.

The subject of wages, working conditions at home or elsewhere, who made what when and where, was of great interest. Everyone wanted to know how others lived, about the poor, and about the rich. And the newspapers catered to both curiosities.

Florence Kelley mentioned to Engels the lack of reliable statistics on American labor conditions, a lack she herself would later address. She could not have foreseen the important role these "facts" and statistics would play in American jurisprudence.

Just about this time, in Zurich in 1885, at the early stages of a the marriage, a coolness arose between Florence Kelley and her father over his delaying publication in America of some letters they were to have published together on working conditions in England. It is not clear whether the original plan was that these letters be published as jointly authored by Congressman Kelley and his daughter, or if they were to carry only her byline.

Later, she bitterly protested that these letters expressed views on free trade, politics, and economics which after her marriage she no longer held. She obliquely accused her father of withholding the publication in order to have the release coincide with his own reelection campaign, a harsh judgment which may not have been true. The altercation between father and daughter was picked up by a gossipy press, and rumors spread that Florence Kelley's husband had blocked the publication of the letters. References to this painful episode in family letters do not survive in the archives. This may have been why the congressman registered under an assumed name at the hotel in New York.

Whatever the emotional dynamic—the new husband, the baby—these two supremely articulate and passionate people who had been voice and ear to one another, for one another, were for the first time silent to one another, a state of affairs which lasted until what must have been an emotional reconciliation in New York just before the birth of Florence Kelley's third child, John, when William Darrah Kelley's health was precarious. Some of the references suggest that Florence Kelley was not in communication with her mother during this estrangement after the family moved to New York; other sources suggest they were in contact.

In 1887 Florence Kelley and Engels were optimistic about the prospect of a large

American audience for the English translation of *Die Lage*. In a single year the American membership in the Knights of Labor increased from 104,000 to 702,000. The word among the European socialists and intellectuals was: the American working class was on the move. Engels wrote that he only wished that Marx could have lived to see it.

May 1, 2013: The count of the dead in Bangladesh continues to climb. People riot in the street, pillory the factory owner, who is caught trying to escape.

About the same time, Engels himself was busy negotiating with British publishers about his own translation of *Das Kapital*. Meanwhile Karl Marx's quasi son-in-law, Dr. Edward Aveling, came to New York on a speaking tour with Marx's daughter Eleanor Marx and precipitated a small scandal among the American socialists. Dr. Aveling had perhaps been promised the right to translate another prominent socialist work when the English translation of *Die Lage* was assigned to Florence Kelley.

At one point Florence Kelley wrote to Engels that she saw herself translating a series of books from the Marxist canon. After the publication of the English translation of *Die Lage*, Engels suggested that Mrs. Wischnewetzky should devote her time to writing articles and pamphlets popularizing the ideas in *Das Kapital* and other seminal socialist writings— presumably including his own. Engels implied it was a waste of time for her to do her own work.

Thanksgiving, November 1998: Zurich. The weather is cold here too. We are visiting friends, stopping first in London. I know nothing of Florence Kelley Wischnewetzky and do not go visit the University of Zurich. Still I remember how clean, how antiseptic Zurich is. It is a beautiful city. We stay at a hotel much beloved by my stepmother.

Florence Kelley and Frederick Engels met twice, once when the Wischnewetzky family was on their way to America and when, with their traveling companion, a German socialist divorcee formerly married to an anarchist and now exiled to England, they paid a call upon Engels in London at 122 Regent Street. At this time the Wischnewetzkys apparently planned to divide their time between Europe and the United States. No commentary or description of the meeting by either party has come down to us. Perhaps they simply did not take to one another, or the meeting was anticlimactic on all sides. Perhaps the baby was fussing, or she was tired. The meeting with no fable took place in September or October 1886.

When Engels came to New York on a speaking tour, Florence Kelley and her husband met Engels at the dock. They never had another extended meeting. Later Florence Kelley chided him for not scheduling time to visit her during his American tour. There seemed little warmth, good will or friendship between them in spite of all the school work.

What is known is that the Wischnewetzkys shed as a traveling companion the German socialist lady divorced from the well-known anarchist, and they arrived in New York City by themselves in the middle of a bitterly contested mayoral campaign in November 1886. Florence Kelley was pregnant with their second child. Margaret was born around December 10, 1886, a few weeks after their arrival in New York. Lazare left for Europe immediately after the birth and was gone for several months. The Wischnewetzky family was not reconciled with William Darrah Kelley, a train ride away in Philadelphia and by that time in failing health.

March 10, 2007: Bright sun, and the snow is melting, turning into dirt-speckled isolated lumps. The thermometer is stuck at the 10 degrees above freezing mark. And I am stuck too. How to channel this river of writing, this cascade of history.

The ghost of Florence Kelley, which emanates from each hurried, visible scratch of her pen across the page of a letter, is abrupt, decisive, practical, always in a hurry, not tarrying over trifles. Even when writing to people with whom she has a close, fond attachment, such as Henry Demarest Lloyd, the expression of affection is restrained.

To her children and her mother, and several female friends, she is openly affectionate and concerned always with their well-being. Admittedly the effusive styles of the present, and other pasts, are not hers, nor characteristic of others of her class and time.

August 25, 1999: First class on "Animal Subjects, Human Regulation." Is property a status, like marriage? If people can be bought and sold, and animals can be bought and sold, are they property? I want to buy a house in Bozeman, Montana. That is property. Are our lives property?

In New York in 1886 when Florence Kelley and her family returned, two national candidates, Henry George and Theodore Roosevelt, both of whom had aspirations to the presidency and one of whom would eventually be president, were running for mayor of New York, as well as a candidate from Tammany Hall, a Republican (the party of Lincoln) and representatives of other factions. The Socialist Labor Party backed Henry George, and an unconvinced Florence Kelley wanted Engels to challenge some of Henry George's platform in his new preface to *Die Lage*, particularly the principal issue of the nationalization of land. Engels wisely demurred.

Florence Kelley was scornful of the writings and public positions taken by Richard Ely, then a professor at Johns Hopkins University, later at the University of Wisconsin. She regarded Henry George as decidedly unscientific, meaning: not following "scientific" socialism. Then the election was over, Henry George was not elected, and the political squabbling and internal divisions between the American socialists continued, always shifting.

September 1, 1999: The students worry about credits for their papers, as they should. If you are arguing for the rights of animals, at least, unlike other clients, they don't talk back or express their own ideas. Of course, they also don't pay or consent to be represented.

The newly arrived Wischnewetzkys gravitated to the local Socialist Labor Party, and the First International, headquartered in Hoboken, New Jersey. Both groups were dominated by recently emigrated Germans whose principal concern was whether political meetings and publications should continue to be in German and be about scientific socialism and communist theory, or whether they should now be in English and directed toward educating the American working man.

Many German socialists in America thought their return to Germany and their ascension to positions of political power in Prussia were imminent and inevitable, in spite of Chancellor Otto von Bismarck's expulsion of the socialists in 1878. Others were convinced that the only hope for socialism and America was the indoctrination and education of American workers in socialist theory in English.

Socialism was the political theory of the times, as if handed down from on high. It seemed to require a great deal of discussion and argument among its advocates and skeptics. Both Wischnewetzkys were for some time after their arrival in New York in the middle of those debates.

There was a great sense that capitalism was all happening here, now. In Chicago there was excitement about the economic activity, and even the skeptical were caught up in it. Everyone in Chicago was mesmerized by the energy. So, William Stead wrote in *If Christ Came to Chicago*:

Marshall Field, the first of the greater gods in the Pantheon of the West, is a born trader. He comes of the true Yankee breed, and he has made his fortune by being quick to perceive that the day of the great store had arrived. What the Louvre and Bon Marche are in Paris, what Whiteleys and Shoolbreds are in London, Marshall Field & Co. are in Chicago. Their wholesale store is one of the sights of the city, and the guidebooks tell with admiration that "Richardson, the eastern architect, received $100,000 for the plans of this stupendous pile." The floor space devoted to the wholesale trade covers twelve acres; the building is 130 feet high, there are thirteen elevators and in this huge hive of industry 1800 employes are constantly employed dispatching the largest wholesale dry goods business in America. In their retail establishment on Wabash there is what is probably the perfection of business capacity directed to the facility of distribution. As the latest finishing touch to the conveniences of this gigantic bazaar, sixty pneumatic tubes, ramifying into all parts of the building, convey cash and return change with almost lightning-like rapidity. A brigade of some 3,000 men and women are employed *behind the counters, and the universal testimony is that the management is far in advance of that of most dry goods stores in Chicago or elsewhere. Merit is readily recognized; promotion comes so rapidly, that the present head of the retail establishment, is still a young man. There is none of the scandal, such as rumor has persistently associated with other dry goods houses and elsewhere. They do not use up extreme youth by employing juvenile cash girls, neither do they pay their female assistants rates of wages which suggest, if they do not enforce, the necessity for supplementing their earnings elsewhere.*

March 5, 2008: Sunny, at last. Even a singing bird outside. Still cold, below freezing, but warm inside. The pressure is rising. No one talks of anything but the election. And it is only March.

On the first day of testimony in the Cook County Courthouse, on that clear day, March 24, 1892, when Florence Kelley had been in Chicago barely three months, Dr. Wischnewetzky's testimony was said to accurately reflect his character, which was called "peculiar." A newspaper reporter described an ordinary-looking man with a heavy red moustache and beard, according to the fashion of the day. Lazare Wischnewetzky, who had been clean-shaven in Zurich, was not unusual with his bright red beard in America.

The testimony that day, a March day without rain—thus today, when these words are written, a slate-colored downpour on March 12, 2007, is perhaps more typical of March in Chicago—the testimony on March 24, 1892, included the deposition of a servant from New York, Mary Murphy, who said the doctor flew into a violent rage if Mrs. Wischnewetzky spoke English to the children or the servants. Although Dr. Wischnewetzky had lived in America for six years and had lofty ambitions to be the founding head of the Medico-Mechanical Zander Institute in New York City, Dr. Wischnewetzky was never easy with the English language.

March 19, 2008: A grey, cold day. The tracery of trees outside the window remain bare lines, light pencil on parchment, waiting for color. Deer look up from the yard. Two generations of deer have given birth in our back yard, the mothers finding a safe haven and apparently jumping the high wire fence with ease.

The Great Writ of habeas corpus was created, preserved, and saved after a period of suspension by Lincoln during the Civil War, and continued to be a legal bastion against tyranny. The Great Writ was the legal mechanism which would allow the Supreme Court of the United States to declare unconstitutional racial discrimination in jury selection. This same writ became a springboard for the Supreme Court recognizing foundational federal principles, such as the right to counsel for criminal defendants and the right to confront accusing witnesses, mostly in capital cases. This small piece of law, a phrase only, was the legal basis for Judge Frank Baker hearing the dispute in which Dr. Lazare Wischnewetzky came from New York to claim possession of his three children from his wife, Florence Kelley Wischnewetzky.

September 21, 1999: How to classify the legislation, and all the new laws: The Animal Welfare Act. What about the snail darter, the ivory poaching, a biodiversity treaty? And it is all law.

The habeas corpus action attracted at least two newspaper reporters, and probably some curious others. There would have been no jury, this being Chancery. There would have been ordinary people there, the witnesses, the parties, some observers, and of course the newspaper reporters.

The testimony on the morning of March 24, 1892, from the deposition of the family's former servant from New York, Mary Murphy, went on to say that while the doctor treated his children with affection in New York, he frequently called Mrs. Wischnewetzky hard names and became enraged at small things.

The domestic distress in the Wischnewetzky household in New York was reported to be acute. The doctor and his wife may have been having deep discussions of philosophy and global justice in Zurich and Heidelberg, and even perhaps in London, but in New York the kitchen budget and unpaid bills for expensive dinners were the principal subject. Many a high-minded European, including some from a distressed European aristocracy, has come to a rude awakening when faced with a practical American wife and unpaid bills from the milkman at the back door.

Economics, big and small, was preoccupying the members of the household on East 76th Street in 1887. The servants, and the rent, and the greengrocer had to be paid before the great questions of Property, Injustice and Labor writ large could be addressed.

In New York in 1886 Helen Campbell, a successful writer, the author of *Prisoners of Poverty: Women Wage-Workers, Their Trades and Their Lives*, lent Florence Kelley $700, the equivalent of a year's earnings for a skilled worker. Florence Kelley and her two babies lived on it while Lazare Wischnewetzky was in Europe finishing his degree. The worry over finances continued for years. And Florence Kelley still received subventions from her mother:

Letter to Caroline Bonsall Kelley, c. June 2, 1892.

. . . The treasures of the box are a delight. I did not know of the existence of the little thimble. Puss [Margaret] sews in a tentative way, and will do so very nicely.

The wrapper is a delight; and the basque will be a beautiful present for Clara and the scrapbook for Ko——, and the trousers for both boys.

103

Give my best love to the boys. Do not worry about my finances, I'll keep you posted. And I think I can manage them myself. <u>I shall not go to any friend. I have not done so.</u> But I told W. [William Jr., her brother] *of Mr. Straus' offer and he approved of it.* [Mr. Straus, her benefactor, had offered to testify against Lazare Wischnewetzky at the 1892 hearing and also offered to defray any financial difficulties she might face.] *I have made no debts but those of which you know <u>and shall make none.</u>*

For a long time others paid for her children's education in private schools, friends of the family, her own friends. William Jr. helped pay the legal fees for Florence Kelley to defend against the habeas corpus filing. Caroline, Will, and Albert all sent money, which, Florence Kelley later wrote, she repaid. Florence Kelley was still taking money from her mother until she left Hull-House.

Perhaps, like so many other couples, the newlyweds argued about money because it was the easy, concrete thing they could argue about. Both were ambitious for a future in America. Lazare Wischnewetzky planned to introduce into the New York market one Dr. Zander's methodology, under the auspices of a new Medico-Mechanical Zander Institute, with himself as the head.

The Zander method of treatment had been developed in Sweden and licensed in other parts of Europe by the 1880s. It consisted of supervised exercise on specially built machines designed to counteract the injurious effects of a sedentary life. Regular mechanical treatment and physical education would keep the body healthy. A Zander Institute did eventually open in New York but not with Dr. Wischnewetzky as director.

The Zander method bears some resemblance to the German gymnasium movement. Regular exercise was the panacea for all ills, and in this the Zander method is not dissimilar to present physical fitness regimes emphasizing running, exercise on machines, and other regimens of fitness, now couched in the discourse of cardiovascular and coronary health, carbohydrates, and calories.

The Zander method consisted of regular workouts claimed to modify defective formation of the thorax and organs, to address afflictions of the nervous system—insomnia, nervousness, neurasthenia, neuralgia, hysteria, chorea (St. Vitus's dance), affections of the heart, chronic gastric and intestinal catarrh, dilation of the stomach, habitual constipation, circulatory disturbances of the liver, amenorrhea, menorrhagia, prolapsus uteri, and many other ailments.

Menus of celebratory occasions at the time describe dinners with eighteen to twenty courses, with wine and brandy being liberally consumed throughout. In the thousands of medical advice columns available then and today, there must be many conditions, whatever name given to them, as opposed to diseases, which would be addressed with positive results by the judicious application of the Zander Medico-Mechanical method and its diet. And, according to Dr. Wischnewetzky, it was all based on science.

June 28, 2006: The young man in my charge, in circus camp today. The sun is shining, and he trots eagerly down the sidewalk. We send him off without worries about smallpox or diphtheria, or kidnapping.

Dr. Zander himself, whom Lazare Wischnewetzky visited in his native Sweden, probably on the trip after Margaret's birth, seems to have been a canny businessman, perhaps not eager to license his highly profitable machines and methodology, or to sign a contract or ship his products without seeing some cash and evidence that the proposed American Medico-Mechanical Zander Institute in New York could actually succeed. Dr. Zander's doubts about licensing to Lazare Wischnewetzky perhaps increased when he actually met the excitable, red-bearded doctor in person. Zander Institutes were flourishing in European cities. A significant new market in America might be negatively affected by a failed first attempt in the potentially lucrative New York market.

March 13, 2007: A few fleeting wispy clouds, and spring, up to 70 today. The window wide open, there are birds. Soon the bees will return. And so another spring, another year. I must get outside.

Treatment in the Zander method consisted of stretching the body on machines which simulated bicycle riding or horseback riding (sidesaddle position for women), performed abdomen kneading (a strange one to imagine done by a machine) and trunk extension (the contemporaneous drawing looks like spinal elongation), and purportedly corrected spinal curvature, a common ailment. Jane Addams suffered from scoliosis, spent months bedridden in a stretching machine, and was told, probably erroneously, that she could never have children. No doubt many people did feel better after physical engagements with these machines, pictured as large presences in empty rooms, an eerie prediction of the hundreds of thousands of stair machines, treadmills and rowing machines standing in empty rooms, while their sweating, heaving spandex-clad adherents exercise elsewhere, or feel guilty sitting or lying prone in the cavernous house.

January 21, 1998, Chicago Tribune: "Texas-Born Drifter, Killer Is Executed."

Lloyd Wayne Hampton, who five years ago forced his execution to be called off at the last minute by filing an appeal, was put to death by lethal injection early Wednesday at Stateville Correctional Center outside Joliet.

Hampton, the 11th person executed under Illinois' 1977 death penalty law, went to his death accepting full responsibility for his criminal acts. . . .

```
"I've been running from myself since I was a small boy in Texas,
and my 44 years have been filled with intense anger and rage. I
blame no one but myself, and I hope my loved ones will forgive
me for the sorrow I have caused them. If God feels I am worthy
of his forgiveness, I'll soon be with my grandparents, brother
and daughter."

The Texas-born drifter confessed in 1990 to torturing, robbing
and murdering a 69-year-old widower in a Downstate motel room.
```

On that March 24 in 1892 the servants testified that on more than one occasion, Dr. Wischnewetzky called his wife vile names and hit her in the face, leaving her face discolored and bruised so that she had to stay indoors for three weeks on one occasion. Perhaps it was better that the estranged and ill congressman, her father, did not know that his adored, highly educated and independent-minded daughter was being beaten and verbally abused by the father of her children.

On the same March day in 1892 in Chicago, Mrs. Wischnewetzky testified that it was dangerous for the moral and physical health and well-being of the children to be subjected to their father's unnatural behavior, meaning the physical and verbal abuse. The children repeated in the nursery the vile language their father used toward his wife, the nursemaid reported. The little children sat through the hearing.

Margaret, the second child of this union, had been born in New York on December 10, 1886, shortly after the family's arrival in America. The Haymarket trial riveted the attention of the nation that summer of 1886. In March 1886 more than 350,000 people across the country had joined a coordinated general strike in support of the eight-hour day.

November 4, 1998: Democrats win in most places, but another Republican, George Ryan, a former Illinois secretary of state, is elected governor, to extend the Republicans' twenty-two-year reign in the Executive Mansion. Of course George Ryan is a supporter of capital punishment and executions. He would not have been elected otherwise.

The eight-hour movement unified specialized workers and craftsmen in the 1880s. So many strikes and labor actions occurred around this time at so many plants that the events were called The Great Upheaval. Its ideological center was the cry for eight hours and its center was Chicago.

March 20, 2008: A pale sun can be seen. Two inches of snow are predicted for tonight. Tomorrow, five inches. The airports will be full of people standing in line to reschedule their flights and sleeping on metal benches designed to be uncomfortable.

In the fall of 1886, when Florence Kelley and her family arrived in New York, the Haymarket defendants, with the exception of the juvenile, had already been sentenced to death. The trial was over in August 1886. The legal case was making its way through the appellate channels to the Supreme Court of Illinois, and eventually it would knock at the door of the Supreme Court of the United States, where it would not be heard. In the meantime the crackdown on labor organizations and the suppression of strikes and meetings in Chicago and other cities was pervasive and successful.

The rigged Haymarket trial was all about bombings and plots to blow up buildings and kill capitalists. The impassioned rhetoric of anarchism was more frightening to the authorities and the public than the actual destruction of one small bomb.

The most vociferous of all terror-talkers, Johann Most, whose work was featured prominently in the prosecution's case in chief at Haymarket, had recently traveled all over the United States giving incendiary speeches in German to audiences of thousands, encouraging his listeners to bomb and kill. More than 5,000 people jammed themselves into Cooper Union's Great Hall in New York City to listen to the high-decibel exhortations in German of the impassioned, deformed, self-proclaimed anarchist Johann Most. Most's books on bomb making included entreaties that his easily made bombs be thrown at capitalists with immediate haste by unjustly treated laborers.

Johann Most himself lived to a ripe age of sixty in spite of being thrown into jail twice, deported twice, and being horsewhipped publicly on a stage by his spurned lover, Emma Goldman. He lived long enough to see the crowds of thousands, who in the early 1880s cheered his enraged exhortations in German to blow up buildings and assassinate capitalists, dwindle to a mere handful a decade later. As a young man Johann Most was obsessed with explosives, and his speeches and writings included very specific instructions on bomb building. As a young man he suffered severe facial scarring from medical mistreatment after a neglected infection, and wore a fiercely luxuriant beard to cover the disfigurement. His appearance as well as his manner were said to be distinctly odd, although he was apparently very attractive to women.

November 10, 1999: Grey, rainy. Last class. The Animal Legal Defense Fund and The Great Ape Project. And thank goodness, it is almost Thanksgiving.

In Most's speeches and writings it was the capitalist bosses, the monopolist railroads, the exploitation of the laborers morning, noon and night. The drama of the Haymarket trial, followed by the public hanging of Spies, Parsons, Engels, and Fischer, after the failure of their legal appeals and petitions for clemency, gripped the country as no other trial and execution would until the Lindbergh case fifty years later. Teddy Roosevelt, camping with his soldiers in the badlands of the Dakotas, burned the anarchists in effigy on the day of the hangings. Only one newspaper and very few public figures were on record as opposing the executions.

March 14, 2007: Yesterday's balmy skies and soft breezes are gone, but it is still warm, and most of the snow has melted. Still so much to be done, and nothing about how to address the 1890s has occurred to me. It's as if I have volunteered to single-handedly resurrect these 1890s writers and their causes.

Lazare Wischnewetzky and his wife may have come back to New York to be part of the great socialist revolution which they saw coming to America, the rising up of the workers against their capitalist oppressors, but in the short run it was economy writ small and domestic politics writ very small which preoccupied them.

According to the testimony of Dr. Wischnewetzky before the Honorable Judge Baker on March 24, 1892, it was economy, economy all the time during the five years when the family lived in New York. Letters from Florence Kelley Wischnewetzky—when she had time to write them—talked about the political infighting between Henry George, the Socialist Labor Party, the Knights of Labor, Terence Powderly, and the disputes and arguments which are and were the stuff of daily politics. But at home, it was how were the bills going to be paid.

The churning American politics pressed Mrs. Wischnewetzky to urge Engels to hurry with his new preface to *Die Lage*. After all, if the working class was going to rise up against its capitalist masters, this book—*The Condition of the Working Class in England in 1844*—even though its subject was working conditions in another country fifty years earlier, might become the manifesto of the new American Revolution. The young Wischnewetzkys had been living in a hothouse of imagined and reimagined revolutionary fervor in the Zurich of exiles, self-described, and would-be revolutionaries. Now they were in the middle of what might be the real one, and they were preoccupied with the petty distractions of everyday life, the small-scale economies of survival in straitened circumstances.

There was no money to be had from the translation of *Die Lage*. This was a labor of love. Nor was finding a publisher proving to be easy. Mrs. Wischnewetzky had begun soliciting American publishers for the work while still in Europe. George Putnam at G.P. Putnam turned it down, although she knew his sister. Finally, Florence Kelley turned for a subvention to her friend Rachel Foster.

Negotiations over the publication of the first English translation of *Die Lage*, and the separate publication of the new preface by Engels, became part of an ongoing imbroglio involving Florence Kelley; Dr. Wischnewetzky; various members of the Socialist Labor Party in New Jersey; Eleanor Marx Aveling, the daughter of Karl Marx; and her unscrupulous and untrustworthy husband, Dr. Edward Aveling.

The arguments over this publication were enmeshed in ongoing, ancillary disputes over whether German should be supplanted by English as the language of political discourse for the Socialist Labor Party and its publications in America. The German immigrants who were in charge at the Hoboken headquarters of the Socialist Labor Party were suspicious of Florence Kelley because her English was too good. She had, after all, grown up and been educated in America. She countered that the party expelled anyone whose English was good.

January 4, 2009: The pink of the sunset is visible from downtown in the winter afternoon. At least we are on the other side of another winter solstice.

The new preface in English that Florence Kelley Wischnewetzky had urged Engels to write was separately published with the financial support of Rachel Foster, who had inherited $100,000 from her mother and was later to become the long-standing assistant to Elizabeth Cady Stanton. Rachel Foster paid the Socialist Labor Party $500 for the printing of twenty thousand copies of the new preface to *Die Lage*. The party spent the money without delivering the agreed-upon product. Furthermore, socialist labor disputes between the Wischnewetzkys and the Executive Committee of the Socialist Labor Party had reached a crisis over another matter, also touching upon Engels himself.

After a series of misunderstandings and jealousies Mr. and Mrs. Wischnewetzky were publicly expelled from the Socialist Labor Party, to their great embarrassment. Mrs. Wischnewetzky found this act characteristic of the "pitiful, untrustworthy mediocrities" who were the leaders of that party.

Meanwhile Engels was deeply affronted over the treatment of Karl Marx's daughter, Eleanor Marx Aveling, and her opportunistic husband, Dr. Edward Aveling, on their American tour, which was being sponsored by the Socialist Labor Party.

For the thirteen weeks of their American speaking tour the Avelings had charged their American hosts thirteen hundred dollars. Aside from the bills for corsages, cigars, and cigarettes, and a two-day wine bill for forty-two dollars, they stayed only at the most expensive hotels (in Chicago at the Sherman). They criticized the German character of the leadership of the American Socialist Party. Their book from the trip, *The Working Class in America*, and Dr. Aveling's book *An American Journey* were and are eminently forgettable.

Aveling had long been known as a crook and a swindler, in spite of Engels's repeated defense of his behavior as being only a "weakness for poetic dreaming." Such dreaming included sticking others with his bar bills and, when he returned from America, raising money in Britain supposedly for the Haymarket defendants and then simply pocketing the receipts. In England many would not attend the socialist gatherings, often at the home of Engels, because of their distrust and dislike for Aveling.

In 1887 the English translation of Marx's *Das Kapital* was published with Aveling's name as co-translator. The reviews were poor, although the book's first printing of five hundred sold out. The consensus was that it was a social history of factory legislation, not a theory of socialism. And then the Avelings quit the British Socialist League.

March 19, 2008: The sun is threatening to come out, the palest of blue shading behind the concrete grey of a winter afternoon. I am still stuck in the 1890s texts.

As to the not-very-theoretical economics of the Wischnewetzky household at 110 E. 76th Street, Mrs. Wischnewetzky testified in court in March 1892 that while living in New York she had contributed to the family's support by translating popular novels and children's books into English from French, German, and Italian. One of the grounds for divorce in Illinois, but not in New York, was nonsupport, in addition to cruelty. The testimony in the habeas corpus hearing constituted a factual basis for a divorce action in Illinois, had Florence Kelley not been ineligible to seek a divorce due to the one-year residency requirement.

Since the estrangement from her father, and also while a student in Zurich, the translation of hack writings had been a principal source of income for Florence Kelley. These were popular novels, bodice-rippers, rags-to-riches stories, many written by women, published by the hundreds in France and Italy, books which sold tens of thousands of copies and made their publishers, and perhaps a few authors, but not their translators, rich. This work was excellent preparation for writing the Factory Inspection Reports.

Chicago in March 1892 supported several editions a day of the *Chicago Tribune* in English, as well as newspapers in German (more than one), Russian, Yiddish, Hebrew, Swedish, Bohemian, and Czech, and regular publications in other languages. It was this vast, rippling American reading audience, reaching across the plains from coast to coast, which Florence Kelley hoped to reach with the publication of the first English edition of *Die Lage*, with its new preface by Engels. It was this audience of readers which was going to rise up and march under the socialist banner.

At the time there seemed an insatiable appetite for ideological writings, no matter how poorly written, as well as for long speeches with statistics, and incoherent evening-length lectures by politicians, would-be elected officials, anarchists, socialists, single taxers, free silver advocates, and men and women who called themselves reformers. Anyone with an opinion, and there were so many with so many passionately held opinions, could and did get a hearing.

November 15, 1998: I have gone to death penalty conferences for over twenty-five years, and never has the atmosphere at a death penalty conference been so electric, so hopeful as here, today, at our law school. More than eight hundred registered, many from the international media.

The scene had everything of the best theatre: it presented a profound human truth challenging conventional thinking and created a unique and surprising visual, spatial and aural environment so that the heart could be reached.

At national death penalty conferences we lawyers from the New Jersey Department of the Public Defender were embarrassed to admit that New Jersey would spend more than a million dollars on the trial of a capital case, with two highly skilled attorneys assigned to each capital defendant from arraignment. The attorneys from Virginia would tell us that $600 was all the state of Virginia would spend for all of the collateral appeals for a person sentenced to death, when the trial ending with a death sentence had been a charade, a travesty of justice.

The rising of the proletariat in the United States was imminent, Engels wrote. When Mr. And Mrs. Wischnewetzky arrived in New York in 1886, William H. Vanderbilt had just inherited $90 million in 1885, making his net worth more than $200 million at a time where there was no inheritance or income tax. Families in the slums of Chicago, as Florence Kelley would later document, were living on five dollars a week or less, if they were lucky enough to be paid for their work. Income disparities were everywhere and highly visible.

The morning of March 24, 1892—the weather was fair, temperature 50 degrees, and all accounts agree, there was no rain—was taken with the opening statements of the attorneys and the reading of depositions from New York.

January 2, 2000: The conundrum of grading. The students can't all be given the highest grade, although some teachers do that. I ask my students how they get their news, how many subscribe to a print copy of a newspaper. Only six read a print newspaper.

On the afternoon of March 24 William D. Kelley Jr., Mrs. Wischnewetzky's older brother from Philadelphia, took the stand and said that Dr. Wischnewetzky's Medico-Mechanical Zander Institute was established with a $20,000 advance from the estate of William Darrah Kelley, his father. And, William Jr. testified, when he demanded half of the income from the institute as repayment—income which was never to materialize—the doctor became so furious than any further communication with him was impossible.

The witness from Philadelphia explained in detail the financial arrangements and money transfers between the Kelley family and the doctor's household in New York as the congressman was dying and his property was being managed by others. William Darrah Kelley's holdings had shrunk considerably from the brief time when he was one of the richest men in Philadelphia. He also supported other family members.

Nor were financial considerations ever absent from Hull-House. The economics of Hull-House were not simple. The monthly residential fee of $21 for room and board did not pay for maintaining all the activities of Hull-House. Thanks to the generosity of the building's owner, the residents of the settlement occupied the building without paying rent. But there were expenses. People had to eat, and others fed.

Helen Culver, the owner of the house, was the niece and heir of the man who built Hull-House and owned the land around it. In 1906 she donated the land under Hull-House and some adjacent lots to Hull-House. The lots were at that time worth more than $75,000. In 1920 Helen Culver created an endowment for Hull-House with another gift of $250,000.

Jane Addams contributed close to $15,000 of her own money to Hull-House during the first four years of its operation, even though some enterprises, such as the summer school, were self-sustaining with fees. Still there were always expenses, such as the construction of a playground ($1,677 cost, $947 donated for the purpose) and the expenses of the ongoing programs and incidental expenses such as that of the creche and its repair at Christmas.

Jane Addams's capital came from an inheritance from her father, in the amount of between $50,000 and $60,000. The importance of this inheritance was it freed her from the necessity to be married. Jane Addams assumed financial responsibility for the children of her sister who died in 1894.

September 2004: My class this fall is on "The Not For Profit Institution." I am spending so much time with trustees and university officers that it seemed I should learn something about the actual law in this area. All everyone seems to talk about is money, how much is raised, how much more needs to be raised. And the tuition for students is already high.

Two substantial outside donors, both women, carried the operating expenses and made the work of Hull-House possible. Over many years beginning in 1891, Mary Rozet Smith contributed more than $115,000 to the maintenance of Hull-House, averaging some $4,000 per year, keeping Jane Addams from "black discouragement." The leaders of the Chicago business community, such as Cyrus McCormick and Julius Rosenthal, actually contributed little, although much was made of their support by them and others.

The other large donor to Hull-House was Louise deKoven Bowen, who contributed more than $540,000, including some $15,000 annually, between 1895 and 1928. Louise deKoven Bowen became associated with Hull-House, like Florence Kelley, in the winter of 1891-92, as a thirty-two-year-old mother of three who was pregnant with her fourth child. Her large fortune derived from her maternal grandfather, who was a Fort Dearborn pioneer and made his money in Chicago real estate. She was an only child.

It was said that when Louise deKoven Bowen was a child her family's carriage was one of the very few to always be attended by liveried footmen. At sixteen she graduated from the Dearborn seminary and at twenty-seven she married a "prominent manufacturer and banker." Her involvement with Hull-House began in 1896 and lasted for her own and Jane Addams's lifetime, and was steady and continuous along with her many other philanthropic interests.

When Jane Addams became seriously ill and incapacitated, she moved into Bowen's home and Louise deKoven Bowen became acting president and then president of Hull-House. She also was engaged in many other reform activities, including lobbying for the establishment of the first juvenile court in 1899.

In 1911 as a memorial to her husband she gave the Hull-House settlement seventy-two acres of land in Waukegan, Illinois, to establish a country club and summer camp for boys from the Hull-House neighborhood, and endowed it as well. Over her lifetime she gave more than a million dollars to Hull-House. She was also very active in the suffrage movement and in the Juvenile Protective Association, writing many of their influential reports herself. Like Florence Kelley she opposed the Equal Rights Amendment in the 1920s because she feared it would invalidate laws passed to protect women.

Louise deKoven Bowen's own memoir was said to report inaccurately that she first heard Jane Addams speak on the Pullman strike. Others recall her coming earlier to Hull-House. Bowen's wealth and respectability in the community balanced the perception that Hull-House was a hotbed of labor agitators. Louise deKoven Bowen was an astute financial manager and was treasurer of Hull-House from 1907 forward.

March 21, 2007: A pelting spring rain, aggravated by the absence of a leaf or a flower. Here in Seattle, the cherry trees are blooming.

Late in life Florence Kelley purchased a summer home in Maine. She kept buying up the surrounding land next to the house near Brooklin, on the rugged Maine coast, on the tip of Naskeag Point near the waters of Eggemoggin Reach. She initially bought an old house near a fishing village on ten acres. At one point she even bought an island, and she eventually owned 100 acres—a great deal of land for a socialist, she remarked. There in August she would live and work, with the company of one assistant from New York or a family member. Her youngest son, John, became attached to boats and settled in Maine for a while as an adult.

The Kelley family home, The Elms, in the outskirts of Philadelphia at 41st and Parrish streets, where Florence Kelley had spent her childhood, later declined in value and had long since been sold by the time of the congressman's death. When Florence Kelley was a child The Elms was so far out of town—four miles from City Hall—that during one year a carriage did not pass by from Thanksgiving to the New Year. By the 1880s, however, The Elms was surrounded by working-class bungalows and was no longer a rich congressman's elegant mansion on the outskirts of town. Now that location is part of the University of Pennsylvania Hospitals.

January 5, 2009: A cold, clear day, snow tomorrow. The city with a lovely glow in the sun. We will soon be gone from here, and perhaps to another city, another place.

In March 1892, William Darrah Kelley Jr. explained to the court and the assembled observers that the Kelley family in Philadelphia paid the rent on the apartment at 110 East 76th Street, allowing the growing Wischnewetzky family to move out of the smaller apartment in Harlem, where Mrs. Wischnewetzky and the children had moved while the doctor was in Europe finishing his degree. The doctor felt the Harlem address was not suitable for a man of his social position. The senior Kelley family provided other family support when more was going out than coming in, and the doctor had no income.

After the reunion in New York, before Florence Kelley's third child, John, was born on January 31, 1888, the ailing congressman gave his daughter $5 for toys for the children, and she bought a Christmas tree to the special delight of Nicholas. Caroline came to stay after John was born. Florence Kelley's recuperation after that delivery was described as slow, and there were the two other young children to care for at home in addition to the new baby.

March 21, 2008: Six inches of snow are predicted. Falling now, tiny wet flakes.

The family rift over money caused name-calling and estrangement before and after the congressman's death, with the demands for money coming from New York and being refused by the caretakers of the Kelley family finances. The estate of William Darrah Kelley had, as is often the case, less money in it, $35,419, than was expected by the heirs. At one point William Jr. said—in one of those remarks which stays hanging in the air—about his sister, Florence, and the Wischnewetzkys' incessant demands for cash: "She is worse than the Tartar!"

William Jr. later became an assistant city solicitor in Philadelphia, a position, his sister bitterly observed during the family troubles, he never would have obtained in a thousand years without his father's name and reputation. William Jr. wrote his sister in 1885, at the time of the strikes but before the Haymarket executions, that he was receiving regular training in riot drill at the Philadelphia City Troop Armory in order to be prepared to shoot down rioting workers. He would play an important role in managing Florence Kelley's unencumbered exit from Chicago, although little record of that remains.

March 22, 2007: Spring! The sky is blue, after a rain so heavy the road was invisible, and hail drummed on the car roof and windshield. Now the 1890s have become focused on Florence Kelley, factory inspector, and what that means.

When William Jr. recovered his health, after Avignon and before Zurich, brother and sister traveled to London. There they were visited by the congressman's old friend, Susan

B. Anthony. Susan B. Anthony suggested that Florence Kelley come and work as her secretary and devote herself to the cause of suffrage for women. Florence Kelley demurred. She was never to do so.

March 5, 2008: Spring seems forever away. Was the winter in Avignon this bleak? Probably worse.

During the London visit to the Kelleys in 1883, Susan B. Anthony's secretary and companion was Rachel Foster, the same Rachel Foster who was to provide $20,000 for the American publication of the ungrateful Engels's new preface to Florence Kelley Wischnewetzky's translation of *Die Lage*.

The parsimonious Engels wanted to know if Rachel Foster retained any property interests in the translated work. Florence Kelley reassured him that she herself retained all of the rights to the translation and that Rachel Foster was now married and too preoccupied by her two daughters to be bothered with socialist propaganda. Perhaps the comment applied to her own frame of mind as well.

April 2, 2007: The sun is shining, a beautiful spring day, full of color and light. A gentle breeze. And the homicide project is finally coming to a conclusion. Time for another project!

Florence Kelley's trip to the Midlands with her brother and father before Zurich included visits to the Black Country, so named because coal mining had left the landscape with a scorched appearance. Then they went to Manchester and visited piece workers in nail and chain factories where much of the most physically dangerous and arduous work was done by women, who could be employed cheaply, while the men stood idle. The working population was living in abject conditions in the mining towns and in the cities.

The trip resulted in Florence Kelley writing a series of letter-essays for the New York Tribune, an assignment arranged by her father, describing the conditions endured by piece workers and what she had observed in the English cities. The congressman delayed the publication of the letters for over a year. This was ostensibly the subject of the later disagreements between them. By that time, Florence Kelley said later, she no longer agreed with her father's strong protectionist position. Most of the letters were eventually published and not under her name.

March 21, 2008: The gentle spring snow of the morning now turning into sleet and ice. A steady accumulation of fluffy white on the outdoor table top.

On the same trip in the summer of 1883, the brother and sister visited the house where Dickens wrote *Bleak House*.

November 6, 2008: Today the grey outside is not dispiriting. We are jubilant!

When Florence Kelley first applied to the University of Zurich, she went to see the beadle, the administrative equivalent to a university registrar, described by Florence Kelley as a staunch Dickensian bureaucrat. He had been a friend to M. Carey Thomas. Along with his wife, the beadle of the University of Zurich waited with M. Carey Thomas while the faculty deliberated on the results of her rigorous oral examination on Anglo-Saxon philology, Anglo-Saxon historical grammar, English historical grammar—each for a quarter of an hour—followed by succeeding oral examinations on German, Gothic, and Old High German philology for three-quarters of an hour, German literature for half an hour, Middle High German for a quarter of an hour, and finally, for half an hour, an oral examination on the development of English literature, the exam concluding exactly as the clock struck six. And as every examiner and examinee knows, in an oral examination the slightest hint of weakness may be instantly probed to the nerve, and forgetfulness or ignorance painfully exposed. The examinations might be rigorous, but there was some humanity in the system, and Dr. M. Carey Thomas passed. That was the standard for academic excellence she established in America at Bryn Mawr, and held others to elsewhere.

March 23, 2007: Another grey spring day, no wind, the three-story green fir tree outside the window, standing, on guard, motionless.

On March 24, 1892, the sensation of the day came in the afternoon when Mrs. Wischnewetzky herself took the stand and testified as to the character of married life in New York. She described meeting the doctor, in a lecture class on politics and economics, when they were students at the University of Zurich in the winter of 1883-84. Her mother, Caroline, and younger brother, Albert, had accompanied her to Zurich, where they all lived in a pleasant pensione. Albert, thirteen, was put in school, where instruction would have probably been in German. In letters from that time Florence Kelley said Zurich was the most beautiful city she had ever seen.

By late 1883 Florence Kelley, who already knew German when she went to Cornell and also studied it there, was attending meetings of the German Social Democratic Party in Zurich, and she joined what she called the Socialist Party in Zurich in 1884. In Zurich there was a socialist newspaper, and party meetings were held regularly. Many Russians, especially Russian Jews, came to Zurich to escape political repression in Russia and its far-reaching hegemony, and the frequent pogroms against the Jews in Russia and what is now Eastern Europe.

January 6, 2009: A cloud of snow engulfs the house. And the roads are pillowed, sounds of movement muffled. The trees resemble Mussorgsky's Russian patriarchs, stately triangular figures in heavy robes of white. The house has become a fortress, a refuge. And it does feel like home, now that we are leaving.

At the habeas corpus hearing the *Chicago Inter Ocean* of March 26, 1892, reported that Mrs. Wischnewetzky testified that she and her husband "worked together in a literary way." Lazare Wischnewetzky furnished her with material for articles she published in the *New York Nation* and the *Overland Monthly*.

In response to a question whether he helped her financially, she replied: "No, he borrowed money off me before the marriage." One reason her father did not approve of the marriage, she said in response to questioning, was "because the Doctor had no visible means of support and had not yet obtained his medical degree."

Their courtship must have been primarily conducted in German, and German was the language of the marriage, in fact and in spirit. There were pensiones and pleasant inns and restaurants in Zurich and later in Heidelberg, where the newlyweds went to continue their studies. As long as they were in a place with a German spirit, the marriage seemed to go well.

When the couple announced their engagement, and later their marriage, they kept it from the University of Zurich for reasons not disclosed.

Most of the women students at Zurich were Russian exiles or Germans, taking degrees in medicine or the sciences, and some were married or formerly married. There was one other American woman graduate student in medicine. It was a joke among the Swiss students that the Russians were so busy planning the revolution that they never noticed if the snowcapped Alps could be seen on a clear day; any beauty which survived in spite of the corruption of capitalist civilization was beneath their notice. The Swiss students boasted that they admitted the oppressed of the earth. And they did.

Some of the refugees made their way to America, several to Chicago. One Russian exile, a translator of Marx and a student of chemistry at the University of Zurich, had been in prison for several years in the Peter and Paul fortress, then sent to Siberia, eventually to escape to America via the Bering Strait. He then met Florence Kelley again, to their mutual amazement, when he was a chemist for the Chicago Board of Health and she was the Illinois factory inspector.

In her *Autobiography* Florence Kelley recounts this meeting; however, one of her biographers notes that the details of this adventurous journey do not match those of the person she identifies, and that the journey matches the published chronicle of another European refugee friend's documented journey to America. There was, however, certainly at least one person whom she met in Illinois, whom she had known in Zurich.

There may have been a generalized bias or a tradition of excluding married women from universities even in Zurich. Perhaps a married woman's enrollment in the university carried the potential of the disapproval or interference of a husband. Women could not vote until very late, in 1970, in Zurich.

February 1998: At Harvard, Yale and Princeton, and other Eastern elite colleges, no women at all were admitted until after the middle of the next century, and strict quotas on Jews resulted in none or very, very few Jewish young men being admitted, in spite of the fact they were graduating with distinction from the most competitive high schools.

In my time the women students from New York flocked to the Cornell School of Home Economics, now retitled the College of Human Ecology, where the tuition was lower, where the students were presumed to be all women, and where they could take a limited number of classes in arts and sciences and find a husband.

Perhaps the young couple just didn't want to reveal the marriage. In the end neither Florence Kelley nor her husband were awarded degrees from the Polytechnicum of the University of Zurich, in spite of all of the studying and lectures attended. His medical degree was from the University of Heidelberg. Florence Kelley's only postgraduate degree was from the Northwestern University School of Law in 1895.

The secret of the engagement was kept from the congressman and he was pained at the news. He and wrote that since neither his advice nor his consent had been asked for, he would not thrust either upon them. He promptly departed for Europe saying he hoped to make his friends believe he had been consulted.

Caroline urged William Jr. to console him, saying that the Russian—he was actually a Polish-Russian Jew, although that was not discussed or perhaps even not revealed to Florence Kelley and certainly not to the family—was not marrying for money or influence since he had enough of both. Apparently not, for either category, at least by the time the Wischnewetzky family was living in New York in 1886.

March 25, 2007: A spring day, breezy, rosy, and a soft sky. The habeas corpus hearing in Judge Baker's courtroom took place 115 years ago today, on a grey day. And still such hearings go on in our courts. Still, the bitter custody battles are immersed in procedural formalities.

After the two-day hearing, Florence Kelley would have been back at Hull-House, licking her wounds with Jane Addams. For Florence Kelley the day after the habeas hearing, there was work to do, finding a way to support herself and her children being the first order of the next day. Not only did she by fiat declare herself to be Mrs. Florence Kelley, after recently insisting to Engels upon the Wischnewetzky name on the title page of the translation of *Die Lage*. She now gave her three children the Kelley name as well, all without the legal right to do so. A legal fiction was created: Mrs. Florence Kelley and the three

Kelley children. She also changed John's name, from John Brown Kelley, after the leader of the slave rebellion, to John Bartram Kelley, giving him her mother's family name.

After the hearing in March 1892 the children went back to Wayside with Henry Demarest Lloyd, Jessie Bross and the nursemaid. On weekends Florence Kelley traveled north to see them on the recently completed streetcar line. It was at Wayside and in the dining room of Hull-House that Florence Kelley came to know John Peter Altgeld.

March 15, 2012: The Ides of March. The weather today, spring and sunshine, in the middle of March. Certainly this weather will not last.

John Peter Altgeld did many good things before, after, and when he was governor of Illinois from 1893 until 1897, in addition to appointing Florence Kelley as the first woman state factory inspector in July 1893. What he became remembered for is the pardoning the three Haymarket defendants, Fielden, Schwab, and Oscar Neebe, the ones who had not been hanged on November 11, 1887, with Parsons, Fischer, Engel, and Spies.

Many people said about John Peter Altgeld that he was the smartest person they had ever known. This was not because he was erudite or highly educated or particularly imposing. He was not a domineering personality, but somehow his intellectual strength, trapped in a sickly body, was communicated. His prose style was only passing good. He was not apparently a mesmerizing speaker, unlike Clarence Darrow or Albert Parsons. Yet he was someone people did not forget when they met him.

March 1, 2007: A breezy, cloudy day, with the chill spring wind waking up all the trees, even the winter-stunned fir tree outside my third-story window, trembling. Now that I regularly drive to Chicago, I pace myself to accommodate the commuter schedules. As darkness falls, on the third floor I hear the steady drone of traffic and the occasional honk. From the third-floor window of this house at night, the time is marked by the pulse of headlights bouncing off trees as the cars stop at the traffic light at the corner on Sheridan Road. The third floor is a quiet place, my own place, my own room. When there are official functions in the house, or it is filled with family members and guests, it is another kind of place, and I am just another guest. This house is only a few miles from where Wayside was, and there is a park there. The woods where Henry Demarest Lloyd regularly rambled with his distinguished visitors have all gone to mansions now.

John Peter Altgeld's parents were part of the great migration of Germans and Prussians and other Europeans to the Americas, but they bore little resemblance, beyond their attachment to the German language, to the socialists and anarchists and political rebels and communists who were exiled to Zurich or London, some of whom then reproduced a wholly reimagined German intellectual environment in London, New York, and, surprisingly, Hoboken and Bayonne, New Jersey.

John Peter Altgeld's father was a wagon maker by trade, and the family eked out a marginal living as tenant farmers in Ohio. They were sharecroppers, and the father never got out of debt until presumably his son became governor of Illinois. Before bankrupting himself in real estate, perhaps the son was able to free the father from his lifelong servitude to his mortgages.

As a boy John Peter Altgeld was hired out as a farm laborer to the neighbors, then came home to do the chores on the family farm. When he was a boy, the father took on additional property and went deeper into debt. The family was never free from worry about money. John Peter Altgeld had a few years at school and managed to learn English against his parents' wishes. He never entirely lost his German accent, and was often teased about it and ridiculed for it by his political opponents.

March 24, 2008: Snow is on the ground, and the house is stone cold. The third day of spring and flurries are expected. Sun rises over the lake, an unexpected beauty of stripes, like the blurry red streaks in a Spanish orange.

During the election campaign of 1892 one of the most controversial and contentious issues was the recent passage of the school bill (called the Edwards Act) in 1889, which mandated compulsory education in English, including reading, writing, history, and geography, for all children up to age 12. A number of religious groups were opposed: the Lutherans didn't want teaching to be in English, the Catholics didn't like the fact that truant officers could inspect parochial schools, and the Jewish educational institutions and parents had their own views about outsiders imposing requirements on their children.

Before his campaign for governor, John Peter Altgeld had approved the education of all children in English, which would have been in accordance with his historical position on universal education. However, during the 1892 campaign for governor he mercilessly denounced his opponent for supporting the Edwards Act, a law he himself not only backed in principle but had probably helped draft.

December 14, 2010: One of the most bitter of cold snaps, 14 degrees, dry, the sidewalk at least dry. My rubber-soled boots stick to the ground. The sky clear, crystalline. And so we walk through the day in new surroundings, not yet at home, but I am grateful to be in the city.

Described as having a voracious appetite of mind, John Peter Altgeld was his whole life an avid reader, as a young man finding books in the houses of neighbors, in churches, in schools, later in the private libraries of judges and lawyers. Like Lincoln, for John Peter Altgeld and his wife, reading was a habit they never forswore. He loved language and poetry and all literature, and political philosophy and the discussion of all kinds of thought. He was himself an engaging philosopher, preoccupied with the big questions which he speculated upon in a dialectic form of discourse fashionable at the time. Strangely his writings, except the Haymarket pardon message, do not convey his passion and are uninteresting, predictable.

John Peter Altgeld never was heard to say a bad word about his father, who whipped him regularly as a boy, locked him out of the house to sleep in the cold if he came home after nine in the evening, and did everything to thwart his education.

After signing up for the Civil War over his father's objections, the sixteen-year-old boy participated in several battles, although later he would brush off his wartime experiences saying that he was just a boy doing what all the boys were doing, following the drums and bugles. That description of war was typical of his good sense. He said that signing the pardon for the anarchists required more bravery than all of the gun-toting and soldiering he did in the Civil War. He must have known pardoning the Haymarket defendants was political suicide. He did it anyway, and criticized the trial as well:

It is further shown here that much of the evidence given at the trial was a pure fabrication; that some of the prominent police officials, in their zeal, not only terrorized ignorant men by throwing them into prison and threatening them with torture if they refused to swear to anything desired, but they offered money and employment to those who would consent to do this. Further, that they deliberately planned to have fictitious conspiracies formed in order that they might get the glory of discovering them.

After a year in the army where he saw many die and many wounded, John Peter Altgeld came back and did his best to get an education, becoming an elementary school teacher of rowdy boys for a time—teaching was about educating himself—before starting on the long trek which was to eventually bring him to Chicago. Briefly, like congressman William Darrah Kelley, he became wealthy through the shrewd purchase of real estate, by getting lucky and riding one of the economic booms. Neither of them thought that acquiring wealth was the most important thing to do. Neither of them had money for long.

March 28, 2007: Rain, iron grey slate skies, and rain, rain, everything the color of the slate roof outside the window. And it is still draughty here even with all the radiators turned up.

Another thing to know about John Peter Altgeld, he was very happily married for thirty years to a woman who was as engaging as he was and who among her other accomplishments—being a musician, well-read, literate, articulate, a college graduate— wrote a fine novel, a story set in the times, about a prairie family and love gone awry. Her father, an educated man and a rich one, didn't want her to marry John Peter Altgeld, and he sent away the young man seeking her hand. John Peter Altgeld then worked his way across several states before winding up in Chicago, sleeping in the fields, hiring himself out as a farm hand for his food and bed. Certainly the young man wasn't prepossessing: totally without financial resources, small and rather shrunken from ill health—probably the illness he contracted in the army—and he had a harelip. Not the desired attributes for the prospective son-in-law of a prosperous, respected gentleman in a small town.

Like her husband, John Peter Altgeld's wife suffered from chronic ill health, and the two of them were frequently unwell and each spent much time devoted to the other's care.

November 5, 2008: A bright day. Warm, unseasonably warm. A day to remember.

John Peter Altgeld himself had two brothers and three sisters who apparently never did anything remarkable or distinguished themselves in any particular way. John Peter Altgeld came to Chicago, after graduating from college, after reading the law with a well-regarded lawyer and judge and being admitted to the Bar of Illinois. He worked briefly as a prosecutor and a county attorney, experience which would serve him well in his dealings with the state legislature.

John Peter Altgeld rode into Chicago on one of the great steam trains heading for the Loop, the way everyone seemed to come to Chicago after 1870—Dreiser's Sister Carrie, tens of thousands from the American South, and then all of the lawyers, architects, crooks, builders, furniture makers, joiners, carpenters, prostitutes, and pimps—everyone who heard there was a party going on in Chicago and money to be made after the Great Fire of 1871, when the Civil War had left much of the rest of the country flat broke, depressed, and uninhabitable. The drumbeat of this economic boom sounded from Virginia to Florida to Germany and Russia, and was heard by the Midwestern farm boys and girls, and sometimes their parents, heard by many who got tired of walking behind the tail of a scrawny mule, pulling a reluctant harvest from an unforgiving rocky soil.

Later, before and after he was governor of Illinois, and richer than he ever thought he would be, his parents and his sisters and brothers came to visit in Chicago. One brother became his business partner.

March 31, 2007: Warm and not a wisp of wind in the branches of the trees. The law school, Florence Kelley's alma mater, now housed in Levy Mayer Hall, remains stuck at twelve in the rankings, although ranked at eight in many categories, to the frustration of the administrators. A great deal of fretting over this.

On the train into Chicago with $100 in his pocket—he had already been practicing law in a small town—John Peter Altgeld fell into conversation with another lawyer who offered the young stranger the use of an empty desk in his own legal office. Another thing that people said about John Peter Altgeld was that it was astonishing he was ever elected governor because doing favors and politicking in the usual sense was contrary to his nature. His nomination was a fluke, one of those unpredictable moments in politics, which occurs once or twice in a century.

Eventually John Peter Altgeld, Clarence Darrow, and Edgar Lee Masters—all master lawyers, all formidable writers, all various kinds of fighters for justice—would share a law office, without being legal partners in the intricate, formal, institutionalized corporate bureaucracy of law firm partnerships today. Edgar Lee Masters became known for writing *Spoon River Anthology* and was hired by Levy Mayer's widow, Rachel Meyer Mayer, to write her husband's biography, a book with curious omissions. Clarence Darrow and Edgar Lee Masters later engaged in a loud public disputes. They did not speak for decades, made fools of themselves, sued one another, and took pains to insult one another in the newspapers long after their association with John Peter Altgeld.

October 12, 2006: Before I am fully awake, when I am lying with my eyes shut, I listen to the sounds from the street outside and guess the time. If there are no sounds, then it is probably before five in the morning. Even before dawn, when the days are short, there will be the rhythm of cars on Sheridan Road, heading downtown.

On a quiet Sunday morning, as day is breaking, if the weather is warm enough and dry, the bicyclists glide by on our quiet side street, and snatches of their conversation float up through our bedroom window open onto the street. Then, a reassuring train whistle at the crossing.

The Schwinn Company had a long and healthy history in Chicago, and bicycling was the rage in Florence Kelley's time. The voices of the cyclists may be loud, or they may be laughing, although the super light bicycles, and their riders in their cartoon bright skin suits may also be as silent as the silver fish sliding beneath the glassy surface of a Montana stream.

They choose this route because our street is empty, has smooth pavement and is just one block off of Sheridan Road. The voices of the cyclists rise and then are quickly gone. The joggers are typically alone and not talking, their ears plugged in to some player attached to their waist. Later the parents and children can be heard walking to school.

In the summer of 1892, after the tumult of the habeas hearing, after Dr. Wischnewetzky and her brother returned home, Florence Kelley finally got her own office, a tiny corner with a window on the second floor of new space at Hull-House. And she soon had a job: she was the special investigator for the Illinois Department of Labor Statistics. There she would have heard the trains, noisier trains than now, and the clinking and clattering of the wagons and streetcars, and always people on the street. Mostly, it seems, she was glad to be where she was, as she said in a letter to her mother:

Florence Kelley, Letter to Caroline Bonsall Kelley, Chicago
June 2, 1892

I think I have been most fortunate to keep perfectly well and my nerves in good order in spite of all of the strain of the trial, which was terrific.

And if I were a little blue and apprehensive, now and then, it would not be surprising particularly as we never see the sun and have had January weather ever since I came here except for a few bright Sundays.

Hull-House bordered on the great slum, and those people and their misery were out on the street. There was no quiet there. There often wasn't enough room in the tenements for all the people who lived there to lie down at night, so some rented rooms for the night only, and others could sleep only in the day, or for a few hours, or in the hallway, and some rooms were rented by the hour.

No one was sleeping in, or lazily stretching their legs in the morning, at Hull-House in the 1890s. The mission of the settlement house was to give assistance to the needy, including food and temporary shelter, to offer educational programs, to care for children and the old and the sick. After much effort a bathhouse was built for the women in the tenements, particularly for the Russian Jewish women for whom there had been no place to take the traditional monthly ritual bath, and so they considered themselves unclean.

This was a noisy neighborhood, full of little children. Florence Kelley was no stranger to the death and maiming of children, and she was right to worry about infecting her own children with smallpox. The children poured out into the street because there were more people inside than there was space for them. The children ran up and down the stairways of the tenements, played in the garbage-filled alleys, skipped among the wheels of the carts, stole pieces of coal from the railway beds, hitched rides on the streetcars, and carried their smaller siblings around on their backs. A child at home was probably caring for another child, but mostly in the Nineteenth Ward the children, both boys and girls, were working, peddling newspapers, running cash, stitching, holding wool, or just begging on the street.

June 25, 1999: Beirut. The sonic boom of the Israeli jets, then the dull thud of bombs. You find out who you are when the gunfire is heard. Swearing loudly, I was the coward under the bed (not a particularly safe place) until we were moved to the basement. The American University has survived so far despite all the wars.

What the women who lived at Hull-House in the 1890s said later about it was that it was like being back in their women's college halls. The women were mostly of that unusual demographic, that crop of early women college graduates not many years away from being students themselves, although many at Hull-House had no formal education.

This is how Florence Kelley's son Nicholas remembered Hull-House:

I have often wished that I could have seen with my present eyes those young women of sixty-five years ago, Miss Addams, whom my mother affectionately called "the gentle Jane," Miss Starr, Miss Lathrop, Miss Barnum, Miss Brockway, and my mother herself. . . . Miss Addams, gentle as she was and matter of fact as she seemed, applied a humane, simple common sense that amounted in its effect to imaginative genius and was firm beyond all imagining. To her every human life was precious and was entitled to high respect, no matter how damaged or wayward it might seem. I never saw Miss Addams angry and never heard of her being angry. My mother once asked her how she could be so calm.

My mother became a resident at Hull House almost at once after we came to Chicago. She had a wonderful flutelike voice, delightful in conversing and in speaking before an audience. She could twinkle with wit and humor but also could give way to anger. She worked very hard to support us children. The time she could find to be with us was precious to her, either visiting us when we were boarded out or having us come to see her at the House. I remember one of those times when she was taking the three of us to her tiny third-floor room, called the "Cell," to read to us from Kipling, whose stories were new and exciting then. On approaching the door, she found sticking out from under the narrow bed the legs of the scrub lady, who was drowning the floor with dirty suds in the name of cleaning it. My mother's storm of anger approached a hurricane. Although I recall only a very few times when I experienced the same thing aimed at me, I remember to this day the invective with which my mother followed a distinguished clergyman who expressed views of which she strongly disapproved.

Many were some kind of teacher, still moist with that longing to make the world a better place: teaching someone English or how to read, or how to ask for more wages. Florence Kelley was always a teacher.

Some were medically trained, including an African American doctor with whom she shared a room at Hull-House for a time, or they themselves had been workers in factories, sometimes being injured there. The lawyers whose names appear in the court filings did not all go to a law school or a college; lawyers read law and were clerks or secretaries to lawyers or judges before being admitted to the bar.

October 11, 2006: What can only be described as a blizzard is raging on the other side of the window, the snow blowing horizontally, and then swirling in a devilish, tornado-shaped vortex. And then a momentary flash of sunshine like a headlight in a fog.

At Hull-House there was always the talk, debate, argument, engagement. Henry Demarest Lloyd and John Peter Altgeld and William Stead all dined at Hull-House, and talked. Later Henry Demarest Lloyd said the talk there, for those who thought and cared about that and what they could do, was the best in Chicago. What others remembered about Florence Kelley was her joy, her wit, as she ran up and down the stairs which grew like wild brambles throughout the house as Hull-House added on to itself, and took over like a wild rose.

January 2, 2009: Now the sunshine bright on the winter landscape, bare without its snow. Every ceremonial occasion is the last time we will do this. And now the children and the grandchildren feel that too, since this has become their home too.

The newspaper in March 1892 reported that Dr. Wischnewetzky did not look like a tyrant, being a man of pleasant appearance with a heavy red mustache and beard, and his hair brushed back straight. This did not seem to be the type of man who would spit in his wife's face. He did not seem to be a person who would do her serious harm.

On the morning of March 24, 1892, he seemed to be greatly affected, as were the newspaper reporters, when his children, Nicholas, Margaret, and John, entered the court. The doctor took the two eldest on his knees and embraced them. The youngest seemed to prefer the company of the people who brought him. That would have been the children's nurse, and perhaps another from the Lloyd household. When it came time to leave the courtroom, the two older children crowded about their father, and were led away only with difficulty.

June 25, 1999: Beirut. At the university hospital all are treated; everyone must leave their guns outside when they enter the hospital. The degrees granted at the medical school are recognized under a special agreement enacted by the New York legislature dating back to the 1920s.

As the Tribune reported under the headline "What the Nurse Told," Clara McDermid told the court that in addition to corroborating that the doctor beat his wife about the face, that her face was bruised and discolored from these blows, that whenever Mrs. Wischnewetzky asked the doctor for money or spoke to him in English, he had a habit of flying into a rage and stomping violently. It was dangerous for the moral and physical health of the children, she testified, for them to be subjected to their father's irrational outbursts.

April 3, 2007: Thunder against a dark sky, a band of pink gold over the lake, shading into grey. The pink promise of tomorrow being fair.

January 7, 2009: Only a handful of days until the new regime comes in. Even the trees seem to be holding their collective breath. It is a kind of miracle that this is what our political system has produced.

The couple lived on what Mrs. Wischnewetzky was paid as a correspondent with the *Philadelphia Times* and earnings from what she described as hack translations into English of French and German and Italian novels. She testified that in New York the doctor had extravagant habits. After borrowing extensively from friends and family, her credit was exhausted, and still he frequently ordered expensive meals from Delmonico's, described in a Chicago newspaper as "a first class eating establishment in New York."

January 3, 2009: Grey, some pale blue streaks. Below freezing, but not as cold as at Christmas.

There was also the matter of Lazare Wischnewetzky's health. The doctor suffered from a serious illness, perhaps rheumatic fever, during the winter of 1888 in New York, requiring the constant care of his wife for six months. He had always been moody and irritable, and had suffered for years from nervous despondency and sleeplessness. His violent deliriums during this illness, however, required regular injections of morphine.

April 24, 1998: Happiness is a wedding. Hope is a wedding. Good fortune is a wedding, where families celebrate and embrace.

Mrs. Wischnewetzky's estrangement from her father and mother continued during this period. The resumption of family relations initiated cash transfers from the older generation to the younger which allowed Mrs. Wischnewetzky to pay the rent and attend the Metropolitan Opera, as well as to enjoy several long carriage drives in Central Park. And Mrs. Wischnewetzky was able to hire two servants with her family's help. Financial assistance from the family of William Darrah Kelley continued in the form of loans and gifts, including the underwriting of a vacation where the doctor was treated with daily baths and massage.

The couple requested an immediate loan of $2,500 with advances into the future, all to be secured by a mortgage for $20,000 on the homestead of Dr. Wischnewetzky's father's estate in Russia, said to be worth $40,000. Neither the mortgage nor the money from Russia ever materialized. Meanwhile Dr. Wischnewetzky spent much of the next year in Europe visiting health resorts, and his wife was in New York with no means of support.

April 5, 2008: The sun. Bright sky, light, everywhere. And 60 degrees. Yesterday, snow flurries predicted but it didn't precipitate. The suspense is unprecedented. Nothing in the news but election madness.

That same year, 1888, saw a visit to America by Frederick Engels during which he was for ten days within two hours of New York and yet he did not find time to arrange for a visit with his translator. There was a silence between them for a while after. So much for gratitude for the years of unremunerated toil over the now successfully published English translation of *Die Lage*, which also had a London edition. Rancor remained over the Aveling matter. The Avelings remained in the news long after their trip to America where, apparently, they drew large crowds in Chicago.

Marx on his deathbed charged Engels with Eleanor Marx Aveling's future welfare, an obligation Engels took seriously. She for a time lived with him, and her husband, Dr. Aveling, was one of many involved with the considerable industry of keeping the flame of Marxism and socialism alive by generating a steady stream of translations and commentary. Indeed there was some suggestion that Dr. Aveling had wanted to translate *Die Lage* himself.

Dr. Aveling was characteristically lax in financial matters, although he was known to have worked assiduously for the socialist movement. He was a womanizer, even while living in a common law union with Eleanor Marx, who called herself Mrs. Aveling although, like many socialists, she often said she did not believe in the institution of marriage. Dr. Aveling was not divorced from his first wife, so marriage to him was not initially a legal option irrespective of her ideological preferences. Nonetheless she called herself Mrs. Aveling.

Dr. Aveling's first legal wife eventually died in 1898, after he had been living with, and been supported by, Eleanor Marx, Engels, and the socialist establishment in one way or another for more than a decade. Soon after his first wife's death, Dr. Aveling married a young actress with whom he had been living secretly. Eleanor Marx discovered this and became desperate with grief. Dr. Aveling then concocted a bizarre joint suicide pact, involving the sequential taking of poisons. Only Eleanor Marx died. No criminal charges were ever brought against Dr. Aveling, who went to live with his actress in New York.

During the time of the dispute over the Avelings' travel expenses in America, Engels never would hear a word of criticism against Dr. Aveling and continued to allot him choice bits of socialist literature to translate. Engels, supported by a sizable income from his father's estate, lived in a comfortable house at 122 Regent Street near Regent's Park, which was a center of the socialist community in London which included authors, English reformers, and German and Russian intellectuals. Americans, such as Henry Demarest Lloyd and William Darrah Kelley, were well-known in this community through their writings.

With this far-flung group, writing was the glue of social cohesion. They all wrote—books and essays, pamphlets or tracts—they published letters in newspapers, others commented upon what they published. They wrote letters to one another about one another, kept the letters and often their own replies. They kept diaries. Then they kept much of their own writings and publications and gave them to libraries and archives. This is how Florence Kelley's letters to Engels ended up in Moscow.

When Engels wrote a new preface to *Die Lage*, it included some remarks which could be interpreted as pointing to deficiencies in the leadership of the Socialist Labor Party, and some members of the Executive Committee in Hoboken took the criticism personally. The Socialist Labor Party didn't like the preface, and they neither endorsed it nor promoted it nor printed it, in spite of having received a subvention for its publication. They kept the money.

There was suspicion among the Hoboken Socialists of the Wischnewetzkys being agents of foreign socialism. Those who resisted the adoption of English distrusted Florence Kelley and her promotion of English as the language for American socialism. The fact that she herself was American and fluent in English was cause for distrust itself. Some suggested she was a spy. It is not clear under whose auspices she would have been spying.

The American Socialist Labor Party proceedings were printed exclusively in German until 1887, and not exclusively in English until 1900. In the meantime Mrs. Wischnewetzky was flogging, without remuneration, the new English preface of *Die Lage* to publishers, distributors, and organizations who had little interest in it. It was surprising how many editors did not want to publish a manuscript by the coauthor of the *Communist Manifesto* at a time when there was a large audience for socialist tracts in America.

One prospective publisher rejected the manuscript, misidentifying the author and saying: "Engels, Engels? Oh! Yes! The man that was hung in Chicago!"

The actual Engels the author, who was alive and well in London, was characterizing his translator in letters to American friends as "a weak woman buffeted by every wind, and someone who translated as a factory." Much ink and warm air was expelled by persons who considered their own opinions worthy on matters both weighty and trivial. The international press commented on the dispute, further aggravating Engels and other supporters of the Avelings. The newspapers regularly included gossipy stories about the comings and goings of notable foreign visitors from a seemingly bottomless reservoir of bulletins about traveling minor European writers and nobility, reporting what they said upon reaching America, what they were wearing, and who was inviting them to dine.

June 16, 1996: So much excitement, so much fuss. And the clothes, much attention to the clothes. A great success, all around.

In New York in 1888, Mrs. Wischnewetzky was twenty-eight years old, the mother of two babies sixteen months apart, and was pregnant again, had little money, a demanding and temperamental husband who made no money, and a manuscript she had spent years translating which no one seemed to want to publish. She was borrowing money from her friends and anyone else—such as an English governess or a relative—who would lend it to pay the household expenses. One friend carefully recorded in her diary the repayment of several hundred dollars with interest. This is when the gap in Florence Kelley's correspondence and diaries begins. The doctor's family had always been far away; at some point his father died and there was talk of an inheritance. Florence Kelley met his mother at some point in Europe. The inheritance never materialized during the marriage.

Eventually with its new preface *Die Lage* was published in an edition of 20,000 copies, funded by Rachel Foster. Thanks to her efforts and with little thanks from Engels, the preface and the translation of *Die Lage* were widely distributed. The capitalist press declared *Die Lage* to be one of the most dangerous publications in recent years, a surprising judgment since *Die Lage* was about England and events taking place more than fifty years earlier. The new English translation of *Die Lage* by Frau Kelley-Wischnewetzky was much praised in Europe. The Socialist Labor Party in Hoboken did nothing to publicize it because of their ongoing dispute with the Wischnewetzkys, and that hurt sales in America.

In the short run, with regard to the small-scale, domestic matters of economy, the children were sick and had to be taken out of the unhealthy air and the heat of the city during the summer. The doctor was trying to establish the Medico-Mechanical Zander Institute in New York City. Henry George was distancing himself from socialist principles in anticipation of his presidential candidacy. The national press was focused again on free trade versus protectionism, Congressman William Darrah Kelley's issue, an issue which never seems to go away. Mrs. Wischnewetzky bitterly described the Republican protectionist press as being at her father's beck and call.

January 3, 2009: The sun is shining, even in the middle of winter. A new day, a new year. And a year of changes, for us, the family, the country.

On the afternoon of March 25, 1892, in Chicago Mrs. Wischnewetzky took the stand and said that when she married the doctor he was a student without an income. She testified that the doctor was never violent toward her personally until just before the birth of their third child in New York. He had always had a violent temper upon the least provocation, and now especially if she spoke English in his presence. Mrs. Wischnewetzky attributed his irritability to worries about the difficulties in establishing the Medico-Mechanical Zander Institute in New York. Perhaps it was an aftereffect of the doses of morphine during his illness.

About this time the doctor took an extended trip to Europe to rest, receive therapeutic treatment, and defend his Wurzberg doctoral dissertation, titled "Some Contributions to the Statistics of the Lower Lip," a paper on the cancers of the lip. The medical practice he sought to establish in New York was not, however, devoted to the treatment of that disease.

June 2, 1999: My book is now out. Our parents' generation didn't so much read the newspapers as ingest them with their morning coffee. They relied upon the newspapers for news, not just for information.

After the doctor returned from a month in Europe, the family moved to a smaller apartment in Harlem, although the doctor believed the apartment was not suitable for someone of his social standing. The family finances continued to be strained. Two babies sixteen months apart, and another pregnancy. Then there was his long and terrible illness, during which he experienced bouts of delusion, according to his wife.

Meanwhile, Florence Kelley was paying newsboys a penny a copy to distribute Engels's preface to *Die Lage*, speaking before clubs such as the National Association of Collegiate Alumnae, which promised to distribute the manuscript to its thousand members across the country, translating for money, and generally promoting her own and Engels's work. Engels wrote from England that she should drop the unpronounceable Wischnewetzky from her byline, because he feared it would harm sales. She replied that was out of the question. Any change of her name she would regard as an infringement of her copyright.

Mrs. Wischnewetzky's interests and friendships in New York had now widened, and both Wischnewetzkys were soon unconditionally reinstated into the Socialist Labor Party and even had a reunion with the Avelings. Engels was planning his visit to America, and much attention was paid by the local socialists to anticipating his comfort and travel. He referred to Mrs. Wischnewetzky in correspondence as "Mother Wischnewetzky" and to the couple as the "Washragskys."

Engels wrote to a mutual friend, saying he did not allow the "little women's rights ladies" to demand gallantry or even, apparently, courtesy. This characterization for someone who had spent years translating and arranging for the publication of his now-unreadable work. He suggested that Florence Kelley spend her time writing popular versions of his own and Marx's work. Instead Mrs. Wischnewetzky turned her attention to her own writing, going back to an old preoccupation, the subject of her Cornell senior thesis: the protection of working children in the labor force.

On the afternoon of March 24, 1892, Mrs. Wischnewetzky testified that the beatings began when she was pregnant with their third child, christened John Brown. During a heavy snowstorm in 1887 during one of her husband's violent spells, as she further testified that afternoon, he raised a heavy Vichy bottle and said, "Get out of the room, I'm afraid I'll do something terrible to you." This threat was probably not expressed in English. Mrs. Wischnewetzky walked the streets of New York in the snow alone that night and did not return.

William Darrah Kelley Sr. had authorized the executor of his estate to advance to his son-in-law such sums as may be necessary to complete the licensing and purchase of the

Zander system. The Elms, where Florence Kelley had grown up, had long ago been sold.

According to the testimony at the habeas corpus hearing, the $20,000 advance to Dr. and Mrs. Wischnewetzky from the estate in 1890 was contested by the executor (not William D. Kelley Jr.) after the congressman's death, when the couple asked for more. The Zander Institute did open for business in 1890 in a respectable office building at 246 Fifth Avenue. The Wischnewetzky family was by then established at 78 West 72nd Street and out of the unsuitable residence in Harlem.

At the hearing Dr. Wischnewetzky claimed the Zander Institute to be on the verge of financial success. The medical societies of New York, New Jersey, or Pennsylvania for this period do not list Dr. Lazare Wischnewetzky as a member.

Mrs. Wischnewetzky further testified that it was during this time after the congressman's death that the doctor struck her in the face so severely that she was badly disfigured and had to be confined to her room for two or three weeks. This for a woman whose professional life consisted of multiple, complex social presentations and interactions: advocacy for the economic independence of women and girls, writing, public speaking about what women and children suffered at the hands of abusive men, all the while negotiating with editors and publishers, selling herself and her work and the work of others—who were sometimes ungrateful—and championing the good which would come with social change. It was a time when hope was maintained in the face of a painfully contradictory reality.

Shortly after the move to the better address at West 72nd Street, the doctor in a fit of violent temper threatened to kill himself, moving forward to the cupboard where he kept his medicines. His wife placed herself in front of the cabinet, and he struck her several times in the face, the marks of which remained for days. "Not only will I continue to beat you," she reported that he said, "but I will teach your son to beat you." That would have been the oldest son, Nicholas.

The testimony in the Chicago court continued: On the anniversary of the death of William Darrah Kelley, January 9, 1891, during a fit of rage the doctor reproached her and her family, using the most vile language. When she left the house and children, the doctor followed her into the street shouting names after her. On that occasion the bruises from where he struck her face did not heal for weeks.

After this beating Mrs. Wischnewetzky showed her bruised face to Thaddeus Wakeman, secretary to the Zander Institute, a Princeton graduate, and a lawyer. He advised reconciliation rather than separation. On another occasion in December 1891 the doctor for no reason struck her in the face with his closed fist while they were walking on Fifth Avenue.

On December 17, 1891, Dr. Wischnewetzky hit her again, spat in her face, and walked out the door. That was when Mrs. Wischnewetzky gathered up her three children and a few belongings and, borrowing money for the fare from an English governess, took the train to Chicago without telling her husband.

November 6, 2008: The yellow trees in the garden are as bright as the sun today, even against a backdrop of a gloomy sky. How do the city and the country survive its politics?

On March 25, 1892, Judge Baker's court was again engaged all day in hearing evidence. In Florence Kelley's papers in the archives from the period there is a bill from 1891 from a New York lawyer which remained unpaid and resubmitted over the years. This bill being, presumably, for legal services to defend against another action in New York for which there is no record. Mrs. Wischnewetzky's testimony of her husband's cruelty and violence toward her remained unwavering under cross-examination by the doctor's attorneys.

She continued to assert that the household in New York was supported by money advanced from her father's estate (the $20,000) as well as income from her hack writings and borrowings from friends, during the time the doctor was seeking to establish the Medico-Mechanical Zander Institute on Fifth Avenue and Twenty-Eighth Street. That would be the establishment of the nonsupport question, grounds for divorce in Illinois at the time.

Dr. Wischnewetzky denied that he had ever used vile or abusive language, or heaped indignities upon her. He said he never struck her intentionally. And he never took money from her in Switzerland because she never had any cash. The doctor did admit to the court that he became angry, enraged, when she spoke English to the children or servants. That would be the cruelty question. He especially disliked hearing the English language when he was tired. As to the quarrel on January 9, 1891, the fault was his wife's failure to provide a key ingredient in a Russian stew when some guests were present for dinner. In the quarrel, he claimed, his wife was the assailant, he the peacemaker. He was pathetic, one news account noted, in telling the story of his grief when he came home and found his wife had left home with the three children.

The witness from New York for the doctor, Thaddeus B. Wakeman, the Princeton-educated lawyer and secretary to Dr. Wischnewetzky's Medico-Mechanical Zander Institute, testified that Mrs. Wischnewetzky did come to him after January 9, 1891, and show him her blackened face. She asked about the advisability of a separation, and he persuaded her to go back to her husband. Attorney Wakeman never heard of any additional domestic difficulties. Nor did Mrs. Wischnewetzky seek his advice again, he said.

Thaddeus B. Wakeman further testified that he had known the family for several years and that the Medico-Mechanical Zander Institute was in 1892 just on the verge of becoming financially viable. The fate of the institute, its financial viability, however, according to Thaddeus B. Wakeman, depended upon whether Dr. Wischnewetzky regained possession of his three children. Mr. Wakeman said he came to Chicago at the behest of the doctor and had tried to persuade Mrs. Wischnewetzky to return to New York with the children. She flatly refused. When he tried to influence her to let the doctor see the children, she refused again. In his view, if Mrs. Wischnewetzky did not return the three children, the Medico-Mechanical Zander Institute was doomed.

December 18, 1998: A reading of my new book in Seattle. The only people in the audience were family, a stray homeless man, and a law school alumnus who came out of the goodness of his heart. And it is dark here early now, as in Chicago.

On cross-examination, Thaddeus Wakeman stated that his interest was primarily on behalf of the creditors of the Medico-Mechanical Zander Institute, that he himself had a financial stake in the institute and thus had a financial interest in the outcome of the proceeding before the court. He described the doctor as a nervous, demonstrative man, insistent upon his views, passionate, but capable of taking advice when the first burst of passion subsided.

On March 26, 1892, Mrs. Wischnewetzky was awarded custody of her three children, the decision of Judge Baker being given late in the evening after a full day of testimony. There were subsequent efforts, which failed, originating in New York, by the doctor to appeal the order and gain custody and bring the children to New York.

On the last day of testimony in the habeas corpus hearing, the doctor expressed great love for his children and said he was unable to live without them. His behavior in court was described as voluble, excitable. At the last moment he asked the court to at least grant him custody of the oldest boy, Nicholas. Mrs. Wischnewetzky's attorneys blocked that move.

After a tearful parting from his children, it was reported that Dr. Wischnewetzky left the courtroom without so much as a glance at his wife. On March 27, 1892, the paper reported that Dr. Wischnewetzky's errand to Chicago had proved fruitless. On April 17, 1892, the last flutter of the official case was heard in Judge Baker's courtroom when the motion was made again by the doctor's attorney to award the father custody of Nicholas. The court commented: "There may be a time when the care of the three children is too arduous a duty for the mother, and their welfare would be served by awarding the father custody. That time was not the present."

The temporary order granting custody of the three children to their mother in Chicago was issued May 9, 1892, although the fight over custody was not over.

Letter from Florence Kelley to her son Nicholas Kelley

July 11, 1906: Pittsfield, Massachusetts

Darling Son, It was the best day of my life, that day twenty one years ago tomorrow which brought you to us. For nothing but good has followed it. The only anxiety you ever caused me was thro' no fault of your own,—when you seemed to be getting small-pox at Miss Whitelaw's; and when you were ill with eyestrain in your Freshman year.

As for the good, it is more than can be said or written. If sons and daughters could only know their power of giving pleasure—and pain—how differently most of them would act. . . . Finally, if you reach the years of your grandfather, old age will have lost its terrors and cancer, one of its blackest shadows, will be under control.

The final order granting custody of her children to Mrs. Florence Kelley signed by Judge Baker is dated May 27, 1892.

November 13, 1998, Chicago Tribune: "Escaping Execution: High-lighting Flaws in the Death Penalty, 31 People Who Survived Death Row Will Gather at Northwestern University."

. . . Highlighting the innocent allows organizers to sidestep the battle over the death penalty in theory—a fight they have been losing—and instead show the world the faces of people who would be dead if the system had run its course.

"I can't imagine how in the face of these people prosecutors can stand up and say the problem with the death penalty is that we don't kill people fast enough," said [Lawrence] Marshall, who teaches law at Northwestern University. "I have friends that I go out to dinner with that if the death penalty was as fast as some prosecutors want it to be, they would be dead."

More than 800 people have registered, far more than were expect-ed. Organizers hope a big media splash will spread the notion that no matter how much sense it makes to some people, the death penalty inevitably means the innocent will die.

November 15, 1998, Chicago Tribune: "Attendees Assail Capital Punishment: Former Death Row Inmates Honored at Conference."

One by one, they marched across the stage, men and women who but for a twist of fate would have marched instead toward a gas cham-ber, an electric chair or a gurney to be injected with poison.

One by one, the 29 stepped up to a microphone. "If the state had its way, I'd be dead today," they intoned, some with defiance, some with a bitterness so deep it seemed to echo in the auditorium.

The joint appearance of the former Death Row inmates was an emotional peak of a three-day conference on innocence and the death penalty at Northwestern University that ends Sunday. The gathering was the first time so many of the 75 Americans known to have been wrongly condemned to death have gathered in one place.

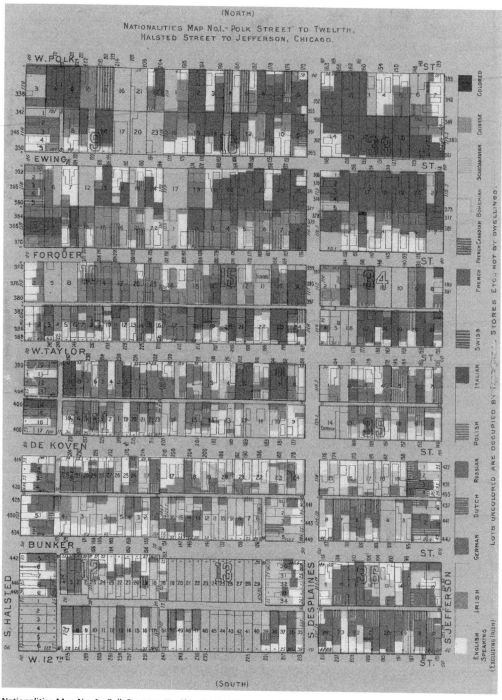

Nationalities Map No. 1 - Polk Street to Twelfth, Halsted Street to Jefferson, Chicago. From *Hull-House Maps and Papers*, published in 1895.

3

The Angels of Reform

The horrors of the slums settle down upon my spirits but only for a few moments at a time. Then I am all right again.

But your loving letters and my exquisite bairns are enough to keep anyone braced up and cheerful. The children are so beautiful physically and so loving and frank, that I have never dreamed of anything like them.

Letter from Florence Kelley to Caroline Bonsall Kelley, Chicago, c. June 1892

"This office makes its initial work that of pure facts. . . . It should be remembered that a bureau of labor cannot solve social or industrial problems, nor can it bring direct returns in a material way to the citizens of a country, but its work must be classed among educational efforts, and by judicious investigations and the fearless publication of the results thereof, it may and should enable the people to more clearly and more fully comprehend many of the problems which now vex them.

Carroll D. Wright, US commissioner of labor, as quoted by Horace G. Waldin in a memorial in the US Congressional Record, February 1909

A Special Investigation of the Slums of Great Cities *was undertaken in the spring of 1893, by the United States Department of Labor, by order of Congress; and Mrs. Florence Kelley, the Special Agent Expert in charge in Chicago, resided at Hull-House while conducting the investigation, the information collected by the government officials was brought within the very doors. . . . Four government schedule men from the 6th of April until the 15th of July 1893 lived at Hull-House and devoted their entire time to examining each house, tenement and room in the designated area.*

Hull-House Maps and Papers

The writer of those words in 1893 is not Florence Kelley but Hull-House resident Agnes Sinclair Holbrook, whose comments introduce *Hull-House Maps and Papers*, published in 1895, after much wrangling and mutual threats of withdrawal and abandonment, by Thomas Y. Crowell & Co. of New York. It was part of a series titled *Crowell's Library on Economics and Politics* edited by Richard T. Ely, PhD, LLD. The book is attributed to "Residents of Hull-House, a Social Settlement at 335 South Halsted Street, Chicago, Ill." And so they were, residents of Hull-House.

Agnes Sinclair Holbook writes the introduction to the maps in *Hull-House Maps and Papers*. The essays are written by different individuals at Hull-House, including Florence Kelley. The genius of the maps is to distill and make comprehensible the river of statistics and data submitted as the *Seventh Special Report of the Commissioner of Labor or The Slums of Baltimore, Chicago, New York, and Philadelphia to the president of the United States and to the US Congress*, by Carroll D. Wright (1840-1909), the first US commissioner of labor (1885-1905). This report is also referred to as *The Slums of Great Cities* when it is reprinted.

January 12, 1999: What is most typical of Chicago, in its novels and in real life, is the persistent fixation on the weather. The dreadful winters, the hot summers. I have not found either so dreadful. For those of us with air conditioning and reliable heat, the weather does not mean suffering. My students from California report: it is eighty degrees in Los Angeles.

The truth is that I am lonely and I have no one to talk to. We seem to spend all of our time at functions, with rich people, the former titans of industry who work downtown and live in mansions in the green suburbs. In my case, the important thing is to show up at these events, where much business gets done. Perhaps the rich are not like us, beyond having more money. Not that I am complaining. We are usually at dinner somewhere, or in pleasant surroundings, but it is a different kind of social relationship, of that there is no doubt. And it is assumed I am present as accompaniment.

Once the children and their nursemaid were settled in Winnetka with the family of Henry Demarest Lloyd, there was the question of employment for the principal breadwinner herself. There was no one else to look to for support, and Florence Kelley had promised everyone, and especially her mother, that she would not borrow any more or go into debt again. These were promises hard kept.

First, Florence Kelley was a resident at Hull-House. At that point Hull-House had not yet grown to the thirteen buildings it was later to encompass. What is striking today about the original house, now a museum, is how small the rooms are, yet how carefully appointed and how graceful their design. It feels like a home. The number of residents was limited to twenty-five, and on occasion included men.

> *The first man resident, he was a son of Horatio C. Burchard, the clergyman of "rum, Romanism, and rebellion" fame and an older relative of Roswell Burchard Perkins, today the assistant secretary of the Department of Health, Education, and Welfare.*
> Nicholas Kelley, *Early Days at Hull House*

Generally, there was a brief probationary period for residency. Residents were required to commit to staying six months. One observer noted: "Thorny people were not admitted." The fees were not large, but not trivial.

Before her federal appointment, on May 23, 1892, Florence Kelley had been named—after volunteering for the job and after Jane Addams engaged in "wirepulling"—as a special agent for the Illinois Bureau of Labor Statistics, to investigate the sweating system in Chicago. The result: a modest job title and what was expected to be a modest report on conditions in the sweatshops for women and children (and men) in the tenements of the Nineteenth Ward, and getting paid, even if it was only a little and for piecework.

September 1999: It is settled: now we will have our conference on Homicide in Chicago 1870-1930 in the fall of next year. The Journal of Criminal Law and Criminology will publish the papers. The data will be sent to researchers across the country, and we will come together, talk about the police records, and write papers, from a variety of academic perspectives. Many distinguished researchers have agreed to write; the new homicide data set demands analysis, attention.

The work for the Illinois Bureau of Labor was a warmup, a prelude to her work of the next year for the US Department of Labor, and preparation and qualification for the later work of being factory inspector. The purpose of it all was to investigate and report upon the living and working conditions, primarily for women and children but for men too, in the sweatshops, factories, and tenements.

Basically, the Hull-House women and their colleagues were inventing for America the practice of social work and legal advocacy for the poor, as it would be practiced for the next hundred years. They were self-appointed advocates for the poor, having been handed a small wedge by a state agency and later by a statute which granted a little of the power of the state to them.

Less than six months after her arrival in Chicago, Florence Kelley earned seventy-eight dollars a month from the Illinois Bureau of Labor Statistics, and fifty cents for each schedule completed. Then, twelve dollars came in sporadically for writing for *The Signal*, described as a labor publication in Champaign, Illinois. Plus, there were periodic remittances of a few British pounds for the sales of the translation of *Die Lage* and some payments for writings in foreign journals. Formerly she wrote about conditions in Europe for the American press; now she wrote about America for European journals.

June 3, 2013: The first beautiful spring day. The legislature has adjourned and they have not addressed the pension issues, gay marriage, or the budget. The speaker holds back the votes, waiting to maximize the political benefit for his daughter, the attorney general, who is considering running for governor. And so nothing gets done, and the fiscal bleeding from prior irresponsible decisions continues.

Florence Kelley was employed in a marginal position as a special investigator for the Illinois Bureau of Labor Statistics. However, after the election of John Peter Altgeld as governor in November 1892, she managed in early 1893 to parlay her position into a job as a special investigator (with Alzina Stevens) for the Joint Legislative Committee of the Illinois legislature. The new legislature was considering a factory inspection statute, and this investigatory report was to be background to the legislation.

The proposed factory inspection statute was drafted at Hull-House by the Hull-House regulars: Florence Kelley, Henry Demarest Lloyd, Jane Addams, and union workers, with input from many others. When Florence Kelley was hired as a special investigator for the *Slums of Great Cities* project, the data for the national project could be used to support the state project, and vice versa. Each gave credibility to the other. The congressional project allowed her to enter the slums as an investigator for the US Congress and to thus establish her legitimacy while developing the factual basis to argue for later state action. No one could keep her out of the Chicago tenements when she was a federal investigator under the authority of the US Congress and the US Department of Labor.

Letter to Henry Demarest Lloyd, Chicago, June 30, 1892

. . . from May 23rd when my [State] Bureau work began to June 23rd, I earned $78.00 from the Bureau and $12.00 from the Signal. (They held over so much of my ms. that the payments for the month were only $3.00, $4.00 and $5.00) Nothing came of the Inter Ocean work for some unexplained reason. However, my current expenses are only $64.00 per month, so that I came out well ahead, so far.

These tasks—the piecemeal investigation for the Illinois Bureau of Labor Statistics, the larger investigation for the Joint Legislative Committee of the Illinois legislature, the work for the US Department of Labor (the filling out of the schedules with demographic and economic data and sending them to Washington)—were essentially all the same task: to document and publish reports, factual reports, mostly statistical reports, about conditions in the slums and tenements of Chicago in 1892, how the people, and especially the women and children working in the factories and sweatshops, lived and worked. And to publish these reports and disseminate the information as widely as possible.

It was first an exercise in counting, in compiling statistics. This was social science, sociology, social work, ethnographic fieldwork, a secular kind of missionary work, and journalism. Florence Kelley and her colleagues would have applied none of those labels. The hope was someone in government would appoint a committee, and then something or nothing would happen, and the work would be forgotten, or not. If someone in a position to do something read the reports, became outraged, perhaps something would happen.

December 4, 2002: Winter is settled in here. And days away from the solstice. Hiding on the third floor and watching the snow fall around is bliss. Albert Parsons, the only American-born Haymarket defendant, the handsome, silver-tongued orator who let his hair go grey when he was in hiding after Haymarket, had not been in contact with his dear wife or their children until the terms of his surrender to the law were negotiated. He was free to walk in the Wisconsin hills, free to make jokes and sing with the family's children. Parsons's lawyer persuaded him to return to be tried, to clear his name, said he would not be executed.

The residency requirement of six months at Hull-House must have been set aside for the four unnamed schedule men from Washington who stayed from April 6 to July 15, 1893, to collect under Florence Kelley's supervision the data for the Chicago part of Carroll Wright's enterprise, the statistical study of *The Slums of Great Cities*. The data collection was going on at the time of the World's Columbian Exposition.

The maps and papers in Hull-House are a visual representation of economic data, literally a graphic display of economic conditions in a neighborhood, and are immediately and intuitively apprehensible still. They are modeled upon maps of ethnicity and poverty in London compiled by Charles Booth, which Florence Kelley would have seen when she visited London and which she acknowledges as a prototype.

Their immediacy of design channels the chaos of detailed statistical information, waterfalls of numbers and graphs which make the viewer forget that economic data points are information collected by real people with some reference to actual people, to what they have and how they live. The maps with their little colored rectangles for houses and buildings, childlike in their charm, and with their enumerated streets, call up an imagined reality of actual streets and houses. Financial and criminal statistics, pages after pages of them, obscure the fact that the data refer to actual people, acts, or lives.

March 15, 1999: The sunny breakfast room at 639 in Evanston. And a kind of peace in the morning. She is dead. There is no use asking if her life would have been happier if she had made other choices, lived somewhere else. Nothing to be done about the remembered unhappiness of the dead. It exists somewhere out in the great void. Hard enough to figure out whether anyone alive, including oneself, is happy. We have no way of knowing how happy was Helen, or anyone else, in March, or April or in the 1890s, or at any time in the future or past. Nor do we even know if that is a proper question. We only know that someone lived, then died, and some writing remains.

In Chicago, then as now, there were laws, lots of laws. The civil society then, as now, was knit together by laws, and held together by the illusion of a law-abiding citizenry. The information reported by Florence Kelley's government inspectors, what she found, what was projected graphically by the maps in *Hull-House Maps and Papers* were the facts. The actual numbers recorded and collected are included as hundreds of tables in the big black tome published by the US Congress. Now those numbers are mostly forgotten because all that remains is data, interesting data, but only statistics.

The maps remain curiously touching; they make comprehensible in a moment how people were distributed in the neighborhood. If people, especially people in a position to make a difference, could not see what the statistics said, nothing would be done. The hand-wringing over conditions in the tenements and sweatshops had been going on for months, years. The maps put the reality, the facts, in a new frame, told the story differently and communicated differently. There was a jauntiness about them, an art which belied the facts of misery.

April 1999: How little I have been moved by the "success" of the book. The publishers did nothing to publicize it. I did everything, and still the sales remained at a minuscule level, by any standard other than an academic one. So it has sold over five thousand copies, but that is far short of the twenty thousand needed for any commercial publisher. An extravagant dinner at the most expensive restaurant in town. How can a bottle of wine cost $800? My taste buds can't distinguish between $100 and $800. Of course that didn't stop me from drinking and feeling guilty nonetheless. To go forward in time, and backward in time, at the same time. . . .

The New Slavery, a report on the tenements and sweatshops, written by Mrs. Thomas Morgan, was published in October 1891, two months before Florence Kelley arrived in Chicago. This pamphlet exposed in detail the extreme conditions in the sweatshops, Florence Kelley wrote Engels, and aroused "a fever of interest," not just in Chicago but also in New York and in the halls of Congress. There was pressure to do something about this, especially in Chicago, especially with the imminence of the Columbian Exposition.

The Chicago City Council in 1891 did much of what was later incorporated into the 1893 Factory and Workshop Inspection Law (or Factory Inspection Law). It did not and could not institute and pay for large-scale, statewide inspections under the authority of the State of Illinois.

January 1999: The Chicago Tribune has published an unprecedented five-part series called "Trial & Error: How Prosecutors Sacrifice Justice to Win" by Ken Armstrong and Maurice Possley. It is a stunning piece of journalism, perfectly placed in a daily city newspaper.

January 10, 1999, Chicago Tribune: Part 1 of 5: "Tipping the Scales: The Verdict: Dishonor" by Ken Armstrong and Maurice Possley.

. . . With impunity, prosecutors across the country have violated their oaths and the law, committing the worst kinds of deception in the most serious of cases. They have prosecuted black men, hiding evidence the real killers were white. They have prosecuted a wife, hiding evidence her husband committed suicide. They have prosecuted parents, hiding evidence their daughter was killed by wild dogs.

They do it to win.

They do it because they won't get punished. They have done it to defendants who came within hours of being executed, only to be exonerated. . . .

Ask judges, defense attorneys, prosecutors and legal scholars why prosecutors cheat, and they often answer with two simple words: To win. . . .

The drive to win is fueled by a variety of factors, including the satisfaction of putting away a dangerous criminal, pleasing the public, and providing justice for victims or their survivors.

When Florence Kelley with members of the Chicago Woman's Club and the Illinois Women's Alliance marched into the City Council and demanded reform in the tenements, they were not bringing the news of unknown conditions, although their march into the City Council was dramatic. In short, Florence Kelley came to Chicago and rode the crest of a wave which had been gathering its strength from a long way out.

The pressure of population from the concentration of recent immigrants in the poorest parts of the cities was part of the urgency. The new immigrants, everyone agreed, would work for the lowest wages and were the least likely to object to their working conditions. This is why they were clumped together in the tenements. Nor was this phenomenon limited to Chicago.

May 3, 2013: Today, after the collapse of the building which killed hundreds of garment workers, mostly women, it is reported that their wages were less than a few pennies an hour. The Bangladeshi city was known as the place with the least government regulation and the lowest wages, with a small presence of unions. The new pope is outraged, says this is slavery.

The Chicago City Council was not a forum for the faint of heart. Johnny Powers, called "Johnny de Pow" because he was for a time the most powerful alderman on the council, was also known as the person who organized the bribes, the payoffs, the "boodle" which the aldermen expected and got in return for passing ordinances and granting franchises favorable to business. Johnny Powers was the alderman for the Nineteenth Ward, the worst slum in Chicago. Later the ward maps would be drawn and redrawn, but the basic structure remained. This is how Johnny Powers was remembered in his obituary in the *Chicago Tribune* on May 20, 1930:

"Johnny de Pow" as he was known on the west side, will be missed not only by chieftains of the Democratic party, but by the poor of the old 19th ward [where he served as alderman for 38 years], now the 25th, whom he did not forget even after quitting politics.

However, the Powers methods of charity were vigorously combated by reform elements—the M.V.L. and Hull-House, for example, Hull-House never could be brought to agree that his distributions of turkeys among his poor constituents at Christmas was real or wise helpfulness.

At the time of *Hull-House Maps and Papers* he was the most powerful alderman in Chicago:

Powers has piloted, either openly or covertly, nearly every boodle ordinance in the city council since the embodiment of the pernicious influence that has dictated municipal legislation for many years. In the Nineteenth, Mr. Powers is not called the Prince of Boodlers. He's called the Chief Mourner. The shadow of sympathetic gloom is always about him. He never jokes; he has forgotten how to smile. He never fails to visit the bedside of the dead, nor to distribute Christmas turkeys to the poor.

Those who know Powers best will tell you that no meaner miser ever rivaled Shylock. The only way he can get votes is by hypocritical posing as a benefactor by filling the role of friend in need when death comes. He has bowed with aldermanic grief at thousands of biers. He is bloodless, personally unattractive. His demeanor is one of timid alertness and anxiety to please, but he is actually autocratic, arrogant, and insolent.

The Chicago Times Herald

As alderman for the Nineteenth Ward, he was the person who controlled the area which was the subject of the research for the *Slums of Great Cities* project and also for the forays into the tenements and factories in preparation for the report for the Illinois Joint Legislative Committee and the preparatory report for the Illinois Bureau of Labor Statistics. Johnny Powers was later locked into a protracted political struggle with Bathhouse John Coughlin, along with Mike Kenna, for control of the City Council.

February 1999: The data for the historical homicide project are all coded, ready to be sent to the researchers. The funding is in place with three separate outside grants. I am persuaded that all 14,000 police cases of homicide from 1870-1930 should be put on a website, whatever that is, and not just sent to the University of Michigan social science research center as a data archive. There will be a law school conference and a journal publication. That is all that I care about. The cases, these police records, will be available as data for future homicide researchers. It all seems to take forever. Perhaps just because it is winter when everything slows down. Mentally we seem to go into hibernation in the winter.

Johnny Powers consolidated his power after being elected for the first time in 1888. When the former political boss of the council was killed in an accident, Powers became his successor with the following maneuver: When the former boss died, no one but Powers knew he had collected some $30,000 in bribes to be distributed among his fellow aldermen for a freshly minted city franchise. Only Powers knew the bribe money was in a safe in the boss's saloon. Powers promptly bought the saloon at a high price, with all the furnishings, took out the safe, distributed the money, and thus established himself as the worthy successor. He then ran the saloon with his aldermanic office on the second floor.

It was Powers who devised the system of selling street franchises block by city block so that those seeking control would always need the vote of each individual alderman and be required to bribe each alderman. He also worked out a system for selling a street franchise several times, pocketing a bribe every time. If a company running a horse car tram wanted to install overhead electric cables, a new franchise was required. Similarly, if an electric car was substituted for horse-drawn streetcars, a new franchise was required, although the vehicles, whether drawn by horses or propelled by electricity, traveled over the same surface. The air rights could be additionally sold for an elevated line, while the ground beneath the street could be sold to a gas or electric company to run power lines or for a tunnel. There was always something in the city to be sold for the benefit of the aldermen.

Here is how the political machinations before the City Council over the street roadway franchises were described by Theodore Dreiser in *The Titan*:

> *On a certain Monday night, therefore, following the Thursday on which, according to the rules of the city council, an ordinance of this character would have to be introduced, the plan, after being publicly broached but this very little while, was quickly considered by the city council and passed. There had been really no time for public discussion. . . . True the newspapers, obedient to this larger financial influence, began to talk of "fair play to the old companies," and the useless mess of two large rival companies in the field when one would serve as well.*

In the novel a political bystander comments: "If the Mayor signs that he should be impeached. There is not a vote in there that has not been purchased."

Johnny Powers was Charles Yerkes's man on the council, the person responsible for rounding up the votes and making sure that certain ordinances and franchises needed by Yerkes were passed. The council assessed Yerkes's property at a value of $1,337 at a time when Yerkes maintained a stable and a private art museum, a bejeweled wife, and a mansion which had a Yellow Room, a palm garden, and a Japanese Room, all described in *The Titan*.

Yerkes bragged that he controlled the city elections. Powers was reported to have warned those who hesitated: "Either you go with us, or you won't get a can of garbage moved out of your ward until Hell freezes over." The garbage franchise was worth more than the garbage, which is why it was the perfect issue for the Hull-House reformers, and why Jane Addams challenged Johnny Powers for his position.

```
May 13, 1999 (Note: correction made to article on May 15), Chi-
cago Tribune: "More Money for the Defense."

. . . The proposed House bill is a companion to legislation al-
ready approved by the Senate about a month ago. It envisions
public defenders tapping the fund to hire expert witnesses, con-
duct forensic investigations, bring in outside legal help, and
generally provide a more level battlefield vis-a-vis the state's
prosecutorial machinery.

Though each of the 11 bungled death penalty cases is unique, a
recurring factor has been inept, bargain-basement legal counsel
during the initial, and crucial, phases of the adjudicatory pro-
cess.
```

Johnny Powers managed Mayor Carter Harrison's 1893 mayoral campaign, larding in to his campaign the organized crime boss Mike McDonald, who set up an office in the campaign headquarters at 137 West Monroe Street, labeled the Committee on City Organization, where all the gamblers came to pay tribute and McDonald summoned them on Democratic Party stationery.

The *Tribune* protested the participation of crooks and boodlers in the Harrison campaign: "If he were elected these are the men who would dictate his policy, control his appointments, and manage the city finances."

The gamblers continued to fill Harrison's campaign chest, some said with $500,000. Meanwhile there was internal squabbling among the crooks with one of the new loyalists, Mike Kenna's partner Bathhouse John, boasting that he had 2,300 new registered voters of his own on the lists.

July 10, 2013: And a beautiful blue sky over a beautiful blue lake. In Bangladesh, where the thousand sweatshop workers died, almost all women, as the building collapsed, the monthly wage was about thirty-five dollars. The person organizing a union was murdered the month before the collapse. The manufacturers association consistently resisted all pressure to raise wages or institute building inspections.

William Stead detailed the delivery of the fat envelopes to Powers's saloon. The furor became worldwide because William Stead was an internationally known journalist, and his reports of corruption in Chicago were firsthand, well-written, and highly credible. No one challenged the accuracy of his scathing accounts. Eventually it was another corrupt city alderman who brought down Johnny Powers, doing what the women at Hull-House could not do.

For this final knock-down, drag-out fight at the end of the decade, garbage was again in the middle of it. Powers came out in favor of the civil service ordinance, another favorite of reformers, after much shouting over whether the civil service law was constitutional. Eventually Powers's rival, Bathhouse John, kept Yerkes's ordinances from passing in order to wrest control of the council from Powers. By 1898 the Hull-House people had moved on to advocate in other forums.

December 14, 2002: When things get bad enough, revolution does seem the only option. The rhetoric of the 1886 anarchists was more inflammatory, more revolutionary than that of al-Qaeda. Their weapons were less deadly.

Florence Kelley left a trail of footprints in the law during the time she was in Chicago. These record only a small part of her life here. Mostly they memorialize her official life, what was caught in the snapshot of a court proceeding. Her time in Chicago was a small part of her entire life. What Florence Kelley was known for, why her name is recognized now, if it is familiar at all, is not because of what she did here as factory inspector but because of what she wrote, because of *Hull-House Maps and Papers*, and because of her work in New York after leaving Chicago.

May 18, 1999: In the sunny breakfast room at 639, surrounded by flowers after surgery. Pain sends you back to your elemental self. Reading Scott Turow got me through the worst of it. The actual surgery was not so bad. The injection for the sample tissue for the biopsy was worse than the surgery. Poor K. went home sick, a limp dishrag. The children are so vulnerable, go down so quickly. Beyond the immediate circle of people you would do anything for, is there anything else? The homicide police files are haunting. They are more about how people lived, rather than about how they died, although ostensibly about that. . . .

The first factory inspection law was passed in Massachusetts in 1866, and between 1885 and 1889, ten more states followed, including New York and Pennsylvania. Illinois had passed an eight-hour law in 1867, but it was never enforced.

The National Labor Union called for equal pay for women in 1869 and 1870. Even though women could not vote, and a women's rights amendment and a suffrage amendment could not get through Congress or the Illinois legislature, there was passionate, committed, if intermittent and sporadic, lobbying on behalf of women during this period. The advocacy for women was both to alleviate their harsh circumstances as sweatshop employees and to promote greater political participation through expanding the vote and removing other barriers.

September 14, 2002: Cyrus McCormick, the son of the Reaper King, who built the family fortune, was pulled out of Princeton by his mother and sent to run the family empire in 1884. His family's influence forced the appointment of the aggressive John Bonfield as police commissioner. Factories and shops spread all over the city in the mid-1880s, and there was a notable increase in patents. McCormick reputedly said: "I regard my employees as I do a machine, to be used to my advantage, and when they are old and of not further use, I cast them in the street."

The law school building which flanks Superior Street is named McCormick Hall, and I walk through it every time I go to work.

Ideas of equality for women and lobbying for a recognition of women's economic contributions were not new ideas of the 1960s and 1970s. These ideas had been put forward regularly in the 1840s, the 1880s, the 1890s, and earlier, in different places at different times. And the fight against them and against their advocates was constant, and resurfaced again and again. Just as one legal change was made, another retrenchment took it back. And so Sarah Pugh's meeting place was burned by a mob, and the reformers found another place to meet.

The economic reports compiled by Florence Kelley and her colleagues for Carroll Wright and for the Illinois Joint Legislative Committee are mostly facts, compilations of statistics. *Hull-House Maps and Papers* is more than that. While present practices for compiling and manipulating quantitative information are vastly more sophisticated, the quantity and quality of basic information collected by these researchers in 1895 is startling, noteworthy.

The Chicago writers and researchers of that time loved to collect and quote statistics.

April 10, 2012: The list of labor unions in Chicago in Moran's Dictionary in 1903 covers more than six columns and four pages beginning with six different amalgamated associations: twenty-three separate unions of carpenters and joiners, two women's unions, and ending with the Woodworkers No. 7, 730 North Campbell Avenue, and the Wood, Wire, and Metal Lathers No. 74, 304 Austin Ave. And these are only the ones affiliated with the Federation of Labor. These may be fragments, partial pictures, but they bloom in the imagination.

Not everyone in 1892 agreed the conditions in the tenements—although everyone agreed they were conditions of social devastation—required government intervention: Johnny Powers opposed the tenement inspection legislation, the building of schools, and the health inspections of the factories in the Nineteenth Ward, and indeed any form of government regulation. Levy Mayer, who would brilliantly orchestrate the constitutional challenge to the Factory and Workshop Inspection Law before the state and federal courts, did not support the effort to clean up sweatshops and document the conditions in the slums. For the business community the conditions in the tenements were an unfortunate, temporary, necessary effect of the invisible hand of economic laws. Differences in predictable economic circumstances were a part of the natural order and necessary for the functioning of the economy. If a few were rich and many were poor, it was because of impersonal forces.

Florence Kelley, Letter to Henry Demarest Lloyd, June 30, 1892

On Monday morning I told 64 Congregational Ministers about our neighbors of the cloak trade. One minister preaches to Henry W. King. [A prominent Chicago philanthropist and the owner of the largest clothing business in the United States. He testified at the US congressional hearing in Chicago in April 1892 to the effect that his firm kept its garment factory in New York because immigrants were inclined to stay there, and thus wages were much lower there than in Chicago.] *He was woe begone when I insisted that H.W.K. is a prop of the system.*

Yesterday six ministers came over to see for themselves. Bisno devoted the afternoon to four of them. When he finished they felt in their vest pockets for tips for him! He slunk away from them insulted beyond words.

He is working at the Athenaeum and will enter Law School in the Fall. Dr. Bayard Holmes will pay his tuition. Alexander McCormick comes over every Wed. eve. to give him some extra coaching.

There is no record at Northwestern School of Law from the 1890s of Abraham Bisno being a student there, nor is there a record of him being admitted to the Bar of Illinois.

After the fact it may seem as if everyone supported what eventually became the operation of a reform, but that is usually not the case and was not the case here. Before the Factory Inspection Law was passed, its opponents were designing strategies to invalidate it should it pass. Meanwhile in 1892 Florence Kelley and her colleagues, with others and especially with the legislators, were going out to see for themselves what the conditions were and what could be done about them.

It was something of a fad for members of the comfortable class to masquerade as laborers, working people, and report on what they found. And there was much interest in these accounts.

Walter Wyckoff, identified as an assistant professor of political economy at Princeton University, disguised himself and joined the laborers to experience firsthand the conditions for the workers and the unemployed as he traveled across the country.

Walter Wyckoff became a temporary laborer in Chicago in April 1892, as Florence Kelley was settling in at Hull-House. He worked on the buildings for the Columbian Exposition on the Midway, set to open in May. Here is his description:

Columbian Anniversary Hotel—No. 1. Chicago, Ill., Wednesday, April 27, 1892

Hundreds of us live all together within this vast enclosure, and have rare occasion to go out except on Sundays, and then only if we choose. We get up in the morning to an eight-hour day of wholesome labor in the open air, and return in the later afternoon with healthy appetites to our temporary "hotel," which is fragrant of clean, raw pine, and stands commandingly on the site of the future "court of honor" near the quiet waters of the lake. About four hundred of us are housed and fed in this one building; men of half a score of nationalities and of as many trades, ranging from expert carpenters and joiners and staff-moulders and steel-workers to the unskilled laborers who work in gangs, under the direction of the landscape-gardeners or, as in my case, on the temporary plank roads which are built for the heavy carting.

Guarded by sentries and high barriers from unsought contact with all beyond, great gangs of us, healthy, robust men, live and labor in a marvelous artificial world. No sight of misery disturbs us, nor of despairing poverty out in vain search for employ-ment. Work is everywhere abundant and well paid and directed with highest skill. And here, amid delicate, web-like frames of steel which are being clothed upon with forms of exquisite beauty, and among broad, dreary wastes of arid dunes and marshy pools which are being transformed by our labor into gardens of flowers and velvet lawns joined by graceful bridges over wide lagoons, we work our eight hours a day in peaceful security and in absolute confidence of our pay. . . .

There was no longer any real difficulty in securing work. The employment-bureaus offered it in abundance in the country, and there was some revival of demand even within the city limits. This by no means solved the problem of the unemployed, how-ever. Many of the men were so weakened by the want and hardship of the winter that they were no longer in condition for effective labor. Some of the bosses who were in need of added hands were obliged to turn men off because of physical incapacity. One instance of this I shall not soon forget. It was when I overheard, early one morning, at a factory-gate, an interview between a would-be laborer and the boss. I knew the applicant for a Russian Jew who had at home an old mother and a wife and two young children to support. He had had intermittent employment throughout the winter in a sweater's den, barely enough to keep them all alive, and, after the hardships of the cold season, he was again in desperate straits for work.

The boss had all but agreed to take him on for some sort of unskilled labor, when, struck evidently by the cadaverous look of the man, he told him to bare his arm. Up went the sleeve of his coat and of his ragged flannel-shirt, exposing a naked arm with the muscles nearly gone, and the blue-white, transparent skin stretched over sinews and the outlines of the bones. Pitiful beyond words was his effort to give a semblance of strength to the biceps which rose faintly to the upward movement of the forearm. But the boss sent him off with an oath and a contemptuous laugh, and I watched the fellow as he turned down the street, facing the fact of his starving family with a despair at his heart which only mortal men can feel and no mortal tongue can speak. . . .

There still remained, however, and apparently in full force, the shrewd gentry who stop pedestrians on the street with apologetic explanations of hard luck and with begging appeals for a small sum wherewith to satisfy immediate wants. . . . A highly profitable trade it often proved, for a dollar a day is a gleaning not at all uncommon to these men, and the more skillful among them can average a dollar and a half. They are rather the sporting spirits among the professionally idle; gambling is their chief diversion, and their contempt for honest work is as genuine as that of a snob.

August 2004: Princeton. I am ready, I am ready although it is difficult, to sell our Princeton house. Seeing it being lived in by people who cared nothing for it, people who didn't treat it as their home, was something I don't want to see again. So, let it be sold. It was our home for twenty-eight years, and a happy place, but time to let it go. We have another home now.

William Wyckoff continues:

But within this chaotic maelstrom of the unemployed, which in every industrial centre seethes with infinite menace to social safety, is always a large element which is not easily classified. . . . The class has to be defined in negative terms. The men are not physically incapable of work, nor are they habitual tramps, nor yet the beggars of the pavements, and they lack utterly the grit for crime. If they have a distinctive, positive characteristic as a class, it is that they are victims of the gregarious instinct. By an attraction which is apparently irresistible to them, they are drawn to congested labor markets, and there they cling, preferring instinctively a life of want and squalor in fellowship with their kind to one of comparative plenty in the intolerable loneliness of the country. . . . Civilization is hard on such men, and their sufferings are none the less real because chiefly due to their incapacity for the struggle for existence.

January 4, 2003: And winter is in our bones. Starting out the new year with a new pen! Find the way to link the historical homicides, the cases, the statistics, with the written and documentary history of the period, including newspaper stories, some sort of reconstruction of that world. . . . That is the task.

Wyckoff's account goes on:

A sharp-eyed, energetical American, who superintends the gangs of unskilled laborers, took me on, and at once assigned me to duty under an Irish sub-boss by the name of O'Shea. . . . Most of us were put in charge of wheel-barrows. These we filled with sand at a neighboring pile and then emptied it in heaps on the road-bed, while the remaining members of the gang spread the sand with shovels to the desired depth before replacing the planks. It was a cloudy morning early in April, with a cold, raw wind blowing in from the lake, and the work, not very fatiguing in itself, kept one comfortably warm until noon. We had a free hour for dinner then. . . .

A large, zinc-lined trough half full of water stood against the wall in an ante-chamber. Here men by the score were washing their hands and faces and drying them near by on roller towels. They then passed singly through the wicket at the dining-room door, where stood a man who punched each boarder's ticket as he entered.

Long wooden tables, heaped with dishes and lined with round-bottom stools, ran the great length of the room. The men took places in the order of their coming, until they had filled one table, when they would begin upon another, and there arose a deafening clatter of knives and forks and dishes and a tumult of mingled speech.

That dinner serves as a good illustration of our fare, both in what it offered and in what it lacked. A bowl of hot soup was at each man's place when he sat down, and, after finishing this, he was given a choice between roast beef and Irish stew. There were potatoes boiled in their jackets, and pork-and-beans, and bread in wide variety and in enormous quantity, and a choice of tea or coffee, and finally a pudding for dessert. Some of this was good, but all of it smacked of wholesale preparation, and appetites nicer than those of workingmen would have found difficulties with the dinner. Even ours were not proof against it all. I was struggling with a slice of tough roast-beef out of which the virtue had been cooked, when suddenly I caught an expression of comical dismay stealing over the ruddy, bristling face of the man opposite me. He was eating a piece of meat from a plate of Irish stew, and he spat it out upon the floor with a deep-drawn oath, and a frank assurance to his neighbors that "the meat was rotten," while his facial muscles were contorted with strong disgust. And the pudding was of such uncertain nature as to recall vividly the oft-repeated saying of a classmate at a college eating-club, that "flies in a pudding are quite as good as currants." Still the pork-and-beans were excellent and the bread and potatoes fine, and the coffee, which was served in large cups with the roast, was not impossible; certainly it was a well-fed crowd which sat smoking for a quarter of an hour or more. . . .

[The author notes that he is urged not to work so quickly.] *"Let up on that, John," they were shouting at me presently. "Go easy with that; there ain't no rush, and you'll make nothing by your pains."*

It was the view which I had heard again and again in gangs of unskilled laborers. One could understand it in a measure among the older men, who could hope at the best only to eke out an existence free from the poor-house to the end. But these and many others from whom it came were relatively young men, with every chance one would suppose, of winning some preferment through effective, energetic work.

October 1, 2004: The Princeton house is sold; the money in escrow, and we must try to buy or rent an apartment in downtown Chicago. We agree: it should be near the law school. We agree: we may never live there, but at least we will own a place in Chicago.

Wyckoff continues:

At five o'clock, the end of the afternoon's labor, we had an hour in which to make lei-surely preparation for a supper which consisted of cold meats in unstinted plenty, and potatoes, and bread, and tea and coffee, and often some stewed fruit with a little cake. After this most of the men loafed in the lobby until bedtime. This sitting-room includes the entire upper floor of a large wing of the building. An enormous base-burner heats it, and serves to render it stifling in the evening, when the men are smoking with every window closed. Games and newspapers strew the tables, and the room is well lighted with electric lamps.

On the same level is the upper section of this main building, where are the sleeping-quarters for the men. The provision here is similar in design to that of a cheap lodging-house; only this is almost immaculate in its cleanliness, and the cabins are large and well ventilated, and the ceilings high and airy, and the berths are supplied with new wire and clean corn-husk mattresses, and with sheets and pillow-cases fragrant from the wash.

June 10, 1999: The breakfast room. People can work in dignity, with support. The most important thing may not be how much they are paid, although that seems to be all anyone talks about. Responsibilities of an academic institution aren't all academic. Every day I wake up and pray that no student will die today. In my course on "Persuasion" we read books and talk about them and then they write, then revise, and write again, and that is worthwhile. There are no wrong opinions, but to have no opinion or thoughts about anything is wrong. The young women law students care about different things than the men, but all want to be lawyers and pass the bar. All I seem to care about is my work, the law, some few institutions, and my children and family in reverse order. I work all the time.

And so, the work continued at Hull-House, as reported by Agnes Sinclair Holbrook:

The entire time of four government schedule men from the 6th of April until the 15th of July, 1893, was devoted to examining each house, tenement, and room in the district, and filling out tenement and family schedules, copies of which are printed at the end of this chapter. These schedules were returned daily to Mrs. Kelley; and before they were forwarded to the Commissioner of Labor at Washington, a copy was made by one of the Hull-House residents, of the nationality of each individual, his wages when employed, and the number of weeks he was idle during the year beginning April 1, 1892.

In recording the nationality of each person, his age, and in the case of the children under ten years of age the nationality of his parents and his attendance at school, were taken into account. All under ten years of age who were not pupils in the public school, and who were not of American extraction, were classified with their parents as foreigners.

Carroll D. Wright, the first US commissioner of labor, had known Florence Kelley for years from her published papers, from conferences in the 1880s, and by reputation. It was a small community of lawyers and activists who investigated conditions regarding child labor in the sweatshops, or worked for regulation of the hours, and then lobbied the state and federal legislatures.

January 19, 2003: Are we doomed to forget? To forget that recent Saturday afternoon in January when the then-governor of Illinois as his last official act as governor stood up, in our very own Lincoln Hall, in Levy Mayer looking at the exonerees and their families, their lawyers, when some of them had been on death row ten, twenty years, and with his words set aside those 150 death sentences. The man, white-haired, with a paunch, looked just like what he was: a downstate Illinois politician. The room was packed with journalists, lawyers, teachers. We all knew it was a moment in history. There was silence.

And so another investigation into an injustice began, the work of chronicling the living and working conditions of every family in the part of the Nineteenth Ward defined as the worst of the slums of Chicago. The investigation was of the wages earned and the ethnicity of every household in the Nineteenth Ward. The discourse was not of discrimination, and certainly not of unconstitutional discrimination. That argument would be made by those opposing the investigations. The question was: should there be any government action at all?

June 30, 1999: Finally all of the coding and data processing on 128 variables on the fourteen thousand historical homicide cases from the old police files is complete. Now the data can be sent to homicide researchers around the country so that they can do what they do, crunch the numbers, write an article for the Journal. There will always be researchers interested in homicide.

In 1892 the investigation was survey research, the compilation of a factual record. There were ten thousand "schedules" to be filled out. Each schedule required a shop visit followed by visits to the homes where the sweatshop workers did the piecework. This job was itself piecework, but of a different character than the piecework done by the button hole makers and the shirt sleeve makers and the cloak lining makers in the tenements. This job was social science research piecework, filling out the schedules, coding them, although they would not have called it that.

The data were written on schedules, or what we would call data collection instruments: the collectors of data put information, or data points, numbers, or checks, in little boxes, then the results were tallied. The schedules are recognizable to us. There wasn't any elaborate system of coding or data analysis. Some of the categories, such as the ethnic identifications, would not be accepted today, but most categories—age of worker, number, age, and gender of people in the family, the amount of money earned in the past week or year—are just simple demographics and economic data on income. The study was transparent and uncluttered. The Hull-House researchers and their helpers from Washington, DC, imposed order, or the illusion of order, upon chaos, for a short period. This is what the Hull-House researchers found and reported in *Hull-House Maps and Papers*:

> *In the Nineteenth Ward the sweaters are Russian Jews and Bohemians; and their employees in the shops are the same nationality, while their home finishers are exclusively Italian—the wives and daughters of the street sweepers and railroad gang hands, who form so large a part of the population of the ward. The garments made here are principally coats, cloaks, trousers, knee-pants, and shirts. There are one hundred and sixty-two shops, employing men, women and children. . . . If the sweater's shop is in a tenement house, it is sometimes—but very rarely—in the ground floor front room, built for a store and lighted by large store windows. But far more commonly it is a basement, or an attic, or a flat over a saloon, or the shed over a stable. All of the tenement houses selected either for shops or home furnishers are of the worst and most crowded description. The staircases are narrow, and are used in common by tenants and garment workers, so that infectious diseases breaking out among the swarming children can scarcely fail to be communicated to garments anywhere under the same roof, because the utmost laxity prevails in the matter of isolation.*

The statistics collected for the US Congress were the facts behind the essays and the maps which became the book *Hull-House Maps and Papers*. The appointment of Florence Kelley as special investigator for the Joint Legislative Committee of the Illinois legislature (charged to consider legislation) was preceded by her short-term appointment as a special investigator for the Illinois Department of Labor in the fall of 1892. Before that there was a very short stint running an employment office for women within Hull-House itself. It turned out no one wanted to hire young women who came for assistance to the Hull-House employment office, and so it was closed.

The investigations, all the statistical compilations, were basically the same enterprise, presenting the facts through the numbers, describing the living and working conditions of people in the sweatshops across the street from Hull-House as precisely, as particularly as possible. The purpose was to show the public, the society which considered itself civilized, a society of law, a society which considered itself just, that it included another society where conditions were cruel, unjust, shocking, intolerable. The government issued findings, and the newspapers reported on it all.

Moran's Dictionary of Chicago (1903) lists twenty-five daily newspapers (in addition to the major ones, the *American* and the *Tribune* and the *Inter Ocean*, there were the *Abend Post*, the *Argus*, the *Drovers' Journal*, *Dziennik Chicagoski*, the *Evening Journal*, and others) and more than 150 weeklies (including the *American Artisan*, the *American Bee Journal*, *Legal News*, *Life*, and *L'Italia*). The newspapers and weeklies are identified as commercial, literary, labor, independent, etc.

January 11, 1999, Chicago Tribune: Part 2 of 5: "The Flip Side of a Fair Trial" by Maurice Possley and Ken Armstrong.

. . . As a result, about once a month, on average, for the past two decades, a conviction has been set aside in Cook County because of a judicial finding of improper conduct by prosecutors. . . .

A Tribune examination of all types of criminal cases since Dec. 31, 1977, found 326 state court convictions in Illinois—207 of them in Cook County—have been reversed because of prosecutor misconduct. Nearly half of the reversals in Cook County were for homicide convictions. In addition, eight defendants in Cook County were sentenced to death and won new sentencing hearings due to prosecutor misbehavior. When new hearings were held, only two resulted in reimposition of a death sentence. . . .

The line between misconduct and hard-nosed lawyering is thin and a matter of integrity and self-control. Misconduct ranges from an overexuberant argument to maliciously hiding evidence of a defendant's innocence.

In the 1890s people did not want to acknowledge how bad things were. They had to be tricked into paying attention. The final *Slums of Great Cities* report to the US Department of Labor was published and presented to the US Congress in 1894. This report is largely forgotten because it is only a compilation of statistics: reliable statistics, interesting statistics, but only statistics. It is a set of statistics about a past no one any longer cares about.

Hull-House Maps and Papers also relies upon statistics for its authenticity. The way in which the categories of jobs are defined has changed: the numbers themselves, the supposedly great indicators of objectivity, are unsupportable because we are no longer in agreement on the categories. The book, however, remains viable, comprehensible as a call for change through the power of the law, the power of the state to right some wrongs. Chronicling the way in which some people lived, by showing those who didn't live that way how their neighbors and countrymen lived, became a legal argument, a piece of advocacy.

March 1999: By the time the fiction book was published, I had lost interest in those stories, being completely wrapped up in Homicide in Chicago, in the coding and preservation of the police records of fourteen thousand homicides in Chicago from 1870-1930. And so it goes. The absorbing part is the doing of it. Of course I was glad for the publication. But it might as well have been written by someone else.

Hull-House Maps and Papers, the book, was actually published after the Illinois Factory and Workshop Inspection Law was passed, due to a series of editorial and publishing delays, and because it took some time to compile the facts and get the essays written. The publication of the book didn't itself influence the passage of the law; however, the group of people working on the book were advocates for the law: their work was known, and they were a political presence.

Hull-House Maps and Papers did not generate the public attention of Stead's *If Christ Came to Chicago*. The two books shared a common purpose: to expose political corruption and the conditions of privation in the tenements. Stead's book gleefully described the greed and follies of politicians. The US Congress's *Special Report*, or *The Slums of Great Cities*, just laid out the facts.

Carroll D. Wright, the man who hired Florence Kelley for the project, is remembered for his research mostly on labor and economics. He is also known for the establishment, at the state and federal level, of a culture which valued the gathering of facts, the generation of reliable statistical investigation and reports within government, a culture which Florence Kelley carried on in Illinois.

January 16, 2009: Record-breaking cold: 17 below zero. The ice forms on the inside of the windows. The trees fortunately are still. A long and angular branch of the ailing redbud tree, a favorite of the cardinals, did break off and is lying like a severed limb on the window ledge outside of the kitchen window.

Carroll Wright was born in Dunbarton, New Hampshire, on July 25, 1840. His father was a pastor and a farmer. At age twenty-two, he left his apprenticeship in the law and enlisted as a private for the Union in the Fourteenth Regiment of the New Hampshire volunteers. His friends who enlisted with him quickly chose him as their officer.

Like John Peter Altgeld, he was sickly and bookish and chose not to spend his life pushing a plow through the rocky, infertile land of his father's farm. The way out of the farm was through education. There were seven children in the family. His further education, and that of others, was available only in private academies. While studying he was also teaching, and eventually because he was smart and a person other people looked up to, he became principal of the Troy, New Hampshire, High School, where the annual tuition was $1.50, probably more than he could afford without working.

These small towns and communities in the North had to raise their quotas of three-year men for the Union. The three-month volunteers having been exhausted, the men for the three-year quotas only came forward when the town supplemented the state and federal bounties with a bit more money for enlistment. In short many, and perhaps Carroll Wright himself, signed up to fight for the Union for the money. Some of the young new recruits worried that the war would be over before they got to the front.

Later, Carroll Wright saw his friends and colleagues slaughtered when promised military support did not appear, or the connecting up of military units was bungled, or when the higher echelons in the Army mismanaged resources. Yet after the war was over he wrote an essay which became a publicly given lecture on Sheridan's campaign. In the lecture he described how "little Phil Sheridan" transformed "black despair and hopeless defeat" into victory. A man who became a leader recognized the same quality in another.

March 18, 1999: In Chicago, people are still interested in the Leopold and Loeb case. There are several ways to pull together these themes. The novel is not the best form for this. My mind wanders. Today is my sister's birthday, and she is out of town when I call. It turns out our library has an extensive archive of original documents from the trial, donated by one of Leopold's later attorneys. Clarence Darrow saved the two from execution. Then their fates diverged. The publisher wants us to include a recent sensational murder; I am against it. That case will not last, will not be remembered.

January 12, 1999, Chicago Tribune: Part 3 of 5: "Prosecution on Trial in DuPage" by Maurice Possley and Ken Armstrong.

With little national fanfare, a most extraordinary trial is scheduled to open next week in the DuPage County courthouse.

Though it has none of the star appeal of the O.J. Simpson case, the trial of three former prosecutors and four current sheriff's deputies accused of framing Rolando Cruz for the murder of 10-year-old Jeanine Nicarico may ultimately be one of the most significant criminal prosecutions of the century.

Both in scope and nature, the case against the prosecutors and detectives is virtually unparalleled in the history of American jurisprudence. While police and prosecutors occasionally have been indicted for misconduct in the past, no other case has alleged a conspiracy to send a man to Death Row and none has alleged that prosecutors perpetuated their deceit for so long.

The charges—conspiring to obstruct justice and perjury—strike at the heart of the American system of justice. If convicted, the three former prosecutors, Patrick King, Robert Kilander and Thomas Knight, would be the first in the nation to be found guilty of a felony for knowingly using false evidence to send an innocent man to Death Row.

Carroll Wright and the other volunteers of the Fourteenth New Hampshire Regiment were dispatched to Washington where they spent a year on guard duty. One of Carroll Wright's assignments in Washington was to police the countryside. He wrote to his mother that he was embarrassed, almost to sympathy with the rebels, by the drunkenness, criminality, and brutality of his fellow Union soldiers.

Wright's abilities soon resulted in his being given special responsibilities, and promotions. The Fourteenth did see combat, and Carroll Wright was eventually to become a staff officer to General Philip Sheridan. An attack of typho-malarial fever resulted in Carroll Wright being sent home as an invalid, missing some critical battles. He returned to the field after ten weeks of recuperation, only to have a relapse.

January 13, 1999, Chicago Tribune: Part 4 of 5: "How Prosecutors Sacrifice Justice to Win; Reversal of Fortune" by Maurice Possley and Ian Armstrong.

. . . "Sitting here today, Mr. Arthur, do you believe that any of the Ford Heights 4—Willie Rainge, Kenny Adams, Verneal Jimerson and Dennis Williams—had any involvement in the murders of Larry Lionberg and Carol Schmal?" asked one of Jimerson's attorneys.

"Yes," [Prosecutor Scott] Arthur said. "I think they did." . . . Arthur clings to his belief even though other men have confessed; even though DNA tests implicated one of those who confessed and eliminated Williams and his friends as suspects; even though prosecution witnesses have either recanted or been discredited, and the scientific evidence at the trial exposed as bunk; even though Williams and his friends have received pardons from the governor and apologies from the state's attorney's office. . . . A case that continues to haunt the Cook County state's attorney's office is the prosecution of the Ford Heights 4, in which four innocent men were convicted and two of them were condemned to die. . . .

A Tribune review of court records shows that prosecutors played fast and loose with the evidence and used long-condemned courtroom tactics to sell juries on a case that was more illusion than truth.

And so Florence Kelley and her colleagues mapped the world in front of them. Sweatshop workers were not encouraged to learn to read or write, to create or control the facts, or even to learn to tell or record the time. Always Florence Kelley and the Hull-House residents were teaching newly arrived immigrants English, to read and write English, especially the women were teaching other women and girls to read, to count, to do sums, to keep a record.

The reports in *Hull-House Maps and Papers* are just the facts:

It is a striking fact that where the better houses prevail as on DeKoven, Bunker, Taylor and Forquer Streets, the street is almost solidly built up; while on Clinton, Jefferson, and Des Plaines the more scattered houses are veritable shells. One feels very clear, however, after long acquaintance with the neighborhood, and after visits to many of the homes, that the poorest of the tiny wooden houses, damp and unwholesome as they may be, offer nothing to compare with the hideousness shut up in the inside rooms of the larger, higher, and to the casual eye the better tenements of the more pretentious aspect.

What we consider facts has changed. The 1895 ethnicity maps would no longer be considered facts, at least in a court of law. The subjects and boundaries remain the same: the census tracts, the ward boundaries have changed, although the practice of drawing the lines by geographic boundaries and demographics has not changed; nor has the highly political process for drawing these electoral boundaries, nor has our method or reason for counting every person changed. The practice of one group judging another by where they live, and where they have come from, has not changed. We measure the poor by the relative standard of the rich. If all are poor, then there are no poor. If many are wealthy, and some obscenely rich, the plight of the poor is worse.

June 25, 1999: The weather is a balm, perfect.

It is true I don't feel this big stone pile of a house built for others, lived in by others, maintained for others is my home, but I am comfortable here now, and the engine of the house, what needs to be done for what we do here, mostly runs smoothly with little more need than the driver lightly steering. My third floor is home, where I am here but not here.

I am transported to 1890s Chicago—the strong intellectual presence of the writers, their descriptions of what they see, the people around them, both in fiction and nonfiction.

All the traveling and all the new people are exciting, but exhausting. Basically, I can have no friends here, because everyone wants something from my husband, or from the institution, or from me.

Carroll D. Wright, known for the precision and accuracy of his statistics, the clarity of his investigations, interrupted his legal studies to go into the army, rose to be colonel, became adjutant to General William Tecumseh Sherman in Virginia, and then returned to Vermont (where he had been in school) and was admitted to the Bar there two years later.

After the war, Carroll Wright moved to Boston, was in private practice, and then elected to the Massachusetts Senate as a Republican in 1871. He was appointed chief of the Massachusetts State Bureau of Statistics, the first such state office. There his reports were said by many to have been the most satisfactory ever published.

In 1885 President Chester Arthur established the US Bureau of Labor with Carroll Wright as its first commissioner, a position he held until 1905. He is remembered by economists for devising a reliable, statistical measure for unemployment, which is still used.

January 15, 2009: The cold is so bitter, twelve below zero, it is painful to step outdoors. The wind chill adds twenty more degrees downward. In the winter of 1893, a hundred thousand homeless men were sleeping on the streets, in the police stations and on the marble floors in City Hall in the coldest winter on record. A year from now I will not be looking out of this ornamental window onto the garden. If the sun can get itself up, I can get up and out. At the law school students will be waiting for me, a good reason to venture downtown.

Carroll Wright became president of both the American Statistical Association and the American Association for the Advancement of Science. As an obituary noted:

He was in a very modest and unaffected manner a sincere devotee of truth, and might well have taken Bacon's words as his motto: "The inquiry of truth, which is the love-making or wooing of it, the knowledge of truth, which is the presence of it, and the belief in truth, which is the enjoying of it, is the sovereign good of human nature."

In 1892 in Chicago, there was a hunger for these facts, a groundswell of passionate interest, whether to clean up Chicago for the World's Columbian Exposition or simply because some civic-minded Chicagoans could no longer tolerate the highly visible disparities. People became rich in the 1880s, some honestly, some not so honestly, and the gap between the rich and poor widened. Then the depression of 1893 came. This when there was no federal income tax, no federal estate tax, and no sales tax. People who accumulated vast wealth could keep it and spend it, mostly on themselves and their families. And in Chicago they did spend it, building themselves grand houses, decorating their carriages and themselves, and traveling, all the while vigorously arguing that any proposed interference from the government would prevent business from thriving in a competitive atmosphere and put a halt to economic enterprise. Some few gave some of their money away. Mostly they left their fortunes to their children.

May 14, 2007: A bright day. Northwestern Law School graduation yesterday in a big convention center. So many happy faces and cameras! All that education now a matter of joyful celebration. The names read out. They come from all over the world, especially Asia now. Sunny, the purple tulips, glorious. These excited young lawyers about to suffer through the bar review, and then the bar examination. And then the world is theirs.

Not that there weren't men and women, and children in 1893, living in equally squalid and destitute conditions in other, smaller cities, or in Paris, London, and Naples, and in rural areas everywhere. There were boys and girls with rickets and tuberculosis in small towns, and girls sold into sex slavery, and babies starving on farms and in the mountains and other places in the United States where it wasn't as visible as on the streets of Chicago.

In Chicago in the winter of 1893 there were one hundred thousand highly visible unemployed men on the streets, while others hid away in mansions designed and furnished with delusions of royalty, their inhabitants in furs and imported lace, people who provided better food and housing for their horses and dogs than was ever to be seen by the children in the tenements.

In Chicago in 1893, there was a deluge of writing about it all. The newspapers were writing about it, outraged about it. They were also writing about what the rich ate and drank, and what members of minor titled European aristocracy said and wore when they came to visit, and exclaimed over the beauty of Chicago. The labor activists yelled about it; and the government agencies issued statistical reports, and people, not just politicians, made speeches about what they saw as the injustices. And some little bit was done. Thus, *Hull-House Maps and Papers* reported:

> *It is a fact of which the public has remained curiously ignorant, that the worst forms of danger to the wearers of garments are found in heavier proportion in the manufacture of expensive custom-made clothing than in the ready-made clothing trade; since there are no inside factories for the manufacture of custom-made clothing, and merchant tailors employ only cutters on their premises, and never have any garments completed there, but always give them out to be finished in the sweatershop, or in the individual tailor's house.*

It was not an absence of law. A compulsory primary school education law in Chicago had been enacted in 1867. No schools were built for children in the tenements after this law was passed. Nineteenth Ward Alderman Johnny Powers did not favor public education. He preferred that children go to Catholic schools, where they would receive training in morality. Many agreed with him. Many did not want their children in free public schools because they did not want people of different nationalities or religious backgrounds to mix. And then there was the question of languages: the fact that public education was in English meant that some children would learn a language their parents did not know.

Nonetheless the push to educate, to inform, continued. As Florence Kelley wrote in the chapter of *Hull-house Maps and Papers* titled "Wage-Earning Children":

> In a discussion of child-labor in Chicago, it may simplify matters to point out, at the outset, what things are not to be looked for. Thus, there is in Chicago virtually no textile industry; and the cotton-mill child of Massachusetts, or the carpet-mill child of Philadelphia, has no counterpart here. There is no industry in which, as in the spinning and weaving of silk, the deft fingers of young children have been for generations regarded as essential. With the large exception of the cigar, tobacco, and paper trades (including both the manufacture of paper boxes and the printing and binding industries), and with the further exception of the utterly disorganized and demoralized garment trades, the industries of Illinois are essentially men's trades.

W.C. Ritchie & Company, the lead plaintiff in the cases challenging the constitutionality of the Factory Inspection Law, was a paper box manufacturer. The men working in the lumber yards, in the slaughterhouses (and many boys, too, standing knee deep in blood and guts while their small fingers picked out gristle and bone chips from the slabs of meat) were not subject to any government oversight. There were pockets of unionized workers there, usually among the indispensable and highly skilled manufacturers of clothing in the tenements that vigorously and mostly successfully opposed any regulation or restriction on their operations, or the examination of conditions in their workplace.

June 15, 2006: The glorious days of late spring continue. My world has expanded and narrowed. Even as the house, which is not my house after all but the university's house, encapsulates my world now. It is our home now. When the family comes, and children are in every room, I want nothing else. I never thought that day would come.

A place, a time, becomes like your skin, your clothes. Not that life was easy in 1890s Chicago. Not that the people were better. Holding a book or a newspaper or a court document from the 1890s, or reading a letter from William Darrah Kelley to his daughter, I hear them and am there.

Our massive, heedless communications over the Internet will never be archived with such accuracy, such loving attention. Nor should they be. So, what, if anything, will be preserved?

Sit down with your manuscript for three hours a day, every day, and a book will be written. You will not be able to stand yourself otherwise.

The women and children working as pieceworkers at home or in the tenement facto-ries sometimes worked under contract, or under no contract, getting paid by the piece. Florence Kelley herself worked for the Illinois Bureau of Labor Statistics under a con-tract for piecework: she was paid fifty cents for every completed schedule of statistical information. The power of the incipient labor organizations was the power to negotiate contracts on behalf of classes of workers for a year or more. Some workers, such as some adult male packinghouse workers, did work under negotiated contracts, and those union members were all white.

Most jobs for women and children were entirely unregulated. There was a massive underground cash economy which avoided any recording of transactions, or taxation. There was no Internal Revenue Service to which income had to be reported. There was no Social Security office keeping track of employer contributions toward a pension. There were no pensions. There were no corporate taxes on profits. There was no corpo-rate income tax. There were no taxes on nonwage earnings. The federal income tax was declared unconstitutional in 1895. Businesses lived without interference by the govern-ment at the state and federal levels, and still complained loudly.

Yet as Wyckoff and others noted: not all workers were in favor of government inter-vention or wanted to join a union in spite of vigorous exhortations by socialists and others:

Two or three times he has asked me to go with him in the evening to meetings which are held near the Fair Grounds, and which are addressed by delegates from the Central La-bor Union. These we have not found very enlightening. There has been a good deal of beer-drinking and much aimless speech, which has grown heated at times in the stress of hostile discussion; and now and then a plain, matter-of-fact workingman has given us an admirable talk on the history of Trades-Unionism and its beneficent results, and the imperative need of organization among workers as the only means of safe-guarding their interests and of meeting on any approach to equal terms, the peculiar economic relations which exist between labor and organized capital. . . . I have tried to explain to him [the author's companion, a master carpenter at the fair], *as well as I understand it, the idea of organization, and the necessity of organization which has grown out of the great industrial change since the middle of the last century. . . . In his experience, work has always had its basis in a personal relation, as, for example, between himself as a contractor and the man whose job he undertook and to whom he looked for payment.*

This new relation between a workman and an impersonal, soulless corporation which hires him, is one that he does not readily grasp. And, for the sake of meeting the new re-lation, this "fusing all the skirts of self," and merging individuality into an organization which attempts to regulate the hours of labor, and its wages, and for whom one shall work, and for whom not, is a thing abhorrent to him.

December 9, 2008: Snow is forecast. But mostly it is cold and damp. Another winter settling in. And in a year we will be out of here. I count the days to the solstice. The voices of the 1890s taunt me. I don't think they would sit idly by and accept what our society has become.

In the middle of the economic turmoil of 1893, government stumbled but continued. Some people, including Florence Kelley, had jobs and got paid. Some got paid for voting. Factories and manufacturing places mostly kept going, although the economic system slowed to a crawl. Those who had money hoarded it and eked the cash out to those they owed, and then to their families.

There were elections. The courts operated, perhaps imperfectly, but the legal system functioned. It didn't shut down. There were coroner's juries, grand juries, petit juries, judges in robes, trials and decisions in cases, passionate and bored lawyers. Lawyers and judges got paid.

There were courtrooms which looked much like courtrooms today: they looked like Protestant churches. The state legislature met and did its work, for better or worse. Governors were elected, and sometimes not reelected. It is a minor miracle that the legal system kept going in that massive economic crisis.

March 20, 2002: So much was preserved. In a corner of the Central Chicago police station a series of clerks recorded homicides, where they happened, who was killed by whom, and what happened afterward. Those clerks' books were preserved, and can be read, and will be able to be read anywhere in the world now.

In 1886 the Knights of Labor had seven hundred thousand members and could turn out thousands for a march; none of them was identified as a Negro, and none were women. Still they could turn out more than a hundred thousand people in support of the eight-hour movement on a given day in May in 1886. The principal activity of the labor organizations was, by their own admission, the conducting of strikes and organizing for strikes, collecting funds to support striking workers, forcing employers to negotiate during a strike.

After Haymarket the eight-hour movement was significantly set back by a systematic crackdown on all labor organizations, usually through the method of hiring police, Pinkerton officers and others to break up union meetings and beat up attendees, especially the leaders and organizers of strikes. Nonetheless in 1893 in Chicago, labor was a force to be reckoned with, as Pullman would prove and as the passage of the Factory Inspection Law proved.

The workers who poured into Chicago for work came from the American South, from the rural areas, from Eastern Europe, from Russia, from the East, and were overwhelmingly young and male. In the summer of 1893 Chicago was like an army camp, with all that implied.

The system of bribing city officials in Chicago was well-entrenched in the 1890s when Florence Kelley and Jane Addams were petitioning the City Council for public schools to be built in the Nineteenth Ward, and for the garbage collectors to make good on their contracts to pick up garbage, contracts which had been paid with city money.

Politics was outwardly all male. Only men were members of the City Council. Only men were elected judges or state's attorneys. The power to prosecute for crimes remained a singular political power, always a threat. Yet people paid attention to these women, and in these early days Jane Addams and Hull-House seemed immune to criticism.

The court system was linked to the city and state government by party control of the election of state officials and judges and prosecutors. The formalities of the law, the structure of filing of cases, of cases going to decision before judges, the mechanics of the enforcement of the law were in theory transparent. The court system remains unchanged in structure, if not in practice.

The grim grey walls of the Criminal Court building have been honey-combed by the busy builders of a patronage system in the center of which the state's attorney sits, surrounded by the satellite of the particular political machine that "put him over." His associates are not—save for a few—his own selections, but represent the ramifications of "the organization," chosen chiefly for their outstanding ability to "deliver" politically in their wards and precincts.

This description of the system for the maintenance of corruption in the city courts and City Council was written by Judge M.L. McKinley, a former chief justice of the Criminal Court of Cook County in 1922-23. The county state's attorney remains at the center of the patronage machine today.

Young lawyers were groomed for political positions by first holding appointed positions, often as assistant county attorneys, or deputy state's attorneys, or lawyers in the Office of the Secretary of State. Typically they would be appointed to fill a temporarily vacant position, then easily elected as incumbents.

November 4, 2010, Chicago Tribune: "Birkett Named to Appellate Court Seat."

DuPage County State's Attorney Joseph Birkett said Wednesday that he has accepted a spot on the 2nd District Appellate Court bench.

Illinois Appellate Court Judge Jack O'Malley, one of nine judges in the district, which covers 13 northern Illinois counties outside Cook County, originally filed to retain his position in the

Nov. 2 general election. However, he withdrew that request Aug. 31, and his tenure as an Appellate Court judge will end Dec. 5.

Birkett, 55, said his appointment is effective Dec. 13. He must run for election in 2012 to retain the post.

He notified his staff of the appointment Wednesday.

Birkett said he contacted Illinois Supreme Court Justice Bob Thomas last month about his interest in seeking a seat on the 2nd District Appellate Court. Thomas notified him Tuesday of his appointment.

Birkett, a Wheaton resident, has been DuPage County state's attorney since 1996 and was the unsuccessful Republican candidate for attorney general in 2002 and lieutenant governor in 2006.

"I can't tell you the pride I have in the office," Birkett said of his tenure as state's attorney. "I've experienced the greatest joys professionally while also the deepest sorrows while working with victims of crime. It's been a honor."

O'Malley, of Harvard, was Cook County state's attorney from 1990 to 1996 and was elected to the Appellate Court in 2000. Incoming DuPage County Board Chairman Dan Cronin will choose Birkett's successor, but his pick must be approved by the board.

William Darrah Kelley came to power under a similar political system in Philadelphia before the Civil War. Those who showed they understood the system and how to cooperate with their sponsors would be put up for election to positions as judges or prosecutors and assured of being elected by their endorsement by the party. Or, those who proved themselves useful were put into government positions where they controlled the awarding of large government contracts to private parties. They then received state or city salaries, hired their relatives or political allies, and put them in line to be on the public payroll. Being on the government payroll was always highly sought after, even in this era before public employment came with health insurance and retirement benefits.

September, 10 2006: Finally, we have the first official meeting of the state Committee to Study the Reform of the Death Penalty. I can't take the title of the committee seriously. The meeting room is in a nondescript State of Illinois office building, like every other state office building I have known. The furniture cheap, the walls unadorned. Apparently, the committee will hold some meetings in Springfield. In spite of the dispiriting beginning, by the end of the day, committee members had shown up, the phone was hooked up, the lights turned on. The people who were supposed to come, came. This committee is a successor to the Commission to Study the Death Penalty appointed by Governor George Ryan.

In 1890s Chicago the political appointees, the lawyers, the clerks, the bailiffs, the civil servants, and the legislators made small salaries, but the opportunities for enrichment through graft, bribes, and outright stealing from the public purse were many and manifold. Plus, no one was ever fired from government, unless the party in power changed. The political machine put people in and kept them there, and made sure they kept receiving their salaries. Jobs were lost when a party was unseated, which was rare.

Judges were former state's attorneys, county prosecutors, or court clerks who were then endorsed for election. Clerks and judges referred cases and clients to lawyers they knew, who had their business with the city and county. Then the cases were heard by judges, who answered to the same political network.

January 14, 1999, Chicago Tribune: Part 5 of 5: "Break Rules, Be Promoted" by Maurice Possley and Ian Armstrong.

As Cook County prosecutors, Carol Pearce McCarthy, Kenneth Wadas and Patrick Quinn drew scathing rebukes from the Illinois Appellate Court for failing to abide by the rules designed to keep prosecutors honest and trials fair.

"Inexcusable," is how the court described McCarthy's misconduct in one case. The state's lawyer disciplinary agency agreed. It took the exceptional step of reprimanding her—but in a way that kept her identity a secret.

"An insult to the court and to the dignity of the trial bar," is what the court called Wadas' trial tactics. Twice, reviewing courts suggested professional disciplinary action might be in order to punish his conduct.

As for Quinn, the court wrote "we can hardly imagine a more obfuscating attempt" to characterize his misleading statements to a jury. Quinn prosecuted a sheriff's deputy for official misconduct—and committed misconduct himself by allowing two witnesses to provide what he knew was misleading testimony, the appellate court ruled.

Collectively, the three prosecutors broke enough rules that nine defendants—four convicted of murder—were granted new trials on appeal, according to court records.

But instead of having their career prospects suffer, all three prosecutors prospered. They were promoted to supervisor in the Cook County state's attorney's office. Then, on the same fall day in 1996, all three were elected judges. . . .

Their path is well traveled. A Tribune analysis of appellate rulings spanning the past two decades turned up 39 other Cook County prosecutors who also became judges after cases they prosecuted were reversed because of misconduct. . . .

Courts have referred numerous prosecutors to the Illinois agency that polices lawyers only to see investigative files get opened and closed with no punishment levied, the Tribune found.

There is little threat of financial penalties from a civil lawsuit because courts have granted prosecutors immunity. Courts, though, have carved out narrow exceptions, and some defendants have won settlements.

The rhetoric may be that legal careers are and were made by talent, but the fact is and was that putting in the time on the lower rungs of the party ladder, showing obedience, is and was often the only indispensable qualification for a job as a judge or a state's attorney. And so the great cornucopia of city and state budgets was there to keep the power structure in place. After all, someone had to do the work, or pretend to do the work, and that person had to be someone who had proved himself trustworthy. The trouble with women in political jobs was not that they couldn't do the work, but that the men didn't trust them.

The mayor of Chicago was the fount of political power, and jobs. Springfield was another world, where a different kind of power was traded, as John Peter Altgeld would discern. In the Nineteenth Ward in 1893 Johnny Powers held the political power, dispensing the jobs, the contracts, and the money. And yet there always were some who didn't just go along, or who did advance because of their abilities. And they could always be pointed to as examples of the integrity of the system, that the system was merit-based.

January 3, 2012: Blue sky, clear, cold, no wind. The winter has announced itself, the pavement spotted from salt with a mirror of ice on top. Just when we had forgotten the bite of it.

The women of Hull-House and their political allies did not have the vote, or much money, or any other external source of political power. The Woman's Christian Temperance Union did have close to a million members, and they supported politicians and were to become their own powerful political force. The Woman's Christian Temperance Union was important in getting passed the US constitutional amendment granting women the right to vote, in addition to the amendment regarding Prohibition. The politics of feminism into the next century included overlaps and divisions between advocates for temperance, advocates for the abolition of slavery and later the rights of Negroes, and advocates for women's suffrage and political participation.

Florence Kelley and Jane Addams mounted a vigorous campaign to unseat Johnny Powers as alderman for the Nineteenth Ward in the 1896 election on the grounds, among others, that the garbage was not being picked up in the ward, although a city contract had been awarded and the city's money paid. The reform candidate supported by Jane Addams and the Hull-House residents received 2,700 votes—not enough to win, but getting that many votes against the machine candidate was considered an achievement.

December 18, 2003, Chicago Tribune: "Ryan Indicted: U.S. Charges Former Governor With Pattern of Corruption; Prosecutor Says Family, Pals Gained."

A sweeping federal indictment of former Gov. George H. Ryan charged Wednesday that he received illegal cash payments, gifts and vacations, and helped his family members reap almost $167,000 in similar benefits—all from a Ryan confidant who made huge illicit profits on state contracts and leases.

During two terms as secretary of state, Ryan allegedly steered contracts and leases to companies that had been extorted for bribes, scuttling internal investigations into his campaign's improper political fundraising practices and personally awarding more than 90 low-digit license plates to cronies and campaign contributors.

The indictment also accuses him of grossly understating his income on four years of federal income tax returns between 1995 and 1998.

Former U.S. Atty. Dan Webb, who is representing Ryan, said in a statement that he was confident the former governor would be exonerated, calling the charges "false, unfair and malicious."

At a packed news conference Wednesday, U.S. Atty. Patrick J. Fitzgerald alleged that Ryan, while governor, had repeatedly lied to federal agents about his knowledge of and involvement in wrongdoing.

"What we're alleging in the indictment is that basically the State of Illinois was for sale, for [Ryan's] friends and family at times," Fitzgerald told reporters. "At times George Ryan stepped into the process to make sure that those interests were taken care of, and that should not be happening."

Many recent immigrants in the Nineteenth Ward refused to vote for a reform candidate, especially one whose principal supporters were women. The incumbents had the powerful promise of keeping things the way they were, or at least not making people worse off. Johnny Powers was effective, a man who listened to and responded promptly to complaints of constituents and gave away favors and food, a turkey at Christmas, and other largesse, jobs for disabled relatives, a bit of cash to tide over the bad times.

Jane Addams commented that he smiled a lot and people liked him, both indispensable qualifications for a politician.

June 23, 2010: I do get a seat in the courtroom, which is crowded with reporters and relatives of interested parties, of which there are many. Whom will Governor Blagojevich pull down with him? His chief of staff, who immediately became a government witness after they were both arrested in a dawn raid, is not a bad guy or a fool. At a class of mine he came and talked about doing work you believe in—then the next month was indicted for being part of the governor's plan to sell Obama's vacant Senate seat.

In 1893 there were plenty of rich people in Chicago. Here is how Theodore Dreiser, who also did careful factual research, described the social scene greeting Frank Cowperwood when he came to Chicago in 1892:

When it came to Chicago, however, and its swirling, increasing life, Aileen [Cowperwood's wife] was much interested. . . . [Cowperwood] asked her to shop in the local stores and tell him about them; and this she did driving around in an open carriage, attractively arrayed, a great brown hat emphasizing her pink-and-white complexion and red-gold hair. On different afternoons of the stay he took her to drive over their principal streets. When Aileen was permitted for the first time to see the spacious beauty and richness of Prairie Avenue, the North Shore Drive, Michigan Avenue, and the new mansions on Ashland Boulevard, set in grassy spaces, the spirit, aspirations, hope, tang of the future of Chicago began to work in her blood as it had in Cowperwood's. All of these rich homes were so very new. The great people of Chicago were all newly rich like themselves. . . .

It was now between five and six, that richest portion of a summer day. It had been very warm, but was now cooling, the shade of the western building-line shadowing the roadway, a moted, wine-like air filling the street. As far as the eye could see were carriages, the one great social diversion of Chicago, because there was otherwise so little opportunity for many to show they had means. The social forces were not as yet clear or harmonious. Jingling harnesses of nickel, silver, and even plated gold were the sign manual of social hope, if not of achievement. Here sped homeward from the city—from the office and manufactory—along this one exceptional southern highway, the Via Appia of the South Side, all the urgent aspirants to notable fortunes. Men of wealth who had met only casually in trade here nodded to each other. Smart daughters, society-bred sons, handsome wives came down-town in traps, Victorias, carriages, and vehicles of the latest design to drive home their trade-weary fathers or brothers, relatives or friends. The air was gay with social hope, a promise of youth and affection, and that fine flush of material life that recreates itself in delight. Lithe, handsome, well-bred animals, singly and in jingling pairs, paced each other down the long, wide, grass-lined street, its fine homes agleam with a rich, complaisant materiality. . . . [Cowperwood's] handsome mustache seemed at this moment to have an especially defiant curl. The pair he was driving was physically perfect, lean and nervous, with spoiled, petted faces. He could not endure poor horse-flesh. He drove as only a horse-lover can, his body bolt upright, his own energy and temperament animating his animals. . . .

There was tingling over his fingers, into the reins, into the horses, a mysterious vibrating current that was his chemical product, the off-giving of his spirit battery that made his horses prance like children. They chafed and tossed their heads and snorted.

These were the people who controlled the city. These were their concerns. What was the prospect for anything changing in 1893?

Florence Kelley wrote in a letter:

If you are to speak as one having authority about social ills, you must suffer from the dirty streets, the universal ugliness, the lack of oxygen in the air you daily breathe, the endless struggle with soot and dust and insufficient water supply, the hanging from the strap of the overcrowded streetcar at the end of your day's work; you must send your children to the nearby wretchedly crowded school, and see them suffer the consequences.

And so she did, at least up to a point. The model for Hull-House, Toynbee Hall, explicitly cast itself as a place where the privileged and educated dedicated themselves to the poor and unfortunate. Hull-House was not so explicit about who was to be a part of the enterprise, and what they were to do there—save souls, save lives, rescue children, all of the above. Nor were all of the Hull-House residents from privileged backgrounds, or even with a formal education. One of the principal reformers, Mary Kenney, a former factory worker and later a journalist, was described as: "Tall, erect, broad shouldered, with ruddy face and shining eyes, she carried hope and confidence withersoever she went."

Toynbee Hall in London was designed as a place where the rich served the poor under the doctrine of service in the Christian ministry. Hull-House was not explicitly associated with a church or specific ministry, although many of its leaders and supporters would have said they were doing Christian work. There were many references to brotherhood.

Walker Evans, another documentarian from another decade, aptly described the religious attitude of his colleague, James Agee:

> His Christianity—if an outsider may try to speak of it—was a punctured and residual remnant, but it was still a naked, root emotion. It was an ex-Church, or non-Church, matter, and it was hardly in evidence. All you saw of it was an ingrained courtesy, an uncourtly courtesy that emanated from him towards everyone, perhaps excepting the smugly rich, the pretentiously genteel, and the police. After a while, in a round-about way, you discovered that, to him, human beings were at least possibly immortal and literally sacred souls.

Foreword to the 1960 edition of *Let Us Now Praise Famous Men*

September 1998: My course this fall is "Murder and Its Consequences," about capital punishment, mostly in New Jersey. We will read state Supreme Court cases involving capital punishment, including Supreme Court of Illinois opinions. We have become friends with a former Illinois Supreme Court justice who was a dissenter, writing a stinging objection in a capital case where the court refused to recognize its own former precedents.

There is an Illinois case I am curious about: State v. Porter. When the class read the opinion, quoting the statements of the defendant, as reported presumably to the police, it seemed to me that there is a false, canned quality to the statements.

One of Jane Addams's biographers wrote of Florence Kelley and Julia Lathrop:

> When both were at Hull-House together, arguing and disagreeing as they often did on the best method of procedure, it is doubtful if any better talk was to be heard anywhere. Prime ministers of Europe, philosophers of all doctrines, labor leaders and great capitalists and unpopular poets and popular novelists and shabby exiles from half the kingdoms of the world visited Hull-House and dined there and listened willingly.

The Nineteenth Ward outside the front door of Hull-House became a living laboratory in which to study child labor, and incidentally the conditions of family life in the tenements, in the 1890s. The passage of the factory inspection statute allowed for a natural experiment concerning the impact of legislation on a social situation, although they would not have used that terminology. *Hull-House Maps and Papers* continues:

The Nineteenth Ward of Chicago is perhaps the best district in all Illinois for a detailed study of child-labor, both because it contains many factories in which children are employed, and because it is the dwelling-place of wage-earning children engaged in all lines of activity.

The Ewing Street Italian colony furnishes a large contingent to the army of bootblacks and newsboys; lads who leave home at 2:30 a.m. to secure the first edition of the morning paper, selling each edition as it appears, and filling the intervals with blacking boots and tossing pennies until, in the winter half of the year, they gather in the Polk Street Night-School, to doze in the warmth or torture the teacher with the gamin tricks acquired by day. For them, school is "a lark," or a peaceful retreat from parental beatings and shrieking juniors at home during the bitter nights of the Chicago winter.

Newsboys, bootblacks, cash-children, candy workers were visible on the street everywhere in every weather and at all times of day. After all, there was no room for them at home because that was where their mothers were doing the piecework on every available flat space while watching over the babies and younger children:

The largest number of children to be found in any factory in Chicago is in a caramel works in this [the Nineteenth] *ward, where there are from one hundred and ten to two hundred little girls, four to twelve boys, and seventy to one hundred adults, according to the season of the year.*

January 2, 2000: The millennium is here. There was no loss of water or power, or even delays at the airports, in spite of all the worries about computerized systems and the date change. What joy to have everyone here. It snowed. We went for walks, and to the aquarium, to the delight of all. And ate, far too much, far too many sweets, we have all gained alarmingly and must go home and start disciplining ourselves once more. Not everyone has jobs, but there are babies, and toddlers running up the stairs and back down again, hiding in the cupboards and secret corners. What could be more joyous than a big old house with windows looking out on the snow, a fire in the fireplace, and the sound of laughter on the stairs.

During the early 1890s, a thousand people came to Hull-House every week. Then it was two thousand. People came for a meal, or a bath, or to go to a meeting, or to literacy or English classes, or brought children to the kindergarten, or dropped off a baby or toddler for a few hours there when they had a deliver a finished garment. These services were almost entirely free. So, Jane Addams describes:

Our very first Christmas at Hull-House, when we as yet knew nothing of child labor, a number of little girls refused the candy which was offered them as part of the Christmas good cheer, saying simply that they "worked in a candy factory and could not bear the sight of it." We discovered that for six weeks they had worked from seven in the morning until nine at night, and they were exhausted as well as satiated. The sharp consciousness of stern economic conditions was thus thrust upon us in the midst of the season of good will.

Jane Addams was a tireless fundraiser, but in practice and as a matter of principle, there was no room in the house for those who did not contribute. The residential fees were small, and there were some fees for other services, for those who could afford them. There was a small fee for classes. Eventually Florence Kelley herself became a successful fundraiser for Hull-House.

October 13, 2000, Chicago Tribune: "Foes of Death Penalty Cite Gains: ABA Says More People Questioning Justice of System."

When the American Bar Association called for a moratorium on the death penalty three years ago, the appeal attracted only a smattering of support. But on Thursday, the president of the 400,000-member lawyers' organization told a Carter Center symposium that the issue is gaining momentum nationwide. "Our system is broken," Florida attorney Martha Barnett said. "A lot of people in the country are beginning to realize we have systemic problems."

Support for re-evaluating capital punishment appears to be mounting in light of the release of a number of inmates from Death Row after new DNA tests proved their innocence or other exonerating evidence came to light. A recent national poll indicates that while 60 percent of the country's voters still support capital punishment, almost half of that support comes with reservations.

For Florence Kelley and Jane Addams, there was always the traveling: to the East Coast to meet with sympathizers and reformers in New York, Boston, and Philadelphia, then to raise money and give a speech to a women's group in Iowa or Portland, Oregon. Always a trip to be prepared for, always a trip ending. And when Florence Kelley became factory inspector there was the traveling throughout Illinois to investigate conditions in the factories while deciding where to prosecute.

April 10, 2012: Beautiful spring day. Cold, and the tulips alongside the city sidewalks are brave but cowering. Perhaps a freeze tonight. They know. The city breathes. The city smiles today. A young woman, skinny legs in jeans, boots above her knees, stacked leather heels, and of course hurrying, hurrying somewhere with a phone held to her ear. Is there anyone on the street this morning who doesn't have a phone on their ear or around their neck? How do people experience where they are?

From 1891 until the passage of the Factory Inspection Law in 1893, there was constant pressure from Hull-House advocates and others on the legislators in Springfield and Chicago to address the conditions in the sweatshops. When John Peter Altgeld was elected governor in 1892, those who had been working on the issue for years realized that factory reform legislation might actually be passed, that something might happen with a new governor. Along with Hull-House associates, the organizations of garment workers and union people—the shirt makers, the custom tailors, the cloak makers and shoemakers, the joiners, and many others—kept up the pressure for abolition by law of the sweating system, or at least introducing some regulation. The registration of women and children in the factories and sweatshops was a beginning. At least there would then be a count of who was working there.

April 23, 2012: Shakespeare's birthday and the birthday of Vladimir Nabokov. A blue sky, and cold. Still the weather is bright, invigorating, although I don't feel invigorated for some reason. I can't blame it on the weather. My own bad temper, insecurities, bad dreams.

One job of the future factory inspector, and of Florence Kelley as she prepared the preliminary investigations which she hoped would be persuasive to the state legislature, was to get as many people as possible to pay attention. As many members of the press who could be persuaded to would then be encouraged to write about and carry forward the factual findings.

The women of Hull-House, and their allies, were everywhere lobbying, and always unified. Suffrage came slowly and not first to Illinois. The right to vote was granted to women in Wyoming in 1890; Colorado in 1893; Idaho and Utah in 1896. Chicago did not grant women suffrage in 1906 in the face of a large campaign to do so. Women could not vote in Illinois until 1913 when a state statute granted suffrage in state and national elections.

November 10, 1998: Glad to be back from the trip to the archives of the American Newspaper Repository in New Hampshire and Vermont. The traveling, the driving, in the snow in an unfamiliar rented car, hunched over the wheel, worried: Would I ever get there? Then a saggy bed in an old-fashioned, old bed and breakfast. The Boston airport a snakes nest of writhing, pulsing ramps.

Nicholson Baker and his family have preserved this newspaper archive as bound sets owned for decades by the British Library. They preserved these papers because it was necessary, because it was the right thing to do. Most libraries destroyed their archival newspaper copies, against donor intent, and contrary to their own mission to preserve a record of the past.

The American Newspaper Repository is located in an abandoned mill, where children no doubt worked in the nineteenth century. It is near water, cavernous, and damp which is a benefit to the newspapers. It was worth it to meet these dedicated people, to see evidence that the Chicago newspapers from the 1890s have survived, at least here. The curse of microfilm defeated for a moment.

The Factory and Workshop Inspection Law did not abolish the sweating system, nor was there the political will to do so. The system was firmly entrenched, and too many people benefited from it for it to be gotten rid of in one stroke by the legislature. The creation of a mechanism for government-authorized inspections nonetheless was the cracking open of a small window.

In *Twenty Years at Hull-House*, Jane Addams recalled that a group of businessmen approached her when the statute was pending in the state legislature. She remembered the incident while reminiscing about her father, a state senator in Illinois:

Of the many things written of my father in that sad August in 1881, when he died, the one I cared for most was written by an old political friend of his who was then editor of a great Chicago daily. He wrote that while there were doubtless many members of the Illinois legislature who during the great contracts of the war time and the demoralizing reconstruction days that followed, had never accepted a bribe, he wished to bear testimony that he personally had known but this one man who had never been offered a bribe because bad men were instinctively afraid of him.

I feel now the hot chagrin with which I recalled this statement during those early efforts of Illinois in which Hull-House joined, to secure the passage of the first factory legislation. I was told by the representatives of an informal association of manufacturers that if the residents of Hull-House would drop this nonsense about a sweatshop bill, of which they knew nothing, certain business men would agree to give fifty thousand dollars within two years to be used for any of the philanthropic activities of the Settlement.

As the fact broke upon me that I was being offered a bribe, the shame was enormously increased by the memory of this statement. What had befallen the daughter of my father that such a thing could happen to her? The salutary reflection that it could not have occurred unless a weakness in myself had permitted it, withheld me at least from an historic display of indignation before the two men making the offer, and I explained as gently as I could that we had no ambition to make Hull-House "the largest institution on the West Side," but that we were much concerned that our neighbors should be protected from untoward conditions of work, and—so much heroics, youth must permit itself—if to accomplish this the destruction of Hull-House was necessary, that we would cheerfully sing a Te Deum on its ruins. The good friend who had invited me to lunch at the Union League Club to meet two of his friends who wanted to talk over the sweat shop bill here kindly intervened, and we all hastened to cover the awkward situation by that scurrying away from ugly morality which seems to be an obligation of social intercourse.

Presumably "the informal association of manufacturers" was what became the Illinois Manufacturers' Association then being organized by Levy Mayer. The factory inspection statute would not have passed without the advocacy of the Hull-House women and the workers organizations, including the very active participation of many women factory workers and union leaders.

The manufacturers and factory owners were disorganized and caught napping until Levy Mayer pulled the whining opposition together into the Illinois Manufacturers' Association. Perhaps Levy Mayer was at the lunch with Jane Addams at the Union League Club, or formulated the bribe.

May 2000: Law school graduation, again. Another crop of lawyers enter the marketplace, cheerfully, optimistically. And so the academic calendar swings through its cycle, too fast. Always a new appointment, a new journey. At least the children now visit. And spring is here, glorious spring again. The house is full of voices. We are busy, too busy, foolishly busy, with little time to sit down and take a breath or think. I escape to the third floor and the nineteenth century, gratefully.

The Law Institute, where Levy Mayer worked as a clerk while waiting to turn twenty-one so that he could be admitted to the Bar, was where the City Hall and the Office of the County Recorder, and all of the remaining legal records were put after the 1871 fire. Lawyers who came to the Law Institute were given access to the library facilities, a desk, and a temporary room assignment. Levy Mayer, the new assistant librarian fresh out of Yale Law School, swept the floor of the office, took care of the modest rooms, and attended to the needs of the lawyers looking for legal authorities and decisions. For this, the industrious young man was paid four dollars a week. The job was worth a fortune.

During his three years there Levy Mayer prepared a catalog for the Law Institute Library and revised two treatises, receiving royalties of twenty-five cents a copy on the sales. In two years 2,500 copies were sold, putting more than $600 in the pocket of the enterprising young lawyer. More important than the money was that he met and ingratiated himself with all the lawyers who came to the institute and made a reputation for himself by helping them find the law and make sense of it.

June 10, 2000: The examination of the historical homicide cases deepens, the coding, the copying, the writing of the introduction, and the planning of the conference. Then, finding the academics to present papers. I walked into the office where everyone was working, and my web designer showed me three hundred photographs from the period. These are stunning additions, pictures of children, horses, streets, police. They will all be placed on the website.

Like Florence Kelley, Levy Mayer wrote for legal magazines and periodicals, getting paid ten to twelve dollars per contribution, or less. As Florence Kelley knew all too well, the publishers were often stingy and slow to pay, but a nimble writer could cobble together a living by writing for several, one and then another, and with a day job. And there was the satisfaction of getting the work out. Lawyers and judges learned your name. Pamphlets and other writings could be sold at public speaking engagements. Mesmerizing speakers such as Florence Kelley and Clarence Darrow drew crowds, and the speakers could cover their expenses by selling the printed copies of past lectures, in addition to charging admission.

There is no evidence that Levy Mayer—at least at this stage of his life—was a commanding public speaker, although he was later to be a compelling appellate advocate and fierce trial attorney. His talent, shown most vividly in retrospect in his organizing of the Illinois Manufacturers' Association, seems to have been in creating networks, building consensus, and persuading squabbling individuals to work together and find a winning legal strategy. This made him rich.

It was the kind of political skill which Florence Kelley and Jane Addams possessed as well. Levy Mayer had one talent which Florence Kelley lacked: he always made sure he was well and adequately paid for his services. Shrewdly, the initial attack upon the Factory Inspection Law included an attack upon the state paying a salary to the factory inspector herself, and her appointment and the appointment of her assistants. The Supreme Court of Illinois dismissed these arguments, but they were part of the fundamental assault upon the very idea that there could be a paid official whose job it was to question business practices. And if he could persuade a lower court to issue an injunction or restraining order, the factory inspectors would have been halted.

March 5, 1999, Chicago Tribune: "Ford Heights 4 Accept $36 Million."

. . . "This county is recognizing the extent of the gross misconduct and the extent of the incredible injuries that these men suffered," said Larry Marshall, a Northwestern law professor who represented one of the men. The settlement, approved by the Cook County Board on Thursday in a closed-door meeting, was described by attorney Flynt Taylor as the largest ever in a civil rights lawsuit concerning police misconduct.

October 1998: Coming back from New Hampshire. The most difficult part of the trip was driving through Boston on the Big Dig, said to have dragged on with inferior workmanship and endless problems because of government graft and corruption in the multimillion-dollar contracts. The trip was a discovery. I got as many pictures as I could, given the short time and other constraints. Many new photographs for the website.

Florence Kelley noted:

The fact of living directly among the wage earners is also an immense help. The municipal arrangements are so wretched that the filth and overcrowding are worse than I have ever seen outside of Naples and the East Side of New York.

The Nineteenth Ward had more than seven thousand children aged six to fourteen, but just 2,579 school places. The extreme economic conditions made possible child labor of the cruelest sort on a large scale. Boys and girls as young as four and five regularly worked as beggars on the streets, with the girls the most visible. Yet, socialism was not popular in this neighborhood. Socialism appealed more to those who didn't need the redistribution of wealth.

Florence Kelley wrote to Engels:

In working class neighborhoods, socialists are seen as bores, nuisances, and professional promoters of discord. Those who stood to benefit the most from socialism, those who had little, showed the least interest in making it happen.

The people in these slums did not share the ideology of the exiles in Zurich, nor their education and intellectual values. Later this would be termed "false consciousness," a term some would consider false itself, since it assumes a monopoly on its opposite, the truth.

Jane Addams reported:

[W]e found it much easier to deal with the first generation of crowded city life than with the second or third. . . . The Italian and Bohemian peasants who live in Chicago still put on their bright holiday clothes on a Sunday and go visit their cousins. They

tramp along with at least a suggestion of having once walked over plowed fields and breathed country air.

March 9, 1999, Chicago Tribune: "$36 Million Can't Remove the Stain on Justice System," by Eric Zorn.

Never has the sum $36 million looked so puny. The case against Cook County for the wrongful prosecution of the Ford Heights Four had become even more powerful than when the men were exonerated and released in 1996, and the extent to which authorities buried the truth and pursued a wicked injustice was never more strong.

The settlement of the civil suit reached Friday ($36 million divided unequally among four defendants, an average of $6 million each after legal fees) looks from here like an excellent bargain for taxpayers. When it came time for a jury to award damages, we would have heard none of this talk of sharing the blame all around or of mistakes sometimes just happen.

The maps in *Hull-House Maps and Papers* have become classics of representation by themselves, irrespective of the persuasive power of their factual content, irrespective of the extremity of the conditions they report, in part because of their jaunty originality, in part because of their importance as singular carriers of unique information, and in no small part because of their arresting symmetry and beauty. Yet, while Florence Kelley's strong personality and artistic power were important, even crucial, to this effort, neither the book nor the political decision of the legislature to create the position of factory inspector and to allow inspections of the tenements in the Nineteenth Ward would have happened had there not been a confluence of unpredictable circumstances.

May 13, 2012: The spring could not be more benign. But nothing to compare with the beauty of Seattle and Victoria Island where ten thousand tulips were in bloom at the famous gardens on another perfect day. Still, home is Chicago now, this changing Chicago, changing around us as our lives change within it.

The Illinois Factory and Workshop Inspection Law would never have been proposed to the legislature or passed had not an unlikely person stepped out of the wings onto the political stage.

John Peter Altgeld was nominated for governor by the Democratic Party in the summer of 1892 and elected in November 1892, taking office in January 1893.

On January 4, 1893, immediately after Altgeld took the governorship, the Illinois legislature convened a joint commission to investigate the conditions in the sweatshops, and Florence Kelley and Alzina Stevens were hired after putting themselves forward to write the report.

That John Peter Altgeld was ever elected governor was improbable, if not astonishing. One of his biographers describes his inauguration:

After the vigorous gubernatorial campaign Altgeld had a complete nervous collapse from exhaustion. "So serious was his affliction that he expected to die before taking office." His inauguration on January 10, 1893, almost killed him. His former opponent even took pity on him and offered Altgeld his arm as they walked slowly to the podium. The atmosphere was so "stifling, other men collapsed from the heat. He looked very pallid, but kept his overcoat on." He couldn't finish his speech. He quit after two or three minutes. He went to the reception which was "riotous" and nearly fainted.

Vice President Elect Adlai E. Stevenson could not get through the crowd to attend the inauguration. Altgeld was ordered to rest, and it was late in the term before the new governor was well enough to pay much attention to the Factory Inspection Law or anything else. Without John Peter Altgeld as governor, there would have been no Factory Inspection Law, no appointment of Florence Kelley as the first state factory inspector, and no *Hull-House Maps and Papers.*

November 4, 1998, Chicago Tribune: "Ryan, Fitzgerald triumph; Democrats Gain Nationally: GOP Keeps Its Lock on Top Job in Springfield."

George H. Ryan was elected Illinois' 39th governor Tuesday, overcoming a strong Chicago and Downstate push for Democrat Glenn Poshard to extend the Republicans' 22-year reign in the Executive Mansion.

Unofficial returns with 94 percent of the precincts reporting showed Ryan, the Republican secretary of state, with 52 percent and Poshard, a five-term Democratic congressman from Marion, with 46 percent.

"It feels very good just to have the 15 months over and have it over," Ryan said late Tuesday. "My main object was winning this election. Absolutely, when you win it makes it all worthwhile. I think we ran a good campaign. I don't know, as I look back on it, if there was anything I would do differently.

"It was never a plan of mine to run for governor. All these things kind of work themselves out, and that's been the story of

my career. If (Gov.) Jim Edgar had decided to run again, I would
have seriously considered retiring."

John Peter Altgeld did not grow up in luxury or come from a position of social privilege. He was born on December 30, 1847, in Germany and was brought to America at three months—a fact his political opponents never let him or any of his supporters forget. He revised his autobiography to list his place of birth as Niederselters, in Nassau, then an independent duchy in Prussia.

He was raised on a hardscrabble farm in the Ohio wilderness where his illiterate German-speaking parents did their best to eke out a living on 140 acres of heavily mortgaged land. His father was a cart maker. They were tenant farmers, basically sharecroppers. There were nine children; most of them died, three in infancy. William, John Peter's brother, was considered the smart one. He died of tuberculosis in his twenties.

May 11, 2007: Blue sky, white clouds. Today anything seems possible. Our fruit tree blossoms immolating themselves in pink all over the front walk. Every birth, every spring, is a miracle, a new beginning, and every death a loss, an ending, a tragedy.

Young Pete, as John Peter Altgeld was called as a young man, was hired out to work on neighbors' farms and also regularly sent to town to sell eggs and butter, then coming back home to do his chores on the family farm. His father was strict and he beat his children. For two summers and one winter, Young Pete attended a little school in the district and sometimes he went to a Sunday school. His parents weren't keen on him learning English; German was the language at home.

July 8, 2013: There is a rumor the Chicago Tribune will split its assets, keep the newspapers separate from the television stations and other media. It is a miracle the newspaper survives as a daily printed paper after the disaster of buyout and bankruptcy.

When he was twelve, John Peter Altgeld's father declared that his son had had enough education. Young Pete didn't object, since he was picked on in school, nicknamed "the little Dutchman," made fun of for his short legs and sprung chest, as well as for his strong German accent. Later the Irishmen he worked with laying track on the railroad on his way to Chicago also called him "the Dutchman," but with less bite. He looked and sounded foreign, or maybe just different.

John Peter Altgeld later said about himself: "If I had to depend upon my looks, I'd have been hung long ago." Perhaps this is what gave him a sympathy for the imprisoned and made him an advocate for the poor and a lifelong opponent of capital punishment. At some point the young man didn't allow his father to take a strap to him any longer. Later people remembered that his mother was a kind and extraordinary woman.

December 10, 1998: Another Christmas coming, another baby, a new member of the family. Some of us will be together. All I can think of at the moment is getting to the end of the semester.

Then, there was Governor Altgeld's hair—apparently a matter of relevance to governors of Illinois—described as "seeming to have been affixed to his skull as if it were a mat." Always cropped short, it grew straight up like corn stubble. There was no way to part it; it just stood straight up and had to be combed straight up or plastered down. Years later, when he was a man of interest to the newspapers, a reporter said: "I never saw hair worn in this style except by boys who had gone swimming and had no comb when they came back."

As if all this were not enough—short stature, bandy legs, a large chest, a strong German accent—he had a slight harelip which affected his speech. Later he covered that upper lip with a mustache. As a young boy he wore coarse, homespun clothes, further cause for ridicule from his schoolmates.

None of this would predict a career in elective politics, not to mention a political career culminating in being elected governor of Illinois, where the smiling kind of personal charm such as that apparently amply possessed by his successor, Governor John Tanner, is said to be indispensable. And as if his physical characteristics were not hindrance enough, John Peter Altgeld had the reputation—even when he was governor—for being unshakably honest. With these attributes he might have been a self-important bore and a prig, but apparently was not.

Florence Kelley at one point wrote to a friend that he had obviously suffered so much and seen so much pain that it was difficult to be around him. Yet the people who worked with him loved him and were fiercely loyal and passionately committed to him, even when they disagreed with what he did. No one thought him a fool or faint of heart. He had a keen, wry sense of observation, and kept a wary account, and his own counsel, about the foibles and foolishness of those around him.

John Peter Altgeld looked and sounded foreign at a time when anti-foreign political agitating sparked deadly riots and bloodshed, not only in Chicago but also in Cincinnati, Louisville and throughout the country. He wasn't Catholic—his family held to the harsh Lutheran tradition—and John Peter Altgeld never presented himself as someone riding forward with the blessing of a higher power. It was a minor miracle that he ever became a leader of a political party or selected for statewide office, and more amazing that he was elected governor. At several points he was a candidate for a higher political office. In his entire political career he never did lose his German accent.

December 15, 1998: People ask how does my teaching here compare with the teaching I did before. They want to know how the students compare. The answer is not simple, since the law students are at a different stage of their education. They are very focused, the law students. They are further evidence, if any were needed, of the deficiencies of education in America at the high school and undergraduate level. They know little history, are unfamiliar with great literature. But they are bright, cheerful people, lively and interesting, eager to work and learn, and generally a pleasure to have in class.

Law and economics were ever the preoccupation of both John Peter Altgeld and Florence Kelley. What we know of her life in Chicago is because of her entanglement in a web of linked official records which ended up being within the domain of the law: her admission and graduation from Northwestern University School of Law; the custody hearing in chancery; the hearings and cases which were part of the legal challenge to the Factory Inspection Law; the factual reports she wrote in preparation for legislation; and then the briefs and papers for the litigation itself, at every level up to the Supreme Court of the United States; and the most fulsome documents of all, the annual reports of the factory inspector to the governor and legislature.

Some of the facts about her time in Chicago, in so far as the stamp of the law vouches for their accuracy, are found in these records. Yet we know there are untrue statements and facts in those legal records, as well. The law—loved, hated, despised, revered—if it does nothing else (and perhaps it does nothing else) has an obligation to write down, to record what people say and what transpires in its realm, once people enter it.

July 5, 1999: The homicide investigations continue. It is hot on the third floor. Going up the stairs my heart beats faster, and walking into the room is always accompanied by an exhale—not a sigh, but the release of a held breath. Just to see the windows, all of them, and that they can be opened, no matter the weather, they can be opened to the outside. The old-fashioned metal peg with the bar, to keep the windows from banging in the wind, and solidly anchor the window to the frame.

The set of handwritten records from 1870-1930 leads to other sources and others and others. An archive with sprouts, and yet complete and orderly of itself.

There is no air conditioning on the third floor. I have a machine I fill with ice cubes, and then a small rattling fan blows a tiny breeze across the ice cubes, a puff of cool air. It is humid, and the sweat pours down my back and falls on the pages where I am writing. The little fan generates a tiny exhale like a mouse breathing beside me in this large space. The sweat sticks my shirt to my back. I am often reading about people in factories. I identify with them, except that I can go downstairs into the air conditioning or step outside into the leafy garden. Waiting for the thunder to dispel that thick, Midwestern stickiness. The rumble of thunder is a letting go, a relief, welcome. Was it then?

When the punishing Civil War was going full strength, Young Pete was thirteen and wanted to answer President Lincoln's call for volunteers. His father refused to let him go. There was no one else to work the land. When the war was older, and he was older, the Ohio Home Guard called for an additional one hundred men to serve for one hundred dollars each for the muster. There was a draft set for each town and the state was required to come up with a certain number of new recruits. The boy was sixteen and he found someone called up who would let him go in his place. Probably he lied about his age. The father kept ninety dollars—a lot of money for a man who made farm carts—and the boy kept ten.

October 1999: This data set of homicide cases is turning into a big research project. The impetus is to get that original data set out to where the researchers can use it. A new homicide data set is always of interest, and this one covers a long period in a place of importance. There is so much more here than murder; each case is a world, a scene crowded with people, alive.

In May 1864, dark days of the war, John Peter Altgeld, not yet seventeen, was in the Union army and went to Washington, DC. In June he reported to General Benjamin Butler, under the command of General Ulysses Grant, just as the Union army was getting ready to finally destroy General Robert E. Lee's army.

John Peter Altgeld later said that his war experience was "nothing of consequence," that he "did not bleed and did not die, but was there; always reported for duty, was always on deck, never shirked and never ran away." He said pardoning the anarchists required much more courage than anything he did on the Civil War battlefield.

Florence Kelley and Jane Addams suffered public criticism for taking a pacifist position during both the Spanish American invasion and the buildup to World War I, although both worked to improve the quality of wartime manufactures for the troops and to rout cheating and fraud among the war manufacturers, protected by special legislation and their friends in the legislatures.

In the army, John Peter Altgeld did come down with the fever, called Chickahominy fever or battlefield fever, a sickness indigenous to the South. Many soldiers died of it. He almost died of it, but after a few weeks in a field hospital, he returned to his regiment, thinking he was cured. The Chickahominy fever—perhaps malaria, from the southern swamps, perhaps some other water-friendly infection—plagued him for the rest of his life. He was never well again for long.

March 27, 2007: A grey sky. Still, warm, balmy. The clumped dirty snow, an afterthought. At least the University of California did not keep out all women, or all Jews. In my father's department, the economics department at Berkeley during the time of the state loyalty oath in California in the 1950s, being a Jew was a cause for suspicion and associated with being a communist. Faculty were summoned to the offices of the chairman and fired—told to clean out their desks by Monday—if they would not sign the state loyalty oath, a law designed to rout communists and socialists from the universities and colleges, a law later declared unconstitutional.

When he returned home from the war, John Peter Altgeld announced over his father's objection that he was going to high school. He also announced that he would no longer suffer his father to beat him with a leather strap. When the next fall came, he lived during the school term with another schoolboy in a little room over a carpenter's shop and tannery. The boys mostly cooked their own food, and his mother brought him eggs, meat and butter or, if she couldn't, a neighbor, Mrs. Pollock, did. Mr. Pollock took Young Pete to a store and outfitted him with a store-made suit and overcoat when he found the young man walking around one cold evening with neither. The same night John Peter transferred to the Pollock barn enough grain to pay for the clothes. Mr. Pollock insisted he didn't want to be paid, but there it was.

For all the reports later of his great intelligence and startling grasp of complex matters, the boy was no whiz at school. He was curious about everything and, once he had learned to read, read everything. As with Lincoln and William Darrah Kelley and Florence Kelley, his passion for reading was lifelong. His town school roommate—one of those who were, perhaps, surprised to see him end up as governor of Illinois—later said Young Pete was a bit stupid with arithmetic and sums. After high school, Young Pete said he wanted to be a schoolteacher and got himself certified. Certainly it wasn't his own academic promise, or the encouragement of his teachers, which urged him in that direction. When he went to work as a teacher, he earned thirty-five dollars a month, all of which went to pay down the mortgage on his father's land.

April 15, 2002, Chicago Tribune: "Ryan's Panel Urges Fixes in Death Penalty: 2-year Study Says Fatal Flaw Exists."

After two years of study, Gov. George Ryan's commission to reform the death penalty has proposed sweeping changes to the state's criminal justice system but ultimately concludes it cannot guarantee that the innocent will no longer be wrongly condemned.

The report, scheduled to be released Monday, does not include a formal recommendation to abolish the death penalty, though a majority of commission members favored scrapping the state's troubled capital punishment system, according to the report obtained by the Tribune.

The proposed reforms would dramatically limit the number of death sentences, with 85 recommendations ranging from videotaping police interrogations—rather than just confessions—to reducing the factors that make someone eligible for the death penalty to 5 from 20. . . .

Most of the commission's proposals require legislative approval and many carry a hefty price tag as lawmakers wrestle with a budget crisis that has forced layoffs.

At age twenty-one John Peter Altgeld was freed of his father's indenture, and in 1869, Young Pete headed out, away from the farm, away from his father, away from everyone he had known. Heading out meant he headed out on foot, tramping toward the West. He had fallen in love before he left, though, with a girl from a better-off family who later sent her to Oberlin College to study music. The girl's father did not find John Peter Altgeld a suitable prospective husband for his daughter, Emma, and he forbade the courtship to continue. And so John Peter Altgeld headed out of town, walking.

July 30, 1999: Finally all the homicide police records have been laboriously copied, and coded for the simple criminological aspects of the homicide: name of victim, name of defendant, characteristics of victim and defendant, circumstances of the crime, date, location, etc., the basic factual attributes of the crime useful and interesting to criminological researchers. For a week, a group of temporary employees, mostly summer students, sat in one big room full of desktop computers and entered the data, and now it is done. The cases are so rich, so expressive. They must be seen. Now the data are in a form where anyone can use them, any researcher can use them and analyze them. We can proceed to the counting and analysis.

Nicholas Kelley, Florence Kelley's oldest child, born in Zurich, later recalled:

There was a time, twenty to twenty-five years ago, when many, beguiled by the new interest of politics and government in these things, were announcing the early demise of settlements. We have not had that funeral yet, and I do not believe it will take place. Settlements are probably more necessary and important now than ever. . . .

When I first was here [at Hull-House], the sidewalks in the neighborhood were made of wood, and the streets were paved with round wooden blocks standing on end. The mothers of households sometimes would dig out these blocks and take them home in their aprons and use them as firewood. Out at the edge of the sidewalk toward the street stood garbage boxes, with the ends sloping inward toward the bottom to make it easier to shovel out the contents, and with the covers hinged across the middle. I recall that toward the end of my time here a policeman shot one of the neighbors who, sitting on his garbage box and perhaps insulting the policeman, refused to get off the box when the guardian of the law ordered him to do so. Until that time the sentiment had been that a man had a right to sit on his own garbage box. . . .

In those early days horse cars ran on Halsted Street. Later cable cars supplanted them. The neighbors worked out something that seemed to be diverting. If they tied a string to something and then dropped the other end of the string into the cable slot, the cable usually would catch it, and the object would go sailing down Halsted Street at the full speed of a cable car. It was not unusual to see a teakettle or an old straw hat or some other incongruous object hastening down the street in this manner.

With ten dollars in his pocket, Young Pete began walking west. The war was over, Lincoln had put in place the Homestead Act, and the railroads were laying down track as the great iron horse moved west. A strong young man could find work. John Peter tramped to Cincinnati, then to Indiana. He worked on farms and pushed on, arrived in Saint Louis with fifteen cents in his pocket, spent five cents for the ferry, then spent the rest on paper and a stamp to write home. If you didn't write a letter no one knew where you were, where you had been or if you were alive or dead.

```
December 15, 2002, Chicago Tribune: "2 Days of Events on Wrong-
ful Convictions."
```

```
Wrongful convictions and the flaws in America's capital-punish-
ment system will be in the spotlight during the next two days in
Chicago.
```

```
The Center on Wrongful Convictions at Northwestern University
School of Law has scheduled speeches, a daylong march and the
premiere of a play on the subject in an effort to draw further
attention to the issue of innocent people being sentenced to
death.
```

On the march, tramping, John Peter found a job as a laborer in a chemical plant. Then he took another job laying track for the Missouri, Kansas and Texas railroad at $3.50 a day, three or four times what he had been making at the chemical factory. And to swing a pick axe put you outside. But under the broiling southwest sun, near Fort Scott, Kansas, he became sick again with the battlefield fever.

The Irish on the line who called him the Dutchman carried him to a hospital where he stayed for weeks while the fever ran its course. The medical people at the hospital where his fellow railroad workers brought him doubted he would recover, but he wouldn't give them his parents' address, telling the doctors he should just be buried in the neighborhood with as little fuss as possible. He didn't want to bother his parents or cause them any expense in bringing his body back home, or anything like that. "Let me just die here," he told them. He was never one to mince words. He had some unfinished business back home, though.

May 1, 2000: I, too, now live in the world of the Web. I worry that all of that information up on the Internet will fall down or be erased one day, with a click, as easily as it was put there. The Internet people don't seem to share this worry, and look bemused when I make such comments.

Impossible to know what someone thought or felt, then or now, but this is what they wrote, and this is what they read. Florence Kelley and Jane Addams read that article in the Chicago Tribune in the octagon at Hull-House on that day. And she certainly wrote that letter. We know that the person who received the letter read it. Who knows if anyone reads any of all those words on the Internet. The sun is shining, another May 1, and I must get outside.

The male students at the law school don't work harder, are not smarter, but are taken more seriously, especially by the male professors.

It was an unusual time, and a special place, Chicago in the 1890s. Decades later, Jane Addams recalled the atmosphere in Chicago before Haymarket, before Florence Kelley's arrival:

[I]n the winter of 1889-1890, by the advice and with the active participation of its leading citizens, the city had reached the conclusion that the only cure for the acts of anarchy was free speech and an open discussion of the ills of which the opponents of government complained. Great open meetings were held every Sunday evening in the recital hall of the then new auditorium . . . and every possible shade of opinion was freely expressed. A man who spoke constantly at these meetings used to be pointed out to the visiting stranger as one who had been involved with the group of convicted anarchists, and who doubtless would have been arrested and tried, but for the accident of his having been in Milwaukee when the explosion occurred.

One cannot imagine such meetings being held in Chicago to-day, nor that such a man should be encouraged to raise his voice in a public assemblage presided over by a leading banker. It is hard to tell just what change has come over our philosophy or over the minds of those citizens who were then convinced that if these conferences had been established earlier, the Haymarket riot and all its sensational results might have been avoided.

In his eighteen-thousand-word message explaining his reasons for pardoning the Haymarket anarchists, the act which killed his political future and which he described as harder than anything he did as a soldier on the Civil War battlefield, Governor John Peter Altgeld, the lawyer, wrote this about the legal decision which upheld the death sentences for the Haymarket defendants:

The judge certainly told the truth when he states that his case was without a precedent, and that no example could be found in the law books to sustain the law as above laid down. For, in all the centuries during which government has been maintained among men, and crime has been punished, no judge in a civilized country has ever laid down such a rule before. The rule was finding the defendants guilty of conspiracy to commit murder, and hence eligible for hanging, although they did not commit or plan the homicidal act.

When John Peter Altgeld finally recovered his health to the point where he could leave the hospital, the young man had spent all the money he had saved from working on the railroad on medicine, and his doctors said he must go live in a cooler, northern climate. The railroad crew with the friends who had brought him to the hospital had moved on.

So he set out tramping again, first to Topeka, Kansas, where he asked to be put up for a night on a farm. Sick again, in mind and body, raving with nightmares, he stayed there three weeks. When that farmer and his neighbors said he must leave and go to an institution, some kind of medical place or asylum, he dragged himself up and out in the middle of the night.

On the road again, he walked a hundred miles with no shoes across the open prairie, and the sickness continued. His feet were bound in rags, his clothes in tatters, and the melancholia was troubling him. He arrived in Saint Joseph, Missouri, with no job and no money, but he wasn't going to go back to his father's farm, even though there were reasons to go back to Ohio.

September 10, 2006: Finally, we have the first official meeting of the Illinois Committee to Study the Reform of the Death Penalty. The meeting room is in a nondescript State of Illinois office building, like every other state office building I have known. Our chairman called the meeting to order. This committee will never have the respect and prestige of the former Commission to Study the Death Penalty appointed by Governor George Ryan, although some of the members are the same. Nor will it have the prestige or effectiveness of the committee formed by the Supreme Court of New Jersey fifteen years ago, to develop statistical evidence for the proportionality review of capital cases. There is a painful disparity between the two government committees. The chief justice of the state Supreme Court of New Jersey held everyone to his own high standards. On this committee, the members make jokes about the stupidity of elected officials.

Still walking, Young Pete collapsed, violently ill, alongside a spring near Savannah, Missouri, a pretty, peaceful town of three thousand in Andrew County with an excellent court, in the middle of rich farmland. After lying in the ditch with chills and the sickness for hours, he dragged himself at dusk to the door of the nearest farmhouse. Most people lived on farms, and the roads between them were unpaved, rutted roads that went on and on. There weren't that many people in the countryside, and they didn't live close to one another.

That night a farmer opened the door and found on his back doorstep a young man, poorly clad, sick and penniless, who spoke with a strong German accent. The young man promised to work on the farm when he got well, and the Andrew County farmer took him in and treated him as a member of the family. Later, that farmer said he had never had a better farm hand, and after a few months when his health returned, the young man had no trouble finding additional work on other farms in that prosperous county. And he earned his keep there.

December 3, 2012: Not cold, but like summer. The warm weather is unnatural, and the swings too big for global warming. Are these extremes what we have brought upon ourselves? Is it time to leave Chicago, or just to leave 1890s Chicago?

When his strength returned, the young man made friends with another family at the county seat, a man who had a library. John Peter Altgeld had the wit to know he needed an education. Finding the books, a library, and someone who knew something about books, was the first task. John Peter soon had a new best friend in the son of this family. They read all the books in the library together, and his new friend corrected his grammar and accent.

When a teacher at the Republican School left in the middle of the term, Young Pete got the job by digging potatoes faster than one of the trustees of the school. He got it in spite of the fact that Andrew County people didn't much like men who had served on the Union side in the war. The other trustee of the school called Pete the greenest, most awkward, and homeliest young man in Savannah. At least it was a distinction. He was called the "Tater Teacher." Later when the person who gave Altgeld the job turned up at the riotous party for his inauguration as governor of Illinois, everyone wondered who he was and why he was there, and when he got a patronage appointment in state government they still were wondering.

February 26, 2013: The lake today a living, breathing bas-relief, a lesson in plate tectonics, as the ice breaks, cracks, and overlaps in huge pieces, as the temperature plummets. The cars crawling on the highway. The office empties out, a lecture is canceled. Nature and the gods once again showing us mere mortals who is stronger. I am remembering the picture of the shaggy pony and the cart, the men in their great coats standing on the ice four miles out, beside the crib, still visible from the drive.

Young Pete won over those who were suspicious of him and made contact with a law-yer and judge—later a member of Congress who would have served with William Darrah Kelley. Soon John Peter was wearing his eyes out reading and copying the law. The judge had come from a similar background and he provided the young man with law books and taught him, encouraged him. It was said he saw the young man as a future son-in-law and law partner.

Now John Peter was teaching at the Republican School, working on his friend's family farm, and reading law at night. Soon he would teach at a better school and go live with the judge, who then took him in his office as a clerk. And he was well, in what must have been a benign climate and a healthy atmosphere. Or perhaps the extreme cold of the winters killed the carriers of diseases or at least tamped down his infection.

In April 1871, a shingle was hung out at that office, J.P. Altgeld, Att'y. The next year at age twenty-four he was appointed city attorney, less than a year after being admitted to the Bar, meaning he handled all the cases in which the city was a party. Now he was referred to in the local newspaper as J.P. Altgeld, Esq., although he owned no land.

June, 2002: The work on the homicide project has a new dimension. We are doing videotaped interviews now, and they will go on the website, too. The life story of a judge, the history of the death penalty in Illinois, and the founding of the Center on Wrongful Convictions.

As city attorney, John Peter Altgeld took cases to the Missouri Supreme Court on causes such as the theft of a black mare with a blaze face, and a guardian who cheated his ward of $2,600 in a bad land deal. The railroads generated enough litigation for every-one and kept the courts busy and the lawyers employed in every kind of suit. Abraham Lincoln, Clarence Darrow, and John Peter Altgeld started out representing the railroads. The railroads paid the bills on time for a new attorney who had no family connections or wealthy friends. Now John Peter Altgeld saw another side of the railroads, from that of the young man laying track.

Then there was a case turning on the issue of whether a Negro woman was property. He argued that she was, under the state law. Out of seven cases to the state Supreme Court, John Peter Altgeld won two.

April 12, 2008: It is steel grey, wet, and predicted to snow tonight. The deer have eaten all the daffodils in the yard, including the especially beautiful ones with the double centers. The airlines have canceled two thousand flights for safety checks. It is a union maneuver. No one will be leaving Chicago.

The faculty whine and complain. Don't they realize they are the last cadre of people with secure jobs?

Now that he was a city attorney, John Peter Altgeld could wear store-bought clothes. Later, it was discovered he had uncharacteristically left unpaid a clothing bill in Savannah. A mustache hid his harelip. And he was getting about socially. The local newspaper reported that in July 1874 he made a trip to Saint Louis, through Illinois, and to Chicago, and came back none the worse for wear.

J.P. Altgeld, Esq., was a rising leader in the community, especially during the Granger revolts, named for the educational and social associations for farmers called Granges. When a collapse of a chain of banking institutions resulted in widespread mortgage foreclosures on farms and other commercial failures, the Midwestern farmers banded together and released a cloud of anti-robber-baron, anti-capitalist public outrage, later called the Granger movement. And John Peter Altgeld was in the middle of it.

April 22, 2008: Suddenly, there is green everywhere. Yesterday spring was here. Today, she is playing hide and seek. The old trees stand still, waiting for her mood.

When J.P. Altgeld, Esq., began practicing law he had lived among the good people of Andrew County for four years. At the county Democratic convention, he emerged as the leader. He was a Democrat, called a Bourbon Democrat. Later he was in a bitter confrontation with Grover Cleveland, supposedly the same kind of Democrat.

He ran for office in 1874 on the Granger ticket. Irrespective of what the party was called, he was in the middle of the same national politics that William Darrah Kelley faced in Philadelphia. The economic conditions were dire, and the voters were angry. Politicians should do something. William Darrah Kelley made a political miscalculation in Philadelphia and opposed the national bank. He had to leave Philadelphia for a while.

At John Peter Altgeld's beginning in politics, it was noticed that nobody went to sleep when he talked. He won his first election and became the prosecuting attorney of Andrew County, a rung up from the city attorney of Savannah. His future in politics, however, was not in Savannah or Andrew County.

J.P. Altgeld, Esq., saw this Granger fever transform into the People's Party, as banks shuttered their doors and foreclosures rolled across the country. These conditions of rolling financial and economic collapse were seen again after the closing of the World's Fair in Chicago in 1893, when John Peter Altgeld was governor of Illinois. He did the best he could with it.

The Panic of 1893 was a true and severe financial panic lasting from May to November, with a run on currency, banks closing, and businesses and manufacturers unable to open because they had no cash to pay workers or buy their materials. The panic included precipitous declines in the stock market, the failure of Wall Street brokerage houses, and the collapse of 158 national banks in 1893, mostly in the South and West of the country.

The panic started in New York and spread, with Chicago as the second trade and financial center immediately feeling the impact. For the first time in July 1893 Chicago banks approved the issuance of clearinghouse loan certificates, foreshadowing their eventual suspension of any cash payments. This meant they gave depositors promises to pay, rather than currency. The Panic of 1893 was followed by an economic depression in employment and prices which lasted until 1897, when John Peter Altgeld was voted out of the governor's office.

The financial markets in Chicago in 1893 were places where people traded stocks or commercial paper, and these were thriving markets:

> *Bucket Shop is a term applied to places outside the stock exchange and Board of Trade, where stock gambling is carried on in a small way, by the aid of the quotations furnished by the instruments of the Gold and Stock Telegraph Company. This is gambling pure and simple, since not a share of stock changes hands, a formality carefully preserved in the regular exchanges, although it is generally understood to be simply "whipping H.S.M. around the stump." A large blackboard is erected on a wall of the bucket shop, and on this board are displayed figures of the latest quotations of all the principal stocks and provisions. Two young men are constantly engaged in changing these figures in obedience to the mandate of a third, who sits at the instrument and announces the fluctuations. On a row of benches and chairs in front of the board sits a crowd of men and boys watching with all the gambler's eagerness the changing quotations. At an office at the end of the room stock privileges are sold, as small a sum as $5 being accepted. When a stock rises or falls enough to wipe out the margin paid, the account is closed. On the other hand, the speculator presents his privilege and collects his money and profit, less a small percentage for the brokerage. The habitués of these rooms are broken down stock brokers and speculators and young men and boys. Many once wealthy men, ruined by stock gambling, may be seen, seedily dressed, hurrying about these places, unable to resist the fascination of the street, and many boys are lured on to ruin by venturing their employers' money.*
>
> *Moran's Dictionary of Chicago*

The financial panic was aggravated in Chicago that summer by the closing of the World's Columbian Exposition, which left unemployed all those itinerant day workers and crafts people who worked at the fair. Businesses and exchanges failed, and several major railroads, with Chicago as their transportation hub, went into receivership. Control of an unprecedented amount of mileage was handed over to the state and federal courts in bankruptcy. During the year ending in June 1894, over 125 railroads went into receivership.

Florence Kelley explained how these bankruptcies functioned in the legal system in a letter from Chicago dated September 16, 1894:

> . . . *The following account will illustrate the matter: ninety-three bankrupt railroad companies are now managed by receivers who have been appointed by judges. These receivers are seen as representatives of the court that appointed them. In many cases the former president of the railway company holds the position, in many others it is a former judge. For example, a judge gave up his seat on the Supreme court of Pennsylvania to take the position of receiver at a bankrupt railway company, with a yearly income of $50,000.*
>
> *It can also happen that a judge who is one of the shareholders of a railroad company has to appoint a receiver. Then if the workers quarrel because of wage cuts, the receiver comes to the judge—who is a shareholder and who has appointed him—to ask for an order prohibiting the workers from striking. Even if a judge owns no stock in the railway company, in a large number of states he might have once worked as a lawyer for the company in question and may hope to be rehired if he is not re-elected. If a judge has issued an injunction, the workers are breaking the law if they insist on striking.*

Baring Brothers in London had prior to the panic of 1893 invested heavily in Argentina and defaulted on liabilities of twenty-one million pounds sterling. Barings was supported by the Bank of England, which borrowed from the Bank of France and the Imperial Bank of Russia to support its losses. And so eventually the house of cards of mutually dependent international interlocking institutional lines of credit collapsed. Some of those in control of financial instruments and deposits made a quick profit, took the money and let the institutions fall around them. Barings survived the nineteenth-century crisis, and subsequent financial panics, only to fail a hundred years later under very similar circumstances.

Whether because of the intolerance of the local community for his religious beliefs or his former military affiliation, or his search for new vistas, or just because his feet were restless, at age twenty-seven in 1875, four years after the Great Fire, John Peter Altgeld got on the train to Chicago with a hundred dollars in his pocket. The story is told that he shared a railroad car with a stranger, a successful businessman in Chicago, who at the end of the train ride offered him free office space for a short time to start his practice. In seventeen years he would be governor and have earned the reputation of being one of the finest lawyers in Chicago.

When he was governor, he didn't forget he was a lawyer first, and somewhere along the way he learned to write. This is his analysis of Judge Gary's work in the Haymarket trial from the 1893 pardon message:

The mass of matter contained in the record and quoted at length in the judge's [later] magazine article, showing the use of seditious and incendiary language, amounts to but little when its source is considered. The two papers in which articles appeared . . . were obscure little sheets, having scarcely any circulation, and the articles themselves were written at times of great public excitement. . . . The apparently seditious utterances were such as are always heard when men imagine they have been wronged, or are excited or partially intoxicated; and the talk of a gigantic anarchist conspiracy is not believed by the then chief of police, as will be shown hereafter, and it is not entitled to serious notice, in view of the fact that, while Chicago had nearly a million inhabitants, the meetings held on the lake front on Sundays during the summer, by these agitators, rarely had fifty people present, and most of these went from mere curiosity, while the meetings held in-doors during the winter were still smaller.

Like Florence Kelley, John Peter Altgeld came to Chicago for a new life, and he left another life. Like Florence Kelley, by the time he got to Chicago John Peter Altgeld was still young, but no neophyte and not naive. He was seasoned and ready for the fray.

Chicago was a destination, a happening, a swirl of people and projects, a city of 400,000 when John Peter Altgeld, not yet thirty, arrived. Its politics were a circus, a game, a hubbub, a knock-down, drag-out fight for money, power, position, respect, only for the thick-skinned and the strong. John Peter Altgeld's nearly penniless tramp across the country—working where he could, where they would have him, escaping when they wanted to lock him up, finding shelter and support where he could, finding teachers and confidence—was excellent preparation for the politics of Illinois and Chicago in the last decade of the nineteenth century.

With a paraphrase of the tale of the Red Hen, the *Chicago Tribune* summed up the political situation:

"Who will clean our streets," asks the neat little housewife.

"I won't," says the Mayor;

"I won't," says the Council;

"I won't," says the Commissioner of Public Works;

"I won't," says the contractor with his gang of intelligent Italians;

"I won't," says the Inspector, who keeps tab on the intelligent Italian vote.

"Then I'll do it myself," says the tidy little housewife.

If there was anything that Chicago had in the 1870s it was work, politics, and workers. Mostly it had work, and capitalists and labor organizations and newspapers, and political parties that held meetings where it could all be talked about, written about, shouted about, or made the subject of law.

It bore some resemblance to the Zurich where Florence Kelley and Lazare Wischnewetzky went to prepare themselves for the revolution, except there was no work for the exiles there, so they had to leave. It bore some resemblance to William Darrah Kelley's prewar Philadelphia.

Bismarck said: "I wish I could go to America if only to see Chicago." His countrymen, including many he exiled for being socialists, came instead.

Everyone came to Chicago expecting something, wanting something. Many came for the revolution. Sometimes people arrived and thought they were coming to a different city. And when they came, fleeing where they came from, they had to figure out how to survive:

All large cities and some small ones in these days have cheap lodging houses in which men may secure a night's lodging at a cost of from ten to twenty-five cents. With the exception of Greater New York, the city of Chicago has a greater number of such houses and a larger floating transient population that any other city in the United States. The reasons for this are many. Situation in the heart of the Mississippi Valley at the foot of Lake Michigan it attracts to itself during a part of the year thousands of harvest hands from the Northwest, deck hands from the lake boats, railway construction laborers, men from the lumber camps of the North, and men from all over the Central West who are employed in seasonal trades of many sorts.

In normal times men of this class who come to Chicago need not long remain unemployed if they wish work. One season trade may soon by fitted into another. The period between the closing of navigation in the autumn and the beginning of work in the lumber camps is not long. In February the ice-cutting season opens and this furnishes employment to thousands of men at a time of year when in many other cities work for unskilled laborers is especially scarce. The growth of Chicago is so rapid and constant that public works and private building practically never cease. One form of work resulting from this growth is what is designated as "wrecking." Old buildings, or sometimes comparatively new and good ones, are torn down to make way for newer and larger structures. The amount of such work in Chicago is considerable and gives employment to large numbers of men. During the course of the ordinary winter there are numerous heavy snowfalls, and the removal of snow from the downtown streets affords temporary employment for hundreds.

One Thousand Homeless Men: A Study of Original Records, by Alice Willard Solenberger

John Peter Altgeld later took his hundred dollars and rented an office in one of the finest buildings in Chicago, the Reaper Block. He partitioned off a corner of his office where he could sleep because he couldn't afford a separate place to live. It was still the 1870s depression, and the young lawyer was neither attractive, rich, prepossessing, nor graceful. Nor did he know anyone. One of his precepts was: "Never ask another lawyer what the law is on any subject. Look it up yourself, it will make you more self-reliant and a better lawyer in the end." Soon he would share an office with other Chicago lawyers who are also remembered for their writings: Edgar Lee Masters and Clarence Darrow.

John Peter Altgeld had no college or university degree. He had to look up all the Latin words and technical terms in the legal dictionary, but his diligence and seriousness impressed even the grizzled old Anglo-Saxon lawyers who controlled the practice of law, once they got past his accent. His first client he snagged by inviting her to come and sit in his office while she was waiting for another lawyer. Then some miscellaneous cases: a dog bite, a divorce, a collection of fees due, and by 1877, he was making a living as a lawyer/solicitor, the law at the time still maintaining the British distinction between law and chancery.

When he made money, he sent some to his father to pay down that persistent mortgage on the farm. Now that he had some money, he was getting about socially and liked to dance, although he was apparently not very good at it. John Peter Altgeld was in Newport, Rhode Island, seeing how the rich lived when the 1877 railroad strike, called the Great Strike of 1877, a precursor to the Pullman strike, shut down the entire Baltimore and Ohio Railroad line and all of Chicago in July.

Chaos followed the strike from Baltimore to Philadelphia, to New York and then to Chicago, where one of the fiercest pitched battles between police and strikers took place at a standoff on the Halsted Street Bridge, as the strikers, mostly boys, went from factory to plant to saloon closing them down one by one, hailing those inside to join the march. And so this boy said to be no older than twelve led the strikers and their followers on to the street until he was dropped by a policeman's bullet on the Halsted Street Bridge. No one who was in Chicago for those days forgot them. Some said it was not the workers who spread the violence but hirelings, Pinkerton men, newly commissioned soldiers and police officers—thugs and goons of the railroads and the business interests, it was said, who were very well-organized and committed to breaking the strike, and to breaking heads.

In his pardon message for the anarchists in June 1893, Altgeld said:

For a number of years prior to the Haymarket affair there had been labor troubles, and in several cases a number of laboring people, guilty of no offense, had been shot down in cold blood by Pinkerton men, and none of the murderers were brought to justice.

The evidence taken at coroner's inquests, and presented here shows that in at least two cases men were fired on and killed when they were running away, and there was consequently no occasion to shoot, yet nobody was punished; that in Chicago there had been a number of strikes in which some of the police not only took sides against the men, but without any authority of law invaded and broke up peaceable meetings, and in scores of cases brutally clubbed people who were guilty of no offense whatever.

The city and the economy had not recovered from the depression and financial panic of the 1870s when Altgeld arrived in 1875, although there were always people who made money, and some made a lot of money in bad times, when banks closed and markets were uncontrolled. The economic power of the country was shifting by geography, by trade, so it became a question of who could adapt, who could survive, who could see what was coming. As one commentator put it:

Every decade after the civil war ended, the number of farms in the South increased, and every decade per capita income [in the South] *fell relative to the national average. In contrast, agriculture in both the "old" and the "new" Midwest was thriving in partnerships with their productivity. For the 1870s onward, both materially and morally, they* [farmers in the Midwest] *were becoming an integral part of the new industrial economy.*

In 1877 at the time of the Great Strike, the property owners and many others headed out of town. The dead bodies of police and strikers were left in the street, and property burned. Soon a regiment of federal troops was in the city to control the "ragged wretches," as they were called, "from the Commune." Marshall Field organized a Citizens' Association to fight communism, and that committee would play an important role in Haymarket and in Pullman. This was probably as close as America came to the revolution foretold by the exiles in Zurich.

William Pinkerton founded a highly profitable business by hiring out strikebreakers and private guards. The police had their ranks swelled by volunteers who were turned into soldiers, in uniform, drilling with their weapons in street maneuvers alongside the police. In 1878 Marshall Field's Citizens' Association presented the city with a gift, a Gatling quick firing gun, which could sweep a street from side to side and mow down a thousand men in a few seconds. This was considered particularly useful in instances of civil disorder. Florence Kelley's brother William Jr. was drilling with the Pennsylvania militia and learning how to shoot down other strikers, in a similar call to action.

Solenberger's 1911 report on homelessness continues:

The homeless man has probably figured as a member of human society since its beginning. . . . The modern tramp also had his prototype in earlier centuries. In fact, in the nomadic days of the race whole nations took to tramping. . . . Previous to the Civil War, the word "tramp" did not appear upon the statute books of any state in the Union. Today nearly all recognize his existence and endeavor to cope with the problem he presents. . . . But for the purpose of this study the term will be used to designate those men of the homeless class who live in cheap lodging houses in the congested part of any large city; and the particular thousand chosen for this study were applicants at the Chicago Bureau of Charities for some form of assistance during the years 1900 to 1903 inclusive. By no means were all of these men really homeless. . . .

On either side of Clark and State Streets on the South Side; on Canal, Desplaines, and Madison Streets on the West Side, and on lower Clark and Wells Streets on the North Side, there are rows of cheap lodging houses. For the man who lacks even the small amount required for admission to these, the Municipal Lodging House doors are always open, and every man who comes to Chicago honestly seeking work knows, or soon finds out, that he will have little difficulty in securing food and shelter without the need of begging for them in the interval before he finds employment. The Municipal Lodging House of Chicago has probably done more extensive work than any other institution of its kind in the country in finding positions for men who apply for lodging. Altogether, no city in the United States offers more favorable opportunities for winter employment for the unskilled, or cheaper food and shelter than does Chicago. It is not strange, therefore, that the city attracts unemployed labor from all over the country.

Among tramps and vagrants also Chicago is a favorite rallying place. It is the greatest railway center in the country; trains from all points of the compass hourly pull into its freight and passenger stations and bring their quota of homeless men. Many of these make it their headquarters for the greater part of the year. The vagrancy laws are as a rule rather laxly enforced and begging is a safe as well as a lucrative business. And here, as in most other large cities, politicians are likely at election times to add to the comfort and security of a floating population whose votes may usually be counted upon in return for small favors. In this as in other cities, too, there are mingling with the less harmful tramps the more dangerous egg men and petty criminals, numbers of whom find it comparatively easy to hide themselves among the homeless throngs in the lodging houses.

In 1877 John Peter Altgeld went home on a family visit, and found his old sweetheart, Emma Ford, who had been sent away to study music at Oberlin and then had returned home, still unmarried. Her father—who had, probably with some justification, strongly objected to Young Pete's courtship—was dead. Later all who knew them commented upon how happy this long union was, although no children were born to the couple. When he predeceased her, she no longer wanted to live.

Mrs. Altgeld, the former Emma Ford, cherished by her father, was tall and handsome, wore clothes beautifully, and was unusually cultured. She could paint, appreciated music, and like her husband was a reader and a writer—the author of more than one novel, including a readable romance called *Sarah's Choice*, or *The Nortons*, a story about the ill-fated romance of a young girl and life on a nineteenth-century farm. She wrote other novels, but the energetic searches of the librarians here find no titles or copies. "Softening" was how others described Emma's effect upon John Peter Altgeld. After their marriage she did her own housework and wondered how they survived because she did not know how to cook.

Meanwhile, the now-busy lawyer John Peter Altgeld had discovered Chicago real estate, and with the help of luck, the changing times, the upswing in the economy, the advice of a few well-connected friends, and his own bold instincts, he was soon what was called well-to-do—surprising especially for a socialist or someone whom some would later call an anarchist. His career bore many similarities to that of William Darrah Kelley, in that he started with nothing and briefly became wealthy and was mostly an underpaid, dedicated public servant, and died with little.

The law was a hardscrabble business for an independent young man with no inherited money or family connections, a man who wasn't going to be bought or keep his unpopular political opinions to himself. But, Altgeld said, at least you could earn a living seated in a chair instead of breaking your back pulling rocks from a stubborn field. A smart lawyer, with a bit of luck and with some other outside factors on his side, such as a willingness to work hard, could make his way.

Eventually the young lawyer had a patron, William C. Goudy, the first president of the Chicago Bar Association, a man upon whose word legislation was killed and judges nominated and elected and state Supreme Court justices appointed. The young lawyer who a few years earlier was a penniless tramp with no shoes was on his way. That real estate would become part of his downfall, but first there was a ride with the money.

John Peter Altgeld, the young lawyer, now married and thirty-two, was entering into real estate deals such as paying $200,000 for 785 acres in Lake View, putting down $30,000, with notes and mortgages for the rest. At one point he owned most of the lots in the valuable Lake View section. Early in the 1880s, he bought lots in the Loop and put up an expensive seven-story office building on Market Street off Jackson. It proved to be an albatross. His over-leveraged investment in this large and unrented office building, the Unity building, was one part of the complicated story of his political downfall when he was governor. He became burdened with debts, which played to the hands of his political enemies.

As in the movement toward war, there came to be a time in Chicago in the early 1890s when everyone seemed to agree that reform of the working and living conditions in the tenements and sweatshops in the Nineteenth Ward was necessary now, without further delay, that these conditions were inconsistent with civilized behavior. Perhaps it was the civic pride from the World's Columbian Exposition, the Great Fair, when twenty-seven million visitors came and marveled at the beauty of Chicago. Just how or when such a coalescence of public sentiment jells and a change becomes inevitable is always shrouded in mystery. The conditions of extreme deprivation found intolerable in the 1890s had long existed, the atrocities and exploitation of children and women were long known and tolerated. But a turning point had been reached. And so there was a groundswell of activity, a rush of shame, a surge in interest, and outrageous conditions known for years were suddenly not to be tolerated.

February 5, 1999, Chicago Tribune: "Porter Freed From Prison."

Anthony Porter, who came within days of being executed by lethal injection last September, walked out of jail Friday after spending nearly 17 years in prison for a double slaying another man now says he committed.

"It feels marvelous to be outside," Porter said after being released about 1 p.m. "I'm free."

Just as Florence Kelley appeared on the scene, and partly but not solely because of her leadership, and then in her official position as state factory inspector, doing something about these conditions was suddenly imperative, and possible in 1892. The economic conditions were a factor, but not the sole explanation. As a historian of the period described it:

Chicago's mighty boom—continuous since the 1840's, with but a pause during the depressed 1890's—spiraled upward until 1929. To the million inhabitants in 1890 another 600,000 were added by 1900, another 500,000 by 1910, and yet another 1,200,000 by 1930, when the total finally leveled off at 3,400,000. Just behind Berlin and ahead of Paris, Chicago was the fourth city in size in the world and second in wealth only to New York. The manufacturing and transportation base of the city's economy continued to flourish. Chicago's banking, commerce, and services (like law, medicine, education, entertainment) dominated the entire Midwest, leaving Saint Louis and Detroit far behind. . . . Despite the heavy influx of unskilled immigrants, the city's occupational force was steadily upgraded.

During the 1892 election John Peter Altgeld was a tireless campaigner. As reported in the unsympathetic *Inter Ocean*, in August 1892, "Judge Altgeld has visited more families, kissed more babies, inspected more dairies and help sit more hens than any man before who wanted to be Governor." Sitting a hen, a lost art, consists of making sure the hen is sitting centered on all of her eggs so that they will all hatch, and making sure that the hen is comfortable in the nest. This practice predates electric incubation. In the political context it presumably means: making sure that everything is going along all right, that the voters are ready to vote, and all details are appropriately addressed so that when the election comes it comes out as expected. As one of his biographers reported:

He was indefatigable. Temperature of ninety-six degrees in the shade found him driving in a horse and buggy over dusty roads to make a meeting in some hamlet of less than a thousand population. . . . He made a point especially of spending considerable time in communities where Germans predominated, and talked German to the men and their Frauen. . . . "To the Germans, the privilege of talking in their native tongue to a man who is the candidate for the highest office in the state is so rare that they never tire of talking about it and marveling at it."

Henry Demarest Lloyd worked for Altgeld's election in 1892. In this campaign John Peter Altgeld was careful not to take too liberal or too pro-labor an approach. His personal spending on the campaign was estimated to be about $100,000—which meant all of his personal wealth—and it was said that he gave up all of his property which was not tied up in the Unity building.

Altgeld was the first foreign-born and the first Chicago resident to be elected governor of Illinois. He received the returns at his home on Frederick Street with his wife.

March 17, 1999, Chicago Tribune: "Kokoraleis' Execution Carried Out: Torn Ryan Agonizes, But Denies Clemency."

Convicted killer Andrew Kokoraleis was put to death by lethal injection at 12:30 a.m. Wednesday, just hours after Gov. George Ryan denied requests for clemency.

The execution followed a day of legal maneuvers that ultimately left the decision to proceed in the hands of Ryan, a longtime supporter of capital punishment who nevertheless agonized for days over the issue.

"I must admit that it is very difficult to hold in your hands the life of any person, even a person who, in the eyes of the many, has acted so horrendously as to have forfeited any right to any consideration of mercy," Ryan said in a statement late Tuesday.

"I have struggled with this issue of the death penalty and still feel that some crimes are so horrendous and so heinous that society has a right to demand the ultimate penalty."

John Peter Altgeld was elected governor in November 1892. The Illinois legislature opened its thirty-eighth session on January 4, 1893. It was described as one of the most corrupt legislatures in the history of Illinois. The new Illinois General Assembly immediately appointed a Joint Special Committee of the Senate and House of Representatives to make their own survey and investigation of the sweatshops. Florence Kelley and Mary E. Kenney spearheaded the investigation and wrote the report.

Later, Florence Kelley wrote to a friend that the committee had been formed as a sop to labor and an excuse for a junket to Chicago for rural legislators. However, the fervor which the two women, and their colleagues, including Abraham Bisno, brought to the task turned it into something else. They personally escorted the legislators to the worst sweatshops and tenements in the Nineteenth Ward, visits irksome to the lawmakers. One legislator refused to enter the tenements, with their vermin and diseases, saying he had young children at home. He was not wrong.

The report, when submitted to the legislature, was so compendious, so compelling and readable, so surprising in its seriousness that it was followed directly by the introduction of legislation limiting the hours of work for women, prohibiting certain kinds of child labor, and establishing a system for factory inspection. In short the report and the investigation which preceded it led, along with a political push across the spectrum of its supporters, to the passage of the Factory and Workshop Inspection Law in the spring of 1893.

The passage of path-breaking law is always a matter of circumstance, chance, and advocacy.

Congressman William Darrah Kelley wrote to his wife, Caroline Bonsall Kelley, on January 31, 1865, as he watched the Congress voting to pass the Thirteenth Amendment:

We are on the eve of voting on the most important question submitted to the House in more than half a century: the proposed amendment to the constitution. The division is so close that each side claims a majority of one or two, and many earnest conferences are taking place on the floor. . . . Warden of Kentucky is on the floor holding forth in much simplified language a last plea from the dying institution of American slavery. Poor fellow he honestly believes that he is defending the constitution. The Supreme Court has adjourned. Chief Justice Chase and his colleagues on the floor. Chatting with them are many leading Senators.

The statute drafted by Florence Kelley and others at Hull-House in the winter of 1893 was simple. It had eight sections and said that children under fourteen could not be employed in sweatshops, that women could not work in factories or tenements for more than eight hours within twenty-four hours. It created the Office of the Factory Inspector and created the position of factory inspector and ten deputy inspectors (of whom five must be women), assigned salaries, appropriated the money to pay them, and gave the inspectors the power and the duty to report to the governor and to prosecute for violations of the act to a magistrate or any court of competent jurisdiction.

All aspects of this law and its implementation were proactive and would be challenged by Levy Mayer and the Illinois Manufacturers' Association as unconstitutional.

The inspectors interpreted this statute as authorizing them to require affidavits signed by a physician as to the health and ages of the workers, and that employers post the hours of work at the factory or tenement. The factory inspectors wrote the regulations saying what was needed. They knew their time in power would be short.

All the new law did in 1893 was to provide the power to inspect working conditions. The inspectors added to their arsenal the power to confiscate and destroy garments, set sanitation standards, require owners of sweatshops to furnish on demand a list of the names and addresses of contractors and workers, set up health and sanitary standards, and—and what they did with this was critical—subject the children in the factories to a medical examination. Then they put the underage children in school. The initial power was no more than the power to investigate, to lay out the facts. As Florence Kelley herself noted:

> There is no hope of a considerable reduction in the number of children employed in sweat-shops under the present provisions of the statute. The sweaters are so irresponsible, so shifting and so numerous, that no small body of inspectors can adequately follow them up, with parents and employees conniving to evade and violate the law, and the board of education declining to enforce the compulsory education law by prosecutions.

> Under the conditions of tenement house manufacture, sweaters are constrained to employ the cheapest possible labor, and their settled policy is to hire children and take the risks. Nothing less than the abolition of tenement house manufacture will, in the opinion of the inspectors, entirely abolish the employment of children in sweat-shops.

Later Florence Kelley would say in the *Fourth Annual Report* in 1896 that "the law didn't, couldn't do enough."

August 20, 2001: The traveling. Sometimes I think it is just so we will think that we are doing something because we are packing for a trip, or coming back from another trip, or planning yet another trip. The dinners, the parties, the people, the parade of people and the hand shaking. It must add up to something or we wouldn't do it. I have to believe that it serves a purpose for the university, does someone some good. We aren't running for office, but it often seems as if we are. Sometimes I get tired on my feet, and tired in the face of smiling, but mostly I believe in the value of the institution, of education. A colleague says: If you have to stand in a receiving line, put your shoes in the freezer for an hour first.

The Factory Inspection Law wasn't extreme in terms of doctrine or legislative initiative. The first factory inspection law had been passed in Massachusetts in 1866. Between 1885 and 1889 other states followed, including New York and Pennsylvania in the late 1880s. What was revolutionary was that someone was set on getting something done.

The Illinois Factory and Workshop Inspection Law was a classic of progressive thinking. It was framed in terms of the public health: the tenements and crowded workshops were to be inspected because they were a danger to the public health. The health of women required special protection. This was the tenet, which caused a deep division in the lobbying for women. Did women need special laws? The emphasis upon cleanliness, the absence of legal terminology, the fact that the law was comprehensible to anyone, were all a giveaway that it had been drafted by women.

Beginning with the magic words of authority, Section 1 of the Factory Inspection Law said:

Be it enacted by the People of the State of Illinois . . . That no room or rooms, apartment or apartments in any tenement or dwelling house . . . shall be used for the manufactures . . . of coats, vests . . . cloaks, shirts . . . except by the immediate members of the family living therein. Every such workshop shall be kept in a cleanly state . . . and each of said articles . . . shall be subject to inspection and examination . . . for the purpose of ascertaining whether said articles . . . are in a cleanly condition and free from vermin and any matter of an infectious and contagious nature.

The statute was structured to be enforced by the Board of Health of the city or state and by the factory inspector and deputy factory inspectors. In the end it was the factory inspectors themselves, not the Board of Health inspectors, who did the inspecting and reporting. Florence Kelley and her allies accused the city health inspectors of being incompetent as well as in dereliction of duty, and after initially cooperating with them as allies, the Hull-House women tried to get the director of the Board of Health removed. They were flamboyant in their allegations of his dereliction of duty, but unsuccessful in getting him fired. The job was left to them. Without the designated factory inspectors there would be no enforcement of the health regulations. They did what they could.

The other provisions of the statute were equally clear:

No child under fourteen years of age shall be employed in any manufacturing establishment, factory or workshop within this State [sec. 4]. . . .

No female shall be employed in any factory or workshop more than eight hours in any one day or forty eight hours in any one week. [sec. 5]

The remainder of the statute appropriated the money to pay the inspectors and gave them the power and the duty to report to the governor and to prosecute.

A violation of the statute was a misdemeanor, and the penalty was a fine. Basically there were no serious criminal penalties, although some of the cases were designated criminal. The cases were brought before a justice of the peace, most coming before Justice of the Peace George Kersten, later the longtime criminal assignment judge who said he had tried a thousand cases during his career. His name comes up repeatedly in the homicide files.

The National Labor Union had called for equal pay for women in 1869 and 1870. The Chicago City Council in 1889-91 had appointed five female factory inspectors, banned child labor for children under fourteen, and limited the hours that women and older children could work to eight. This city legislation was potentially stronger than the Factory Inspection Law, although limited to the city jurisdiction.

It was the threat of enforcement under the Factory Inspection Law which the factory owners and the newly formed Illinois Manufacturers' Association feared. A law on the books which was never enforced, and where there was no money and no prospect of it being enforced, was no threat. The statute books are filled with such laws. A law by itself is nothing but words. No one thought the City Council would enforce its ordinances or enforce its mandatory school attendance law, and they were right.

October 20, 2009: O'Hare again, back at O'Hare. We spend too much time here. Too much time waiting for a plane to go. Suddenly the banners, the signs, the flags: Chicago 2016, which were everywhere, all gone, not a trace or a sign of them. As if it never happened, as if the whole city had not been drunk on the prospect of having the Olympics in Chicago.

Many in the Nineteenth Ward preferred their children and certainly their women to be working rather than going to school or learning English in classes at Hull-House. Literacy training, which took the women in the sweatshops away from earning money with piecework, was not popular. The idea that if women were educated they would raise questions about their circumstances was also not a new idea nor confined to the 1890s tenements. The unapologetic political activism of the women of Hull-House was offensive to many. Not all the working women in Chicago were in the tenements, and many of these women also did not want a new law. As one of the contemporaneous scholars noted:

There are over one hundred thousand self-supporting women in Chicago. Many more than half of these belong to the class known as "working girls." The great part of them live at home, else many would not live on the wages they receive. . . .

It is estimated that three out of every forty Chicago working girls have someone depending on them. For example, there is a girl in a paper-box factory on Michigan Av-

enue who, working by the piece, is able to make from five to seven dollars per week. She supports a sick mother, an aged father, and a worthless brother who works but a small part of the time. She has worked for three years at this factory, which employs two hundred and fifty girls, many of them under school age. They work from half-past seven o'clock in the morning until six in the evening, with half an hour lunch time. Wages are from two and a half dollars to seven dollars per week. Forewomen receive nine and ten dollars per week. There are girls here who have worked six and seven years without other vacation than Thanksgiving Day, Fourth of July, and the usual holidays.

Ritchie & Company, the first named party in the case challenging the Factory and Workshop Inspection Law, was one of the largest employers of these women, a paper box manufacturer.

Hull-House itself was a demonstration of its radical intentions, with its offerings of free food, shelter, clean water, playgrounds, public baths, literacy classes, and child care services. The women of Hull-House were very clear about what they saw and what they thought needed fixing.

This, from the introduction to *Hull-House Maps and Papers*:

The smart frontage is a mere screen, not only for the individual houses, but for the street as a whole. Rear tenements and alleys form the core of the district, and it is there that the densest crowds of the most wretched and destitute congregate. Little idea can be given of the filthy and rotten tenements, the dingy courts and tumble-down sheds, the foul stables and dilapidated outhouses, the broken sewer-pipes, the piles of garbage fairly alive with diseased odors, and of the numbers of children filling every nook, working and playing in every room, eating and sleeping in every window-sill, pouring in and out of every door, and seemingly literally to pave every scrap of "yard." In one block the writer numbered over seventy-five children in the open street; but the effort proved futile when she tried to keep the count of little people surging in and out of passage-ways, and up and down outside staircases, like a veritable stream of life. . . .

It is customary for the lower floor of the rear houses to be used as a stable and outhouse, while the upper rooms serve entire families as a place for eating, sleeping, being born and dying. Where there are alleys the refuse and manure are sometimes removed; where there are none, it would seem they accumulate undisturbed. In front of each house stand garbage-receivers,—wooden boxes repulsive to every sense, even when as clear as their office will permit, shocking to both mind and instinct when rotten, overfilled, and broken, as they often are. Fruit-stands help fill up the sordid streets, and ice-cream carts drive a thriving trade. One hears little English spoken, and the faces and manners met with are very foreign. People are noticeably undersized and unhealthy, as well to the average observer as to the trained eye of the physician. Especially do the many workers in the tailoring-trades look dwarfed and ill-fed; they walk with a peculiar stooping gait, and their narrow chests and cramped hands are unmistakable evidence of their calling. Tuberculosis prevails, especially in diseases of the lungs and intestine, and deformity is not unusual. The mortality among children is great, and many babies look starved and wan.

September 1, 2001: The heat has broken, and it is raining. The windows open, the smell of the garden fresh, exhilarating. The sky a changing velvet tapestry of blue and white. Across the sky the occasional silver slash of a plane, seeming to crawl across the expanse of blue. Tomorrow predicted to be the same.

Garbage collection was the perfect cause for Hull-House. Uncollected garbage had an impact every day upon health, welfare, and aesthetics, and was in theory a part of expected city services, if there were any services actually delivered to the residents of this part of the city. It had an effect upon the smells, the quality of the air people breathed day in and day out, and the allowed persistent presence of rats and vermin which were disease carriers in the tenements. It was an issue with little ideological baggage: who could be against garbage being picked up? And it was another example of outright fraud on the part of the City Council.

September 13, 2001: A fine day, the sky is blue, the sun is bright. Silence. And not a plane in the sky. Our world is altered forever.

After a few months in Chicago, Florence Kelley's soft-voiced but electric style of public speaking, as well as her magnetic personality and her demonstrated commitment, made her prominent among the advocates for the cause whose day had come. Soon she was featured as the only woman on the podium with other longtime advocates for the causes which she had elsewhere come to identify as her own.

It was said that those who heard her speak did not forget her. One young woman wrote a master's thesis about Florence Kelley's rhetorical style and reported that she heard Florence Kelley speak once and immediately changed the direction of her studies and her life.

The initial research on the sweating system by Florence Kelley was published as the Illinois Labor Statistics Bureau's *Seventh Annual Report*, a report not listed under her byline. This report is a foreshadowing of the annual factory inspection reports. The spine of these reports was the same as that for her research on child labor laws at the Library of Congress as a Cornell undergraduate. The purpose was to bring the facts forward and present them in a context with law. Henry Demarest Lloyd's method was the same. The newspapers were critical allies. With the emergence of the outrageous facts would come the institutional alliances and the political will, at the national and state level, and the solidification of the opposition. Before Florence Kelley's bedraggled arrival in Chicago, more than a few civic-minded women and men had already been pressuring the City Council to do something about the conditions in the tenements, especially with regard to child labor. And soon Levy Mayer would organize the opposition.

March 22, 2001: Fog, rain, cold. Snow predicted. Living in Chicago is like living in Dickens's London. The fog of Bleak House, the fog of the law.

The women's organizations that confronted the City Council and other public agencies were not immune to the usual kinds of political infighting and jealousies. The disputes over the Women's Bureau of the Great Fair resulted in Jane Addams and Florence Kelley and others resigning from the board because of their disagreements over the way labor and slavery were portrayed in the Women's Building at the fair. In the decade that Florence Kelley lived at Hull-House, however, an unusual level of cooperation was maintained among astonishingly varied groups. For the factory legislation to pass, a broad spectrum of support was required, and a large lobbying effort.

Like Florence Kelley, Henry Demarest Lloyd was a person of action. Nine years separated them, but their methods of persuasion were similar, as were their persistence and their uncanny ability to turn facts into advocacy, and then into political action. They were close friends, confidants, co-conspirators in reform, and allies. Henry Demarest Lloyd considered standing for an elective office, but never did. However, he frequently argued before courts and public officials, agencies, and the US Congress, and the line drawn between politics, legal representation, and advocacy was often blurred. Florence Kelley never ran for an elected government position.

Putting an eight-hour limit for women workers was a throwing down of the gauntlet to business and manufacturers, especially when put on the back of legislation for factory inspections. Any regulation of conditions in the factories was anathema to business. Florence Kelley, at least, considered the eight-hour provision for women to be a prelude to an eight-hour provision for all workers.

Without the energy and brilliant organizational talents of Levy Mayer, the business and manufacturing community might not have been able to mount a credible, systematic, whole-scale constitutional challenge to the Factory Inspection Law. The threat of anarchy, and the invocation of an organized Haymarket and Pullman, was their strongest rhetorical weapon.

September 13, 2013: The specter of a teachers strike looms. It will happen. The Chicago Public Schools will close. The weather fine, the mood in the city, dark, gloomy, watchful.

Nicholas Kelley continues his remembrance of Hull-House:

My acquaintance with Hull House began in 1891, in its second year, when as a small boy of six I came here with my mother and my younger sister and brother. . . . I have always loved the memories of those days and of the men and women who were here then and of the Henry Demarest Lloyds in Winnetka, with whom I spent much of the time when I was not here at Hull House. I look back with pleasure even to the times when we children were boarded out with Mrs. William Russell Carey Wright, the wonderful mother of Frank Lloyd Wright, the architect, and sister of the distinguished Unitarian parson of those days, Jenkin Lloyd Jones. I long have believed that I was blessed with the best bringing-up and educating of anybody that I have known of my time. As I have thought it over recently, I have found that the secret was those eight years here in Chicago at Hull House and with the Lloyds.

Nothing else is like a good settlement, and Hull House in those early days was the settlement of settlements. Every day held an adventure of some kind. Everything was important. It was serious, sometimes deadly serious, but at the same time it was gay and amusing, and it could be hilarious.

Wayside, the country home of Henry Demarest Lloyd and his wife, Jessie Bross Lloyd, has been described as a place full of high spirits, helpfulness, and the joy of people who were living and working together for something they believed in. Regularly, a dozen to thirty people would sit together at table, white and black, genteel and simple, workers and college presidents, seamstresses and carpenters, immigrants and illiterates, all at table, together. In short, it was like Hull-House. As at Hull-House, the economics of the Lloyd household were sometimes precarious.

The Lloyds weren't Quakers, but there were similarities between Wayside and the Quaker atmosphere in which Florence Kelley's mother, Caroline, was raised, and The Elms, William Darrah Kelley's family home in Philadelphia where Florence Kelley was raised. These people valued achievement, both political and intellectual, and sought the company of others with the same sympathies and accomplishment. They were not rich, nor were they poor. If they had little, they had their pride. Staying afloat economically challenged their ingenuity, and they gave generously of their time and resources, especially to the poor.

In September 1872, Horace White, editor of the Chicago Tribune, had offered a job to the recent law graduate Henry Demarest Lloyd, who followed Horace Greeley's advice to young men and went west, although he had a good position at the *New York Evening Post*.

His sister and biographer, Caro, offers this account:

Chicago, recovering from the great fire of October, 1871, was in a chaotic state. Business was starting anew, hammer and trowel were reconstructing a city on the ashes of the old. From the stable and conservative East, where, in university and lecture room, he had studied the principles of political economy, he was now transported to a vast commercial hive, where the practical side of life was uppermost.

The Tribune *was at that time Liberal Republican in bias and ranked as the leading paper of the North-West and one of the best in the country. He entered upon his apprenticeship with misgivings. His first post was as a paragraph writer.*

Jessie Bross was the only surviving daughter of the *Tribune* publisher William Bross. Jessie had refused to go east to college after the fire, instead staying in Chicago and assisting the Relief and Aid Society in distributing food and clothing which had been donated from all over the world, including from places as far away as India. In 1871 she was vice president of the Chicago Philosophical Society. They seemed destined for one another. Henry Demarest Lloyd's biographer continues:

These were days of exaltation, as well, for he was now deeply in love. Among the new friends was Miss Jessie Bross, a prominent figure in the brilliant coterie of Chicago's young people. Her father, William Bross, popularly knows as "Deacon Bross," had come from the East in 1848, when Chicago was little more than a village, and his daughter but four years old. A schoolmaster in youth, he became in Chicago bookseller, publisher, journalist, and, with John L. Scripps, founded the Free Press, afterwards merged in the Tribune. Of the latter paper he was one-quarter owner, and all his life active in its management. From 1865 to 1869 he served as Lieutenant-Governor of Illinois, and during his term, Illinois being the first State in the Union to ratify the Thirteenth Amendment to the Constitution, in February, 1865, Mr. Bross, as presiding officer of the Senate, was the first to sign it. Miss Bross had therefore grown up with the city and seemed indeed to typify its exuberant energy and enthusiasm. She possessed rare social charm and as her father's companion had met and counted as friends men and women of mark. When a girl, for instance, during President Lincoln's administration, she went with her father to call at the White House, but the President was "too busy" to see callers. Walking away, Governor Bross heard his name, and turning, saw the President at an upper window. "Bross, Bross," he was calling, "bring Jessie back; I want to talk to her!" Bereft of home and fortune in a few hours by the great fire, she was obliged to stand in line with her basket waiting to get the provisions meted out to each citizen. But belonging to the privileged few who were quickest to recuperate, she bent her energies to relief work.

Take Saturday, for instance [she wrote], *I started out at nine o'clock, riding till twelve in the open buggy of a kind friend. . . . I visited ten families who needed relief. . . .*

Everything needed to wear and to eat was delivered from our unpretending establishment, from a pound of tea for a poor old woman over seventy, to a pair of mittens for a three year old. After lunch I wrote a petition to the common council which my father and another friend signed, to ask that honourable body for a free license for a poor burnt-out Frenchman to peddle coffee and spices. . . . Besides trying to collect bills for a burnt-out curler and dyer of feathers, which added to the long details already written make up a day's work. . . .

It was while still immersed in this work that she met the young journalist. What he saw through her eyes of these distressing conditions made a profound impression on him.

They married in 1873, a time of another great financial panic and banking crisis. The Bross family funds were frozen in the panic, and the couple were married at the Bross family home as a result, on Christmas 1873. Florence Kelley would have not yet entered Cornell University.

Jessie Bross regarded her husband's causes as the center of his life, and thus the center of her life. His health was delicate. He suffered from insomnia. She made it possible for him to be an effective advocate, by creating a home in which he would work in the morning, enjoy varied company and conversation at the midday meal, and then in the afternoon take a brisk ten-mile walk through the woods nearby, with whoever could keep up with him. Then a quiet family meal in the evening.

May 2008: My husband cannot believe that this financial giant of an institution, one hundred years old, which he was so proud to be part of, is now nothing, its stock is now nothing. The television news shows the workers carrying out their cardboard boxes and hailing a cab. Their stock is worth nothing. Their pensions are gone; their options are under water. This is a big thud and will reverberate throughout the system, and not just in New York.

The workers came to Wayside and their leaders came, and foreign visitors, and government people, and Jessie Bross welcomed them all and created an atmosphere of distinction and peaceful comfort which was said to be unequaled, except perhaps at Hull-House itself, where Henry Demarest Lloyd frequently dined if he was in town. Ellen Gates said that she had never seen a husband and wife who were so mutually worthy of each other.

For example, after six weeks of enjoying the art of the Renaissance and other pleasures Europe had to offer the traveler, in Venice Jessie Bross Lloyd became deathly ill with typhoid. For a month her life was in the balance, and Henry Demarest Lloyd nursed her back to health. When she was well enough to travel, she went home and insisted that Henry join his oldest brother, a playwright, for a tour of the British Isles, which was in a ferment of socialist political activity.

Economic conditions in Britain were bleak; families were starving and men out of work. The factory owners were intransigent and would not raise wages. While the men remained idle, the women and children went to work for lower wages to support the family. The two brothers made their own investigation of the facts and conditions in England and Ireland and then wrote their friends about it. Both Henry Demarest Lloyd and Florence Kelley were indoctrinated by the conditions they saw in Britain, and the indifference of public and private institutions.

On this trip with his brother David D. Lloyd, Lloyd went to the House of Commons, talked to politicians, writers, and editors, attended a huge socialist meeting and heard the legendary and imposing William Morris speak. His reports back were widely distributed and discussed.

February 26, 2013: Truly the lake today is an ever-changing ivory canvas, of ice, of snow, of different kinds and densities of whites, and always about the light and dark.

Jessie Bross Lloyd was a new woman of the 1880s, a friend of Frances Willard, an admirer of Emerson, an heiress and a leader in Chicago society: like Jane Austen's Emma, she was "handsome, clever and rich," beautiful, energetic, and smart. When Florence Kelley arrived Henry Demarest Lloyd had just published a series of passionate articles in the *Tribune*, describing the conditions among the miners locked out by the mine owners in Spring Valley, Illinois, an unrestrained indictment of the indifference and hypocrisy of business, capitalism, the mine owners. His advocacy was to continue in *Wealth Against Commonwealth:*

> *For one hundred years or so our economic theory has been one of industrial government by the self-interest of the individual. Political government by self-interest of the individual we call anarchy. . . . [America has become a society of] mausoleums in which we bury the dead rich, slums in which we bury the living poor. . . . We are very poor. The striking feature of our economic condition is our poverty, not our wealth. We make ourselves rich by appropriating the property of others by methods which lessen the total property of all. . . . Modern wealth more and more resembles the winning of speculators in bread during famine—worse, for to make the money it makes the famine.*

As Florence Kelley and Henry Demarest Lloyd saw it, Americans naively believed that man was naturally good and that the rich and powerful would use their wealth to help mankind. In fact, the rich and powerful Florence Kelley and Henry Demarest Lloyd saw cared little or nothing for helping mankind or the poor and were more radical in their political interventions than the poor, who had little time for utopias or planning. Those with the wealth believed no one, especially no government, should interfere with how they did their business and made their money. Nor should there be any tax or other encumbrance or restrictions upon what they or their companies did with their massive accumulations of capital or how they paid or treated their employees. It was all the operation of impersonal economic forces.

March 2012: The economic divisions of the country are greater than ever. The gap between the rich and the poor is larger than ever, with the wealthiest few accounting for the largest proportion and the largest amount of capital in history. The top three percent of Americans are richer than several important nation states.

America's new wealth, Lloyd said, is too great for the old forms of government. Meaning, the disequilibrium between the accumulation of political power in the hands of the rich was not moderated by the old forms of personal responsibility, or by the old rules of government. Lloyd came to believe charity by the rich would never address the wretched working and living conditions of the poor. And government was too weak and not motivated to change these circumstances. Business had managed to thwart every legal restraint upon businesses proposed to the legislature.

The American Economic Association did not stoop to review Henry Demarest Lloyd's *Wealth Against Commonwealth*, although it was widely read and commented upon in the United States and Britain. A conservative economist subsidized by John D. Rockefeller was hired by Columbia University to attack the book in academic journals, which he did to little effect. When the 1893 depression hit Chicago with a vengeance, there was too much reality to be argued away by economic theorists.

Inherent in the ideology of the free market, and the Darwinian idea that the rich represented the survival of the fittest, was the assumption that the poor, immigrants, and industrial workers were inferior, that they deserved to be at the bottom and were unworthy of the franchise or education. For those who believed in the benign rule of the free hand and free markets, any attempt to improve working conditions for the poor was a conspiracy, probably a foreign conspiracy, a socialist or anarchist conspiracy, and should be suppressed.

September 2009: People reassure themselves that the banking system, the entire capitalist financial system did not collapse. There was not much time for celebrating on January 1, 2009.

The protection of property and making sure those who had the wealth kept it was the bulwark and the foundation of the law, the legal system, and morality. Levy Mayer was outspoken on the subject: the purpose of the law was to provide rules that business could rely upon, and to create and maintain conditions for a predictable and dependable commercial atmosphere. He was the most articulate advocate of this position.

The presidential election of 1896 posed two legendary figures in a debate over a technical aspect of monetary policy, which resulted in an inflamed, confusing rhetoric. Wrapped up in the debate over free trade and protective tariffs, the issue of whether the American dollar should be backed by gold or some combination of gold and silver was the issue with symbolic value.

The most vocal thought they understood it. In fact no one knew what the long-term economic effect of this proposed change to the currency would be. If the US currency was "taken off" the gold standard, or if bimetallism, a currency standard based on both gold and silver, were to be adopted the effect was a matter of speculation. No one had a clear idea of how it would work.

If Christ Came to Chicago was published with a drawing of an angry Christ driving out the money changers on the cover. It sold seventy thousand copies on the day it was published. On the back cover was a map, similar to the maps in *Hull-House Maps and Papers*, showing the names and locations of the more notorious brothels and saloons.

William Stead's book caused such a flurry of discussion and outrage that he hired a hall and spoke about his investigations and what he found when he went out and talked to people in Chicago. This public meeting resulted in the founding of the still-active Civic Federation of Chicago. This same body issued an admonitory analysis of the Illinois pension situation after 2008.

If Christ Came to Chicago was the new journalism of 1893: factual reporting, interviews with prominent citizens and ordinary people, and vehement Christian preaching. William Stead exhorted William Randolph Hearst to give soul to his sensational journalism.

December 11, 2011: Blue skies, and another exoneration. Illinois is now the example of cynical, unethical prosecutions, and then what dedicated lawyers can accomplish, as well as a watchword for legal blundering. And it took years to uncover these injustices. Whatever the reason, the winters in the Midwest are more benign than the 1960s where twenty degrees below zero would come and sit down on you for days, pushing the breath from your chest.

Henry Demarest Lloyd and his colleagues, not only Florence Kelley, were crusaders for a new and an honest social order. They dissented, in print and from the podium, from the consensus of lawyers who considered the hanging Judge Gary from the Haymarket trial a hero.

Henry Demarest Lloyd describes how Judge Gary was introduced at the celebratory Christmas Bar Association Dinner after the death sentences were imposed:

Mr. Wirt Dexter is reported to have said at the Bar Association dinner December 27, 1887, responding to the toast, "Why are you a lawyer?": "Let me call your attention to our relation to the State. We [the legal profession] offer the bulwark of a conservative element, in that we believe the State exists by contract. How needful is this bulwark at the present time I need not say, with the deep unrest that exists about us. When men armed with destructive theories seek their enforcement, which would speedily make for us an earthly hell, other professions will expostulate, but the law—and I say it with Judge Gary sitting in our midst—will hang." (Great applause.) "I mention his name in obedience to an impulse of the heart too strong to resist, for I don't believe he will ever know how we feel towards him and how we love him." (Applause)

Henry Demarest Lloyd continued:

By this speech Judge Gary and the Bar Association, which applauded him to the echo, are egging on the monopolists in their lamentable attempt—sure to fail—to break up the trade-unions in order to force the disunited and helpless workers to make their contracts as "individuals" with employers massed into corporations and unions of corporations with uncounted millions of capital. He and the applauding Bar say to the combinations of capital: "Your offence is light." To the combinations of labour: "We will break you down." . . . The historian of that posterity which, as Howells finely says, "judges the judgments of courts," will pay particular attention to this speech . . . and will see in it a flood of light pouring backward.

By September 1893, seventy-four railroads had declared bankruptcy; then there was a bond crisis, followed by a stock market crash. The poor from the countryside poured into the city looking for work. The World's Columbian Exposition closed in August 1893. Hull-House became a shelter for homeless women in one of the most bitterly cold winters in memory, or since.

The great city Florence Kelley found to be so welcoming, intelligent and generous could be cruel. When a hundred thousand unemployed men were sleeping on the streets, in police stations, and in City Hall, the public debate in the newspapers and lecture halls was whether offering the poor seventy-five cents a day to sweep the streets would permanently lower wages and kill the financial incentive for the poor to seek work.

James McCosh, a Princeton professor of philosophy—a building on the Princeton campus is named for him—wrote in 1892: "God has bestowed upon us certain powers and gifts which no one is at liberty to take from us or interfere with. All attempts to deprive us of them is theft. Under the same head may be placed all purposes to deprive us of the right to earn property or to use it as we see fit."

Levy Mayer would have agreed. Property and the protection of property were the purpose and principle of the United States Constitution and of the law.

Henry Demarest Lloyd challenged the new business elite, richer than ever, more arrogant than ever, who in spite of their pro-business rhetoric were hobbling new industries with layers of debt with non-transparent financial maneuvers and pocketing quick profits at the expense of the people who did the work. Shadow companies were created to shield ownership of assets so that debt could be leveraged, paper sold, and the profits for those who created the debt for that purpose taken out. The layers of inscrutable financial transactions were created to hide the transfer of large amounts of wealth to those who created the financial paper, bonds and stocks, in shell companies which didn't make anything or do anything but temporarily hold paper profits.

And so, in 1893 Theodore Dreiser described the fictional Mr. Judah Anderson, president of the Lake City National Bank, the largest financial institution in the city, with deposits of over $14 million:

> *Long familiarity with the banking world and great affairs generally had given a rich finish to the ease and force which the latter naturally possessed. He looked strangely replete for a man of thirty-six—suave, steady, incisive, with eyes as fine as those of a Newfoundland or a Collie and as innocent and winsome. They were wonderful eyes, soft and spring-like at times, glowing with a rich human understanding which on an instant could harden and flash lightning. Deceptive eyes, unreadable, but alluring alike to men and to women in all walks and conditions of life.*

Henry Demarest Lloyd was as good as his principles. He left his comfortable house in Winnetka and went to live with the locked-out miners in Spring Hill, eventually assisting in brokering a settlement in addition to reporting on the conditions there. This is how Caro Lloyd describes the episode:

> *In 1889 Illinois became the scene of a death-dealing combat to that end [to break the labor unions], in Spring Valley and its rich coal mines. On one side stood corporations representing $500,000,000, while on the other were miners with wives and children, bearing on their gaunt faces a look of bewilderment, "wondering why they must die."*

> *Back in 1884 the "enterprise" had started. Fields covering the coal were bought from "uninformed farmers," a city map drawn, alluring advertisement circulated, and agents sent abroad. As men of the best business talent of the country were leaders, lots sold well and in six months two hundred thousand dollars had been realized on land costing less than twenty thousand. Thrifty and intelligent miners, picked men of the country, attracted by the promise of "steady work," settled there, many selling their*

homes to reinvest their all in Spring Valley. The coal fields were extended and trades-
man, clergymen, doctors came, until there were 5,000 people, and the estate became the
largest of any coal mining company in the world. Full of faith the miners bought lots
on monthly payments and built homes, getting their material from the company. Thus
began the bright days. But there was one cloud. No matter how hard they worked, they
could not make the wages promised. Their accounts at the month's end after deducting
the bill at the company's store, the payment on the lots, the cost of oil and sharpening of
tools, showed little or no surplus.

One day shortly before Christmas, 1888, without warning, with no whisper of strike
from the union into which the men had organised, the company told one third of the
miners to take away their tools and not return. They had been earning just enough
to keep alive and were now kept from starving by the generosity of those still at work.
"The whole population," said Lloyd, "staggered through that winter as best they could."
In April, again without notice, the remaining workers were locked out and the com-
pany's store closed. Then began slow starvation. . . . The public had become aware of
the trouble through the press, but had been erroneously informed that it was a strike
instead of a lockout. . . . In September, Lloyd went to learn the facts first hand.

There must be a new day, a new democracy, Henry Demarest Lloyd argued, which
would depose the rule of the monopolists and remove the power of money from politics.
In this new day ideas of right and justice and humanity would override the corruption
of politics by money and the influence of the big corporate interests over politicians.
His research laid bare the corruption at the heart of the state politics, as business people
bribed and bought the votes and the power to pass laws protecting business in the state
legislatures, the US Congress, and then have them upheld in the courts where judges
were elected. A new Christian order must, he argued, substitute the general welfare and
social justice for the vast enrichment of the few.

The defenders of property, however, remained intransigent. Henry Demarest Lloyd
quoted Judge Gary from his speech to the Chicago Bar Association:

"The monopolies of capital are a mischief which calls for a remedy but the burden from
them upon the individual is so light as to scarcely be felt. Corruption in office adds tem-
porary burden to taxes, and frauds at elections put the wrong men in office. But none of
these evils, unless in very rare instances, deprives anybody of the necessities of life. The
tyranny under which labor groans stops industry and takes bread from the mouths of
hungry women and children. What can we do to break it down?"

As Henry Demarest Lloyd said:

Enveloped in several passages of Judge Gary's utterances can be traced the unborn outlines of the judicial opinion [in Haymarket], *fully conceived and waiting for the time of delivery, holding that in case of a conflict between strikers and Pinkertons or other mercenaries of business every member of the trade-union which ordered the strike is guilty of murder if anyone be killed. "The law is (my) common sense"* . . .

In an interview in the daily Tribune, of January 21, 1888, on the subject of railway passes, Judge Gary gave utterance to the following views, which throw a search-light on his relations to the railway corporations, which are the most powerful and most constant litigents in our courts.

"I have always accepted passes, and probably always shall. I only regret that I can't get more. The passage and enforcement of the Inter-State Commerce law has ruined all my passes that were good for anything, and I would not give much for a pass that will not take a man outside the State of Illinois. If any one has any suspicion that my possession of these passes is liable to influence my judgment, why they are welcome to such suspicion, that's all. . . ."

A railway president, head of one of the most important western roads, Mr. A.B. Stickney, tells very frankly and succinctly . . . that passes are given by the railways, "to legislators, the executive offers, the judicial officers, and to all the clerks, and employes of the several departments of state, then to county boards and the various county officials, clerks and employes; then to that very numerous class known as 'political workers,' and finally to every person supposed to be able to do something to aid a railway company in case of political or judicial emergency, or, if not so propitiated, to do harm."

In plain English they are meant to be bribes.

Jane Addams saw the settlement house in Chicago as an application of the principle of the higher conscience—a term they used to describe the basic human motivation to do good. When the Supreme Court of Illinois rejected the appeal of the death sentences imposed on the Haymarket defendants in September 1887, the opinion was written by Justice Benjamin Magruder, who was to write the opinion regarding the constitutionality of the hours provision of the factory inspection statute in March 1895.

January 31, 2000, Chicago Tribune: "Ryan Suspends Death Penalty: Illinois First State to Impose Moratorium on Executions."

Denouncing a system that is "so fraught with error and has come so close to the ultimate nightmare," Gov. George Ryan declared a moratorium Monday on the death penalty in Illinois, marking the first time any state has taken such dramatic action.

"Until I can be sure that everyone sentenced to death in Illinois is truly guilty, until I can be sure with moral certainty that no innocent man or woman is facing a lethal injection, no one will meet that fate," Ryan told a throng of reporters.

Ryan decried the state's "shameful record of convicting innocent people and putting them on Death Row" and repeatedly referred to the 13 condemned inmates who have been cleared since Illinois reinstated capital punishment in 1977, one more than the number of inmates the state has executed.

January 31, 2000, Chicago Tribune: " 'My Concern Is Saving Lives, Innocent Lives.' "

The following are excerpts from Gov. George Ryan's announcement Monday of a moratorium on the death penalty in Illinois and from his comments during questioning afterward:

I want to make it clear there are a lot of people in Illinois, including myself, who feel the death penalty is an appropriate punishment. . . . .There's going to be a lot of folks who are firm believers in the death penalty who may not agree with what I'm doing here today. But I am the fellow who has to make the ultimate decision whether someone is injected with a poison that's going to take their life. . . .

My concern is saving lives, innocent lives, and (saving) people from being prosecuted and convicted and possibly put to death.

John Peter Altgeld first offered the job of factory inspector to Henry Demarest Lloyd, who suggested that Florence Kelley be appointed instead.

And so the governor did, on July 12, 1893, making Florence Kelley the first female statewide factory inspector in the country and the first woman to hold statewide office in Illinois.

Her work had already long since begun.

Looking south, Administration Building from Wooded Isle Bridge; World's Columbian Exposition, Chicago, IL. Source: ICHi-25087. Chicago History Museum. Reproduction of photographic print.

4

In the Middle of It

The whole scheme of this autobiography and its apparently systemless system—only apparently systemless, for it is not that. It is a deliberate system and the law of the system is that I shall talk about the matter which for the moment interests me, and cast it aside and talk about something else the moment its interest for me is exhausted. It is a system which follows no charted course and is not going to follow any such course. It is a system which is a complete and purposed jumble—a course which begins nowhere, follows no specified route, and can never reach an end when I am alive.

Mark Twain, *Autobiography*, quoted in *Mark Twain*, Charles Neider, editor

Jane Addams: *Do not seek to do good, but only to understand life.*

July 1, 1894.

Dear Sir: I have the honor to submit herewith a special report on tenement house manufacture in Chicago during the small-pox epidemic of 1894, according to your instruction of June 25th.

Yours very truly, Florence Kelley,

State Factory Inspector.

This enforcement of the newly enacted Factory and Workshop Inspection Law consisted of visiting the tenements and getting lists of the workshops, then going there, identifying smallpox cases and reporting them, under the authority of sections 1 & 2 of the statute. The first task was the counting:

> As there are in Chicago between 950 and 1,000 licensed shops and about 25,000 other rooms in which garments are manufactured, it would be a hopeless task for any body of inspectors.

The factory inspector was in place, the *Smallpox Report* presented, and, in the meantime, the research and preparation for the publication of the book *Hull-House Maps and Papers* continued. The research for the US Department of Labor on the *Slums of Great Cities* project had already allowed Florence Kelley and her associates into the slums and tenements to do the demographics and economic research, which would become the basis for everything that followed, which was also basically counting. The inspections under the Factory and Workshop Inspection Law were a continuation of that work under a different source of legal authority and with a different statutory purpose, but the same social purpose.

The narratives for the factory inspection reports became background for the prosecutions, then became the visual presentations, the maps, in *Hull-House Maps and Papers*, transforming the demographic and wage information from the *Slums of Great Cities* project into something else.

The research process was described in *Hull-House Maps and Papers*:

> The great interest and significance attached to Mr. Charles Booth's maps of London have served as warm encouragement; and although the eyes of the world do not centre upon this third of a square mile in the heart of Chicago as upon East London when looking for the very essence of misery, and although the ground examined here is very circumscribed compared with the vast area covered by Mr. Booth's incomparable studies, the two works have much in common . . . [aiming to be] a photographic reproduction of Chicago's poorest quarters. . . . The manner of investigation has been painstaking, and the facts set forth are as trustworthy as personal inquiry and intelligent effort could make them. . . .

> Although the experience in similar investigation and long residence in the neighborhood enabled the expert in charge to get at all particulars with more accuracy than could have attended the most conscientious efforts of a novice, it is inevitable that error should have crept in. Carelessness and indifference on the part of those questioned are undoubtedly frequent, and change of occupation as well as irregularity of employ-

ment entail some confusion and uncertainty. Then, too, the length of time covered by the investigation is so great—one year—that neither buildings nor tenants remain the same throughout. . . .

The determination to turn on the searchlight of inquiry must be steady and persistent to accomplish definite results, and all spasmodic and sensational throbs of interest are ineffectual as well as unjustifiable. The painful nature of minute investigation, and the personal impertinence of many of the questions asked, would be unendurable and unpardonable were it not for the conviction that the public conscience when roused must demand better surroundings for the most inert and long-suffering citizens of the commonwealth. Merely to state symptoms and go no farther would be idle; but to state symptoms in order to ascertain the nature of the disease, and apply, it may be, its cure, is not only scientific, but in the highest sense humanitarian.

As a manifesto for this enterprise, these comments by Agnes Sinclair Holbrook could serve as the credo for any piece of social or economic research or artistic enterprise. It is an articulation of the motivation behind painstaking efforts to find out what is there, what the facts are. This investigation seems to have been carried on with sweet cooperation at Hull-House during 1894 and continuing through the publication of *Hull-House Maps and Papers* in 1895. The continuing relevance of the book has meant that the eyes of the world have over the century remained focused on this third of a square mile in Chicago whose portrait is preserved in those writings.

February 25, 2009: The morning is bleak. At least a little warmer, even if a grey sky. How slowly and yet how quickly one's attitude changes. Now that there is a date certain for our leaving, my glance is sturdily backward. Just changing the prospect for the next few years gives a different view of the present, of the moment, of the past, of where we are now. The boys must continue to come here during the summer, for their education and because we need them. The goals of education have changed little: to prepare the young to be citizens of the world they have been born into, not our world, not Florence Kelley's world, not a world any of us know or can foresee. So much is taken for granted: the civil order and economic stability.

To impose control on an otherwise unbearable human reality, and to endure daily a face-to-face confrontation with human suffering and misery, seems to have inspired the clarity of this writing, the precision of the artful drawing of the maps, the plain and straightforward language of description, the absence of preaching, all of which hands this work down to us pristine, as if it were a shield of hammered gold. To address directly the injustices lifted the spirit and was more tolerable than to observe and do nothing.

March 9, 2000, Chicago Tribune: "Ryan Sets Up Panel to Study Death Penalty."

Five weeks after declaring a moratorium on executions, Gov. George Ryan has put together a panel to study the death penalty system in Illinois, drawing both defense lawyers and prosecutors, as well as high-profile names like former U.S. Sen. Paul Simon and lawyer-novelist Scott Turow.

The panel, which Ryan is expected to announce Thursday morning, also includes Frank McGarr, the former federal judge who spent five years as the Northern District of Illinois' chief judge, and former U.S. Atty. Thomas Sullivan.

The research on *Hull-House Maps and Papers* and the investigations of the factory inspectors took place in the middle of the world of politics. For all the purity of purpose of the occupants of Hull-House, everyone working on the book, on the legislation, and everyone doing the factory inspections themselves, understood this was a political enterprise. The language of human suffering, of natural rights, the invocation of principles of justice, may have been lofty, but the reality of getting the bill passed, then of going into the factories and tenements and getting the inspections done in spite of the vociferous, physical opposition, was the politics of the street. The Hull-House women and their allies proved adept at both parts of the job, the high-minded rhetoric, the inspirational appeal to higher purpose, and the nitty-gritty of pressuring legislators and other government officials who had the power to make law, and the pushing and shoving in the streets of the tenements to get inside the sweatshops.

The passage of the Factory and Workshop Inspection Law had galvanized the opponents of government regulation. The opponents formed a state organization, the Illinois Manufacturers' Association, which after its founding in Illinois moved to Washington, DC, to become a powerful and well-funded national lobbying organization for the same principle: that business and commercial activities should not be interfered with or regulated by government.

February 26, 2013: Today the lake is a rippling, heaving surface of muddy green water. The ice sculptures of yesterday vanished like the cubes in last night's water glass. The mood also different, darker, more restless. The waves moving away from the breakwater, heavy, incessant.

The National Association of Manufacturers in Washington represented business interests before Congress for decades: opposing Social Security legislation, offering reasons to vote against any form of regulation of business and banking, opposing unemployment insurance and all of the proposals of the New Deal, and lobbying against other welfare provisions, including any form of unemployment insurance and any safety regulation of the conditions of the workplace. In 1895, with the litigation challenging the factory inspection statute successfully concluded, from its perspective, the Illinois Manufacturers' Association devoted itself to opposing provisions requiring fire escape ladders in any factory building above two stories and any state-imposed safety regulations or building codes.

February 3, 2006, Chicago Tribune: "A Christmas Card Defense; Defense Case Opens With Details of Gifts From Governor's Staff."

After 17 weeks of fighting back in a case that painted former Gov. George Ryan as a corrupt politician who schemed with friends and family to enrich themselves, Ryan's attorneys Thursday finally began to present their side of the story on their terms. . . .

Shortly after prosecutors rested their case, Ryan's defense offered testimony from a longtime secretary who swore that each Christmas Ryan legally accepted thousands of dollars in cash gifts from his staff.

The testimony was intended to answer a prosecution charge that Ryan mysteriously carried around wads of cash but rarely made bank withdrawals.

But on cross-examination, the prosecution quickly raised questions about whether Ryan had solicited contributions from employees and why Ryan would accept cash from janitors and other low-level staffers.

"So he was willing to take cash from anyone in the office who was willing to give it to him, is that right?" Assistant U.S. Atty. Joel Levin asked Vicki Easley, Ryan's former secretary. . . .

On the first day of its case, the defense called Easley to show that during Ryan's four years as governor and eight years as secretary of state, he received an estimated $1,500 to $4,000 in cash each year in a Christmas gift card from staffers. . . .

The gifts came from department heads to janitors, students and receptionists, she said.

The list of contributors allowed Ryan to know who hadn't given money as well, she conceded.

Levy Mayer brought together the manufacturers and business interests opposed to the Factory Inspection Law and masterminded the legal challenge to it. He went on to become one of the richest and most influential lawyers in Chicago, representing commercial leaders for the rest of his life and serving as a longtime personal counselor to Philip Armour. Strangely, the official biography of Levy Mayer, commissioned by his widow and written by the skillful and respected writer Edgar Lee Masters, makes no mention of the 1895 factory inspection litigation, although it was one of Levy Mayer's great triumphs in litigation.

Florence Kelley wrote in her *Autobiography* thirty years later:

The Illinois Association of Manufacturers established in 1893 seems not to have been in working order until after the new law took effect in July, or to have been too feeble to make any timely opposition. No sooner, however, had we begun to enforce the statute against violators in the tenement houses, by urging their employers to cut off supplies during the epidemic, warning them that goods found in the presence of infection would be summarily destroyed, than many workers showed us letters from the Manufacturers' Association promising protection if they were molested by inspectors who were, the letters said, operating under a new law clearly unconstitutional.

The Factory Inspection Law did not actually do much. It authorized the inspectors to enter tenement factories and report upon conditions there. Then factory inspectors could cite violators and impose a small fine. Florence Kelley took advantage of this new authority to report upon the outbreak of smallpox in the tenements, upon the request of Governor John Peter Altgeld. If people couldn't be interested in the conditions in the sweatshops for themselves, perhaps the report of a fatal, disfiguring, highly communicable disease running rampant in the tenements would get the attention of the public.

December 7, 2012: Pearl Harbor Day. I remember Pearl Harbor, the news event. I was standing in line at the newsstand, probably with my father, and I remember seeing the headlines and people exclaiming, whispering the news. It was a cold, damp morning in Berkeley, California, like today in Chicago. I was a kid, standing in line waiting for bubblegum, which was scarce. My father was buying the special edition of the newspaper, probably the San Francisco Chronicle, issued for Pearl Harbor.

February 1, 2000, Chicago Tribune: Editorial: "Fix This Broken System."

Gov. George Ryan's surprising move to declare a moratorium on executions in Illinois invites cynical speculation as to his motives and the timing of the decision. But whatever the motive, the governor's action is wise and welcome. . . .

His office largely credits the governor's 180-degree change of heart to the Tribune's five-part series: "The Failure of the Death Penalty in Illinois." . . .

Then there's Illinois' chilling scorecard on executions since the death penalty was reinstated in 1977: 12 men executed—but 13 Death Row inmates, like Porter, cleared.

The courage of Ryan's decision lies in that, despite all the near-misses, the death penalty is still popular within his own Republican Party—including with presidential front-runner George W. Bush, whose home state of Texas leads the country in executions.

It is also favored by this newspaper and by a wide majority of Illinois voters.

In a democracy the will of the people, the outrage of the people, is needed if there is to be a change from a status quo which benefits many who have much to lose from any change in the system. Then, perhaps people would rather not know. People would rather not know how bad it is out there. People would rather not know about injustice, brutality, lying by the government. The question becomes how to get the attention of the public—so, Florence Kelley reported in the specially commissioned *Report on Smallpox*:

A random search among a thousand shops and 25,000 to 30,000 other rooms being out of the question . . . we made . . . immediate inspection of shops in and near infected premises. In the course of these inspections we found so many cases of small-pox which had not been reported to us that we soon ceased to depend on the city hall lists alone. . . . The disease was overwhelmingly epidemic in the Polish and Bohemian district from 16th street south to the river. . . . The prejudice against vaccination, which is obstinate and widespread among the population in this part of the city, contributed largely to the spread of small-pox.

Florence Kelley's children, Nicholas, Margaret, and John, ages nine, seven, and six in 1894, were living at Wayside with the family of Henry Demarest Lloyd and Jessie Bross Lloyd. Florence Kelley's repeated exposure to smallpox during the summer of 1894, although she was vaccinated, kept her away from them for weeks at a time. Ko spent the summer at the Lloyds' home on Rhode Island, where he went almost every summer for the rest of Florence Kelley's time in Chicago, and later as well. In September 1894 Margaret and John became residents at the Hillside Home School in Wisconsin.

During the summer of 1894 Jane Addams wrote, "The Dr. is prowling about the children constantly." Perhaps Dr. Wischnewetzky hoped to reopen the custody proceedings. Perhaps that is a reason Florence Kelley did not go ahead with divorce proceedings, which she would have been eligible to do after a year of residency.

December 14, 2010: Today the city of Chicago is again addressing questions of residency. Those who wish to stop the candidacy of Rahm Emanuel for mayor have filed petitions and complaints saying that when Emanuel left town to be chief of staff at the White House for President Barack Obama, he gave up his legal residency in Chicago and thus is not eligible to run. It is a maneuver worthy of the 1890s politicians.

Every morning, in every weather—the sunshine, the rain, the snow, and the wind, the always-present wind, sometimes so strong it is hard to stand against it—every morning, or afternoon, I step out of my apartment onto the pavement of Chicago Avenue, and every morning no matter what the time of day or the weather, there are people on the streets of Chicago. Mostly we are all going to work or coming back from work.

At 6 a.m. there are women, some men but mostly women, in blue and purple medical scrubs coming off or going onto a shift at one of the hospitals. They wear the rubber sandals. Looking through our windows facing east, I can see the red sun of the morning or the snow hitting the buildings. I see the dark, wet street below. At dawn a lone yellow taxi scutters along the shining street between the buildings.

People live in cities because they want to be with other people, to watch other people, to see what everyone is doing. That is why people live in cities. The same beggar woman in a head scarf and long robe, her head bowed, holding the same sign every morning: help me and my children. I have lost everything.

Levy Mayer was born in Virginia in 1858, the child of 1855 Jewish immigrants from Bavaria, where at that time only Catholics were allowed to engage in public worship or pursue trades and professions. His parents came to Chicago from the American South after the Civil War when all commerce and society was decimated there. Levy Mayer's unlikely paid skilled biographer, Edgar Lee Masters, was another well-known Chicago lawyer, who for a time shared office space with John Peter Altgeld and Clarence Darrow. Edgar Lee Masters's *Spoon River Anthology* is a chronicle of small-town life in the nineteenth century read by generations of twentieth-century American high school students, and now largely forgotten.

Levy Mayer, the architect and counsel for the Illinois Manufacturers' Association, the man who crafted the legal strategy challenging the Factory Inspection Law to the Supreme Court of Illinois, was, like Florence Kelley, a person with strong political opinions: he was against direct election of senators, against the primary system for nominating public officials, and against the income tax.

The cardinal principles of American democracy were, Levy Mayer believed, individual liberty and noninterference with business, and these were *his* guiding principles. Levy Mayer hated socialism and abhorred the dreams of populism. John Peter Altgeld's political principles were anathema. In his view, any government regulation of business was intolerable interference with the free hand of the market. The National Association of Manufacturers would continue to support this position in Washington, DC, long after Levy Mayer had disappeared from the scene.

March 7, 2000, Chicago Tribune: "Death Penalty Support Erodes: Many Back Life Term as an Alternative."

The number of Illinois voters who support the death penalty is declining, and large numbers of them favor life in prison without parole as an alternative to execution, according to a new Tribune poll.

Support for capital punishment among registered voters has fallen to 58 percent from 76 percent in an August 1994 Tribune poll and from 63 percent a year ago, the poll found.

When respondents were asked to choose whether murder cases should be punished by the death penalty or life in prison without possibility of parole, support for capital punishment eroded further, the poll found, with 43 percent supporting the death penalty and 41 percent favoring life without parole.

The numbers mirror a similar decline nationwide. A Gallup poll released last month showed that 66 percent of Americans support capital punishment, down from 80 percent six years ago.

Levy Mayer himself was a better businessman than most of the heads of the companies and manufacturing firms whom he cobbled together to form the Illinois Manufacturers' Association. The law was or should be a business, he believed. The business of the law was to lay down and then to enforce reasonable rules for manufacturers and businesses to conduct business, to protect property, so that business could operate under the protection of the predictability of the rule of law. The purpose of the law was to facilitate commerce, to support contracts, to make it easy for business to prosper. And if a law placed a burden or a tax on the profits or making of money by commercial people, then that law should be overruled or eliminated.

March 22, 2009: Sunshine. Still unclear where we will go next. Tennis this morning. Great to move on the tennis court. Not great to move from a large house after fifteen years of accumulation. Don't let numbers fool you. There are facts, and then there are facts. The numbers are not facts. A few small green shoots. Nothing green on the trees yet. Spring is not here. That is a fact.

Levy Mayer's most famous legal victory, representing the defendants in the Iroquois fire cases, showed his talents. On December 30, 1903, more than 500 people, mostly mothers and young children, died in a flash fire in the Iroquois Theatre in the Loop, a theater where none of the required city and state safety and warning systems were functioning. The owners admitted that the theater was in violation of the code and that they had illegally locked exits. None of the defendants represented by Levy Mayer served a day in jail or paid a court-imposed fine, although many of those who died were from wealthy, prominent families.

Levy Mayer's handling of these cases, after more than 500 indictments for homicide were brought against the theater owners, after the filing of hundreds of wrongful death actions, was brilliant. First he persuaded the courts to hear the cases outside of Chicago, and then he succeeded in delaying and delaying the litigation until the cases came before more sympathetic judges in nearby counties. There were some unreported out-of-court settlements, but no damage claims awarded by a jury, and no theater owners went to jail. The mayor spent a night in jail, but all the manslaughter charges were put aside.

When financial panic struck Chicago in 1893, Levy Mayer was the attorney for one of the largest failing financial institutions, the National Bank of Illinois. He devoted his professional life and his considerable intelligence and influence to opposing organized labor, to recruiting strike-breakers, and to preventing or thwarting the goals of striking workers. Government-authorized factory inspections, and having reform-minded meddlers coming into the sweatshops, were exactly the kind of state interference with business which should be stopped, according to Levy Mayer and the Illinois Manufacturers' Association. The courts were the way to accomplish that. Eventually the economic interests of the property holders would bring about any needed change, he believed. If people worked under difficult circumstances, they had the liberty to leave. If manufacturers could make money in hard times only by offering sub-subsistence wages, the market ruled.

June 24, 2008: Another perfect summer day. The air is perfumed. The visiting boy goes off so cheerfully. Unless it does not matter that a child is robbed of her childhood, if that does not matter, even if that child has long ago grown up, and died, then nothing matters, or makes sense.

Florence Kelley's *Smallpox Report* in 1894 records cases by street, for the streets on a grid were how the city was organized after the fire in 1871, and that was how the inspectors did their work, methodically, street by street, block by block. Conditions were extreme, she reported:

> *It is impossible to induce people as sorely in need as the garment-workers of Chicago, to suspend work during three weeks merely because some fellow tenant in a crowded tenement house has a sick child. And he must be both a sanguine optimist and comfortably ignorant of the ways of the dwellers in tenements, who expects of them any such reasonable precaution as isolation of the patient. Indeed, the intimacy bred of overcrowding is increased in times of sickness, and neighbors help with the nursing, sit up with the dead, and attend the funeral, with dogged disregard of the infectious nature of the malady.*

This is Florence Kelley, the wife of a physician and the daughter of a judge and legislator, speaking. And it is Florence Kelley the realist.

September 18, 2008: This is panic. Banks are afraid of a run on currency. Will people never learn? Government officials make reassuring pronouncements. No one believes them.

Always precocious, like Florence Kelley, always the bright, adored child, Levy Mayer was enrolled in the Jewish Training School, where some of the students later had a connection to Hull-House. The Jewish Training School was established in Chicago to educate the boys and girls of recent Jewish immigrants.

At age twelve Levy Mayer went on to Chicago High School, then on Monroe Street near Halsted, a special exception being made to admit him at that age. He received grades of 84-90 in Latin, 82-96 in Greek, 97-99 in spelling, and as high as 97 in rhetoric. His deportment average was 99. The representation of Levy Mayer's praised deportment can be seen in the serenity of his bearing and his calm face in the portrait by Leopold Seyffert of Chicago, which today stares back in the entrance lobby of Levy Mayer Hall, filling the block between Chicago Avenue and Superior Street, which in 1926 became the first autonomous home of the Northwestern University School of Law.

June 15, 2008: My office is to be moved to the eighth floor and out of Levy Mayer Hall. Some renovation needed in the ceilings, they say. Maybe they just want me out of there. I am happy to go, and the eighth floor where all the clinics are has beautiful views. And a friendly atmosphere. Everyone is very welcoming. No one hides behind a closed door.

Although the budget of the Factory Inspector's Office and Florence Kelley's salary were small, by the spring of 1894 momentum had been built by the convergence of several different projects, many emanating from Hull-House and all centered on reporting on the working and living conditions in the tenements in the Nineteenth Ward. The smallpox epidemic and the economic crisis after the closing of the World's Fair added impetus. In the 1890s Florence Kelley and Jane Addams had political support across a spectrum of social classes, and momentum had been built by recent overlapping, cumulative efforts to reform the sweating system nationally and locally.

Most of the reform work at Hull-House was accomplished by socialists helped by the philanthropy of the civic-minded rich. Louise de Koven Bowen, the longtime treasurer and supporter of Hull-House, was the daughter of a millionaire and lived in a forty-room mansion on Astor Street. Her mother had been the third white child born in the rebuilt Fort Dearborn; her grandmother rode to Chicago on a covered wagon with a rifle across her knees.

As a young girl Louise de Koven took up a collection for a girl she saw being injured in a street accident. She was so outraged when she saw the conditions in the tenements where the injured girl lived that she started a social club for poor young people in the basement of her parents' mansion.

The work of the factory inspectors began immediately after the law took effect in 1893, and continued:

June 6, 1894—Joseph Mathous, 469 W. 19ᵗʰ street, coatmaker for Nicoll the Tailor, Adams and Clark streets. Inspectors Kelley and Merz.

This shop is in the first floor rear of a three story tenement house, Mathous living on the premises, shop not properly separated from his living rooms. The inspectors found thirteen persons at work, and six coats completed, or in process of manufacture, or in bundles not yet opened. The addresses of the thirteen employés were taken, and it was found that all were living on streets where small-pox was epidemic.

During this inspection a child was removed from 463 W. 19ᵗʰ street to the pest-house, the fifth case taken from that house. The ambulance and the Health Department carriage stood at the door forty minutes, while a crowd gathered, made up of school children, work people from the neighboring shops, and friends of the patient's family. The little patient was finally carried to the ambulance through a surging crowd of primary school children who pressed about the physicians and drivers, eagerly curious to see how the sick child looked. There were no police in sight, and when the patient had been carried away groups of neighbors stood talking of the large number of cases that had occurred in the block, and the uselessness of precautionary measure, since "small-pox comes from Heaven, and has nothing to do with making scratches on children's arms."

Like Jane Addams and Henry Demarest Lloyd, Florence Kelley accepted many speaking engagements and during 1894 she also taught English to young workers at night. They read William Morris's *News From Nowhere*, Thomas More's *Utopia*, and Engels's *Development of Socialism From Utopia to Science*. And so they learned English. Meanwhile Florence Kelley's own cash was so low she lived day by day on her wages, like her subjects, wearing old, worn clothes, mismatched silk stockings in need of darning, and often walking miles because she could not afford the streetcar. Tramping up and down the stairs in the tenements regularly left her feet so swollen that she came home to soak them in a large tub for the evening.

September 4, 2004: My third-floor studio stretches half the length of the house and has two sets of windows, mostly open, and bright tables, covered with papers and books and photographs. At five in the morning, or earlier, the pulse of the cars can be heard on Sheridan Road—swish, swish, as they glide downtown.

What Florence Kelley later called the "bewildering absence of contemporary hostility" to the enactment of the Factory and Workshop Inspection statute was short-lived and probably attributable to the fact that no one expected any meaningful enforcement. Statutes had been passed by the Illinois legislature or by the Chicago City Council for universal primary education, or banning child labor, or for protection against fire in theaters, and no one thought that any enforcement of such laws would take place. And if a law proved troublesome to those with influence—the business people, the manufacturers, the bankers, the streetcar magnates—the legislators could repeal the law or the courts could be persuaded to make it toothless. And they did.

> July 13, 2001, Chicago Tribune: "State Court Issues Rules to Hasten Death Row Appeals."
>
> The state Supreme Court on Thursday issued new rules designed to streamline and speed the appeals process for Death Row inmates. . . .
>
> "This court has engaged in exhaustive efforts to balance the concerns of fairness and justice with the need for finality in postconviction proceedings in death-penalty cases," Justice Major Harding wrote in Thursday's majority opinion.

The *First Annual Report of the Factory Inspectors of Illinois* was presented to Governor John Peter Altgeld on December 15, 1893, and covers just the first five months of the law. Enforcement was investigation and a reporting of the facts, followed by a reporting of the first prosecutions for a misdemeanor. The prohibition against the employment of children under 14 in the statute was a straightforward place to start with enforcement.

One of Florence Kelley's first official acts as factory inspector was to obtain a ruling from the attorney general of Illinois that the hours and child labor provisions of the statute applied to factories and workshops outside of the trades mentioned specifically in the statute. In other words, the statute's provisions were not restricted to the factories in the garment trades. The first countermove of the fledgling Illinois Manufacturers' Association was to suggest that the act applied only to the clothing manufacturers. The factory inspector won the first skirmish.

The *First Annual Report* contains statistical tables, lists of the factories and workshops visited, including names and addresses and what was found there, and a compilation of analogous statutes from other states. It was a foreshadowing of the Brandeis Brief which Florence Kelley and her future colleague, Josephine Goldmark, would invent for the Supreme Court of the United States a decade later.

Actually the statute itself gave little power for enforcement. All the inspectors could do was enter the factories and report on what they found there. They interpreted the statute as giving them the authority to ask for affidavits stating the age of workers, to make health examinations, and to issue small fines for violations. They interpreted their authority as giving them the power to put underaged children in school. As Florence Kelley described it:

Among the first work of the inspectors was a careful canvass of the sewing, metal stamping, woodworking, book-binding, box, candy, tobacco and cigar trades, and the discharge of a large number of children under fourteen years of age.

As with any challenge to a system, the first effect of the new law was a negative effect, to put out of work a sizable number of children who were discovered to have been working illegally. The candy manufacturers were the largest employers of children, especially during the holiday season. Later Florence Kelley would find large numbers of children working illegally at the Illinois Glass Works in Alton, Illinois. One of the most bitter confrontations under the statute was to take place there.

September 9, 2001, Chicago Tribune: "State Judges Get Lesson in Capital Cases: Death Penalty Reforms Mandate Special Training."

. . . Many of those attending the seminar—designed to keep them abreast of the latest case law and rules applicable to death penalty trials—have never presided over a capital case, but all could hear such cases in the future.

Mistakes in such cases have the highest stakes: Innocent people have been convicted, and the guilty are sometimes freed because verdicts are reversed due to trial error. So now, the state high court has decided that training might better prepare judges with a role in such life-and-death decisions. . . .

But among the most progressive changes is the mandatory judicial training, which no other state has adopted. Every two years, any state judge in Illinois who may have to hear a capital case must attend a Supreme Court class. . . .

The class scoured the new rules of procedure handed down in January, and it also reviewed current case law governing capital trials. Judges were presented with hypothetical situations and then asked to vote on electronic keypads as to how they would rule.

Seconds later, the vote breakdown would appear on the screen in the front of the room, and the instructors would go over the answers.

Requiring an age affidavit to be filed with the factory inspector resulted in many children being withdrawn from employment, under fear of prosecution, and also a brisk trade in forged affidavits. The factory inspector sought assistance of a doctor from the College of Physicians and Surgeons of Chicago, as well as a female doctor from Hull-House, to make free, thorough medical examinations of the children, including an eye test, a hearing test, and measurements of weight, height, curvature of the spine, and other common disfigurements and injuries.

February 10, 2007: I admit then, I am committed to the abolition of capital punishment, without moral ambiguity. It is simply wrong, unjust, by any perspective. Like slavery, it is simply unjust. I am long past argument. The Illinois Reform Committee is bogged down and opposed to any kind of serious systematic research. In today's meeting the other members said they considered any systematic data collection to be "only a matter of interesting academic research, suitable for an academic article or discussion, and not relevant here."

Of course if there is no systematic data collection by this committee, or a reliable compilation of facts by someone, everyone will simply be able to make factually incorrect statements without contradiction. We will never see the day in governmental bodies such as this when factual research determines policy.

Since I am an academic, however, I will conduct the academic study for myself, even by myself, with my own research funds. In New Jersey not only the prosecutors but also similarly the head of the public defender appellate section opposed that systematic data collection, saying it only would hurt our clients. It turned out that the systematic factual record of prosecutions for murder became proportionality review, the issue the Supreme Court of New Jersey used to delay executions, and the sole surviving legal issue in the crawl toward abolition.

If the child was of age and found able to continue work, the child was granted a health certificate. If the child was under age, or found unhealthy and unfit to work, that child was ordered to be discharged from employment. The enforcement of the statute required conscientious doctors willing to work for nothing. The doctor must volunteer to do the examination and be willing to go to the tenement factory to inspect the child and the conditions in the factory. But, Florence Kelley wrote, that was not enough:

Thus a healthy child may wish to enter a cracker bakery, and unless the physician visits it, and sees the dwarfish boys slowly roasting before the ovens, in the midst of an unguarded belting and shafting (a danger to health which men refuse to incur), he may be inclined to grant the certificate, and thereby deprive the child of the only safeguard to his health which the State affords him.

The charge for fake certificates by real doctors ran from fifty cents to two dollars, and fake documents by real or fake doctors were not difficult to obtain. Florence Kelley later concluded that this section of the law may have been unenforceable, in spite of the donation of free medical examinations by Drs. Josephine Milligan and Bayard Holmes, and the faithful work of Dr. Holmes's medical students under his direction.

There were three Dr. Holmeses in Chicago in 1893. This was not the notorious murderer H.H. Holmes. Dr. Holmes, a teacher working with Florence Kelley, wrote:

The wider reward of those students only being "a widened knowledge of the physique of children of the wage-earning class."

Florence Kelley taught always, believing before and after Hull-House, that knowledge is power, that the facts would set people free, and control over the keys to the world must be wrested from those who want to keep control of the facts and the law for themselves. Teaching one person to read may be the most important contribution any teacher can make, whether the reading is technical, scientific, or just the words of others. A person who can read can find what she needs to know, about her world or another's. Otherwise it is starting all over again for every generation. Where and how the knowledge is kept, and who has access to it, is always critical. Many don't want women and girls to learn to read, then and now. As they say now: it is a contested space.

October 2, 2007: The weather today, a dense fog advisory, but in the 60s and later in the week in the 80s. Last night driving up from downtown the sunset against the buildings showed dark buildings as the cutouts against a sky of grey, pink, rose. The sunset reminds me of another place, another time, other sunsets. People in 1894 woke up, looked outside, and saw the sun, heard the rain speaking to them. The earliest and the latest gods were the weather gods. The apocalypse, the judgment day, is always floods, rain, thunder and lightning.

In the *First Annual Report* Florence Kelley wrote that her first year of experience under the statute convinced the inspectors of the inadequacy of the law: it should be amended to prohibit, as the law of Ohio had done since 1890, the employment of any child under sixteen at any job "whereby their lives and limbs may be endangered, or their health injured, or their morals likely to be impaired."

Thus the Ohio law prohibited the employment of any child at "swing belts, or to adjust the belt of any machinery, circular or band saws, wood shapers, wood joiners, stamping machines in sheet metal and tin ware manufacturing, stamping machines in washer and nut factories."

Prohibitions on the employment of teenagers are remembered by some as reasons they could not be hired for the summer, if under sixteen, as waiters, or in their fathers' factories hauling boxes, and instead worked for tips as caddies at the local golf club.

The report continues: "The hazards to children persist in operating rolling mill machinery, or stripping or working tobacco, or in preparing the composite for matches, or dipping dyeing materials, or packing matches. Nor should children be employed in any capacity in the manufacture of paints, colors or white lead."

Manufacturers were always and remain eager to employ children. Children are cheaper, they protest less about unsanitary conditions or the absence of toilets, and when injured go away more quietly. After the children, women are cheaper, protest less, and go away when they are injured, as if they deserve nothing more than that.

February 20, 2009: A day to say a grateful adieu. The winter has set in with new stubbornness. California is far away, although only yesterday. Cold again, snow predicted for tonight and tomorrow all day. The sky pale, struggling for a bit of blue, now turning grey, and then a hard white. Something metallic about the cold. And soon we will be out of here.

The numbers, the facts, would tell the story. And when people heard the facts, they would act. Among the many statistics Florence Kelley quoted was the finding that 59,878 new school places would be required in the fall of 1892 if the promise of universal primary education was to be met in the poor wards. The lack of instant communication—telegraph and telephone connections were sporadic and inconvenient—meant that no one from New York or Washington would immediately receive the release of every detail of the *Special Report* or the *Slums of Great Cities*. New York could, however, read in the newspapers about what was being done in Chicago. Florence Kelley always understood that no change would come without publicity and a groundswell of outrage. As the new factory inspector, she was a person whose name was recognized, and she knew the value of newspapers. Get the news out, lift the rock and let the world see what was crawling underneath—if it could be persuaded to look.

February 28, 2011: No snow. Another manuscript, another working day. Still the governor has not signed the bill. The sun climbs the ladder of the horizon and crawls across a leaden sky. Any day there could be the murder of a policeman, or the rape or torture of a murdered child, the horror all over the television and the front pages, in color. And no governor could sign. Today, followed on the street by a man in a business suit asking strangers if they could see the star of Bethlehem over his head.

When the Factory and Workshop Inspection Law passed in Illinois in 1893, it was unique in the country because it created a department with jurisdiction throughout the state with regard to goods made in tenements and factories. There were factory inspectors in other states, but usually their authority was confined to cities or to a small part of industry. After 1893 in Illinois, owners of goods produced under the sweating—or outsourcing—system were required to produce on demand the names and addresses of contractors and those who worked at home. That wasn't written into the law. It was an interpretation of what was required.

Florence Kelley and her colleagues, some medically trained, some doctors, some women or men who had worked in, and been injured in, factories, were the band of inspectors who went and looked, armed only with the authority of a slim new law saying there should be an "inspection" of factories.

March 6, 2009: A day to believe in. Sunshine, clouds. Forecast for rain all weekend. Today fresh air, today breath. Tomorrow rain. Always coming back to the same questions, the same events. The past changes every time you look at it.

And yet somehow even in the tenements, under the most straitened circumstances, the human heart kept beating. People fought, oppressed one another, loved one another, performed acts of gratuitous kindness and generosity, or cruelty, and were born and died under conditions which anyone today would find intolerable to read about. Such conditions are replicated today in many places, including parts of Chicago. So Jane Addams observed:

> *I was detained late one evening in an office building by a prolonged committee meeting of the Board of Education. As I came out at eleven o'clock, I met in the corridor of the fourteenth floor a woman I knew, on her knees scrubbing the marble tiling. As she straightened up to greet me, she seemed so wet from her feet up to her chin, that I hastily inquired the cause. Her reply was that she left home at five o'clock every night and had no opportunity for six hours to nurse her baby. Her mother's milk mingled with the very water with which she scrubbed until she should return at midnight heated and exhausted, to feed her screaming child with what remained within her breasts.*

People came to Chicago in the 1880s and 1890s for the same reasons that people come today to Mumbai or Rio de Janeiro or still Chicago. They are mostly young, mostly energetic, the migrants. They are families. Sometimes they come out of desperation. Sometimes they just come with hope. They are still coming. The cities are where we live together in the twenty-first century.

And so the factory inspectors did their work in 1893:

The Women's Protective Association of Chicago brought to our attention a pop-corn factory, the owner of which was being prosecuted for a criminal assault upon one of the children in his employ. The man was tried and upon a technicality acquitted. The evidence adduced proved the unspeakably low moral tone of the place. Meanwhile his factory upon inspection proved to be a cellar, with sanitary arrangements which were an outrage upon all decency. Here he employed a foreman, a forewoman, and six little girls under sixteen years of age, of whom two were orphans wholly dependent upon themselves for support. Of these one child had no relations except a brother eight years old, now in a charitable institution. The little girl had been earning her way since she was twelve years old, boarding with a woman who absorbed the child's entire earnings. The second orphan girl had no relatives except a sister. . . . The discharged orphans were turned over to the compulsory department of the Board of Education and School Children's Aid society, with a recommendation for especial attention. . . . But here, as in cases previously cited, the inadequacy of the present law, and the need of amendment, is demonstrated.

The mood of the *First Annual Report* is mostly hopeful. This is a lawyer speaking of the need for amendment to the law, although Florence Kelley's law degree would not be conferred until June 1895, with admission to the Bar of Illinois to follow automatically soon after. The power of enforcement was primarily in the age provision. The age and hours provisions of the law were the most specific, the easiest to document. The power of enforcement was principally a threat. If the inspectors could show that the children working in the factory were under fourteen, nothing else need be proved. The violation of the age provision was the fact with the least ambiguity, but many children did not know their age. This led to children bringing in false certifications as to their age. The health and safety violations were always more ambiguous, required a medical examination and diagnosis of the adverse condition.

August 8, 2000: Evanston. I dreamed a perfect plot, about a woman, a man, who run a taxi stand. In Chicago. There is a literary agent involved, and huge fees in a confidential trade are negotiated in a cab with the driver listening. I woke up laughing. The next family visits over Labor Day with the nieces and nephews and their children. I don't know any of them but want to welcome them. What else is this big house and beautiful garden for? And there is a recent family tragedy to recover from.

What inspection meant and where it could lead were in the will and the hands of the enforcers. The factory inspectors could do no more than find employers in violation of one of the law's provisions and impose a paltry fine. Their most powerful weapon was the threat imposed by their sheer presence and that they might come back, that they could report.

As the factory inspection reports detail, the employers in violation usually simply paid the small fine and then went back to doing what they had been doing before, or they moved to escape further inspection. What was a health certificate, after all, but a piece of paper, a kind of license, something to post on a wooden door so that the factory managers could proceed. The health certificate could be forged, and was.

The individual factory inspection reports include the date and address for the place of enforcement, a description of what someone saw at a particular place and time. The reports are a record of someone coming and looking, of some busybody interfering, a record that someone was not going to just let it go. And if the press would report it, or the facts could come before a judge, there might be the possibility of something being changed. The *First Annual Report* continues:

> *The medical examinations made in this office preliminary to granting health certificates reveal an incredible degree of filth of clothing and person. The children taken from the candy factories were especially shocking in this respect, and demonstrated anew the urgent need of bathing facilities both in the working-man's home, where bath-tubs seem to be unknown, and in numerous and accessible swimming-baths, where a plunge can follow the day's work.*

> *Boys are found handling candy with open sores upon their hands, and girls wrapping and packing it whose arms were covered with an eruption which is a direct consequence of filth. Boys from knee-pants shops have presented themselves so covered with vermin as to render a close examination almost impossible.*

Florence Kelley and her colleagues at Hull-House were called the Sanitarians—it was not a compliment—because of their obsessive attention to soap, bathing, ventilation, and fresh air. So much of what they saw could be immediately ameliorated by fresh air and water and a good scrub. The plumbing in the tenements was rudimentary; most tenements had outside water closets. The maintenance of the city sewer system in the tenements was sporadic, at best.

The general rule was the lower the economic conditions, the less the political influence, the worse the plumbing, the less likely the garbage was to be collected. The availability of clean, running water in the Nineteenth Ward was a luxury, and still is in most parts of the world. The outhouse in the tenements was typically rare, usually behind the building where the animals lived. Rotting food and garbage littered the streets and alleys. A contractor with the city had been paid a good amount, with a cut to Johnny Powers, to pick up the garbage three times a week in the Nineteenth Ward. The garbage was picked up once a month at best.

September 19, 2007: A breezy, cool day, and class today. I feel pressed, overwhelmed. As the fall marches in, tempo and pace are increased. Always coming back to the same material. Events happen at a time and place. Legal actors attempt to intervene and derail or push forward events, and then impose their own structure on time. In this sense, the law is like theater which imposes its own formal structure on persons and events, and corrals them to exist at a specific time and place. At a point certain it will all be over. The curtain will come down. The judgment will be entered. A death will occur. This allows the observer, and the participants, to share the illusion of control over time.

The attraction of the saloons for men and their sons, and for the women who went there or solicited there (some saloons let in women), was that the saloons had running water, heat, toilets better than a cold outhouse, and a place to wash up. The saloons got men out of where they lived, away from the smell of decomposing food, the spectre of human waste in the larger and smaller sense, away from crying women and children, away from the vermin and the stench of themselves and those others crowded in with them who couldn't wash themselves or their clothes. There were even some all-female saloons.

The saloons did offer the free lunch, even sometimes to people who were not buying beer, until there was a vigorous political campaign against the free lunch. It was the ploughman's lunch: a piece of bread, a piece of cheese, and some soup. During the 1890s, and especially in the 1893 depression, the police offered the homeless a bowl of soup and the floor of the police station to sleep on, and a cup of coffee in the morning before they had to move on. The poor were crowded in their spaces, jammed into rooms or hallways, crammed together in basements, shared space by the hour, rooms thrown together with chinks in their walls, rooms without heat rented by the hour.

If the conditions in the tenements were deplorable, those in the working men's warehouses, or single men's, single night occupancy hostels or hotels were worse. William Stead, like Sherman Hoar and William Wyckoff, disguised himself as an ordinary worker to see for himself:

According to the best authorities, the floating population [of young men without permanent places to live] is about 30,000 single men, who are living [in 1893] in lodging houses. . . . Within a stone's throw of one of Chicago's best private hotels can be found one of these lodging houses. It is a small, one-storied frame structure. Its sleeping accommodation consists of one hundred and fifty beds, which occupy the ground floor and the basement. Upon entering the front door one is almost overcome by the odor, which more resembles that of a long disused tomb than that of a human dwelling place. Pushing open the door the "office and parlor" is entered. Here in a room twenty-five by thirty feet were to be seen, a short time ago, crowded round a stove, twenty-seven men, whose clothing was more conspicuous by its variety and filthiness than by its adequateness. . . .

Stepping to the desk the visitor asked the price of a night's lodging, and after being told deposited a dime. . . . Following the direction pointed out, the investigator entered the sleeping room.

Yet, Stead reported, when someone who had been successful in setting up healthy, cheap municipal lodging houses in London and Glasgow tried to persuade the City Council to issue regulations addressing the conditions in these houses, he was told there were no bribes (boodle) in it for the aldermen. Thus the City Council would not issue regulations, or inspect, or do anything about these conditions which were well-known to the city and to everyone else.

September 18, 2007: A glorious fall day. Golden, the light is like spun gold. Everyone trying to put the best face on it, but discouraged. This is bad news, a shadow on the future. Of course death is inevitable, but we think of it always as far away, distant, even as we age. Such are our unreasonable, unjustified expectations, to live to a ripe age. Every day we get up, start the day, ignoring the reality that we are steadily marching towards our own deaths or, worse, the deaths of our loved ones. The most difficult, unspeakable, unthinkable, and yet endured often in the 1890s, and even now, the death of a child.

In January 1894 Florence Kelley mailed an ultimatum to every manufacturer in the state announcing her intention to arrest and prosecute violators of the eight-hour provision of the factory inspection statute. The economic depression, she argued, helped her. The argument was: shorter hours would require the hiring of more people, if the same amount of work was to be accomplished and the manufacturers were to keep production at the same level, therefore the new hours restriction would employ more workers.

The Illinois Manufacturers' Association, first called the Illinois Manufacturers' Protective Association, collected dues and immediately promised to pay the expenses and legal fees of anyone arrested for violating the eight-hour provision for women workers.

By May 1894 the Illinois Manufacturers' Association had selected cases to defend and had given $4,000 in legal fees to Levy Mayer.

Jane Addams describes how this politics came to interfere with support for Hull-House:

> Up to that time, our history had been as the minor piece of the early church. We had had the most generous interpretation of our efforts. Of course, many people were indifferent to the idea of the settlement; others looked on with tolerant and sometimes cynical amusement which we would often encounter in a good story related at our own expense; but all this was remote and unreal to us and we were sure that if the critics could but touch "the life of the people," they would understand.

> The situation changed markedly after the Pullman strike, and our efforts to secure factory legislation later brought upon us a certain amount of distrust and suspicion; until then we had been considered merely a kindly philanthropic undertaking whose new form gave us a certain idealistic glamour. But sterner tests were coming.

The regulations under the new statute required that work areas be separate from living quarters, free from vermin (lice, mice, rats, cockroaches, and other creatures) and infectious and contagious matter (as the public health doctors then understood those), that no one under fourteen be employed and that the employer furnish proof of age for workers under sixteen, that the number of hours for female workers be limited to eight per day and forty-eight per week, and, most important, the law designated inspectors to report on violations of these provisions.

Initially inspections were delayed because of legal wrangling over what kind of factories could be inspected. Certainly included were shops making coats, vests, trousers, overalls, knee pants, cloaks, shirts, ladies' waists (blouses), purses, feathers, artificial flowers, and cigars. As Florence Kelley reports:

> Although the law prohibits absolutely the employment of any child under 14 years of age in manufacture, yet the children under 14 years can never be wholly kept out of the factories and workshops until they are kept in school. At present the school attendance law is almost useless, at least in Chicago, where the largest number of children have been found at work.

The biggest single employer of children in the state was the Illinois Glass Works in Alton, near Saint Louis. It took a while for Florence Kelley and her inspectors to get to them. The battle over inspections with them was bitter and protracted. Inspections were fiercely resisted by the company with the support of the local newspapers, the Illinois

Manufacturers' Association, and others. The Illinois Glass Works fought hard against any inspection of its buildings, any regulation or interference by the government, any scrutiny of working conditions inside its plant. The *Chicago Tribune*, never a bystander, charged that factory inspectors were merely a front for labor organizers. And the history and political leanings of the factory inspectors were in that direction. The manufacturers threatened suits for trespass in retaliation for the announcement of a scheduled inspection of the plant sweatshop.

In the meantime the inspectors sharpened their skills on the local manufacturers:

Thus, a recent night inspection of work given out from one of the largest cloak manufacturies in the west resulted as follows: the garment maker was found in his tenement dwelling in the rear of a factory. With his family, a wife and four indescribably filthy children, he occupies a kitchen and two bedrooms. The farther bedroom could be entered only by passing through the other rooms. This farther bedroom, where the man was found at work, was 7 X 7 X 8 feet, and contained a bed, a machine, one chair, a reeking lamp and two men. The bed seemed not to have been made up in weeks; and in the bed, in a heap, there lay two overcoats, two hats, a mass of bed-covers, and nine fine tan-color capes trimmed with ecru lace, a tenth cape being on the machine in the process of stitching. The whole dwelling was found to be crawling with vermin, and the capes were not free from it.

In her *Autobiography* Florence Kelley reports that after being appointed factory inspector she took herself to the Office of the State's Attorney in Cook County and laid before the young lawyer there evidence concerning a young boy illegally employed gilding cheap picture frames with a poisonous fluid, who had lost the use of his right arm as a consequence. There was no legal responsibility for this on the part of the employer. All the law could do was impose a fine of twenty dollars under the factory inspection statute for employing a child without a proper age certificate.

July 8, 2003: Unlike my grandmother who took a six-month sea voyage, met her husband, the underage ship's doctor, and changed her life, we take many small business trips on airplanes, to the east, to California, Florida. Our air carrier has been crippled by strikes, is on the verge of insolvency, reports staggering losses year after year as fuel costs rise and billions of dollars in loans come due. Bankruptcy actually does protect it, especially from its own unions and creditors.

The young assistant state's attorney replied that he would never get to such a case in a year and that next she would be asking him to sue Marshall Field himself. Florence Kelley writes that she went and enrolled at Northwestern University School of Law the next day.

Actually, that account in the *Autobiography* must not be accurate. According to admissions records, Florence Kelley signed up for courses at Northwestern University School of Law within a few months of her arrival in Chicago, although she did not take the classes, perhaps because she could not afford the fee for matriculation. And as to the retort that she would next be wanting to sue Marshall Field, when the law took effect she already had met with him and was aware of tenement workers delivering goods to his store. Marshall Field's stated objection to the Factory Inspection Law—that he could not take honest labor away from the honest widow who was required to work at home—caused Florence Kelley to comment (but not to his face) that the only such person she had encountered meriting that description earned so little at the sweatshop making goods for Marshall Field's that the widow had to take her meals for free at Hull-House.

Marshall Field remained a powerful and formidable adversary; his role in suppressing demonstrations and sending armed militia to put down riots is well-documented in both Pullman and Haymarket. His public statements may have been couched in concern for the needs of the poor widows, but his methods were those of Pinkerton and the hired strike-breakers who smashed heads and killed anonymously, without fear of arrest or prosecution. He refused to let his female clerks, who worked ten hours at a stretch, sit or take a break during their shifts.

No matter when she began, by 1894 Florence Kelley was enrolled in evening classes at Northwestern University School of Law. She was given credit for some of her graduate classes in Zurich and for her published work on child labor laws in Washington (her Cornell senior thesis). Nor was she the first or the only woman in her class. Mabelle Thatcher Little graduated from Northwestern School of Law with Florence Kelley in 1895 and practiced with her husband for years. Together they published a leading law journal.

October 2004: My law students come from all over the country, and the world. Admissions are competitive, and the answering voices often accented. A female student said in class this week: "Well, that was in the 19th century when we know women didn't work."

Basically all the factory inspectors could do was count the number of children working illegally, count the injuries, count the hours women worked, count the sick, and then report. And so they did:

The condition of the sweaters' victim is a conclusive refutation of the ubiquitous argument that poverty is the result of crime, vice, intemperance, sloth and unthrift; for the Jewish sweaters' victims are probably more temperate, hard-working, and avaricious than any equally large body of wage-earners in America. Drunkenness is unknown among them. So great is their eagerness to improve the social condition of their chil-

251

dren, that they willingly suffer the utmost privation of clothing, food, and lodging, for the sake of keeping their boys in school. Yet the reward of work at their trade is grinding poverty, ending only in death or escape to some more hopeful occupation.

Levy Mayer's family was such a family, one which did everything to keep its smart boys in school. In Bavaria there were many laws against minorities, not only Jews, laws against certain groups purchasing and owning real estate and holding government positions. Levy Mayer's family came from the same part of Europe as John Peter Altgeld's family, leaving for similar reasons but under different circumstances. This same crucible produced and pushed out Louis Brandeis's highly educated family, and others like them, whose emigration was chronicled by one of Florence Kelley's biographers. The Mayer family had more education and more resources than John Peter Altgeld's family. The Mayer family went to Richmond, Virginia, after arriving in New York, because Levy Mayer's mother had a brother who was already established there. Yet circumstances of relocation were never simple. Virginia in 1858 was in the middle of its own political maelstrom, as reported by Levy Mayer's biographer, Edgar Lee Masters.

In New York, Governor [Horatio] Seymour had vetoed a prohibitory law, but that only rendered more active the temperance men in that state. And everywhere it was found that the anti-slavery men had united with the cause of prohibition. It was also the days of distrust of Roman Catholicism and the era of the Know Nothing Party, which was devoted to attacks upon aliens and Catholics. When the war between the States came on, the new home in Richmond had lost whatever illusory appeal it had for these immigrants from Bavaria. On March 1, 1862, Jefferson Davis, the President of the Southern Confederacy, proclaimed martial law in the city of Richmond and the adjoining country to a distance of ten miles, and at the same time he had suspended the privilege of the writ of habeas corpus. The execution of this law had been placed in the hands of General [John] Winder, and he was invested with almost unlimited power. He prohibited the distillation of spiritous liquors and closed all liquor shops. Extraordinary arrests of law-abiding citizens were made, capricious actions of tyranny were committed and their victims were left without redress. He established an abominable passport system, arrested editors and closed up the offices of newspapers. It was a reign of terror. Beginning with July 1, 1863, the campaign of Gettysburg was waged, and General Lee was hurled back from his invasion of the North. Then, on September 15, 1863, President Lincoln suspended the writ of habeas corpus in the North.

To escape this tyrannous turmoil, Henry Mayer and his wife decided to leave the South and to go to Chicago. After great difficulty in securing necessary passports and after some delays in getting through the military lines, they reached New York and took their way to the capital of the Mid-West, which at this time had a population of 160,000 people.

The family arrived in Chicago when Levy Mayer was five. The Mayer family settled on the Northwestern Plank Road, later Milwaukee Avenue, where Levy Mayer's father set up a small business as a pants maker. Between the Great Plank Roads were large sections of open prairie. The Plank Roads were literally planks of wood put down over mud and ice and snow, and they ran as straight spokes to the hub of the city—the courthouse, City Hall, and the commercial activities which grew up around them. The courthouse needed bail bondsmen and a jail. City Hall always needed a notary, and both needed lawyers nearby. Lawyers needed their clothes tailored and cleaned, and the judges, the lawyers, the bail bondsmen, the jailors, and everyone else with business in court had to eat and sleep and have a place to drink and talk and negotiate nearby.

Levy Mayer's older brother David had entered business and supported his younger brother when it was time for him to attend Yale College and then Yale Law School. David paid his younger brother's expenses to go to Yale at age sixteen in 1874, persuading the institution to waive its requirement that entering students must be eighteen.

At that time Yale College required a bond to be paid to the president and fellows of the college before a student could matriculate, and David Mayer put forward that bond. While at Yale Levy Mayer wrote voluminous letters, took copious notes on his reading, and kept close accounts of his expenditures. At that time there were two classes at Yale Law School: the junior class and the senior class. Levy Mayer prepared himself for law study after college by corresponding with members of the faculty.

The Mayer family would have been very aware of their Jewish neighbors in the tenements. Some of the families in the tenements sent their children to the Jewish Training School, where Levy Mayer had briefly been a student. These circumstances, reported in *Hull-House Maps and Papers*, would have been familiar to Levy Mayer's family:

> *I have found myself on Bunker Street a brick tenement house filled with Bohemian and Jewish tenants engaged in the tailoring trade and in peddling. In the ground floor, front flat, which was exceedingly clean, I found a tailor at work one Sunday afternoon upon a broadcloth dress-coat belonging to an evening suit of the finest quality, such as sell for $70 to $100. On a bed about five feet from the table at which the tailor was working, his son lay dying of typhoid-fever. The boy died on the following day; and the coat when finished was returned to the merchant tailor and delivered to the customer without fumigation or other precaution.*

In 1894 the legal cases challenging the Factory Inspection Law were making their way through the system. Levy Mayer, attorney for the factory owners, and Colonel John W.

Ela and Andrew A. Bruce, attorneys for Mrs. Florence Kelley and the State of Illinois, stipulated before Judge Sears on April 21, 1894, that thirteen of the cases tried before Justice of the Peace George Kersten should be sent at once to the Supreme Court of Illinois for a decision on the constitutionality of the statute.

April 10, 2012: The sky shining blue and white, the perfect spring day. Will I ever finish this manuscript? There is too much to know about these people, this period, and no bottom or end to the writing and research.

George Kersten had been appointed a justice of the peace by Mayor Carter H. Harrison Sr. in 1883, three years before he was admitted to the Bar. Born in the Smokey Hollow section of old Chicago, he attended public schools and later was a student at Standau and Wiedinger's German-American Institute. During his time as justice of the peace and his subsequent term on the Circuit Court bench, he tried more than 100,000 cases and sentenced several notorious defendants to death. He also served as assignment judge, which meant he was in the very powerful position of deciding who would decide what cases. He was the judge in many of the factory inspection prosecutions, and his name appears often in the homicide files.

June 16, 1999: The subset of 345 abortion cases within the fourteen thousand homicide reports to the police from 1870-1930 offer an opportunity for analysis. Chicago was, apparently, the abortion capital of the Midwest, with posters in small towns and rural areas telling girls "in trouble" where to go. Another revolution brought by the great railroad.

The thirteen defendants, those being charged with violating the Factory Inspection Law, represented by Mr. Levy Mayer, included Joseph E. Tilt, owner of a boot and shoe factory; William E. Ritchie, owner of a paper box factory; Bunte Bros. and Spohr, candymakers; and Strauss, Eisendrath and Drom, a clothing establishment. The Ritchie box company was to become the lead, named defendant.

As a history of the Illinois Manufacturers' Association, founded in August 1893, described:

Child labor, the Association considered, was an excellent preventive of delinquency and crime. There were thousands of boys in Chicago alone who were unfit for further schoolwork, who would be roaming the streets "wild as rabbits" if the [proposed federal law prohibiting child labor] present law were enacted. Manufacturers News reported numerous stories of young boys denied employment because of child labor laws who ultimately became hardened criminals.

The association was very active in the immigration debate of the 1920s, lobbying for the legislation which first imposed national origins quotas. The explicit purpose of the law was to restrict immigration largely to western and northern Europeans, excluding southern Europeans, Russians, and people from Asia and Africa.

Florence Kelley's *First Annual Report* noted that women and children constituted 37 percent of Chicago's industrial workforce and could be found in every occupation. Three of the twenty-one meatpacking companies employed only children. As Florence Kelley commented: "It is not a crime to kill a child in Illinois."

In 1877 Levy Mayer returned to Chicago, a young man recently graduated from Yale College and Yale Law School. He had to wait until he was twenty-one to be allowed to practice law, the one occasion when an age requirement was not waived in his favor. At that time schoolhouses and other temporary quarters were being used as courts because Chicago was still rebuilding after the Great Fire. Although the courts were in makeshift quarters, there was plenty of work for lawyers after the fire. Legal records, tax warrants, deeds, and titles to property, the legal foundation for ownership and the legal basis for economic relations, had to be reestablished. Lawyers from all over the country poured into Chicago in the middle of an economic boom which lasted, with only a few bumps downward, until the panic and depression of 1893.

May 18, 2000: Another law graduation, another glorious day. The robed students march up on stage to get their degrees. The graduating women almost without exception are wearing spike heels to walk across the stage. One young woman who has been working on the homicide project, visibly very pregnant. Her husband stands at the back of the audience holding another child. When the students ask me when is a good time to have a baby in terms of your career, I answer: there is no good time to have a baby for your career.

We sit as faculty members in our colorful robes, looking serious, as if we know something secret, something the students don't know. We don't know anything. Maybe we know how to keep our jobs.

Levy Mayer put his temporary disqualification to good use and became an assistant librarian for the Chicago Law Institute, where City Hall and the Office of the County Recorder had been placed after the fire. Lawyers who came to the Law Institute were given access to the library, a desk, and temporary accommodation, meaning: a room with a bed. One of Levy Mayer's jobs was to take care of the rooms for the lawyers—including sweeping the floors and making sure there was clean linen for the beds.

His job also was to help the lawyers find legal documents and authorities. For this he was paid four dollars a week. In this job he met and worked with every lawyer and property owner with legal business in Chicago. They all came to know him and rely upon him.

During his three years at the Chicago Law Institute he prepared a catalog of the Law Institute Library and revised two legal treatises, receiving royalties of twenty-five cents on every copy sold. In two years 2,500 copies were sold, demonstrating not for the last time his considerable intellectual energy and entrepreneurial skill.

March 14, 2009: The sunshine bright, we are fooled into thinking winter is over. A few stubborn clumps of snow hiding under the bushes. There will be more snow before spring is really here. In the meantime, from the third floor of the house it is all a landscape laid out below. Documents from the nineteenth century cover every available flat space. This book has become the coming together of these scattered records, writings and documents. I am at home with this varied, contradictory array. Every day is a day closer to our leaving this house, and for me this space.

At the time Levy Mayer worked at the Law Institute all of the official reports of the Supreme Court of Illinois numbered only some seventy-five volumes, and the federal reports were comparably inconsiderable, especially given that many of the pages in those 150-odd volumes would be formal, formulaic, and repetitive, or blank, or filled with titles, or surplusage, as the lawyers like to say. One person at that time could master and keep up with all of the federal and state court reports, the changes in doctrines, the precedents, the new statutes and the case holdings, as they were published. Levy Mayer made himself useful to all the lawyers and made a name for himself as an encyclopedic resource, and this was to serve him well in the future.

In 1876 there were 1,025 lawyers in Chicago. When it came time to form the Illinois Manufacturers' Association seventeen years later, his reputation was well-established. Levy Mayer initially organized the association for the sole purpose of spearheading the fight against the Factory Inspection Law and against the work of Florence Kelley and her staff. He was the first counsel to the organization. He shrewdly recognized that the challenge to the statute would be more credible if it were on behalf of an association of business people, rather than being brought by a single business or manufacturer. For all of his professional life he was counsel to the great commercial interests in Chicago, a reliable advisor during later armed confrontations between labor and business.

August 18, 2011: Another clear day. The Blue Angels are doing their aerial acrobatics overhead, and the blue sky provides the perfect backdrop. They fly upside down and around, and in formation, and the large crowd on the edge of the lake is mesmerized. Better to waste the fuel and manpower on foolish display than expend it in killing civilians.

Florence Kelley made enforcement of the compulsory education law part of the factory inspection mandate:

A little girl thirteen years of age, found at 120 West Taylor Street (Baumgarten's knee pants shop) sewing on buttons in the bedroom of the sweater's family, was discharged. She is a Russian Jewess three years in this country, and does not know her letters. She was taken bodily to the Jewish Training School and entered as a pupil.

The Jewish Training School of Chicago was founded with an initial grant of $20,000 from Mr. Leon Mandel in May 1888, to maintain a kindergarten for children too young to attend public school, a kitchen garden and sewing school for older girls, and a manual training school where boys might learn to love work, find out for what kind of work they were best fitted, and receive that preparation and assistance which would make them intelligent, skillful, competent workers, in that department best suited to their abilities.

The school was housed in a handsome four-story building, designed by Adler and Sullivan and made possible by private donations, located on Judd Street between Clinton and Jefferson, in the immediate neighborhood where most of the children in the tenements lived. Many who became prominent in Chicago public life had parents and grandparents who attended that school or were themselves pupils at the school.

October 2000: Another official event, another large gathering. Many Jews in the city remember bitterly the anti-Semitic traditions of our institution. For some of them it was a personal experience: they were not welcome at Christian fraternities. They want that memory replaced by something with their name prominently displayed.

The Russian Jews who emigrated to Chicago in large numbers in the 1880s established the Jewish Training School to teach the English language and familiarize the new arrivals with American methods and institutions. The school's curriculum was designed to equip the sons and daughters of the Jewish poor with the power of making a healthy, honest and honorable livelihood and to equip them with the desire to live in a respectable and self-respecting manner. It was in short a trade school.

For economic and religious reasons the newly arrived Russian Jews huddled together in what became known as the Ghetto. A city within a city was built up where living conditions were such that if a building were removed, each person would have had less than a square yard upon which to stand. The founders of the Jewish Training School believed that centuries of persecution and restrictions in occupations suffered by Jews in Russia and eastern Europe had rendered the newcomers unfit to grapple with the conditions under which they now lived, and thus these immigrant children needed special instruction.

June 21, 2011: On the streets of Chicago at 7 a.m., everyone is doing what they are supposed to be doing, going to school, going to work. Except the homeless woman who sleeps in the entranceway next door. She is folding her blanket and moving on for the day. The official start of summer is 12:16 today, and it is hot. But inside the temperature is steadily and artificially set at comfortable. Outside the office window at 12:16 p.m. the boats are bobbing in the harbor, their decks covered with beer-drinking, nearly naked sunbathers, who hop from boat to boat and occasionally jump into the lake to cool off.

The Jewish Training School's curriculum was based upon corrective measures and training in handwork. From its founding the school accepted both boys and girls, and one goal was to train these children for as many elementary trade activities as possible, in order for them to find out their bent. The academic work was to be as practical as possible. For the girls the school sought to connect them with domestic and commercial worlds, in other words to find jobs as servants or in the shops. It was not preparation for the professions, although at the time there were prominent Jews in business and in all the professions. This is how the Jewish Training School described its purpose:

> *The past decade has brought to Chicago thousands upon thousands of Jewish emigrants from the most benighted and degrading sections of Europe. They had come hither but little affected by modern culture, ignorant of our language and ignorant of the grand opportunities this free country offers its citizens; and almost without exception, they have domiciled themselves in wretched dwelling-houses in one section of the city, where they have created their own ghetto. It is as natural as night that the small quarters in which large families are domiciled should be unclean, and that those in whom persecution abroad developed a hereditary tendency to trading should in this country make a livelihood by peddling or by unskilled labor.*

> *This is an unfortunate state of affairs, but, endeavor all we will, it is barely possible to do much for the permanent social improvement of the adults. We must leave it to the free institutions of this country to improve them as best they may. But the children we can influence. These saplings can still be bent. Of them we can make clean, honest, useful, educated Americans.*

The first factory inspectors found illiteracy and lack of education throughout the tenements and sweatshops, not just among the Jewish immigrants:

> *Greek, Italian, Bohemian, Polish and Russian children are constantly encountered who speak no English, hundreds of whom cannot read nor write in any language. Children who cannot spell their name or the name of the street in which they live are found at work every day by the deputies. . . . In Massachusetts every child must attend some school throughout the period during which the public schools, are in session until four-*

teen years of age. . . . New York goes even farther, and empowers her inspectors to order peremptorily the discharge of any child under sixteen years of age who cannot read and write simple sentences in the English language. . . . Nor do the children who are deprived of school life receive at work any technical training which might in part compensate for their loss.

A different kind of ill health for children was associated with each trade: in the garment industries children were prone to tuberculosis and curvature of the spine; in cigar shops, nicotine poisoning; in paper box factories, arsenic poisoning; in stamping works, poisoning from acid fumes; in laundries, curved spines and exhaustion from the heat and dampness; in the glassworks, rheumatism, burns, tuberculosis, exhaustion, and blindness from glass particles.

Once again, William Stead captures the scene:

The first impression which a stranger receives on arriving in Chicago is that of the dirt, the danger and the inconvenience of the streets. Those accustomed to the care that is taken in civilized cities to keep the roadway level and safe for teams and carriages stand simply aghast at the way the thorough fares are corduroyed by ill-laid, old fashioned street car line, the gauge of which projects so much above the body of a rail on which the traffic runs as to be perpetually wrenching wheels off the axle. . . . Here cuddled is the climax of reckless incompetence in city management, the supreme example of the sacrifice of public safety, public property and public convenience to the interests of great corporations. . . .

If a stranger's first impression of Chicago is that of the barbarous gridironed streets, his second is that of the multitude of mutilated people whom he meets on crutches. Excepting immediately after a great war, I have never seen so many mutilated fragments of humanity as one finds in Chicago.

Every year children were killed and maimed in factory accidents, and it was no crime. The factory owners protected themselves by having parents sign blanket releases discharging factory owners from any responsibility and by requiring workers (many of whom were illiterate in English) to carry cards they could not read with instructions on how to handle dangerous equipment and a description of hazards, followed by an assumption of risk clause. A state statute limited liability for injuries in factories to $5,000.

February 14, 2009: Valentine's Day. Where are my sweethearts? New snow and everything is white and shining. Not far from this day in 1892 Florence Kelley and Alzina Stevens led a band of Illinois state legislators through the sweatshops in the Nineteenth Ward to show why factory inspection legislation was needed. The legislator who refused to enter the tenements at home was not foolish. His name is not in the record.

Inspection—being able to take a look—was how the statute was enforced. Enforcement was met with evasion, as well as direct opposition. The factory inspectors also encountered practices they didn't expect, another reason to look at what is actually going on. The *First Annual Report* continues:

> *A surprising thing developed by the use of the affidavits is the migratory method pursued by the employed children. Our very thorough complete system of handling the registers, records and affidavits, enables us to trace a child changing its place of work and also to note the number of changes in any one place. I cite one instance typical of all: On August 22 [1893], I inspected a candy factory, where I found eighty children under 16. For sixty three of these affidavits had been filed, of which I found forty-three correct and twenty worthless because improperly made out. The forty-three correct affidavits were stamped, seventeen children unprovided with affidavits were sent home, and twenty defective affidavits were returned to the children, who were given until the next day to get them right. On September 8, another inspector visited this factory and found seventy-one children at work with sixty-five affidavits awaiting inspection. Only one of these bore the stamp of my previous inspection, two weeks before. The seventy children were a new lot, and all but one of the children I had found in this place had taken their affidavits and flitted off to other work. In the same factory on September 11—only three days later, and one of those a Sunday—a third inspector found 119 children, and, of course, new records and an almost total change in the register were again necessary.*

While the children were migrating, on the lam, seeking to remain employed, evading the enforcement restrictions if they could, their parents, if there were parents, were doing the same. In 1893 the city was in the middle of an economic crisis: bank closings, foreclosures, a run on the currency, and the laying off of workers as economic activity ground to a halt. Often the children found employment, even if the wages were meager, more easily than the adults. Just get someone to bring in some money. The term cascading effect, or downward spiral, to describe the collapse of an economic system implies more order in the pattern than that harsh reality, which resembled chaos. The few, mostly church-run social service centers were overwhelmed. People fought against the waves of economic losses and drowned. The researchers on homelessness described what they found:

> *A.B. was a printer, aged 35; married and with four children. He had a good work record in his home city; he drank occasionally but not to excess and he was paying in installments for a home of his own when his wife, quite suddenly, died. Being unable to find a*

capable housekeeper he soon broke up his home and placed his children in institutions. In his intolerable loneliness following this action, he thought that he would be happier if he could go to some new place and find employment. He set out with this intention.

These case histories of the homeless on the streets were gathered by Mrs. Alice Willard Solenberger during 1900-03 from interviews. This was one of several social investigations of homelessness and unemployment generated by agencies or academic projects. The original researcher herself died before the study was complete, or at least the last chapter was not complete, as is explained by the introduction, written by another woman who sees the research to its publication as the book *One Thousand Homeless Men*. These studies at universities represented the beginning of the academic part of social study and social work. Hull-House was the symbolic and actual center for many of these enterprises, and *Hull-House Maps and Papers* its prototype. Most of this research was done by women, well-educated women who were paid little or nothing.

September 26, 2007: Grey outside and a chill. Yesterday uncharacteristically warm. Chicago has the feel and bustle of a city celebrating itself. The talk is of the Olympics and how the games would be another World's Columbian Exposition. When the Olympics come to Chicago, the world will come and be agape at the beauty of our city, the city leaders say. There are plans to revive Burnham's plan.

In 1893, people wanted to know who the homeless were, and the social service people and the reformers set themselves to find out. The public debate was over whether the homeless on the street were simply shiftless and lazy or whether there were other reasons they could not or did not find work.

William Stead describes a single men's hotel in 1893 when a bed could be had for a dime:

Saying he would like to retire, a doorway at the farther end of the room was pointed out, and he was told in a far from civil tone to take his choice of any of the beds. Following the direction pointed out, the investigator entered the sleeping room. For a few moments it was impossible to see anything in the place, the only light coming from a dirty lamp at the farther end of the room, which was about fifty by twenty-five feet in dimensions; while the darkness was made more apparent by the smoke from a dozen pipes of the men who were lying in the beds and smoking. The arrangement of the room was certainly unique in character. The beds consisted of a piece of canvas, which was fastened to the wall on one side, while on the other they were supported on upright wooden poles, which ran from the floor to the ceiling. They were arranged in tiers, four deep, and the covering on each bed consisted simply in one thin blanket, which in several cases was reeking with vermin. In the center of the room was a large stove filled with blazing wood which only served to dispel any breath of air which might by inadvertence have entered the apartment. In this place one hundred and fifty men sleep, no precaution being taken whatever to prevent the spread of any disease which may be brought in by any of the lodgers.

And so these women researchers set out to chronicle the statistical data, and the life stories, of *One Thousand Homeless Men* in Chicago at the time of the 1893 depression. The story of A.B., the inadvertent tramp, continues:

But failing to secure work, and even more restless and lonely in this city than in his own, he went on to another. Still not finding work he went to a third city, and in the meantime drinking considerably and becoming daily more shabby in appearance. When his money was exhausted he began to beat his way from city to city, constantly associating with tramps both on the railroads and in the cheap lodging houses. Within a few months he no longer even made a pretense of seeking work but frankly dropped to the level of the men with whom he traveled.

When we knew him this man had been drifting and wandering aimlessly about the country for four years. He was sodden with whiskey and so degraded physically, mentally and morally that it was difficult to believe he had ever been the clean and useful citizen, with a family and a home of his own, which correspondence with his home city proved him to have been less than five years before. We did our best to save this man who had once been so well worth saving, but we did not succeed.

Given that there were neither automobiles nor airplanes, it is remarkable how far and how often men and many women traveled from one city to another to seek stability and work. This was the culture of tramping, or beating, as it was called, a way across the country, sometimes on foot and sometimes on the rails. It was established as soon as the railroads were built. Sometimes women disguised themselves as men and rode the rails. The social service agencies in Chicago regularly put women and orphans on the train to somewhere else, when they turned up homeless in Chicago.

The World's Fair brought hundreds of thousands to Chicago for work. When it closed, there was no work and nowhere to go, and many stayed, living on the streets, and many others went back to tramping. There was no work where they came from; at least a man could sleep on the floor of the police station and have a cup of coffee in the morning in Chicago.

Later a noted economist analyzing the panic and depression of 1893 wrote:

It is interesting to note an article in the London Statist, *July 23, 1892, which in effect predicted a gold run and bank panic in the U.S. The prediction was in response to the wave of selling of U.S. securities by Englishmen, which was explained by lack of confidence in the U.S. due to the monetary situation. The predicted disaster was to start with a run on banks, then a run on the Treasury, after which gold hoarding was to occur and lead to a premium on gold and finally a panic and disaster. While the events in the 1893 panic did not follow exactly the pattern predicted, all the events alluded to occurred in the Spring and Summer of 1893.*

Florence Kelley's inspections as factory inspector began in the tenements in the summer of 1893 and soon branched out to the rest of the state. A smallpox epidemic presented a special occasion for inspections and garnered public support for them.

The Illinois Glass Works in Alton refused to allow the factory inspectors in. Instead of helping the poor, the *Alton Evening Telegraph* said, the factory inspectors were enforcing a law passed by demagogues.

Florence Kelley replied to the company's characterizations in the *First Annual Report*, saying that the children working in the glass plant were "ill-fed, ill-clothed . . . and in many cases unable to work without stimulants. Boys of 7 to 10 years old chew tobacco habitually, and boys 10 to 14 are in some cases habitual drinkers of the beer and whiskey which are freely sold just across the street from the [glass] works."

Governor John Peter Altgeld, who had firsthand experience of child labor, refused to back down on the matter of enforcement of the statute at the Glass Works. However, he did testily ask Florence Kelley not to be so confrontational in doing her job, although that was not the language he used.

November 28, 2004: So generous, so kind, so talented, and now so suddenly dead, the painter Ed Paschke. He told me I could have an image from any painting for the cover of my book. His son said: "What he got from his father he gave to me, and that was the feeling that everything might at any time disappear. So he worked six days a week, and on Sunday he sat around the house making drawings with a bad ballpoint pen. . . . "

As for the widows and orphans, often held up by business as the justification for not regulating child labor, Florence Kelley retorted that the only one she had found at the Illinois Glass Works "was a blind woman who was being supported by her sons seven and nine because the plant supervisor had denied her compensation and told her to send her children out to work instead."

These disputes over facts were aired at length in the local newspapers. Meanwhile the Illinois Glass Works continued to take a hard line and referred to the state factory inspector, Florence Kelley, as "demented." She had heard, and would hear, worse.

The Factory Inspection Law designated children as the subject of its protection, its excuse for intervention, but it also targeted the lying men and women who gathered up orphans and deserted children from the poorhouses of surrounding counties, and from nearby Saint Louis, saying on the affidavits that these children were fourteen when they were in fact seven to ten years old. These "guardians" of the orphans often lived on barges, could float the purchased children downriver, away from where anyone could check on them, and then take all of the forty cents a day the children earned at the Glass Works while providing minimal food and shelter. The children, especially the young boys, became part of the floating army of the unemployed.

July 13, 2013: A visit to a family who adopted a Vietnamese boy who was severely deprived in an orphanage overseas. He has made remarkable progress: he can now speak, feed himself, and throw a ball. It is a miracle, and the result of years of devotion.

Surely, Florence Kelley and her assistants believed, if the good people of Chicago knew of such practices, they would not tolerate them.

It is a matter of rarest occurrence to find a set of children who have been working together two months in any factory. They are here to-day, and gone to-morrow; and, while their very instability saves them, perhaps, from the specific poison of each trade, it promises an army of incapables to be supported as tramps and paupers. The child who handles arsenical paper in a box factory long enough becomes a helpless invalid.

Levy Mayer's client, Ritchie & Company, was one of the largest of the many paper box manufacturers in Illinois. All the factory inspector's prosecution could do, after all, was call the attention of the judiciary and the public to the violation of the law. And so the first cases prosecuted under the new factory inspection statute proceeded:

Wertheimer, Samuel, before Justice Eberhardt November 14; cloak maker at 535 W. Sixteenth Street for Joseph Beifeld & Co.; charged with employing two children under sixteen years of age without affidavits; first jury trial under the law; found guilty and fined $3 and costs upon first charge; trial on the second charge in same court on November 24; defendant again asked for a jury trial, and jury again fined him $3 and costs.

Some were jury trials in Chancery, although equity courts typically did not have juries. The defendants asked for juries, expecting either the legal skill of their lawyer or popular hostility to the statute to predispose juries to their side. They usually lost.

In the flush of optimism after the statute was passed, some thought that much would change. However, the fines were minimal, and the manufacturers just paid the fine and continued what they were doing. On the other side, if one of the law's purposes was to educate, the reports of the inspections, the dissemination of the official reports and the newspaper stories did accomplish that.

This is how John Peter Altgeld described the law, and what the law could do, in a speech:

The administration of justice, or rather of the laws, is better than it has ever been; but it is only a struggling toward the right, only a blind groping in the darkness toward light. . . . The wrongs done in the courts of justice themselves are so great that they cry to heaven. . . . The wrongs done by government are so great that they can be measured only by the eye of omniscience.

The chronicle of the homeless man who lost his wife continues:

In the course of his wandering he had broken his left arm and, because of the condition of his system through the use of whiskey, the bone could not be made to knit, and he could never hope to recover use of the arm. In spite of this handicap, however, we felt that if he could be persuaded to give up his habits of drink and of wandering, the man might again possibly become self-supporting. We appealed to him through his love for the children he had abandoned, and he agreed to stop tramping and to take a drink cure. We furnished him with new clothing and he went to an institution where he remained for about two weeks; then he left and wandered onto the road again without returning to the Bureau office.

The boys taken from the orphan asylums for a small fee and drifted down river on barges to the Illinois Glass Works were called blowers' dogs. Their job was to run from the glass blower to the furnace and back again, to cut the molten glass off, give it to the blower, and to carry water to the blowers. The furnaces ran all night. The injuries from the unguarded machinery were many, especially to unwary, untrained and exhausted children. There was always the dripping molten glass, and glass shards on the floor where the barefoot children ran.

Florence Kelley reported in 1893:

The class of little children whom I taught in the Polk street night school last winter was made up of Italian boys and girls, ten, eleven and twelve years old, children so wholly illiterate that they were struggling with the bats, cats and rats in the opening pages of the primer. In November and December a large number of them left the night school because the candy factory in which they spent their days began to work overtime, and my pupils worked in it from 7 a.m. to 9 p.m., with a half hour for dinner and no sup-per, a working week of eighty-two hours. I used to see them going home long after 9 o'clock at night. This year this factory worked eight hours except and during two weeks, when it worked ten.

June 13, 2008: The spring means driving around the axle-wrenching potholes on the streets. The economic news remains grim. One giant bank after another in grave trouble.

The near-collapse of the English banking house of Baring Brothers in 1890 precipitated the collapse of other banks and financial institutions, as the great financial empires built upon mutual credit came down, first slowly, and then precipitously with a great crash. The comparative size of that system and the present systems is: in 2006 the gross national product of the United States was over $13 trillion; in 1893 the gross national product was close to $29 billion, and it shrank to $27 billion in 1894.

In the 1890s the political debate was about tariffs and about how gold and silver should be held as the basis for paper currency. The political debate over tariffs and protectionism, over how much the United States should be part of the global economy, was no more informed than such debates are today. The 1890s was a time when the federal government debt increased, when the balance of trade shifted to negative, and the value of the dollar in comparison to other currencies fluctuated wildly. The economic analysis of the 1893 depression continues:

For fourteen years, 1878-1892, only an insignificant amount of gold was paid out by the treasury [of the United States] in the redemption of legal tender notes; the total amount of gold in the treasury increased almost steadily and continuously from $140,000,000 on January 1, 1879, to $300,000,000 in 1891.

The rapid diminution of that to $190 million gold reserves on June 30, 1891, continued with a further fall in gold reserves to $95 million in 1893 and $64 million in 1894, and that represented a run on the U.S. Treasury.

The failure of the great English banking-house of Baring Brothers in 1890 brought a considerable withdrawal of English capital invested in the United States; and an unhealthy and inflated industrial development in this country was stimulated by the new tariff.

The McKinley Tariff of 1890 was faulted, as was the Sherman Silver Act of 1890, which authorized the purchase of silver and the issuing of silver-backed treasury notes as legal tender. The government declared its intention to maintain the two metals on a parity.

The enactment of these two statutes within a few weeks of each other resulted in a greater than anticipated exchange of gold for currency in the US, and the net assets of the government were sharply and quickly reduced. The quality of the government assets was also quickly reduced as the proportion of gold reserves dwindled. The decreased amount of the government gold reserve assumed a magnified importance and was watched daily for ups and downs. For most people these were effects of something occurring somewhere else; the immediate result was that people could not get their money from their bank deposits, or they were unemployed, or they were on the streets with nothing to eat.

Meanwhile, the factory inspectors continued to do their work and report on the special new circumstances of the smallpox epidemic, as requested by the new governor:

May 12, 1894—David Schwartz, 704 W. 18ᵗʰ street, cloak maker for F. Siegel & Bro., 222-228 Market street. Inspectors Kelley and Bisno.

This shop is in the basement of the rear house on the lot with windows opening on the alley. On this date seven persons were employed in the shop. The inspectors found the yellow card [marking the presence of smallpox] *posted on a door inside the front house. They immediately made an inventory of the goods in the shop, finding one hundred and twenty-five cloaks for children in process of manufacture and in bundles, and two of the persons in the shop unvaccinated. The shop was then ordered closed. The inspectors learning that there were ten families, sixty five persons, living on this lot, proceeded to examine the arms of the persons then on the premises, forty in all. Of these forty persons they found eighteen vaccinated. In one family they found four children in different stages of the disease. One flat was locked and darkened and access to it would not be gained. Subsequently it was ascertained that there was small-pox there also. As an illustration of the total absence of quarantine it may be mentioned. . . .*

Monday, May 14, Inspectors Kelley and Bisno again visited the premises, 704 W. 18ᵗʰ street, and found everything as before, except that the yellow card had been removed to the outside door.

Yet somehow people continued on. They rode the streetcars to look for work. The boats full of immigrants still came, perhaps because it was worse elsewhere and because they believed there was at least hope here. And once the journeys started it was not easy to turn back or reverse course, even if you didn't know how or where it would end. When there was nothing to eat and no work, the children went out on the streets and begged, or worked or sold themselves. The women bore children, fed and cared for them, and the children died—40 percent of the children in the Nineteenth Ward did not reach the age of five. And the women continued working. The *Smallpox Report* detailed:

. . . that while this inspection of arms [for proof of vaccination] *was going on, a milk-man came through the houses serving milk to the ten families, and two children came*

home from their day's work in a candy factory, to which they had gone from rooms adjoining those occupied by the four sick children.

The inspectors did what they could.

Inspector Kelley telephoned [Health] *Commissioner* [Arthur] *Reynolds of the four cases of small-pox at this number in addition to the case indicated by the yellow card, and asked that an immediate official diagnosis be made of the cases, and the tenants all vaccinated.*

The hardship continued, economic conditions worsened, and people went on. Everyone who could, kept working throughout the epidemic. Some people died; some left town. Hull-House fed more people. More than a thousand people a week came through Hull-House. Jane Addams and others somehow found the money somewhere to keep it going. The doors were always open.

March 1, 2009: The weather in San Francisco the day before yesterday was perfect: bright sunshine, a light breeze, in the 60s. Walking beside the San Francisco Bay in the Mediterranean light, a tonic. The next day in Chicago, the snow is swirling. Last night we landed with no difficulty, and the temperature was 26 degrees. California was hard hit by the recession, but sunshine undercuts the misery. The homeless in the tents aren't shivering.

Meanwhile, at the national level, the depression of 1893 was deepening; the government seemed hapless, the banks and financial institutions took whatever money they could and closed the doors, as analyzed by Professor Davis Rich Dewey, of the Massachusetts Institute of Technology, in *Financial History of the United States*:

Fortunately the internal revenue receipts maintained their customary level with something to spare; but increased appropriations, due largely to the passage of a dependent pension bill in 1890, cut deep into the funds of the treasury. In 1890 the surplus was $105,344,000; in 1891, $37,239,000; in 1892, $9,914,000; in 1893, $2,341,000; but in 1894 appeared a deficit amounting to $69,803,000.

Within the national government itself, intense effort was put to stop the cycle. The levers of government control were few, and the mechanism for how to stem an economic collapse inscrutable. For individuals, there was no Social Security, no welfare, no Medicaid or Medicare, no federal or state unemployment insurance. Help for the homeless and the starving and the unemployed, help for the children on the street came from a few private agencies, most linked to churches, or from no one. The rich locked their doors to the poor or went away. That the state now paid for factory inspectors to intervene, only to report on conditions and violations of the hours regulations, when nothing could be done, seemed to many a dangerous interference with the invisible hand.

January 3, 2013: The pension situation in Illinois is the worst in the country, but none of the states, except those with oil and gas, is doing well. Certainly the governing of Illinois is a disgrace.

Florence Kelley, Henry Demarest Lloyd, and others made speeches about the greed of monopolists. The demands upon the resources of the charitable institutions increased. The poor, the unemployed, the men on the street, the begging children were everywhere in Chicago in 1893 and 1894.

February 26, 2011: Again snow, after the champagne of the California sun. Still the governor has not signed the abolition bill. The attorney general of the state has gone on record as saying the governor shouldn't sign. The pressure from all the elected state's attorneys, especially from the Cook County state's attorney, is unremitting. They see jobs, budgets going out the window.

The investigators writing the report on *One Thousand Homeless Men* hoped to shed some light on why many people were homeless by looking at who was on the streets or in the homeless encampment. It was an enterprise similar to the effort to chronicle the conditions in the tenements.

The fact that thousands and tens of thousands of boys, unemployed workmen, tramps and vagrants are stealing rides on the railroads and traveling about the country without personal expense is one with which we all are familiar, but that a second very large army of wanderers is traveling from Maine to California . . . with its transportation paid out of charity funds, is a fact which is probably not so well known.

The most striking differences which exist between the two armies of wanderers, are, first, that the "paid for" group included hundreds if not thousands of women and children, which among those who beat their way women are so rare as to be almost unknown. . . .

A most interesting chapter might be written about the tramp-women and the tramp-families on the road, figures as familiar to charity workers as men tramps, and whose restoration to normal living present even more serious and difficult problems.

What could one American citizen do in the face of systemwide collapse? Florence Kelley's son John writes his mother in an undated letter probably from 1907 from Phoenix, Arizona, where he has been working as a night clerk at the Hotel Adams—described on its letterhead as "new and Modern in every respect" and "built of brick and brown stone":

Dear Mother...

If you look at the market reports you will see that copper is selling at from twelve to thirteen cents a lb. You will find (on another sheet) that the mines will probably resume work at any time from the first to the last of next year, according to the ideas of the different reports. I don't know how the slump affects New York but I do know that there are five hundred men sleeping in the streets in Phoenix. I have only been good and hungry once in my life, I went sixty hours between meals in Jerome. The next time I do that, you can take a mallet like Baldwin's old friend advised his son to do. The mines are daily turning off men. Small construction projects are closing down, railroad men say they can't be sure that the railroad construction work won't stop at any time and little Johnny isn't leaving three meals a day for a wild goose chase.

William Darrah Kelley had witnessed firsthand the ravaged economy in the post-Civil War South. His mother and her children had suffered when his father dropped dead on the street and she was left penniless in an earlier economic recession. For William Darrah Kelley these events further confirmed his commitment to protective tariffs. Institutions such as Hull-House could do little, although their contributions of food and shelter and a bath were significant to many, postponing, forestalling homelessness, starvation or just offering a moment of hope and an exchange of kindness. This is how Jane Addams described it:

The administration of charity in Chicago during the winter following the World's Fair had been of necessity most difficult, for, although large sums had been given to the temporary relief organization which endeavored to care for the thousands of destitute strangers stranded in the city, we all worked under a sense of desperate need and a paralyzing consciousness that our best efforts were most inadequate to the situation.

During the many relief visits I paid that winter in tenement houses and miserable lodgings, I was constantly shadowed by a certain sense of shame that I should be comfortable in the midst of such distress. This resulted at times in a curious reaction against all the educational and philanthropic activities in which I had been engaged. In the face of the desperate hunger and need, these could not but seem futile and superficial. The hard winter in Chicago had turned the thoughts of many of us to these stern matters. A young friend of mine who came daily to Hull-House consulted me in regard to going into the paper warehouse belonging to her father that she might there sort rags with the Polish girls; another young girl took a place in a sweatshop for a month, doing her work so simply and thoroughly that the proprietor had no notion that she had not been driven there by need; still two others worked in a shoe factory; —and all this happened before such adventures were undertaken in order to procure literary material.

Jane Addams was so profoundly distressed by what she saw around herself and Hull-House in the winter of 1893 after the fair that she took herself to visit Leo Tolstoy at his estate, Yasnaya Polyana, to consult him about adapting to the American context his efforts to relieve unspeakable distress and want in Moscow in the winter of 1881. Yet Russia had no solutions to these economic and political problems, and people carried on, and the privileged and famous left records of what they did and felt:

Yalta, March 27, 1894 Anton Chekhov to Alexei Suvorin

Greetings!! For almost a month now I've been living in Yalta, ever so boring Yalta, at the Hotel Russian, Room 39. Room 38 is occupied by Abarinova [who played a central part in the original unsuccessful production of "The Seagull"], *your favorite actress. We're having spring weather, it is warm and sunny, and the sea is as it should be, but the people are excruciatingly dull, dreary and lackluster. It was stupid of me to sacrifice all of March to the Crimea. . . . Maybe it's because I've given up smoking, but Tolstoy's moral philosophy has ceased to move me; down deep I'm hostile to it, which is of course unfair. I have peasant blood flowing in my veins, and I'm not the one to be impressed with peasant virtues. I acquired my belief in progress while still a child; I couldn't help believing in it, because the difference between the period when they flogged me and the period when they stopped flogging me was enormous. I've always loved intelligent people, heightened sensibilities, courtesy and wit, and paid as little attention to whether people pick their corns or have suffocatingly smelly footcloths as to whether young ladies walk around in the morning with curlpapers on. . . . Prudence and justice tell me there is more love to mankind in electricity and steam than in chastity and abstention from meat. War is an evil and the court system is an evil, but it doesn't follow that I should wear bast shoes and sleep on a stove alongside the hired hand and his wife.*

March 13, 2009: Finally the days are longer. The day begins with hope when the sun shines. The sun must have been shining some of the time despite the smog in 1893. Yesterday, 14 degrees, snow falling. I tiptoed over the ice to the Water Tower and then to the big, black Hancock building, rumored to be the object of terrorist threats. People on the street are stern, wrapped up, muffled up against the cold, in their bright puffy coats and colorful scarves, their feet laced up in all kinds of boots, as if it were January. The economic news is pessimistic still, the light is a spring light, a blue-tinged light. Seasonal affective disorder: a depression occurring in the winter months, when darkness descends and the daylight is less than half of the twenty-four hours. Good company, laughter is the best remedy.

The severe economic crisis in America in 1893 continued, as Dewey writes:

Although the president attempted by a specific declaration to make clear the harmonious purpose of the administration that redemption would continue in gold, public apprehension would not be allayed. Whatever might be the wishes of the administration, it was feared that it would not have power to carry them out; particularly when it was announced in April, 1893, that the gold reserve had been drawn down to $96,000,000 by redeeming the treasury notes of 1890.

At this juncture of financial and commercial difficulties, in June, 1893, the British government closed the mints in India to the free coinage of silver. The price of silver bullion fell promptly and rapidly, and, while such a decline might on another occasion have produced no immediately serious consequences to the treasury, it came at a moment when public opinion, at least in the Eastern States, was aroused to a belief that the entire financial problem was associated with the coinage of silver; and it thus furnished one of the contributory forces which drove the commercial community into a state of panic.

This economic crisis set the stage for the presidential election of 1896. The Hull-House residents supported the reelection of the governor. After Altgeld had commuted the sentences of the three living Haymarket defendants, however, his political capital vanished as quickly as the capital reserves of the state banks. Still, he always said later, he had no regrets about that decision. Pullman was yet to come. The financial panic was acute in Chicago:

It was not until June 30, 1893, when the panic was well under way, that a special session of Congress was called for August 7. . . . So far as the treasury was concerned, the mischief had been done . . . . Thus on December 1, 1893, the actual net balance in the treasury above the gold reserve, pledged funds and agency accounts was only $11,038,488. Trade and industry had been disorganized; the panic of 1893 extended into every department of industrial life. In December, 1893, the comptroller of the currency announced the failure during the year of 158 national banks, 172 state banks, 177 private banks, 47 savings banks, 13 loan and trust companies, and 6 mortgage companies . . . . The fright of depositors was general and the shrinkage in deposits enormous; bank clearings were the lowest since 1885.

Fear and loss of confidence in the economy spread quickly. To this day no one understands the dynamic, or how to stop a panic. It is an epidemic, like smallpox. People can make a show of confidence, of confronting the panic, or the plague, but can't deliver government results. Public confidence in the economic system is the oxygen which holds the system together, and when it becomes scarce or disappears, the gasping begins. And then the question is, can life support get there in time?

> *The production of coal, both anthracite and bituminous, fell off. . . . New railway construction almost ceased; in 1894 there were 156 railways, operating a mileage of nearly 39,000 miles, in the hands of receivers; among them were three great railway systems,— the Erie, Northern Pacific, and Union Pacific. The total capitalization in the hands of receivers was about $2,500,000,000, or one fourth of the railway capital of the country. . . . The problem of the unemployed became general; special committees were organized in nearly all of the large cities to provide food, and in many places relief work by public bodies was instituted.*

December 29, 2011: The most glorious bright blue sky, and sunshine. Everyone gone now. Finally the economic news is not completely bleak.

A committee of the fortunate has never dealt in a satisfactory way with correcting what befalls the poor. The members of a committee gather together and drink their coffee around a serious, square-cornered table, frowning and nodding over how little can be done, how hard it is to understand the deplorable lack of motivation and moral fiber among the poor. Soon it is time to adjourn for lunch.

July 9, 2008: Another perfect summer day. Anger remains, and fear. How can well-meaning people in power make such a mess of it. This is what democracy brought. For me, the excitement of a new writing project. There seems to be little to admire about our current government. I so retreat into the past. The collapse of the markets continues, spreads around the world.

In the debate over what to do about the 100,000 people sleeping on the streets in the brutally harsh winter of 1893, the question was whether offering the poor the opportunity to sweep the streets for seventy-five cents a day would damage their incentive to seek regular employment.

Florence Kelley observed in the *Second Annual Report*:

> *Of the 8,130 wage-earning children in Illinois some are orphans and half orphans, but a large majority are the children of men employed in industries without strong labor organizations; such as laborers, lumber shovers, or employees in the garment trades.*

> *In hundreds of cases during 1893-4 the children left school and went to work because the father, previously the sole support of the family, was now among the unemployed. This is a lasting injury wrought by every industrial crisis; for the children so withdrawn from school are ashamed to return, after a prolonged absence, to a lower class;*

and having tasted the excitement of factory life and partial self-support are unfitted for anything else. The growth of child labor during these months has been very marked, the demand for children increasing in the universal effort to reduce expenses by cutting wages, so that it was a matter of common remark that in any given trade in which children were employed, that factory was busiest which employed fewest adults.

March 19, 2009: Sunshine. Nothing but sunshine for the next three days. To find the strength of the green shoot pushing up in the yard. People love stories. These serious institutions, all of those buildings, will they survive? Probably not as we know it here, now. Our education continues.

The *Second Annual Report* continues:

Although the law prohibited absolutely the employment of any child under 14 years of age in manufacture, the children under 14 years can never be wholly kept out of the factories and workshops until they are kept in school. At present the school attendance law is almost useless, at least in Chicago where the largest number of children have been found at work. . . .

Although the Chicago Board of Education employs attendance agents, yet children leave school to sell papers; to carry cash in stores and telegrams and messages in streets; to peddle black boots, "tend the baby," or merely to idle about. Unruly children are expelled from school to suit the convenience of teachers. Principals of schools have sent to the inspectors children 11 years old, with the written request that permits be granted to enable the children to go to work (in violation of the factory law) because in each case the child is "incorrigible." As no factory can be a better place for a child 11 years old than a reasonably good school, this request voices the desire of the principal to be relieved of the trouble of the child. . . . The last school census, 1894, shows 6,887 children between the ages of 7 and 14 years, in Chicago alone, who attend no school.

For Florence Kelley, concern for her own children was always present, always uppermost in her mind. If they were not with her, which was most of the time, then they were under someone else's care, or at school, until they grew up and went off to college. Always on her mind: where were they?

September 1, 2012: There will be a teachers strike. What's the Board of Education supposed to do? There is no money to balance the budget, yet people expect to be paid and to get raises and pensions.

In spite of the prohibition against children at Hull-House, Florence Kelley's children spent much time there. The longtime residents became aunts, uncles, surrogate parents. And even though Florence Kelley knew everyone, had contacts with everyone, it wasn't always straightforward or easy to find a decent boarding school, especially if there was no money to pay for the school fees.

Briefly in the summer of 1893 she brought the children and her mother to live in an apartment near Hull-House. However, sending the children to school in the Nineteenth Ward was consigning them to typhoid, smallpox, and other diseases carried by rats, pigs and sick human beings. She had seen too many children die to do that to her own children. Yet the alternatives were not perfect:

To Florence Kelley, Jan. 10, 1897

Dear Mrs. Kelley [on the letterhead of the Hillside Home School, where John and Margaret were enrolled as boarders]—*Yours of Dec. 29ᵗʰ was duly received—We were quite pained at its contents—for we had worked faithfully with your children—and it was, to say the least, rather depressing to have the result so poor.*

I. I had intended getting return tickets for the children—but in handing the ten dollars to Mr. James I failed to specify round trips—and he did not purchase them—However John's shoes have grown out and I will use it for that and as you have otherwise directed.

II. I do not know what more we can do to have them brush their teeth than we have done, except as you suggest stand by them until they have brushed them. Margaret has been "sent from the breakfast table" more than once, last time to clean her teeth. Our girls usually do not require such constant oversight in that, as our boys—they clean their teeth as they wash their hands.

III. John's clothes are properly laundried although I seem to contradict you in making the statement. His bedding is changed twice a week sometimes three times. His straw mattress changed every week—when he first came and put out on the grass between times, because there was such an odor that it penetrated the whole chamber. . . . Those trousers you mentioned were washed the week before his return but winter-drying of such garments invariably leave streaks and besides the stains even on the bed clothes are hard to remove even with "the boiling."

You are greatly mistaken if you think we scrimp his washing because we do not charge extra for it for really John's washing has been larger than any little boy's in school.

IV. Few days before he went home John complained of chilblains and we told Mrs. Ketchin to soak them in hot water and apply kerosene to them—which is really quite efficacious.

V. Your fears that John's devotion to Hillside is because of the license that is his—as in-dicated by "the state of teeth, his feet and trousers" is entirely ungrounded.

The little lad loves the <u>natural</u> out of door life that is his—and it is not at all <u>lawless</u> in-side or out—and the teachers all remark how much he has <u>improved</u> since he has been here, not only in health but in what tells for character we see it.

Signed, Jane Lloyd Jones

September 10, 2012: Sunshine, clear, blue skies, a wisp of cloud, and the Chicago public school teachers, all twenty-six thousand of them, are on strike. They don't have a choice. The union has called the strike and whether or not you are a member of the union, you pay the union dues and you are on strike. The parents bring some of their children to our office on the lake, where they color and draw and stare into their electronic devices.

Chicago in the late 1880s and after, in spite of Haymarket, was still the place where organized labor was strong and workers could be turned out for a strike or a march. The collapse of the railroads during the economic crisis of 1893 presented an opportunity for the critics of capitalism, especially those as eloquent as Henry Demarest Lloyd, to show how heedless and greedy the owners and management of the railroads had been as they bribed government officials and forced contracts to establish their monopolistic hold on tracks and land across the country, while paying labor as little as possible. The newspa-pers and magazines were critical to exposing these abuses.

In 1894 Coxey's army of the unemployed marched from Colorado to Ohio and on to Washington. Economic distress was further aggravated by the failure of the American corn crop in 1894. The demand for American wheat in Europe fell off as Europe suffered its own economic depression. Wheat on Western farms in America sold for less than fifty cents a bushel, an extraordinary low price.

June 21, 2011: The first day of summer. It is hot, humid, in the high 80s. Putting one foot in front of another is the best I can do today. The sky is blue, but the air thick. There are people on the street, always, going places, going to school, going to work. Stepped out into the traffic, up the elevator in the bowels of the big black building, and I am here, pen in hand. A wom-an, her head down, wearing a headscarf, sitting on a blanket, a hand-lettered sign propped up: "Lost my job, need to feed 3 children."

Henry Demarest Lloyd, Richard Ely, Florence Kelley, Jane Addams, and others chal-lenged in the 1890s the orthodoxy of the blind rule of the free market, the unseen hand, with the consequent inevitability of poverty and the sharply skewed distribution of wealth and resources. Richard Ely, the editor of the series which published *Hull-House*

Maps and Papers, attacked laissez-faire capitalism, and for his publicly expressed views lost his academic job at Johns Hopkins and almost lost his next academic job at the University of Wisconsin.

March 20, 2009: Sunshine again, although not warm. Today the plans for moving. I will no longer see the trees, today swaying gently outside my window.

Florence Kelley had been no particular admirer of Richard Ely's views when she was in Europe, but they were mostly on the same side of the ideological spectrum by the time she came to Chicago. The new progressive agenda posited a society run by a central government headed by a new breed of intellectuals and technocrats. The new technocrats were to be immune from the greed and irresponsibility so evident in government and industry in the 1890s. There was the hope that government could change.

In 1892 after being run out by Johns Hopkins for his views, Ely formed a School of Economics, Political Science and History at the University of Wisconsin. Florence Kelley asked him about an academic job there when she arrived in Chicago. This was the new ethical economics, in contrast to unbridled capitalism, which, it was alleged, had brought about in 1893 the miseries and disenfranchisement of the working class, the obscene self-enrichment of the monopolists, and the subservience and corruption of government officials as businessmen and monopolists unapologetically bought the votes of aldermen, legislators, judges, governors and anyone in government who controlled resources.

December 30, 2011: A shiny, rainy day. Chicago still the proud, the beautiful city, and still the same issues. The revolution came, it just wasn't the revolution they expected.

Government had resources to sell, or lease, and the elected officials were eager to sell, to get the cash. The corrupt in politics, which seemed to be the majority of politicians, made sure that the resources of the country and the city and the state went to profit those who bribed them or made them rich. The relationships were so blatant that it required little investigation to uncover the flow of advantage from government officials to commercial people, in contracts, in grants of franchises, and in the trading of jobs.

December 6, 2012: Springfield, Illinois. The weather a bit chilly. Government is the only game here, and museums and monuments to Abraham Lincoln reminding us and the schoolchildren, we do have history. The traffic pours in on one street at nine, and pours out in the opposite direction on a parallel street at five. Then the streets are empty. Riding the train to Chicago reminds me that John Peter Altgeld, Frank Cowperwood, Theodore Dreiser, and Florence Kelley herself all rode the great steam train to the center of Chicago, as did the millions who were part of the great migration.

It was a rare day in Springfield when the legislature passed a law such as the Illinois Factory and Workshop Inspection Law, whose purpose was to protect those with no money, no recognized rights, and few supporters. The poor and the accused have no friends in government. A new order based upon social justice, the general welfare, and the principles of Christianity must emerge, Jane Addams and Henry Demarest Lloyd argued. Their eloquence and example brought many along with them.

January 2007: Another semester begins. Levy Mayer Hall seems like my place now, and the big old stone house in Evanston has become our only home. The work of this state committee is much like the work for the state in New Jersey. It is slow; there are always obstacles to budging a bureaucracy, to implement even the smallest change.

In Illinois the state's attorneys have been bringing capital murder charges and running for election on the basis of executions and death sentences for decades, if not centuries. The judges, similarly. They are elected. Why should comfortable government officials, with a salary, a pension, and health benefits risk all that for a will of the wisp, someone else's idea of reform, someone else's grand ideas of what is right or wrong, someone else's notion of justice?

This economic reality is unchanged.

The court administrators, the police, and the public defenders are laced into the system too. The government funnels money to bureaucrats, professionals, and not just in salaries but also with institutional monetary incentives, paying for programs, buildings, equipment, and offices. What do the reformers have to offer except fewer jobs? A pure heart, a clear conscience? People would rather have health insurance.

The fact that government salaries are not large does not mean that there aren't people lining up for those jobs, especially if they come with the power to hire others, or transfer assets to others, or to sell public assets, and these days if they come with health insurance.

Championing the rights of labor to organize and strike for better working conditions became the immediate, practical application of humanitarian, democratic ethics for Florence Kelley, Henry Demarest Lloyd, and Jane Addams. Richard Ely, as a faculty member of a university, had to tread more carefully. The pseudo-science of the simple-minded ideology of the free market created, Henry Demarest Lloyd said, the fiction of a free contract and the false gospel of competition.

When Henry Demarest Lloyd toured the tenements and saw how families lived, he sat on the curb and wept, and then devoted his purse, his pen, and his voice to the children whom he found to be the most cruelly exploited. Florence Kelley was with him then, in fact and in spirit. If nothing else, protect the children, for their childhood is so brief, and once gone, gone forever.

Her son John wrote to his mother from boarding school:

October 9, 1899, Hillside, Wisconsin.

My Dear Mother,

I hope you are very well as I am. I wrote my letter on the 6th but it got lost so I am writing another.

The weather is very nice now only it looks like rain. Uncle James is going to husk this week he thinks. The leaves are all changing the colors. It is very dry now and the roads are very dusty. Everything is pretty now. Yesterday, Miss Elsie preached. I didn't understand the sermon for I never do. Saturday I helped Uncle James. In the morning I picked up potatoes. A little baby died in the morning too. It was Mrs. Hickok's little baby. I think we are haveing Indian summer now. If we don't have rain pretty soon we wont have any skating for the pond is not a foot deep and is getting shallower every day. I like to skate very much and will be glad when the ice comes. I am sure I want to work for Uncle James again next summer. I liked it very much last summer there was a great deal of fun in it. Does Ko ride his wheel very much nowadays? I get horseback rides by going up to Uncle James and bringing horses down.

Goodbye with a lot of love, John

P.S. Give Ko my love

Like Florence Kelley, Henry Demarest Lloyd considered his work to be the study of economics, although he refused to join the American Economic Association, founded by Richard Ely and a colleague and today remaining the leading association of the profession, because he thought the association was too close to business interests and the monopolies.

May 1, 2013: Thousands of demonstrators before government offices in Dhaka on Workers' Day, protesting the collapse of the factory building where more than 400 garment workers are reported to have died. The factory workers were ordered to report to work after seeing cracks in the walls and saying they were afraid to go to work. Other workers refused to enter the building. Today, summer weather, and a march on behalf of the undocumented at City Hall.

Hundreds of people came to Henry Demarest Lloyd's well-advertised public addresses and were moved to action, or speech themselves. This ability to move people, which Florence Kelley also possessed, is not easy to apprehend from the surviving written work. His particular target was the hyper-individualism of the super-rich. He attacked the gospel of free and unregulated competition, when those who benefited from it did not themselves operate in a competitive environment but bribed their way to legitimacy and crushed their competitors with dishonest trade practices. An ethics which sanctioned the distribution of the country's vast virgin wealth and resources to the few, and consigned the many to destitution, a situation the churches and philanthropies signed on to in exchange for a pittance of charity from the rich, was no system of ethics at all, he and his colleagues at Hull-House argued.

The old questions never were put to rest. On November 17, 1894, seven years after the hanging of the Haymarket defendants for, among other things, being in possession of his incendiary, bomb-the-rich book, Johann Most spoke to a large crowd at the Haymarket memorial, exhorting his listeners to direct violence. Most came again to Chicago to speak in 1895. No one interfered with him.

March 11, 2009: Still cold, still freezing. But the presence of some sun. The sun changes everything. In Chicago winter is never over by March 11, but the sun temporarily transforms the world outside the window, and the world inside my head.

In spite of the backlash after Haymarket, many social enterprises to benefit workers and the poor, as well as lectures by outspoken reformers, continued at Hull-House and elsewhere during the 1890s and were well attended. On Friday nights Florence Kelley taught German. Hull-House had college extension classes offering thirty-two courses to 182 students. There was a free concert and lecture series on Thursday night which included speakers such as Thomas Dewey. The Butler Art Gallery at Hull-House attracted three hundred people a day. On Sunday afternoons free events showcased musicians and music clubs. All together about a thousand visitors and volunteers came to Hull-House each day.

January 8, 2009: A bright and chilly thirteen-degree day. Even the bushes look startled. And we are waiting. Knowing this is our last year makes everything poignant, and yet hurried. Waiting for the other shoe to drop.

The People's Social Science Club at Hall-House considered "The Industrial Problem." Sigmund Zeisler, one of the lawyers for the Haymarket defendants, talked about the jury system. There were fourteen other clubs, mostly for girls. The exploitation of young women workers, and not just in the thriving prostitution trade, continued. There were two hundred thousand women working in Chicago. At Hull-House a few young women were taught to read and how to manage their paltry wages, which usually went to someone else. Most of the young women were supporting a parent or a disabled family member.

In 1891-92 the annual operating expenses of Hull-House had grown to $12,140, of which residence fees covered only $738. Jane Addams needed to raise $11,402 to balance the budget, and find other resources.

June 5, 2009: Somehow all the work will get done, in this beautiful weather. And we will be gone, out of this house, if not out of Chicago. There would be vast changes in the civil order, a revolutionary change in working conditions, but the changes would not be the one envisioned by the champions of labor in 1894.

These "General Comments" introducing *Hull-House Maps and Papers* by Agnes Sinclair Holbrook are a manifesto for all the Hull-House research enterprises. The subject: how people in the poorest sections of the state and city, in the factories, and in the tenements, in the glass works, lived and worked:

In classifying the people from so many corners of the earth, an effort has been made to distinguish between the groups forming different elements in social and industrial life, without confusing the mind by separate recognition of the people of every country. . . .

Italians, if present, are invariably found in the rear tenements, and the same is true of Russian and Polish Jews; however, in most cases where one apartment contains Italians or Jews, the whole tenement house is given over to them; for the arrival of either one is followed by the prompt departure of all tenants of other nationality who can manage to get quarters elsewhere, in much the same way that the appearance of a cheap money is the signal for a scarcity of dearer coins. It is rare that one will find Italians and Jews in the same house, moreover; for the lofty disdain with which the Dago regards the Sheeny cannot be measured except by the scornful contempt with which the Sheeny scans the Dago.

The reports in *Hull-House Maps and Papers* exert control over an otherwise unbearable reality and are a direct confrontation with human suffering and misery. The beauty and precision of its language, the simplicity and art of the maps, the absence of preaching deliver this work to us shining in its clarity. The polished edges of language, the gentle drawings and maps, catch the light and are startling, as in turning into a shadowed corridor and coming face-to-face with a full-length mirror: e.g., in describing the color coding of the maps:

The white lots that are so numerous east of the rivers indicate brothels. These houses are separately classed, both because their numbers and whereabouts are of importance, and because it would be unfortunate to confuse them with laboring-people by estimating their incomes in the same way. . . . The most interesting fact brought out by the investigation in this connection is that the brothels in this section are almost invari-

ably occupied by American girls. A comparison of the nationality-map with the one under consideration will make this plain. Few of the girls are entered on the schedules as Chicago-born, and the great majority come from the central-eastern States. There are many colored women among them, and in some houses the whites and blacks are mixed. Only such places as report themselves brothels are so entered in the maps, the many doubtful "dressmakers" in the same region being classified as wage-earners, according to their own statements. There are no declared brothels in the region west of the river.

September 10, 2001: The day starts out as a pleasant day, a sunny day, a quiet day, and in New York also, and in Washington, DC.

Many of the brothels and gambling houses in the area of protected illegal enterprises were controlled by prominent aldermen and city officials. Johnny Powers, the alderman for the Nineteenth Ward, owned a saloon and located his political office on the second floor there. The brothels and gambling houses, called resorts, funneled cash, both as taxes and as bribes, to many businesses, and to the aldermen, police, and city officials.

A well-publicized but short-lived closing of the Levee vice district in 1912 briefly interrupted the flow of this cash. The women's organizations, the Woman's Christian Temperance Union, and other civic organizations marched, made speeches, and carried placards and signs, and some of the resorts were briefly closed. The women who organized the social services briefly gained custody of some of the young girls in the resorts, and after detoxification tried to send them away from the city.

Programs to rehabilitate prostitutes and set up the young women in other trades elsewhere proliferated and were generally unsuccessful. There was a brisk trade in mail-order brides in the territories. Cocaine, morphine, marijuana, opium, laudanum, and other drugs, as well as cheap and expensive alcohol, were readily available in the Levee and elsewhere in the city. The great push for the prohibition of the sale of alcohol was part of the women's political agenda to clean up the houses of prostitution and the gambling resorts.

Women reformers were a visible, vocal presence at the state legislature, before the City Council and at other places of government. Although women didn't vote, the legislators recognized them as a political force. Unionized tradeswomen and other women workers as well as the Hull-House women and their supporters were critical to passing the 1893 factory inspection statute.

June 13, 2008: Another day, another page, another sentence. Weather: grey, rainy. The Florence Kelley website has thousands of documents, a chronology, photographs. Sloshing through the mud and garbage in the unpaved streets in the 19ᵗʰ Ward in heavy garments was what they did. And they didn't wear pants. How could they do what they did in those clothes, even granting that there were hundreds of laundries and, in Chicago alone, thousands of laundresses. My students wear high heels to interviews and at graduation.

Professor Richard Ely published *Hull-House Maps and Papers* as Volume Five of his series on economics and politics. It is available on the Internet, all the other volumes seeming to have sunk into obscurity. Florence Kelley would have preferred to publish the essays in a German journal devoted to legislation. When Professor Ely balked at publishing the hand-drawn colored maps along with the text, Florence Kelley threatened to withdraw the book from publication altogether. The maps were originally included in a pocket and printed on a folded, colored, light cardboard backing, an appendix for an extra price. Although the essays do not all contain her byline, the entire book carries her imprint. There would never have been a book without her.

March 15, 2009: The Ides of March, and so clear, so benign. Possible to believe anything: that there will be no more snow this winter. That the problems of the homeless will be solved. Anything is possible, and one thing certain: we will be out of this house in months.

The book sold well, but the Boston publishers, Jane Addams remarked a bit wistfully, did not consider it worthy of a second printing. It has since been reprinted many times and has never been out of print.

Turning the impersonal demographic information from the survey for the United States Department of Labor into the graphic display of the colored maps accompanied by the essays was a stroke of genius. The information is delivered to us free of the constraints of explanation of the original research. The color key is simple and beautifully precise. The maps are as timeless and expressive as a nineteenth-century landscape painting. Nor are they purely abstract. They continue to have content, important human content, surprising content. Meanwhile, overlapping with work on the book, the work of the new factory inspectors continued:

Among the reasons for concealment [of a smallpox case], *the chief are the fear of the pest-house and financial loss. Parents dread to see suffering little children carried away to a pest-house where 70 per cent of all the patients die, and they resort to extraordinary measures such as hiding sick children in coffee-sacks, locking them in water closets, or smuggling them away to remote suburbs wrapped as bundles of coats and transported in street-cars filled with unsuspected fellow-passengers. In some cases an entire flat has been darkened and locked for days together, the parents coming and going in the small hours of the night, while they nursed their children through the plague, and neighboring tenants upon the same floor believed the whole family had gone away. In other cases, doors and windows were barricaded as well as locked and bolted, and the health officers were obliged to break down the doors. . . . And the politics was not quietening down.*

What is necessary to know about Pullman in 1894 is that everyone in this narrative is involved in the events: John Peter Altgeld, Carroll Wright, Jane Addams, Henry Demarest Lloyd, George Pullman. Also a new cast of characters walks on the stage, most notably Eugene V. Debs, who then has connections to all the others. Plus, certain national players such as the president of the United States and his attorney general are important legal actors and play a role, not a constructive one, in the unfolding events.

The events were dramatic. There was a strike, followed by a lockout. The Pullman idea was to remove discontented industrial workers from a dirty, unhealthy city slum and relocate them in a beautiful, clean, self-sufficient town, a company town where the company owned everything and billed for everything: the houses the workers rented, the stores where food was sold, the water, the heat, and everything else needed to live there. The management of Pullman told the workers how to vote and made sure the vote was delivered. The workers were contract workers. What at first was a pleasant option when the economy turned down became a prison.

The town of Pullman was founded in part in response to the 1877 railroad strike, which shut down the newly linked national rail system, with violence spreading from Philadelphia west to Chicago. The town with its corporate autonomy was carefully designed to be self-regulating on the 4,000 acres near to, but outside of, the jurisdiction of the City of Chicago. Later a challenge was brought under the principle of *quo warranto* alleging that the provisions of Pullman went beyond the authority of the corporation's charter, lawyers after the fact looking for a legal foothold. Eventually, the town was ordered to sell the buildings and its other holdings. By the time that lawsuit was concluded, however, the Pullman strike was long over, the political disputes concluded, and most of the dramatic events forgotten.

September 15, 2013: The strike of the Chicago Teachers Union continues to close all of the Chicago public schools. The City of Chicago is broke, but stakeholders behave as if it were not true.

George Pullman was a builder, not always with the best judgment, known for having a temper, and a significant backer of the lying Police Captain Michael Schaack, who traversed the country making money by lecturing and selling his book about the conspiracy of Haymarket.

George Pullman was a vice president of the Law and Order League after the railroad strike of 1877, an officer and founding member of the Commercial Club, and one of the business leaders who helped win the World's Columbian Exposition for Chicago. The Pullman Palace Cars were his design, and the company of his making. The Pullman cars transformed rail travel.

December 9, 2008, Chicago Tribune: "Arrested: Blagojevich Tried to Sell Senate Seat in 'Political Corruption Crime Spree'; Lt. Gov.: Blagojevich Should Step Aside."

Gov. Rod Blagojevich and his chief of staff, John Harris, were arrested Tuesday for what U.S. Atty. Patrick Fitzgerald called a "political corruption crime spree" that included attempts to sell the U.S. Senate seat vacated by President-elect Barack Obama.

Blagojevich and Harris were named in a federal criminal complaint that alleged a wide-ranging criminal conspiracy aimed at providing financial benefits to the governor, his political fund and to his wife, First Lady Patricia Blagojevich.

Blagojevich was taken into federal custody by FBI agents at his North Side home Tuesday morning—one day shy of his 52nd birthday.

George Pullman housed his workers in clean brick houses and integrated life and work to facilitate the construction of his truly visionary Palace Sleeping Cars. The planned community in spite of its capitalist foundations offered a warped preview of what could go horribly wrong in the planned centralized communities of the Soviet Union and China decades later. Yet anyone who had been in the tenements had to grant that the cleanliness and order of Pullman were an improvement. Perhaps not being allowed to walk on the grass was a small price to pay for clean running water and indoor plumbing. Still, people's spirits were starved, and there was a punishment for nonconformity. Richard Ely was one of the first to call the Pullman idea paternalistic.

June 23, 2011: Blustery. Clouds, a little wind. It will rain. When things are going too well, stay quiet and hope the gods won't notice you and how well everything is going. They are jealous, the gods.

George Pullman's formal education stopped after fourth grade, but not for lack of family resources. Unlike John Peter Altgeld's father, his family, especially his mother, wanted him to continue his education. The boy, however, didn't like school and was a born salesman. He went to work for his uncle, soon showing an uncommon aptitude for business. Like many other Americans he was fascinated by the rapidly growing railroads—their organization, combinations, their domination of industrial production.

April 26, 2008: Really, I wish for nothing more. I am happy. To take care of him, them, to get my work out. Some day I will look at the rest of the letters. I am the beneficiary of good fortune.

George Pullman's father had patented a machine for moving buildings, and the father's business in New York grew when the federal government decided to widen the Erie Canal, requiring a number of houses and buildings to be moved. This was the business which George Pullman, as a young man of twenty-right, brought to Chicago in 1859 when the city had just decided to raise and pave the streets and install a sewage system in the central business district. George Pullman won the contract to raise and move the five-story brick Matteson House, one of Chicago's prominent hotels. He went on to move other buildings, lifting up and moving structures on an entire city block.

December 16, 2002, Chicago Tribune: "Former Inmates Press Ryan; 36 Ex-Death Row Prisoners Stand for Commutations."

. . . The men, all former prisoners who were freed from Death Row, were the key figures at the National Gathering of the Death Row Exonerated. The program clearly was organized for one purpose—an emotional appeal to outgoing Gov. George Ryan to commute the death sentences of more than 140 people on Illinois' Death Row before he leaves office on Jan. 13. . . .

"You can make a decision that will change the course of a nation," said Rev. Jesse Jackson, advising Ryan, as if the governor were present at the conference, which he wasn't.

The story is told that soon after coming to Chicago, George Pullman booked an overnight trip to New York and found the sleeping accommodations intolerable: ugly, unpleasant, uncomfortable, and stifling. He later said the long, sleepless night spent on a top bunk in his clothes with two others in the same cubicle sparked the design and the impetus to build his luxurious Pullman Palace Car. The cars featured cherry wood paneling, single beds, closets, individual heaters, and lower, more comfortable seats which were made up into beds at night by the invariably Negro Pullman porters, who went on themselves to create a unique and contradictory history, now recorded and memorialized in advertisements, photos, books, and film. Many a Hollywood heroine and hero booked their overnight passage on the Pullman cars, or met by chance and fell in love to the rumbling rhythm of the Pullman trains. The Pullman cars glamorized rail travel and made it a luxury.

July 4, 2006: The weather is fine. We take the children to fireworks. The whole town of Evanston comes to sit on the damp, grassy slope and watch.

The sleeping cars were introduced in August 1859. Thanks to George Pullman's vigorous promotion, the special cars were included in the funeral train which slowly carried the body of Abraham Lincoln back from Washington, DC, to Springfield, Illinois. George Pullman, like many others, however, had paid for a substitute to take his place in the Union army during the Civil War. He recognized the unprecedented opportunity of having his cars be part of the ceremonial train—its slow journey observed by Jane Addams's family and hundreds of thousands of others—carrying Lincoln home.

March 8, 2009: My Illinois Committee to Study the Reform of the Death Penalty seems to be completely preoccupied with trivial procedures, such as complying with the state open meetings laws. Some members want the committee to do nothing, and they are winning the day. They say the death penalty is fixed and we should leave things as they are. Why are we even bothering to meet, if the result of the meetings is going to be a committee report which says nothing, does nothing, changes nothing. The elected county prosecutors, the elected judges, the elected legislators have always won the day on these issues in these settings. They remain firmly entrenched as does capital punishment. They show up and just resist. They will probably win again, just by delaying. The prime legal tactic, delay, is still effective. People will just get tired and go away.

The incorporation of the Pullman company took place in 1869. Surviving the Great Fire, which destroyed his offices, and the panic of 1873, which depleted his capital when a bank he invested in failed, George Pullman was soon on his feet again and was lionized as one of Chicago's corporate leaders. He relocated his new corporate headquarters opposite the Chicago Club so that he could join the Millionaires Table every day for the business lunch. He was very involved in the post-Haymarket civic events.

Although he never ran for elective office, George Pullman was a national figure, a loyal member of the party of Lincoln. He and his new wife frequently stayed at the White House as guests of President Grant and his wife. Mrs. Pullman and President Grant's wife jointly hosted social events at the White House.

March 9, 2009: The calendar and the weather march inexorably forward. After the fact no one wants to go back and correct the record. Today: grey, foggy. Not cold. But wintry. Everywhere grey. The weekend lost to some stomach ailment. The economy is in free fall. Our president under siege, as if it were his fault. Where did Florence Kelley and her associates find the strength to ignore so much of what was so obviously wrong and misunderstood, and concentrate upon the things they could do something about?

The Pullman family mansion was on Prairie Avenue. When the family traveled to Rhode Island for the summer, where the Lloyd family also spent their summers, it took several private train cars to carry everything needed for their holiday: themselves, their servants, their clothes, their linens, their pets. Even the family pony, as well as food for the journey, table linens and silver, went in the special train.

December 17, 2002, Chicago Tribune: "March From Death Row: Ex-Inmates Carry Plea to Governor From Stateville."

. . . And with that, at 4:40 a.m., Gauger took the first step of a 37-mile relay walk joined by more than three dozen other freed Death Row inmates. Each former prisoner walked one or two miles with a singular purpose: He was a messenger charged with delivering a letter to Gov. George Ryan imploring the governor to commute the death sentences of all inmates on Illinois' Death Row to life without parole.

The Pullman town opened on January 1, 1881, on a two-square-mile tract of unincorporated private land, rented to the company. The town was beautiful: the buildings were neat, the houses heated and watertight, grass grew in the public places, and everything was very clean.

Central to the town—modestly named for George Pullman himself, as was the company—was a 350-ton, 2,400-horsepower Corliss steam engine, which Florence Kelley would have seen when taken by her father to the Philadelphia Centennial Exposition in 1876. The engine had been shipped in pieces in thirty-five railway cars to Pullman, where it was reassembled, placed on a platform, and used to power the factory. It was dedicated by Florence Pullman, George Pullman's favorite daughter. The town's sole hotel with its iconic spire was named for her. When George Pullman came to Pullman, he always stayed in the Hotel Florence in his special suite.

March 2, 2013: Today a new pattern on the lake: little cubes of ice and snow, a tapestry, a knobby knit sweater, bubble wrap.

The design and comprehensive plan of the Pullman town was revolutionary. Control of the residents and workers was through their wages, and by having every aspect of their life funneled through the Pullman Palace Car Company. In a February 1885 article in

Harper's Weekly magazine, Richard Ely commented that Pullman was not just a company town, but a revolutionary approach to social management. He was right, and one of the few to dissent from the general public enthusiasm for the enterprise.

Was it not reasonable to believe that the Pullman town, with its tidy single-family houses, orderly rental units, its wide streets named for the captains of industry, was an improvement over the hell-holes described by William Stead, the *Factory Inspection Annual Reports* and *Hull-House Maps and Papers*? And if it was all based on profit, for the Pullman Palace Car Company, what was wrong with that?

March 5, 2011: A drizzly Chicago day, not really rain, not snow. Cold. A day to stay indoors and look for color indoors. A day which makes you think of graves, and gods. Now that we are part of the cement and steel of the urban community, I miss the grass and flowers at our old house. The new hospital next door is now entirely faced with handsome stone except for the bottom floor, for which something decorative is planned. Its most distinctive feature, the imprint of a child's hand stenciled into the façade.

By 1893 the population of the town was more than twelve thousand, about half of whom worked for the company. The Pullman cars required specialized workers, carpenters, furniture makers, and sewers, as well as the iron and steel kind of railroad workers. The railroads as a whole employed hundreds of thousands, in direct and secondary industries. If the company town had been run by the government, the enterprise would have been called communism.

After a visit Richard Ely concluded that the town was feudal and George Pullman like a benevolent Russian czar or the German kaiser. It was long before 1917.

January 19, 2003: Our governor knew he was making history. Still, there was a weariness in his eyes behind the rimless glasses. The exonerated look bewildered. No one can quite believe it happened. I don't believe it was a cynical act of political expedience. It was an unprecedented act, the commutation of all 150-plus death sentences.

Eugene V. Debs was twenty-four, years younger than George Pullman, the child of immigrants from Alsace—where the families of Levy Mayer and John Peter Altgeld came from—and raised in Indiana. He had no talent for the family's small grocery business; in fact he had no talent for business of any kind. He quit school at age fourteen, to the distress of his parents, and went to work for the railroad. Attractive and companionable, he first rode the rails and moved up in the ranks to be a railway fireman, then becoming the recording secretary to the local Brotherhood of Locomotive Firemen. Soon he was the editor of a national labor magazine, and as the unions grew and became more powerful, he rose within the fractious leadership.

October 2, 2004: The written text, and then we hear the words in our heads. If it were possible to know how the music evokes the words of the song. I can't help but think that if Albert Parsons had been a woman he would not have allowed himself to be hanged. He would have confessed, even if the confession were false. Instead of singing "Annie Laurie."

In a disastrous—for the union—railroad strike of 1888 against the Chicago, Burlington and Quincy Railroad, engineers and firemen walked out and were replaced by the company with unemployed workers. The union sought unsuccessfully to boycott all trains and were enjoined from doing so by the company with the authority of a court order behind them. It was a dress rehearsal for Pullman, an enormous failure for labor, and fresh in the mind of Eugene V. Debs in 1894.

April 2009: Our reform death penalty commission meets, decides nothing. We talk, have no consensus. Agree to meet next time. Another set of hearings is scheduled. No one's mind will be changed by the evidence or by the work of the committee. A report will be issued. No one will read the report. The arguments have long lost relevancy.

On June 20, 1893, as Florence Kelley was waiting to be appointed factory inspector, the American Railway Union was founded in Chicago with Eugene V. Debs as its president and a new policy of opening its doors to all white men who worked for the railroad. The exclusion of Negroes had been contested but was not overturned. The union ranks immediately swelled to 150,000 members and 465 locals, and with an attitude of confrontation. In the spring of 1894 the union successfully challenged the Great Northern Railroad Company after three successive pay cuts in eight months. It was the warmup for the confrontation at Pullman in 1894.

September 5, 2009: A day to believe in labor—the people who gave you the weekend. Forecast for rain all weekend. Today the sun is shining.

Pullman became the new forum for the never-ending disputes between labor and management over hours and wages. Conflict simmered for years before blood ran in the streets and mayhem ensued. There was not one precipitating incident, but a cascading series of events.

First there was the strike in Pullman itself (May 11, 1894). Then a boycott by the union was called (June 20) declaring that union members would no longer (as of June 26) handle any trains with Pullman cars. Rail traffic ground to a halt. The company responded by getting an injunction in federal court against the boycott. The federal troops were called in allegedly to get the trains running so that the mail could be delivered. Eugene V. Debs, the fiery union leader, was put in jail for ignoring the federal injunction, and that got him out of the way.

March 10, 2009: The calendar and the weather are indisputable, and everything else a fact subject to dispute. Today: grey, foggy. Not cold. Perhaps someone else would say cold. No one seems to be able to prevent the spreading of this vast economic meltdown. We watch in disbelief as financial institutions which have survived for centuries fall into insolvency, and their fired employees pour onto the streets with their laptops and briefcases. They are still in bankers' uniforms, black suits, white shirts for men and women, carrying out their personal belongings in cardboard boxes.

The federal judiciary was a minor player mostly on the Chicago scene in Florence Kelley's time, unless there was an event, such as Pullman, which pulled in federal officials, such as the president and his attorney general, and pitted them against the state courts, the mayor of Chicago, and the governor of Illinois. The civil society was generally held together by a truce between these mostly independent legal actors. The society, the social order, and its many political incarnations rumbled on, and sometimes rode over the actors who played their roles within the structured legal institutions. There was "the rule of law," although the law was imposed and its mandates carried out within imperfect, flawed legal institutions.

July 3, 2003: The homicide project is turning into a project on the history of Chicago and the history of criminology. The 1877 strike was a real strike, against the power of the technology and the great industrial innovation. The railroads provided a target for the revolutionaries, as they systematically shut down all railroad traffic across the country. The place names are familiar: Canal Street, Desplaines, the Halsted Street Bridge.

During the Pullman strike both sides used every lever they could to reach all the available legal systems: filing state and federal injunctions, invoking the recent recognition of the right to strike, the city and the police calling upon their authority to arm a local militia, the calling in of federal troops by the US attorney general who had been counsel for the railroads, the ad hoc intervention of elected state judges to make rulings on behalf of both sides, the jailing of Debs on the order of the court, and more and more. It was a battle in the law and over the law, and within the theater of the law, and about whose law would prevail. Finally the law of no law, the law of civil disorder prevailed.

March 15, 2009: Another Ides of March. Today, blue sky and wisps of clouds. Threads of clouds, fooling us. Today in quiet Evanston the clouds of war, a very real war abroad, seem far away, even as geographical distances as a matter of practicality diminish daily. Our bodies stay in a time and place, while our fingers travel the world. It is an illusion, this geographical travel over the world while staying at home.

The term "capital" had since the Middle Ages been used by William Blackstone and others to describe the stock with which a company or person enters into business. The "capital letter," a letter of credit with a bank or another holder of wealth, guaranteed the availability of money to back an enterprise. The term capitalism later came to describe the political and economic system in which private wealth is used in the production and distribution of goods and services.

May 10, 2013: The Bangladesh factory disaster is now being described as the worst factory disaster in history, with more than 1,100 dead. Many are buried in rubble without identification. Most of the people killed were women. There must have been children working in the factory who died, although the newspapers haven't mentioned them.

George Pullman was both the chief stockholder and the chief executive officer of the Pullman Palace Car Company. Eugene V. Debs was a former railroad worker and president of the American Railway Union, the largest national railway union. The railroads were one of the largest employers in the country. In that sense it was a classic confrontation between capital and labor.

Although it is still referred to as "the Pullman strike," the civil disruption was not a typical strike, although the role of the union was critical. The events were triggered by the very real economic depression of 1893. The tide of public opinion, which had been enthusiastic about the Pullman idea, as it was called, started to turn as reports of destitution, suffering, privation, and starvation began to surface. These were no longer conditions of the workman's paradise. The term slavery was used. Pullman workers could not leave because they owed their future wages to the company store to pay back rent on their houses and assessments for food and utilities. George Pullman left town, evacuated his servants, locked his silver in the company vault, and ordered armed guards to surround his home.

October 2013: The teachers strike is settled. Both sides claim victory. My students and I struggle to understand the lines of legal authority in the bureaucratic administrative structure, overlapping city, state, and federal laws, and reams of incomprehensible regulations. The Chicago Public Schools website is dense with statistics and detailed descriptions. The relationships between the legal entities are inscrutable.

Irrespective of the principles and who believed what about the town's purpose, or who was at fault after the close of the World's Fair, the deepening economic depression of 1893 resulted in many Pullman residents being caught between layoffs and wage reductions while the mandatory payments continued for rent. In the spring of 1894 a third of the Pullman workers joined Debs's union, and a workers' grievance committee was formed.

February 28, 2011: And still it goes on, the winter. Grey, even the lake grey. The waves run up along the breakwater, like live things. The lobbying by both sides is intense but mostly unreported, anecdotal. We wait for the governor to sign.

The Pullman strike was called initially to protest a cut in wages by management when rents imposed by the company and other costs to the workers remained unchanged and the company continued to pay its 6 percent dividend to shareholders.

Later the specially constituted strike commission heard days of testimony regarding the suffering of workers' families trapped in contracts which sent all their wages as debt back to the company, while the workers could not afford food. The protests met the intractable opposition and iron will of George Pullman, who refused to rescind the wage cuts.

An uneasy peace reigned at Pullman in May and June of 1894. An eerie stillness settled over the town, commentators noted. The Railway Union vice president exhorted the strikers not to drink, nor to use threats or intimidation, nor to use force against anyone who went to work against the boycott. Things always start out calmly, reasonably, with people predicting it will all be over soon. The huge car works on the north edge of Pullman were initially undamaged. The workers themselves placed three hundred men around the plant to guard the property from hoodlums and thieves who might take advantage of the circumstance, they said. The company saw it as intimidation.

There was a strike fund, and a trading company donated twenty-five thousand pounds of beef and an equal amount of flour to feed the strikers. Doctors donated their services, and individuals dropped off contributions, some small, such as a box of hats or chewing tobacco. The strikers wore white ribbons and met nightly in open assembly.

Eugene Debs called George Pullman paternalistic and said the workers should figure out how to take care of themselves. Company officials and their supporters wore miniature American flags on their lapels and held their meetings in the Hotel Florence. Many workers were Civil War veterans and resented the implications of their adversaries adopting the flag.

As June dragged into July, the company continued to resist arbitration. The company implied that it had been overpaying wages in the past and said it would prefer to close for six months rather than pay higher wages and run the plant at a loss. Debs worried that the general economic depression and large numbers of unemployed would undermine the strike, in spite of the union's official optimism. Meanwhile a report to the June 15 union convention noted that wage reductions at Pullman were 30 to 70 percent, while corporate dividends were unchanged. The company consistently refused to lower the rents on company houses or reduce dividends.

Jennie Curtis, a Pullman seamstress who, along with others in the girls' local, made the drapes, carpets, and seat coverings and other luxurious trappings for the Palace Cars, told the union convention that after her father, also a Pullman employee, died, deductions for his back rent continued from her biweekly paycheck, leaving her with nine or ten dollars to live on for the whole month, from which she paid seven dollars for room and board.

The labor convention approached George Pullman with another request for arbitration. The company refused, referring to the team of workers sent forward as former employees, as people with no different status from that of the man on the sidewalk. Nor did the workers appreciate hearing arbitration being referred to as the creation of a dictatorship and that George Pullman's own submission to such demands would be making himself and the entire railway industry hostage to the demands of a dictator. The newspaper cartoons portrayed Debs wearing a crown.

The attorney general of the United States, Richard Olney, a corporate lawyer who represented and served on the boards of several leading railroad companies, on July 2, 1894, issued a federal injunction restraining the American Railway Union and its leader, Eugene V. Debs, from interfering with national railroad traffic. Federal troops were ordered down from Fort Sheridan over the objection of John Peter Altgeld and the mayor of Chicago, John P. Hopkins, himself a former Pullman employee. Ten years later in a talk at Princeton University—he is buried in the small town cemetery near the university—Richard Olney called the Pullman events a "conspiracy." All together President Grover Cleveland sent two-thirds of the entire US Army, some sixteen thousand troops, to deal with the strike and its anticipated anarchy.

Sheridan Road is so named because it was the route the troops took on July 3 when they marched from Fort Sheridan, thirty miles north, to downtown Chicago to camp on the shores of the lake. The pretext was that the federal post office had called for help, but the mail was not stopped or delayed. President Cleveland ordered the troops to march on Chicago on the advice of his attorney general, whose principal clients had been the Burlington and Santa Fe railroads.

General Nelson Miles of the U.S. Army set up his headquarters in the Pullman Building. He hired spies to infiltrate union meetings and told his troops to fire upon rioters, as needed. In his view this was the Paris Commune of 1791. The white ribbons worn by the Pullman strikers annoyed him. George Pullman stayed out of town for the whole episode. The presence of five thousand uniformed troops living in tents alongside the lake infuriated the Pullman workers and their supporters.

The federal troops arrived around midnight on July 4, 1894. Violence broke out; more than seven hundred railroad cars were set alight; factories were emptied of workers; looting broke out.

On July 5, a raging fire burned down the temporary buildings of the World's Fair in Jackson Park. Rioters were shot and themselves shot at police. Maria Bach, a seventeen-year-old girl standing on a roof watching the demonstration, was killed by a stray bullet.

The federal troops and marshals and the police decided to send out the mail from six federal stations. The railroad General Managers Association and George Pullman held fast. The elite businessmen played an important role behind the scenes. Debs was in jail—and the boycott fell. On July 18, the federal troops left. It was all over except the assessments after, and the counting up of the losses.

May 3, 1999: In the middle of the night a dream of remembered whole streets, scenes, and games from childhood; people forgotten about for decades appeared full blown in the dreams with their names. And so, a drawer of the mind opens, and is surprisingly, suddenly filled with interior photographs. Then it is gone.

At the time of the Pullman events, Jane Addams was thirty-four and Florence Kelley was thirty-five. Hull-House, which started as one old house, three outbuildings, and a bathhouse less than five years earlier, was the intellectual and social center for reform politics in Chicago, and, some argued, the rest of the country.

Both Jane Addams and Florence Kelley were thoroughly immersed in the small and large group politics of labor's challenges to large employers who, with the overwhelming support of the state and federal courts, broke up demonstrations and declared strikes, collective action, and organizing workers unconstitutional restrictions upon property. The courts, the legislature, the governor, and the City Council were mostly aligned with the commercial elite, and that was considered good for business. The reformers were supported by and lived within that community, not outside of it.

After the strike was over, Jane Addams, speaking from her position on the newly formed Civic Federation of Chicago, would characterize George Pullman as a modern King Lear. George Pullman categorically refused to negotiate with his workers, correctly perceiving that his whole grand design, the interlocking Pullman factory and town, and his ties to the entire railroad industry were under attack. The action was between a great business monopoly, its diehard and intransigent leader, and the firebrand head of a new and insurgent railway union with 150,000 members, fresh from a recent triumph elsewhere. The strike called out 125,000 workers, and twenty railroads were completely shut down. What remains of those events now, in addition to the contemporaneous incendiary journalistic reports, is the hundreds of pages of testimony in Washington and Chicago before the Strike Commission and the conclusion that it all might have been avoided with negotiation.

Jane Addams described the events as "a drama which epitomized and, at the same time, challenged the code of social ethics under which we live, for a quick series of unusual events had dispelled the good nature which in happier times enveloped the ugliness of the industrial situation."

Once again Jane Addams captured the moment: law enforcement can never by itself guarantee civil order, and if the citizens do not trust those who have been empowered to uphold the law, civil disorder reigns. A city of diverse people living side by side and peacefully sharing the streets suddenly, or not so suddenly, turns the public space into a place where rocks are thrown, railroad cars are torched, flames rise in the sky, shots ring out and are returned, dead bodies are on the street; people who can run away and hide, do so. And the civil order is gone. There is no law then.

At the end of the day, however, the reasons and the justifications, the fault, the excuses, and what was said or explained afterward mattered little: civil order, peace on the streets, had been destroyed and the memory of that lasted, and the threat of it persisted.

March 19, 2009: The weather, briefly glorious. This kind of skin cancer is supposed to be highly treatable. It is always a matter of fate as to who lives to an old age and who dies young. When my students ask, I reply: yes, marry, if you have that partner; yes, have babies when you are young and healthy; yes, it will hurt you professionally, and in the long run that won't matter. As the economists say: in the long run we'll all be dead.

The events so disrupted the civil order that a national panel was convened afterward to investigate the strike. This Strike Commission was headed by Carroll D. Wright, the head of the *Slums of Great Cities* project, which had hired Florence Kelley soon after her arrival. After many days and hundreds of pages of testimony, the commission concluded that George Pullman should have gone to arbitration. Some testimony emphasized the looting mobs; others the disproportionate military response with fixed bayonets and cavalry charges. The rich, the powerful, and many others left town or hid indoors during the days of violence, remembering 1877.

One introductory sentence from Carroll Wright's commission report sets out how the commission defined its inquiry:

These great losses and many crimes; the vast numbers, strength and resources of the labor that contended under the leadership of the American Railway Union upon one side and the Pullman Palace Car Company and the General Managers' Association upon the other; the attitude of labor towards capital, disclosed in its readiness to strike sympathetically; the determination of capital to crush the strike rather than accept any peaceable solution through conciliation, arbitration or otherwise; the certainty with which vast strikes let loose the disreputable to burn, plunder, and even murder; the conversion of industrious and law-abiding men into idlers, law breakers, or associates of criminals; the want brought to many innocent families, the transformation of rail-

road yards, tracks, and stations, as well as busy marts of trade, into armed camps; the possibilities of future strikes on more extended lines of union against even great combinations of capital—all are factors bearing upon the present industrial situation which need to be thoroughly understood by the people and be wisely and prudently treated by the government.

Whatever else you may wish to say about these events or this commission, someone, probably Carroll D. Wright himself, knew how to build a sentence within the structure of the English language.

Hearings were held in Chicago beginning on August 14, 1894, and adjourned on August 30, all proceedings being open to the public. An additional day of public proceedings was held in Washington, DC, on September 26.

Jane Addams testified. Florence Kelley did not; it is not recorded who was asked to testify but did not. The total number of witnesses examined in Chicago was 107; two additional witnesses appeared in Washington.

The report, the transcript of testimony before the commission, and its recommendations number 681 pages and read like the serious public inquiry it was:

[Commissioner Worthington to George Pullman] . . . *I was only trying to get a bird's eye view of its* [the company's] *success in this, as I understand it, that with a stock ranging from $1,000,000 to $36,000,000 in twenty-seven years, and with undivided profits amounting to $25,000,000 and with dividends paid upon that stock of never less than 8 per cent and as high as 12 per cent, you would naturally conclude it was a good financial operation?*

Ans. [George Pullman] *Yes; well, let me say right there—*

[Commissioner Worthington] *These are practically the facts, are they not?*

Ans. [George Pullman] *Let me say right there—let me qualify that—the $25,000,000 is not an absolute addition. Out of that $25,000,000 would come any depreciation of property.*

The testimony of Eugene V. Debs had been solicited earlier:

In connection with the same matter I would like to state that a great deal of fault has been found on account of the action of the employees on the Santa Fe system. They have been often very harshly criticized on account of striking there, the contention being that they struck without any cause; no reduction of wages had been made on the Santa Fe system, and therefore it was grossly unjust that they should strike.

The fact is, and was, that the Santa Fe company had been in arrears to these employees from two to almost four months for their wages. I was over the system myself, and know that a great many employees were on the verge of starvation, because they were not getting their wages from the company. At one time, as the Gentlemen of the Commission remember, Governor Waite, of Colorado, was called upon to intercede with the Federal authorities to compel the Santa Fe receiver to make at least a partial payment of wages to prevent the employees from suffering, and they were actually on the verge of starvation. Many of the employees were actually suffering, simply because their wages were withheld by the company.

[Commissioner Kernan] What do you know as to how able the company or the receivers were to pay them at that time?

Ans. [Eugene V. Debs] Of my own knowledge I know nothing about their ability to pay their wages.

March 17, 2008: A grey-blue sky. Still, no wind. A squirrel hanging upside down and working the tiny metal lever of the bird feeder with his feet to spill seed. Not one leaf, or one sprout. Yet in a few weeks all will be green. The miracle of new leaves.

Eugene V. Debs continued his narrative of events, as requested by Commissioner Carroll D. Wright:

On the 26th day of June, pursuant to the order of the convention, the employees began to refuse to haul Pullman cars. The officers of the American Railway Union established temporary headquarters at Ulrich's Hall. They were very careful to instruct the men, or to advise the men, rather, in our advisory capacity, not to take this action anywhere unless it was sanctioned by the majority of employees and they felt strong enough to make it effectual.

We said, it is not wise for a few men to create trouble, and not to strike unless it is sanctioned by a majority of the employees, and unless it was certain that the employees of the body will stand by you in so doing. The committees came from all yards, and from all roads to confer with us. . . .

All the meetings were held in the city of Chicago, and there were a great many. All of us were addressing from two to six meetings a day, and all the meetings that were held were held with open doors. We did not hold a secret meeting during the entire trouble, not one. . . . We did not hold a meeting but what we admonished employees under all circumstances to maintain order. We said, we want to win as becomes men; we want to win as becomes law-abiding citizens; we have got a right to quit in a body, and our right ends there; the railroad companies have the right to employ men to take our places, and their rights begin there, and we have no right to interfere . . . .

[Commissioner Kernan] *Where is that record that shows those instructions were given to the committee?*

Ans. [Eugene V. Debs] *There is no record of that except the record that could be made by the affidavits of the committee themselves, and that could be produced. . . .*

[Commissioner Wright] *You mean it is on record, because it is a fact which can be proven.*

Ans. [Eugene V. Debs] *Yes, sir.*

June 10, 2013: Finally, a spring day. No settlement in Springfield over the pension issue. The unions have taken the position that the state should just find the money. The states, the cities and the counties are the only ones left who employ unionized workers these days. And the state has no more credit or credibility.

The conclusion of Carroll Wright's Strike Commission was that the violence could have been averted with mediation and that George Pullman's stubbornness and unwillingness to modify any company rules in response to the economic privation of the workers sparked the boycott, which led to national unrest. The commission recommended the formation of a National Strike Commission. Whoever was at fault, mutual civil trust had broken down. The term anarchy was bandied about. The government's response was described as analogous to Lincoln's response at Fort Sumter.

In the middle of it all, the assassin of Mayor Carter Harrison, the insane person who shot the sitting mayor just before the closing of the World's Fair, was hanged on July 13, 1894. The issue of capital punishment was never far from issues of political dissent and defiance of state authority. Capital punishment was and is a symbol of the state's power, the ultimate power to kill.

Clarence Darrow, one of the defense attorneys for the clearly guilty assassin, then took up the defense of Eugene V. Debs. A number of Hull-House residents, especially Mary Kenney, supported Debs in his days of despair in jail.

Alzina Stevens, Florence Kelley's chief deputy, protected Debs after the Pullman events and stood by him to keep him from drowning his depression in drink, she said, when he could bear it no more, shielding him from the press and others until he was himself again.

Later Debs, along with Altgeld, supported the loser, William Jennings Bryan, in the presidential election of 1896. The rallying cry in the election was bimetallism, or the issue of whether the US dollar should be backed by silver and gold. The political debates over bimetallism were passionate and ill-informed and now incomprehensible. Debs later became the first Social Democratic Party candidate for president in 1900.

On November 14, 1894, the United States Strike Commission, Carroll D. Wright, ex-officio chairman, John D. Kernan, commissioner, Nicholas E. Worthington, commissioner, presented its report to Grover Cleveland, president—the man who had authorized the ordering in of federal troops—the report to be subsequently forwarded to the Senate and House of Representatives. The $5,000 appropriated proved amply sufficient for all expenses of the commission.

Carroll Wright's commission set the cost of destroyed property at $700,000 and the cost to the railroads at more than $4.5 million. The loss of wages to Pullman workers was more than $350,000, and more than $3 million to all railroad workers. Those who come after the fact think they can understand such events if a dollar value or a number can be assigned to the losses. Certainly this was some kind of out-and-out war, even if no one would call it a civil war, or class war, or anarchy. There were heavy losses, on all sides, and to the civic culture.

February 2005: New York City. It is cold and grey, but exciting. The city is electrified by the Gates project. Everything is Gates orange, and the city is alive with the celebration. I knew working here would fundamentally change my views about art, and it has. My job is to talk to people in the park, answer questions, keep an eye on the installations. Everything from: "I've live lived my whole life in New York City and never been to Central Park" to "Yes, ten of us came from Sweden to see this."

The Pullman strike began as a relatively limited work stoppage to protest repeated wage cuts and then became the largest, most famous strike in American history. Chicago in July 1894 was a city under martial law and an armed camp. Everyone who was anybody was asked for their opinion by the commission and gave it. Once again Carroll D. Wright was the voice of sanity who got the work done in a responsible and serious manner. General Miles, the leader of the federal forces called in to suppress the strike over the objection of Governor John Peter Altgeld, advocated many other government interventions, including the forcible restriction of immigration and the large ruralization (i.e., shipping those unemployed in the cities to the countryside) of the population. Nor were such views aberrant. This appeared in a respectable academic journal:

Year after year Europe pours into the United States multitudes of degenerate human beings, who, incited by the freedom of American institutions . . . immediately give free rein to their atavistic imaginations, and . . . plunge into anarchy and lawlessness. These people are savages and should not be treated as civilized beings.

A newly formed Immigration Restriction League had as its purpose the exclusion of elements undesirable for citizenship. The recent economic crisis had aggravated economic disparities, accentuated the differences between rich and poor, and polarized political allegiances. As one commentator put it:

The most abiding effect of the panic of 1893 was the sudden and complete severance with our commercial past . . . the happy-go-lucky methods of buying and selling, the unquestioned belief in regularly recurring cycles of boom and speculation, the lack of economy in production and the extravagance in distribution . . . and the blind confidence that the future was an inexhaustible fund, against which we could always draw in the way of constant multiplication of machinery and of factories.

Hard times make for radical legislation and strained, conservative court opinions. By a 5-to-4 decision the Supreme Court of the United States declared the federal income tax unconstitutional in 1895. Western states adopted laws to postpone foreclosure, federal bankruptcy legislation passed in 1898, and the midterm elections overwhelmingly elected Republicans with the issues of tariffs and taxation remaining central until 1896 and after. Sentiments about populism, communism, and the value of silver played a large role in William Jennings Bryan losing the presidency in 1896. The country congratulated itself on narrowly escaping the scourge of the dreaded Altgeldism and reform politics. A year later Altgeld himself was defeated for a second term as governor.

One hundred twenty years later, we have only some numbers and a few facts about the strike: the number of people shot and fatally wounded: 12 (although not all of them show up in the police records); the number arrested by the police: 515; the number arrested under United States statutes and against whom indictments were found: 71; the number arrested against whom indictments were not found: 119; the total number of US troops, militia, extra deputy marshals, extra deputy sheriffs, and members of the police force of Chicago called up and involved in the events: 14,186. This would be just in Chicago. That more than two-thirds of the entire United States military force was employed in responding to these events is noteworthy. And so Carroll Wright's commission recorded what happened according to the people who were there or observed it, as in a trial. And there were only statistics at the end.

March 18, 2009: My sister's birthday. I still remember when she and her best friend had a club excluding me. How silly to remember such hurts. Yesterday, the weather pulled me outside for a walk. After a morning of stillness, in the afternoon a lively breeze waking up the trees. Leaving is on my mind. Perhaps leaving Chicago.

The Hillside Home School, established in 1886 in the Helena Valley near Spring Green, Wisconsin, had a distinguished pedigree. Frank Lloyd Wright's biographer, Meryle Secrest, provided some background: The school was conceived of and run by Frank Lloyd Wright's unmarried aunts, Nell and Jane Lloyd Jones, who inherited the family farm and homestead of their settler parents. Nell was forty-one, Jane thirty-eight: "Both held themselves in the stylish swanlike manner, their waistlines corseted, wearing the ruffled trains and bustles, the silks and satins, that were all the rage in the 1880s. In short, they were women of some consequence in the world, but they had lost none of their Lloyd Jones idealism."

From the outset the school took children of all ages as boarders. It ran the farm, and each child had his own plot to till and knew each cow and horse by name. Nature walks, picnics, horseback riding, and football were offered. The school was coeducational from its founding and there were dances taught by a slippered dancing master. Sleigh rides, skating parties, and theatricals were common. Boys were expected to learn "womanly" arts, such as seam stitching and sock darning, this being controversial.

Because of the family background there was great interest in design, and for a time the school was housed in the Lloyd Jones family chapel, the architecturally significant Unity Chapel, Frank Lloyd Wright's first building.

The charismatic family member Uncle Jenkin lectured around the country and was a colleague of Jane Addams, Susan B. Anthony, Booker T. Washington, and others, many of whom appeared frequently at Hull-House.

The school and the family were severely threatened when in 1907 another Lloyd Jones uncle, James, died attempting to rescue two farm owners unwisely guiding a heavy threshing machine engine across a small bridge over a dry stream bed. This much-beloved uncle had been buying up small farms in the valley in a progressive desire to improve and mechanize farming to scale. The loans were co-signed by the family, and when the depression of the 1890s came the prices of crops were more than halved. Mortgages went in arrears, creditors were at the gate, and the family's possessions were sold. Nevertheless, in 1907, when Margaret and John were gone, the school had expanded to a hundred teachers and pupils. Uncle James Lloyd Jones's debts were more than $65,000, a sizable sum, and the school declared bankruptcy in 1909.

The Lloyd Joneses were among the early settlers, who endured terrifying ocean crossings, some taking three months with multiple returns to port and landing at surprising destinations, only to arrive in New York to be swindled by Welsh-speaking petty criminals and then lose the rest of their savings to money changers. And all that before they struck out for Wisconsin, where some fifty family members eventually settled in the 1850s close to one another in the Valley, buying forty-acre parcels for $1.25 an acre. Nor was this rich farmland, but stony ground covered with trees, with unreliable water in winter, turning into mosquito-filled marshland in the hot summer, breeding grounds for malaria, fever, and ague. The Welsh immigrants came to build a "kingdom of walls," and their language was indeed a foreign language when they landed in America. And almost immediately, the family's efforts turned to establishing a community and running a school.

At home there had been attacks upon the Rebecca Raiders, men wearing wigs and dressed as women who rode through the countryside demolishing state-imposed road tolls. These were Welsh revolutionaries who came seeking a legendary tribe of Welsh-speaking Indians, descendants of a medieval Welsh prince whom returning travelers claimed to have met.

The exploits of these adventuresome, courageous, accident-prone and often unlucky people were rightly the stuff of legend. The horrors of the ocean crossing alone, where passengers were encouraged to bring their own food which soon ran out when ships went astray or lost their sails in a storm, would have deterred any but the strong and determined. Their national identity as rebellious Welsh nationalists seems to have been critical to survival, as it was a driving force in their leaving. In short, they had a great deal in common with the later immigrants from Romania and Eastern Europe, and with the Jews.

When Florence Kelley moved to New York, Ko, who was almost fourteen, became the child of Hull-House, more than ever.

Letter from Alice Hamilton to Florence Kelley, June 2, 1899

. . . My letter stopped there though I cannot remember what interrupted it, but I know I had not another minute for writing before I left . . . . Ko says that he has written you about this last indisposition and his unlikely encounter with Mrs. Vance's dog. Don't worry about that at all. His leg was pretty much bruised but the skin was broken in a place the size of a large pin-head and I squeezed out the blood immediately and cauterized with some carbolic so that I am sure no germs escaped. And the dog is a perfectly healthy fox terrier who has a way of snapping at anybody who does not know him. They usually have him tied, so I suppose this is why we have not encountered him before. . . . Ko had the nurse inspect his leg and there was absolutely no infection. He stood the cauterizing in a way that made me feel like crying. I can't tell you how I felt when I said good-bye to him. One can say good-bye to grown people for a few years and feel that one will see them again, but Ko won't be Ko when I see him again. He stayed for my last lunch and risked being late for school, which pleased me immensely. And I think he really hates to have to go. But children can't be as fond of you as you are of them, do you think that they can?

The House is going to be very empty soon and Mrs. Addams will have a lonely time of it until you come.

Margaret, too, spent holidays from Hillside at Hull-House. This to her grandmother Caroline on December 24, 1899:

We went right home and saw a lovely Christmas tree at which Miss Ellen Gates Starr was Santa Claus, just think of her being Santa Claus. . . . Mama has given me my choice of a watch or camera and I am nearly distracted for I don't know which to take.

January 1, 2013: Home after ten days on the beach. Mostly people behaved and got on. The trip was long. And we will all soon forget the joy of it. I realize this, why don't they? Life is too short to squabble with your loved ones, especially about money.

John, the youngest, also spent school holidays at Hull-House as he grew older.

Hillside Home House Wisconsin, Jan. 6, 1901

My Dear Mother,

I hope you are well as I am.

I had a great time at Hull House as you must know by this time I have written so many letters.

I thank you very much for the five dollars.

I got a fine pocket book from Miss Addams a dandy knife from Miss Benedict a dollar from miss Waite and one from Miss Herman and three from Miss Smith. At first she intended to give me five but she thought better of it I guess and so I gave back the five Uncle Bert sent me, and say I haven't the slightest idea what Uncle Bert looks like. I haven't seen him for so long, you will not have to send me money for quite a while because I saved my Christmas money and have it here. I mean I saved most of it.

I went to three plays in Chicago. The first one I saw was Sherlock Holmes which a detective play and was great. That was Mr. Smith's present to Stanley and I. We had two dollar seats. Then Mr. Tivos took Stanley and I to see "Rob Roy" play at the "Studebecker" by the Castle Square and was good. It was about the Highlander and Prince Charles. Then Stanley and I took Mr. T to see that play Hamlet which was also grand but would give a fellow the nightmare for a week.

I read "Ivanhoe" this vacation with Stanley and I think it was fine only the Templar thought to much of himself and Athelstan thought to much of his stomach.

I am reading the "Talisman" now and have just got to where the daffy hermit takes sir Keneth up to that room where he sees his girl but it don't say how she got there. I think the hermit should wear something better than goat skins if he had money enough to keep all that fine silver and all that kind of stuff.

When I came back the pony was so full of life that I was almost afraid to ride her. I have been growing stronger lately than I ever dreamed of. I like to work better than ever it is making me so much healthier and although that is not saying much. I don't know what I'd do if it weren't for the pony. I can have more fun with her than and any boy in the school she's so quick to learn and remember everything I teach her.

Good by with love from John.

P.S. I got 99 in our last Latin quiz this letter is long but I could say more but it is time to go to sleep, so good night.

November 22, 2008: At the New York Public Library: The hard cardboard boxes with their black metal staples, a testament to the will to preserve a record of lives, and to remember. The silence of reverence. The pale green new folders, the labels handwritten in pencil. Some of the letters in ink completely legible from a century ago. The paper crepe-paper thin. Others, as if dropped in water, only a blank piece of paper with water marks and pale, illegible lines. The sturdy thick oak tables probably the same vintage as the letters.

Whose handwriting can I recognize? I know Florence Kelley's now, although it varies depending upon the amount of hurry. I regret the coming of the typewriter to her correspondence, even though every letter has her own recognizable prose style even with the typewriter. The typewriter and the styles of typewriting, still, are much more distinctive, individual, than the faceless fonts of word processing.

Florence Kelley takes a typing class and says, now I can get a job as a secretary for nine dollars a week. Caroline Bonsall Kelley's written voice is distinctive, intelligent. And she uses ink which lasts, so that her letters, which are among the oldest, nonetheless remain legible and evocative. The curious practice of not only writing on both sides, but of turning over the letter and writing over the earlier page with lines of text going in the perpendicular direction. Yet legible. You can read the lines over the lines of the letter. The brain can process that as a separate message, on a separate line. Caroline Bonsall Kelley's voice on the page is alive, passionate, warm.

This is to her husband who writes her from the floor of the Congress and says he wishes she were there for the historic moment of the passage of the Thirteenth Amendment:

Write to me as often as you can for my only consolation in your absence is, that you write so much more affectionately than you talk to me. . . . Good night and God bless you. Your affectionate wife, October 27, 1856.

January 12, 2003, Chicago Tribune: "Clemency for All: Ryan Commutes 164 Death Sentences to Life in Prison Without Parole; 'There Is No Honorable Way to Kill,' He Says," by Maurice Possley and Steve Mills.

Declaring the state's capital punishment system "haunted by the demon of error" and citing the state legislature's failure to reform it, Gov. George Ryan on Saturday commuted the sentences of every inmate on Illinois' Death Row.

With two days left as governor, Ryan issued a blanket commutation that converted every death sentence to life in prison without parole—164 inmates, including four women.

"Because the Illinois death penalty system is arbitrary and capricious—and therefore immoral—I no longer shall tinker with the machinery of death," Ryan said, borrowing the words of the late U.S. Supreme Court Justice Harry Blackmun. "I won't stand for it. . . . I had to act."

On 24 April 2013, Rana Plaza, an eight-story commercial building, collapsed in Savar, a sub-district in the Greater Dhaka Area, the capital of Bangladesh. The search for the dead ended on 13 May with a death toll of 1,129. Approximately 2,515 injured people were rescued from the building alive. Source: Wikimedia Creative Commons.

5

Losing the Battle, Winning the War

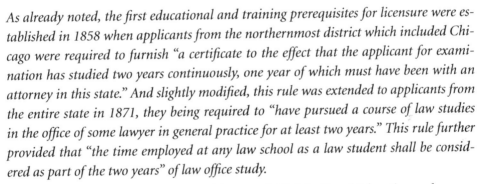

As already noted, the first educational and training prerequisites for licensure were es-tablished in 1858 when applicants from the northernmost district which included Chi-cago were required to furnish "a certificate to the effect that the applicant for exami-nation has studied two years continuously, one year of which must have been with an attorney in this state." And slightly modified, this rule was extended to applicants from the entire state in 1871, they being required to "have pursued a course of law studies in the office of some lawyer in general practice for at least two years." This rule further provided that "the time employed at any law school as a law student shall be consid-ered as part of the two years" of law office study.

(citing Sup. Ct. R. 85, 53 Ill. xvii [1871].) James D. Heiple, "Legal Education and Admission to the Bar: The Illinois Experience," 12 *S. Ill. U. L.J.* 123, 1987-88.

Florence Kelley wrote to a friend soon after her appointment as factory inspector:

All big businesses are "on bail" or have accepted the eight hour day. There are 18 law suits pending to enforce the eight hour law, and it should be established permanently by Easter. That the companies in the Stockyards adopted the eight hour day and reduced their hiring of underage children was a tremendous harbinger of an early victory.

In March 1895 Florence Kelley rented rooms at the Leland Hotel in Springfield, Illinois, to prepare her *Third Annual Report of the Factory Inspectors* to the governor and the legislature and to wait for the opinion of the Supreme Court of Illinois in the case challenging the constitutionality of the Factory Inspection Law. The opinion, Ritchie v. People, was handed down on March 14, 1895.

Levy Mayer and the Illinois Manufacturers' Association had challenged the entire Factory Inspection Law, the restrictions placed upon the hours women could work, the age provisions prohibiting children under fourteen from working, the legal authority for the inspections, the requirement of health certificates, the funding of the office, the appointment of Florence Kelley as factory inspector, the payment of Florence Kelley as factory inspector, the payment of the assistant inspectors, and each and every provision of the statute and its regulations.

September 2008: The state committee to review capital punishment now meets regularly. The procedural rules are cumbersome: certain offices, such as the governor, have the power to appoint. I am appointed by the head of the General Assembly, at the suggestion of our clinic. People come on and off the committee. One member was indicted and resigned, another appointed member never comes to meetings, another says his other commitments don't allow him to come.

Each new appointment seems to tilt the balance in favor of the state's attorneys and the prosecution. The Governor's Commission Report in 2003 made sweeping recommendations for reform, and nothing happened. The legislature did nothing, felt they needed to do nothing. What can this committee say five years after the former governor's commission said everything that needed to be said? The public is sick of the issue. We will hold hearings, take testimony, and write a report. No one will pay the slightest attention. Another exercise in government wheel spinning and futility.

Levy Mayer and the Illinois Manufacturers' Association intended to have the entire statute declared unconstitutional, so that there would be no enforcement, no inspections, no health affidavits, no yanking children out of the factories and putting them in school, no certification required that the boys and girls were old enough to be legally working, no government inspection for smallpox, and no interference of any kind by any government official with the operation of any manufacturing business or factory, including the tenement sweatshops. The public outrage prompting the passing of legislation had been about the conditions in the sweatshops and tenements, and about the dwarfed children at the sewing treadles, but the law applied to other establishments as well.

Procedurally, the Factory Inspection Law was challenged by the plaintiffs in error, meaning that the constitutional challenge was brought by the manufacturers who had been fined and convicted of misdemeanors under the statute and other similarly situated plaintiffs. They included the paper box manufacturer William C. Ritchie of Ritchie (W.C.) & Company. The statute had mixed criminal and civil jurisdiction: allowing for the imposition of fines and the conviction of a misdemeanor. Some cases were heard by a justice of the peace; others went before a trial court judge and a jury. The appellants challenged the constitutional validity of the entire statute, first to the trial court, by bringing a writ of error after a fine or conviction, then being certified immediately to the Supreme Court of Illinois, under the authority of the same writ of error, and finally to the United States Supreme Court. The basis for the writ of error was that the statute was in violation of the state and federal constitutions.

April 22, 2012: The most perfect spring weather. Today a celebration and a tree planting at the Hull-House Museum, whose address is now 800 S. Halsted Street, not 335 Halsted, the address in Hull-House Maps and Papers. *The street system of Chicago has gone through several renumberings since 1893. The Hull-House dining room, re-created according to the design of the original, is the site for a luncheon consisting of recipes from the nineteenth-century Hull-House kitchen. How delicious everything is.*

A story is told that Jane Addams had never tasted garlic until she tried spaghetti Bolognese in the Italian neighborhood of the 19th Ward. Now, in spite of the surrounding six-lane expressways, Hull-House remains standing, its character intact, the integrity of the original building preserved. It is as if the silhouette of the nineteenth-century home was stenciled on the present Halsted Street. The preservation of rooms, of objects, with pictures and signs, is respectful but not deadly. The rooms are surprisingly small. We have become profligate with space, heat and water. The house still feels like a home. It could not accommodate all twenty-one residents now, because its ancillary buildings have been torn down.

On the way back my car was gradually surrounded, as if by water rising, by a marching band, floats, and women and children in pink ribbons and green costumes. Some sense of the old Greek neighborhood has survived, in spite of the cruelty of the Daley expressways which cut through the old neighborhoods like an apple corer.

People will find a way to distill something of their heritage, or what they have heard of where they came from, or where their parents came from, or of the lives lived by their grandparents, even if all they have is a crystal necklace, a pair of leather gloves, a photograph of anonymous old people frowning into the portrait camera: what people remember may be a color, a word, the taste of a special food, a smell of spice, a snatch of song.

Hull-House now faces a three-story concrete parking lot for the University of Illinois campus on Halsted Street. Hull-House no longer looks out on the worst slum in America; that slum now is to the west and the south. That is where the children who cannot read and do not know their names or letters now live, in the shadow of their gun battles. Hull-House the museum faces toward the skyscrapers of downtown Chicago.

On the street are students, of every identification, an especially large and varied proportion of Asians. Halsted Street is still broad, still a great plank street, leading into the heart of the downtown, although now it goes under and over the expressways.

The city bus stops right across the street, and there are people, old people, young people, infirm people, white people, Hispanic people, women with collapsing ankles, covered women, and young girls snapping gum, waiting for it. They are all staring at their cellphones. There is a new phone app which tells how many minutes before the next Halsted Street bus is due.

This is how the proceedings, the facts determined in the trial below, and the legal issues were presented to the Supreme Court of Illinois in Ritchie v. People:

> *April 20, 1894, appearance of parties in criminal court; defendant waives jury; defendant found guilty and fined $5; motion for a new trial; motion overruled; objection and exception by defendant.*
>
> *Judgment on finding.*
>
> *Defendant fined $5 and costs; objection and exception to judgment; appeal prayed and allowed to the Supreme court of Illinois, southern Grand Division. . . .*
>
> *Mollie Fach, a witness for the people, testified:*
>
> *I live at 39 Miller street, worked for defendant, February 23, 1894, for wages, in his paper box factory in Chicago, by the piece, nine and three quarter hours; was paid by the number of boxes I made; worked from 10 minutes after seven to twelve, with half an hour for dinner, and from half-past twelve to twenty-five minutes after five; had ten minutes to get ready to go home, and twenty-five minutes to six we left the shop; am twenty-seven years old; support myself, and am not married. . . ; I try to make as many boxes as I can, because I want to earn more money; . . . have never objected or been unwilling to work the hours indicated; don't know that I would work longer hours; was willing to work more than eight hours because I was anxious to earn as much money as possible; the more money I can earn the better able I am to support myself. . . .*
>
> *[I] could quit at the end of nine and three-quarters hours if I would ask permission; have to work according to the rules and hours prescribed in the factory; would work as much as the others did, week after week. . . .*
>
> *Defendant submitted propositions of law as follows: As a matter of law, we ask the*

court hold that the act of the legislation . . . approved June 17, 1893, and each and every section thereof is illegal and void. . . .

The finding is contrary to the constitution of Illinois; the finding is contrary to the constitution of the United States and the amendments thereto.

(Ritchie v. People, Abstract of Record at trial)

Although the matter appeared before a justice of the peace, it was designated criminal, and there was an option of a jury trial. To expedite the appeal, Florence Kelley as factory inspector agreed to stipulate to certain facts and to suspend some further prosecutions pending the decision on the constitutionality of the statute by the Supreme Court of Illinois. At a certain point there was no reason to gather more testimony or facts. The facts were simple enough: did these women work more than eight hours a day, the limit stipulated in the statute? Was the child employed under the age of fourteen? The cases brought to the Supreme Court of Illinois didn't even include facts about health of the working children or the conditions in the factories and tenements. Not all prosecutions were suspended during the appeal to the Supreme Court of Illinois: proceedings against the Illinois Glass Works continued.

In January 1894, the last of the actions against W.C. Ritchie & Company for violations of the hours rules and the child labor provisions were filed. Eventually there would be nine plaintiffs.

January 3, 2009: A bright day as if it were fall. The city sparkles. On the street everyone seems to be hurrying to an important meeting. Perhaps they are just going for lunch. The atmosphere of hurry implies that serious business is afoot. I, too, bustle into the taxi, go through all of the identification rituals to be admitted to the big law firm office, a picture ID, to be on a list, in order to enter the glass and steel high-rise office building on the river where the capital punishment reform study committee meets today.

The work of the death penalty reform committee goes forward, although it is not clear what that work is. None of the members of the committee is interested in research. They are lawyers, and lawyers don't believe in research. Actually they become uncomfortable when I ask embarrassing questions about what we know or don't know, or when I suggest that we should collect reliable data about questions such as where the money has gone and the pattern of capital prosecutions across countries.

The lawyers think that "arguments," whatever those are, will win the day in the courts and legislature. Why bother with research, even if it produces facts, and facts can be evidence? Every conceivable argument about the death penalty has been heard and is familiar to anyone who has seriously considered this question, and certainly to all members of this commit-

tee. We are long past argument. And so I am in the middle, a lawyer, but not their kind of lawyer, a researcher, a writer, an academic, a word which is pejorative here. Calling something "academic" is a reason to dismiss it as a fact. Ironically, the academics don't count me as their own either.

Today we met in the sumptuous conference room of our chair's private law firm, windows taller than we are, a dark polished table big enough to seat twenty for dinner, the shine of chrome, stale fruit, weak coffee. We are a bunch of shuffling people, almost all men, mostly lawyers who have spent their lives in state government, or as country prosecutors, or as administrators. They squirm here in these luxurious surroundings, as I do, as we pour our coffee, pinch the free fruit, not available at our other workplaces, deliberate over the stale pastries, and argue our stale positions on capital punishment.

The first jury conviction under the Factory and Workshop Inspection Law was of a sweater employed by Beifield & Co. Joseph Beifield was the treasurer of the Illinois Manufacturers' Association. Although the penalties and fines under the statute were small, minimal even, Levy Mayer had brought together the disorganized manufacturers into an association, collected dues, and built the comprehensive challenge to the statute as a whole, and to everything that Florence Kelley and her associates did and strived to do.

As Florence Kelley was writing in the *Annual Report* that the statute must be strengthened to be effective, the Illinois Manufacturers' Association was doing its best to bring the entire operation of factory and tenement inspection to a halt. As far as the business community was concerned, the statute was a declaration of war by the unions and the workers.

February 18, 2005, Mumbai: The dwarfish girl in a filthy dress, like the brilliant actress she is, catches my eye, changes her expression to pitiable, scratches at the closed window of our car, stalled at a traffic light in the sulphurous streets of Mumbai. Scratch, scratch, then her fingers scooping air into her mouth. "Feed me. Give me money." Her expression: alert, smart, calculating, changing in an instant to a frown of despair, a downturn of her sweet child's mouth.

Our Indian driver rolls down the window and motions her away gently, not unkindly, and turns and apologizes to us. She turns and with a motion of her head signals over her shoulder to two comrades working the parallel lanes of stymied traffic. We four, the Indian driver, our local host in a Western suit, and the two sweating American visitors on the plastic-covered back seat, stare straight ahead, not responding, pretending not to see, fixated on some imaginary still point ahead of the dusty line of cars.

The hosts, the people who escort us everywhere, are often women, highly educated women. The drivers are always men.

Our Indian host says she made a decision long ago about the limbless beggars and the blinking beggar children with the clotted eyelashes, the toothless women holding up blind babies: "I used to give them money," she says, "but the mothers spend it on cocaine and the babies aren't even theirs. They are common beggar babies, the newspaper says, and then they are left to die, and they get another one. If they are too fat, she says, they throw them away."

The air is pungent from the window being rolled down even for a moment. The air conditioning in the car labors with whirs and creaks to maintain a damp, perfumed mist for our comfort.

Outside the ancient, beautiful temple a filthy boy, he looks six and is probably eight, stands on bare feet without moving and weeps piteously, not shrieking, not screaming. He just stands and cries and cries. Four skinny men, not so clean themselves, squat with their bony knees up, behind an array of religious trinkets set out on a blanket. Why doesn't someone pick him up? Just pick him up.

The *Chicago Tribune* accused the factory inspectors of being no more than labor organizers under the guise of government officials. Certainly the sympathies of the Hull-House reformers were in that direction. The critics had a point. As the decade continued, Jane Addams, who had enjoyed unqualified support in Chicago, was beginning to be criticized: Hull-House was too radical, was harboring people like Florence Kelley, who was a socialist, or worse.

September 9, 2012: The most glorious morning. Last night a helicopter on the roof outside our window was bringing a child to the new $800 million children's hospital. A momentary blaze of lights, orange, green, red, bright white, then the whirr, then silence. There are stairs from the helipad to the hospital. The silence is punctuated by the sound of drums from a museum party across the street. Bright orange flames flash intermittently, a fire eater as entertainment for the party.

Florence Kelley's agreeing in May 1894 to suspend all prosecutions for hours violations under the 1893 statute, pending the decision of the Supreme Court of Illinois, was a procedural victory for Levy Mayer. Neither side wanted to waste time and money on repetitive prosecutions. Both sides wanted the matter resolved before the next gubernatorial election. Levy Mayer's substantial contribution was to organize the business community and to articulate the legal challenge in such a way that it could not be ignored.

Florence Kelley and her assistant inspectors started investigations immediately after her appointment. Prosecutions and inspections continued throughout 1893, 1894 and 1895 under other provisions of the statute. The convictions came fast. In the fall of 1894, only a year after the law was enacted, there had been twenty-five convictions for the employment of underage children in a variety of manufacturing industries: tailors, meat-packers, candy manufacturers, cigar factories, garment makers, and furniture makers. The decision of the factory inspectors to continue with prosecutions for violations of the child labor provisions during the appeal was strategically astute. That would be the part of the statute which had the most support, the part the court was least likely to get rid of. It was also the part dearest to Florence Kelley's heart.

December 11, 2013: Winter weather, 26 degrees, but clean, and clear skies. Sunrise in a coal-black sky at 7 a.m. Only days to solstice.

The last prosecution for the violation of the hours provision was against a watchmaking factory. Once again, the trial took place before a judge without a jury. The defendant manufacturers waived their right to a jury trial, either because they thought a jury would not be sympathetic to them or simply to speed things along. This may have been a strategic decision by Levy Mayer, to bypass the jury and to get to the high court more quickly. A jury conviction would not have any more legal weight than a conviction without a jury, as far as the constitutional challenge was concerned. There was no provision for damages, only the paltry fine.

Florence Kelley and the state, and her inspectors and helpers, also had an interest in having the constitutionality of the statute settled. Florence Kelley was advocating for an increase in the powers of the factory inspector, and the sooner the litigation was resolved, the sooner the governor and the factory inspector could go back to the legislature and ask for stronger legislation for more serious penalties and greater powers of enforcement. The investigators had done their homework. The facts were clear. Many were in violation of the statute. The position of the Illinois Manufacturers' Association was also clear: that all the current practices and conditions of employment were legal, and the statute, unconstitutional.

August 3, 2012: A noisy, bright thunderstorm last night. Today, hot, sunny. Still a drought for the farmers, but all the buildings downtown are gleaming. Cities now are people walking fast, looking like they know where they are going. I am going to a quiet place with no windows where I will enter the nineteenth century once again.

This was the procedure in 1894 for challenging the constitutionality of the state Factory Inspection Law. The underlying complaint charged that on a certain day in February

1894, for example, the plaintiff in error employed a certain adult female of more than eighteen years old for more than eight hours. That fact established guilt for a violation of Section 5, the hours provision of the statute. The cited factory owner appeared to plead. The waiver of the jury trial quickly resulted in a judge finding the cited manufacturer guilty of a violation of the Factory Inspection Law, with the imposition of the small fine (usually five dollars) and costs.

The appellant was called the plaintiff in error because the appeal was under a common law writ of error. The writ of error is one of the traditional common law writs fundamental to the British common law, brought to the colonies from Britain, just as the writ of habeas corpus was. A writ called for the bringing into court of a person or party. This tradition is described by Pollock and Maitland's *History of English Law: Before the Time of Edward I* in 1895:

> *Closely connected with the introduction of trial by inquest is the growth of that system of original writs which is soon to become the ground-plan of all civil justice. For a long time past the king at the instance of complainants has issued writs, which either bade their adversaries appear in the royal court to answer the complaint, or else committed their causes to the care of the sheriff or of the feudal lord and commanded that right should be done to them in the county court or the seignorial court. Such writs were wont to specify with some particularity the subject-matter of the complaint.*

Hence the factory inspection case before the Supreme Court of Illinois is captioned: *W.D. Ritchie, plaintiff in error, versus People*. The other party, of course, is the People, or the State, defending the constitutionality of the state statute, which gave Florence Kelley and her associates the authority to knock on the door and enter the premises of the tenement manufacturers and large factories such as the glass works in Alton.

The procedural posture of the case is that the manufacturers are bringing the matter to the Supreme Court of Illinois as an appeal in law via the common law writ of error. And if the statute were found to be unconstitutional, there would be no legal authority for Florence Kelley and the factory inspectors to report on or fine for any violations. It is the allegation that the statute gives the authority for inspection, reporting, and prosecution. It is the hours provision and the age provision which allow the inspectors to pull the children out of the tenements and enroll them in school under the school attendance law.

February 14, 2008: The national economy is shaking. People are predicting economic hardship and unemployment in America not seen since the 1930s, or earlier.

Tonight coming home alone, driving into the large, dark driveway, I encountered a figure, a muffled figure, walking on the side lawn. "Who are you?" I called. A woman approached the open car window, a woman of uncertain age, wrapped in a scarf. "I used to live here," she said, then quickly walked away down the driveway and onto the street. Someone has been taking our mail and throwing it on the ground. Perhaps it is she.

In 1902-03 Margaret Kelley attended the Young Ladies' Seminary at Ferry Hall in Lake Forest, Illinois, an elite preparatory school known for its support of social causes. Frances Perkins, the first female Cabinet member in the United States, and an acolyte of Florence Kelley's, taught there in 1904.

Florence Kelley writes to Nicholas: "What is Mr. Lloyd writing?" and says "my chief occupation is writing things for immediate publication, and this makes a poor correspondent." The writers always want to know what the other writers are writing.

October 3, 2007: Class today. Another glorious fall day. The Arctic ice cap may be melting, but the weather here is surprisingly beautiful. We have never had a family birthday where we are so aware of the fragility of life. A loved one hangs on with yet another round of punishing treatment, paid for by the state.

The justice of the peace or the trial court judge was asked by each factory owner convicted to hold the entire factory inspection statute unconstitutional, each and every section illegal and void. The trial court refused to so hold; thus there was an appealable ruling.

The Illinois Manufacturers' Association first tried the tactic of arguing that the statute applied only to cigar manufacturers and clothing manufacturers. Governor Altgeld's attorney general, M.T. Moloney, who later argued the constitutional case for the state before the Supreme Court of Illinois, had already at Florence Kelley's request, immediately after her appointment, ruled that the statute applied broadly to all manufacturers.

Then the Illinois Manufacturers' Association argued that government had no authority at all to legislate regarding the conditions of employment or the hours worked under the mandate of protecting the public health, or under the state's authority to protect specially the health of women and children, or under any other constitutional authority. In their view, the authority to regulate violated the police powers of the state. Finally the Illinois Manufacturers' Association argued that the statute violated principles of due process and freedom to contract and control one's liberty for individuals under the Fourteenth Amendment to the federal Constitution, which had been used to challenge the practice of slavery.

This debate over whether the state legislature or the US Congress could legislate to protect the health of certain classes of citizens would continue for decades, be argued in cases before a number of other state supreme courts, and be the explicit subject of decision by the Supreme Court of the United States.

There were other arguments against the constitutionality of the factory inspection statute, including that it violated the "single subject" rule, a highly technical Illinois constitutional requirement that no statute address more than one subject. This doctrine allowed the court to declare unconstitutional a statute on the basis of a finding that the statute impermissibly covered two subjects: technical procedural grounds with no substantive component, grounds incomprehensible to the public and mysterious to many lawyers. If there were nothing else, this doctrine was useful to judges inclined to declare a politically controversial statute unconstitutional without a substantive explanation. In this case a ruling by the Supreme Court of Illinois that the statute violated the "single subject" rule might simply have resulted in the legislature rewriting the statute, assuming that a majority still could be found. A violation of the single subject rule could be corrected by the state legislature.

February 15, 2008: Though the Committee to Study the Reform of the Death Penalty seems hamstrung in its ability to recommend any change, new details about the working of the Illinois capital punishment system are emerging at our public hearings, where attendance is small, usually limited to those testifying and to the committee members. The testimony is overwhelmingly from those opposed to capital punishment, although everyone is bored with this and knows that such testimony is irrelevant.

The state's attorneys are uncompromising: each of the 101 elected state's attorneys from the 101 other counties in the state has the discretion, and should have the discretion, which is unreviewable, to declare a murder case capital and to bring it to trial, or not. The state's attorneys on the committee always make sure the abolitionists testifying are identified on the record as such, and always ask pointed questions about their opinions on the death penalty to discredit their testimony on the record in advance.

The present Supreme Court of Illinois will never declare the capital punishment system unconstitutional. Nor will the federal courts in Illinois. Still, certain facts about patterns and practices in capital cases are now irrefutable and a matter of public record. Even if the final report of this committee is not noteworthy, the testimony and findings of the committee will be available for later challenges to the system. It will be possible to find the committee reports and the transcripts of these hearings all online. No one will have to go to the library. If anyone cares enough to look.

Admission to the Bar in Illinois had been formalized for some time when Florence Kelley was admitted in June 1895. Some took examinations; however, graduation from a respected law school, such as the School of Law at Northwestern University, was deemed sufficient for admission also. There was no character and fitness test formalized. Prospective lawyers were "interviewed" by members of the Bar; sometimes these interviews took place in saloons. Florence Kelley would have had enough respected members of the Bar to vouch for her.

In the June 13, 1878, *Chicago Tribune* the results of the examination for admission to the Bar in Springfield were reported for the first time. The appellate court had formally adopted rules requiring applicants who had pursued a course of study for two years in school, or in the office of a lawyer, and had filed certificates of moral character to present themselves in open court for examination. Tuesday of each week in term was dedicated to these examinations. The names of those who passed were forwarded to the Supreme Court. Of the examination reported on June 13, 1878, twenty-five passed and seven did not; only the names and towns of residence of those who passed were reported.

May 10, 2008: The fact that the Illinois Bar gave me so much trouble about the five months when it could have been argued I wasn't practicing law is an indication, if one were needed, that the purpose of the Bar is to keep down the number of lawyers in the state.

At the time when Levy Mayer worked at the Chicago Law Institute and began practice in 1876, there were 1,025 lawyers in Illinois and the Bar was increasing at the rate of about fifty lawyers a year. The statutes were compiled every year and tracked the legislative session of that year. In addition there were few legal publications or outlets for additional commentary or opinion, except through self-published pamphlets or newspaper editorials, or a small number of magazines. When Henry Demarest Lloyd published an article in *The Atlantic*, it was read. There are now about three thousand new members of the Illinois Bar every year, and there are approximately thirty thousand lawyers in the state.

Treatises on the central legal topics—contracts, property, crime—included annotations, margin notes, and references to cases and statutes which were printed with wide margins left blank so that the learned lawyers and judges could write their own notes right next to the text of the law. When a judge's library burned, it was the loss of his education, his stored wisdom, a loss of the opportunity for others to become educated by his education, in addition to the loss of authoritative books.

A distinguished legal and judicial scholar was embedded in books, often literally surrounded by his library. Education was through the published and written word. There was a well-established oral tradition of legal and political oratory. The Supreme Court of the United States was far away, as was the Congress, and both rarely needed to be taken into account for state legal questions and both typically had little interest in what went on in state legal forums.

It was highly unusual when a member of the US Congress would come to Chicago to hold hearings on conditions in the city. The legal game here was typically played in the rings of the Chicago circus: the state and county courts, the state's attorney's offices, the state legislature and agencies, and the governor's office. The moneyed people supported various state politicians, and the city ward bosses, the City Council, the mayor, and the party in power controlled the beehive of city and state bureaucracies. It wasn't that state law trumped local law, although it sometimes had the technical authority to do so. It was a question of deference. For the most part city officials could confidently ignore what went on in Springfield and expect that Springfield would ignore them, and they could ignore the US Congress and US Supreme Court as well.

December 5, 2012: Springfield is flat, so very flat. Some of the historic buildings decorated. The new Lincoln museum, grand, shaped like the White House in miniature. The Leland Hotel where Florence Kelley stayed has not been torn down. There are pictures of the building with the Leland Hotel sign on the Web. The building is no longer a hotel.

In Springfield the governor's office, the two houses of the state legislature and the Supreme Court of Illinois were in the 1890s the ostensible locus of power. All were closely attuned to Chicago and its politics. In times of economic boom and bust, the hands controlling the political power turned on the money and the patronage—or some would say the jobs and the bribes. Lawyers were always at the center of these politics. When Florence Kelley arrived in 1891 the merry-go-round of Chicago politics had been going full tilt since the Great Fire and earlier. The city was up and running again soon after the fire in 1871, partly because so many found a reason to leave where they were and come to Chicago. Chicago built and built.

On April 4, 1892, Congress held hearings for the specifically designated congressional subcommittee in Chicago over the conditions in the Chicago sweatshops. After hearing testimony on the conditions in the sweatshops, and receiving a report from Mrs. T.J. Morgan and hearing testimony from Abraham Bisno, the subcommittee called upon representatives of the business community.

April 22, 2012: A blustery day, spring in Chicago. Today to the Hull-House Museum. If Mrs. T.J. Morgan did much of what Florence Kelley did—conducted factory inspections in the tenements, wrote an influential report, testified before the congressional committee, worked with women factory inspectors under the authority of the City Council—why is she not the talismanic figure of reform?

In 1892 during these congressional hearings in Chicago it was proposed to outlaw all manufacturing in dwellings and institute a federal licensing system, under the authority of the commerce clause of the US Constitution, with inspection and reporting requirements imposed at the federal level.

Abraham Bisno testified that he was a cloak maker in business for eleven years, making eleven dollars per week and working sixty hours a week: "The sweat shops are in basements and attics, and the nuisance was brought about because people can work longer than in a factory."

This allows us to pinpoint Abraham Bisno's presence in Chicago as dating from at least 1881. In other words he would have been in Chicago for Haymarket, for the strikes and events preceding Haymarket, and for the Haymarket trial and the hangings. In 1891 Abraham Bisno identifies himself as president of the Chicago Cloak Makers' Union, but he doesn't so identify himself at the congressional hearings in 1892.

The Congressional Committee on Labor suggested instituting a system for monitoring conditions in factories by tagging garments as inspected under a federal law issued by Congress as part of its authority to regulate interstate commerce. There was precedent for this. Decades later a national system to assure the uniform treatment of items of clothing similar to what was proposed in 1892 was adopted. Florence Kelly in New York and the International Ladies' Garment Workers and many others spent decades advocating for such a system, and eventually it was put in place. During wartime Florence Kelley argued for standards for military uniforms and exposed corruption in the manufacture of wartime goods.

At the hearings in 1892 this is the testimony of Mr. King, whom Florence Kelley identifies to Henry Demarest Lloyd as the manufacturer who controls the largest number of sweatshops in the tenements.

I am against interfering with our business in any manner, shape, or form. We would rather go out of business. To the objections made by the other witnesses to the tagging or numbering plan, I add that I object very materially; and before we would submit to anything of that kind we would sell out and go out of business because it would place us at the mercy of a lot of tailors who want to be bribed by both parties. . . .

Q: Your answer is, Mr. King, that you object to any interference with your business by the Government of the United States?

A. Yes, sir.

This is not a manufacturer with a small operation but one whose business was valued between $2 million and $3 million annually. In the Nineteenth Ward, three-quarters of the employees were women and a significant fraction were children.

May 2, 2009: The first real spring day. Sun, blue sky. Yesterday, May Day, the worker's day. We are out of here in three months. I am not ready to leave. Nothing is packed, and everyone wants to have a farewell dinner for us, although we say we are just going downtown, which is true.

In 1867 an Illinois statute was enacted saying that the ordinary working day was eight hours. However, an exception provided that individual employers and employees could contract away from the eight-hours provision, so the legal stricture was of no use as a tool to address the conditions in the sweatshops. Employers simply made sure there was some sort of written "contract" or agreement, whether with the parents of the working children or with the workers themselves. These contracts signed by prospective employees typically included clauses promising not to take legal action if injured or not to challenge the number of hours worked.

In 1889 there was a city ordinance saying that children under fifteen could not work with machinery, and their workday was limited to eight hours. On June 26, 1890, the city passed an ordinance saying that no child under fourteen was to be employed, but exemptions were allowed if the children had a work permit. There was an exception that children could work if they were supporting a widowed or disabled parent. In short, employers and parents could contract away the provisions protecting children. And they did. And most of the working children were giving everything they earned to a parent or relative.

January 9, 2009, Chicago Tribune: "Full House to Vote Next on Whether to Oust Governor."

The Illinois House should impeach Gov. Blagojevich for abusing his power, mismanaging Illinois government and committing possible criminal acts, a special committee concluded Thursday.

The House could vote Friday to make Blagojevich the first governor impeached in the long, sordid history of Illinois politics. Impeachment in the House would trigger a Senate trial to decide whether the second-term Democrat should be removed from office.

The 21-member committee voted unanimously to recommend impeachment. Many called it "a sad day" for Illinois, but Rep. Bill Black disagreed.

"I think this is a good, glad, happy day for Illinois because it points out that nobody is above the law," the Danville Republican said.

In 1889 the Illinois General Assembly passed a compulsory education act, saying children ages eight to fourteen must be in school not less than twelve weeks of the year. In 1891, although women did not have the vote, the Illinois Women's Alliance secured passage of a city ordinance empowering the commissioner of health to appoint five women factory inspectors.

September 10, 2009: The squabbling on the capital punishment reform committee continues. The work of the committee seems after the fact since the Ryan Commission, which was a much more distinguished committee than we are, has already said everything that needed to be said about what needed to be done about capital punishment in Illinois.

Our committee members seem most interested in declaring the capital punishment system "fixed," so that executions can proceed. As long as judges are elected and legislators are afraid of being defeated by being labeled soft on crime or anti-gun, the present situation will continue. No one now holding a state office thinks the death penalty will ever be abolished in Illinois, even though it is an example of the worst kind of government policy. So we stumble forward with no change. What is the point of our formal hearings, of the taking of testimony, or of writing reports when nothing changes? The committee's authority will expire, and nothing will have been accomplished.

During the months of waiting for the decision of the Supreme Court of Illinois, Florence Kelley continued the investigation and prosecutions of the Illinois Glass Works in Alton. At the Illinois Glass Works, it was underage boys, the blowers' dogs, not women, who were the focus of her attention. The Illinois Glass Works was the largest single employer of children in the state. And the conditions of their employment, abysmal. Basically, the children were taken from orphanages and sold into slavery.

After the factory inspections started in 1893, the returns were initially reasons for optimism: the stockyards unilaterally and dramatically instituted an eight-hour day for their ten thousand employees, men, women, and children. The eight-hour day was a symbol for both sides: a thinly veiled threat to strike, demand higher wages, and limit the authority of the factory owners. The catch phrase for the unions in hard economic times was "eight for ten," meaning: reduce the number of hours worked from ten to eight without a reduction in pay, thus increasing the per-hour pay for workers.

The eight-hour provision for women in the factory inspection statute applied more widely than the analogous provisions in the factory inspection laws of other states, some of which had been held to be constitutional by state high courts on the grounds that the state could legitimately legislate on matters related to health and that state legislatures could pass laws to protect the health of women.

May 5, 2009: The panic of moving, of leaving the green, the trees, the view, the grass. The panic of leaving what is now finally our home. For decades, almost ever since we have been a family, we have lived in a house. And yet as life changes go, this is not such a drastic one, or a bad one. We have been extraordinarily lucky. Lucky to live here now, to work here, lucky to have lived in this house for as long as we did, lucky to be here in this part of this society where peace primarily reigned, lucky to be part of a great educational institution.

The argument for the hours provisions for women only was that working women required special legislation to protect their health, because they were mothers or potentially mothers. Thus, to limit working hours for women only was a legitimate exercise of the police power of the state, an act to protect the health of some of its citizens. This line of argument was sharply criticized by feminists later. The arguments for the constitutionality of the state's ability to regulate specially for women to protect women more than men because of their special needs and vulnerability were seen by some as part of a fabric of gender discrimination which, under the guise of protection, actually gave a legal rationale for excluding women from economic and political activities, such as serving on juries, thus contributing to the exclusion of women from the highest reaches of politics and the professions. This argument continued throughout the nineteenth and twentieth centuries and was at the heart of the debates over the Equal Rights Amendment and civil rights legislation in the 1920s and later.

The position of the manufacturers was that the state had no authority to interfere in any way with the terms or working conditions imposed by employers upon any employees, not just women. Levy Mayer was correct in perceiving that it was the entire system of sweatshop labor which was being challenged under the guise of finding violations of the hours provisions and child labor provisions in the factory and workshop inspection statute.

Meanwhile, Florence Kelley's own children were in school in the country in Wisconsin.

Hillside Home School, January 30, 1901, Margaret Kelley to her grandmother, Caroline:

John is trying to clean all the snow off the ice on the pond so that the skating will be good for everyone. Early last week they succeeded in clearing away several inches of snow and had only one afternoon of good skating when all their work was undone by heavy snowfall. They do not seem to be discouraged in the least, however. . . . John and I are worried as we have not heard a word from Momma since we came back at Christmas time and which is now four weeks. We don't feel quite as secure a[s] we did before she had the diphtheria and didn't write us a word for six weeks but of course we hope very much that nothing is wrong.

Lovingly Margaret.

Levy Mayer cleverly attacked the law on both state and federal constitutional grounds: if the political climate under which the law was passed remained, a state constitutional interpretation striking down the law could be reversed by a state constitutional amendment or an amendment to the state statute. A decision based upon principles of federal constitutional law would not be subject to reversal by the state legislature or state courts.

The same strategy in reverse was successfully adopted in the challenge to the reimposition of the death penalty in New Jersey: an interpretation of disproportionality in the selection of death-eligible cases for capital prosecutions, and their disposition, was held by the Supreme Court of New Jersey to be unconstitutional on independent state grounds under the state constitution. This ruling came down after the Supreme Court of the United States held that racial disproportionality in the application of capital punishment would not be considered a violation of the Constitution of the United States.

October 5, 2010: A new United States Supreme Court term begins, with formality, with pomp, and all the pretense needed to prop up the illusion of the rule of law.

After all of the motions and hearings and trials and inspections, after all the marching through the tenements, after the momentary jubilation over the passage of the statute, the case challenging the law, Ritchie v. People, came to rest in the lap of the Supreme Court of Illinois.

Who were the seven white men, justices of the Supreme Court of Illinois in 1895, the men who decided the constitutionality of the Factory and Workshop Inspection Law? How did they come to be sitting on the Supreme Court of Illinois in 1895?

November 10, 2010: My class of two-year JDs is very rambunctious. They consider themselves superior to everyone. At the last class I ask a sitting justice of the Supreme Court of Illinois to come and talk to the class. They are appropriately respectable, mostly, to the justice, who is very charming.

The justices of the Supreme Court of Illinois were elected, as they still are today. It was the custom that they live in Springfield during the term of the court, having their meals together, discussing the cases, assigning and reading the draft opinions, all in a Spartan setting similar to a summer camp or university residence hall. This practice remains today. The seven justices of the Supreme Court of Illinois live in Springfield during term, eat their meals together, and discuss the pending cases during their residency. Visits from spouses are not encouraged.

In 1893 they were a group of men whose paths to the court varied. All but one of them sported extensive, well-barbered facial hair. They were men of their times.

May 10, 2007: The Florence Kelley Project continues to evolve. The librarians and archivists of the Supreme Court of Illinois continue to find legal materials from the 1890s litigation. We will put everything on the Web. The legal procedures have changed not at all. The lawyers were better writers then.

The justice who wrote the opinion for the court in the *Ritchie* case, Benjamin Drake Magruder, was not chief justice at the time, although he did serve as chief justice of the Supreme Court of Illinois in 1891, 1896, and 1902. Benjamin Magruder was, however, the author of the opinion of the court in the Haymarket case, which the court referred to as the Anarchist Case. The assignment of opinion is made by the chief justice, if he is in the majority. In the Haymarket case and in the *Ritchie* case the opinion was unanimous.

December 23, 2003, Chicago Tribune: "Ryan Pleads Not Guilty; Former Governor Vows to Fight Corruption Charges."

Embarking on the most important campaign of his life, a defiant former Gov. George Ryan said Tuesday he was "absolutely not guilty" of federal corruption charges, then dug in for a lengthy court battle.

"I'm not going to give up. I'm going to fight. I'm going to fight hard," Ryan told reporters after he pleaded not guilty in U.S. District Court to an 18-count indictment alleging he received illegal payoffs and steered lucrative contracts to friends who peddled their influence on his behalf.

"I will not plea bargain," Ryan said. "I'll go to trial and establish my innocence."

In a news conference after the arraignment, Ryan's lawyer, former U.S. Atty. Dan Webb, said the indictment against Ryan was based on a string of "innocent acts that are nothing more than the fabric of what goes on in Illinois politics and Illinois government."

Webb said Ryan committed no crimes, and that prosecutors have been unable to find even one witness who will testify that he pocketed corrupt payments or bribes during his 4-year tenure as governor and 8 years as secretary of state.

"That's a huge defect in the government's case," Webb said,"
and one which I'm confident will be the basis for a 'not guilty'
determination by a jury."

Benjamin Magruder was born in Mississippi before the Civil War and was sent up east to Yale for his undergraduate degree. He came back to the University of Louisiana, New Orleans, for an LLB and was valedictorian of his law school class in 1858. Like so many others, he came to practice law in Chicago in 1861, drawn by the magnet of the economic boom in the city. There were many reasons to leave the foundering state of Mississippi in 1861.

He became master in chancery in Cook County in 1868 and was elected to the Supreme Court of Illinois in 1885, just before Haymarket, in time to take the responsibility and write the unanimous opinion upholding the imposition of the death sentences for all the adult Haymarket defendants for conspiracy to commit murder. If the dice had rolled differently, he might have served on the Supreme Court of the United States with his Yale Law classmate, Justice David Josiah Brewer, who served from 1889 until his death in 1910.

October 1, 2007: The back garden is tamped down for the winter, but some vibrant colors remain: the deep red of the weeping maple, the dark defensive green of the fir tree, the work-manlike grey of the thick oak. The man who oversees the garden, this garden, has been doing it for decades; he knows every tree, every bush. It is his garden. Gently, he puts aside any suggestions for change.

Justices on the Supreme Court of Illinois were not always elected. The first Illinois Constitution of 1818 provided in Article IV that there would be four justices of the newly formed Supreme Court, with appellate and some original jurisdiction for mandamus and revenue. They were to be appointed by a joint ballot of both branches of the General Assembly (as it was then and still is called), and then served under a commission from the governor, holding office during good behavior with periodic assignments to ride circuit in several counties. They were still riding circuit in 1895.

The 1848 constitution reduced the number of Supreme Court justices from four to three and added a requirement that the state should be partitioned into three grand divisions, as nearly equally as possible, and the qualified electors of each division should elect one justice for a term of nine years. In other words, only the voters from that division could vote for the justice from their division. After the first election the General Assembly would have the power to provide for the election of these justices by the whole state.

April 12, 2008: It is steel grey, raining, and supposed to snow tonight. O'Hare will be a middle-class refugee camp with 5,000 stranded travelers sleeping in cots. The young sleep on the floor. Everyone draining down the stocks of overpriced snacks and putting pressure on the bathrooms. But these stringent circumstances for the airplane travelers are temporary, hence bearable. And the stranded passengers do have access to running water, electricity and plumbing, and everyone believes the planes will fly again sometime soon. They are not living in that deprived position forever, for the foreseeable future. The accounts of the forced marches in war, in mass dislocations, unimaginable.

Decisions of the three-judge Supreme Court historically required a quorum of two. This division of the state for the purposes of guaranteed geographic representation on the Supreme Court remains in effect today, some believe to the detriment of the quality of the court. Chicago dominated the politics of the state. The purpose for required geographic representations outside of Chicago was to limit the power of Chicago politicians.

Meanwhile, family life continued for Florence Kelley:

Hillside, May 6, Wisconsin: [The envelope is stamped May 6, 1902.]

Dear Grandma:

. . . I got up at 4 o'clock this morning and went out on the hills for violets to send away. I did not find many flowers but had one of the most beautiful walks I ever in my life had, everything was covered with dew and the bird songs were beautiful. . . . I love to hear from you when you feel like writing and hope you are well and pleasantly situated.

Lovingly, Margaret K.

The 1870 constitution provided that all judges and justices be directly elected. The participation of the legislature in the election of judges was removed. The 1870 constitution additionally provided that the Supreme Court of Illinois would consist of seven judges, three of whom were to be selected from the First District (which included Chicago), and one each from the Second, Third, Fourth, and Fifth judicial districts. Four justices would thereafter constitute a quorum, so that the three justices from the First District (which included Chicago) could not operate as a bloc and dominate the court.

The justices select a chief justice from among themselves at the beginning of each term, for one year and they continue to do so. The chief justice has the power to assign the writing of the opinion, if he is in the majority. The structure of judicial elections introduced by the constitution of 1870 would have been a recent memory to the members of the Supreme Court of Illinois and citizens of the 1890s.

In some states the chief justice is appointed for a number of years, or is elected or confirmed separately for a length of term, or the position rotates. The chief justice is typically the administrative head of the entire court system in the state, as the chief justice of the United States is the titular head of the entire federal court system. Thus, the chief justice has authority beyond that of the other justices. During the 1980s the Supreme Court of New Jersey would never have developed its extensive jurisprudence of proportionality review in capital cases without the leadership and will of then-Chief Justice Robert Wilentz. The practice in Illinois of having a chief justice who is elected every year is distinctive, not typical, and weakens the authority of the chief justice.

October 5, 2007: Always returning from a trip, planning for the next trip, then returning to the same tasks, the same rooms, the same rattle of the heater, the same draught from the window. The rhythm of the school year gives structure to the time. Always glad to be on my third floor surrounded by my books, old papers, and research. Usually glad to be in my office downtown at the law school, surrounded by the bustle of the students, feeling their mounting anxiety as the semester draws toward examinations.

Then, home after the traveling, the endless traveling, the habits of life take over: what side of the bed you get up from, what you eat for breakfast. Always the anxiety of the planes: will the plane be late, will the weather cause cancellations.

This time to New York and a conference on medical ethics and lethal injection. In Illinois the legislature will never get rid of the death penalty because of a technicality such as that involving lethal injection as a method, even though that litigation has been an excuse to halt executions in several states. Too many state legislators are former prosecutors. No one in Illinois would run for office, either as an elected judge, an elected prosecutor, or a governor saying they were against the death penalty. It would be an open invitation to an attack from the gun lobby and the fear-of-criminals lobby. These are low-turnout elections where single-issue lobbyists are effective. Our law school colleague who ran for governor says now that refusing to support the death penalty is what defeated her.

Plus, the fabric of the criminal law is held together by the traditions and special rules and procedures for the death penalty: the earliest state criminal codes and British statutes didn't define crimes, they simply set out what crimes were capital offenses. Then all the special capital provisions come into play: the rules governing capital juries, in the United States the special statutory aggravating and mitigating factors, and then the rules governing the conduct of the participants in the trial, defense attorneys, judges, and prosecutors. Everyone keyed to the fact that a life is at stake, at least theoretically. Makes us lawyers feel important. Nor am I immune. The death penalty attracts high-quality, serious scholarship. But what a waste of talent and energy, not to mention money.

The weather in Springfield in March 1895 was cold, cloudy with traces of snow, on the day the opinion in *Ritchie* was announced. In Chicago it was a bit colder. The weather in Chicago was measured every day by Mannasso, Optician, at the Tribune building and reported by the *Chicago Tribune*. The *Tribune* reported the weather on March 15, 1895, for the previous day for Illinois: "(light snow) lower and upper Michigan (fair, slightly warmer) as well as for Wisconsin, Nebraska, Iowa, South Dakota, North Dakota and Montana." Many who lived in Chicago had relatives, friends, lovers in these distant places. Or they might be considering traveling there themselves.

On the day the decision was announced, March 14, 1895, handed down in Mount Vernon, not in Springfield, it was a hard 20 degrees in Springfield, and in Chicago the knife was out at fifteen degrees. The word around Hull-House was that the law was going down.

October 20, 2007: Two days ago a tornado warning. These extreme weather patterns have become more frequent. The trees starting to color finally, a stripe of yellow, a siren call of orange from a modest bush.

The electoral process for judges included in the 1870 constitution required that all judges, including justices of the Supreme Court of Illinois, be nominated at a party convention or primary and elected at a general election after an election in their respective judicial districts. In other words, only the people in the district could vote for the justice nominated by the party in the early stages. This procedure ensured continuing party control. The justices of the Supreme Court were elected, but not directly elected, and did not run at large in the whole state.

The political bosses retained the threat of pulling the justices from a future nomination, no matter how popular they were. This cemented the control of the selection of judges in the hands of the party politicians. The political parties and the political machine controlled nominations for the state judiciary, the county prosecutors (the state's attorneys), the state legislators, and other state and local offices. And when a party official wanted a favor, or an outcome, or some pressure was put on a judge or a state official or a county prosecutor, it wasn't necessary to remind the official that the nomination procedure would soon be coming around again.

October 17, 2010, Chicago Tribune: "Change of Subject—Column Goes Wrong: Simple Correction Isn't Enough," by Eric Zorn.

Apologies to DuPage County State's Attorney Joe Birkett.

My column Friday greatly and unfairly overstated the potential financial benefit to him if he were to be appointed associate Circuit Court judge before Jan. 1, and was based on the assumption that he had applied for such a vacancy, as he told reporters last month that he was planning to do. And though we published a short correction in Saturday's paper, I want to set the record straight and explain what went wrong.

Birkett, 55, has worked for 29 years in the county prosecutor's office in Wheaton, and has led that office since 1996. On Sept. 28 he told reporters he was "in the process of filling out the application" for an entry-level vacancy on the Circuit Court, which would have required him to step down halfway through his fourth term. . . .

Thursday, Illinois Municipal Retirement Fund executive director Louis Kosiba told me, and I reported, that if Birkett were to have been appointed to the bench before Jan. 1, he would be allowed to "double dip," or collect from the state both his prosecutor's pension—$137,520, roughly 80 percent of his current salary—and his judge's salary of $169,893. But if he were to have been appointed after Jan. 1, he would have had to defer collecting his pensions until after he retires from government work altogether.

This turns out not to be true, as Kosiba explained Friday in a follow-up call. The double-dip deadline does not, as he said he thought, apply to existing government employees, even those who change state jobs and join different pension programs.

And therefore it was wrong of me to strongly suggest that Birkett was in a hurry to leave his high-profile, influential position for an obscure job presiding over minor matters in order to be sure to reap the advantages of getting a state pension plus a state salary at the same time, a perfectly legal practice, by the way.

No matter when he might make his hoped-for transition to the bench, he will be able to double-dip, though anyone who becomes a judge after Jan. 1 will be enrolled in a somewhat less lucrative pension plan.

Birkett took strong exception in our conversation Friday to the implication that money might be motivating any of his career decisions. "I sacrificed a lucrative career in the private sector to stay here," he said, referring to the prosecutor's office. "I could be making millions of dollars" a year.

The process for electing justices to the Illinois courts typically was: a temporary appointment to the state judiciary after a retirement (perhaps voluntary, perhaps not) followed by the election of the justice who runs as an incumbent. The appointment to fill a vacancy may have been a reward for service to the party, and it came with the expectation of almost certain election as an incumbent later.

After the election to the Supreme Court of Illinois and the lower appellate court, there is a retention election. In Illinois, judges and justices are almost always retained by election. Recently the retention elections for Supreme Court justices in the states have become highly contentious, with large amounts of money spent on these campaigns, sometimes after a justice's overturning a death sentence on constitutional grounds or a controversial opinion on abortion or gay marriage. In Illinois large amounts of money are now spent on judicial elections, including retention elections.

April 22, 2012: A blowy day, a familiar kind of weather in Chicago. Birkett was responsible for the repeated prosecution and death sentences imposed upon persons who were later found not to have committed the murders for which they were sentenced to death. The prosecutors in these cases were found at trial to have withheld exonerating evidence, even to the point of withholding evidence that another person had confessed to the murder. After the retention election Birkett's judgeship will be secure for six years.

Benjamin Drake Magruder was born in 1838 in Natchez, Mississippi. Both his mother and his father, a professor, were from the North. He was educated at home until age fourteen when he entered Yale University, graduating at age eighteen in 1856.

Justice Magruder's legal training after Yale was at the University of Louisiana's Department of Law, and he was admitted to the bar in Memphis, Tennessee, where he practiced for several years. When the Civil War broke out in 1861, he moved to Chicago, where he developed a private legal practice.

One of Magruder's partners in Chicago was a former partner of an influential judge, and upon recommendation of this partner, Magruder was appointed to be master of the Superior Court of Cook County, where he served for sixteen years.

In 1885 Magruder ran for the Supreme Court of Illinois, having been named by the Republican Party to succeed a recently deceased justice. The Democrats also supported him, and he ran unopposed in 1885, was reelected in 1888 and 1897, and nominated by the Republicans in 1906.

Justice Benjamin Magruder, the author of the Haymarket opinion and the opinion in the *Ritchie* case, was not reelected in 1906 after serving twenty-one years on the Supreme Court of Illinois. He was "cruelly turned out to earn his living as a practicing lawyer at age 68," as the *Chicago Tribune* put it, noting that men do not accumulate fortunes on the

Supreme Court bench. Perhaps, the comment by the *Tribune* implied, in comparison to the wealth that could be gained elsewhere, for example, by holding other public offices in Illinois.

When a friend asked the impecunious former Governor Altgeld, himself a former judge, how he could have turned down a million-dollar bribe from Charles Yerkes to sign the street railway legislation, which had passed the legislature without difficulty allegedly after many bribes, Altgeld replied: "It was only half a million dollars." Altgeld later said the fictional account of the offering of the bribe in Theodore Dreiser's *The Titan* was essentially correct—the description of an emissary coming to the governor and leaving a briefcase with cash in his office and asking him to lock it up, and saying that no one would inquire about it. Except that the amount of the bribe offered was not a million dollars, Altgeld said, but half a million.

It was said about Benjamin Magruder that too much work and old age impaired his usefulness. When he was not renominated he had ceased to be the predominant member of the court he once was. The comment was that he had worn himself out in public service.

November 9, 2010: Another breathtakingly beautiful day. Why is Henry Demarest Lloyd forgotten? He was a brilliant prose stylist—when not being too doctrinaire—a passionate advocate. The issues are unchanged. He did not flinch at going himself to live for months among the locked-out miners at Spring Valley. Is it because he was stigmatized as a "communist" or a "socialist" long before the McCarthy hearings?

Justice Magruder left his entire estate of $40,000 to his unmarried niece, who had come from her home in San Antonio, Texas, to care for him and make bearable by her kindly treatment and sweet disposition his lonely and desolate life after the death of his wife. Justice Magruder's niece was the daughter of J.B. Magruder, presumably the brother of the Yale-educated justice, who was head of a preparatory school in San Antonio. Miss Lizzie Magruder asked to be released from a teaching contract at the art department at Emerson College in Texas and offered to come to her uncle's rescue three months after her aunt's death. The release from contract was granted, and Lizzie Magruder was her uncle's companion and caretaker until his death.

March 30, 2009: Missed the snow, yesterday, by being in New York. New York is strange now, and I am always glad to return to Chicago. The New York Public Library archives are a haven of silence in the city's tumult. In Chicago the heavy, wet snow broke branches, caused power outages, and wrapped the houses and cars in white, reminding people who had forgotten that we are hostage to the weather, to the gods. And that a storm can be magnificent.

"He never mentioned the will to me," Lizzie Magruder told a representative of the press after Justice Magruder's death.

The headline on the newspaper story was: "Kindness Given Rich Reward." She notified Judge Magruder's son of the arrangement leaving everything to her, and he responded that he was satisfied with the disposition of the property, which included a house at 7 Washington Place, a lot in Evanston, a building with a store at 517 East Washington in Springfield, an insurance policy of $5,000, a bank account, a law library, and the furnishings of a law office.

After the disclosure of the contents of the will, Lizzie Magruder was confined to her room on the verge of nervous prostration from grief over her uncle's death and the excitement of recent events. True, as was pointed out in Justice Magruder's obituary, men do not become rich from service on the Supreme Court of Illinois, but they may accumulate some modest property. This was long before Social Security, unemployment insurance, state retirement pensions, disability funds, or state paid health insurance.

Lizzie said she would stay and maintain the old house. The death was April 21, 1910. The story in the paper about Justice Magruder's will did not appear until May. She then returned to Texas—where she had no doubt been sorely missed—for the summer. The will further provided that the income from another commercial property in Chicago would go to support a son, Henry Latham Magruder, described as an invalid.

June 8, 2011: It is definitely true that the Midwest winters were harsher in the 1960s. The cabdriver in Iowa City confirmed this. He has been driving cabs in Iowa City for forty years, and he corroborated my memory of some soul-destroying cold in Iowa in the 1960s. As I waited for a bus in Iowa City as a student when I was pregnant and could not close my coat, the wind simply whipped aside the unbuttoned coat and the cold immediately knifed into all that awkward flesh, including the new life. Now we rarely see 20 degrees below zero and never for two weeks at a time.

Of the court sitting in 1895 when Ritchie v. People was decided, three began their terms in 1888: Baker, Wilkin and Bailey.

Jacob W. Wilkin, chief justice when Florence Kelley's factory inspection case was decided in 1895, was a member of the Supreme Court of Illinois for eighteen years and lived to the then relatively ripe old age of seventy. He was chief justice a second time in 1901. Before he was to be made chief justice for a second time he died of Bright's disease. Justice Wilkin was born in 1837 in Newark, Licking County, Ohio, receiving his undergraduate degree at McKendree College and then reading law under Judge John Scholfield, who was influential in shaping the professional careers of many prominent lawyers.

The lawyers, like the financiers, the builders, the businessmen, the prostitutes, the thieves, the carpenters, the maids, the barbers were typically not born in Chicago but were drawn to the spinning vortex of Chicago, and there found their sponsors and supporters.

Judge Wilkin's father was a builder, then a farmer in Illinois. Judge Wilkin had eight brothers and sisters, and all worked on the land. His legal career was postponed by the outbreak of the Civil War, when he enlisted after college as a private for the Clark County volunteers. He later was elected captain in the 130th Illinois.

Judge Wilkin served with General Grant during the Vicksburg campaign, guarding the general's headquarters. He then was transferred to General Robert Ransom and remained in command of his company until the fall of 1865.

He was promoted in the military and then resigned to go to the Bar in 1866. Wilkin and Scholfield were in private practice together until Scholfield became a member of the Supreme Court of Illinois in 1873.

In 1880 Jacob Wilkin was elected to the Fourth Judicial Circuit, and reelected in 1885. He was then appointed to the appellate court where he served until 1888. In 1888 Wilkin was elected to the Supreme Court of Illinois representing the Third District, following a vacancy, being reelected in 1897 and 1906. He served nineteen years on the Supreme Court of Illinois, twice serving as chief justice, and died in office.

He married twice and had five children, three of whom survived him. His first marriage, after his return from the Civil War, was to the daughter of a prominent Illinois judge.

Justice Wilkin was a member of the Masons and other civic societies, an active Republican, a presidential elector, and said to be a deeply religious man, a man of great simplicity and an old Southern gentleman, although he fought with General Grant.

February 15, 2008: Finally I get to see Springfield, Illinois. And it is cold. The Death Penalty Reform Committee will take testimony in the Capitol. The downstate prosecutors and defense attorneys can be spared a trip to Chicago and present their testimony in Springfield. I take the opportunity to look at the old Supreme Court of Illinois, a place of wood and velvet, and quiet, where Florence Kelley might have heard the argument in the factory inspection case.

The chairman drives, we chat, and it is a pleasant, if boring, drive through flat Illinois farm country. This is the court where Abraham Lincoln practiced law. This is the farm country of the last century.

At the hearing several hitherto-unacknowledged facts emerge, such as: the fact that the state's attorneys never return the money for capital prosecutions when the notice of prosecution is unilaterally withdrawn by the state's attorney and the case does not go to trial as a capital case. In other words the state's attorneys have a large financial incentive to declare a case capital pre-trial, and then withdraw the designation just before trial. The public defenders and appointed counsel also have a financial incentive to go along. As soon as a case is declared capital, all the bills are paid by the state, upon approval by the trial court judge.

Under the tiny so-called reform statute enacted in 2003, money can be withdrawn from the state, as opposed to the county coffers, to pay for the entire investigation and all the preparation for the expenses of a capital trial. The Office of the State's Attorney, and the defense counsel, which is typically appointed counsel in private practice, counsel appointed by the trial judge, can both have the state pick up all their bills without ever going to capital trial.

The trial court judge in the capital case appoints the defense counsel from a list of lawyers eligible to practice in capital cases. The lawyers in private practice can take hundreds of thousands of dollars in fees, subject to the approval of the trial judge. The public defenders benefit because their office is spared the expense of preparing the case for trial. No one really wants a full capital trial, except perhaps private counsel who can continue to bill large fees for all the expenses of going to capital trial and build a reputation for the next case. The testimony at the hearing was that some judges from some counties approved everything and others approved almost no special expense. Why should any attorney risk contradicting a judge who controls the purse strings and might not appoint him next time? And both lawyers can and do contribute to the judge's campaign funds.

For the judges the incentives are also in the direction of approving all submitted expenses: what judge would want to be overturned on the grounds that his ruling was a constitutional violation of due process because he was saving money? Plus the judge has the publicity of a capital case, and that is useful at election time. So the bureaucratic momentum is for a sham capital case.

Florence Kelley in the *Third Annual Report of the Factory Inspectors* includes the entire *Ritchie* opinion, as well as reprinting again the statute and some proposed legislation regarding expanding protection of child workers. The briefs for the case were included in the *Second Annual Report.*

Florence Kelley in the *Third Annual Report*, submitted December 31, 1895, comments:

The new feature introduced into the body of American legal precedent by this decision is the Court's assumption that it is not exclusively a matter of the constitution of Illinois. . . . The Court, however, makes the fourteenth amendment to the Constitution of the United States the basis of its decision. If this position were sound, all efforts for legislative restriction of the working day would be wasted, and there is no prospect of any immediate change in the Constitution of the United States. [The report goes on to note that the ten-hour laws in other states have been upheld.]

It remained for the Supreme Court of Illinois to discover that the amendment to the Constitution of the United States passed to guarantee the negro from oppression, has become an insuperable obstacle to the protection of women and children. Nor is it reasonable to suppose that this unique interpretation of the Fourteenth Amendment will be permanently maintained, even in Illinois. . . .

When the observation of a few more years has convinced the medical profession, the philanthropists, and the educators, as experience has already convinced the factory employés themselves, that it is a life and death matter to the young people who form so large a proportion of their number, to have a working day of reasonable length guaranteed by law, it will be found possible to rescue the Fourteenth Amendment to the Constitution of the United States from the perverted application upon which this decision rests. We may hope that Ritchie v. The People will then be added to the revered decisions in which the Supreme Court of Illinois is so rich.

The *Ritchie* opinion held that the hours provision in Section 5 of the statute, as applied to adult women, was unconstitutional. The holding has never been reversed by the Supreme Court of Illinois, although it is no longer considered precedential. Nor has the opinion in the Haymarket case ever been reversed. Neither is considered good law or followed.

May 8, 2011: Beautiful, now raining, and I have worn my leather jacket. My mischievous grandson has put some apps on my phone, and I don't know what they are or how to get rid of them.

The men on the Supreme Court of Illinois who were considering the constitutional arguments in *Ritchie v. People* when Florence Kelley was renting a room at the Leland Hotel in Springfield and writing her *Third Annual Report*, were closer to the generation of William Darrah Kelley than they were to the women in their thirties who lived at Hull-House. Like William Darrah Kelley, these men had direct personal experience with the devastation of the Civil War and its aftermath. Either they had served in the military themselves, or had a family member who did. They knew firsthand the economic and civil catastrophes of that war.

December 11, 2011: Blue skies and clear. They say the mild temperatures are global warming, but that fact is disputed, subject to much argument. Another exoneration, another death sentence uncovered which was imposed upon a man who did not commit the murder. Il-

linois is now the national example of what dedicated pro bono lawyers and students can accomplish with skill and good luck, and how bad lawyers, irresponsible prosecutors and defense attorneys, and corrupt police put innocent people in jail. Illinois, after decades of being the example of how you could hit your head on the wall forever and nothing would change, is now a place where the exonerations are rolling in and challenging public complacency. It has taken years, and much more than circumstance, although the role of fortune is important. No one, not even their attorneys, believed so many could be exonerated in one state in such a short time.

The repercussions of the collective national trauma, its long remaining imprint, for this and overlapping generations of the Civil War, is perhaps matched in recent history only by the social and civic devastation which the First World War was for the British, French, and Germans: generations of men gone; vast swaths of property destroyed and rendered toxic; buildings, factories, industry laid waste; hundreds of thousands of women and children and civilians senselessly killed, maimed, or uprooted; families destroyed by the loss of loved ones; entire cities leveled; the countryside a wasteland. The survivors, people who had formerly lived a reasonable civil life in their country, in their city and countryside, where expectations were generally met, were thrown into entirely new, often desperate circumstances, to find their way, or not.

Those who escaped death never forgot this destruction and the halting, slow rebuilding. The threat of a return to civil anarchy or unrest, if by strikers and bomb throwers, would have resonated differently and seemed imminent to these jurists. The members of this 1895 court had seen the country come unstuck once. Perhaps two or three generations must pass before the collective memory of the horror of war, of the madness of no government or an irrational government, is forgotten, and people are willing to take up the weapons of war again, or listen to the clarion call for change, a call for destruction of the status quo.

December 20, 2008: One more Christmas in this house. We look for a skating rink and find an indoor one. In Princeton, only a few times and always unexpectedly, usually in January or February, the conditions on the lake would be unpredictably perfect for skating, safe, the lake smooth, frozen across with dark ice. On a rare occasion it was possible to skate all the way to the next town, looking down through the black ice along the lake's edge at branches, translucent pale leaves or whole trees black beneath the surface.

The entire town would come out to the lake: the butcher, the milkman, the car mechanic, the tree trimmer, the exterminator, the gas station owner, the clerk at the cheese department of the grocery store, and if you had children who had gone through the school system, you saw families you hadn't seen since kindergarten. Mothers propped children up between their legs, overbundled, crying children in merry hats, babies being rolled across the ice in strollers or prams, many a bawling toddler sitting splat on the ice in bright pants, wearing a nubby hat with a red tassel, a pink scarf, its complement gloves dangling on a string. And so the community could see itself, as if in an old-fashioned painting, with everyone doing something their ancestors had done. If you could skate, you did. If you couldn't, you watched. Smiling, everyone smiling, glad to be outside on the ice in the winter.

Jacob W. Wilkin took an active part in the siege at Vicksburg, serving on special duty at General Grant's headquarters. The siege of Vicksburg was a brutal encounter with the reality of war. In addition to Vicksburg, the later Justice Wilkin was in all of the pitched battles of the Red River campaign and at the battle of Sabine Cross Roads where the general in charge of the troops was wounded and the adjutant general was killed.

Jacob Wilkin also was in the Mobile campaign and at the surrender of Mobile, Alabama. Not only were Civil War soldiers and their commanders often surrounded by chaos, confusion, and violence, but they also witnessed the unremitting wholescale destruction of property and lives, often without explanation or justification. The war was a continuous assault upon a man's sensibilities and rationality. Even the victors wrote of witnessing senseless carnage. Peace, even peace which was not on your terms or of your making, was a deliverance from fighting.

December 20, 2008: How wonderful the skating on the lake was. Surprisingly upright and adept older couples, arm in arm, in long coats, even the occasional fur muff, swooping by at a clip. The teenagers turning the outing, every outing, every occasion, into a contest, a game. Laughing as they fall down, they chase one another, pull at each other, or cling together. Some startlingly swift skaters—one spindly scientist who hadn't been seen in the academic halls for years, flicking over the ice in racing skates. He is bent perpendicular in the Canadian style on the extra long, thin speed skates, hands clasped behind his back in the racing posture, dark blue scarf flying behind, face down to the ice catching no one's eye, a blur from the past, skating on remembered strength.

My own Canadian grandmother, whom I cannot envision, my father's mother, was said to have been an expert skater, and her suitor, my grandfather, who seemed as an old man to have no grace, had once been a wonderful speed skater, and they had danced on the ice during their courtship on the frozen ponds and lakes of Ontario.

Jacob Wilkin came to the Supreme Court after Benjamin Magruder's opinion upholding the death sentences in the anarchist cases and after the Haymarket executions themselves. When his wife predeceased him in 1883 with no children, he remarried after a few years to a worthy "lady of Marshall" and was survived by their three or four children—the uncertainty as to the number of children belongs to the writer of his Crawford County obituary. He was survived more certainly by his two brothers, one a minister, the other the clerk of the Circuit Court. The writer of the obituary said the judge was recognized all over the state as a just and upright man, a Christian gentleman, honored and beloved by all with whom he came in contact.

July 30, 2012: A beautiful day, but humid. Summer, and a nice part of summer. There will be outdoor music. Always the busyness, the busyness to go here, to go there, so that at the end of the day you are tired enough to sleep. At least I have this to come back to. If it is not what you do, or what you think, or what you feel, then how does what you write matter, or give comfort?

For a number of summers while Florence Kelley lived at Hull-House, Nicholas went enthusiastically to Sakonnet, Rhode Island, to stay with the Lloyds. When Jessie Bross Lloyd suggested that Margaret join him there, Florence Kelley described to Nicholas the regimen for girls at Sakonnet:

Beloved son, Burn this! . . .

As I understand the standard of Demeanor for Damsels at Sakonnet requires . . . :

Perfect Punctuality at meals;

Exquisite Order of Room at all Hours;

Imperturbable affability towards Elders, Domestics, Bores together with Distinguished Reserve towards persons of the male Sex.

Devotion towards an Elder Brother;

Daily Enthusiastic Dishwashing and Bedmaking. . . .

Justice Jesse J. Phillips was a year older than Justice Magruder, born in 1837 in Montgomery County, Illinois, and like Justice Wilkin he served with the Union army in the Civil War. He was wounded in the battle of Shiloh. By the end of the war he had risen to the rank of brigadier general.

Justice Phillips was first elected judge of the Fifth District in 1879, joining the Supreme Court of Illinois in 1893, where he remained until his death from pneumonia in 1901. He was only a couple of years on the court when the constitutional challenge to the Factory and Workshop Inspection Law was heard.

Striking in appearance with long, shoulder-length hair and an erect and commanding presence, Jesse Phillips was said to attract attention in any gathering. On the Supreme

Court he succeeded Justice Scholfield, in whose chambers Justice Wilkin and many others read law.

> September 20, 2005, Chicago Tribune: "Ryan Confident as Trial Begins."
>
> A relaxed and smiling George Ryan came to federal court Monday and listened intently as his legal team and federal prosecutors began the job of finding a jury to hear the evidence in the former governor's racketeering trial.
>
> "Good morning, good morning," Ryan said, arriving in the courtroom and greeting reporters in a hearty voice. "You had to get up early this morning—all of you."

Justice Phillips was called an Illinois War Democrat, meaning that when the secession of the Southern states took place, support for Lincoln and for the Union was stronger than party loyalty to the Democrats. A complicated set of political accommodations was contrived for the War Democrats. The border states, including Illinois, were torn by the conflict in "bleeding Kansas" after 1854, when both sides of what was to become the Civil War, or the war between the states, sought to settle disputes over the reach of slave holding by acts of Congress. In 1861 Caroline Bonsall Kelley was shipping clothes to "bleeding Kansas" for the relief effort after the war. People do what they can, when they can.

October 1, 2007: The Supreme Court opens today, being constituted as a body newly dominated by a conservative majority. The most recent appointments sandbagged their way through the mildest of Senate questioning. Today a grey day, cool. A day when winter simply lies in wait. Someone has been stealing our mail again. Envelopes are strewn all over the front porch. A large check has gone missing. The mail will be temporarily diverted.

The former Whig Party collapsed in the ongoing dispute over the status of slavery in the border states, leaving northern Democrats to form the Republican Party, unalterably opposed to slavery, which did well in the elections of 1856. This was the bitter political fight which in Philadelphia sent the abolitionist, anti-national bank William Darrah Kelley fleeing to Boston. The Democrats then became the dominant party of Southern secessionists.

Justice Phillips wrote an opinion for the Supreme Court of Illinois said to take "advanced grounds against the legitimacy of monopolies." This apparently led to him being considered briefly as a running mate for William Jennings Bryan on the presidential ticket in 1896. His obituaries describe him as an able and incorruptible judge, this apparently a noteworthy attribute.

Meanwhile, Margaret and John continued to be at the Hillside School as their mother carried out her duties.

Ferry Hall Seminary (Lake Forrest, Il.) Dec. 17

Dear Grandma . . . I am the same Basket-Ball fiend that I was the winter I was in New York and have been playing ever since I came here and yesterday we played the only match game we are allowed to play this year so the excitement here was great. We had the good fortune to win and no one has calmed down to her normal state yet. We have had the most remarkable Indian summer which lasted until just about a week ago and there have been only three or four wintry days. There was quite a heavy snowfall last week and there are still many traces of it about.

When Abraham Lincoln became president in 1860, he was elected without a single Southern electoral vote. The Supreme Court of the United States in 1857 had declared that citizens, that is, white men who met the property and other qualifications of citizenship and could vote, possessed unlimited rights to hold slaves as property throughout the Union, as well as, of course, throughout the South before the Civil War, in the territories and border states. It was a question of liberty, due process, and property, after all, and a man—that is, an upright white male citizen—could not be deprived of what he paid good money for, his property, even if that property was a human being, his slave, or the hours of work of his employee. Liberty and property together were the fundamental rights guaranteed by the Constitution.

September 29, 2005, Chicago Tribune: "Battle Lines Are Drawn; Opening Statements at Historic Trial Paint Contrasting Images of Governor."

The historic trial of former Gov. George Ryan opened Wednesday with the once gruff and commanding leader of the state cast by prosecutors as a crooked pol greasing the palms of a "chosen few" and by the defense as a simple family man who never took a corrupt nickel.

Ryan strode into court with the same confidence he exhibited as governor, greeting the packed gallery of spectators with warm hellos before taking his seat at the defense table.

The prosecutor portrayed Ryan as a politician who betrayed the public trust, doling out a slew of state contracts and leases to friends who rewarded Ryan and his family with gifts, vacations and money.

Dan Webb, Ryan's chief lawyer, pounded away at the perceived Achilles' heel of the government's case, telling jurors that "not a single, solitary witness" will testify that Ryan ever pocketed a corrupt dollar while in office.

The trial—the first of a former governor in Illinois in three decades—opened in a courtroom packed with spectators and reporters, many of whom waited more than 1-1/2 hours to get a seat.

When it came to the constitutionality of the factory inspection statute, the abolitionists' arguments about the sanctity of liberty and property were turned into an argument about the sanctity of the freedom to contract. This argument, artfully put forward by Levy Mayer on behalf of the Illinois Manufacturers' Association, said that women, who did not have the right to vote or act independently in many areas, and indeed were restricted by law with regard to the ownership of property and its disposition, could not be deprived of the right to independently contract for the hours and conditions of their labor, irrespective of the conditions of contract. Thus, the legislature could not impose limits or regulate with regard to the number of hours that women could work in the sweatshops.

The Supreme Court of Illinois in 1895 in *Ritchie* summarized this position:

The privilege of contracting is both a liberty and property right. Liberty includes the right to acquire property, and that means and includes the right to make and enforce contracts. The right to use, buy and sell property and contract in respect thereto is protected by the constitution. Labor is property, and the laborer has the same right to sell his labor, and to contract with reference thereto, as has any other property owner. In this country the legislature has no power to prevent persons who are sui juris from making their own contracts, nor can it interfere with the freedom of contract between the workman and the employer. The right to labor or employ labor, and make contracts in respect thereto upon such terms as may be agreed upon between the parties, is included in the constitutional guaranty above quoted. The protection of property is one of the objects for which free governments are instituted among men.

Ironically, because the opinion was based upon federal constitutional law, it opened the door for the principles upheld by the Supreme Court of Illinois opinion in *Ritchie* to be reconsidered in the Supreme Court of the United States's later case regarding the constitutionality of a ten-hour provision applicable to laundry women in Oregon. In 1895 the trend was in the direction of state courts invalidating state regulatory legislation, although some state supreme courts, as was pointed out in the defendant brief, upheld similar or even more far-reaching state regulatory provisions, on grounds of state constitutional law.

September 1, 2009: A bright day, a day in which winter is put off. Nightmares. A drowning, then a submarine. Tears. But then forgotten, what was it about, the dream. Anxious, afraid, for no waking or rational reason. The weather today: a glorious refutation of fear, no cloud in the sky, the weather mocking the dream. A comfort to wake up to our sun, after dreams in the dark. The outside world reassuring by just seeming to be there, even if the sky is an illusion, mysterious. I miss the small roses, pink smiles along the walkway. I had never loved flowers before, or spent time just being with them. The construction of the children's hospital outside our bedroom window continues. A monument to civic aspirations to protect children, an enterprise the community can support.

Young men, such as Justices Wilkin and Phillips, answered President Lincoln's initial 1861 call for 75,000 new troops for the Union army. Carroll Wright and other eager young soldiers worried that they would not see battle, and the war would be over before they could shoot their rifles. As ever, the promise, the expectation, was that the war would end quickly, with a successful rapid march to the capital of the enemy (here, Richmond, Virginia), then a quick surrender, and with little bloodshed, death, harm, or direct military action. Later in the bloodiest, most desperate days of the war, Lincoln called for 500,000 more troops on July 18, 1864. For the next several generations of Americans, the Civil War was the defining, watershed event, the one for which everything else would be before or after, and the event by which every citizen was judged.

September 9, 2009: The archives of the New York Public Library. A rainy day. Always New York is colder than Chicago in spirit, the rain more pelting, the people on the street—so many of them speaking languages which are not English. The manuscript reading room is now another familiar place, its serious silence, the whispering librarians, the taking of my purse and the tiny stub of a pencil and one piece of paper issued. A temple to reading and writing.

Florence Kelley's archives have recently been separated from those of her son, Nicholas Kelley, for many years an attorney with the Chrysler Corporation.

I am grateful to the archivists who create the finding aid, the people who put all those letters and documents into the pale numbered folders with their penciled identities. Once again I regret the widespread adoption of the typewriter. The handwritten letters from Caroline to her husband and daughter, from the 1880s, the letters of Sarah Pugh in the 1860s, and Florence Kelley's own handwritten correspondence with her father, her mother, her children, and their handwritten replies express vastly more than the typed letters, no matter the words.

Levy Mayer's family moved to Chicago at the beginning of the plans for secession when it became clear the fabric of civil society in the South was rapidly disintegrating. There were no opportunities for an energetic recent immigrant in a state imposing martial law. Again, the impetus for migration was varied and multiple.

June 17, 2011: At the New York Public Library Archives. The metal railing, the walkway, the catwalk, which encircles the room and allows access to the higher shelves. The reverent quiet, as in a hospital. Only whispers allowed. Many sit with earphones plugged into computers. The walls decorated, ornate, sedate. The desks, solid, workmanlike, golden, sturdy oak. The rustle of tiny movements. Pens not allowed. Your own pencils not allowed, a holdover. A church in which to worship the haphazard surviving remnants of the past. I, however, am still writing my manuscript by hand.

The Civil War battles were bloody, brutal and long, and both military and civilian suffering and casualties were unending. More people died in the Civil War than in all subsequent wars of the United States combined. The totals have recently been revised to over 750,000. People's remembrances of the Civil War were of blood and severed limbs and moaning on the battlefield, the gases of death, the sacking of cities, and devastation of the countryside, images, smells, and scenes which were torpid, vivid, and unforgettable. After the war stopped, the losses, deaths, and permanent injuries didn't go away but were calculated, the tally added in of burned or ruined buildings, the crippled and permanently invalided men and women, the missing sons and daughters and the constant pain of absence and loss of a family member, the unhealed wounds.

The South was too broken even to count; its losses are all estimates. Illinois and Chicago were relatively unscathed because no invasions or battles took place in the state. After the fire in 1871 the city was immediately focused on its rebuilding, even though less than half of the city was destroyed. The fire became a symbol and an excuse for building, for expansion, to make everything new, higher, more shining. Help and cash poured in from around the world. For those who had been surrounded by the devastation of the Civil War, the rebuilding after the fire was a relief from the relentless grief of the war's aftermath, an intoxication with hope.

January 2006: The winter settling in, again. The icy roads, the dark, cold house. It seems as if we have been here forever. While this can't continue forever, the pretense is always that the end is not yet.

Our universities, like our legal system, require loving attention. It is a miracle they survive at all. Yet there is much impetus, and inertia, to preserve them. So many depend upon the legal system and the universities, not just for education, not just for a matter to be settled, but for their support, for jobs, to inculcate values, for order and stability, for the symbol of continuity. Yet so much time and money in both institutions is wasted, or devoted to the ancillary, to what is not important.

The battle of Antietam stopped Lee's invasion of the capital in Washington at the cost of twelve thousand Union casualties, with a corresponding toll of nine thousand Confederate casualties. Casualties reported in Civil War battles meant deaths. In the Civil War the wounded additionally died, often slowly and painfully, or languished in primitive battlefield hospitals until they were killed by disease or infection. The mules and stretcher bearers, when they could get to the wretched wounded hours or days after the battle, dragged away those who hadn't bled to death, and perhaps did them no favor.

One of Lincoln's stymied generals sacrificed 12,500 men in a failed offensive at Fredericksburg, Virginia. It was said that the heartless General Grant, who ordered every plant and animal killed or burned as he marched through the South, could not himself tolerate the eating of meat unless it was very well-cooked, while the ebullient Sherman—himself an admirable prose stylist—embraced the cruelty of war, saying it could not be otherwise.

In the early days of the war, both sides foolishly lived in the expectation of an early, quick victory. In the Union, resistance to the war and the draft rose as injuries and deaths mounted. Meanwhile, some Confederate governors were ignoring their new central leaders. Inflation in the South spiraled and the newly minted Confederate currency was worth less every day. Easy to start a war, order the munitions, recruit or draft the soldiers, spend the public money, send the young men eager to carry guns off to fight. Putting the invaded land back together is more complicated. Easy to point a rifle and shoot, hard to reestablish a civil society.

The economic devastation was complete in the South, but substantial deprivation occurred in the North and in the border states. Some buccaneers made money selling arms, food, or horses, but most farmers, professionals, lawyers, and business people became poorer as civil society ground to a halt. Many soldiers left farms or small towns, and in their absence no one was there to take care of the barn, the store, the land, the animals, or the women and children. Crops were not planted or harvested, or were confiscated for the army. Working farm animals were taken away or killed, sometimes eaten by soldiers. In the South the entire agriculture and many cities were destroyed, and the people who might have rebuilt them dead, gone as soldiers, or escaped as slaves. So the country stumbled forward with its bitter after-politics, with nothing solved, because it had no choice.

November 3, 2004, Chicago Tribune: "Obama Sails to Senate Win; Obama Scores a Record Landslide."

Democrat Barack Obama, a state legislator whose compelling personal story and stirring message of opportunity and inclusion
propelled him to national prominence, swept to a historic and
decisive victory Tuesday in Illinois' U.S. Senate race.

In defeating Republican Alan Keyes by the largest margin ever in
a Senate contest here, the 43-year-old Obama becomes the only
African-American elected this year to the world's most powerful
legislative body and only the third since Reconstruction.

Conservative War Democrats in Lincoln's Cabinet criticized Lincoln's tyranny in pursuing the war. His Cabinet contained some who had been Confederate supporters. It was
Lincoln's genius as a politician that not only could he listen to dissent and criticism, but
he found a way to win over his most passionate, principled adversaries.

In Illinois, debate over the election of Lincoln and what was seen as Lincoln's war was
vigorous and ongoing throughout the Civil War and after. Lincoln countermanded his
military commanders who in 1861 issued field orders emancipating slaves. Instead he
attempted to allow border state slaveholders to accept compensation for runaway slaves.
He made an ill-fated attempt to colonize freed slaves on an island off of Haiti.

General Sherman ordered that freedmen be given land in freehold on the Outer
Banks of the Carolinas. The Emancipation Proclamation on September 22, 1862, freed
no slaves. What it did on its effective date of January 1, 1863, was allow the invading
Union army to be an army of liberation as it conquered Southern territory, opening the
Union army to Negro soldiers.

*June 17, 2011: At the New York Public Library Archives. The letters, I am concentrating on
the letters, to her, from her, from the children, to the children.*

As late as 1863 the military momentum continued to be with the Confederacy. Both
Britain and France signaled that they might recognize the Confederacy as an independent state. As General Lee moved north into Pennsylvania, the Union army engaged
them over three days at Gettysburg on July 2-4, 1863, in a battle which resulted in a total
of forty-three thousand deaths and finally a weak Union victory. At the war's end, April
9, 1865, the grand totals were 360,000 Union dead, 275,000 wounded, 258,000 Confederate dead, at least 100,000 Confederate wounded. These figures were not abstractions or
distant memories to the men passing judgment on the Illinois Factory and Workshop
Inspection Law. The law was seen as a bastion against violence and anarchy. Strikes and
marches and public demonstrations were threats to peace. Strikers were on the side of violence and chaos, for many of that generation.

June, 10 2007: Our government committee on the death penalty is meeting now on a regular basis, and at some point a report will issue. The trick is to have someone pay attention to the reports, to the revelations of an outrage. The trick is to have the reports persuade someone. Why assume good sense will prevail? The rivers and oceans of government reports are mostly forgotten.

The siege of Vicksburg, on the banks of the Mississippi River, where Justice Wilkin was a staff member on special assignment to General Grant, lasted six weeks and resulted in the collapse of the town and garrison on July 4, 1863. It was a turning point, opening the entire Mississippi valley to Union conquest because Vicksburg was strategically located on what was repeatedly referred to as an oxbow curve of the great river, its port vital to the supply of arms and food to the entire Confederacy. The fall of Vicksburg was the beginning of the end for the Confederacy.

And yet, people forget war and history tends to repeat itself. And there were always some places, such as Chicago, which were relatively unscarred and quickly recovered economically. This is how William Stead described the city in 1893:

I have studied autocracy in Russia and Theocracy in Rome, and I must say that nowhere, not even in Russia, in the first year of the reaction occasioned by the murder of the late Tzar, have I struck more abject submission to a more soulless despotism than that which prevails among the masses of the so-called free American citizens, when they are face to face with the omnipotent power of the corporations. "Wealth," said a workman bitterly to me the other day, "has subjugated everything. It has gagged the press; it has bought up the legislature; it has corrupted the judges. Even on the universities it is laying its golden finger. The churches are in its grasp. Go where you will, up and down this country. You will find our citizens paralyzed by a sense of their own impotence."

The siege of Vicksburg was not accomplished easily or quickly. After unsuccessful attempts by the hotheaded Union naval officer David Farragut to reduce the Confederate garrison, and another unsuccessful attempt to dig a bypass canal in the great Mississippi River, after both Grant and Sherman sustained significant losses at Holly Springs and Chickasaw Bayou—such bucolic names for places of carnage—after Grant was repulsed in two bloody assaults on Vicksburg's main defenses in May 1863, Grant managed to lay siege to the city and garrison. That meant nothing and no person came in or out of the besieged city: no food, no animals, no supplies, no soldiers, no civilians. And the carnage from constant bombardment by cannons was unremitting. The Union army camped outside the city and waited, the army of over seventy thousand hunkering down, rustling and settling itself like a vulture shifting from one leg to another, standing and watching, waiting for its prey to slowly die. Meanwhile those in the besieged Vicksburg retreated into caves and began to eat the rats.

November 3, 2004, Chicago Tribune: "Obama Sails to Senate Win; Obama Scores a Record Landslide."

. . . Obama beat a crowded field in the Democratic primary after the campaign of early frontrunner Blair Hull, a multimillionaire securities trader who spent heavily on his effort, unraveled amid revelations that Hull had once been accused of domestic violence by an ex-wife.

Then Jack Ryan, the GOP primary winner, dropped out of the race in July amid the release of embarrassing allegations in his previously sealed divorce file that he had tried to pressure his ex-wife into having sex in public at sex clubs.

After several false starts trying to find a replacement for Ryan, Republicans finally turned to Keyes, a fiery conservative from Maryland. He fanned controversy by charging that Obama was a socialist and proclaiming that Jesus wouldn't vote for the Democrat because of his position on abortion.

The people who survived the siege of Vicksburg told of round-the-clock assaults, starvation, and of eating insects, birds, worms, or any other plant or living thing they could find. Not until 1945 would the town celebrate the national holiday of the 4th of July because of its association with the surrender of the city. At the end of the siege Confederate General Pendleton surrendered himself, 2,166 Confederate officers, and 27,230 enlisted men and turned over 172 cannons and 60,000 rifles.

The surrender of Vicksburg marked Grant's ascension to overall command of the Union army, the cementing of his reputation for strategic brilliance, and ultimately to his two terms as president of the United States, in 1868 and 1872. His second term was characterized by economic depression and scandal. The history of the war was told in numbers, but remembered in lost lives, destruction of the civil order, starvation, and death, and it sowed fear and an existential distrust and hatred of the enemy in the hearts of those who survived. The war was not over when the peace treaty was signed.

November 7, 2007, Chicago Tribune: "Unbowed, Unrepentant; Convicted Ex-Governor Loses Bid to Stay Free During the Appeal, Continues to Maintain Innocence."

With his last hope for staying out of prison dashed, former Gov. George Ryan defiantly proclaimed Tuesday that he would go

to prison "with a clear conscience" and vowed to overturn his
sweeping corruption conviction.

The 73-year-old Republican has battled to remain free since his
conviction 18 months ago as his lawyers filed a series of so-far-
unsuccessful appeals.

But on Tuesday, U.S. Supreme Court Justice John Paul Stevens refused to extend Ryan's bail any longer, forcing him to report to
prison Wednesday to begin serving his 6 1/2 year sentence. Stevens offered no comment in his order.

"Tomorrow I embark in a new journey in my life," Ryan told reporters Tuesday evening outside his two-story brown brick house
in Kankakee. "I do so with a firm faith in God and my family. We
will continue in our fight."

Even distant historians describe the Union advance to Atlanta, and then deeper into
the South, as being obtained only at the price of brutal battles in the period just before
Atlanta fell and Lincoln was reelected in November 1864. Then after the war there was
the question of how to pay for it all, and how to rebuild the war-torn states and unite the
country.

Most of the federal revenue after the war was provided by high tariffs on imports, up
to 50 percent on some durable goods and industrial commodities such as steel. This was
how the government paid its debts. Once again the question of tariffs, exports, and imports was at the forefront of debates on national policy. The question was where to find
the money to pay for what the government had already spent on the war.

*October 1, 2006: The crows which used to roost in the tall oak tree by the dozens, fifty or
eighty at one time on an outstretched branch, have been felled by the crow disease. There are
none in the big oak tree now. Winter is in the air, tantalizing, brisk, admonitory, and opening the window is an act of rebellion. At the outside entrance to the house last night someone
came in, there is no lock on the door, and took some fruit that had been left in the hallway
pantry outside the back door; scattered orange peels were all over the back lawn.*

Justice Jesse J. Phillips saw action in several Civil War battles. His horse was shot out
from under him as he was leading a desperate Union charge. He was severely wounded
and never recovered the full ability to walk. His striking appearance, his erect, military
bearing, his black shoulder-length hair, army moustache, and "imperial"—a small beard
flowing beneath the lower lip—made him instantly recognizable in Springfield, a commanding figure as he made his distinctive, gimpy way about the capital. His war wounds

required him to walk with crutches, but he was always ready to forget his own suffering, the obituary writers said, to let down his judicial demeanor, to relax and enter heartily into the spirit of jollity and good fellowship. In other words, like many a military man, he drank. In a war there is often good reason to drink.

September 12, 2007: Good class today. Last night at dinner, a white-tablecloth restaurant, tears raised by the anxious discussion of money, the future, and too much wine. Choking, seated at a candlelit table by a window on the street as the rain came down. There are still men and women, and some children, some drunk or crazy, some ragged or toothless, begging on the streets of Chicago. Overheard in a city park from a young, strong man: "I can make $400 a day hustling, why should I put up with this?" Women sitting on the sidewalk with a baby on a blanket, it could be Africa or India. The cars glide by smoothly while the rain taps on the window, as if the cars were part of the veil of water and people weren't dying somewhere abroad under our name, or in the alleys of Chicago. If the draft were reinstated this war would not be tolerated.

General Grant himself was reported to be drunk on several public occasions during and after the war. And yet at least for some generals and some soldiers, there was the exhilaration of war, being drunk on the excitement of it, drunk on the killing, the clarity of it.

General Sherman wrote:

To be at the head of a strong column of troops, in the execution of some task that requires brain, is the highest pleasure of war—a grim one and terrible, but which leaves on the mind and memory the strongest mark; to detect the weak point in the enemy's lines; to break through with vehemence and thus lead to victory; or to discover some key-point and hold it with tenacity; or to do some other distinct act which is afterward recognized as the real cause of success. These all become matters that are never forgotten. . . . Every attempt to make war easy and safe will result in humiliation and disaster.

These are the words of the man who planned and carried out the destruction of all roads, houses, and animals on the march to Atlanta to make Georgia howl, and he did. Sherman was not pleased when at the end of the war it was proposed that Negroes be given the vote, saying that the problem was not to enlarge the franchise but to curtail it. Whereas General Grant hated politics and did not understand how to operate in the world of scheming, decisive, manipulative men: the result was political disaster during his presidency, especially in the second term.

At Appomattox, on a whim, without forethought, General Grant let the Confederate officers return home with their horses, side arms, and personal property. He loved horses and would not eat chicken or any other creature that walked on two legs, and only ate beef very well-cooked. The sight of a suffering animal greatly agitated him. Hundreds of thousands of horses died in the Civil War. Later he told a biographer that, unlike Sherman, he never went into battle willingly or with enthusiasm. He said he was always glad when it was over, and he never wanted to command another army. This from the general who is credited with winning the war for the Union. General Sherman, whose mental stability was at times in question, would have gone back into battle the next day, every day.

September 2, 2008: Once again, the academic year begins with some fanfare. How easy our life is since it is structured by the school year, by the patterns of admission, graduation, examinations, making the roles and duties clear. It is like being in any system, an army in peacetime, a court, a juvenile home, a boarding school. Someone knows what to do and when it must be done. The civil legal system in peacetime is propped up by a similar bureaucratic order, the routines of filing, of trials, judgments. And how does a legal system survive a war?

Justice Jesse Phillips was described as an almost extinct kind of man, knight-like in his fidelity to personal honor. To women he was the essence of old-fashioned gallantry, and although his temper was quick and hot, his judicial demeanor was calm and his rulings said to be fair. None of the obituaries mention a wife, or children, or family members who lived with him or cared for him.

A solemn news report on March 3, 1900, reported his attending doctors saying he had no hope for recovering from pneumonia. They did not expect him to live more than two or three days. He died eleven months later, February 2, 1901, remaining on the state high court until his death at 63.

These seven justices of the Supreme Court of Illinois were asked to issue an opinion on the federal constitutionality of the state Factory Inspection Law. And they did:

The right to acquire, possess and protect property includes the right to make reasonable contracts. And when an owner is deprived of one of the attributes of property, like the right to make contracts, he is deprived of his property within the meaning of the constitution. The fundamental rights of Englishmen, brought to this country by its original settlers and wrested from time to time in the progress of history from the sovereigns of the English nation, have been reduced by Blackstone to three principal or primary articles: "the right of personal security, the right of personal liberty, and the right of private property." The right to contract is the only way by which a person can rightfully acquire property by his own labor. "Of all the 'rights of persons' it is the most essential to human happiness."

Ritchie v. People, 1895, citations omitted

October 18, 2007: A stormy, blustery day, with heavy grey clouds blowing about. We march ahead, giving way here and there, not thinking much.

Justice Joseph M. Bailey, fifteen years younger than Justices Phillips and Wilkin, was of a different generation, but shared some commonalities with other members of the court. He, too, died while still sitting on the court, at age 62.

Justice Bailey grew up on his father's farm in New York, graduated from the University of Rochester, read law in the chambers of a Rochester lawyer—Rochester at that time being a thriving commercial city on the Erie Canal—and was admitted to the Bar at the early age of 22, before moving to Freeport, Illinois.

The general rule then was that being admitted to the Bar in one state was sufficient to practice in another. Attorneys from other states could be admitted in Illinois, it was reported on November 10, 1897, "if it appears to the Board of Examiners of this state that the requirements for admission were equal to those of Illinois." By 1897 rules for admission had been issued by the Supreme Court of Illinois and a state Board of Law Examiners was in place. Application for admission was presented in open court. The state Board of Law Examiners, consisting of five members of the Bar in good standing for five years, conducted and supervised the examinations and reported on the qualifications of candidates. Each examiner was appointed for three years.

The examinations, both written and oral, were to be conducted as uniformly as possible across the state. The subjects were the ordinary legal subjects, the common law of property, contracts, torts, and crime, the principles of the constitution of this state and the United States. A fee of $10 was required, and the applicant was required to be a resident of the state and a citizen of the United States, or having declared his intention of becoming a citizen, and to be of good moral character. For Florence Kelley her former political associations might have caused a problem, but apparently didn't. There were a number of other members of the Bar of Illinois who were prominent unapologetic socialists.

Each applicant had to present evidence of a preliminary general education, graduation from high school, and three years of law study in an established law school, or having been under tuition of one or more licensed lawyers.

The new rules, it was said, would prevent many ignorant and worthless persons from becoming lawyers. "A great amount of litigation is caused by the carelessness and ignorance of lawyers and by suits stirred up by disreputable lawyers," the attorney Julius Rosenthal reported in 1897, "and judges are not receiving the proper and full assistance from members of the bar."

January 5, 2009: I remain dumbfounded by the election. The excitement and disbelief are dampened by the economic crisis. Still, a feeling of hope is pervasive. I did not think it would ever happen. This is the only home we have now, and we must soon leave.

Rarely but occasionally the Illinois legislature would hold impeachment trials: a trial for the impeachment of Justice Theophilus Smith, who had studied in the law offices of Aaron Burr, was held before the Illinois legislature in 1831-32. The Supreme Court of Illinois was much embroiled in the contentious politics of the 1850s and 1860s, and it was not until the 1870s constitutional convention that some of the political battles were settled for a time. It remains almost impossible to remove an incompetent or corrupt judge, even when the Bar finds the judge incompetent or with a conflicting interest.

Justice Bailey was elected to the Illinois House of Representatives, then elected to the Circuit Court for 1877-80, when he was elected to the Supreme Court from his district. He served in the court until his death in 1895. He did not live long after *Ritchie* was decided. He had been chief justice during the 1892-93 term.

In *Ritchie* the court ruled:

It has been held that a woman is both a "citizen" and a "person" within the meaning of this section. The privileges and immunities here referred to are, in general, "protection by the government, with the right to acquire and possess property of every kind, and to pursue and obtain happiness and safety, subject, nevertheless, to such restraints as the government may prescribe for the general good of the whole." As a citizen, a woman has the right to acquire and possess property of every kind. As a "person," she has the right to claim the benefit of the constitutional provision that she shall not be deprived of life, liberty or property without due process of law. Involved in these rights thus guaranteed to her is the right to make and enforce contracts. The law accords to her, as to every other citizen, the natural right to gain a livelihood by intelligence, honesty and industry in the arts, the sciences, the professions or other vocations. Before the law, her right to a choice of vocations cannot be said to be denied or abridged on account of sex.

Justice Joseph Bailey was also a presidential elector and a trustee of the University of Chicago. In 1850 he married a woman from New York. They had five children: two who died in infancy; a daughter, Anna; a son, Charles, described as a successful lawyer in Sioux Falls, South Dakota; and Joseph Jr. Justice Bailey's wife, Anna, was said to be prominent in charitable and religious work in Freeport and the founder of the first kindergarten there.

The court continues:

The tendency of legislation in this State has been to recognize the rights of woman in the particulars here specified. The Act of 1867, as above quoted, by the use of the words, "he or she," plainly declares that no woman shall be prevented by anything therein contained from working as many hours overtime or extra hours as she may agree; and thereby recognizes her right to contract for more than eight hours of work in one day.

An Act approved March 22, 1872, entitled "An Act to secure freedom in the selection of an occupation," etc., provides that "no person shall be precluded or debarred from any occupation, profession or employment (except military) on account of sex." (1 Starr & Cur. Ann. Stat. page 1056). [113] The Married Woman's Act of 1874 authorizes a married woman to sue and be sued without joining her husband, and provides that contracts may be made and liabilities incurred by her and enforced against her to the same extent and in the same manner as if she were unmarried, and that she may receive, use and possess her own earnings, and sue for the same in her own name, free from the interference of her husband, or his creditors. (Rev. Stat. Ill. chap. 68, secs. 1, 6 and 7.)

A Republican and a Baptist, Justice Bailey was a thirty-third-degree Mason who made the Masonic pilgrimage of Europe with the Apollo Commandery—a ceremonial journey undertaken by Masons who reached the highest level in the order. He received honorary doctorates from the University of Chicago and from his alma mater, the University of Rochester.

January 2009: The family has left; the house is creaking, stiff, cold. The final round of academic ceremonies. It has all gone quickly, too quickly. The city is so itself, so full of itself, so proud, so silly in its pride, like a teenager. Risible, irresistible, a teenager astonished at the stubble poking out on its upper lip.

A fellow Supreme Court justice who served with Justice Bailey for six years described him as a model judge, combining the widest learning with unwearied industry and the loftiest integrity, noted for his powers of reach and keen analysis. After the day's business when others were devoting themselves to domestic pleasures, the light would be seen on in Justice Bailey's room and the rapid click of his typewriting machine heard. Justice Bailey was always beforehand in his work. When the court met he would have read exactly as many opinions as there had been cases referred to him, being not only painstakingly thorough but prompt as well. In judicial conference, he was said to be persistent and aggressive, but not opinionated, always ready to yield to legal authority.

March 7, 2011: The Honorable Justice Sonia Sotomayor of the Supreme Court of the United States is visiting our School of Law today. The women of Hull-House, and especially Florence Kelley, would have been proud to welcome to our law school the first Hispanic woman, and the third woman, to be appointed to the Supreme Court of the United States. The men and women in the reception area, who are mostly Hispanic, have dressed up in clothes with a Spanish style in honor of her presence. She spoke about her family and the confirmation, in a way no man would have spoken about himself.

One justice commented that whatever acerbity might exist on the court—Justice Magruder could jump on Justice Bailey and roast him unmercifully—Justice Bailey never let it ruffle him more than a fly might bother him by landing on his shoulder. He was a temperate man, and while the court was not composed of intemperate men, sometimes whiskey would be passed around, and while others took a drink he did not join them or rebuke those who did.

> *Attention is also called to the above mentioned Act of March 22, 1872, which makes an exception of military service, and provides that nothing in the Act shall be construed as requiring any female to work on streets, or roads, or serve on juries. But, without stopping to comment upon measures of this character, it is sufficient to say that what is said in reference to them has no application to the Act of 1893. That Act is not based upon the theory, that the manufacture of clothing, wearing apparel and other articles is an improper occupation for women to be engaged in. It does not inhibit their employment in factories or workshops. On the contrary, it recognizes such places as proper for them to work in by permitting their labor therein during eight hours of each day. The question here is not whether a particular employment is a proper one for the use of female labor, but the question is whether, in an employment which is conceded to be lawful in itself and suitable for woman to engage in, she shall be deprived of the right to determine for herself how many hours she can and may work during each day. There is no reasonable ground—at least none which has been made manifest to us in the arguments of counsel—for fixing upon eight hours in one day as the limit within which woman can work without injury to her physique, and beyond which, if she work, injury will necessarily follow.*
>
> Ritchie v. People (internal citations omitted)

April 27, 2013: A real spring day, with sunshine and blue sky, and everyone on the street smiling. In Beijing now the smog is so thick that it is a health hazard for children.

With Judge George Moran, who compiled and published the 1903 *Dictionary of Chicago*, Justice Bailey started the Chicago College of Law and devoted a portion of his time to teaching there. These labors never interfered with his judicial duties. He was driven to that work, the work of teaching, it was said, by the feeling of necessity to make more provision for his family. His teaching was described by a colleague as not debilitating, but rather a recreation.

```
February 3, 2009, Chicago Tribune: "Blagojevich Lightly Roasted
by Letterman: Former Governor Sticks to Talking Points During
'Late Night' Appearance."
```

From the time he walked through the curtain on "The Late Show with David Letterman" Tuesday, ex-Gov. Rod Blagojevich was a walking punch line, drawing big laughs when he maintained he'll be vindicated and fidgeting under a folksy-yet-savvy grilling from the host.

"I've been wanting to be on your show in the worst way for the longest time," Blagojevich said.

"Well, you're on in the worst way, believe me," said a well-prepared Letterman, who went on to ask the famously coiffed politician if he uses "shampoo and conditioner."

Justice Bailey's unnamed, unidentified illness was known for some time before his death, but not known to be extreme. A large man, weighing some 250 pounds, late in his life he learned to ride a bicycle to reduce his flesh, riding fifteen miles a day. His judicial colleagues warned that he was overdoing it, but he was rather boastful of the good it had done for him. He thought his health had been permanently injured by being in a courtroom which had been kept too warm.

It is not the nature of the things done, but the sex of the persons doing them, which is made the basis of the claim that the Act is a measure for the promotion of the public health. It is sought to sustain the Act as an exercise of the police power upon the alleged ground, that it is designed to protect woman on account of her sex and physique. It will not be denied, that woman is entitled to the same rights, under the constitution, to make contracts with reference to her labor as are secured thereby to men. The first section of the fourteenth amendment to the constitution of the United States provides: "No State shall make or enforce any law which shall abridge the privileges or immunities of citizens of the United States, nor shall any State deprive any person of life, liberty or property without due process of law, nor deny to any person within its jurisdiction the equal protection of the law."

Ritchie v. People (continued)

When he was on the three-man appellate court, the two other judges, one of whom suffered from rheumatism, kept the room "hot enough to fry eggs," Justice Bailey said. And he, as the youngest, the kid, had to stand it. He had an attack every year of a skin disorder as a result, and the excessive heat caused insomnia, but then Judge Bailey would continue to sit after court adjourned reading French, of which he was uncommonly fond. His health was very seriously impaired three years before his death by the untimely death at age 34 of one of his sons, a banker and a promising young man.

May 8, 2009: Spring has finally come. Everything is in bloom, the daffodils, the tulips, everywhere but in our yard; the deer and squirrels have eaten them all. A conspiracy among the rabbits and deer so that I would not miss the flowers so much. The wet, black tree branches now dipped in green fuzz. The miracle of earth's awakening again.

Justice David J. Baker was also of the generation reaching manhood before the Civil War, having been born in 1834, living past his Supreme Court tenure, from 1888-97, to drop dead in his law office in 1899 after returning from lunch and while talking with his son and law partner. His wife entered the law office a few moments later, swooned from the shock and fell to the floor.

November 7, 2007, Chicago Tribune: "Ex-Gov. Ryan Arrives at Prison."

Former Gov. George Ryan slipped through a back gate at a rural federal prison Wednesday, avoiding any fanfare as he began serving a 6 1/2-year corruption sentence.

The 73-year-old Republican entered the correctional center about noon, said Bureau of Prisons spokeswoman Felicia Ponce, and managed to avoid a throng of media awaiting his arrival at the main entrance.

Justice Baker was an Illinois man, born in Kaskaskia, Randolph County, and receiving a BA from Shurtleff College in Upper Alton. He came up through politics, like so many others, serving as mayor of Cairo, then being elected as circuit judge for the Nineteenth District from 1869-73, then being elected for the Twenty-Sixth Judicial Circuit, and serving there until 1878, each judicial circuit being its own political world.

May 12, 2009: Still everything is in bloom. Pink, yellow, green. Rain in the future, always, in Chicago. To sit in the garden in the middle of the flowers, colors, the smell of the earth, the clouds, the sky. Why the endless busyness? The economic situation offers no comfort. Are we to believe the entire world economic system was on the verge of collapse? Meanwhile government stumbles on.

He was appointed to fill a vacancy on the Supreme Court of Illinois in July 1878, returned to the Circuit Court in June 1879, then came back to the Supreme Court in 1888, where he remained until June 1897, when he was defeated for reelection. He was chief justice from June 1893 to June 1894, missing being chief justice for the *Ritchie* decision.

After his 1897 defeat for reelection, Justice Baker moved to Chicago, where he was said to have the respect of scores of Chicago lawyers. His office was visited daily by those wishing opinions on important cases or interpretations of vital points of law. He lived at

5517 Cornell Avenue with his wife and five children, who survived him. At his death he was 65, but said to look much younger. He was a close friend of R.J. Oglesby, the governor whom Henry Demarest Lloyd unsuccessfully petitioned to commute the death sentences of the Haymarket defendants.

Stenographic Report of the Testimony of State's Attorney Joe Birkett before the Capital Punishment Reform Study Committee, Public Hearing, January 26, 2009, 100 West Randolph Street, Chicago, Illinois.

. . . There are many, many guarantees and layers of safety that are in place in Illinois that this committee has probably not even heard about. . . . We also recognize, just like our predecessors, that there was a crisis of confidence in the death penalty here in Illinois and other states as well that in large measure did have to do with the decisions which were being made. . . .

We recognize that there was this crisis in confidence, but we also recognize that the law depends on public confidence and support for its effectiveness. While it is clear that most ordinary citizens continue to support capital punishment, it is equally clear and important that resources be devoted not only to discovering the sources of error but also finding out whether or not an innocent person had been executed. Well, that's been done. That has been done; and, thankfully, there's no evidence in the modern era that any innocent person has been executed. . . .

On that topic, you have to be very careful with statistics. I know you're attempting to gather statistics. There's a lot you're not going to learn from the sheet. And one of the things that we talked about in the Death Penalty Decision Guidelines is the investigative responsibility and the authority that the State's Attorneys have. . . .

The argument should be about the morality of capital punishment and justice, not cost. The debate over cost is a charade. It is a charade.

State's Attorney Birkett would be named to the Appellate Court on November 4, 2010.

In 1902 after moving to New York, Florence Kelley continued to return to Hull-House, still her spiritual home. Her mother, Caroline, by then dependent, was living in an apartment on the lake in Chicago. Florence Kelley's daughter, Margaret, in boarding school and not old enough for college, visited her grandmother when she came to stay over school holidays at Hull-House.

Even though he was now at school elsewhere, Nicholas came to visit Hull-House on his school vacations and was very much a favorite with the longtime residents, who considered him their boy. Florence Kelley came to Hull-House, as if returning home, when she could.

June 30, 2008: Two boys, nine and eleven, are visiting. So gentle, so sweet, so freckled. The quality of love does not change. We are unused to all that youth and energy. The boys laughed, we all laughed ourselves silly at the theater, at a Roman comedy, the language by Shakespeare, and then brilliantly reset by a Chicago writer in the London Blitz, and played for laughs joyfully, exuberantly. Today, a perfect Chicago summer day.

Justice Joseph N. Carter came from Kentucky, born in that border state in 1843, a few years later than his colleagues on the bench who fought in the Civil War. He did serve three months as a private in Company A of the 70th Illinois Infantry in 1862. He was awarded a BA from Illinois College in Jacksonville in 1866 and an LLB from the University of Michigan in 1868, then admitted to the Illinois Bar in 1869 and began practice in Quincy, Illinois.

Like his colleague Justice Bailey, Justice Carter went to the state Supreme Court after being elected to the Illinois House, where he served from 1878-82. He sat on the Supreme Court from June 1894 to June 1903, being elected chief justice by his colleagues on the court from June 1898 to June 1899.

Justice Carter's first election to the Supreme Court of Illinois in June 1894 was described as a hustle, with the Republican Carter carrying the day in a heavily Democratic fourth judicial district. The Democratic candidate had been nominated after a three-day fight in an ugly and quarrelsome party convention, whereas Carter was unanimously nominated by acclamation at the Republican convention, being recognized, it was said, all over Illinois as one of the foremost jurists of the day.

Both candidates thoroughly canvassed the judicial district during that election. . .

April 16, 2012: A cloudy, gloomy day, a grey day, but broody, interesting. Last night a bright and noisy Midwestern thunderstorm, the skies lit as if with a torch, and when we came out of the theater puddles everywhere and the scent of the fresh rain. . . .We are still here, here in Chicago, in spite of all the false starts to go elsewhere.

. . . although no public meetings were held as they worked to get out the vote on that Election Day in June 1894, at a time when farmers were busy in the fields. The Democrats feared loss of support in the rural districts because of public apathy and disaffection with the party.

Something always needed to be done on a farm: a stall to be mucked out, a sick cow, a horse with a loose shoe, a broken piece of farm equipment to be repaired, a floor to be mopped, a shirtwaist torn or overalls to be mended at the knee, tomatoes and fruits to be put in jars for winter, and, when time permitted, children to be taught to read.

Yet some farms were more cheerful places than others, just as some homes were joyful, even absent indoor plumbing or electricity, even in the face of tragedy, just as the presence of luxury, comfort, and convenience does not ensure happiness. As Florence Kelley wrote to a friend: "I have been happy in the simplest of circumstances, and miserable when surrounded in luxury." Families endured, carried on, celebrated or grieved together. And some were mean-spirited and miserable and some were joyful, in the same circumstance. And some gave up, and some carried on.

June 23, 2008: John Adams spoke eloquently about music, about learning, and why we go to universities to learn and to preserve what has been learned before. Libraries are changing, must learn to change, but must retain their function of holding, distributing, and passing on knowledge, data, and information, and remain within the great institutions dedicated to teaching, to preserve for the next generation what is known. I am skeptical that it will all be safe and available forever on the Web. There must be some physical reservoirs for this complicated knowledge, technology, and science, the art of language, music, and dance, where we can all come to bathe, and soothe and fortify ourselves, and drink deeply from the words of those who came before. Most of the people celebrating the university, its arts and sciences, are relatively secure, while the collapse of the housing bubble continues to destroy value and leave others in society with crippling debt.

Hull-House had grown so large, Florence Kelley wrote to Nicholas in 1902, she hardly recognized it when she came back to visit. Clarence Darrow came to dinner, she wrote, and was raising money for John Peter Altgeld's widow. After Governor Altgeld refused the bribe from Yerkes, he borrowed money from Yerkes on a regular loan and paid it back, while still in debt from overextending his credit for the Unity building.

Emma Ford Altgeld was desolate without him, and the governor had left no estate. She didn't long outlive him, dying childless, but much beloved, on March 29, 1915.

Theodore Dreiser in *The Titan* described the economic collapse of the stock market in the 1890s:

On August 4, 1896, the city of Chicago, and for that matter the entire financial world, was startled and amazed by the collapse of American Match, one of the strongest of market securities, and the coincident failure of Messrs. Hull and Stackpole, its ostensible promoters, for twenty millions. As early as eleven o'clock of the preceding day the banking and brokerage world of Chicago, trading in this stock, was fully aware that something untoward was on foot in connection with it. Owing to the high price at which the stock was "protected," and the need of money to liquidate, blocks of this stock from all parts of the country were being rushed to the market with the hope of realizing before the ultimate break. About the stock-exchange, which frowned like a gray fortress at the foot of LaSalle Street, all was excitement—as though a giant anthill had been ruthlessly disturbed. Clerks and messengers hurried to and fro in confused and apparently aimless directions. Brokers whose supply of American Match had been apparently exhausted on the previous day now appeared on 'change bright and early, and at the clang of the gong began to offer the stock in sizable lots of from two hundred to five hundred shares.

"Clarence Darrow had gotten quite fat," Florence Kelley wrote to Nicholas, by then away at boarding school and preparing—with some trepidation—to go to Harvard College as an undergraduate. At his 45th Class of 1906 reunion he reports that he lives in the same homes that he has lived in since 1927 and runs the Holstein Dairy Farm in New Jersey which he started in 1922. He continues to spend summers in Sakonnet Point, Little Compton, R.I. (where he spent summers with the Lloyd family as a child), and he continues to ride horses with Russian colonels in the same small indoor ring in which he began to ride with them in 1931.

To his surviving Harvard classmates, Nicholas reports that he flew to Europe in 1946 with the president and the Chrysler Export Corporation, visited European capitals, and had legal businesses with the Earl of Roseberry and Sir Patrick Hastings. He notes: "As I write this, Chrysler Corporation again is making war material and preparing to make a great deal here." The date would presumably be around 1951.

His official alumni record lists his father as Lazare Wischnicwetezy, a different spelling from that used by his mother, implying some contact with the family.

He was initially admitted provisionally at Harvard as a special student. It took Florence Kelley's legendary persuasive powers and the calling upon friendship with influential people in Cambridge to get him admitted, conditional for the first year upon his academic performance. And Harvard was expensive. Nicholas's entry into Harvard College was facilitated by a windfall of cash from an unexpected source.

June 12, 2012: A pleasant breeze off the lake. Today, the foreign students come for orientation. A small lunch for them in the room off the entry hall where Levy Mayer's portrait presides and emanates an atmosphere of seriousness. International students come to study law for a year and then return, or not, to their home country. If only they knew how strange our legal system often seems to those of us in the middle of it whose job it is to prop it up.

In this election of 1894, the towns in his Judicial District, except Quincy, Judge Carter's hometown, were mostly Republican. The party disputes were bitter, and the stakes were high. Judge Carter was a splendid campaigner, and his supporters and friends received words of encouragement from every county in the electoral district in spite of the majority being Democrats, not from his party. Meanwhile the Democrats made the strongest possible appeal to the electorate for aid, financial and otherwise.

When Judge Carter won his seat on the Supreme Court as a Republican, it was described as a rout of the Democratic patronage politicians who, in a recently gerrymandered district, had exercised authority in a high-handed way and parceled out among themselves the bounty of contracts and jobs at state and federal institutions, including the Post Office. The Democratic Party workers were admonished to arrive early and work late on Election Day. Even the Roman Catholic Church sent out a circular asking the flock to vote for Carter's opponent, their best friend. As ever the election was more about the bounty to be had from government offices, and who controlled the public purse, than about the substance of the issues.

July 1, 2008: Another summer day, made perfect by the fact that the boys are here. One in summer school and the other in circus camp. Rain forecast for tomorrow. Thousands are still coming to the homicide website. We didn't anticipate the genealogists, the people looking for their ancestors by name in the handwritten police records of murder. Or that so many were interested in murder, any murder.

On Election Day in June 1894 the Democrats were out in force with carriages and complete lists of all voters who could be counted upon to vote for their nominee. The carriages were paid for by assessments on the employees at the state institutions, where employment was controlled by the party in power. The carriages were sent for early, and the election proved they brought to the polls men who voted for the Republican Carter, instead of his Democratic opponent, whom they had been brought to vote for.

The Republicans for Carter hired no carriages, but some brought their own buggies to the polls and did what they could with them, and with volunteers. It was said that if the Republicans had done as the Democrats, they would have gained another two hundred votes. As it was, Judge Carter won by 4,650 votes, in a district which two years earlier in 1892 gave the Democrats a seven-thousand-vote majority.

It was the first Republican majority returned in that district in fifteen years, and congratulations poured in from all Republicans. The win was attributed to dissatisfaction with the Democratic administration in Washington, DC, where a Republican majority also was returned for the first time in fifteen years.

Sometimes the voters can outsmart the politicians, and a clever plan to bring out the vote on Election Day can win.

April 12, 2009: Cold, rainy. The Monday after Easter, which fell on the same weekend as Passover this year. We remember when the grandchildren ran over the back lawn, and the squirrels had eaten all of the chocolate eggs hidden in the bushes.

The Republicans, the party for Carter, held firm to the principle of nonpartisanship for the judiciary and dispensed with party apparatus, such as the party committees. Instead, they ran a noiseless campaign. A Carter literary bureau was established in each school district, and the managers kept abreast of affairs in every school district in the twelve counties in the judicial district. A few men were trusted with getting out the vote, and the managers did not betray their plan by work or look, as the typewriters click-clicked away all day. The party managers had a perfect political organization by school district in the countryside, and block by block in the towns. It was all done through personal letters. The Democrats smelled a mouse a few days before the vote and made a desperate effort to get out their certain votes, but to no avail.

Word of the disgraceful political scramble at the Democratic convention counted against the Democrats, as did the rampant bossism. People were disgusted. Half a dozen bosses held a meeting and without caucus or convention authorized the Democratic candidate to select whomever he wanted, his own delegates, to the judicial convention. The Republicans after Carter's election hoped to elect a congressman from their new fifteenth district.

October 17, 2007: The still outside in the night. Our great city blanketed under its weather, and a microcosm because the planet is groaning under its weather, mismanagement, human waste, an explosion of population, and the aftereffects of ever-present human folly. Still, if a child woke up to a beautiful day and felt glad, without reason, that is a reason to live.

The opinion of the Supreme Court of Illinois continued:

But the police power of the State can only be permitted to limit or abridge such a fundamental right as the right to make contracts, when the exercise of such power is necessary to promote the health, comfort, welfare or safety of society or the public; and it is questionable whether it can be exercised to prevent injury to the individual engaged in a particular calling.

During the week the *Ritchie* decision was handed down, Florence Kelley wrote her Northwestern Law School evidence professor, John Henry Wigmore, not yet dean, asking for permission to take her law school examinations later because she was detained on business in Springfield. Permission was granted.

And so on March 14, 1895, the Supreme Court of Illinois issued its opinion in the *Ritchie* case in Mount Vernon, Illinois, declaring the eight-hour provision for women unconstitutional, and a corner was turned. The mood, the times, had changed. And no amount of high-minded, moralistic preaching about the suffering of the poor was going to carry the day.

November 12, 2007: As November comes, and with it the promise of Thanksgiving. This house, which I never thought I could love, has become a family place. When it was built, it occupied the entire block. There was a carriage house, converted into a separate house before we arrived, and there was a little shed in the back and goats were kept there. They say a man, "the goat man," lived in a little shed in the back. Then the big lot was split up, pieces sold off after the war. At least all of the great old trees were not cut down.

Levy Mayer's attack upon the appropriation for the factory inspector was strategically astute. There could be no enforcement without government salaries to pay the inspectors. After the *Ritchie* decision in Illinois, the factory inspector in New York City was quoted as saying that the Illinois decision, in spite of its being grounded in principles of federal constitutional law, had no impact on the enforcement of the factory inspection law in New York because the New York law was a general law, a ten-hour law, applying only to minors. The other relevant law in New York was already upheld by the highest court in the state restricting the number of hours employees can work for corporations chartered by the state, a law directed at the railroads.

January 4, 2009: V.S. Naipaul says writers waste time writing in journals. I disagree, although it can be procrastination, and I never look at the journal entries or come back to them. There is something comforting about sitting down in the morning, facing the empty page with a favorite pen, and writing, just writing about what kind of morning it is, an announcement of consciousness. The better the writer, the better the journal. All real writers keep journals or a notebook. Every writer I have ever known does, has, and will, and I will. It is not a tweet, or a blog, it is a conversation with the page. Are you there, today.

Alfred M. Craig was an Irishman from Illinois whose father came from Philadelphia and perhaps knew his contemporary William Darrah Kelley. The family initially went to Kentucky, but, unwilling to live in a slave state, they moved to Illinois. Born in 1831, he was brought up on a farm, and attended school only in the winter and worked on the family farm in the summer. The long summer school vacations still in place throughout much of America have their origin in the fact that children were needed to work in the fields to bring in the harvest on the family farm in the summer.

Alfred Craig eventually went to Knox College. Farm boys and girls learn early that sitting, or better lying down, and reading or writing is more liberating to the imagination than forking hay into bales, or pushing cows reluctant to walk, or chasing ornery horses who can show their rumps and kick. Growing up on a farm there was a strong incentive to find a way to spend time reading and writing, to be with books, to dream of studying law, making a life of holding a pen and paper. Better than flicking the reins for eight hours in the sun staring at the tail of a mule. The law, a profession of sitting and talking, of clean shoes and a white shirt, of being someone other people listened to, had many attractions.

October 27, 2007: A fall day, grey and wet. To touch the evanescent reality, the fleeting cloud, the dying flower. To give evil a name. To be able to pinpoint, to say with accuracy what happened, is happening. To understand what a fact is. To control by writing. Courts do that. Novels do that. Poems do that. Otherwise, where does thought go? Don't ask where all the writing goes, where all the notebooks go.

After graduating from college Alfred Craig read law in Lewistown, Illinois, and was admitted to the Bar a year later. The justices of the Supreme Court of Illinois, deciding the factory inspection cases, ruling upon whether the state could inspect conditions in the urban tenements and city sweatshops, were mostly rural people from modest backgrounds, traditional people, small-town lawyers who went into politics, like John Peter Altgeld. They were church people. Their upbringing and backgrounds were typical of the country at the time: most Americans did not grow up or live in cities in the 1890s. Their education may have been sporadic; they believed in a God. The lawyers on the Supreme Court of Illinois in 1895 may have been impressed with Levy Mayer's urban sophistication, with his degree from Yale, even if they were suspicious of him being educated in the East and being a Jew. Perhaps this is why the Yale-educated Justice Magruder was chosen to write the opinion, because he was seen as the intellectual equal of Levy Mayer.

April 24, 2007: Spring has come, spent its few days, and there is much to celebrate. Our school is thriving; the students seem enthusiastic and diligent. Everyone is healthy. The students mostly love the law, love the studying, welcome the hurdles which are part of their education. They say they don't want to be in private practice, that they want to be in public service, but few will end up there.

Alfred Craig opened a law office in Knoxville, Illinois, the county seat, where you would need to be if you were going to make a living as a small-town lawyer representing clients before the county bar, where everyone knew everyone, and everyone knew who did what. People came to town expecting to find the lawyers at or near the courthouse and to be able to hire a lawyer on the spot.

April 28, 2013: Our one day of spring is gone. The worst factory disaster in memory has occurred. In Bangladesh, hundreds dead, having been told to come to work when large cracks had appeared in a poorly built multi-story building. The big American clothing companies seek to distance themselves; the owner of the building is in hiding. The factory workers, who pointed out the cracks in the wall to the management, were told either come to work tomorrow, or don't come to work the next day.

Alfred Craig soon built what was described as a large and lucrative practice, his skill and erudition being demonstrated, it was said, by the fact that he never lost a case at court. This compliment is considered by some to be only an indication that the lawyer never took on a difficult case, a close case. In 1856 he was appointed state's attorney for Knox County, then elected county judge in 1860, a typical route to the higher court still. In 1869 he was selected to go to the convention which wrote the Illinois Constitution of 1870. At the constitutional convention he was chairman of the Committee on Counties.

Levy Mayer's parents came to Chicago before the city was choked by bituminous coal, at a time when views from the cupola of the proud new courthouse encompassed the entire city, north, south, and west. To the east the Great Lake of Michigan with its water pumping station four miles offshore; to the north the forests and small towns; to the south the great river and the lumberyards and industry there, the ships on the river and in the harbors of the lake; to the west it was possible to see the city grow overnight before your eyes along the great plank roads all leading to the hub, the center, the heart of the city: City Hall and the Cook County Courthouse.

September 5, 2010: A new project: the history of the Northwestern University School of Law. It is a logical outgrowth of the Florence Kelley investigations. On May 8, 1925, a groundbreaking and dedication ceremony was held on the site of what would be the new home of the School of Law of Northwestern University on the new Alexander McKinlock Memorial Campus opening onto Lake Michigan and its beach and occupying several blocks from Huron and Erie streets to Chicago Avenue.

The new home of the School of Law would be called Levy Mayer Hall. The celebration commemorated a gift of $500,000 from Levy Mayer's widow, Rachel Meyer Mayer, a woman noted for her philanthropy, especially for her support of Jewish charities and social service organizations, as her daughter would be similarly known, and who commissioned the Levy Mayer biography to be written by the poet and lawyer Edgar Lee Masters. Perhaps she instructed him to leave out the story of her husband's role in the successful challenge to the factory inspection statute and his work against everything Hull-House stood for. There is much detail in the book about the Iroquois fire case, in which he represented the theater owners.

Justice Craig, who started life as a poor farm boy, became president of the Bank of Galesburg, owned extensive and rich land holdings, married the daughter of a prominent attorney, and was survived by two of his four children, a druggist and a lawyer. His son Alfred Craig was elected to the Supreme Court of Illinois in 1913, having followed his father to Knox College, and after graduation taking further education at the University of Notre Dame.

Alfred Craig, the father, who was on the court at the time of the factory inspection case, was a member of the Supreme Court of Illinois for 27 years, each time being returned with a larger majority. Before going on the Supreme Court he successfully prosecuted a notorious murder which ended with the only hanging to take place in Knox County. This was the last case he tried.

First elected to the Supreme Court in 1873, and returning to it in 1901, Justice Craig owned several large farms. He was called the farmer-judge because he was always solicitous of the interests of farmers. Described by contemporaries as well-preserved and with a keen intellect, he was urged to consider national office because of his abilities. On the free coinage issue, the gold and silver choice, the burning question of the 1896 election, he took the position that the silver dollar ought to be equal to the gold dollar and that the US government ought to coin all its own ore and reject foreign imports.

January 25, 2008: A stormy day, warm. Almost summery, but grey. Last night: piano music for the left hand played with wonderful artistry. Never ask where all the beautiful piano playing goes. I admire the theater people, the actors, the playwrights: they never moan about how quickly what they make vanishes. Writers are spoiled, clasping the physical book, captivated by the century-old newspaper clipping. As if the physical thing meant something.

These were the seven men Levy Mayer confronted when he put forward the arguments that the Factory Inspection Law was unconstitutional, under the federal constitution. He crafted that argument, and his rhetoric carried the day.

From Ritchie v. People:

But aside from its partial and discriminating character, this enactment is a purely arbitrary restriction upon the fundamental right of the citizen to control his or her own time and faculties. It substitutes the judgment of the legislature for the judgment of the employer and employee in a matter about which they are competent to agree with each other. It assumes to dictate to what extent the capacity to labor may be exercised by the employee, and takes away the right of private judgment as to the amount and duration of the labor to be put forth in a specified period. When the legislature thus undertakes to impose an unreasonable and unnecessary burden upon any one citizen or class of citizens, it transcends the authority entrusted to it by the constitution, even though it imposes the same burden upon all other citizens or classes of citizens.

In the same year that Ritchie v. People was decided, undermining much of the work Florence Kelley and her associates had dedicated themselves to, on June 12, 1895, almost three months to the day after the decision was handed down, Florence Kelley graduated from Northwestern University School of Law and soon was admitted to the Bar of Illinois. Her name was published in the *Tribune* announcing her ascendancy to the Bar of Illinois.

April 20, 2009: The editors of the Journal *are right: the article isn't ready. But postponing it, especially now when I am distracted with moving, is disappointing. I wanted the piece out this year, while I am still on the State Committee so that I can use the published article as leverage on the committee. Well, it will just come out later, and be the better for it. I want it finished now but it isn't ready.*

While staying at the Leland Hotel in Springfield in the winter and in March of 1895, Florence Kelley was in the midst of a protracted battle against the Illinois Glass Works in Alton.

The boys at the glass works had the same job as the blowers' dogs whom Florence Kelley had seen as a child when her father, William Darrah Kelley, took her to a glass factory in Pennsylvania. Contrary to the assertions of the factory owners, these boys never became glass blowers. They endured serious burns, lung problems, and other permanent injuries. The jobs for boys in the glass works were not positions of apprenticeship. Apprenticeships in the Alton glass factory, leading to union-protected, salaried jobs, were reserved for the glass blowers' sons, who were never employed as blowers' dogs but instead went to school. The men who were glass blowers in the union joined with the manufacturer in resisting protections for these servient children, said they needed their assistance, didn't seem to care that they were underage boys.

May 10, 2009: Mother's Day, and fair with dark clouds. To be outside in the clear air is exhilarating, a luxury, a privilege, as is our whole life here.

Jane Addams described Florence Kelley's energy in pursing the mission to gain some protection for the children in the factories as "dismaying" as she "issued her order with the same negligence of appearance that she showed in throwing her clothes on in the morning like some daughter of Minerva and Mars sallying forth to war." And so she was.

The Illinois Glass Works fought back with no holds barred, in the family way: pulling hair, gouging eyes by arguing that the underage boys were supporting widows, by threatening to shut down all or part of its furnaces in retaliation to the proposed inspections, by saying they would lay off all the men and boys in the middle of winter, and by vilifying Florence Kelley and her workers in the local newspapers.

Florence Kelley called upon Governor John P. Altgeld, and after a public hearing a compromise was negotiated, although Altgeld did ask her to moderate her demands. Still the Illinois Glass Works resisted every inspection, every proposed regulation. Finally, she reported in the *Fourth Annual Report*, the Illinois Glass Works was in compliance at least with regard to not employing boys under the age of fourteen. That the glass works was compliant with some of the regulations was a large triumph.

May 11, 2009: Cloudy. All the white flowering fruit trees in bloom. It seems that our future is uncertain still. In the end only the end is certain for all of us, and that only as an abstraction, and not known by us.

The result of the settlement with the glass works: boys under 12 would be dismissed within a month, and older boys later. Those whom their wages supported, the families of the boys who were employed, and the townspeople in Alton were not happy. But the sitting governor said the Factory Inspection Law, at that very moment being reviewed by the Supreme Court of Illinois, must be respected, even if every shop and factory in the state closed down.

When a court is engaged in making a pronouncement which will be politically controversial, when a court dredges deep and far afield for the precedent to reach its conclusion, then that court will couch its decision in the language of technicality and obfuscation. In Illinois the single subject rule of constitutional interpretation is the perfect refuge for such legal obscurantism. The general rule is that a piece of legislation shall have only one subject. The legal argument was that the provision for salaries of the factory inspectors and for other remedies, such as inspections, violated the single-subject rule. So the Supreme Court of Illinois in *Ritchie* gravely addressed that topic, with its convoluted definition of what constitutes a single subject:

> *The title of the act not only does not mention the pay of the legislature and the salaries of the government officers, but it does not mention the salaries of the inspectors. The word "therefor"* [in the statute] *does not necessarily imply that the appropriation is for the salaries of the inspectors. Non Constat, so far as the title expresses to the contrary, that the inspectors were not to act without salaries. . . . If it were not for section 16* [a state constitutional provision stating: "The General Assembly shall make no appropriation of money out of the treasury in any private law. Bills making appropriation for the pay of members and officers of the General Assembly, and *for the salaries of the government shall contain no provision on any other subject*" (italics as cited in opinion)], *it might be said that the salaries of the inspectors were a necessary expense incidental to the execution of the law, and properly included in the title, though not expressly named therein. But sections 16 and 13 are in the same article of the constitution, and both use the word "subject," which evidently has the same meaning in each.*

The question, therefore, whether the matter of the salaries of state officers is an independent subject is not a matter of construction, because the [Illinois] *Constitution itself, by the language used in section 16, defines and sets apart appropriations for such salaries as a subject, which is distinct and separate from all others, and cannot be included in any other.*

Much technical jargon and the poor syntax are evident in this part of the opinion. This is not the soaring rhetoric of earlier constitutional arguments. A general rule prevails: if there is a court opinion which is difficult to understand, with convoluted diction and syntax, interlarded with rhetorical citations to obscure sources or Latin references, that opinion was probably controversial, politically fraught, and forged on a rickety consensus. At the end of the day, however, the court did not use the single-subject rule to declare the entire statute unconstitutional.

Our conclusion is, that section 5 of the Act of 1893 ["no female shall be employed in any factory or workshop more than eight hours in any one day, or forty-eight hours in any one week"], *and the first clause of section 10* [regarding payment of factory inspectors] *thereof, are void and unconstitutional for the reason here stated.*

A court can control the reality for a brief period with its language, with pronouncements. The lawyers are like children coming to plead for a favor from a parent, the judge, for what they see is their due, to be given a ruling for good behavior. The lawyers must convince the judge that they are worthy of being treated seriously, like adults, and to win, by having the argument decided in their favor. The judges sometimes do reward their favorite children.

November 2007: It is astonishing how much petty conflict can be generated over who will have what bedroom, when children should go to bed, or who shall control a student organization or an office arrangement. Perhaps people just enjoy quarreling, that it reminds them of when they were children and quarreled as sisters and brothers.

The appellate court judges are the grandparents, with more grey hair, in many courts with grey wigs, in theory wiser, sterner, answering to another higher order, the principled rule of law, unlikely to rule on the basis of what happened in the fray below, but nonetheless not completely above it, knowing the parties, able to make a correction for justice.

And so the seven justices of the Supreme Court of Illinois took the opportunity to remove a powerful arm of the Factory and Workshop Inspection Law without declaring the whole statute unconstitutional. They could make the business community happy but not give in entirely to its demands, in spite of Levy Mayer's clever arguments. Unlike the opinion by Justice Magruder in the anarchist case, this opinion was not a complete victory for business.

March 15, 2007: The semester rolling to its close. The students glad the worst of winter is over. The education pits them one against the other, for the prizes, for the recognition, but they recognize their commonality in privilege. This is what higher education has become, but we are a magnet for the world. Whatever we are doing, the rest of the world wants to be let into the game.

On March 14, 1895, when the Supreme Court of Illinois issued its opinion declaring the eight-hour provision for women unconstitutional, it was a watershed. Something was over. Florence Kelley could protest in her *Third Annual Report* that only one section of the law—the eight-hour provision for women—had been declared unconstitutional and that the rest of the law was still in place, and that was correct. But the tide had turned. The Supreme Court could say it was not declaring unconstitutional the protection against employing girls under fourteen, or against factory inspection generally, but the word had gone out. The law had not been upheld. These seven men decided as a group, as a court, that they would not stand fully behind the law.

April 16, 2009: The weather, blue skies, not warm, but bright, so bright. It lifts the spirit. The law school library remains a refuge. The relentlessness of time's passing is unforgiving.

The court opinion in *Ritchie* concludes:

Section 5 of the Act of 1893 is broad enough to include married women and adult single women, as well as minors. As a general thing, it is the province of the legislature to determine what regulations are necessary to protect the public health and secure the public safety and welfare. But inasmuch as sex is no bar, under the constitution and the law, to the endowment of woman with the fundamental and inalienable rights of liberty and property which include the right to make her own contracts, the mere fact of sex will not justify the legislature in putting forth the police power of the State for the purpose of limiting her exercise of those rights, unless the courts are able to see, that there is some fair, just and reasonable connection between such limitation and the public health, safety or welfare proposed to be secured by it.

June 7, 2013: The political system in Illinois seems paralyzed. The only bill the legislature passed was the concealed-carry gun bill. Nothing on pensions, nothing on budget. The governor is threatening to call them back in session. But what good will that do, if the legislators can't agree on any legislation? The state is broke, and no one will take responsibility.

How the courts fit a ruling into the competing demands of the system is never simple:

Our conclusion is, that section 5 of the Act of 1893, and the first clause of section 10 thereof, are void and unconstitutional for the reasons here stated. These are the only portions of the Act, which have been attacked in the argument of counsel. No reason has been pointed out why they are not distinct and separable from the balance of the Act. The rule is that, where a part of a statute is unconstitutional, the remainder will not be declared to be unconstitutional also, if the two are distinct and separable so that the latter may stand, though the former become of no effect. We do not wish to be understood by anything herein said as holding that section five (5) would be invalid if it was limited in its terms to females who are minors.

Ritchie v. People

This part of the opinion was an invitation to the legislature to act, to amend the provision to apply only to minors. The legislature didn't act. Nor did it act to provide greater protection for children.

May 10, 2009: I have found a co-conspirator in state government in the search for facts on the cost of capital punishment, and been sent an astonishing set of data. Pages and pages of numbers, details on years, cases, counties, about how the millions of dollars appropriated by the legislature, a stopgap to avoid abolition, money supposed to ensure fairness in the prosecution of capital cases has actually been spent. Sometimes luck just comes your way. Not that I didn't spend months tracking down these data, asking for the numbers, while my fellow members of the state capital punishment reform committee told me I was wasting my time. And so the postponement of the article on the cost of capital punishment is a piece of good fortune, after all. It can now include these startling facts.

Jane Addams, Florence Kelley, and the other political activists knew the political mood had shifted in 1895. The book *Hull-House Maps and Papers*, like Jane Addams's own book, would carry on the fight, inspiring generations.

As Jane Addams remembered later:

At the end of five years the residents of Hull-House published some first found facts and our reflections thereon in a book called Hull-House Maps and Papers. The maps were taken from information collected by one of the residents [Florence Kelley] for the United States Bureau of Labor in the investigation into "the slums of the great cities" and the papers treated various neighborhood matters with candor and genuine concern if not with skill.

Jane Addams's *Twenty Years at Hull-House* was first published in 1910. The book is meditative, reflective, and still read and still in print. The writing and publication of *Hull-House Maps and Papers* in 1895 was compressed into three years. It has the immediacy and disjointedness of a report being prepared under deadline, with an eye on its release to the press in order to have an impact on public opinion. Its moods hopeful, exultant, with the excitement of new research.

Levy Mayer had taken a ragtag group of factory owners and manufacturers, made them pay dues, and turned them into a highly effective advocacy group, an organization with a mission. The fight went on elsewhere, and then moved to New York. The legal battles continued, moved to other places, at other times. Florence Kelley noted in her *Fourth Annual Report*:

> *The rigid enforcement of the law has convinced the inspectors that the attempt to protect the health of the community while maintaining tenement-house manufacture is a hopeless one. No staff of inspectors, however large and well equipped, can grapple successfully with the essential evils of tenement-house manufacture in great cities, where the garment trades tend increasingly to concentrate. . . .*

> *The present regulation places all responsibility for garment manufacture in tenement-house shops upon contractors, who are in all respects irresponsible, and none upon wholesale manufacturers. It involves this irresponsible middle-man as employer; the small and scattered groups incapable, by reason of their numerical weakness, of insisting upon wholesome conditions of work; the concealment of infection (the interests of the landlord and his tenants, of the sweater and his victims, coinciding in this respect, and often obtaining the connivance of a physician of the same race and religion), the economic impossibility of wholesome surroundings for employes, and, finally, the home finisher, the most dangerous and wretched link in this chain.*

The organization Levy Mayer created went on to become a national lobbying organization, a major player on the Washington scene in the next century, representing manufacturers and consistently opposing government regulation of business in any way.

April 14, 2009: Grey. Grey. Grey. And rainy. Cold. Nothing to attract a person to go outside. The tracery of the branches of the tree still bare, the black line of limbs. All I see now is the end of our time here. How can all of that research on the nineteenth century be packed up in boxes? Never ask what is next, only what is now.

The law school alumni and Elbert H. Gary, class of 1867, donated funds, in addition to those bequeathed by Levy Mayer's widow, for the construction of the law school building with its main entrance opening onto Chicago Avenue, the grassy courtyard behind, then a second entrance onto Superior Street. At that time, the building, Levy Mayer Hall, was on the shores of the lake. There was no Lake Shore Drive. The academic building and its grassy courtyard, completed in 1926, marked the graceful terminus of seven decades of transiency for the school, as the author of the dedication ceremony's commemorative book commented. The author was John Henry Wigmore himself, with his wife being thanked for much of the decoration and accoutrements of the inside of the building.

May 2, 2008: The clinic offices have been opened on the eighth floor of Rubloff, the newer building attached to Levy Mayer Hall in the 1970s. My new office will be there. The administration has decided that my office on the second floor of Levy Mayer needs to be renovated. I am happy enough to move upstairs. The views of the lake are spectacular, and all the offices for lawyers are the same size, which suits my sensibilities. Moving is an annoyance, but will soon be over.

The old-world charm of Levy Mayer Hall, its dark wood paneling, the leaded windows, the colored glass inserts, remains Levy Mayer's legacy. The class gifts commemorated with a stained-glass panel in the leaded windows of Lincoln Hall, the ornamentation, the chimes, all repeatedly the subject of trivia questions for new law students. The English Inns of Court were the model. Lincoln Hall is a replica of the British House of Commons in London and is expressive of the popular image of the formality of law. Movies and television shows about lawyers are filmed here.

April 28, 2009: First, grey and rain. Then sunshine, now grey again. Cold. The weather demands our attention. Demands we look elsewhere.

The faculty under Wigmore's leadership contributed to the design of the special desks for Lincoln Hall, the aisles wide enough so that no one would be disturbed if someone left. Surely it mattered to that 1926 Faculty of Law Committee on Building, and to the law alumni trustees, that their names were emblazoned in the light purple and gold Dedication Handbook. The entire building, the leaded windows, the stone floors, the dark wood was designed to create an atmosphere of authority, solemnity, reverence. The eighth-floor clinic, on the other hand, is designed like a modern law office with large windows, carpeting, bland furniture, a circular design where everyone mills about.

April 28, 2013: When Governor George Ryan spoke at Lincoln Hall, the deep trough of the center of that august setting was filled with television cameras and reporters.

George Ryan's speech announcing the commutations on January 11, 2003, was broadcast around the world:

Four years ago I was sworn in as the 39th governor of Illinois. That was just four short years ago—that's when I was a firm believer in the American System of Justice and the death penalty. I believed that the ultimate penalty for the taking of a life was administrated in a just and fair manner.

Today, three days before I end my term as governor, I stand before you to explain my frustrations and deep concerns about both the administration and the penalty of death.

It is fitting that we are gathered here today at Northwestern University with the students, teachers, lawyers and investigators who first shed light on the sorrowful condition of Illinois' death penalty system.

In Lincoln Hall of the Northwestern University School of Law, Governor George Ryan commuted the death sentences of all death-row inmates in Illinois, an unprecedented act in American jurisprudence. In that vaulted ceremonial hall, packed with journalists, family members of the exonerated, and photographers, the mood was jubilant, celebratory, solemn, disbelieving and emotional, and the stately hall lived up to the occasion, which never could have been foreseen by John Henry Wigmore or his wife.

January 11, 2003: Governor George Ryan's commutation speech is his last official act in office. He has the full attention of the audience, including myself; we know we are witnessing a historic occasion.

I grew up in Kankakee, which even today is still a small Midwestern town, a place where people tend to know each other. Steve Small was a neighbor. I watched him grow up. He would baby-sit my young children—which was not for the faint of heart since Lura Lynn and I had six children, five of them under the age of three. He was a bright young man who helped run the family business. He got married and he and his wife had three children of their own. Lura Lynn was especially close to him and his family. We took comfort in knowing he was there for us and we for him.

One September midnight he received a call at his home. There had been a break-in at the nearby house he was renovating. But as he left his house, he was seized at gunpoint by kidnappers. His captors buried him alive in a shallow hole. He suffocated to death before police could find him.

His killer led investigators to where Steve's body was buried. The killer, Danny Edwards, was also from my hometown. He now sits on death row. I also know his family. I share this story with you so that you know I do not come to this as a neophyte without having experienced a small bit of the bitter pill the survivors of murder must swallow.

My responsibilities and obligations are more than my neighbors and my family. I represent all the people of Illinois, like it or not. The decision I make about our criminal justice system is felt not only here, but the world over.

No woman is listed among the board of trustees on the Committee on Building in 1927, or on the faculty of law itself, nor among the architects, the builders, the engineers for heating, lighting, and ventilation for Levy Mayer Hall. A note in the program says that at a meeting of the Faculty of Law, held Monday Evening, September 20, 1926 (in the absence of the dean, John Henry Wigmore), a resolution was adopted to acknowledge the indebtedness of the faculty to the devoted interest of Mrs. John Henry Wigmore for suggestions on the decoration and interior arrangement, and from whose advice the faculty has consistently profited throughout the construction. The statue of St. Ives, the patron saint of the legal profession, still sits with his back to the wall, guarding Levy Mayer's portrait in the entrance lobby.

We have come very close to having our state Supreme Court rule our death penalty statute—the one that I helped enact in 1977—unconstitutional. Former state Supreme Court Justice Seymour Simon wrote to me that it was only happenstance that our statute was not struck down by the state's high court. When he joined the bench in 1980, three other justices had already said Illinois' death penalty was unconstitutional. But they got cold feet when a case came along to revisit the question. One judge wrote that he wanted to wait and see if the Supreme Court of the United States would rule on the constitutionality of the new Illinois law. Another said precedent required him to follow the old state Supreme Court ruling with which he disagreed.

Even a pharmacist knows that doesn't make sense. We wouldn't have a death penalty today, and we all wouldn't be struggling with this issue, if those votes had been different. How arbitrary.

March 4, 2011: Rain, grey. In class this week, a state Supreme Court justice is our guest.

Children digging with pick axes on a Chicago street; Chicago, IL. Source: ICHi-52108. Chicago History Museum. Reproduction of photographic print, photographer unknown.

6

At the Library

Father had taught me to read when I was seven years old, in a terrible little book with woodcuts of children no older than myself, balancing with their arms heavy loads of wet clay on their heads, in brickyards in England. They looked like little gnomes and trolls, with crooked legs, and splay feet large out of all proportion to their dwarfed frames. The text told of the hardships they were then suffering, nearly two decades after Lord Shaftesbury's bill to shorten the working hours of women and children in English factories had been enacted by Parliament. When my mother and grandmother remonstrated with him for darkening the mind of a young child with such dismal ideas, he replied seriously that life can never be right for all the children until the cherished boys and girls are taught to know the facts in the lives of their less fortunate contemporaries.

Florence Kelley, *Autobiography*

The large outstanding figures of one generation are commonly no more than shadows (when they are even that) to its successor. . . . Outside a little group of surviving friends, associates, and followers, there are probably few today to whom the name of John P. Altgeld is significant or even familiar. . . . He belongs with what is called the dead past, which we in America bury more speedily and with less reverence than any other people. But, as the sages frequently remind us, the past is never dead—"at last it is all that lives."

Harry Barnard, *Eagle Forgotten*

After being fired as chief factory inspector in August 1897, Florence Kelley found herself four months later working as a part-time librarian in the evening for the John Crerar Library, a special reference collection primarily devoted to science, established with more than $400,000 from the estate of John Crerar. It was the only job she could get. Governor John Tanner, who defeated John Peter Altgeld in 1896, told her he would reappoint her, then fired her with no notice or explanation. He appointed in her place a lawyer who had worked twenty-five years for the Illinois Glass Works. Governor Tanner asked the head of the glass works, who had said the child labor provisions in the law would not be enforced in his company, to recommend someone, and he did. This factory employed the largest number of children in the state and was often in defiance of the law. It recommended a loyal employee.

Florence Kelley sought another job in Chicago with the help of everyone she knew. The search was long, proving once again: even if you know everyone and have done good work in your previous job, even if you are eminently qualified, or overqualified, sometimes you just can't get a job.

The job she seems to have really wanted was that of factory inspector for the State of New York. With Jane Addams, she went to see Theodore Roosevelt, recently elected governor of New York. Initially after not having time to see Florence Kelley, Governor Roosevelt could not deny Jane Addams, and he gave an audience to the two of them.

Governor Roosevelt told Florence Kelley how much her work in Illinois as factory inspector was admired in New York. Later, he wrote to a colleague that he could not risk appointing her because she was tainted with "Altgeldism." Instead, the governor appointed as factory inspector an elevator operator in Albany who was recommended by a state legislator, telling the elevator operator he should contact Florence Kelley, who "knew more about the work of a factory inspector than anyone."

Then, continuing their search for a job, Jane Addams and Florence Kelley went to see President William McKinley.

During this meeting, President McKinley had tears in his eyes when he remembered William Darrah Kelley. The two women asked for Florence Kelley to be appointed as staff to a federal industrial commission investigating the sources of violence between labor and industrialists. President McKinley did not appoint Florence Kelley to the position.

Later, Florence Kelley replied to Governor Richard Yates, the governor of Illinois from 1901-05, when he offered her the position of assistant chief factory inspector:

To one who has faithfully performed the duties of Chief Factory Inspector of the State of Illinois, the offer of the position of Assistant Chief Inspector cannot be presented otherwise than as an affront.

June 10, 2011: Iowa City. The weather is glorious, although apparently severe thunder and rain have delayed some traveling to the Iowa Writers' Workshop seventy-fifth reunion. To superimpose a literary work on top of another literary work, as Christo and Jeanne-Claude's the Gates Project put a work of art (the eleven thousand orange fabric gates themselves) on top of another work of art, Central Park itself with its gates.

To put historic legal events on top of earlier legal events which show the same patterns: the passionate idealized idea of reform, then the messy, dirty lobbying for legislation, the initial implementation, the challenge, the rhythm of the back and forth in courts, and all in the warp and weave of the law, the politics, and the economic reality of the times.

A joy to be with people who value writing, think writing—even poetry—is an activity worth engaging in. From the horse's mouth: "Three hours a day, six days a week, go to the same place, perhaps at the same time, and a book will be written. You won't be able to stand yourself being idle. It will have to be done!"

Certainly you won't be able to stand yourself being idle at your writing place. And so you will write. Something. Surely Florence Kelley knew this.

The groundbreaking for Levy Mayer Hall was on May 8, 1925, when the new building was dedicated with a gift of $500,000 from the estate of Levy Mayer, who was at the time of his death in 1922 one of the most successful lawyers in Chicago. His principal clients were the liquor industry and theater owners. The gossip was: he represented the mob, especially during Prohibition. The then-dean of the Northwestern Law School, John Henry Wigmore, probably negotiated the gift with Levy Mayer's widow, Rachel Meyer Mayer.

June 17, 2011: The New York Public Library Archives. Most are copying onto their laptops, copying the documents, the letters, the bound volumes, the ledgers. I cruise in the neatly organized pale file folders, never know what I am looking for until I find it, am insufficiently prepared. Sometimes I come here just to read the letters, copy some and make notes about others with the tiny stub of a pencil and the single sheet of blank paper which the very helpful archivists provide. The pencil, most awkward. Really I am here just reminding myself of what I am doing.

In Levy Mayer's biography there is an extensive exposition of the Iroquois fire case in which Levy Mayer represented the theater owners. First, Levy Mayer was successful in moving the case out of Cook County, then in delaying all civil proceedings for years, in spite of the fact that after the tragedy the mayor of Chicago was briefly jailed and indicted on more than 500 counts of manslaughter. All criminal indictments, another set of manslaughter counts against the theater owners, were eventually dismissed.

Levy Mayer died on August 14, 1922, in the apartment in the Blackstone Hotel where he had lived for many years with his mistress. At the time of his death, his wife, a daughter, and the family chauffeur—one of whose descendants fifty years later spontaneously contacted this author—were traveling in Europe. The chauffeur regularly accompanied the ladies on trips to Europe, to make arrangements at hotels and restaurants, to take care of everything, as well as to drive, according to his descendant. Perhaps the ladies didn't drive, or not in Europe, and there may have been a drinking issue as well. Due to the unavailability of air travel, it took days for the wife and daughter to arrive back in Chicago after Levy Mayer's unexpected death.

January 4, 2009: When you know you must move, to go to another place, a part of your heart is left behind. To set aside the dearly held but false view that one's own contribution is crucial, irreplaceable.

The Iroquois fire case first introduced Levy Mayer to the theater owners and then to the liquor distributors, since the two industries were closely tied. He eventually represented the whiskey trust in a case challenging Congress's passage of Prohibition which went all the way to the Supreme Court of the United States, Hamilton v. Kentucky Distilleries & Warehouse Co., 251 146 (argued Nov. 20, 1919, decided Dec. 15, 1919). Levy Mayer argued the case himself before the Supreme Court, and lost.

Representing the Kentucky distillers, Levy Mayer and Mr. William Marshall Bullitt, for the appellees, argued that Congress had no power to prohibit the sale of whiskey except during wartime under special legislation. The case was brought after the armistice in World War I.

Supreme Court Justice Louis Brandeis, appointed to the court in 1916 by President Woodrow Wilson long after the Illinois factory inspection case and serving until 1939, delivered the unanimous opinion of the court. It is the rare case where Levy Mayer's name appears on an official court record.

The Supreme Court of the United States case, Hamilton v. Kentucky Distilleries, considered whether the armistice with Germany on November 11, 1918, invalidated the War Time Prohibition Act. The plaintiffs were successful below in seeking an injunction, and the case was certified directly to the high court. The plaintiffs argued that the act prohibiting the sale of liquor amounted to the taking of private property without compensation. The court found that if a state could take private property without compensation, then the federal government could, under the Fourteenth Amendment. Noting that the president retained control of the railroads, the final link in the chain of supply determining the price of numerous commodities, the opinion noted that the "possible abuse of power" is not an argument against the existence of the power itself and that every "reasonable intendment" must be made in favor of the validity of the statute. Nor did the subsequent adoption of the Eighteenth Amendment establishing Prohibition trump the statute. The War Time Prohibition Act was held to be valid and still in force. The argument that the United States lacked the police power to do this failed. There was no Fourteenth Amendment violation. The argument harks back to Levy Mayer's strategy in the *Ritchie* case.

May 15, 2013: The United States manufacturers who now admit that goods for them were being made in the collapsed building in Bangladesh are now protesting that they had no knowledge of these conditions and are calling for some sort of agreement between manufacturers to protect against future disasters. Their protestations of ignorance ring false.

Toward the end of Carroll Wright's life, he completed the Eleventh United States Census. As his health was failing, the presidency of Clark University was created for him with the idea that the work should not be so hard. His *New York Times* obituary noted: "He went on as determinedly as before, however, and during his administration as Head that institution prospered."

Abraham Bisno's daughter, Beatrice Bisno, wrote a biographical novel based upon her father's life and work, titled *Tomorrow's Bread*, published by the Jewish Publication Society of America, Philadelphia, in 1938. The book was chosen for the Edwin Wolf Award for the best novel of Jewish interest. In the novel there is a character named Myra Jones who lives at a settlement house called Smith House. Myra Jones is in charge of factory inspection in the city; she has translated a Marxist work and was formerly married to a Jewish doctor. There is also a character who is described as the founder of the settlement house.

The character of Sam Kerenski, the radical Jewish Marxist labor organizer, seemingly modeled upon Bisno himself, the author's father, calls strikes, goes to jail, gets bailed out, and devotes his life to improving the lot of workers. The events reported are dramatic if not factually reliable.

The novel tells the story of the labor organizer's two marriages, his many marital infidelities and love affairs, and his work as an organizer of garment workers in New York as well as Chicago. Abraham Bisno was a principal force behind the creation of the International Ladies' Garment Workers' Union. There is little that is personal in the novel about the protagonist's interaction with Myra Jones and the others at "Smith" House. At one point in the novel Sam Kerenski inquires about the sex lives of the women at the settlement house and is told by a man, who bears some resemblance to Henry Demarest Lloyd, that perhaps they are all celibate.

June 18, 2011: The archives of the New York Public Library, again. The father of Florence Kelley's mother, Caroline, dies Nov. 5, 1838, of apoplexy on the street. Leaves five small chil-

dren who had previously lost their mother. This is when Caroline is taken in, adopted by Sarah Pugh's family (Box 14, Folder 16). A testimonial to Caroline's father, an obituary in beautifully ornate handwriting, mounted on heavy decorated paper. He must have been a remarkable man, for she was a remarkable woman. The memorial statement is serious, heartfelt, and beautifully presented and preserved.

In 1902-03 Margaret Kelley attended the Young Ladies' Seminary at Ferry Hall in Lake Forest, Illinois, an elite preparatory school known for its support of social causes. Margaret, however, was to graduate from Brookline High School in Brookline, Massachusetts.

America in the 1890s was a country where every kind of moral, political, and social question (except same-sex marriage) was on the agenda for discussion: terrorism; getting rid of the remnants of slavery; all varieties of the God question; what to do about the know-nothings, aliens, and immigrants; the poor quality and incompetence of politicians; restrictions on the franchise; whom to let in or kick out of the country; the changes brought by technology and machines, and especially the revolution brought by the railroads, the iron horse; anarchism and what to do with the anarchists; the pros and cons of capitalism and wealth; the unabashed corruption and greed of public officials; how children should be educated and raised; the autonomy of women; and the ideal structure of the family.

Anarchists and terrorism were not a theoretical threat: the assassinations of heads of state and political leaders by anarchists and mad people occurred in Europe and America, including the assassinations of President McKinley in 1901 and the mayor of Chicago in 1893.

In the 1890s people in the public arena, people running for office, took positions on political questions such as the excesses among the wealthy, the desperate condition of children in the tenements, the extremes of poverty and whom to blame for them, the improvident nature of the country's involvement in international wars, the scandals and ignorance of the government officials in Washington—these issues now considered too controversial to be discussed in public by most politicians running for office.

The trauma of the Civil War was over, the armed confrontations among the troops stopped, but little was settled. An exhausted and disillusioned citizenry looked up, saw pain, devastation, and economic collapse everywhere, and went on. And while slavery may have been legally abolished, the social, economic, and political status of Negroes and former slaves remained a matter of large and small conflict for generations.

November 10, 2012: A sudden thunderstorm, after a warm morning. Now black clouds, the upending of a bowl of water from the sky. People scattering to the shelter of the eaves of tall buildings. Then quiet.

By 1900 Florence Kelley had moved back to New York:

New York City, Jan. 19, 1901. It is bitterly cold, but clear and fine. . . . As I write, the air is full of sunshine and snow—the first snow of the season—both together. It is a wonderful winter.

This also from Florence Kelley in New York: "We are drafting a child labor law, a compulsory education law, and a license law for newsboys."

After Florence Kelley moved to New York, Nicholas went to be an "all-round handy lad" for the Trenton, Bristol and Philadelphia Street Railway Company in Bristol, Pennsylvania, while awaiting admission to Harvard College.

While visiting in Massachusetts Florence Kelley had approached a family friend about boarding John in their home while he attended the Bussey Institution—a small undergraduate school of agriculture and horticulture in Boston founded in 1872. And so everyone in the family was moving on from Chicago, leaving Hull-House.

Florence Kelley writes to Nicholas:

June 29, 02 Chicago

Ko Darling. I am writing in the octagon. The sun is shining for the second time in three weeks. Margaret is reading the morning papers in front of the grate fire in the next room. John is at breakfast with Mr. Riddle, the very nice parole officer. After dinner, we are going to see Grandma.

On July 6th Mr. Twose and John will start for Boston together where Mr. Twose will enter John at Bussey, as a regular student if he can, otherwise as a special student. . . . But I need to know your dates! Have you no Harvard catalog?

John did not do well at the Bussey Institution; Florence Kelley then tried to place him at the Sachs Collegiate Institute in New York, later known as the Franklin School, and more recently as the Dwight School, a school founded in 1872 by a brother of one of the founders of Goldman Sachs.

Caroline Bonsall Kelley was spending the summer of 1902 at the Chicago Beach Hotel in Hyde Park. George Twose, a British Hull-House resident, taught wood working and theater at Hull-House. William D. Kelley Jr., Florence Kelley's older brother, was the person generally in charge of the family affairs and finances. Her younger brother, Albert, was also watching out for her welfare. Still, a parent always has a lot of arranging to do when there are young people to be placed in appropriate educational institutions.

Florence Kelley writes to Nicholas from New York:

A wonderful piece of good fortune has come to Margaret. Mrs. Glendower Evans has asked her to be Miss Fuller's successor; to live with her and go to the Latin School. . . . Mrs. Evans has been looking for a Secretary since Miss Fuller's marriage. . . . Margaret is delighted with the idea and resumes the idea of college with fortitude. She will have her home; and will be companion and secretary. I shall keep on with her allowance for books and clothes. . . . There is no more interesting house in Boston! You know where it is, on the same row with the Brandeis' and around the corner from Miss Rose Lamb's. . . . I love to think you are taking Margaret to shows!

Lawyers say: my profession makes my words, my speech more important than the words of others because they are the words of the law. Most of those whose whereabouts and words are reported solemnly in the contemporaneous newspapers are now deeply forgotten.

Margaret enrolls in Smith College in September 1905. Her mother cautions her: "It runs in our blood to be leaders. You will find yourself one without setting out to be one. And your jests will count. A keen wit is a terrible weapon. So don't jest with your contemporaries about serious things as you could safely do with my contemporaries."

The law which so often thinks it is about something else: distributing property, meting out punishment, bringing order to chaos, righting a wrong, returning property to its legitimate owner, and always first wrapping itself in self-important language, is always first about making a record, reporting who was in the room at a particular time and place, and what the ostensible matter was.

The law is a guide in a cemetery of unmarked graves, a series of faded snapshots taken in a court at a time and place and preserved in a handwritten ledger, or in print, in a book, or a volume, or now in the cloud, for as long as the court records and newspapers, or this technology, survives. Unlikely our words will be accessible in one hundred years.

June 1, 2013: If we can't even read the computer files of two years ago, why should we assume anyone will be able to access any record of our civilization or anything we wrote? When the Internet falls from the sky from its own weight, from carrying so much trivia and detail, it won't hit the ground as print.

Dr. Alice Hamilton, who was part of Florence Kelley's original factory inspection group, discovered during a typhoid epidemic that the common fly, in great supply around the rotting garbage in the Nineteenth Ward, was an important carrier of the disease. This discovery was a contribution to the control of typhoid. During her long career, Alice Hamilton reported on industrial diseases and workplace infirmities to the eye at Pullman and other locations, and systematically documented that painters contracted lead poisoning from their work.

Elizabeth Morgan, author of *The New Slavery* report for the Chicago City Council before Florence Kelley's arrival in December 1891, was one of the first women to obtain membership in the Knights of Labor, joining Local Assembly No. 1789. She was the head of a small group of Chicago women who organized the Ladies Federal Labor Union No. 2703 in June 1888.

Both Elizabeth Morgan and her husband, Thomas Morgan, a leader of the Socialist Labor Party in Chicago, who at one point ran for mayor of Chicago, emigrated from Britain, where they had been factory workers, in the 1880s. The mixed trades union of women Elizabeth Morgan organized included clerks, book binders, candy makers, typists, dress makers, music teachers, gum makers, and other female workers. The union was chartered by the American Federation of Labor and recognized with a state legal charter. It later transformed itself into a women's advocacy group.

January 4, 2013: Something about a city in winter, the white light, how the city pulls itself around itself, as if the tall buildings tilt in and the sidewalks roll up at the curb. Today, very cold, and flecks of snow. More predicted for tomorrow. And yet the city holds its head high, is bright, alert.

In 1892 Elizabeth Morgan organized women watch makers in Elgin and shoemakers. The Ladies Federal Labor Union had twenty-three craft unions with their own legal charters. On November 2, 1888, the Chicago Women's Alliance was formed. In 1889 the Illinois General Assembly passed a new compulsory education act, mandating that children aged seven to fourteen must attend at least sixteen weeks of school or fines would be issued. A woman was appointed to the Chicago Board of Education.

October 17, 2012: My law students and I go the public meeting of the Board of Education, which takes place in a packed meeting room resembling a court. The members of the board sit on a raised platform, like judges, and look down on the parade of people who come to present their grievances, their applications for some sort of dispensation to the board. They are mostly asking for things that the board has no power to do. Nor is this is the forum where serious discussion takes place, where legal arguments are heard, or where decisions are made. The complaints are nonetheless real: the children don't learn what they need to know, the teaching is inadequate. Some of the best, as well as the worst, public schools in the country are in Chicago.

Parents never stop worrying about the children's education and welfare. John writes to his mother on stationery from the Hotel Adams in Phoenix, Arizona. No legible date. He is an adult. It's the year 1907.

Dear Mother,

Your last letter was the first cold thing I've had since I've been up against it. You blithely stated that you hoped that next time I wrote I would tell you that I had an outdoor job in the line of promotion. I can't at present fulfill your wishes. . . .

The mines are daily turning off men. Small construction projects are closing down, railroad men say they can't be sure that the railroad construction work won't stop at any time and little Johnny isn't leaving three meals a day for a wild goose chase. Isn't. Isn't.

I am looking for work every afternoon. I have run across jobs that looked pretty fine from the outside but I haven't found anything solid yet. I had an offer to camp at a shut down mine, and have a horse and gun, and four dollars a day for doing it. The horse and gun were to be turned in. The only apparent drawback was the isolation.

I was on the point of jumping at it when I stumbled on the information that the company owed the last man four hundred dollars wages. They lack ready money and made him take out shares. The mine not worth much and if it is, he has the controlling interest by this time. I am not living thirty miles from the nearest ranch for the pleasure of riding horseback and shooting quail.

I also turned down an offer to travel for a ladies wearing apparel concern. I may have been foolish but I don't believe that I'd be able to do it without grinning and of course the grin would be misconstrued and any prospective buyers would think I was handing them a gold brick.

Three days after I left Jerome five hundred men were turned away. A couple of hundred got here at about the time I got this job. There were thirty applications the day I clinched it.

I wouldn't have said anything about this but for your letter. I gather that you misunderstood the situation.

Love to ko. He never answered the letter I wrote him c/o of his agents. Love from J.

June 2011: The New York Public Library Archives. As a young man, John migrates south and then west, works as a cowboy, a horse handler, ending up for a while in Denver in hard times. Working in a rodeo, he breaks a leg. He then is hired as a night clerk at a hotel. His mother periodically sends him money, but reluctantly, perhaps remembering her own propensity to borrow. Later he will be a sailor, a journalist, and become involved in a political campaign on the West Coast, all the while writing about what it is like where he is, there, then. The writing gene passing from William Darrah Kelley, through Florence Kelley, to John Bartram Kelley. What he leaves: a strange, shredded spiritualist manuscript in the Cornell

University archives, too fragile to copy or mail via inter-library loan. Yet, John's idealism, his trenchant prose style, his passion seem to resemble hers. His letters are vivid, personal, glimpses of a long-gone world and web of relationships.

Another letter, later, on the letterhead of the Ford Hotel: "Strictly First Class," Corner of Washington Street and Second Avenue, in Denver. The same year, 1907.

Dearest Mother

I am still hunting a job but it is really very discouraging. I might get a job carrying letters but I can't stand the walking. [John is still suffering from his broken leg.]

I've left the Adams as I can't afford to pay three a day and it would be foolish to spend it even if I could.

Somehow I feel as though the manager played me dirty in getting his old friend out without saying a word about it. But it's all in a lifetime and I don't get it any rougher than the rest of us. If it wasn't for your check I guess I'd be pretty hungry about now.

I don't like to go to a rooming house because so many sick people are in there. Still I guess I'll be all right before long and earning my living. I've got to be. This perpetual spending where you can't think what to do when the money is gone gets on one's nerves. And I've got to get a job if it's only cleaning streets.

I'll try to write a more cheerful letter next time. My mail may still go to the Adams as I call for it there.

Miss Lilian is really very nice and I'm glad to have met her.

Your loving son, John Bartram Kelley.

In August 1891, before Florence Kelley's arrival in Chicago, Abraham Bisno, president of the Chicago Cloak Makers' Union, reported that the General Assembly had set up a committee, including two residents of Hull-House. Elizabeth Morgan's report on "the sweating system" was completed September 6, 1891. Florence Kelley didn't come to Chicago and introduce the issue of the sweatshops and child labor. The issue was already on the table.

The public outcry was fueled by a fear (a realistic fear) of wearing contaminated garments: clothing infected with smallpox, diphtheria, scarlet fever, and typhoid. Elizabeth Morgan sent her report to the US Congress, and this is what triggered the congressional investigation in Chicago in April 1892.

Soon after Abraham Bisno's arrival in Chicago around 1881, he became active in union organizing. His own autobiography may not be accurate about the chronology.

The legal record does show him testifying about the conditions in the sweatshops before the US congressional committee in Chicago, and there he refers to his arrival as a boy of sixteen.

June 2008: Back from Doha. I am not inclined to travel there again, and not just because of the long journey. The educational enterprise is impressive, as is the input from our own institution.

A visit to a court in Doha, where after some effort I finally found someone who could translate for me, revealed much that was surprising: including, many Western-dressed (most, but not all, wearing head scarves) women lawyers among the lawyers standing and waiting. The lawyers are waiting for the functionary present in every court system: the court clerk or bailiff or assignment judge, the immediately recognizable person sitting behind an enormous stack of files, the person whose job it is to tell the lawyers when their cases will be heard, and by which judge. For Florence Kelley's factory inspection cases, that position was held by Judge Kersten.

Such a person is always enormously powerful. In Doha, he was a British-educated Sudanese lawyer of the old school, polite, trained, skilled, with a dark, pockmarked face, perhaps scarred by smallpox. Like most of the professionals in Doha, the court bailiff is not a native of the country.

And so the children carry on the legacy of their parents, or not. On January 21, 1920, a special grand jury in Chicago that had been investigating "red" activities in Cook County returned indictments against William Bross Lloyd, described as a "millionaire socialist," and thirty-seven other alleged members of the Communist Party. The return of the grand jury was made before well-known Cook County State's Attorney Robert E. Crowe. Those indicted were members of the national executive committee of the Communist Party, including three women. They were charged with conspiring to overthrow the government. Once again, conspiracy theory proved useful as a vehicle for the prosecution.

The indictments were an outgrowth of raids by agents of the state's attorney on New Year's Eve, twenty-four hours before a national roundup of reds was launched. The arrests were part of a large national campaign to incarcerate or deport communists under the authority of newly enacted state and federal statutes criminalizing being a member of the Communist Party and plotting the overthrow the government.

This attack upon reds and socialists led to riots and the closing of many political organizations. Over the years there were periodic attacks upon Florence Kelley for her socialist affiliations and views.

June 18, 2011: New York Public Library Archives. The picture of Hull-House in 1893 (Box 14, Folder 21) shows a large, imposing structure. And yet Jane Addams always refers to it as being a gracious home. The house stands squarely against the elements, windows stolidly facing out in a direct confrontation with the weather. This is a house whose presence makes a statement about its permanence. No wonder Jane Addams and Ellen Gates Starr fell in love with it and wanted it for their new settlement house, to be their home.

William Lloyd was the oldest of the Lloyd children, a few years older than Nicholas Kelley, and, with his siblings, a lifelong friend of the Kelley family. Described in a news account as a "millionaire resident of Evanston," William Bross Lloyd was a sergeant-at-arms of the Communist Labor Party. His indictment was partly based on a statement he made in newspaper interviews after the roundup of other reds. He proclaimed himself as the "reddest of the red," basically challenging the state's attorney to arrest him.

Cases were brought against an additional eighty-six members of the Communist Party and thirty-eight members of the Industrial Workers of the World, based on indictments returned by a single grand jury. Some of the indictments were stricken with leave to reinstate, meaning they could be revived if additional evidence were to be found. The assistant state's attorney explained that in the previous IWW cases most of the men indicted had been convicted on similar federal charges before Judge Kenesaw Mountain Landis in federal court, and thus the state prosecutors were unnecessary, although not barred by double jeopardy.

William Bross Lloyd was eventually released on bond of $3,000, on order of Illinois Supreme Court Justice Carter in November 1921 after a conviction at the trial court in September 1919. The appeal was expedited. Justice George Sutherland of the Supreme Court of the United States refused to take further action in the case. After being accused of fleeing to Michigan after the conviction, William Lloyd did surrender a few days later to the authorities and was taken to Joliet prison.

The trial lasted ten weeks. One of the chief witnesses was Ole Hanson, a former mayor of Seattle, which had had a general strike a year earlier. One of Lloyd's offenses was that he had driven down State Street in Chicago with both a red flag and an American flag flying from his car. The jury was out only a few hours before coming back with a verdict of guilty. Lloyd was given a sentence of one to five years and fined $2,000. All twenty of his codefendants were also convicted.

The case went to the Supreme Court of Illinois as People v. William Bross Lloyd, et al., plaintiffs in error, 304 Ill. 23 (October 5, 1922). William Bross Lloyd was represented by Clarence Darrow.

The Supreme Court of Illinois upheld the verdicts.

June 18, 2011: The New York Public Library Archives. In the letters, there are many from John. He misspells words, omits parts of sentences, writes awkwardly. Sometimes others are writing for him from school. When he is at the Hillside School his mother wants him to get a goat for a pet, because it is cheap. He wants a pony. His love of horses and his familiarity with them will be lifelong. His first pony, which he loves, is named Bonito. Correspondence with his mother continues until her death since both are often traveling. It is he who comes and brings her from Maine to Philadelphia when she is dying.

Margaret loves clothes and is reported to be handsome, tall, and with a striking carriage. There are few pictures of Margaret in the archives.

There are many stiff letters from Florence Kelley's older brother, William Darrah Kelley Jr., the same whom she took care of in Avignon and who later came to testify in Chicago at the habeas hearing. William Darrah Kelley Jr. as the oldest brother becomes the person who handles the money and is responsible for keeping track of the family. His letters are dutiful, careful, reporting on the health of their mother, other relatives and friends, his own family's health, the deaths of family friends, other items of interest. The tone of these letters is flat, somewhat lifeless. He often is apologetic, as if he were frowning as he writes.

Chief Justice Orrin Carter—the son of the Justice Carter who was on the Supreme Court of Illinois when the factory inspection case was decided—dissented from the opinion of the Supreme Court of Illinois upholding the convictions of the "reds" and saying this about the legislation enacted by the Illinois General Assembly which made it a crime to advocate the overthrow of the government:

The law of this State enacted in 1919 is so drastic and far-reaching in its provisions that many public utterances of the great leaders in our past history would have been punishable under its provisions. Had this law then been in force, parts of President Lincoln's first inaugural address could have been suppressed from publication. . . . This law of 1919 not only seems to be intended to prevent any acts that would attempt to change the existing laws by force but to prevent all wild or foolish talk advocating such changes, and to suppress all public utterances, whether wise or unwise, advocating changes that may result in an attempt to bring about such changes by force. Legislative enactments or decisions of courts cannot prevent people from believing that laws should be changed. . . . Other rulings of the trial court might well be considered so objectionable as to justify a reversal of this verdict, but aside from all other questions it seems to me that under the well settled rules of law, under the constitution of 1870, governing freedom of speech, this Overthrow Statute of 1919 should be considered so vague and general and so clearly against the American doctrine of freedom of speech as to be held unconstitutional. [Carter, J. dissenting, People v. Lloyd, 304 Il. 23, 136 N.E. 505 (1922)]

Governor Len Small, on November 29, 1922, pardoned sixteen of the twenty defendants. One had fled to Russia; another forfeited bond; two others died during the pendency of the appeal. Lloyd did go to prison, but not for long; there is a newspaper report of his release from Joliet.

June 18, 2013: The story of the eighty-ninth Illinois exoneration made the front page of the Chicago Tribune this morning. Our lawyers were remarkably restrained in their commentary upon the prosecutors, police, and judges who imposed and upheld the conviction and imprisonment of an innocent person.

In the novel based upon his life, the character based upon Abraham Bisno, Kerenski, is admitted to the Bar. However, no record has been found verifying Bisno's admission to the Bar in Illinois or New York. Nor could any record be found of his applying to or taking classes at Northwestern University School of Law, although at one point Florence Kelley mentions in a letter that Bisno is about to start law classes.

Bisno's outspoken advocacy did not interfere with his many public speaking appearances, including at Northwestern University. The firebrand anarchist Johann Most, openly advocating violence against individuals and the authorities, spoke freely in Chicago several times, as did the Marx-Avelings, again without interference or prosecution. The sudden change of mood culminating in the arrest of the reds across the country in 1919 remains striking.

The *Chicago Daily Law Bulletin* reports on November 7, 2012:

Two Illinois Supreme Court justices won big electoral victories Tuesday, potentially paving the way for an era of stability on the seven-person bench. . . .

The victory for the 63-year-old Democrat [Justice Mary Jane Theis] ensures her party maintains a majority on the court through at least 2018, barring any unexpected departures or retirements.

March 2008: For our Northwestern law students now, few will not pass the Bar. The bar review course efficiently prepares students for the exam. The state bar associations have outsourced the enterprise to professional testers who worry about how to outsmart the bar candidates. Some say an intelligent, diligent student could pass the bar without ever going to law school, just by taking the bar review course. Many very profitable businesses prepare students for the Bar and for the admissions test for law schools. Recent graduates and law students are employed in the business of preparing students for the tests. The promise of the high salaries, a promise not always kept, drives many to the elite schools. More than one successful entrepreneur says all her contacts, all her initial funding came from people associated with her Ivy League college.

By 1901 John Peter Altgeld was devoting himself to the practice of law and had joined the firm of Darrow and Thompson, where Clarence Darrow was making money. John Peter Altgeld did not think a true public servant should be employed by anyone, or serve anyone, but the people.

January 2, 2009: The family has departed in different directions. The house is eerily quiet, the children gone, only the mounds of wet towels, the empty refrigerators, the dishwashers full, cupboards empty, the wastebaskets overflowing with Kleenex. If only they didn't have to take a plane to get here.

We swam in an igloo, because something was broken in the pool house so the inside of the pool housing became encrusted with ice as the steam rose off the uncovered, heated pool and froze as it met the freezing walls. It was the coldest December in years. So we were polar bears jumping into the pool, poking our heads above the steaming blue surface, then running to shower through the unheated corridor in our wet bathing suits and up the stairs.

A lot of laughter. They will always have, I hope, laughter among and with each other, and in their lives. So soon the alliances are set, so soon the character, the personality is formed. Remember the giggles, the laughter on the stairs, the laughter at the table, if nothing else.

On March 11, 1902, John Peter Altgeld had spent all day in trial before Judge Kohlsaat in Chancery Court arguing against an injunction which had been imposed upon a union engaged in a strike against the Pennsylvania railroad. At the end of the day, he continued on to Joliet for a speaking engagement, before a meeting called by sympathizers of the Boers (against the British colonists) in what was described as "distant country in Africa."

Unknown to the man himself, a secret pact among his friends had been formed ensuring that Altgeld should never be allowed to travel alone. A friend who later became a judge was supposed to accompany Altgeld to Joliet that evening, but he could not for some reason, and another friend went instead. Altgeld admitted to being tired on the train and remembered that in the excitement of the trial he had forgotten to eat any lunch, contrary to his regular habit of having a substantial lunch, usually including two pieces of pie for dessert.

In the train diner, he ate a large steak even though his own rule was that a person about to engage in public speaking should never eat before a performance. He felt better for the steak. But when he arrived at Joliet, he again complained of being tired. Initially he could not get into his room at the Hotel Munroe. The best room in the hotel had been set aside for him and it was not ready. Finally when he was settled in a room, a newspaper editor wanted to interview him, so there was no time to rest, and then he proceeded to his event to speak.

January 14, 2013: Finally it is cold, but clear, and blue skies. Many at the office sick with the flu. I have avoided a funeral on the excuse that a talk has to be prepared. I instead gave away about forty books from my private library, some sort of an achievement. Why would anyone want to contribute to the glut and write another one?

A chorus was scheduled to sing before Altgeld's speech, and it did. Then Altgeld spoke vigorously for forty-five minutes, while perspiring heavily and wiping his forehead repeatedly throughout.

In his closing he said:

I am not discouraged. Things will right themselves. The pendulum swings one way and then the other. But the steady pull of gravitation is towards the center of the earth. . . . The gravitation of eternal justice is upward toward the throne of God. Any political institution if it is going to endure must be plumb with that line of justice.

When the next speaker talked, Altgeld said he felt dizzy and then staggered as he stepped off the stage. Then he was seized with a violent attack of vomiting. He was laid on the stage for an hour before it was considered advisable to move him.

The Illinois Medical Society was holding its annual banquet in Joliet, and several doctors came in response to the call. They found him in a coma, but they revived him to the point that he recognized one of the doctors and engaged in some banter over the most efficient way to unbutton his shirt.

Then the newspaper reporters came. Altgeld asked them to forbear from reporting on his illness in the newspapers in order not to alarm his wife. At midnight Clarence Darrow was sent for, and in the early morning John Peter Altgeld was pronounced dead. Even his old enemy the *Chicago Tribune* had nothing but praise for him in its report of his death:

Friends of Mr. Altgeld say that he had begun to express a desire to quit the practice of law and that he was dissatisfied with it. . . . He never, according to these friends, had been more active than during the few days just preceding his death. His movements in the last few days illustrate this. On Saturday night he spoke in Buffalo. On Monday and Tuesday he appeared in the federal courts, and Tuesday night he was speaking in Joliet.

As it is affirmed that every one of Mr. Altgeld's addresses represented much care, forethought, and preparation, these occasions became a strain for him. Each address was carefully written by him and changed and then dictated to a stenographer, during which process he learned it by rote and could repeat it line for line.

January 5, 2013: A grey and desolate, cold day in Chicago, in the teens, and waiting for snow. The traffic piled up on the highway. Dark at five, even though the solstice is behind us.

At his funeral, it was said, the scene was "a bleak landscape stretching away from his open grave, fierce March winds bearing down the bitter cold of a northern blizzard as they howled through the leafless trees, tumbling waves beating on the nearby shore of the angry Lake, and a lowering but not altogether sunless sky overhanging the scene."

Jane Addams and Clarence Darrow were the only outside speakers at Altgeld's funeral. His casket was carried to the Chicago Public Library to lie in state. As one account described it, forty thousand to fifty thousand people stood in a double line in the pouring rain to pay him tribute:

All day long they stood, in imperceptibly moving line: the common people, care-worn, toil-stained, wet to their thinly covered skins, men and women and children together, waiting to look upon the dead face of the man who had borne their troubles in his heart.

Then, the work, and everyone's lives, continued:

June 21st Saturday (1902)

Florence Kelley to her mother, Caroline

Your letter of the 17th came yesterday with the check for which please accept my heartfelt thanks. But I am at a loss to imagine how you make both ends meet and still give me so much help!

We have had a very happy week. The exams went off well and the last two days of festivities have been charming.

Margaret is the most beautiful girl I ever saw. I suppose every mother's only daughter is so in the maternal eyes. But Margaret's figure is so willowy that I think she must be very much as you were when a girl. Although her dresses are very simple she wears them with a distinction amazing in a chick of her years. The commencement was yesterday, and the dance last evening and, this morning nearly everyone went home.

There has been a heavy rain and the country is looking its loveliest.

Dear John blossomed out in long, white duck pants and a picque blouse-shirt with high collar. He was so happy that he illumined his part of the hall with his radiance.

I think we shall leave here on July 7th for Rockford, where our address will be Rockford College until July 15th. Then I shall start on a journey among the factories.

We have not yet had one uncomfortably hot day this summer. While I have been well of my diphtheria for some time, I am only now accumulating reserve strength. I feel very well and sleep an amount truly astonishing to the children.

I cannot help thinking that you will be the better for getting away from the Biddies!

I only hope you may find a nice place. This will reach you at Bryn Mawr, but I do not know about the next letter after this.

Please give my love to Mrs. Lloyd and to Bert when you see him. It is a great comfort to think of him in his new office. Ko seems to be staying all this month in Boston. I am sorry he is not at the sea-shore, but Mrs. Lloyd's good food and coddling will certainly not come amiss after the wintery frugality.

Your loving FK.

P.S. Please give me Will's address. I have lost the box number.

December 19, 2012: It looks and feels like snow in Chicago today, about 30 degrees, crisp, crinkling the nose. Too much time in the hospital. Health is the most important thing to be grateful for, for life. And how vigorously we deny, repress the fleetingness of it all. We must resist that recognition or we could not go on. Only religious mystics, or poets, can keep the inevitability, the capriciousness of death in the forefront of their consciousness all the time. Poetry, the worship of some god, brings relief. The grey backdrop to the somber concrete hospital buildings makes them look like the fortresses they are against the winter, against the grey skies, and our fear.

When Florence Kelley moved to New York in 1899, Nicholas came with her. Margaret and John stayed at the Hillside School as boarders. The children spent all of August and September of 1899 at Hull-House. Jane Addams became even closer to Margaret. In December 1899, the Kelley family was together at Hull-House for Christmas. By then Florence Kelley was living in New York and working at the National Consumers' League.

August 2009: I did not expect it, but the happiest memories of living here, and of that big old house, are of Christmases there.

This year the ceremony of it and the occasion were enough to make everyone feel something, if not a religious feeling. And when it snowed, the house and garden were blanketed; no one had to go anywhere, and there was a fire in the fireplace.

Later, the children said, there were so many places to hide there, including the secret hiding place behind the paneling beneath the stairs.

In the 1920s still about a thousand people a month came to Hull-House. In 1925 six thousand paid showers and twelve thousand baths were taken there. Benny Goodman played in the Hull-House Boys Band, and there were lessons in piano, violin, organ, drama.

There were more than sixty clubs and classes, including classes in serving and dress making. It was the oldest settlement music school in the country. Drama was a method of education, the method with instant, universal appeal. Free classes in citizenship were offered after the 1906 naturalization law required applicants to have some knowledge of history in preparation to receive citizenship papers.

Sunday, June 11, 2006: The tenement house museum in New York is on Orchard Street, a few blocks from the Henry Street Settlement where Florence Kelley lived after Hull-House. The rooms with their many layers of wallpaper, small, dark, outdoor plumbing, but actually the rooms not as small as I expected. By the 1920s Mexicans had become the largest ethnic group surrounding Hull-House. Many were skilled artisans.

Late in 1904 Florence Kelley spent Christmas with a friend down the street from where the Brandeis family lived in Cambridge, Massachusetts. She had all three children with her. It was the home of Mrs. Ellen Glendower, who was to hire Margaret as a personal secretary. Margaret worked two years there before enrolling in Smith College.

"You can't think what this means to me, to have my children, all of them with me. Such a thing has rarely happened in my life," Florence Kelley wrote in a letter of thanks to Mrs. Glendower.

November 19, 2012: Another fine day, just a few white clouds. Another trip planned. This is how we distract ourselves.

And always, how are the young people? So easy to be lulled into the mindset: everything will continue, everything will be fine. Even with the most assiduous care, preparation, tragedy happens, history happens, lives are upended, expectations scratched. The ancient Greeks knew the gods are vengeful.

In New York Florence Kelley did not forget the stinging defeat handed down by the Supreme Court of Illinois in *Ritchie*. In addition to her service on advisory boards and commissions on workplace conditions, especially with regard to women and children, an opportunity presented itself in 1907. The Oregon Supreme Court upheld the constitutionality of a state statute limiting the working hours of women in laundries and "similar establishments" to ten hours in a day. The law actually said "manufacturing, mechanical establishments, and laundries." In other words, it was a statute similar to the hours provision of the Illinois factory inspection statute that the Supreme Court of Illinois had struck down in 1895, except that the number was ten hours, not eight. And the law was simply an hours law.

A prosecution had been brought under the law against an overseer at Curt Muller's Grand Laundry in Portland for requiring Mrs. Elmer Gocher to work more than ten hours. He was found guilty of a misdemeanor and fined ten dollars. The conviction was appealed. The structure of the case was very similar to the challenge to the Illinois Factory and Workshop Inspection Law.

The justification for the Oregon statute limiting work hours was to protect the health of the women, the same as the justification for the hours provision in Illinois. Louis Brandeis agreed to take the case *pro bono* and was insistent upon representing the state of Oregon, not simply on being *amicus*, so that he could control the litigation. From the outset he wanted the case to be centered on upholding the legislation as a protection for women's health. Brandeis was determined to structure the argument before the Supreme Court of the United States as one based upon facts, scientific research, and documented damage to women's health due to long hours and overwork. If another lawyer had been in charge of the litigation, it would have been structured differently.

February 10, 2010: Where is everyone today, in the winter dark? The semester has started; the students are cheerful, gleefully complaining about the weather. They call their mothers in California and report the subzeros.

Brandeis proposed to put these issues before the court in a new way. His argument and brief marked a radical departure in the defense of protective labor laws. The defense of the statute as constitutional confined itself to tangible human elements: the health, welfare, and economic efficiency of women.

In a brief of more than 100 pages, he devoted only two to the legal aspect of the case, and over 100 to a new kind of testimony: mankind's experience, physical and moral, with respect to women in industry and their working conditions and hours. The document was made up from the accumulated mass of British and continental factory inspectors' reports, commissions, and legislative findings, as well as the findings of medical men and economists.

When it came down, the decision in the Oregon case was no narrow victory. It was the most sweeping decision ever rendered by the Supreme Court of the United States in relation to working conditions and hours. In a word, the highest court in the nation rejected the fiction of the free contract as regards the working woman and declared that "the evil effects of overwork upon her and her future children justify legislation to protect her from the greed as well as the passion of men." The new method of argument had amply justified itself.

There was another advantage to the Oregon statute as a vehicle for challenging in another venue the holding in *Ritchie*. There were basically no laundry men, so the statute did not result in any real discrimination against male workers. The statute had been supported on appeal by the Oregon Consumers' League, which then along with the Oregon attorney general brought the appeal to the Supreme Court of the United States. This was a group that Florence Kelley had assisted in founding. Perhaps she had a part in drafting the Oregon statute. None of her biographers mention her playing that role, but she did consult with the Oregon Consumers' League and other state chapters, and she did travel to Portland on behalf of the league several times before 1907 to help found the Oregon chapter.

March 17, 2012: The streets of Chicago are filled with young couples, laughing, families, young women and men, everyone wearing green, silly green paper hats, green vests. Many are not sober. The temperance people had something. Today the Chicago River will be dyed green. The weather a balmy eighty degrees, the city is sparkling after yesterday's noisy thunderstorm. It is a party, a citywide party, a very drunken party.

Laundry women were not a small or invisible segment of the class of working women, yet this Oregon statute did not carry the political baggage of the challenges to the hours legislation regarding tenement workers in the clothing industry in Illinois. The Oregon statute simply limited the number of hours worked by women in laundries (as well as manufacturers and similar establishments) to ten. There was nothing in the statute creating a state bureaucracy, nothing about inspections, epidemics, or people paid to enforce the statute. It was simply an hours provision, and it applied only to women.

The results of challenges to similar statutes regarding workplace conditions were mixed at the state supreme court level. *Ritchie*, with its unequivocal rhetoric and reliance upon federal constitutional law, continued to carry considerable influence more than ten years after it was decided by the Supreme Court of Illinois.

July 2008: It is hot, and the city in the summer throbs with sweaty energy. Everyone complains about the heat, but actually it is mostly pleasant. We have the garden and can sit outside in the evening and in the morning.

The work of the Illinois Committee to Study the Reform of the Death Penalty continues, with little accomplished. The committee meets, we hear testimony. The state's attorneys and the attorney general remain stubbornly opposed to any changes in current practices. They sing the same song: the death penalty statute has been reformed; the practices which led to wrongful convictions have been removed. No change is necessary. And since the prosecutors are a majority of the committee members, our final report will be formulaic, toothless. Stacking the deck with prosecutors on the committee has been an effective strategy.

The Consumers' League of Oregon notified the National Consumers' League as soon as the Supreme Court of the United States decided to take the case. When word of the decision of the Supreme Court of Oregon reached the board members of the National Consumers' League in New York, one of the men on the board recommended that Florence Kelley go see one Mr. Joseph Choate, described as "the foremost lawyer" in the city, a former ambassador to China, to enlist his aid in arguing the case before the Supreme Court of the United States.

National Board Secretary Florence Kelley was not happy that this overture to a well-known New York attorney had been made by a board member of the league without consulting her while she was away on a speaking trip. She had someone else in mind. Now there was a delicate dilemma: how to put off the distinguished member of the New York Bar, and a friend of a board member, from taking the appeal to the Supreme Court of the United States without offending him or the member of her board who had contacted him.

March 25, 2012: We might be living in California next. Today a California day: blue skies, breezy. Everyone running, walking by the lake. The softness of the spring air, so distinctive. I'm wondering, what has happened to those educational institutions of the late nineteenth century? They have certainly changed. McKendree College, Knox College, the Chicago College of Law, founded by Judge Thomas Moran and Justice Joseph Bailey—the schools attended by the judges and lawyers in Florence Kelley's time.

Florence Kelley and Josephine Goldmark called upon the same distinguished Mr. Choate at his convenience in his luxurious private law offices. The conversation began with some complimentary references to Mrs. Kelley's father.

As Josephine Goldmark recalled the scene in her biography of Florence Kelley: Mr. Choate first emphasized how busy he was, and much pressed for time. What did this Oregon law do after all, the lawyer said in his booming voice: "A law prohibiting more than ten hours a day in laundry work? Big, strong, laundry women," he continued. "Why shouldn't they work longer?"

Florence Kelley saw her opportunity and jumped in immediately: "Why not indeed?" she replied in her most charming and agreeable manner. She apologized for taking the time and attention of such a busy, important man for such a small matter. The two women promptly exited before the discussion would be extended and the lawyer be given a chance to reconsider.

June 18, 2011: The New York Public Library Archives. A church where the past is worshipped. Outside New York has more tourists and more languages are heard than ever: Chinese, Korean,

French, Russian, German, Spanish, Arabic. A group of women in full-length black Muslim dress, and head scarves, walking briskly into Saks Fifth Avenue across the street.

Before his appointment to the Supreme Court of the United States, Louis Brandeis was already well-known as a champion of workers. In 1908 he urged a comprehensive system of social insurance against the hazard of industrial accidents, illness, old age, and unemployment. He also was Josephine Goldmark's brother-in-law.

Florence Kelley knew she wanted Louis Brandeis to argue the case for the Oregon Consumers' League and for the National Consumers' League as soon as she heard the Supreme Court of the United States had agreed to hear the case. After their visit to Mr. Choate, Josephine Goldmark and Florence Kelley left for Boston to visit Louis Brandeis at his home, to ask him to take the case. While the ruling by the Oregon Supreme Court upheld the hours statute, the specter of the US Supreme Court's precedent loomed large, and *Ritchie* remained an obstacle.

April 29, 2012: The day after, and the day after, and the day after. Grey, rainy. Italics for direct first-person voice, the direct quotes from a printed source are once more removed and need another style of presentation. These are the words which have come down to us. How to judge the truthfulness, or even the simple factual accuracy of any statement from the past? The statements regarding "thoughts" or "feelings" or even the holding of "opinions" are unknowable, even if written down. At the time they existed as a dialogue in a heart or mind. Yet, there is something called the ring of truth which can be heard in these accounts.

Louis Brandeis had become radicalized in 1892 by Mary Kenney's description of the armed violence between steelworkers and management in Homestead, Pennsylvania, near Pittsburgh, when Andrew Carnegie decided not to renew his company's contract with the steelworkers and refused to deal with the union. Mary Kenney, the same woman who was Florence Kelley's colleague at Hull-House, traveled to the scene and later described to Brandeis the wall with apertures for guns that the company had mounted around the mill.

The contract expired; wages were slashed; the steelworkers went on strike. Henry Clay Frick, the company manager, hired Pinkerton guards and sailed up the Ohio River to protect the strikebreakers who had been hired by the company.

A pitched battle ensued, with most of the casualties being taken by the strikers. Louis Brandeis, who was at the time preparing an early course on business law for the Massachusetts Institute of Technology, said that he "saw at once that the common law, built up under simpler conditions of living, gave an inadequate basis for the adjustment of the complex relations of the modern factory system."

Louis Brandeis had met Mary Kenney through his friendship with his neighbor in Cambridge, Mrs. Glendower Evans (the same family friend whom Florence Kelley visited with her children at Christmas in 1904). Mary Kenney was at the time, in addition to being a labor organizer and advocate, a reporter on labor matters for the *Boston Globe*.

Louis Brandeis's biographer, Philippa Strum, describes the evolution of his views:

It was the shock of that armed battle, where "organized capital hired a private army to shoot at organized labor for resisting an arbitrary cut in wages," which urged Brandeis to begin a searching study of the relations of labor and industry. He came to the conclusion that law was a dynamic entity, reflecting changing social conditions, and must keep pace with the new phenomenon of highly concentrated capital if it were to have moral authority. In the Homestead Mill matter the law upheld Carnegie's right to hire armed troops, while denying the union the right to organize. Nor would that have been an unusual alignment of the law.

In his private practice Brandeis's clients were mostly small manufacturers or retail merchants. His parents were part of that large and influential group of 1848 Prussians who left Germany. They were not socialists or radicals; however, they brought to America their commitment to education, an intellectual life, and justice.

In Boston, after Florence Kelley's presentation to him of the case, Louis Brandeis agreed to represent the Oregon Consumers' League and the National Consumers' League, to write the brief and do the oral argument before the Supreme Court of the United States, on two conditions: first, that the attorney general of Oregon must invite him to defend the law on behalf of the State of Oregon, and second, that the two women from the National Consumers' League, Josephine Goldmark and Florence Kelley, must compile a compendium of all facts published by anyone with expert knowledge of "industry in its relation to women's hours of labor, such as factory inspectors, physicians, trades unions, economists, social workers." And this factual research must be accomplished in two weeks. The brief was also to include a compendium of relevant and analogous laws.

Their work cut out for them, Florence Kelley, Josephine Goldmark, and a few others gave up all other engagements to devote their entire time to this research. Industrial medicine had yet to be founded by Dr. Alice Hamilton and others, but there were medical studies and other reports on the effect of long hours on women's health.

January 10, 2012: Former Governor George Ryan is due to be released from prison imminently. He is in his late 70s, but his parole officers say he can't get out until there is a work release plan for him. One of the legal battles after his conviction was whether he could keep his state pensions. His wife died while he was in prison.

As they prepared their brief, the New York Public Library and the Columbia University Library were their archive and resource. The women were allowed to take out any reference works they needed. Initially they were not permitted to take out the British Sessional Papers, and it was there that they found extensive documentation from British factory inspectors dating to 1833, records comparing experience with long and short hours. French, German, Italian, and Belgian reports were consulted, as well as reports from Massachusetts.

Skeptics said such a compendium would never be read through by the justices of the Supreme Court of the United States. Mr. Brandeis, however, was pleased with the voluminous research presented to him a short time later. He wrote a brief with just a few pages of legal argument and attached this compendium of "facts of common knowledge." This was a bold and unprecedented move. Louis Brandeis credited Josephine Goldmark, identifying her as his assistant since she was not a lawyer. Florence Kelley's name does not appear anywhere in the brief or in the litigation.

November 9, 2012: Like spring, blue skies, white clouds, mild temperatures, the weather mocking us for expecting some heaven-sent reprieve. Meanwhile New York has a record snowstorm; New Jersey is buried, all traffic stopped, buried houses, cars. People could hardly get out to vote, yet they did. Flat-out exhausted from standing for four hours in a huge, milling crowd, waiting, waiting. But worth it.

Louis Brandeis's unusual brief caused a stir in the legal community, with factions strongly in favor of and strongly opposed to its style of presenting facts, the facts themselves and their relevance, and its minimal argument about the law. The brief was much discussed in academic circles. Both Louis Brandeis and the Oregon attorney general argued in person before the Supreme Court of the United States.

On February 24, 1909, the Supreme Court of the United States unanimously held the Oregon ten-hour law constitutional. The form of the brief was cited with approval by Justice Brewer in his opinion in Muller v. Oregon, 208 U.S. 412 (1908), which Florence Kelley immediately and correctly branded as "epoch making." Brandeis's brief immediately became even more in demand in law schools and university libraries, and was followed. A new form of legal argument had been created.

November 10, 2012: And now I am felled with the flu, even after having a flu shot, and can not drag myself out of bed. It must have been four hours in the crowd, the foreign crowd with new germs. Or getting on another plane. The relief, the happiness nonetheless is a consolation.

What remained then was to bring the issue back to the Supreme Court of Illinois. After Muller v. Oregon, Florence Kelley and Josephine Goldmark applied for a grant from the Russell Sage Foundation and over the period of 1908 to 1909 collected additional medical and scientific reports from around the world on the experience of working long hours in factories and its effect upon women's health. The new research, as well as all that was gathered for the brief in Muller, was made available to all labor people defending women's hours laws, and Louis Brandeis stood ready to enter a case in another state with a brief as *amicus* in hand, upon invitation of the attorney general of the state in question. The research was later published as a book by Josephine Goldmark.

The women were punctilious in their deference to the state officials. Josephine Goldmark recalled many spirited meetings in attorneys' offices around the country, meetings flavored with "picturesque language and shrouded in the most rank cigar smoke." They always got their invitation to join the challenges, however, in Virginia, Michigan, Louisiana, California, Illinois, Washington, and Ohio. The battle continued with renewed energy in support of protective legislation for women, regarding not just hours, but conditions of night work and the specific conditions for women workers in hospitals and factories.

January 10, 2012: Grey, rain forecast, but no snow yet in Chicago. Something is changing in the air. There was snow in Indiana and Michigan. The evident incompetence of government continues, with the state legislature and governor being unable to figure out how to get out of the pension debts irresponsibly created by unions, legislators, and others whose only concern seems to have been getting reelected.

Illinois was of course of special concern for Florence Kelley. The mood had shifted again in Illinois, and a ten-hour law modeled upon the Oregon statute was quickly passed by the state legislature after the Supreme Court of the United States handed down *Muller*. An injunction against the enforcement of the new statute was immediately sought by Ritchie & Company, the paper box manufacturer that was the lead plaintiff in the original challenge to the hours provision in the 1893 factory inspection statute. This would become the first case after *Muller* to bring the federal constitutional issues before a state supreme court. Florence Kelley quickly secured the participation of Louis Brandeis for the oral argument before the Supreme Court of Illinois and to submit a brief on the merits. An Illinois lawyer of distinction, a newly appointed ambassador to China, was also engaged.

February 6, 2013: Winter has arrived in a fury, making majestic patterns in ice on the surface of the lake, bold strokes in the night.

Mr. Brandeis's brief again contained only a few pages of legal argument, the rest of the brief being a compendium of facts. Levy Mayer did not represent the factory owners, although the Illinois Manufacturers' Association brought the litigation again. The factual part of the brief in Illinois was even more extensive than the brief presented to the Supreme Court of the United States in *Muller*, due to additional research by Florence Kelley and Josephine Goldmark supported by the Russell Sage Foundation. The factual appendix was more than 600 pages, a compendium of scientific and medical research and relevant laws from around the world.

Louis Brandeis made an arduous journey by train from Washington, DC, in bitter winter weather to lead the oral argument in Springfield. He had obtained a three-day adjournment of an important US Senate investigation in order to personally argue the case before the Supreme Court of Illinois. The paper box manufacturer and the Illinois Manufacturers' Association were represented by William Duff Haynie of Haynie and Lust. Levy Mayer wisely left the legal work to others.

On April 21, 1910, the Supreme Court of Illinois handed down its decision in the second *Ritchie* case (Ritchie v. Wayman, 244 Ill. 509 [1910]). The court upheld the new Illinois ten-hour law on the basis of the same federal constitutional principles as in the earlier *Ritchie* case. The court did not overrule its earlier decision in the factory inspection case, however, although the earlier decision was in effect overruled. The Supreme Court of Illinois similarly never overruled its opinion in the Haymarket case, even though the holding, the imposition of the death penalty for conspiracy to commit a murder, had long since been discredited. Both opinions—the first *Ritchie* opinion and the Haymarket judgment—were unanimous rulings written by Justice Benjamin Magruder, the Yale graduate on the court.

After the decision upholding the ten-hour law in Illinois was handed down, Florence Kelley commented in her National Consumers' League *Annual Report*:

> If the National Consumers' League had done no other useful thing besides its contribution towards this decision, our eleven years of existence would be justified by this alone. . . . The old Ritchie decision has been for fifteen years a baneful influence in every industrial state in the Republic, always raising the question whether, after all, it was wise to spend energy in trying to get legislation of this character when the courts were likely to hold it contrary to the state if not the federal constitution.

Florence Kelley printed a large edition of the winning Illinois brief, after raising money for it with a special fund, and made the brief available to advocates around the country.

May 30, 2013: The deaths of more than 1,100 workers in the Bangladesh factory collapse have now fallen out of the headlines and will soon be forgotten. A newspaper photograph of the owner, attempting to flee over the border, shows him being carried away in handcuffs. An investigation has been ordered.

After the Triangle Shirtwaist Factory fire in 1911 when nearly 150 young women died from fire and asphyxiation in a New York factory where the doors were locked and there were inadequate fire escapes, Frances Perkins created a commission which in its investigations into working conditions for women went far beyond an examination of fire hazards and the particulars of the Triangle fire.

November 19, 2012: On this lovely day, I can feel it, we are on our way out. There will come a time when we will no longer live in Chicago, but just keep a footprint here, perhaps. I hope this departure is to start a new adventure, not for reasons of infirmity or an inability to keep up with the city's pounding rhythms.

The collaboration among Louis Brandeis, Florence Kelley, Josephine Goldmark, and the National Consumers' League lasted until Brandeis's appointment as justice of the Supreme Court of the United States. Florence Kelley and Brandeis were not always in agreement; however, there was a mutual respect.

Louis Dembitz Brandeis's confirmation battle still ranks as among the most bitter and intensely fought in the history of the court. Four months after his name was submitted on January 28, 1916, he was confirmed as a justice of the Supreme Court of the United States.

Known as the "people's lawyer," Brandeis came to Harvard Law School directly from Annen-Realschule in Dresden, Germany, graduating two years later at the head of his class at Harvard Law. A partner in Warren and Brandeis (when the traditional Boston firms would not take a Jew), he soon amassed a fortune of $3 million in practice. While in practice, Brandeis also took cases such as Muller v. Oregon and its successors *pro bono*. The opinion in Muller v. Oregon was unanimous. Brandeis's advice to presidential candidate Woodrow Wilson was influential in shaping the future president's position on economic and social issues.

Woodrow Wilson first wanted to appoint Brandeis as attorney general, but the opposition of the Boston Bar was so vociferous, this plan did not succeed. Robert La Follette was an ally, calling Brandeis a "progressive." Most of the opposition was simply anti-Semitism. Opposition included the former head of the NAACP, the president of the Organized Bar, and President Abbott Lowell of Harvard, who circulated an anti-Brandeis petition signed by "50 proper Bostonians." Also opposed were the *Wall Street Journal*, the *Nation*, and the *New York Times*. Supporters were few and included Felix Frankfurter, eight of the eleven members of the Harvard Law School faculty, and onetime Harvard President Charles Eliot.

The final vote before the Senate was 47-22, and 10-8 in favor at the Senate Judiciary Committee. Former President William Howard Taft was vehemently opposed, wanting the nomination for himself.

Brandeis retired from the court at eighty-three in 1939. He was the first justice to cite law reviews and other nontraditional sources in his opinions. He served on the court fifteen and a half years with Oliver Wendell Holmes. William O. Douglas succeeded him.

The kind of blatant anti-Semitism opposing Brandeis's appointment was demonstrated by his Supreme Court colleague Justice James McReynolds, who refused to speak to Brandeis for three years following his appointment. McReynolds deliberately absented himself from Brandeis's retirement celebration and would not have his picture taken with him.

When Benjamin Cardozo was sworn in, in 1932, Justice McReynolds read a newspaper throughout the ceremony, muttering, "another one." McReynolds never spoke to Cardozo at all. He would stalk from the conference table when Brandeis spoke, listen outside the door, then return. He wouldn't sit next to Brandeis during Supreme Court conferences, nor would he attend Frankfurter's robing ceremonies in 1939, commenting: "My God, another Jew on the court." McReynolds never sided with Wilson on any significant issue involving government activity.

October 29, 2012: Cool, bracing, blue sky. Clouds. Chicago and its spectacular weather, and we are still here.

New York remained a center of labor politics, and Florence Kelley, Josephine Goldmark, Abraham Bisno, and Francis Perkins were in the middle of it. The New York attorney general incorporated much of Francis Perkins's *Triangle Fire Commission Report* in his brief in support of a proposed law regulating night work for women. Later a brief was submitted by the New York assistant attorney general to the Supreme Court of the United States, successfully arguing in support of a New York statute regulating night work for women. The same legal strategy as Brandeis used in his brief in *Muller*—framing an argument based upon a compendium of "facts in the common knowledge," the marshaling of references to the laws in other states—was used in a series of minimum-wage cases and many other cases involving protective legislation. The "Brandeis Brief" became an institution.

All of the worker protection laws were vehemently and consistently opposed by state manufacturers and then business associations, organizations such as the Chambers of Commerce, and what became the National Association of Manufacturers, which had morphed out of Levy Mayer's Illinois Manufacturers' Association. Opposed as unlawful interference with business were state regulations, such as fire escape laws, factory inspection laws, minimum-wage laws, sanitation regulations, ventilation requirements, unemployment insurance provisions, safety regulations on machinery, and many other health and safety regulations.

An observer, Judge William Hitz of DC, himself a distinguished jurist, wrote of Brandeis's oral argument before the Supreme Court of the United States in the minimum-wage case: "When Brandeis began to speak, the court showed all the inertia and elemental hostility which courts cherish for a new thought, or a new right or even a new remedy for an old wrong, but he visibly lifted all this burden, and without orationizing or chewing of the rag he reached them all."

Florence Kelley was to say of Brandeis's many appearances on behalf of the National Consumers' League that no case was decided adversely in which he took part in oral argument or supplied a brief.

When Louis Brandeis summarily disposed of the constitutional arguments put forward by Levy Mayer as the advocate in *Hamilton*, the whiskey case, Brandeis relished the punctilious details about the placement of the word "thereafter" and the conclusions that Congress had not exceeded its police power, that the court may not inquire into the motives of Congress, and that there had been no Fourteenth Amendment violation in passing the statute Levy Mayer argued was unconstitutional.

April 24, 2006: A birth, and a girl at last. And all is well. Of course we have all known that the baby was a girl. A girl after five grandsons. She will be petted and spoiled, at least for some time. What joy!

In 1897 Margaret was eleven. Mary Rozet Smith paid her boarding school tuition in 1897-98 and 1898-99 and "will go on doing so as many years as may be necessary," Florence Kelley told her mother. Margaret was often at odds with her mother's view of what she should do with her life.

"Margaret is a handsome creature," Jane Addams wrote Mary Smith, "but her attitude when she found out her Semitic ancestry was pathetic, none the less so for its absurdity." Jane Addams reported that Margaret wept copiously when informed that her father was a Jew.

The Wischnewetzkys were living at 110 East 76th Street when Margaret was born. The best date for her birth seems to be around December 4, 1886. December 10, 1886, is the date of a letter after the birth describing the mother's slow convalescence. Lazare Wischnewetzky left for Europe on December 4, 1886, and Florence Kelley wrote that he left immediately after Margaret's birth.

October 17, 2009: The still outside in the middle of the night. I suspect the night was never still at Hull-House, at 335 Halsted Street. We who are clever enough to see beyond our own solar system can't take care of our own small, insignificant backyard in the heavens. We govern ourselves poorly. People get away with murder and worse. Our state committee on the death penalty will put out its report, and no one will pay any attention. At least my research will be published independently, thanks to the law school journal. I publish what I found and what I think, to set the record straight for anyone who cares to look.

Theodore Dreiser's Frank Cowperwood in *The Financier, The Titan,* and *The Genius* was closely modeled upon Charles Yerkes, the 1890s Chicago streetcar magnate, and also upon himself. Certain details were changed such as the length of time that Charles Yerkes spent in prison before coming to Chicago, the details of some of the complications of the financial shenanigans regarding the loans and stock paper for the street railways, as Yerkes schemed to create inventive and deceptive financing and drain the cash from that highly profitable business. The passengers complained about terrible service and crowded cars, and pedestrians were routinely maimed and killed, but the street railways made money for their owners and for a while for their bond holders.

Also changed by Dreiser, for the purposes of a different story, were the details of what happened subsequently to Charles Yerkes's second wife and to his last very young, very beautiful mistress, who was Yerkes's ward and the daughter of an American courtesan, as in the novel. The ending of the real-life story was altered for the novel.

The women fared better in real life than they did in the Dreiser novels: Charles Yerkes's rejected second wife, whose beauty is described with such loving detail in the novel, in real life subsequently married a successful writer and playwright twenty-five years her junior. Apparently they enjoyed themselves for many years living in prosperity in Hollywood. As for the actual child mistress, who was indeed Yerkes's ward, she left him and decamped to London with a good amount of his money. After he died, she was prominent in London society, remarried, and was able to obstruct, at least for some time, the publication in London of *The Titan,* which describes how Cowperwood (Yerkes) courts her by essentially buying off her courtesan mother. After several decades of living abroad, she returned to America, and the customs office in New York listed her as declaring more than $800,000 worth of personal jewelry. The widow seems to have thrived.

The letters from John to his mother continue:

Sept. 4, 1900

Hillside Wis.

I have been driving Lotty and Leah all summer and when I came think over the goat plan I decided that there would be a good deal of money wasted for I don't think I would care anything about them after a little while.

The goats would cost eight dollars apiece the harness six and the wagon twelve or fifteen which would nearly forty dollars. Then I talked to Aunt Jenny and Aunt Nell about a *pony and they said I could work for all but the amount of board the goats take which would be ten dollars. There is a man in Spring Green who had a little black bronco is a very good pony. He has been held at forty dollars all summer until Saturday and then a drover came he a pony match one this man had so he put the price down to $30. For one day.*

Uncle James said that if you didn't want me to keep him he could sell him wright away because I got him a such a bargain it would be easy. Now the only additional expense the saddle and bridle which would about three dollars. This is more than you bargained for but if you agree I would like it as a Christmas present.

Good by with love from John

P.S. Dear Mother would you see if I could have most of my Christmas presents in money.

The ruling of the Supreme Court of the United States, Muller v. Oregon, in 1909 made constitutional history. The Illinois court's reliance on federal constitutional law in *Ritchie I* turned out to be a boomerang which circled right back to hit the Supreme Court of Illinois when the Supreme Court of the United States upheld on federal constitutional grounds the analogous Oregon statute against a due process, Fourteenth Amendment challenge.

May 2, 2009: The first beautiful spring day.

The rapid growth of the Bar in Illinois reflected the growth in wealth and economic activity in the city. Levy Mayer was prescient with his emphasis upon the law being a business: the business of law was and is to maintain the social structure and uphold those rules and customs which peaceably order people's actions and behaviors in a civil society, whose rules are transparent and predictably interpreted. Many hope the law does more.

Jane Addams, Florence Kelley, and the others knew the political mood had shifted after 1895. It was to swing back again in 1909. John Peter Altgeld and Florence Kelley's advocacy for more stringent legislation protecting child workers in 1895 failed in the Illinois legislature, in spite of Governor Altgeld calling the General Assembly back for a special summer session. Nonetheless, before being fired, Florence Kelley and her lieutenants prosecuted 542 violations in 1895 and 520 in 1896, after the *Ritchie* decision. The *Third Annual Report of the Factory Inspector*, the most comprehensive, if not the most optimistic (that would be the *Second Annual Report*), was published in February 1896. The fight moved to New York with Florence Kelley.

January 19, 2010: Altgeld Gardens is now the homicide capital of Chicago. Jane Addams has her name attached to an ugly expressway which slices through and has destroyed the ethnic neighborhoods of Chicago surrounding Hull-House, in order to deliver cars, trucks, buses, and taxis to downtown Chicago, the Loop, where the Yerkes overhead track still circles the heart of the city where the state government, the courts, and the tall, shining buildings packed with lawyers continue to stand.

William Stead, the gifted writer, the author of *If Christ Came to Chicago* which caused such a stir at its publication in 1893, was, in addition to being a minister and preacher, a dedicated spiritualist, much beloved of the many mediums and spiritualists who practiced in London and throughout Europe and America.

William Stead did go down with the Titanic. He was reported to be helping others into lifeboats as the ship sank, rather than joining the unseemly scramble for a seat for himself. Before his fateful end he had written an account of a large ship hitting an iceberg in a sentimental novel titled *From the Old World to the New*. After Stead's death a number of psychics claimed to have received messages from him, and some claimed they had warned him psychically of his impending death at sea. The captain of the ship which went down in the North Atlantic in Stead's novel is named Edward J. Smith, the same name as the captain of the Titanic. Some of Stead's most rhapsodic descriptions of Chicago were written before he ever visited the city in 1893.

August 23, 2009: All day, lawyerlike things, some involving writing, most just talking, on the phone, endless emails. Getting lost in the computer. Every semester, my students teach me again online legal research. All day my hair flying away in the heat, as if scattered thoughts were flying out of my brain. A hot day, all day inside. I miss my third floor where I could sit, and sweat, and have the illusion I was doing something other than wasting time in meetings, talking, talking, without anything happening.

It turns out the state attorney general's office has its own pot of funds for capital cases, about $900,000 a year which doesn't even come out of the capital litigation trust fund. Another hidden prop of the current system.

August 17, 2010, Chicago Tribune: "Blagojevich Convicted on 1 of 24 Counts."

As governor, Rod Blagojevich was a personal and political riddle, and the muddled end Tuesday to his summer-long federal corruption trial did little to clear up the mystery.

After 14 days of deliberations, the six-man, six-woman jury convicted Blagojevich on just one of the 24 felony counts he faced—a charge that he had lied to FBI agents about his intense involvement in campaign fundraising. . . .

Still, the lone conviction makes Democrat Blagojevich the second former Illinois governor in four years to be convicted in federal court of wrongdoing and the fourth since 1973.

Stead's popular spiritualism included being an "automatic writer": that is, a person who receives messages from an absent or dead person and writes them down automatically as messages, either directly from the deceased or from a distant living person. This was a popular occupation. Stead conducted a "live" interview with one Lady Brooke while he was on a railway carriage in Dover and the interviewee was at a castle in northern Scotland. This feat was reported in the Sunday *Chicago Tribune* in November 1893, in a face-to-face interview with Stead. The astounded reporter commented: "I must say, Mr. Stead, that this opens up a new and bewildering vista of journalistic possibilities." A Scottish commentator remarked upon Stead's writing on spiritualism: "It's a bit like Haggis—there's a good deal of confused feeding in it."

Stead was a dedicated feminist, and when he founded a newspaper, he staffed it mainly with women, which was then considered startling. He was welcome at Hull-House.

January 11, 2013: Rainy, wet, but not cold. The winter greyness imparts a kind of hopelessness. In a hurry, to a huge glass office building of lawyers, security elaborate, high ceilings, glass, marble: during the meeting break I get lost in the unmarked corridors looking for a bathroom. Huge, heavy doors of impressive wood close silently, leaving me in tall, empty corridors looking at more closed doors. The meeting is about writers and a museum dedicated to Chicago writers. Empty conference rooms in the middle of glass office buildings of the city. You can look out and see other cavernous, empty offices. This one, the law firm which Levy Mayer founded and which still bears his name, and which prospers in spite of its apparently temporary excess office holdings in downtown real estate.

Courts keep chaos at bay by being rigid about procedures, by locking down what comes in and what comes out, by characterizing the limited or highly formalized reality presented as immutable fact which is then turned into a rule of law. The lawyers know they are just pretending there are verifiable facts. Florence Kelley pushed the boundaries far, the boundaries between fact and law, pushed the legal system to recognize some facts as illegal.

March 6, 2013, Chicago Tribune: "Dawn Clark Netsch 1926-2013: An Illinois Trailblazer; Unabashed Liberal Was a Woman of Firsts—in Law Class, as State Officeholder, as Governor Candidate."

Dawn Clark Netsch was a political pathfinder for generations of Illinois women, the first to hold statewide office and the first nominated by a major party for governor.

As a lawmaker, Mrs. Netsch was an ardent supporter of the Equal
Rights Amendment, abortion rights, time off work for medical
care of family members, banning handguns, gay rights and elimi-
nating the death penalty.

Edgar criticized her opposition to the death penalty as being
soft on crime. . . .

In a heavily Republican year, locally and nationally, Edgar won
with 64 percent of the vote to 34 percent for Mrs. Netsch.

As Jane Addams knew, to get such a large proportion of a losing vote was a triumph, and of course, Dawn Clark Netsch wasn't the first woman to hold a statewide office in Illinois, as she would have been well aware.

October 27, 2009: A real fall day, wet, but not really raining, just glowering. To capture the evanescent reality, to pinpoint the weather, as if to stop it. To give evil an name. To understand what a fact is. To control by writing it down.

Facts collected for one purpose, to enforce a bold law, are now available for other purposes. The list of trades which in the factory inspection reports is used to classify businesses for the purpose of showing who was arrested, who was under indictment, who was prosecuted, is now a record of what work was, where men and women went to work, of whom would be found in the factories. The 1890s factory inspection reports tell us what the factories looked like, how they smelled, and what people were doing when they were at the factories. The result: evidence. The legal system's tolerance for the conditions brought to its attention speaks for itself, then, now.

June 17, 2013: The weather, unseasonably cold. Another exoneration announced today. A woman who spent years in jail for the murder of her son because the trial court judge would not admit eyewitness testimony from another son saying the child strangled himself accidentally. And yet no bitterness was expressed at the press conference. No blame assigned. The lawyers were restrained. It is the eighty-ninth exoneration in Cook County, nor do I think Illinois is unusual. We just have lawyers and students doing investigations.

The indexing system in the factory inspection reports, like the indexing at the office of the clerk of the courts, the indexing of briefs, the indexing of the police files, and the indexing in libraries is, was highly efficient. One revolution of the Internet is the elimination of all those prior systems of classification, of information retrieval, all that time in law school spent understanding key numbers, now irrelevant. The law now lies nestled even deeper within the great, capacious English language.

Florence Kelley looked to the New York factory inspectors and their reports and to the employment maps in London for models. Yet it is not their efficiency that preserves these reports or explains why they were used in arguments before the Supreme Court of the United States. At the end of the day what remains is the power of the words and images describing how people lived and worked: the circumstances of how real people lived, what they did, what they looked like, how they survived. The artful language carrying the human experience, the outrage, the pity. This is where we came from, although we arrived in our own lives without preparation or knowledge of this.

October 28, 2007: The date arrived at by counting backward from Wednesday, which is the 31st. And a beautiful bright day it is. The sun shining, our glorious sun. The fall colors out.

John's correspondence with his mother continues:

Hillside Wis. Sept. 29, 1899

My Dear Mother,

I hope you are very well as I am. The weather is very nice and clear and cool. We boys play train nearly all the time before and after school.

The leaves are beginning to change already.

I hope we will have good skating this winter. I wish I could have a pair of skates this winter. Could I send Margaret after them in St. Paul? Would that be all right?

We are having South American in Geography and all kinds of fractions in Arithmetic.

I chase the cow up to the barn every afternoon. There is a cow that first had a calf the other day and she is in a different pasture from the rest of the cows.

I think I would like to work in the same way next year that I did this year.

I had a pretty good time this summer.

Give my love to Ko and tell me how he is too busy to write.

How does Ko like it and how do you like New York? Does Ko ever go swimming?

Good bye with a lot of love from John

P.S. The grapes have all gone.

In the middle of leaving, moving on, getting her affairs straightened out in 1899, for Florence Kelley the children remain at the forefront of her consciousness, always.

Ko did finally matriculate at Harvard College with the help of his mother's friends. At one point Florence Kelley goes to Boston and meets with the dean of Harvard College and is told that her son may enter Harvard not in the freshman class but only as a "special student," taking courses in botany and geology, with the understanding that if he does well he can continue as a regular student the following year. And he does well and graduates from Harvard Law too. If they had known he had a Jewish father, they might not have admitted him at all. His son also goes to Harvard.

Mary Roset Smith paid Nicholas's tuition at Harvard. Florence Kelley said she didn't mind accepting this generosity, which was freely offered and equally freely accepted. When Nicholas went to Harvard, the then fourteen-year-old John Kelley was preparing to leave the Hillside Home School for another establishment, and Margaret was also leaving for another school.

June 17, 2011: At the New York Public Library Archives. Letters from Caroline from 1845 in her delicate, meticulous handwriting, unstamped covers. July 7, 1845, with additional writing across lines on the page. Perfectly legible.

Margaret continued as a student at Ferry Hall.

Ferry Hall Seminary

Dear Grandma (Jan. 28)

. . . The new semester begins Monday and my troubles began in earnest today when we had the first of our mid-year examinations. I am sure that John and Ko are having the same horror. It does seem a useless kind of agony after all, doesn't it?. . .

I do not care at all about going to college but I do not know how Mother feels about it. As I am certainly not going to teach but intend to join that estimable corps which you so admire and approve, the trained nurses. It seems the only thing open to girls except teaching and I am so thoroughly tired and sick of going to school that I would never make a success of that so what is the use of Mother's going to all the anxiety and expense of sending me to college.

March 5, 2010: Soccer these days seems to require the parents to be driving all the time, in winter, on slippery roads. Every weekend, three times a week after school, practice, what they live for.

According to one of her biographers, after her return to America, Florence Kelley published her most radical and doctrinaire opinions in German journals. The publisher for such socialist views was Heinrich Braun, whose Jewish identity and socialist views blocked the possibility of an academic career for himself in Germany. As did many others, he believed statistical data created a common ground for all reformers, socialists and non-socialists alike.

Since Florence Kelley's own English version of these German articles no longer exists, the printed German version has been translated into English by her acolytes. Given Florence Kelley's facility with German, she may have originally written the articles in German, and there may never have been an earlier English version.

May 2009: The inexorable rhythm of transition. Let the move be over so that life and work can continue.

When Florence Kelley moved to New York for the job at the National Consumers' League, John and Margaret stayed at the Hillside School.

June 4, 1900 Hillside Wis.

My Dear Mother

Hope you are very well as I am. I was very much surprised to receive this letter because just last week I wrote and told you the very questions you asked. I would like or rather I need two wastes or I mean blouses and one white waiste for the dance. Margaret says I ought to wear a high collar but I don't care much and I'll have it for you to decide that. I wear "14" size shirt waistes and "15" blouse. Perhaps you had better get both of them "15-1/2."

The next thing and the thing I most hate to ask for is a new suit.

Margaret says that she thinks a dark one would be nicest but whichever you think best bring.

Good by with love from John.

P.S. I think you know how I hate to ask for things and I would not ask at all if it was not nessisary.

August 10, 2012: A wonderfully stormy day, with majestic clouds and thunder and pelting rain, then blue sky. We fly tomorrow, and it is supposed to be fine.

May 3, 2011, Chicago Tribune: "Jury Hears He's a Crook or Victim: After Jury Seated, Opening Remarks Hint at Streamlined Corruption Case for Retrial."

. . . Opening statements saw Blagojevich painted by prosecutors as a schemer who betrayed the state. To the defense, he was a naive blabber who didn't make a corrupt nickel.

But most notable this time was the government's effort to portray Blagojevich's talking as a crime in and of itself. . . .

"He was going to shake down the man who was going to become president of the United States," charged Niewoehner. . . .

Goldstein said Blagojevich was the true victim in the case, beset upon by people hoping to pry favors from him that he never granted and who sometimes invented damning testimony to please prosecutors.

William Darrah Kelley died in Washington, DC, on January 9, 1890. After a memorial service in the House of Representatives, his body was taken in a special train car to be buried in the family plot in Philadelphia. His daughter Mrs. Wischnewetzky was not reported to be one of the family members at his bedside at his death. The records do not show if she was present for the memorial service in the capital or at the internment in Philadelphia. Later his widow, Caroline Bonsall Kelley, transferred the remains of their five children who had died in childhood to that same family plot in Philadelphia. The post-burial reception was at the home of Florence Kelley's older half-sister, the child of William Kelley from his first marriage. This half-sister had spent some of her childhood at the Elms.

We want to believe that there are some for whom the moral compass never wavers. They, these special people, always are pointed toward true north, morally speaking. They know the good and are always on its side, pursuing it, working to further it because it does exist, if only because of their belief in it. Such people are basically Platonists, believing in the immutable nature of the Good. We would like to believe this especially about our lawyers.

The divorce action in 1900 grants Florence Kelley permanent custody of the three children and says she can revert to the name Florence Kelley as her legal name. In fact the children had been in her custody since 1892, although they rarely lived with her, and she had used the name Florence Kelley without interruption since her arrival in Chicago. Later the children, especially Nicholas, claimed Hull-House as their memory of childhood, and all took the Kelley name.

In the divorce action in Chicago in 1899 and 1900, Florence Kelley lies on the record and claims to be a legal resident of Illinois, although she has already moved to New York, accepted a position there, and begun work as the first general secretary of the National Consumers' League. She may be lying again on the record when she says that she has no idea where her husband, Dr. Wischnewetzky, is, or where the final notice of the pending divorce action should be served.

She may be lying in claiming that there was no answer or acknowledgment of the summons, the notice of service of the action for divorce filed at the last known address of the doctor. The proof of service goes to an address in New York City and comes back unknown. However, at the time her younger brother, Albert, is actually negotiating with the doctor over untangling the couple's joint ownership of some property. The doctor does not want to make any trouble, Albert writes; he seems to be docile, tractable, eager to avoid publicity.

November 18, 1899, Department of Law, City of Philadelphia

My dear sister,

. . . I am so glad some decisive steps are about to be taken. Now for business. I will see the distinguished foreigner next week after Thursday. Up to that time I shall be actually engaged in court. It would suit me best to meet him on Friday morning but I shall leave time and place to him. If you will send me his address at once I will communicate with him and send you a copy of my letter. Neither Mr. W. or I attach any importance to your having accepted money from him beyond the fact that you were very lucky to get J. We think that the fact that it was put to use for his son meets any point that might be raised. I should not care to have you present at our interview for if he said anything I did not like I fear I should lose control of myself and incontiently punch him. Please therefore send me his address at once and any suggestion you may have to offer and believe me my dear sister to be,

Your loving brother,

Bert

The principals perhaps were engaged in veiled discussions before going ahead with the divorce. That Judge Frank Baker could continue to have jurisdiction over the case at the divorce was critical. The law must get its business done.

If these are lies, lies sworn to under oath, they are the lies of expediency, lies required because the law did not allow her to finish the job of disentanglement in the earlier proceedings. The proceedings could have been reopened by the doctor. He could have claimed fraud in his exclusion from the proceedings.

Florence Kelley's brother Albert met with the doctor over the distribution of jointly held property which could not be settled until a divorce was final.

October 13, 1902, Law Offices of George Qumtard Horwitz, Philadelphia

I am sending you by mail the blocks sent me by Paul, Enochs & Co., and I enclose the agreement. I have your note from Boston and am delighted to hear how well Ko is fixed. Mother was safely transported to Mrs. Lyons on Saturday, and I know you will be glad to learn that the deal of which I spoke to you when you were here, has been closed and as soon as the final legal details have been attended to, the fund will be ready for *distribution and should make a handsome sum. The amount is not yet certain but it can't possibly be less than $10,000 and it may reach $20,000. So Ko and John can join clubs galore if they want to, I will write you of conditions as I find them at Bryn Mawr.*

Au revoir dear Sister,

Your loving brother,

B.

This windfall of cash went to pay some of Nicholas's expenses at Harvard, although those were also paid by Florence Kelley's friends. Thanks to the money after the divorce, Florence Kelley told Nicholas to buy a new coat. She wrote him that she did not want him to be embarrassed among his Harvard friends by wearing shabby clothes.

If Florence Kelley had moved to New York without being divorced, Lazare Wischnewetzky could have claimed custody or visitation with the children, who never did live with her in New York City. And he arguably could have claimed half of whatever salary she earned or property owned. She also might have been responsible for supporting him, under the law.

Clarence Darrow was not one of the regulars at the Hull-House dining room table. He disdained much of the work of the educated women of Hull-House and sometimes had a sneer for who they were and their womanly exhortations and enterprises. And they did not approve of his drinking alcohol and womanizing. Clarence Darrow was never the ally to Hull-House that Henry Demarest Lloyd and John Peter Altgeld were. Jane Addams, Florence Kelley, and Clarence Darrow were also competitors. They occupied the same public turf and plied the same trade, making their living through public speaking, writing, always with a political agenda as they stood on the public platform, taking a position in the center of highly publicized controversy. Like all competitors, they all kept a close eye on one another.

Not all the Hull-House residents, or Florence Kelley's co-workers, were educated or had gone to a college. Some were completely self-taught. Florence Kelley herself was largely educated at home to protect her health, as she describes in her *Autobiography*:

Because I never went regularly to school, and encouraged by his interest I began then, at the age of ten years and wholly without guidance, to read Father's library through, starting at the ceiling, at the southwest corner of the study and continuing the process whenever we were at home until, at the age of seventeen, I entered Cornell University.

This dramatic account, she notes later, is questioned by some family members. Some of the women who worked with Florence Kelley on the various research enterprises or as factory inspectors were anonymous residents at Hull-House who helped out. Copying all the schedules every evening before sending the originals to Washington was done by unsung helpers whose names we will never know. Those copies may be in a library archive somewhere in Chicago or Washington. Nor do we know the names of the four "schedule men" from Washington who lived at Hull-House from April to July of 1894 and completed the survey of the tenements and slums for Carroll D. Wright.

Abraham Bisno became a Hull-House regular. Later he remarked, "People who did not belong to our class took an interest in our lot in life." And about Florence Kelley, he said, "She talked with me as though I were equal. The fact that she was a Yankee and I a jew seemed to make no difference to her."

"Hull House had grown so large," Florence Kelley wrote to Nicholas in 1902. Clarence Darrow came to dinner and was raising money for John Peter Altgeld's widow. The governor left no estate. Clarence Darrow had raised enough, some $9,000, so that Emma Ford could stay in the house where they had lived together. Darrow was working on raising enough for a stipend. "Clarence Darrow had gotten quite fat," Florence Kelley wrote to her oldest son and confidant, Nicholas, now away at boarding school, and preparing—with some anxiety—to go to Harvard.

The end of some of these stories is known. Florence Kelley, the sickly child who devoted much of her life to trying to protect other disabled, helpless or sickly children, lived to a robust age, dying at seventy-two in her childhood city of Philadelphia in 1932, after a sickness of several weeks. She had wanted to die in her favorite place, Brooklin, Maine, but she was brought back to her old home city by her son John and died there in a hospital. She lived long enough and hopefully was able to understand that Jane Addams became the first woman to win the Nobel Peace Prize in 1931.

October 5, 2007: Awake in the middle of the night, I don't open my eyes and only listen. If there are no sounds from the street, no cars, and just the occasional crack of a branch, no rapidly approaching and receding voices, no footsteps on the walk, it must not be the morning. I don't allow my eyes to open, to check whether there is a ribbon of daylight beneath the shade and therefore it must be daybreak. Two grandchildren and their mother coming today. The good thing about time passing, new children in the family. All the fruit, the cheese, the preparation of the food, the tasting, the cooking, the smells in the kitchen, the anticipation, as good as or better than the actual eating. The children grow; their parents also.

Henry Demarest Lloyd, now largely unread, was relentless in his attacks upon the irresponsible members of his social class and upon corrupt or inept government officials. In 1883 he exposed the speculative rigging of futures markets in commodities, attacking the manipulation of financial paper as abominable gambling and the artificial manufacturing of prices, while the criminal rich continued to sell adulterated grain and provisions. He pointed out that Philip Armour—for whom Levy Mayer would act as private attorney and adviser for decades—depressed the prices of produce and provisions during harvest and manipulated them artificially afterward to the injury of farmers, merchants, and consumers.

The *Chicago Tribune* continued to remain firmly in the camp of the economically powerful, where it steadfastly remained for decades and through most of the next century. On February 28, 1885, Henry Demarest Lloyd and his wife, Jessie, saved Joseph Medill and his father-in-law the embarrassment and public confrontation which would have resulted from Medill firing him. He never wrote for the *Tribune* again.

September 18, 2012: A celebration of the New Year, the Jewish New Year, at a large and commodious Jewish country club in the middle of Chicago. Through the tangle of torn-up streets, of course we are lost or turned around. The distance is only a few miles from downtown Chicago, but it takes us over an hour to drive there. Then a heavy rain, on the green pampered golf course in the middle of the city where trees, many old, proud trees, are standing as accoutrements of the improbable golf course.

The irony: an extravagant, energy-wasting country club was built by Jews kept out of other clubs decades ago in the middle of the city. Now it is stately and an island of green itself. Trees are preserved, and there is an oasis, watered, manicured, in the middle of the concrete city, even if it is a fairway, even if it is again restricted.

Across the long table, laden with delicacies, as well as with the many traditional courses, the college-age young catch up: "What I want is an Indian nose ring with a little silver chain which attaches to my earring!"

The speaker's hair is black on the top, then a blond couple of inches, then pink at the bottom where the curls start.

Their grandfather is in a wheelchair. The anesthetic for surgery sets the old people back. You can see it in their eyes. The fear, but dampened, dulled by the promise of no pain soon.

The grandfather's grandfather was taken as a child to the Jewish Training School on Judd Street. I have seen the picture.

Driving home in the warm rain, maneuvering down one-way streets, and across another. To get across the river, to find a way through or over the ugly, dangerous expressways. Over the Halsted Street viaduct where the hand-to-hand battle between strikers and police of 1877 took place, led by a twelve-year-old boy shot dead in the confrontation.

The circle interchange, every year the locus of dozens of car accidents, is to be avoided at all costs. It is legendary among city planners as a great failure.

Considering how many bad governmental decisions affecting thousands, costing millions, are made every day—and that is leaving out war, or armed rebellion, deliberate killings—it is a miracle that the species and our city have survived to this point.

Levy Mayer Hall still occupies an entire block at the lake with its coveted wood-paneled offices overlooking Chicago Avenue and Superior Street, some with views of Lake Michigan. Levy Mayer was the sole home of the School of Law until the 1970s when the Rubloff building expanded the footprint and merged with the American Bar Association building, later itself to be occupied by the Northwestern University School of Law clinics and the administrative offices of the Northwestern School of Medicine. Rubloff's name is associated with large public structures all over Chicago. Said to be pious and industrious, a Jew with no children, Rubloff left the residual of his estate, which turned out to be enormous, to the great public institutions of Chicago.

Rachel Meyer Mayer was a dutiful widow and burnished her husband's posthumous image with the large, dark portrait by Leopold Seyffert in the entrance hall to his building, the portrait showing a handsome, sartorial, serious, scholarly-looking man. He stares back with the well-tailored, restrained demeanor of a successful litigator. This portrait faces the not-at-all flattering portrait of herself. Both portraits hang outside what was once the Law School Student Lounge, Lowden Hall, with a portrait of Frank Lowden, a former governor of Illinois, over the stone fireplace. Lowden Hall has kept its dark wooden benches and paneling, each detail of decoration overseen by John Henry Wigmore and his wife.

At the groundbreaking for Levy Mayer Hall on May 8, 1927, present were Mayor William Dever, the reform-minded mayor of Chicago, some of the faculty of the School of Law, and Dean John Henry Wigmore, as well as students, university administrators and alumni.

The groundbreaking exercises were conducted by Brigadier General Nathan William MacChesney, whose name remains on a bright fourth-floor, recently refurbished seminar room in the south wing of the Levy Mayer building. At the dedication ceremony in 1927, there was live music and a short address by the president of the university, Walter Dill Scott. John Henry Wigmore lined the walls of Levy Mayer Hall with drawings and cartoons of courts and lawyers, pictures from Japan and Europe, collected during his extensive overseas travel. He and his wife were childless, like John Peter Altgeld and Emma Ford. John Henry Wigmore spent time and taught at Tokyo University in Japan and traveled to China, South America, and elsewhere.

John Henry Wigmore's wood-paneled office on the other side of the entrance lobby is where I prefer to teach my classes: it looks out through leaded windows onto the grassy courtyard of the old Quadrangle Garden, where a redbud tree still attracts the occasional cardinal. The dedication in 1927 also commemorated the Elbert H. Gary Law Library, critical to the institution's intellectual strength and dominance.

October 9, 2007: The children, the grandchildren gone to their real homes across the county. The toys in the yard. The weather bright. As if there were no fall. Why should anyone care whether Florence Kelley and Jane Addams dined with Henry Demarest Lloyd, Jessie Bross Lloyd and their charming children? Yet I do.

Florence Kelley would never, could never be part of those teams of men who fought in gladiatorial combat in the courtrooms of Chicago.

Men and women fought the factory inspection fight side by side: Henry Demarest Lloyd, Florence Kelley, John Peter Altgeld, Abraham Bisno, Jane Addams, Mary Kenney. Florence Kelley correctly predicted that Altgeld would lose his reelection bid, but she was unpleasantly surprised to be fired herself in August 1897. The Illinois Glass Works before its prosecution had employed several hundred boys aged seven and eight, many of them taken from orphanages, and the man appointed to succeed Florence Kelley, Louis Arrington, had been convicted of violating the law he was later appointed to enforce. Later Florence Kelley wrote: "Throughout his term there were no prosecutions against glass manufacturers, nor was the child labor law strengthened."

It must have been with the sentiment of revenge being a dish best served cold that Governor Tanner fired Florence Kelley as factory inspector. Nonetheless, after all the editorials and attacks, lies and false allegations that the company could not proceed, would not proceed, without child workers, at the end of her tenure as factory inspector the Illinois Glass Works in Alton was operating in compliance with the Factory Inspection Law.

October 15, 2007: Rain predicted. Drizzle over the weekend. I find what this book is about as I write it. The postponements, the procrastinations seem endless. There is too much competition for my attention. The young people ungoverned, soon to be ungovernable, arrived with lice in their heads, causing amused consternation and a necessary delousing. Shades of the nineteenth century.

Henry Demarest Lloyd died of pneumonia in 1902 after a week of intense political activities surrounding the owning and operation of the Milwaukee (Saint Louis) streetcar franchises, issues which mirrored those in Chicago. Today the hurrying lawyer climbing into a taxi on Washington and State streets can look up and see the varying sizes of the scaffolding supporting the elevated tracks, a relic of Yerkes's attempt to solidify his monopoly by forcing all lines to follow his singular gauge.

June 27, 2011: A freckle-faced grandson looking Irish enough to be a nineteenth-century immigrant, with his slim new $900 computer slipped lovingly into his backpack, begins pro-

gramming camp today. There are eighteen in the class, and only two girls. More than half Asian, probably half of those raised in the United States. He is in love with his computer, which recognizes him by reading his fingerprint. The stock exchange crash was on June 27, 1893, 108 years ago today.

At the time of the divorce action in Chicago in 1899, Albert Kelley reassured his sister that the doctor had no intention of interfering with the divorce. Indeed he was eager to complete the formalities regarding the jointly held property, which had increased in value in the intervening decade, so that the money could be dispersed. The doctor apparently needed the money. Albert writes:

Letter to Dr. L. Wis, etc. Hotel Cambridge, New York November 20th, 1899

My sister informs me that as a result of an unexpected interview with you she has learned that you desire to make some provision for her. She has referred the matter to me and I hasten to ask you to make any proposition that you may have to make to me.

So in the end it came down to the marriage being about property after all, but not about grand themes of property or economics.

Philadelphia, March 29th, 1900

My dear sister,

I wired you today for the name and addresses of your Chicago attorney and I fear you may have been somewhat startled but I assure you there is no cause for that. I was called up on the "phone" today by Dr. w. who has been over here with a patient, he says, and who wanted to talk to me. Accordingly I met the gentleman at his hotel and had a three quarters of an hour talk with him. He seemed docile enough and most anxious that proceedings should at once commence, he to provide the wherewithal. He wanted to accept his cheque for $500 at once, to be used in the proceedings but this, for obvious reasons, I refused to permit. I should write to him this afternoon to send the money to the West End.

Your loving Brother,

Bert

A final sighting of Lazare Wischnewetzky, after the divorce, after Florence Kelley moved to New York, occurs and is preserved in an archive of an obscure newspaper published in Frederick, Maryland, on November 2, 1907. A young widow, described as being of "striking appearance," after taking her seat in a crowded streetcar, was reported to be "accosted" by a Dr. Wischnewetzky, identified as a medical specialist, whom she had never seen before, when she was bothering no one and simply looking out the window.

The newspaper account reports that Dr. Wischnewetzky, who had been watching her narrowly from his seat near hers, suddenly arose and began to denounce her in a loud, excited manner, shaking his finger in her face, saying: "I have been studying your type, and I have been studying you. It is such women as you who corrupt the morals of the young men and women of our cities, who send them to perdition. I saw you nudging the man next to you."

Some passengers came to the widow's rescue. The police were called and arrested the doctor, who said at his arraignment that every time he went into a streetcar women began edging up to him and elbowing him to attract his attention. The doctor was sent to Bellevue for observation. No further report of the incident has been found.

Perhaps he became an irrational person, perhaps he was not always so. In the original habeas corpus filings in 1892 there is testimony regarding the neural state, neurasthenia, of Doctor Wischnewetsky and testimony as to the neural state, gloom, and possible depression of Mrs. Wischnewetzky.

There is no obvious indication in the Nicholas Kelley letters whether the adult Nicholas Kelley and his children had any contact with the doctor. Later in his life Nicholas has some involvement with Russians, and the original source of that connection is not clear.

And then the cruelest blow:

Letter from Ellen G. Starr, Chicopee, Mass. September 30, 1905

My dear friend,

Just this afternoon I have heard about Margaret! And to think of my sitting here, so near you, and not knowing. Mr. Gunn sent me the notice saying he hoped I could tell him that it was not our Miss Kelley. I telephoned to Northampton, and got Mrs. Sessions. But she did not know where you were going.

I am glad Margaret was with Mrs. S. the last few days. She is a beautiful, large, calm soul.

My brother-in-law asked me to say how glad he would have been to help you in any way. He read the notice last night, but I was not in the room, and my sister said it could not be your Margaret. She did not know this Dana, nor that she was at Smith.

Margaret was so beautiful in June. I spoke of it to many people, & thought of writing you. I had never seen anyone grow so much in grace. Her manner was cordial & interested and she was gay & dignified at the same time, & just. Mrs. Trowbridge came to see me one day, and was charmed with her. She asked Margaret about the Jones School and Margaret's way of answering was so frank and at the same time so fair, that Mrs.

T. relied on her judgment as if she had been an equal in age. She spoke of it several times afterwards, how attractive she was.

I will not ask you to tell me about it. I am going back to the House soon, and Jane will tell me.

I go back to the children's babyhood. It seems such a little time since. I thought of it last summer, and rejoiced for you that they had all grown up to be so fine.

Mrs. Hamline said one day "Whatever Mrs. Kelley has had to suffer it is worth it." Of course it is worth it. You have been wonderful; and you are wonderful, now. I have no doubt. I am very sad for you.

I met Dr. Gardiner, Mrs. Evans' brother, at Woods Hole. He spoke of Miss Kelley's tact; said that she slipped away unobserved, whenever he and his sister might wish any conversation apart, and then was very agreeable and charming at other times. He said a great deal, quite spontaneously in praise of her, which of course gave me pleasure.

Give my love to Ko and John. I am thankful you have them. You know, I am sure, what is in my heart.

Always lovingly yours,

Ellen G. Starr.

Margaret died while a student at Smith College. Her death was caused by either a heart attack or an aneurism. It was unexpected, completely. Florence Kelley's biographer said: "Her face was like stone afterwards."

The revolution in work and in the workplace did indeed come, for many, if not for everyone, and it created unimagined opportunities for making even more money for the rich, the privileged skilled. Even the worldwide poor had the chance to benefit. Almost overnight it seemed there was worldwide access to literacy, to the acquisition of technical training. No longer would elite educational institutions have a monopoly in science or technical training, or in access to libraries and the literature of the world, or to the learning of English. It wasn't the revolution that Florence Kelley or Henry Demarest Lloyd or Clarence Darrow or Frederick Engels expected, but it is a revolution, and of work, and of the workplace.

Much of her time in New York Florence Kelley lived at the Henry Street Settlement House, a place like Hull-House but not the center of a national and international community, or perhaps the times had simply changed. The National Consumers' League became her community.

Florence Kelley opposed the Equal Rights Amendment in the 1920s after decades of devoting herself to advocating for women's political suffrage and political participation.

New Delhi, January 12, 2011: The people who live here call this cold, the middle 50s. It is damp. From the Chicago perspective of a dreary, endless, bone-chilling winter it is warm in India, twenty degrees above freezing. The air is grey, and the greasy smog, the particulate industrial exhalations can be felt immediately, in the lungs, on your face, in the hair. It leaves a slime. Everyone complains about it, and everyone says that someone must do something about it. 1890s Chicago must have been like this, or worse, the black cloud overhanging the city—coal dust—seen as people approached the city on the train.

New Delhi, built in 1911 as the colonial capital, is not the newest city in the region. Out by the airport a new city has sprung up just in the last few years, a new city already of several million, and dozens of shining skyscrapers. Chicago is the old world now. China and India are the new world, their young populations taking over the world by Internet, and building, building, building.

The hotel where we are staying is old, beautiful; except for the large photographs of colonial India lining the corridors, it could be anywhere. In Beijing the air pollution and the traffic are said to be worse than here, now.

When we venture outside, everyone is pushing ahead, the couples on the streets, teetering motorcycles inching their way through. The women, some with baskets on their heads, a fold of sari held up to the mouth, striding alongside the crawling traffic, many gaining on the sulphurous ribbons of cars which inch forward as a single living entity. The men, too, striding forward, sometimes in the traditional baggy pants, mostly in cheap European-style ready-to-wear, the pale synthetic shirts, the narrow-hipped polymer trousers, and European-style leather shoes. The women never in European-style trousers. In the crawling, honking, moving globs of people and machines, and an occasional goat, everyone is muffled up, their shoulders wrapped in a grey or dun-colored scarf, their heads down. Some men wear a grey or dark skullcap, sometimes with a narrow stripe, reminiscent of a boatsman's cap. These men will never shovel coal into the maw of a river steamer or steer a soft-nosed fishing boat out to a lobster bed. Their work is a different kind of work. On the streets, the occasional steaming cooking pot, a squatting man in dingy white poking the embers with a stick.

In the cars, mostly there is a male driver sitting forward, giving full attention to inching forward, moving with the others, leaving a space between the lines. There is little honking here, less than on State Street at a red light at rush hour. The men, and some women, in the back seat on their cellphones, iPods, or computers, or reading a newspaper.

The Delhi air is thick, brown, acrid, chokingly heavy. Everyone has the Delhi cough. The pretty-faced beggar girls—eight or six, carrying a two-year-old in rags—scratch at the back-seat window, hold their hands up, put their fingers together, and hold them to their mouths, sometimes they point to the younger one, perhaps asleep, perhaps blind—

chocolates, money, rice, anything. Occasionally a window rolls down quickly and some coins, or a few wadded notes, are put in the little hands, then the window is quickly rolled up again.

Some old, very thin men, their beards straggly and stained, lean on a stick, hold their fingers in the same position, fingers to the mouth, tap the car window. At night people sleep on the sidewalk or in the gutter. In Chicago the begging style at present is to hold the hand open, the receptacle for the coins and bills, on the street, the hand lettering on a piece of cardboard: VETERAN, NO FOOD.

The sweet-faced, hard-eyed girls in the little ragged dresses, grey, blue, red, keep moving. If one of those girls could survive to adulthood in the modern world with that determination, that stamina intact, whatever its dark source, with some luck she may find riches in a world beyond our imagining. To be hungry in a society where wealth is everywhere visible, the shining cars, the gold-flecked saris, the tall, shining office buildings, the guarded mansions, does not always make for success.

Newspapers here make money, are published in more than one language, each day the news read by many and read aloud in the market. The boys, ten, twelve, bringing the tea around to the offices are one or two steps up the ladder. At least they work inside and can get something to eat.

Also stymied in the traffic are the covered mini-taxis, the very small covered vans, with two facing benches inside, where women hold children, and men with dark, stern faces stare out the open canvas back as we all wait for the great stagnant river of traffic to crawl forward. A man leans out of a van, blows out his nose onto the ground.

If a toddler smiles, its eyes shining, I will wave. But a wave is not what they want. The children wear not-very-clean T-shirts, the universal garment, but never worn by women here. No matter how ragged and unkempt, no matter how dirty, the women wear the sari. There are no drunks visible on the street, and rarely is anyone seen to be smoking. Nor does anyone carry a paper or plastic cup or a water bottle. There are some open tents where men sit in a circle smoking something from a water pipe. On the sidewalks, everyone walking purposefully.

January 9, 2011: In the tiny cubicle in the luxurious hotel in Delhi where the guests receive their email, after a long, silent wait I log onto to my mail. The Illinois General Assembly has passed the bill abolishing the death penalty. The Journal students write saying the legislators are citing our article in the debate. Maybe statistics can carry the day after all. I never thought the legislation would get this far. There are others waiting patiently to use this very slow computer. Astonishing, I must tell someone, certainly not the tourists waiting to print out their airline reservations. . . . The Illinois legislature has actually passed a bill abolishing the death penalty in Illinois. I have to tell someone. So I clasp my hands together and tell the

English couple having trouble printing their boarding passes.

We don't know the weather in Philadelphia on Florence Kelley's tenth birthday, the day she walked into her father's library at the Elms, the neighborhood so isolated that no moving object, no carriage, would pass the house from Thanksgiving until Easter, on the day she began to make her acquaintance with books "in good earnest." It was the day she began to educate herself and vowed to read all the books in her father's library:

> *The top shelf was filled chiefly with modestly bound, small volumes of the Family Library. Though I understood almost nothing in these books of so-called Natural Science, and there were no illustrations to help, I did learn the names of Newton, Galileo, Giordano Bruno, Kepler, Copernicus, and a few other astronomers, chemists and physicists whom I thereafter revered indiscriminately, classing them all with Dr. Priestley, who was a friend of Benjamin Franklin and, as will presently appear, a hero of the family.*

> *Walter Scott, in nine large volumes of bad print, stood on a high shelf and was early reached. He saw me well along through the year of my twelfth birthday, partly because we left home in September and did not return until the following spring. That winter the Library of Congress afforded Dickens and Thackeray, along with Miss Alcott and Horatio Alger.*

> *At home there was little poetry beyond Shakespeare, Milton, Byron, Goldsmith and several anthologies dear to my memory. But there were long shelves of history. Full sets of the writings of President Madison and Daniel Webster's orations, and the histories of Bancroft, Prescott and Francis Parkman, alone must have weighed hundreds of pounds.*

> *Emerson's essays and Dr. Channing's sermons midway down the shelves, were identified, by their dates, with Father's sojourn in Boston as a young jeweler specializing in enameling. . . . Fortunately for me, Emerson, Channing, Burke, Carlyle, Goodwin and Herbert Spenser were near the floor, and I was nearly fifteen when I arrived at them.*

March 4, 2011: Back in Chicago. The governor has said his plans had changed, and he would sign the bill abolishing the death penalty in Illinois in Springfield on Tuesday, that would be March 8, 2011. Today it is raining, but not a hard rain. We wait. Anything could happen between now and Tuesday to stop the signing.

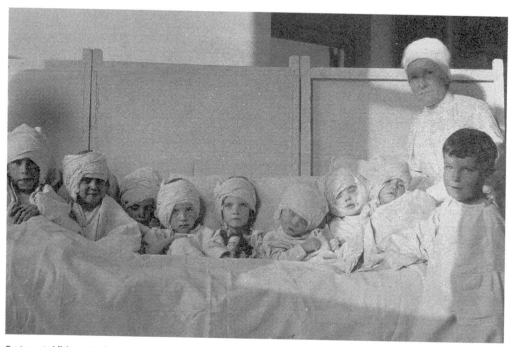

Post-mastoiditis surgical patients (young children) at Cook County Contagion Hospital; Chicago, IL (G1986:484). Source: ICHi-26997. Chicago History Museum.

Afterward – At the End of the Day

January 12, 2011, Chicago Tribune: "Historic Measure Awaits Quinn's Signature."

Springfield—Gov. Pat Quinn now has to decide the fate of the death penalty in Illinois, a state whose troubling record of condemning innocent men to death row put it at the center of the national debate over capital punishment.

The Democratic-led Senate on Tuesday approved legislation to end the death penalty in Illinois by a vote of 35-22, with two senators voting present. The House approved the measure a week earlier, and now it's up to Quinn.

In the end, it was a matter for Springfield, and in spite of the exonerations, the economic straits Illinois found itself in, the vote in the Senate was not overwhelming. The cost issues played a role, although the abolition came before the news about the Illinois pension debts reached a crescendo. It would not have passed the Senate if certain Illinois senators who were not running for reelection had not been there to vote for abolition and not had to face opponents labeling them as soft on crime.

March 10, 2011, Chicago Tribune: "Illinois Bans Death Penalty: Quinn Commutes 15 Sentences to Life, Angering Some Victims'

Families. System Lost Support Amid Revelation Innocent Men Were Nearly Executed; Moral Arguments Gave Way to Concern About Mistakes," by Steve Mills.

If there was one moment when Illinois' death penalty began to die, it was on Feb. 5, 1999, when a man named Anthony Porter walked out of jail a free man.

Sitting in the governor's mansion George Ryan watched Porter's release on television and wondered how a man could come within 50 hours of being executed, only to be set free by the efforts of a journalism professor, his students and a private investigator.

And yet it happened, has happened elsewhere. What was different this time was that people looked at the system.

March 10, 2011, Chicago Tribune: "Illinois Bans Death Penalty: Impossible to Create System Free of Bias, Governor Says," by Ray Long and Todd Wilson.

Springfield—Gov. Pat Quinn turned to the Bible for wisdom. He drew strength from the writings of the late Cardinal Joseph Bernardin. And he pored over the impassioned pleas from families of murder victims who begged him to give them a chance at closure.

Finally after two months of struggling with what he said is the hardest decision he's had to make as governor, Quinn decided over the weekend to abolish the death penalty in Illinois and clear out death row.

"It is impossible to create a perfect system, free of all mistakes," Quinn said Wednesday, moments after signing the death penalty ban into law. "I think it's the right and just thing to abolish the death penalty and punish those who commit heinous crimes—evil people—with life in prison without parole or any chance of release."

And so, it did matter who was governor, as it mattered who was governor at the time of the Ryan commutations, as it mattered who was governor when John Peter Altgeld introduced, supported, then signed the factory inspection legislation in 1893. And the governor held up our research article, with its statistics on cost and waste, at the signing ceremony. Quinn's predecessor as governor had another fate in store for him, a fate entwined with the legal system in a different context. He might not have signed the legislation, even if it had gone through the legislature during his administration, which would have been unlikely.

As with so many other instances of "reform," or legal change, leading up to the governor's signing of the abolition bill, there were many places where it could have been derailed, and the many, many people—lawyers, exonerated defendants, and others—who had worked for this change for decades would have been disappointed once again. Many of those who hold public office who always opposed the abolition have not changed their minds about the death penalty. The political opposition, reinforced by the 102 state's attorney's offices throughout the state, remained unwavering.

The budgetary issues—that the prosecution of capital cases and their appeals cost so much more—could not be denied and became the seemingly objective reason to repeal. For some, however, the view that cost was irrelevant persisted, because the issue was one of morality and biblical punishment, not expediency, not practicality.

Looking back on the years when I would go in and out of writing this book, while becoming increasingly involved in reform efforts in Illinois, what I think about now is how familiar these nineteenth-century reform efforts seemed. Then, as now, there were the many conundrums: Why isn't this book about Elizabeth Morgan? Mrs. Elizabeth Morgan founded a women's union, marched, lobbied, did everything Florence Kelley did and more. What she didn't do was write *Hull-House Maps and Papers*, which is still in print, in spite of its idiosyncratic form, in spite of some of its dated attitudes. *Hull-House Maps and Papers*, published in 1895, remains vital, readable, urgent, insistent, suffused with the passion for justice. While it does not carry Florence Kelley's byline, except for her chapter, her influence is everywhere apparent, right down to the listing of the author as "the residents of Hull-House."

Why is the work of Henry Demarest Lloyd largely forgotten? His books and articles are not dated substantively. He and his wife tirelessly worked for social justice, yet today few know his name. Lawyers who did far less than he remain in the collective memory, yet he and his work are largely forgotten. Perhaps this story will rekindle some interest in him and the remarkable work he did on behalf of workers, miners, laborers, and children. He and his family deserve to be rediscovered.

For me, the fact that Florence Kelley was an 1882 graduate of Cornell University caught my interest, as did the more astounding fact, which I only became aware of after the research on Chicago was well along, that she was an 1895 graduate of Northwestern University School of Law, the law school where I was teaching.

There was a sequence of public and private events which were the life we were leading in Chicago and Evanston, and they occurred at a specific time and place. At a certain point, after some agonizing about the diary entries for the narrative of the near present, it became clear to me that although autobiographical, they should not be sequential:

while alive a writer has control over time on the page. It is possible to imagine forward, to imagine backward, and everything in between in no particular order, to imagine into another's life, the world of the past, and into another galaxy. During the writing there is no present except the words falling on the page.

After death, time travel is impossible.

When people die, they lose the ability to move through time and place: therefore the Florence Kelley narrative had to be roughly chronological, roughly sequential, because the events of her life are over and cannot be changed. The diary of the person now composing Florence Kelley's biography can jump from the present to the distant past, from Chicago to India to New York, to the future, and back to the near present, to a different present and a different past. For that is how we live, what it means to be alive. And when Florence Kelley was alive, that was true for her also. She lived in her past, her future, her present.

My own story, our experiences, our version of the events of our lives can be rearranged, the past retold, and set out upon these pages. So the diary entries are jumbled, deliberately, sometimes, but not always, contemporaneous, with some entries reflecting our presence in Evanston, family time in the old president's house, or events elsewhere. Other entries chronicle events elsewhere in Chicago, some entries take note of momentous events beyond our small world. Time passed differently in Evanston than it did in Chicago, and always there was the traveling between the two. So the diary entries became purposely sporadic, incomplete, passing glimpses only of our lives, what we witnessed. For that was our fragmented experience, partially remembered.

Imposing order on Florence Kelley's written recollections, the chronology of her family life, her preoccupations, imposed her priorities upon mine. Her focus on the law focused mine. What she did, her work and the work of her colleagues, was a constant reminder of the evanescent triumph and fleeting character of legal reform, of the fragility of the possibility of legal change.

We know much about Florence Kelley, her family, and what she did as factory inspector in Illinois, and before and after her coming to Illinois. Yet much about her life is not now available, and perhaps has been concealed, with letters and diaries destroyed. The family papers include many letters, but many others are not there. Letters and diaries from the period of family estrangement are missing.

Her biographers address the public person. The private one, a person who made a strong impression on so many, is protected. Or, perhaps it is just that the keeping of the family records was haphazard. A scrapbook of clippings and memorabilia of Hull-House at the New York Public Library Archives has become brittle, with many of the newspaper clippings torn, brown and illegible. Not so with some other letters and documents, such as a vellum remembrance of Caroline Bonsall Kelley's father, written for a service after his untimely death more than 150 years ago. Not only is it physically well-preserved, because of the quality of the paper used, but because of its beautiful language it remains fresh: the remembrance of the man by his loved ones recalls him vividly to life. In some letters the handwriting has become so ghostly there is no more than a faint blue shadow on a blank page. Others, even those dating from the 1860s, are completely legible.

Florence Kelley's children and family members who took it upon themselves to preserve her public reputation may have feared that remnants of her allegiances to socialists or communists would only provide fodder for those intent upon destroying her work and her legacy. That the ruling of the Supreme Court of Illinois in Ritchie v. People (1895) was never overruled, even though it became a legal nullity after Muller v. Oregon in 1908, is testament to the continuous presence of her adversaries.

In her several biographies, the details of the 1892 custody hearing and the 1899 divorce, even though the transcripts of the proceeding are public records and available, the fact of the abusive husband being Jewish and the many contradictory affiliations with socialists or communists are played down or reframed by her admiring chroniclers. She herself wrote her *Autobiography* allegedly in response to the attacks upon her reputation by the Daughters of the American Revolution and others, political attacks upon socialists and communists in government which were present before and after World War I, and con- tinued well into the Cold War era and beyond.

The exception to this caution is the biography *Florence Kelley: The Making of a Social Pioneer* (1966) by Dorothy Rose Blumberg, herself a prominent socialist. Blumberg's book is based in part upon the discovery of the correspondence between Florence Kelley and Frederick Engels, available on microfilm from the Institute of Marxism-Leninism in Moscow. Dorothy Rose Blumberg does not hesitate to document the political affiliations, and her book is not published by a commercial press. Dorothy Rose Blumberg was the only person to serve a prison sentence for a violation of the Smith Act; her biographer is proud about Florence Kelley's socialist loyalties. Her husband, a professor at Rutgers, the State University of New Jersey, was also prosecuted under the Smith Act but did not go to prison.

For me, at the end of the day, I was not interested in the political affiliations, or the labeling as socialist, communist, or whether her politics were controversial or not. It seemed to me the least interesting aspect of her work and her writings. I found the doc- trinaire diatribes, the ideological fealty to Marx and Engels and the others to be expend- able. It bored me, and I had no interest in whether one or the other was right or wrong, as a matter of theory or doctrine. That writing was all tedious.

Similarly I was not particularly interested in Florence Kelley's disputes with Richard

Ely, or even in her arguments over principle with her father, except insofar as they affected their father-daughter relationship. For me, these were dated disputes; it was the relationship which was timeless. By contrast, Florence Kelley's outrage at conditions in the tenements and the sweatshops, or at the plight of boys at the Illinois Glass Works, was fresh, heart-rending, and universally relevant. This was the plight of exploited children now and everywhere.

In New York in 1886, Florence Kelley and Lazare Wischnewetzky and the Socialist Labor Party, the party the Wischnewetzkys became involved with, backed Henry George for mayor of New York. He is now remembered as "the single taxer," what is now called a "flat tax," a reform recommendation which continues to appear in the political platforms of renegade candidates for higher office. The idea is an old and tired idea.

Florence Kelley became disillusioned with Henry George. Then that tumultuous election was over. Henry George was not elected. Political divisions deepened and became more embittered as Haymarket and its long aftermath exacerbated the deep social and economic divisions between organized labor and the business and financial community. Then came the election of 1896 and the "free silver" debate, a contradictory, incomprehensible, economically questionable exchange of arguments over a hypothetical change in the way national currency was backed by the central bank. This was a classic example of an irrational debate over a change in economic policy which was symbolic, at best, if it was anything. This debate could never be resolved, as each side dug itself deeper into its own position.

As in the many nineteenth-century debates over immigration policy and export and tax policy, advocates rarely disclosed their assumptions, the sources of their data, or the foundations for their projections; thus judging the "accuracy" of their arguments is virtually impossible. The free silver debate was characterized by an especially large quantum of unverifiable assumptions and assertions. Even John Peter Altgeld seemed to be in a quandary. The immigration debates were always about where someone was coming from, literally and figuratively. The abusive name-calling was familiar, except different groups were receiving and giving the insults.

What surprised me was how little I was interested in this rhetoric, and who took what sides, although the debates were carried on with great passion and at great length by our principal characters in the public forums and correspondence. The political debates, the arguments, were about issues of importance, yet their circumstances limited them. The truthfulness of the assertions put forward were indeterminable. What was left was not the right or wrong of this or that position, but what people did, and what their lives were. Others more knowledgeable than I have detailed the role Florence Kelley played in the ideology and politics of her time. My sense was that in Chicago she was extremely cautious about getting caught in political crossfire, although as a young woman she was not hesitant in expressing her political allegiances. The political fight for the Factory Inspection Law explicitly dragged in the contentious politics of the eight-hour movement.

The more research I did, the more I found out about Florence Kelley's time in Chicago, basically from 1892-99, the more I came to believe that her biographers did not fully address the context of being factory inspector in Chicago and in Illinois. After all, her biographers were all from New York or the East Coast. I concede that her time in New York as general secretary of the National Consumers' League was longer and more important in terms of large national political events. Still, the Chicago part of her life, her attachment to Hull House in its prime, and their claiming her as their own, were a special part of her life as a reformer and of the history of the city. The direct application of a new law addressed to the issues of poverty and economic desperation was also unique, then and now, and created a natural experiment to measure the effect of a statutory change. Her admission to the Illinois Bar and her graduation from Northwestern University School of Law in 1895 were a symbol of her deep commitment to working for social change through the law.

Looking for Levy Mayer through the formal legal system yielded few records. Ritchie v. People, the 1895 case decided by the Supreme Court of Illinois, was a triumph for him and a serious setback to the reformers. None of the available records indicate how much the family paid for Edgar Lee Masters to write the biography of Levy Mayer. While Yale University Press published the book, it doesn't claim copyright and doesn't list it among its publications. It was a strange choice for a biographer, since the political attitudes of Levy Mayer would have been counter to those of Edgar Lee Masters, if the company they kept is an indication of political affiliation.

Interestingly, in a commissioned biography, where the author presumably had access to family letters and other professional papers, there is no description of the litigation leading up to Ritchie v. People or the beginnings of the Illinois Manufacturers' Association, or of Levy Mayer's personal and professional triumph over Florence Kelley in the factory inspection litigation before the Supreme Court of Illinois. We can only speculate that his widow—who commissioned the biography, as well as his fine portrait in the entrance lobby of Levy Mayer Hall—did not want that story told.

The successor firm to the law firm he founded, which still carries his name, did not have any letters or court records from his cases. A telephone call to a distant, elderly relative resulted in no new information about the family. The closest I ever came to making direct contact with the family was when Levy Mayer's wife's chauffeur's granddaughter contacted me, after discovering my Chicago historical homicide website, and said that she remembered her grandfather talking about being with the wife and daughter in

France at the time of Levy Mayer's unexpected death.

For the second *Ritchie* litigation before the Supreme Court of Illinois, a case which was clearly going down because of its similarity to the recent Supreme Court of the United States opinion in Muller v. Oregon, Levy Mayer wisely did not represent the Illinois Manufacturers' Association on the appeal. Louis Brandeis, having won *Muller* before the Supreme Court of the United States, traveled through a blizzard to come to Illinois to win again before the Supreme Court of Illinois in Springfield.

In 1995 when we arrived in Chicago, the local economy was strong, the university was thriving, the city was once more reinventing itself and its image. Chicago was once again where everything was happening. In my own area of expertise, the capital punishment system, Illinois and Chicago were initially static, and then suddenly everything was called into question by the set of rolling exonerations of persons on death row in Illinois. These cases originated in investigations which had been going on for years, many of them being brought by the Northwestern School of Law faculty and staff. Events and persons outside of Chicago were also influential.

No one involved in the abolition movement believed that abolition would actually happen in Illinois, until it did. Unpredictable changes in government authority and office holders made a difference, and there was a perceptible, also unexpected, change in the mood of the public. This was true in New Jersey and other states, as well. There had long been a strong and active reform community of lawyers and judges in Chicago, and they had been hitting walls for decades. Judges and prosecutors who ran for election and reelection on the basis of their reputation for being tough on crime were not going to give up capital cases without a fight.

Starting in 1998, however, in Illinois the ground shifted under everyone's feet, beginning with the exoneration of Anthony Porter, whose death sentence had been upheld twice by the Supreme Court of Illinois. Anthony Porter was a few days from execution when an appeal filed on the collateral issue of his competency to be executed, based upon a single overlooked school report in his file, allowed for the time to reveal his innocence and unravel the entire case. Such is the serendipity of the law. Timing is everything, and individual pieces of a case can come together with external circumstances and events in an unpredictable way. No one would have predicted that Governor George Ryan, who had always supported capital punishment, would be the government official to declare an unprecedented moratorium on executions, and later commute the death sentences of more than 150 persons on death row in 2003.

As the new century turned, national politics was again in a state of upheaval. The destruction of the World Trade Center on September 11, 2001, profoundly changed American politics at home and abroad, changes which are still reverberating through the society and the legal system. The Great Recession came in 2008 and continued. Two foreign wars, neither of which was going well, soured the mood of national optimism. The country became obsessed with the presidential campaign. Barack Obama came onto the political scene with the energy, and unstoppable force and beauty, of a great nineteenth-century Chicago steam engine. He created hope, then stepped into a quagmire.

There were many reasons for Florence Kelley to be divorced, and divorce was not difficult in Chicago in the 1890s, yet she did not seek a divorce until she moved to New York and took a new job in 1899. In Chicago in the 1890s, legal grounds for divorce included non-support and "incompatibility," as well as desertion and cruelty and others not difficult to prove. The question is: why didn't she do it earlier?

She may have worried that if she brought a divorce action in Chicago, Lazare Wischnewetzky would have come into court and challenged her custody of the children. This challenge might have succeeded since she traveled a great deal and the children were not in fact living with her most of the time. Nor is there any reliable background information as to how Florence Kelley's custody case continued to be assigned to the unusual Judge Baker, who kept jurisdiction over the case until the divorce was finally granted in 1900. Perhaps there was an understanding, or the case remained open, or there was some manipulation of a docket, but however it happened, that judge was critical to the case.

When Florence Kelley moved to New York there were other considerations beyond the legal custody for the children. Had Florence Kelley not been divorced from Lazare Wischnewetzky and had they both been living in New York, he arguably could have claimed half of her property, or half of what she earned. She also could have been responsible for his support and care. Before moving to New York, Florence Kelley needed the law's finality on the facts of marriage, to finish the job of disentanglement, which as a matter of personal relationships had been finished years ago. In addition, as she was a public figure in New York, it would have been at the very least awkward to have a husband, especially a disreputable husband, on the scene.

The archives and letters preserved do not indicate whether Nicholas or John Kelley had any relationship with their father after their mother moved to New York. I suspect Nicholas did have some relationship with his father, since at a certain point he has an elaborate relationship with a group of visiting Poles. That might have involved some connections to his father's family, or it might have been coincidental.

While Florence Kelley was absorbed in the factory inspection fight, Margaret and John were boarders at the very interesting Hillside School. She never forgot them, reduced her expectations for them, or seemed unaware of their needs and their love. Nonetheless, they reported themselves lonely. When she had diphtheria and didn't write for six weeks, or when she didn't visit because she didn't want to expose them to smallpox, although she herself was vaccinated, the children missed her. Like the children of many preoccupied parents, they were self-sufficient, but they missed her.

The sudden death of Margaret remains heartbreaking and mysterious. A heart ailment, or the kind of fatal aneurysm to which young women seem particularly susceptible, seems to have been the cause. From the letters, it seems Margaret lingered for a few days, although her mother was not able to reach her before her death, and that would be consistent with that kind of medical event. There is no recovery from the loss of a child.

Florence Kelley was unwavering in her commitment to higher education, lobbying for her oldest son to go to Harvard, talking to various high-status persons about what needed to be done for him to be admitted to Harvard as a provisional student, while teaching reading to illiterate immigrants herself. She may have been a socialist for herself, but she wanted her son to be part of the educated elite. Florence Kelley had no illusions about the character of the elite institutions and whom they served, calling them shamelessly irresponsible on social issues. She didn't send Nicholas to Harvard under the illusion that he could change Harvard. She seems to have wanted him to have and use the full arsenal of social status to accomplish his goals, just as she had.

Not only did Nicholas attend Harvard College and Harvard Law, but his son Nicholas Kelley Jr. was Harvard '31 and Harvard Law '35. Nicholas's daughter Florence attended Smith College ('34) and graduated from Yale Law School ('37). Another son, Augustus Maverick, began at Harvard ('31-'33) but graduated from the University of Chicago ('35). Nicholas practiced law in a private firm and presented himself publicly as Florence Kelley's son.

For a time he was in private practice, then his principal legal job was as counsel to the Chrysler Corporation, where he played a role in the planning and construction of the Chrysler Building. His obituary mentions his long-standing contributions on many not-for-profit boards, including the board of the National Consumers' League.

Nicholas Kelley first set up the Nicholas Kelley Archive as a collection of his own papers, including his mother's papers, at the New York Public Library Archives. The library subsequently set apart Florence Kelley's papers, creating a separate archive for her, since she is the one whom people find of interest.

The family history of William Darrah Kelley and Caroline Bonsall Kelley is emblematic of the times and intriguing, not just because Florence Kelley was a part of it. The Philadelphia Quakers were extraordinary in their public service, dedication to others, commitment to education, and in creating what seems to be a culture of kindness and respect within the family.

Unlike Nicholas, John, the youngest, did not take to schooling. However, he became a charming writer, had a hard time supporting himself, was always involved in journalism and politics. He went from school to school, probably had dyslexia, we would say today, never settled down, eventually married and then separated. Along the way he became an accomplished yachtsman, a journalist, and reported on various political campaigns and social movements around the country. He spent time in Maine at the family home. John seemed to inherit his mother's passion for justice, her vivacious attractiveness, as well as her political ideology. When he remained unemployed in Colorado during an economic depression, he wrote bitterly of the hopelessness of the people on the food lines, of the impossibility of anyone getting a job, of the fact that he couldn't afford medical care. When his mother was dying, he went to Maine and brought her to a hospital in Philadelphia.

It is Nicholas who kept, perhaps partially destroyed, and then donated his mother's letters, diaries, and papers, first to Columbia University and then to the New York Public Library Archives, which performed the Herculean task of ordering them and cataloging them. William Darrah Kelley Jr. and Albert Kelley also kept family records and watched over the family welfare and legal matters. William Darrah Kelley Jr.'s only deviation from rectitude as an adult seems to have been being named as a co-respondent in a controversial divorce action himself. For the rest, the young man who suffered the unexplained blindness which brought his sister to Europe and changed her life seems to have led a relatively conventional, stable professional life primarily as an attorney for an insurance company.

Soon into the writing of this manuscript it became clear that the time of the deep past moved at a different pace from the time of the present, or of the recent past. Florence Kelley was in Chicago for less than ten years, and much of that time was spent traveling elsewhere. As I described the pulse of our life here, sought to find the beat of the legal reform effort of the 1890s, I looked for synchronicities.

Our time here has now stretched into twenty years, almost twice as long as Florence Kelley's time in Chicago, although a good bit of her time, and ours, was spent on the road. Yet in so many ways Florence Kelley's time here in Chicago was the distillation of everything she was before and afterward, and so it was for us and our family.

This book ends with Florence Kelley, formerly the factory inspector in Illinois, working as a part-time librarian in the evening at the John Crerar Library, after being fired for doing too good a job by the new governor, John Tanner, in August 1897. This is not the end of her story. Florence Kelley did go on to accomplish many things at the National Consumers' League in New York and on the national stage. She remained embedded in national politics and social advocacy for the rest of her life, especially with regard to the protection of children and child workers. The story of her life after Chicago is told by others.

I began this book because it seemed to me that none of Florence Kelley's three biographies, excellent as they were, nor her own autobiography, re-created the context for what she did during that decade of the 1890s in Chicago. *Hull-House Maps and Papers* then became the center of my ruminations upon what lasts, what remains of our work, our lives. Neither the book nor the many different research projects which form its factual basis would have happened without her. It is a tribute and an evocation of Hull-House, along with that other great book inspired by the same community, Jane Addams's *Twenty Years at Hull-House*. Both are steeped in their time and the very personal experience of their authors, and thus are also timeless. A reader now cares little for the time-bound character of the facts in both books, but because the writing, the voice of the person detailing that world, speaks to us so clearly, so personally, so irresistibly, both books are still read today.

These women did not have the vote, nor did they wear pants or enjoy other conveniences of modern life, such as dishwashers, computers, cellphones, or washing machines, or the freedom to get in a car and drive away. A whole book could be written about the history of laundry and laundry workers, including the Chinese, in America and the role played by laundry women and other working women in landmark legislation and court cases, such as Muller v. Oregon. That book will be written by someone else. Like the joiners and the fifty varieties of woodworkers found in *Moran's Dictionary of Chicago*, some of those jobs are gone forever. Yet everyone still has to figure out how to get the clothes clean, and wonder where the clothes we wear are manufactured, and find a place to sleep and how to pay for food.

Several unanswered questions remain: Why isn't Mrs. Elizabeth Morgan the central figure in this book? In addition to everything else she did, Elizabeth Morgan organized the first chartered women's union for the Knights of Labor. Elizabeth Morgan marched, gave fiery speeches and was everywhere this issue was in the public eye. So why isn't this book titled *Elizabeth Morgan, Factory Inspector in 1890s Chicago*? Elizabeth Morgan had a compelling and dramatic life story: working in a factory as an uneducated young girl, then leaving Britain with her husband who was also a factory worker (although he later became a lawyer) and coming to Chicago to join the revolution. But again, it is always Elizabeth Morgan and her husband. He takes center stage even when she is doing something remarkable for women and women workers in the wings.

Part of the answer may be that her public personage was overshadowed by that of her flamboyant, ambitious husband who left an extensive archive about himself to the University of Chicago, a small part of which is devoted to her. Thomas Morgan ran for mayor, was the head of various incarnations of the Socialist Labor Party, went to jail, gave rabble-rousing speeches, and was present and loudly heard on all of the issues all of the time. Elizabeth Morgan was always Mrs. Thomas Morgan. Elizabeth Morgan temporarily stepped out of the fray to raise her children, but then she came back stronger and more active than ever and left a record of astonishing advocacy and achievement, for women, for workers, and for labor.

While Elizabeth Morgan was apparently a passionate speaker, she was not mesmerizing as a speaker, as Florence Kelley was. People listened to Florence Kelley and changed their lives. More important to me, Elizabeth Morgan was not a brilliant prose stylist. Someone who cares or knows nothing about labor, nineteenth-century Chicago, the plight of child workers, and the abject conditions in the tenements can be immediately captivated by *Hull-House Maps and Papers* and by the four *Factory Inspection Annual Reports*, written by Florence Kelley.

Then, there seems to be another inescapable reality: social class. Elizabeth Morgan's background was "authentic." Elizabeth Morgan had actually been a worker in a factory, grew up without education, and knew firsthand the desolation and destitution of being a powerless worker and what workers suffered. Perhaps that was not always an advantage. Similarly, Abraham Bisno, who clearly had a powerful and attractive personality and was a successful labor organizer, perceived himself to be pigeon-holed by his social class and the fact of being a Jew.

Florence Kelley was accepted everywhere and could do what she had to do in any social circumstance or gathering. She went to the tenements herself and talked to people there, and she sipped tea and brought in money from the ladies and gentlemen of Chicago, Boston, and New York. She wasn't intimidated by Louis Brandeis, Johnny Powers, or Theodore Roosevelt.

Henry Demarest Lloyd and Jane Addams had that same advantage, coming perhaps from the same source: an upbringing among people who knew who they were and apologized to no one. They could be criticized for their elitist attitudes, but all three seemed to have earned the trust and respect of their fellows and associates up and down the social, economic, and political ladder. That, too, is a gift.

As for some of their statements or attitudes, which may resonate in the present as condescending, intolerant, supercilious, or worse, I leave those judgments to others. They got things done. Part of the strength of these nineteenth-century people was that they were what we now would call "judgmental": if a child was starving in the street or developing a bent spine over a sewing machine and not learning to read, that was wrong, plain and simple. And they didn't hesitate to say so. Their words and deeds or ideas can be delivered without blemish or scar to the next generation, or the generation after that, who will, at the end of the day, make of us all what they will.

My purpose was always to clear away the distracting debris from their writings, their work, and their lives: ignore the tedious ideological rants; edit out the lecturing, no matter how well-intentioned or for whom it was intended; bypass the commemorative, celebratory speeches and accolades by them or about them (and how little those have changed over the century); find that small voice, that spark of individual humanity in the arc of their lives or in their words. I strived to capture the moment of the colored light in the sky in 1890s Chicago and in the present.

Finally, it wasn't just that we were left with so many records, and that they were so eloquent, which made these people and this period magical, special, alive. These same people—Henry Demarest Lloyd, Jane Addams, Abraham Bisno, Mr. and Mrs. Morgan, and many others—remained in Chicago continuing the various political and social fights after Florence Kelley left for New York in 1899, even though for a while the air seemed to have escaped from the balloon after the *Ritchie* decision, after John Peter Altgeld was defeated for a second term as governor.

So much of what they fought for in the 1890s is still here: the same ideas, the same reform agenda, the same passionate outrage over the same conditions which have remained only moderately changed, the same press for the organization of workers, the same push to erode the concentration of power and wealth in the hands of a few. Yet something changed after the turn of the century. In 1909, the temper of the times had changed again, and then the dynamic leading up to World War I took over. There is little about the temperance movement in this account, although that was a movement dominated by women, as was the movement for suffrage for women. Both overlapped with the lobbying for all the different varieties of labor reform. That history has been and will continue to be told by many scholars more expert and knowledgeable than I.

Once I was deep into the records and archives, the story of Florence Kelley became a story about the law. It was incidental that she received a law degree, although that it was from Northwestern University School of Law made me smile. That she herself became a subtle and accomplished advocate is amply demonstrated by her handling of the aftermath of the *Ritchie* case and the taking of the same issues to the Supreme Court of the United States in Muller v. Oregon a decade later. She developed into an extraordinary advocate: cunning, sensitive to the times, unwavering in her commitment.

Then the theme emerged of how much of her life could be discovered. The more I found of the official records and papers, the letters, the diaries, the biographies, the more these came to seem like a constructed record. Some of this was because the cases were carefully planned "test cases," designed to elicit a ruling on a matter of constitutional law from a high court. I became interested in the longevity of any legal change. Does any legal reform stick, or are large external pressures—a coming war, a national depression, the momentum and feedback of an economic boom—overwhelming, so that the reformer is simply tossing a twig into the stream?

If a person devotes her or his life to legal reform or social change, what happens when that life is over? Is history just the parade of who happens to occupy the positions of power? A transformative individual, a Barack Obama, a Carroll Wright, a Jane Addams, or a John Peter Altgeld, may appear once in a generation, but for the most part it is people going in and out of their institutional boxes, proceeding with their heads down doing the best they can in their time with what is possible while they are there. Assuming there is a civil government that functions, that there are legislatures—more or less corrupt, or functioning—governors, courts, and lawyers who proceed under the authority of the law, all the rest of us can do is try to keep going.

Striking to me as my research into Florence Kelley's legacy continued was how unchanged the institutions, procedures, and framework for the law were. The legislatures still passed laws, and they were challenged and brought before courts in the same way in the 1890s as now. And those ideas of revolution, did they survive? The vocabulary of revolution, and its apostles, have changed little. The rhetoric of justice and its specific goals have changed little.

A revolution came and is still in progress, and it has been a revolution in work and the terms of employment, but it isn't the revolution Florence Kelley and Lazare Wischnewetzky and the socialists in Bayonne, New Jersey, and New York City were expecting. Who could have predicted that all those offices and factories would be filled with people staring at lighted screens? And so the story that gripped me became larger, and smaller.

Who were these people, and what traces of them and their work remain a hundred years later? I became less interested in the big ideas and more interested in the fact that they were mothers and fathers, as well as leaders and writers. How did they manage their family lives, and how did the times manage their lives? We can't see it, but the world around us structures all of our lives, presenting opportunities, taking them away, the accident of birth determining much of what we are and do.

What about the children, their children, did they carry on the parents' work, or rebel and separate themselves? If these mothers and fathers were out giving speeches, camping out and supporting labor actions, or counting the twisted spines of the dwarfish girls bending over the sewing machines in the sweatshops, who was taking care of their own children? And so it did circle back to being a story about the women, as women, and their children. Inescapable was the fact that the availability of cheap domestic labor, most of it supplied by women, was a prerequisite for all of these people to do what they did.

August 7, 2012: Another broody day, as we wait for rain through the record drought. Still, for the city dwellers, it is blue skies, a few wisps of cheesecloth clouds, and a breeze off the lake.

The newspaper, the *Chicago Tribune*, was published continuously during the last century, along with many other newspapers now mostly gone, and into the present. The role and character of the paper has changed many times. The role it has played in the politics of legal reform in the city was important in the 1890s and is still important, even as the authority of newspapers has diminished greatly in the age of the Internet. Still the *Tribune* is an ever-present public voice, reporting the news, deciding what deserves our attention, still, as we scan the opinions and political allegiances of its editors. In the movement leading to the abolition of the death penalty, the *Chicago Tribune*, and its prize-winning, indefatigable staff reporters and editors, played an irreplaceable role in the lead-up to abolition.

The offices of the law are largely unchanged: the Cook County courts, the Supreme Court of Illinois, the thousands of other legal decision makers, the institutions of the Justice of the Peace, the United States senators and members of the US House of Representatives, the Supreme Court of the United States, the Chicago Police Department, the Office of the Mayor of Chicago and the Governor of Illinois all have remained surprisingly stable as institutions, in spite of dramatic changes in the behavior and reputations of the individuals leading those institutions. And the heightened importance of the words of the justices of the Supreme Court of Illinois and the U.S. Supreme Court is also unchanged.

The courts continue to hear cases; disputes are brought before judges and juries at all levels and a resolution of some matter is sought. The quality of justice dispensed and the individual idiosyncrasies of meting it out and bringing the matter to court change over time. Individuals, powerful, ordinary, poor, and rich, come and go in the public space, sometimes reluctantly. The quality of the judiciary and the individual lawyers varies enormously, at all levels, in all courts, within all jurisdictions.

Lawyers and judges play their roles throughout with more or less integrity, intelligence, honesty, and humility. It is a miracle that the legal system survives as a system, given the unremitting onslaughts on its principles. As time went on, and my attachment to this project deepened, I became less interested in putting labels on people or their work. In fact, the opposite. They were reformers, lawyers, journalists, legal advocates, all at once, and their opinions changed, and were in some sense irrelevant to what they did. Their motivation seemed to come from some deeply felt humanistic core, rather than from a commitment to a particular ideology.

Then and now, schemes for reform, for change, for revolution, or for just maintaining the stability of the status quo, or for getting rich, or becoming powerful were and are everywhere. Sometimes they are realized, sometimes aborted, and sometimes, remarkably, they bear fruit. This book turned itself into the stories of some of the people on the ground who were living in the middle of all of this history in Chicago in the 1890s and later.

Part of the story of the law is the story of legal education, who controls who will become lawyers, judges, professors of law. Florence Kelley's experience at the University of Zurich, and that of her Cornell colleague Dr. M. Carey Thomas, were unusual only because these women were persistent and one university presented the opportunity. Our renowned educational institutions, the professional schools and the graduate schools, have, like our courts, been remarkable survivors as institutions. The great schools and universities of Chicago are bedrock, the foundation for philanthropy, art, culture, and science. They must be acknowledged as part of the landscape, like our Great Lake, buffeted by storms, suffering the whims of fortune, beautiful against the blue horizon when calm prevails, occasionally damaged by chance, or by irresponsibility.

The politics of Illinois and Chicago is with us still. Can one person, even a remarkable person like John Peter Altgeld or Florence Kelley, make any lasting change? There is no escape from politics within the law, nor does politics ever escape the tangle of economic interests or the greed and acquisitiveness of daily business. In Chicago the economic boom of the 1880s was followed by the economic collapse of 1893, and the technology boom of the 1990s was followed by the shock of the September 11, 2001, attacks, their economic and political consequences, another building and housing boom, the bursting of that credit bubble, and ripples from other international political events. The mechanics of the stock market, the technology available to banks and financial institutions may be new, but the enterprise (to make and keep as much wealth as possible) is as old as recorded time, as is the attempt to regulate it.

Through it all, in the 1890s, in this century and the last one, people go on, trying to make sense of their lives, some trying to make a difference, some concentrating on surviving. Politics, large and small, goes on and shapes the law: people run for office, get elected or not, serve, sometimes they cheat and steal, and get caught and thrown out of office and sent to prison. Sometimes they try to do some good, as they see that. Sometimes they steal votes, bribe legal authorities, and get away with it. Throughout the older period and in the present there is a similarity of patterns: the gradations of human behavior, good and bad, have changed little. Only the levers have changed.

Our numbers have grown exponentially; there are so many of us. Our wealth has reached unimagined levels, and its disproportionate distribution within our own country and internationally would be a source of astonishment and despair to the denizens of Hull-House. The methods of management, the tools, have changed, but what people do, and did, what they want seem to have changed little: some try to remedy what they see as injustices; others phrase it in terms of the fight against intrusions of government. Some are builders, some tear down and set explosions.

And the women, what about the women, their children, and their families? For every article, every book, every testament to Florence Kelley, Jane Addams, Henry Demarest Lloyd, and the reformers for whom Hull-House was home and spiritual center, there were also unsung women who got up in the morning, looked out the window and took note of the weather on a given day in Chicago before going to do what they could. What happened to their work? They also gave their lives to their work. Did anything stick?

The people from the 1890s were irresistible as subjects because of their difference from us, and their similarities to us. They raised all the big questions. Remnants of their great buildings, displays of their wealth, their writings, are here still. The great libraries, the overhead lines of the street railways, the courthouses are still here. Of course there were and are no answers to the big questions, which is no reason not to keep asking them.

Being here, unexpectedly, living in the middle of this extraordinary city, being part of one of its great educational institutions, at a time of historical vibrancy, I became absorbed in these people's lives as a way to make sense of our lives, as a way to understand the trajectory of national economics and politics now, and as I watched social norms changing before our eyes every day. If I could understand them, I thought, perhaps I could see who we had become.

The comparisons were frequently uncomfortable. They were so clear about what was important: justice, the protection of the children, the poor and powerless, honesty in law and politics. They knew they were making history. They wrote about themselves and their own with varying degrees of candor and sophistication, or honesty, and left much for us to puzzle over.

I was grateful that so many of them were memorable prose stylists. Indeed, I was impatient with those who weren't. One purpose of this book became to rescue some part of their narrative accounts, to revive what was alive from its sometimes dated context. It was a constant challenge to find the relevant facts, the speaking facts, the reliable sources, to disentangle the truth from the cant. There are storehouses of diaries, documents, books, newspapers, legal records, letters, more or less available, saved by our great libraries, educational institutions, and court archivists. Some of the accounts of their world were buried in a book or government report long forgotten. The job was to cut away the pretension, the dross, the self-aggrandizement, the claims of virtue or right which ring hollow now. Some of the most moving, the most trenchant of these writings were buried in long-forgotten official government reports. *Hull-House Maps and Papers* and the rich detail of Florence Kelley's four annual *Factory Inspection Reports* are breathtaking, and remain the original inspiration for this book. One purpose of this effort is to lead others back to those original documents, to let their imaginations fly into the tumult of this history, and find the heartache, the joy, the outrage and the mess of politics of 1890s Chicago, and then reflect upon our own.

Image of a large group of children standing under showers over the street in Chicago, Illinois. Source: DN-0076144, Chicago Daily News negatives collection, Chicago History Museum.

Notes for Further Reading

Biographical Material on Florence Kelley

The Autobiography of Florence Kelley: Notes of Sixty Years was originally published as a series of autobiographical sketches in *The Survey* in 1927. See, e.g., "I Go to Work." *The Survey*, Vol. 58 (June 1, 1927): 271-274, 301. A more recent reprinting of the entire work is edited by Kathryn Kish Sklar (Chicago: Illinois Labor History Society/Charles H. Kerr Publishing, 1986).

There are three very different published biographies of Florence Kelley.

The most detailed, recent, and scholarly is *Florence Kelley and the Nation's Work: The Rise of Women's Political Culture, 1830-1900* by Kathryn Kish Sklar, the first of a projected two-volume biography (New Haven: Yale University Press, 1995). This biography includes a detailed annotation of Florence Kelley's publications, and references to archives and libraries with relevant materials, available with permission on the Florence Kelley website at Northwestern University (florencekelley.northwestern.edu). Volume 1 ends with Florence Kelley going to New York to be secretary at the National Consumers' League. Volume 2 is forthcoming.

Each of the three biographies lists its own sources and archives, and since all, with the exception of the Sklar book, were published before the availability of sources through the Internet, they are principally references to archives of letters and family papers in research libraries.

The biography by Dorothy Rose Blumberg, *Florence Kelly: The Making of a Social Pioneer* (New York: Augustus M. Kelley, 1966), is unusual because the author discovered a trove of letters in German exchanged between Frederick Engels and Florence Kelley which went undiscovered in Russia until the end of the Cold War. This biography is especially strong on the family history and Florence Kelley's relationship with her father. The bibliographic entry in Blumberg for the correspondence with Engels reads: "Letters from Florence Kelley-Wischnewetzky to Frederick Engels, Dec. 5–1884 to Dec. 31–1894. On microfilm. From Archiv, IML, Fond I, Opis 5 (Archive, Institute of Marxism-Leninism, Fund I, Schedule 5)." See also other sources in the bibliography in the Blumberg biography.

Josephine Clara Goldmark's *Impatient Crusader: Florence Kelley's Life Story*, the biography by Florence Kelley's colleague at the National Consumers' League (Westport, Connecticut: Praeger, 1976), is a valuable resource especially on the litigation leading to the United States Supreme Court case Muller v. Oregon [208 U.S. 412 (1908)] brought by Louis D. Brandeis on behalf of the National Consumers' League.

Josephine Goldmark herself played an important part in this litigation, and was herself a scholar and author on the subject of labor history, the history of immigration, and other topics relevant to Florence Kelley and her work. See Josephine Goldmark, *Fatigue and Efficiency: A Study in Industry* (New York: Russell Sage Foundation, 1912). This book contains the research for the Brandeis brief in Muller v. Oregon and later research on the subject that was made available to advocates involved in litigation in similar cases throughout the country.

The Kathryn Kish Sklar biography has an extensive compilation of the Florence Kelley publications and translations. The book referred to repeatedly in this narrative as *Die Lage* is Frederick Engels's *The Condition of the Working-Class in England in 1844, With Preface Written in 1892* translated by Florence Kelley Wischnewetzky (New York: John W. Lovell, 1887). The edition used for this book was published in 1926 in London by George Allen & Unwin Ltd.

Florence Kelley's letters have been collected and published as *The Selected Letters of Florence Kelley, 1869-1931* edited by Kathryn Kish Sklar and Beverly Wilson Palmer (Urbana-Champaign: University of Illinois Press, 2009).

The Florence Kelley Archive at the New York Public Library is an extensive collection of letters and papers donated by her oldest son, Nicholas Kelley. A useful finding aid to that archive is available on the New York Public Library website.

Factory Inspection Reports and Other Legal Materials

The annual reports of the factory inspectors of Illinois from 1893 to 1899, as well as the *First Special Report of the Factory Inspectors of Illinois on Small-Pox in the Tenement House Sweat-Shops of Chicago*, are available on the website The Life and Times of Florence Kelley in Chicago, 1891-1899 (florencekelley.northwestern.edu).

The annual reports of the Department of Health of the City of Chicago are also available on the Florence Kelley in Chicago website.

The brief and transcripts of the Ritchie v. People case are available on the Florence Kelley in Chicago website. The Supreme Court of Illinois opinion is quoted extensively in the *Third Annual Factory Inspectors Report* and is available on the website as well.

Josephine Goldmark, Florence Kelley's colleague and friend at the National Consumers' League, tells the story of the original Brandeis Brief and the final chapter of the litigation involving the 1893 Factory and Workshop Inspection Law, which was challenged in Ritchie v. People. Louis Brandeis was married to Josephine Goldmark's sister.

In addition to being Florence Kelley's partner for the first Brandeis Brief, Josephine Goldmark chronicled the history of immigration of those who fled Austria and Prussia after the revolution of 1848 and the repressions later introduced by Chancellor Otto Von Bismarck in *Pilgrims of '48*. The edition used for this book was published in Manchester, New Hampshire, by Ayer Company Publishers in 1930.

For the details and dates of Justice Brandeis's confirmation, see Henry Julian Abraham's *Justices, Presidents, and Senators: A History of the U.S. Supreme Court Appointments From Washington to Clinton*, 4th ed. (Lanham: Rowman & Littlefield Publishers, 1999). Also see *Louis D. Brandeis: Justice for the People* by Philippa Strum (Cambridge: Harvard University Press, 1984).

The constitutional history of the challenge to labor laws of these several decades, and into the twentieth century, has been extensively analyzed and documented elsewhere by commentators and academics with various political views. None disputes the jurisprudential importance of the first Brandeis Brief submitted to the Supreme Court of the United States in that case, the brief prepared by Florence Kelley and Josephine Goldmark.

The *Slums of Great Cities* Project and Other Government Documents

The *Slums of Great Cities* project was the result of a joint resolution of the Congress of the United States approved on July 20, 1892.

Originally the national study of the slums was to include sixteen cities, but Congress pared the appropriations to $20,000, and only four cities were included: Chicago, Baltimore, New York, and Philadelphia.

The commissioner of labor, Carroll D. Wright, led the project, which resulted in the "Seventh Special Report of the Commissioner of Labor" of *The Slums of Baltimore, Chicago, New York, and Philadelphia* (Washington: Government Printing Office, 1894). This report has been reprinted as *The Slums of Great Cities* (New York: Garrett Press, 1970).

Carroll D. Wright was also the author of *The Industrial Evolution of the United States* (New York: Chautauqua-Century Press, 1895).

For biographical information on Carroll D. Wright, see James Leiby's *Carroll Wright and Labor Reform* (Cambridge: Harvard University Press, 1960). There is a Congressional Memorial to him and his work after his death in February 1909 as well as several obituaries and published tributes to him. Carroll D. Wright is remembered for setting up the first state Bureau of Labor Statistics in Massachusetts and assisting in the establishment of similar offices in other states. He was the first US commissioner of labor. Carroll D. Wright commissioned Florence Kelley to undertake the Chicago part of the *Slums of Great Cities* study. Florence Kelley was the special agent expert in charge of the investigation of the slums in Chicago.

Original data collection instruments were included in the original publication of *Hull-House Maps and Papers* and are available on the Florence Kelley website. These were presumably the data collection instruments used for the *Slums of Great Cities* project, as Agnes Sinclair Holbrook's introductory comments to *Hull-House Maps and Papers* refer to the "four government schedule men" living at Hull-House for six weeks.

Political interest in the conditions of the sweatshops was not confined to Chicago, to Illinois, or even to the cities. There were other reports and activities before the US Congress, including resolutions to investigate the sweatshops: see "Resolutions introduced to investigate sweating system of tenement house labor" (Feb. 5, 1892, reported with amendment), House Document Citation: H.misdoc.71 (52nd Congress, 2nd session): Committee on Manufactures. House.

The national investigation that followed involved hearings in Chicago on April 4 and 5, 1892, in Boston on April 12 and 13, 1892, and in New York City on December 19, 1892.

The report compiled after these hearings was House Report 52-2309, published as *Report of the Committee on Manufactures on the Sweating Systems: Investigation of Sweating System of Labor, With Testimony* (Washington, DC: Government Printing Office, 1893).

Jane Addams and Hull-House

Jane Addams's *Twenty Years at Hull-House* (New York: Macmillan, 1911) is one of her many publications. It is available in a number of reprinted editions, some of which include the original illustrations.

There is extensive biographical literature and scholarly commentary on Jane Addams, Hull-House, and the collection of people in the Hull-House community in the 1890s and later. A good place to start is Louise W. Knight's *Citizen: Jane Addams and the Struggle for Democracy* (Chicago: University of Chicago Press, 2005) and Jean Bethke Elshtain's *Jane Addams and the Dream of American Democracy* (New York: Basic Books, 2002), as well as the bibliographies and archives cited therein. Further information on Jane Addams and Hull-House can be found in the bibliography on the Florence Kelley website.

Hull-House Maps and Papers by the Residents of Hull-House, a Social Settlement, is available in a recently reprinted edition (Urbana-Champaign: University of Illinois Press, 2007).

The quotations from Nicholas Kelley's remembrances of Hull-House are from a speech he gave at a celebratory dinner which was reprinted for private circulation: Nicholas Kelley, "Early Days at Hull House," reprinted for private circulation from *The Social Service Review*, Vol. XXVIII, No. 4 (December 1954).

For additional background on the economics of Hull-House, see *The Jane Addams Papers, Vol. 1 1860-1881* edited by Mary Lynn McCree Bryan, Barbara Bair, and Maree de Angury (Urbana-Champaign: University of Illinois Press, 2002) and "Who Funded Hull-House?" by Kathryn Kish Sklar in *Lady Bountiful Revisited: Women, Philanthropy, and Power* edited by Kathleen D. McCarthy (New Brunswick and London: Rutgers University Press, 1990).

The Kelley Family

The letters from the Kelley children and the correspondence with the principal of the Hillside Home School are in the New York Public Library Archives Florence Kelley Collection, as are the letters from Florence Kelley herself, her friends and associates, and letters to and from friends and family members, such as William Darrah Kelley, Caroline Bonsall Kelley, William Darrah Kelley Jr., Ellen Gates Starr, and Jane Addams, all cataloged by date and author in the finding aid available at the New York Public Library website.

The congressman William Darrah Kelley, Florence Kelley's father, is the subject of two PhD dissertations. "William Kelley: The Congressional Years, 1861-1890" by Nicklas, F. Williams, PhD, Northern Illinois University, 1983, and "William Darrah Kelley: The Ante-Bellum Years" by Greco, Michael Robert, PhD, Johns Hopkins University, 1974.

There are many remembrances of William Darrah Kelley by his colleagues and tributes to him after his death in the Congressional Record and elsewhere.

Henry Demarest Lloyd

The many writings and publications of Henry Demarest Lloyd are available through libraries and now from online resources. The articles originally published in the *Atlantic Monthly* on the Spring Hill Mine lockout, titled "The Story of a Great Monopoly" (March 1881), were reprinted in many newspapers and eventually printed as a book, *A Strike of Millionaires Against Miners or The Story of Spring Valley, An Open Letter to the Millionaires* (Chicago: Belford-Clarke Company, 1890). Henry Demarest Lloyd lived with the starving, locked-out miners for months and then testified at congressional hearings on the matter.

Henry Demarest Lloyd's sister, Caro Lloyd, published a two-volume biography of him in 1912 which includes extensive quotations from his writings and letters, as well as commentary by others: *Henry Demarest Lloyd, A Biography, 1847-1903, Volume One and Volume Two*, by Caro Lloyd (New York and London: G.P. Putnam's Sons, 1912).

Henry Demarest Lloyd's work as a legal reformer is the subject of Richard Digby-Junger's *The Journalist as Reformer: Henry Demarest Lloyd and Wealth Against Commonwealth* (Westport, Connecticut: Praeger, 1996). Another biography is by E. Jay Jernigan, *Henry Demarest Lloyd* (Boston: Twayne Publishers, 1977).

"An Exposure of Judge Gary" by Henry D. Lloyd was published as a leaflet issued by the Chicago Trade and Labor Assembly, reproducing a letter dated Sunday, November 5, 1893, from Mr. Lloyd. This letter is included in the Caro Lloyd biography. The leaflet was intended to aid in the defeat of Judge Joseph Gary who in 1893 was running for the Illinois Court of Appeals. He was not defeated.

The Henry Demarest Lloyd papers are archived at the Wisconsin Historical Society in Madison. The same archive has the papers of Richard T. Ely.

Other Background

In addition to many articles, political analyses, and his own extensive publications, John Peter Altgeld is the subject of two major biographies: *Eagle Forgotten: The Life of John Peter Altgeld* by Harry Barnard (Indianapolis: Bobbs-Merrill Company, 1938) and *Altgeld of Illinois: A Record of His Life and Labor* by Waldo R. Browne (New York: B.W. Huebsch, 1924). Governor John Peter Altgeld's pardon message for the Haymarket defendants is available in a number of print editions and online.

Abraham Bisno's life story is told in *Abraham Bisno, Union Pioneer: An Autobiographical Account of Bisno's Early Life and the Beginnings of Unionism in the Women's Garment Industry* (Madison: University of Wisconsin Press, 1967). The origins of the manuscript are described in a publisher's note as follows: "Sometime during the years 1924-1926, Bisno dictated to three typists his account of his early life and the beginning of unionism in the women's garment industry." Abraham Bisno's grandson Sidney Bisno used the manuscript as a basis for a thesis for a master of arts degree at the University of California, Los Angeles. Abraham Bisno's daughter Beatrice Bisno wrote a novel based upon her father's life: *Tomorrow's Bread* (Philadelphia: Jewish Publication Society of America, 1938).

There are several books on Karl Marx's daughters, Dr. Edward Aveling, and the writers, editors, and activists who were part of a social group surrounding Frederick Engels in 1880s London. See, eg, *Marx's daughters: Eleanor Marx, Rosa Luxemburg, Angelica Balabanoff* by Ronald Florence, 1st ed. (New York: Dial Press, 1975).

The source of biographical information for Levy Mayer is from *Levy Mayer and the New Industrial Era: A Biography* by Edgar Lee Masters (New Haven, 1927).

Background on Levy Mayer and the Illinois Manufacturers' Association and its founding

461

can be found in *A History of the Illinois Manufacturers' Association* by Alfred H. Kelly, PhD (University of Chicago Libraries, 1940).

Biographical details about Elizabeth Morgan are found in "Elizabeth Morgan, Crusader for Labor Reform" by Ralph Scharnau, *Labor History*, Vol. 14, No. 3 (Summer 1973). The University of Chicago Regenstein Library has a substantial collection of the papers of Thomas Morgan and Elizabeth Morgan.

Sources on Chicago History in the 1890s

The *Chicago Tribune*, the *New York Times*, and contemporaneous and local newspapers remain invaluable resources for obituaries and background articles. For references to archives, see sources listed under Bibliography on the Florence Kelley website.

A valuable and highly readable resource is the official report of the 1894 Pullman Strike Commission: *Report on the Chicago Strike of June-July 1894 by the United States Strike Commission* (Washington: Government Printing Office, 1895).

If Christ Came to Chicago by William Stead (Chicago: Laird & Lee, 1894) remains in print and is the source of many colorful descriptions of people and places in Chicago in the 1890s. One reprinted edition was published in Evanston, Illinois, by Chicago Historical Bookworks in 1990.

William Stead also wrote a vivid description of Chicago before ever coming to the city: "From the Old World to the New." It is the last portion of Chapter 7 of *From the Old World to the New; or, A Christmas Story of the World's Fair, 1893* and reprinted in Martin Gardner ed., *The Wreck of the Titanic Foretold?* (Buffalo: Prometheus Books, 1986). The chapter in the Stead novel does indeed describe an encounter with icebergs of a large ocean-going vessel in the North Atlantic, and the rescue and revival from the dead of a person stranded on an iceberg who communicates with a person on the ship by extra-sensory perception and automatic writing.

Moran's Dictionary of Chicago and Its Vicinity With Map of Chicago and Its Environs: An Alphabetically Arranged Dictionary, Comprising All of the Interests That Contribute to Chicago's Greatness, George E. Moran, Publisher and Proprietor (Chicago: 1616 Masonic Temple Building, 1903), is the source of many lists and alphabetical entries offering a glimpse of the world of 1890s Chicago. *Moran's Dictionary of Chicago* includes a map of

Chicago and its environs from the turn of the 20th century, an alphabetically arranged list of groups, newspapers, official court locations, and other useful information. The publication includes evocative, contemporaneous pictures and advertisements for hotels and railroads and other commercial establishments. George E. Moran was for a time a law partner of Justice Joseph M. Bailey, who sat on the Illinois Supreme Court for the *Ritchie* decision in 1895.

The Workers: An Experiment in Reality by Walter A. Wyckoff, assistant professor of political economy at Princeton University (New York: Charles Scribner's Sons, 1898), is a narrative account of a contemporaneous observer. In Chapter VI, "A Road Builder on the World's Fair Grounds," Wyckoff describes working in Chicago for the Columbian Exhibition. His obituary describes him as a distinguished philosopher.

The system for the maintenance of corruption and centralizing power in the political party in the city courts and council at the turn of the century was described by Judge M.L. McKinley, a chief justice of the Criminal Court of Cook County in 1922-23, and published as the pamphlet titled "Crime and the Civic Cancer—Graft" and by the *Chicago Daily News* in 1923. It is available on the Chicago Homicide website: Homicide in Chicago 1870-1930 (homicide.northwestern.edu).

One Thousand Homeless Men: A Study of Original Records by Alice Willard Solenberger (New York: Survey Associates Inc./Russell Sage Foundation, 1911) is an early, serious social science study of homelessness based upon interviews and the turn-of-the-century records of the Chicago Bureau of Charities. It is available on the Chicago Homicide website and has been reprinted. This was one of several social science studies published by the Russell Sage Foundation.

Katherine A. Jones's *Working Girls of Chicago: Their Wages, Their Homes, and Their Summer Outings* (Pamphlet, September 1891) is an uncollected pamphlet on the fascinating topic of who the working girls of Chicago were and how they lived. A more detailed scholarly study is: *Women Adrift: Independent Wage Earners in Chicago, 1880-1930* by Joanne J. Meyerowitz (Chicago: University of Chicago Press, 1991). The bibliography for this book and selections from it are available on the Florence Kelley in Chicago website.

There are a number of academic histories of Illinois and Chicago. See, eg, Bessie Louise Pierce, *A History of Chicago* (New York: Alfred A. Knopf, 1937-57).

In addition to its own fascinating narrative, there is an extensive bibliography in Carl S. Smith's *Chicago and the American Literary Imagination 1880-1920* (Chicago: University of Chicago Press, 1984).

Also see Richard J. Jensen, *Illinois: A History*, pp. 89-90 (Urbana-Champaign: University of Illinois Press, 2001).

There are also many incidental special reports and documents, such as *The Second Annual Report of the Executive Board of the Jewish Training School of Chicago*, Joseph Stolz, secretary (173 Monroe Street, Chicago: S. Ettinger, Printer, 1891).

Legal History

The quotation regarding the history of the common law writs is from Sir Frederick Pollock and Frederic William Maitland's *History of English Law: Before the Time of Edward I: Volume I* (Cambridge: Cambridge University Press, 1895). Chapter VI, "The Age of Glanvill," describes the development of the common law system under Henry II in the twelfth century.

James D. Heiple, "Legal Education and Admission to the Bar: The Illinois Experience," *Southern Illinois University Law Journal*, Vol. 12 (Fall 1987): 123-151.

Economic History

The following general and specialized books, among others, provided background:

The Depression of the Nineties by Charles Hoffman (Westport, Connecticut: Greenwood Publishing, 1970).

Financial History of the United States by Davis Rich Dewey (New York: Longmans, Green and Co., 1934).

Cornell University

The 1870 announcement of classes being open to women at Cornell University had been sent to William Darrah Kelley, and according to Florence Kelley's *Autobiography*, she found the announcement in his study wastebasket and promptly began studying for the entrance examination.

In addition to Florence Kelley's account of her years at Cornell in her *Autobiography*, there are many memoirs, letters, and biographical and autobiographical accounts of the educational experiences of these young university women who were students at Cornell University in the last decades of the nineteenth century. See, e.g., *The Power and Passion of M. Carey Thomas* by Helen Lefkowitz Horowitz (Urbana-Champaign: University of Illinois Press, 1999). Cornell University alumni offices can provide additional references to memoirs, letters, and family archives.

Other References

The novels of Theodore Dreiser describing Chicago in the 1890s were an invaluable resource. See, e.g., *The Titan* by Theodore Dreiser (New York: John Lane Publishing, 1914). See also *Sister Carrie* by Theodore Dreiser (New York: Doubleday, 1900). Both books are reprinted in many other editions.

The quotations from Mark Twain are in *Mark Twain* by Charles Neider (New York: Horizon Press, 1967). Neider quotes from his own edited version of *The Autobiography of Mark Twain* (New York: Harper, 1959).

Let Us Now Praise Famous Men by James Agee and Walker Evans (Boston: Mariner Books, 2001). This book was originally printed in 1940, but Evans's quote about Agee comes from his Foreword to the 1960 edition.

The Great Trial of the Chicago Anarchists by Dyer D. Lum (New York: Arno Press and the New York Times, 1969). This book includes large sections from the original records of the trial.

Anton Chekhov's letter to Alexei Suvorin (dated March 27, 1894) is from *Anton Chekhov's Life and Thought* translated by Michael Henry Heim (Evanston: Northwestern University Press, 1976).

The Pullman Case: The Clash of Labor and Capital in Industrial America by David Ray Papke (Lawrence: University Press of Kansas, 1999).

Image of horse drawn carts stopped on a commercial street in Chicago, Illinois, during a Teamsters Strike. DN-0003842, Chicago Daily News negatives collection, Chicago History Museum.

Acknowledgements

This book has been ten years in the writing, and there are many, many people to thank. The research and the writing would not have been possible without the help of many at Northwestern University and its School of Law. First, Dean David E. Van Zandt consistently provided support for this research, and his successor Dean Daniel B. Rodriguez continued that support.

Staff members of the Pritzker Legal Research Center at the Northwestern University School of Law, especially the librarians Marcia G. Lehr and Pegeen G. Bassett and their team, have been invaluable and steadfast helpers, consistently patient, knowledgeable, and critical. The Northwestern University Library, particularly Sarah M. Pritchard, dean of libraries, Charles Deering, McCormick University librarian, and Kevin B. Leonard, archivist, have provided wonderful assistance. I hope at some point all the librarians will forgive me for having so many books out at the same time. The continued support of the university administration, President Morton O. Schapiro and President Emeritus Henry Bienen, is irreplaceable, and I am very grateful for it.

This research started as background for the Chicago Historical Homicide Project, and all those who supported that work—the John D. and Catherine T. MacArthur Foundation, the Robert R. McCormick Foundation, the Joyce Foundation—must be thanked again. Thanks to the Chicago History Museum and its marvelously rich archives.

I am very grateful for the generosity and hospitality of Nicholson Baker and his wife, Margaret Brentano, for welcoming me to the American Newspaper Repository and for taking the time to find contemporaneous articles about Florence Kelley in the only continuous print copy of the Chicago Tribune available at that time.

At an early stage Paula and Howard Trienens and Sidley Austin LLP provided a substantial grant for this project, and I remain greatly in their debt. The project would not have proceeded, could not have proceeded without that critical aid coming at a critical time. Thank you again. Tom Morsch, the most careful of readers, provided invaluable advice and commentary, for which I am most grateful.

I am very grateful to Lookingglass Theatre, its executive director, Rachel Kraft, and then-board chair Lisa Green for providing shelter for me and my sprawling boxes of notes and books at a critical point during the composition. Thanks to all of the many people who love Chicago and just helped; Chicago is a village. I am very grateful to Mellody Hobson for always believing in me and the worth of my projects.

Staff support at Northwestern University has been immeasurable: my current faculty assistant, Maryanne Martinez, has provided much expertise and help, as did my former faculty assistant, Juana Haskin. Special thanks to Rita Kathleen Mosevich for her unwavering enthusiasm and assistance. Adolfo Gomez, and other staff at the Bluhm Legal Clinic, as well as its director, Thomas F. Geraghty, and the executive director of the Center on Wrongful Convictions, Rob Warden, as well as Jennifer B. Linzer, assistant director, have all been wonderful throughout. Also very helpful were Dolores Kennedy of the Center on Wrongful Convictions and many other staff at the Bluhm Legal Clinic. It is an honor to work here among you. Student assistants and interns were numerous, over a number of summers and terms. Kelsey E. Bleiweiss, Northwestern 2013, provided expert, knowledgeable assistance over the course of a year. Her editorial skills were superior to those commonly found at professional places. Farhad A. Fatakia, Northwestern University School of Law 2016, similarly was in the trenches with us during the last stages and editing in the summer of 2013. Andrea Ryken, Northwestern School of Law 2014, and Zach Sommers pitched in and battled alongside the rest of us. And I know I am leaving out many others, to whom I offer sincere thanks without naming you individually. I am truly appreciative of all you have done, and thank you for your patience. Nancy Watkins provided much-needed editorial review.

There is one person whose unflagging support was indispensable to this project and to all of the other research projects I have engaged in since coming to Northwestern. That is Mark Swindle, Web Designer. Not only did Mark Swindle drag me, metaphorically speaking, kicking and screaming onto the Internet, persuading me to put the homicide data set on the Web, but his patience, understanding, and shining intelligence have been more than support. They have been and are inspirational. His putting the Chicago Daily News photographs on the Homicide in Chicago website and then others on the Florence

Kelley website made those sites come alive. The beautiful designs of those websites are a gift to all of us. Nor were the technical aspects of the designs trivial. I am very grateful for the originality and beauty of that work.

There are so many people to thank, and so many people who made this book possible. I know I have not mentioned as many individuals and institutions as I should have, so a blanket thanks and note of appreciation will have to suffice for the moment. Of course, any errors, mistakes, and omissions, and I am sure there are many, are my responsibility.

Leigh Buchanan Bienen is a writer, advocate, and teacher whose areas of expertise include capital punishment, sex crimes, and legal reform. In addition to many legal articles, her books include *The Left-Handed Marriage* (fiction), *Crimes of the Century* (with Gil Geis) (nonfiction), *Murder and Its Consequences* (essays on capital punishment), and stories and essays in *TriQuarterly* and other literary journals. She has three daughters, currently teaches at Northwestern School of Law and lives in Chicago with her husband, Henry Bienen, president emeritus of Northwestern University. In addition, she has developed three law-related websites: homicide.northwestern.edu, florencekelley.northwestern.edu and illinoismurderindictments.law.northwestern.edu.